PENGUIN 🐧 CLASSICS

PENGUIN ENGLISH POETS
GENERAL EDITOR: CHRISTOPHER RICKS

WILLIAM BLAKE:
THE COMPLETE POEMS

WILLIAM BLAKE was born in Broad Street in 1757, the son of a London hosier. Having attended Henry Parr's drawing school in the Strand, he was in 1772 apprenticed to Henry Basire, engraver to the Society of Antiquaries, and later was admitted as a student to the Royal Academy, where he exhibited in 1780. He married Catherine Boucher in 1782 and in 1783 published *Poetical Sketches*. The first of his 'illuminated books' was *Songs of Innocence* (1789), which, like *The Book of Thel* (published in the same year), has as its main themes the celebration of innocence and its inviolability.

Blake sets out his ideas more fully in his chief prose work, *The Marriage of Heaven and Hell* (1791), which proclaims his lifelong belief in the moral primacy of the imagination. But in *Songs of Experience* (1794) he recognizes the power of repression, and in a series of short narrative poems he looks for mankind's redemption from oppression through a resurgence of imaginative life. By 1797 he was ready for epic; *Vala* was never finished, but in *Milton* and *Jerusalem* he presents his renewed vision of reconciliation among the warring fragments of humanity. Other striking poems of his middle years are the lyrics of the Pickering Manuscript, and *The Everlasting Gospel*, but in the last years of his life he expressed himself in drawing rather than poetry.

Little of Blake's work was published on conventional form. He combined his vocations as poet and graphic artist to produce books that are visually stunning. He also designed illustrations of works by other poets and devised his own technique for producing large watercolour illustrations and colour-printed drawings. Blake died in 1827, 'an Old Man feeble & tottering but not in Spirit & Life not in the Real Man The Imagination which Liveth for Ever'.

ALICIA OSTRIKER is Professor of English at Rutgers University, New Brunswick, New Jersey, USA.

WILLIAM BLAKE

The Complete Poems

Edited by
ALICIA OSTRIKER

PENGUIN BOOKS

PENGUIN BOOKS

Published by the Penguin Group
Penguin Books Ltd, 80 Strand, London WC2R 0RL, England
Penguin Group (USA), Inc., 375 Hudson Street, New York, New York 10014, USA
Penguin Books Australia Ltd, 250 Camberwell Road, Camberwell, Victoria 3124, Australia
Penguin Books Canada Ltd, 10 Alcorn Avenue, Toronto, Ontario, Canada M4V 3B2
Penguin Books India (P) Ltd, 11 Community Centre, Panchsheel Park, New Delhi – 110 017, India
Penguin Books (NZ) Ltd, Cnr Rosedale and Airborne Roads, Albany, Auckland, New Zealand
Penguin Books (South Africa) (Pty) Ltd, 24 Sturdee Avenue, Rosebank 2196, South Africa

Penguin Books Ltd, Registered Offices: 80 Strand, London WC2R 0RL, England

www.penguin.com

First published 1977
Reprinted with revised Further Reading 2004
28

Editorial material copyright © Alicia Ostriker, 1977, 2004

Printed in England by Clays Ltd, St Ives plc
Filmset in Monotype Ehrhardt

ISBN-13: 978-0-140-42215-3

www.greenpenguin.co.uk

Contents

Preface

William Blake is the rebel *par excellence* of English poetry, who sets his face against convention and restriction of every sort, glorifies untrammelled inspiration and defends the artist's liberty, in matters of literary format as well as in his religious, political and social ideas. Almost none of his work was published in conventional printed form. Pursuing his vocations as poet and graphic artist simultaneously, he printed most of it himself, with text (in his own orthography) and illustrations commonly intertwined, by a method of etching he invented for the purpose. Copies of individual works often vary, not only in the character of the water-colour tintings he gave them, but also in the order of the plates and in words or lines which appear in some copies but are deleted in others. Blake's spelling, punctuation and grammar obey his individual temperament. Many of his poems, including some major ones, exist only in much-revised manuscript form.

No conventionally type-set edition of Blake's poetry can compete, either in beauty or in clarity, with the original illuminated books produced by the poet; neither can it suggest the full complexity of the texts in manuscript. Given these limitations, however, the intention of this edition is to reproduce the work with as much fidelity as possible to the forms in which he wrote it. 'Improvement makes strait roads; but the crooked roads without Improvement are roads of Genius,' Blake remarked. Intrigued readers may be lured onward to the originals, or to the many excellent facsimile editions of them which fortunately exist today.

Spelling, grammar, punctuation. Most readers will not be troubled by Blake's often archaic or eccentric spelling, his frequent use of capitalization for emphasis, his predilection for the rapid '&' as opposed to the conventional 'and', and his sometimes crude grammar. These peculiarities have usually been accepted by Blake's editors and readers alike as quirky but charming. A greater stumbling-block is Blake's punctuation, which is at all times idiosyncratic, and at some times, particularly in the manuscript poems, virtually non-existent. Most standard editions of Blake have supplied a conventional punctuation, but to alter in this matter is clearly to distort. I have therefore followed the procedure of David V. Erdman in *The Poetry and Prose of William Blake*, retaining the poet's punctuation and non-punctuation intact. As a rule, any punctuation mark may be taken simply as a sign for a greater or lesser *pause* in the flow of language, rather than as an indicator of grammatical relationships. With a little relaxation and practice, the reader will find that this is less difficult than it appears at first, and finally that it may create a sense of freedom and buoyancy, and an openness of syntactic construction, which bring considerable aesthetic and intellectual pleasure.

Revisions. In the presentation of textual variations, emendations, revisions, etc., a distinction is made between Blake's manuscript poems and his finished work. For poems which Blake published (or had published or printed for him) in any form, and which we may thus suppose to be finished, the relatively few variations which exist are presented in the Notes. For poems which exist only in manuscript form, this material is incorporated in the text through italics and brackets, reproducing as far as possible the condition of the texts in their 'workshop' state, with successive stages of revision evident as one reads along. The assumption here is that unfinished poems should not be presented to the eye as if they were finished, and vice versa; and that the reader will benefit from an opportunity to sense Blake's verse both as working process and as completed product. In this respect, the innovative and successful procedure of Geoffrey Keynes's Nonesuch and Oxford editions of the *Complete Writings* is followed with gratitude.

Texts. The texts on which the present edition is based are those of David V. Erdman, *The Poetry and Prose of William Blake*, Doubleday, 1970. This volume should be consulted for complete detail in regard to Blake's revisions, and for full discussion of textual complexities. There are some changes, particularly in punctuation. The marks '!', '?', ':' and ';' are often difficult to distinguish in Blake's calligraphy. Erdman commonly transcribes '!' where I find a colon or semi-colon. Blake's full stops and commas are also difficult to tell apart, and he is rather skimpy about the latter. Thus in works where both '.' and ',' appear, they are retained (but the readings sometimes disagree with Erdman's). In works where '.' alone appears, and is evidently doing service for both conventional '.' and conventional ',' in the original, the present text follows what normal grammar and syntax would require. Another change is that Night VII [b] of *The Four Zoas*, which Erdman believes was 'supplanted by VII [a]', is here placed within the text rather than as an appendix, following the argument made by several scholars that Blake never definitively rejected this portion of the manuscript. A final alteration is that the *Songs of Experience*, which Blake printed in 1794, are here placed just after the *Songs of Innocence* (1789), for the reader's convenience.

Notes and Dictionary of Proper Names. The Notes attempt to clarify what is difficult in Blake's poetry, and to indicate where passages from the Bible, Milton and other sources seem necessary to explain a text or enrich our understanding of its implications. The Dictionary of Proper Names defines recurrent terms in Blake's symbolic systems.

To express my gratitude to the multitude of Blake scholars who have shaped my comprehension of his poetry would be impossible. I have at each step walked particularly in the tracks of Geoffrey Keynes, David Erdman, G. E. Bentley, Jr, S. Foster Damon, Northrop Frye, Harold Bloom and W. H. Stevenson, and have gained knowledge and insight from many other commentators. I owe special thanks to Professor Erdman for assistance with texts and guidance through the labyrinths of the Notebook; to Morton Paley for advice on *Jerusalem*; and to James McGowan for the use of unpublished research on *Poetical Sketches*.

EDITORIAL MARKS

Material marked [thus] indicates editorial interpolation.

Material marked [*thus*] indicates a word, phrase or passage deleted, erased or emended in the manuscript.

Material marked [*thus/ and so*] indicates successive deletions within a passage, followed by a final accepted version.

Material marked [*thus (this) and so*] indicates a deletion within a passage that was afterwards itself deleted.

? preceding a word indicates an uncertain reading.

Table of Dates

1757   William Blake born on 28 November at 28 Broad St, London, to James Blake, a hosier, and Catherine Blake. Older brother James was born 1753; other siblings were John (b. 1760), Richard (b. 1762, died in infancy), Catherine Elizabeth (b. 1764), Robert (1767).

1765–7   Sees his first vision, a tree filled with angels on Peckham Rye, at the age of eight or ten; his father threatens to thrash him for lying, but his mother intercedes.

1767–8   Begins to attend Henry Parrs's drawing school in the Strand.

1772   Apprenticed to the engraver Henry Basire.

1774   After arguments with other apprentices, sent to do drawings in Westminster Abbey for Basire.

1775   Beginning of the American War of Independence.

1779   Apprenticeship ended. Admitted as a student in the Royal Academy, under G. M. Moser. Friendship with fellow artists George Cumberland, John Flaxman, Thomas Stothard.

1780   Exhibits at Royal Academy. Witnesses Gordon No-Popery riots and the burning of Newgate Prison. Engraving plates for bookseller Joseph Johnson.

1782   Marries Catherine Boucher (b. 1762).

1783   *Poetical Sketches* printed for Blake by Flaxman and Rev. A. S. Mathew, but not publicly distributed.

1784   Father's death; partnership with James Parker in a print-shop at 27 Broad St.

1785   Dissolves partnership, moves to 28 Poland St.

1787   Death of Robert Blake, whose spirit Blake sees rise through the ceiling 'clapping its hands for joy'. Friendship with painter Henry Fuseli.

1788   *All Religions are One* and *There is No Natural Religion* printed.

1789   *Tiriel* written. *Thel* and *Songs of Innocence* engraved. William and Catherine attend first London meeting of Swedenborgian New Church. Outbreak of French Revolution.

1790   *Marriage of Heaven and Hell* probably begun.

1791   *French Revolution* proofs printed for Joseph Johnson. Begins engravings for John Stedman's anti-slavery *Narrative of a five years' expedition against the Revolted Negroes of Surinam* (pub. 1796). Bill to abolish the slave trade rejected in Commons. *Visions of the Daughters of Albion* probably begun. William and Catherine move to 13 Hercules Buildings, Lambeth.

1792–3   Invasion of France stopped at Valmy. 'A Song of Liberty' written.

1793   Execution of Louis XVI. Britain declares war against France. *America* and *Visions* engraved.

1794   *Songs of Innocence and of Experience* issued in a combined volume. *Europe* and *Book of Urizen* engraved.

1795   *Song of Los*, *Book of Ahania* and *Book of Los* engraved.

1796–7   Engravings for Young's *Night Thoughts*; the work was not well received.

1797   *Vala* begun. Illustrations and dedicatory poem for Gray's poems.

1798   Wordsworth and Coleridge publish *Lyrical Ballads*.

1800   William Hayley, on Flaxman's recommendation, commissions engravings from Blake. Thomas Butts becomes Blake's friend and patron. 16 September, William and Catherine move to Hayley's cottage in Felpham, Sussex.

1800–1802 Felpham residence, work on engravings and miniatures for Hayley, increasing dissatisfaction on Blake's part. *Vala* continued, *Milton* begun.

1802 Peace of Amiens.

1803 10 May, renewal of war with France. 12 August, Blake ejects the dragoon Schofield from his garden, and is charged with sedition. Returns to London, takes rooms at 17 South Molton St.

1804 10 January, sedition trial; Blake acquitted. *Milton* completed. *Jerusalem* probably begun.

1805 Publisher Robert Cromek commissions designs for Blair's *Grave* from Blake, but afterwards gives the engraving work to Schiavonetti.

1807 Stothard exhibits *Canterbury Pilgrims* painting; Blake believes the idea stolen from him.

1808 Blair's *Grave* published, Blake's designs attacked by Hunt in *The Examiner*.

1809 Blake's exhibition of his paintings, accompanied by the *Descriptive Catalogue*, proves a failure. *The Examiner* calls him an 'unfortunate lunatic'. Years of increased obscurity follow, although Flaxman and Butts continue to befriend Blake.

1814 Engraving Flaxman's designs for *Hesiod*.

1815 Napoleonic wars end. Blake engraving Wedgwood china designs.

1816 *L'Allegro* and *Il Penseroso* designs.

1818 Probable date of 'Everlasting Gospel' fragments in Notebook. Water-colours of *Job* commissioned by Butts. Friendship with the young artist John Linnell. Linnell and a group of others, calling themselves 'The Ancients', will become Blake's admirers and supporters in his last years.

1820 *Jerusalem* engraved. Woodcuts for Thornton's *Virgil*.

1822 *The Ghost of Abel* engraved.

1824 Friendship with Samuel Palmer. Linnell commissions Dante designs.

1825 The diarist Crabb Robinson visits Blake and records his conversation.

1827 12 April, writes to Cumberland: 'I have been very near the Gates of Death & have returned very weak & an Old Man feeble & tottering but not in Spirit & Life not in the Real Man The Imagination which Liveth for Ever.' 12 August, Blake dies.

Further Reading

EDITIONS

Geoffrey Keynes (ed.), *The Complete Writings of William Blake*, Oxford University Press, 1966.

Geoffrey Keynes (ed.), *The Letters of William Blake, with Related Documents*, 1968; 3rd edn, Oxford University Press, 1980.

David V. Erdman (ed.), *The Poetry and Prose of William Blake*, Doubleday, New York, 1970. Commentary by Harold Bloom. Rev. edn, University of California Press, 1982.

W. H. S. Stevenson (ed.), *The Poems of William Blake*, Longman, 1971. Text by Erdman. Fully annotated.

David Bindman, assisted by Deirdre Tooney, *Complete Graphic Works of William Blake*, Putnam, 1978.

FACSIMILE EDITIONS

Among the many facsimile editions of Blake's illuminated writings, of particular excellence and value are the series done by W. Muir, printed by the Blake Press at Edmonton in the 1880s, and those printed for the William Blake Trust by the Trianon Press, London, during the 1950s through to the 1970s. Each volume of the latter contains a bibliographical note by Geoffrey Keynes. *The Illuminated Blake*, annotated by David V. Erdman, Doubleday, 1974, presents Blake's complete illuminated works in black and white, with commentary, in a single volume. Most recently, Princeton University Press has published, under the general editorship of David Bindman, *The Illuminated Books of William Blake*, under the titles *Jerusalem*, *Songs of Innocence and Experience*, *The Early Illuminated Books*, *The Continental Prophecies*, *Milton, a Poem* and *The Urizen Books*. Each volume includes colour reproductions of the original plates, transcriptions of the text, and plate-by-plate commentaries.

Facsimile editions of texts in manuscript form are:

Tiriel. Facsimile and Transcript of the Manuscript, Reproduction of the Drawings, and a Commentary on the Poem, ed. G. E. Bentley, Jr, Oxford University Press, 1967.

The Notebook of William Blake (facsimile and transcription), ed. Geoffrey Keynes, Nonesuch, 1935.

The Notebook of William Blake: A Photographic and Typographic Facsimile, ed. David V. Erdman, Oxford University Press, 1973.

Vala; or, The Four Zoas. A Facsimile of the Manuscript, a Transcript and a Study of its Growth and Significance, ed. G. E. Bentley, Jr, Oxford University Press, 1963.

The Four Zoas: A Photographic Facsimile of the Manuscript with Commentary on the Illuminations, ed. Cettina Tramontane Magno and David V. Erdman, Bucknell University Press, 1987.

BIOGRAPHY

Peter Ackroyd, *Blake*, Sinclair-Stevenson, 1995.

G. E. Bentley, Jr, *Blake Records*, Oxford University Press, 1969. *Supplement*, 1988.

—— *Stranger from Paradise: A Biography of William Blake*, Yale University Press, 2001.

Alexander Gilchrist, *Life of William Blake, 'Pictor Ignotus'*, 2 vols., 1863; Everyman, 1945.

James King, *William Blake: His Life*, Weidenfield and Nicolson, 1991.

Mona Wilson, *The Life of William Blake*, 1927, ed. Geoffrey Keynes, Oxford University Press, 1971.

CRITICAL STUDIES

G. E. Bentley, Jr, *William Blake: The Critical Heritage*, Routledge, 1975.

Harold Bloom, *Blake's Apocalypse: A Study in Poetic Argument*, Doubleday, 1963.

Helen P. Bruder, *William Blake and the Daughters of Albion*, Macmillan, 1997.

Tristanne J. Connolly, *William Blake and the Body*, Palgrave Macmillan, 2002.

S. Foster Damon, *William Blake, His Philosophy and Symbols*, London, 1924.

Leopold Damrosch, *Symbol and Truth in Blake's Myth*, Princeton University Press, 1980.

Jackie DiSalvo, *War of the Titans: Blake's Critique of Milton and the Politics of Religion*, University of Pittsburgh Press, 1984.

Morris Eaves, *William Blake's Theory of Art*, Princeton University Press, 1982.

—— *The Counter-Arts Conspiracy: Art and Industry in the Age of Blake*, Cornell University Press, 1992.

T. S. Eliot, 'Blake', in *The Sacred Wood: Essays on Poetry and Criticism*, London, 1920; reprinted as 'William Blake' in *Selected Essays*, Faber, 1932.

David V. Erdman, *Blake: Prophet Against Empire, A Poet's Interpretation of the History of His Own Times*, Princton University Press, 1954.

Michael Ferber, *The Social Vision of William Blake*, Princeton University Press, 1985.

—— *The Poetry of William Blake*, Penguin, 1991.

Harold Fisch, *The Biblical Presence in Shakespeare, Milton and Blake: A Comparative Study*, Clarendon Press, 1999.

Northrop Frye, *Fearful Symmetry: A Study of William Blake*, Princeton University Press, 1947.

David Fuller, *Blake's Heroic Argument*, Methuen, 1988.

Robert F. Gleckner, *The Piper and the Bard: A Study of William Blake*, Wayne State University Press, 1959. (Blake's early work through *Visions of the Daughters of Albion*.)

Heather Glen, *Vision and Disenchantment: Blake's Songs and Wordsworth's Lyrical Ballads*, Cambridge University Press, 1983.

Nelson Hilton (ed.), *Essential Articles for the Study of William Blake, 1970–1984*, Archon Books, 1986.

E. D. Hirsch, Jr, *Innocence and Experience: An Introduction to Blake*, Yale University Press, 1964.

Christopher Z. Hobson, *Blake and Homosexuality*, Palgrave Macmillan, 2000.

James Joyce, 'William Blake', in *The Critical Writings of James Joyce*, ed. E. Mason and R. Ellman, Faber, 1959.

Zachary Leader, *Reading Blake's Songs*, Routledge Kegan Paul, 1981.

Margaret Ruth Lowery, *Windows of the Morning: A Critical Study of William Blake's 'Poetical Sketches'*, Oxford University Press, 1940.

Kathleen Lundeen, *Knight of the Living Dead: William Blake and the Problem of Ontology*, Association of University Presses, 2000.

John Mee, *Dangerous Enthusiasm: William Blake and the Culture of Radicalism in the 1790s*, Clarendon Press, 1992.

Josephine Miles, 'The Language of William Blake', in *Eras and Modes in English Poetry*, University of California Press, 1957.

Dan Miller, Mark Bracher and Donal Ault (eds.), *Blake and the Argument of Method*, Duke University Press, 1987.

W. J. T. Mitchell, *Blake's Composite Art: A Study of the Illuminated Poetry*, Princeton University Press, 1978.

Alicia Ostriker, *Vision and Verse in William Blake*, University of Wisconsin Press, 1965.

Morton Paley, *Energy and the Imagination: A Study of the Development of Blake's Thought*, Oxford University Press, 1970.

Morton Paley (ed.), *Twentieth Century Interpretations of Songs of Innocence and Experience*, Prentice-Hall, 1969.

Kathleen Raine, *Blake and Tradition*, 2 vols., Princeton University Press, 1968.

Algernon Charles Swinburne, *William Blake: A Critical Essay*, 1868.

Leslie Tannenbaum, *Biblical Tradition in Blake's Early Prophecies: The Great Code of Art*, Princeton University Press, 1982.

Joseph Viscomi, *Blake and the Idea of the Book*, Princeton University Press, 1993.

W. B. Yeats, 'William Blake and the Imagination', in *Ideas of Good and Evil*, 1903. Reprinted in *Essays and Introductions*, Macmillan, 1961.

Paul Youngquist, *Madness and Blake's Myth*, Pennsylvania State University Press, 1989.

REFERENCE WORKS

G. E. Bentley, Jr, and Martin Nurmi, *A Blake Bibliography*, University of Minnesota Press, 1964.

S. Foster Damon, *A Blake Dictionary: The Ideas and Symbols of William Blake*, Brown University Press, 1965; new edn with Forward and annotated bibliography by Morris Eaves, 1988.

David V. Erdman, et al., *A Concordance to the Writings of William Blake*, 2 vols., Cornell University Press, 1967.

Mary Lynn Johnson, 'William Blake' in *The English Romantic Poets: A Review of Research and Criticism*, ed. Frank Jordan, Modern Language Association, 1985.

Geoffrey Keynes, *William Blake's Illuminated Books: A Census*, New York, 1953.

The Poems

Miscellaneous Poems

TO SPRING

O thou, with dewy locks, who lookest down
Thro' the clear windows of the morning; turn
Thine angel eyes upon our western isle,
Which in full choir hails thy approach, O Spring!

The hills tell each other, and the list'ning
Vallies hear; all our longing eyes are turned
Up to thy bright pavillions: issue forth,
And let thy holy feet visit our clime.

Come o'er the eastern hills, and let our winds
Kiss thy perfumed garments; let us taste   10
Thy morn and evening breath; scatter thy pearls
Upon our love-sick land that mourns for thee.

O deck her forth with thy fair fingers; pour
Thy soft kisses on her bosom; and put
Thy golden crown upon her languish'd head,
Whose modest tresses were bound up for thee!

TO SUMMER

O thou, who passest thro' our vallies in
Thy strength, curb thy fierce steeds, allay the heat
That flames from their large nostrils! thou, O Summer,
Oft pitched'st here thy golden tent, and oft

Beneath our oaks hast slept, while we beheld
With joy, thy ruddy limbs and flourishing hair.

Beneath our thickest shades we oft have heard
Thy voice, when noon upon his fervid car
Rode o'er the deep of heaven; beside our springs
Sit down, and in our mossy vallies, on   10
Some bank beside a river clear, throw thy
Silk draperies off, and rush into the stream:
Our vallies love the Summer in his pride.

Our bards are fam'd who strike the silver wire:
Our youth are bolder than the southern swains:
Our maidens fairer in the sprightly dance:
We lack not songs, nor instruments of joy,
Nor echoes sweet, nor waters clear as heaven,
Nor laurel wreaths against the sultry heat.

TO AUTUMN

O Autumn, laden with fruit, and stained
With the blood of the grape, pass not, but sit
Beneath my shady roof, there thou may'st rest,
And tune thy jolly voice to my fresh pipe;
And all the daughters of the year shall dance!
Sing now the lusty song of fruits and flowers.

'The narrow bud opens her beauties to
'The sun, and love runs in her thrilling veins;
'Blossoms hang round the brows of morning, and
'Flourish down the bright cheek of modest eve,
'Till clust'ring Summer breaks forth into singing,   10
'And feather'd clouds strew flowers round her head.

'The spirits of the air live on the smells
'Of fruit; and joy, with pinions light, roves round
'The gardens, or sits singing in the trees.'
Thus sang the jolly Autumn as he sat,
Then rose, girded himself, and o'er the bleak
Hills fled from our sight; but left his golden load.

TO WINTER

O Winter! bar thine adamantine doors:
The north is thine; there hast thou built thy dark
Deep-founded habitation. Shake not thy roofs,
Nor bend thy pillars with thine iron car.

He hears me not, but o'er the yawning deep
Rides heavy; his storms are unchain'd; sheathed
In ribbed steel, I dare not lift mine eyes;
For he hath rear'd his sceptre o'er the world.

Lo! now the direful monster, whose skin clings
To his strong bones, strides o'er the groaning rocks: 10
He withers all in silence, and his hand
Unclothes the earth, and freezes up frail life.

He takes his seat upon the cliffs, the mariner
Cries in vain. Poor little wretch! that deal'st
With storms; till heaven smiles, and the monster
Is driv'n yelling to his caves beneath mount Hecla.

TO THE EVENING STAR

Thou fair-hair'd angel of the evening,
Now, while the sun rests on the mountains, light
Thy bright torch of love; thy radiant crown
Put on, and smile upon our evening bed!
Smile on our loves; and, while thou drawest the
Blue curtains of the sky, scatter thy silver dew
On every flower that shuts its sweet eyes
In timely sleep. Let thy west wind sleep on
The lake; speak si[l]ence with thy glimmering eyes,
And wash the dusk with silver. Soon, full soon,   10
Dost thou withdraw; then the wolf rages wide,
And the lion glares thro' the dun forest:
The fleeces of our flocks are cover'd with
Thy sacred dew: protect them with thine influence.

TO MORNING

O holy virgin! clad in purest white,
Unlock heav'n's golden gates, and issue forth;
Awake the dawn that sleeps in heaven; let light
Rise from the chambers of the east, and bring
The honied dew that cometh on waking day.
O radiant morning, salute the sun,
Rouz'd like a huntsman to the chace; and, with
Thy buskin'd feet, appear upon our hills.

FAIR ELENOR

The bell struck one, and shook the silent tower;
The graves give up their dead: fair Elenor
Walk'd by the castle gate, and looked in.
A hollow groan ran thro' the dreary vaults.

She shriek'd aloud, and sunk upon the steps
On the cold stone her pale cheek. Sickly smells
Of death, issue as from a sepulchre,
And all is silent but the sighing vaults.

Chill death withdraws his hand, and she revives;
Amaz'd, she finds herself upon her feet,   10
And, like a ghost, thro' narrow passages
Walking, feeling the cold walls with her hands.

Fancy returns, and now she thinks of bones,
And grinning skulls, and corruptible death,
Wrap'd in his shroud; and now, fancies she hears
Deep sighs, and sees pale sickly ghosts gliding.

At length, no fancy, but reality
Distracts her. A rushing sound, and the feet
Of one that fled, approaches – Ellen stood,
Like a dumb statue, froze to stone with fear.   20

The wretch approaches, crying, 'The deed is done;
'Take this, and send it by whom thou wilt send;
'It is my life – send it to Elenor: –
'He's dead, and howling after me for blood!

'Take this,' he cry'd; and thrust into her arms
A wet napkin, wrap'd about; then rush'd
Past, howling: she receiv'd into her arms
Pale death, and follow'd on the wings of fear.

They pass'd swift thro' the outer gate; the wretch,
Howling, leap'd o'er the wall into the moat,　　　　　30
Stifling in mud. Fair Ellen pass'd the bridge,
And heard a gloomy voice cry, 'Is it done?'

As the deer wounded Ellen flew over
The pathless plain; as the arrows that fly
By night; destruction flies, and strikes in darkness,
She fled from fear, till at her house arriv'd.

Her maids await her; on her bed she falls,
That bed of joy, where erst her lord hath press'd:
'Ah, woman's fear!' she cry'd; 'Ah, cursed duke!
'Ah, my dear lord! ah, wretched Elenor!　　　　　40

'My lord was like a flower upon the brows
'Of lusty May! Ah, life as frail as flower!
'O ghastly death! withdraw thy cruel hand,
'Seek'st thou that flow'r to deck thy horrid temples?

'My lord was like a star, in highest heav'n
'Drawn down to earth by spells and wickedness:
'My lord was like the opening eyes of day,
'When western winds creep softly o'er the flowers:

'But he is darken'd; like the summer's noon,
'Clouded; fall'n like the stately tree, cut down;　　　　　50
'The breath of heaven dwelt among his leaves.
'O Elenor, weak woman, fill'd with woe!'

Thus having spoke, she raised up her head,
And saw the bloody napkin by her side,
Which in her arms she brought; and now, tenfold
More terrified, saw it unfold itself.

Her eyes were fix'd; the bloody cloth unfolds,
Disclosing to her sight the murder'd head
Of her dear lord, all ghastly pale, clotted
With gory blood; it groan'd, and thus it spake: 60

'O Elenor, behold thy husband's head,
'Who, sleeping on the stones of yonder tower
'Was 'reft of life by the accursed duke!
'A hired villain turn'd my sleep to death!

'O Elenor, beware the cursed duke,
'O give not him thy hand, now I am dead;
'He seeks thy love; who, coward, in the night,
'Hired a villain to bereave my life.'

She sat with dead cold limbs, stiffen'd to stone;
She took the gory head up in her arms;   70
She kiss'd the pale lips; she had no tears to shed;
She hugg'd it to her breast, and groan'd her last.

SONG

How sweet I roam'd from field to field,
    And tasted all the summer's pride,
'Till I the prince of love beheld,
    Who in the sunny beams did glide!

He shew'd me lilies for my hair,
    And blushing roses for my brow;
He led me through his gardens fair,
    Where all his golden pleasures grow.

With sweet May dews my wings were wet,
    And Phoebus fir'd my vocal rage;   10
He caught me in his silken net,
    And shut me in his golden cage.

He loves to sit and hear me sing,
    Then, laughing, sports and plays with me;
Then stretches out my golden wing,
    And mocks my loss of liberty.

SONG

My silks and fine array,
    My smiles and languish'd air,
By love are driv'n away;
    And mournful lean Despair
Brings me yew to deck my grave:
Such end true lovers have.

His face is fair as heav'n,
    When springing buds unfold;
O why to him was't giv'n,
    Whose heart is wintry cold?   10
His breast is love's all worship'd tomb,
Where all love's pilgrims come.

Bring me an axe and spade,
    Bring me a winding sheet;
When I my grave have made,
    Let winds and tempests beat:
Then down I'll lie, as cold as clay.
True love doth pass away!

SONG

Love and harmony combine,
And around our souls intwine,
While thy branches mix with mine,
And our roots together join.

Joys upon our branches sit,
Chirping loud, and singing sweet;
Like gentle streams beneath our feet
Innocence and virtue meet.

Thou the golden fruit dost bear,
I am clad in flowers fair;   10
Thy sweet boughs perfume the air,
And the turtle buildeth there.

There she sits and feeds her young,
Sweet I hear her mournful song;
And thy lovely leaves among,
There is love: I hear his tongue.

There his charming nest doth lay,
There he sleeps the night away;
There he sports along the day,
And doth among our branches play.   20

SONG

I love the jocund dance,
  The softly-breathing song,
Where innocent eyes do glance,
  And where lisps the maiden's tongue.

I love the laughing vale,
  I love the echoing hill,
Where mirth does never fail,
  And the jolly swain laughs his fill.

I love the pleasant cot,
  I love the innocent bow'r.   10
Where white and brown is our lot,
  Or fruit in the mid-day hour.

I love the oaken seat,
  Beneath the oaken tree,
Where all the old villagers meet,
  And laugh our sports to see.

I love our neighbours all,
  But, Kitty, I better love thee;
And love them I ever shall;
  But thou art all to me.   20

SONG

Memory, hither come,
  And tune your merry notes;
And, while upon the wind,
  Your music floats,
I'll pore upon the stream,
Where sighing lovers dream,
And fish for fancies as they pass
Within the watery glass.

I'll drink of the clear stream,
  And hear the linnet's song;
And there I'll lie and dream
  The day along:
And, when night comes, I'll go
  To places fit for woe;
Walking along the darken'd valley,
  With silent Melancholy.

MAD SONG

The wild winds weep,
  And the night is a-cold;
Come hither, Sleep,
  And my griefs infold:
But lo! the morning peeps
  Over the eastern steeps,
And the rustling birds of dawn
The earth do scorn.

Lo! to the vault
  Of paved heaven,
With sorrow fraught
  My notes are driven:
They strike the ear of night,
  Make weep the eyes of day;
They make mad the roaring winds,
  And with tempests play.

10

10

Like a fiend in a cloud
  With howling woe,
After night I do croud,
  And with night will go;
I turn my back to the east,   20
From whence comforts have increas'd;
For light doth seize my brain
With frantic pain.

SONG

Fresh from the dewy hill, the merry year
Smiles on my head, and mounts his flaming car;
Round my young brows the laurel wreathes a shade,
And rising glories beam around my head.

My feet are wing'd, while o'er the dewy lawn,
I meet my maiden, risen like the morn:
Oh bless those holy feet, like angels' feet;
Oh bless those limbs, beaming with heav'nly light!

Like as an angel glitt'ring in the sky,
In times of innocence, and holy joy;   10
The joyful shepherd stops his grateful song,
To hear the music of an angel's tongue.

So when she speaks, the voice of Heaven I hear
So when we walk, nothing impure comes near;
Each field seems Eden, and each calm retreat;
Each village seems the haunt of holy feet.

But that sweet village where my black-ey'd maid,
Closes her eyes in sleep beneath night's shade:
Whene'er I enter, more than mortal fire
Burns in my soul, and does my song inspire.   20

SONG

When early morn walks forth in sober grey;
Then to my black ey'd maid I haste away,
When evening sits beneath her dusky bow'r,

And gently sighs away the silent hour;
The village bell alarms, away I go;
And the vale darkens at my pensive woe.

To that sweet village, where my black ey'd maid
Doth drop a tear beneath the silent shade,
I turn my eyes; and, pensive as I go,
Curse my black stars, and bless my pleasing woe.   10

Oft when the summer sleeps among the trees,
Whisp'ring faint murmurs to the scanty breeze,
I walk the village round; if at her side
A youth doth walk in stolen joy and pride,
I curse my stars in bitter grief and woe,
That made my love so high, and me so low.

O should she e'er prove false, his limbs I'd tear,
And throw all pity on the burning air;
I'd curse bright fortune for my mixed lot,
And then I'd die in peace, and be forgot.   20

TO THE MUSES

Whether on Ida's shady brow,
    Or in the chambers of the East,
The chambers of the sun, that now
    From antient melody have ceas'd;

Whether in Heav'n ye wander fair,
    Or the green corners of the earth,
Or the blue regions of the air,
    Where the melodious winds have birth;

Whether on chrystal rocks ye rove,
    Beneath the bosom of the sea   10
Wand'ring in many a coral grove,
    Fair Nine, forsaking Poetry!

How have you left the antient love
    That bards of old enjoy'd in you!
The languid strings do scarcely move!
    The sound is forc'd, the notes are few!

GWIN, KING OF NORWAY

Come, Kings, and listen to my song,
    When Gwin, the son of Nore,
Over the nations of the North
    His cruel sceptre bore:

The Nobles of the land did feed
    Upon the hungry Poor;
They tear the poor man's lamb, and drive
    The needy from their door!

The land is desolate; our wives
    And children cry for bread;   10
Arise, and pull the tyrant down;
    Let Gwin be humbled.

Gordred the giant rous'd himself
    From sleeping in his cave;
He shook the hills, and in the clouds
    The troubl'd banners wave.

Beneath them roll'd, like tempests black,
    The num'rous sons of blood;
Like lions' whelps, roaring abroad,
    Seeking their nightly food.   20

Down Bleron's hills they dreadful rush,
    Their cry ascends the clouds;
The trampling horse, and clanging arms
    Like rushing mighty floods!

Their wives and children, weeping loud,
    Follow in wild array,
Howling like ghosts, furious as wolves
    In the bleak wintry day.

'Pull down the tyrant to the dust,
    'Let Gwin be humbled,'   30
They cry; 'and let ten thousand lives
    'Pay for the tyrant's head.'

From tow'r to tow'r the watchmen cry,
  'O Gwin, the son of Nore,
'Arouse thyself! the nations black,
  'Like clouds, come rolling o'er!'

Gwin rear'd his shield, his palace shakes,
  His chiefs come rushing round;
Each, like an awful thunder cloud,
  With voice of solemn sound.   40

Like reared stones around a grave
  They stand around the King;
Then suddenly each seiz'd his spear,
  And clashing steel does ring.

The husbandman does leave his plow,
  To wade thro' fields of gore;
The merchant binds his brows in steel,
  And leaves the trading shore:

The shepherd leaves his mellow pipe,
  And sounds the trumpet shrill;   50
The workman throws his hammer down
  To heave the bloody bill.

Like the tall ghost of Barraton,
  Who sports in stormy sky,
Gwin leads his host as black as night,
  When pestilence does fly.

With horses and with chariots –
  And all his spearmen bold,
March to the sound of mournful song,
  Like clouds around him roll'd.   60

Gwin lifts his hand – the nations halt;
  'Prepare for war,' he cries –
Gordred appears! – his frowning brow
  Troubles our northern skies.

The armies stand, like balances
    Held in th' Almighty's hand; –
'Gwin, thou hast fill'd thy measure up,
    'Thou'rt swept from out the land.'

And now the raging armies rush'd,
    Like warring mighty seas;   70
The Heav'ns are shook with roaring war,
    The dust ascends the skies!

Earth smokes with blood, and groans, and shakes,
    To drink her children's gore,
A sea of blood; nor can the eye
    See to the trembling shore!

And on the verge of this wild sea
    Famine and death doth cry;
The cries of women and of babes.
    Over the field doth fly.   80

The King is seen raging afar;
    With all his men of might;
Like blazing comets, scattering death
    Thro' the red fev'rous night.

Beneath his arm like sheep they die,
    And groan upon the plain;
The battle faints, and bloody men
    Fight upon hills of slain.

Now death is sick, and riven men
    Labour and toil for life;   90
Steed rolls on steed, and shield on shield,
    Sunk in this sea of strife!

The god of war is drunk with blood,
    The earth doth faint and fail;
The stench of blood makes sick the heav'ns;
    Ghosts glut the throat of hell!

O what have Kings to answer for,
  Before that awful throne!
When thousand deaths for vengeance cry,
  And ghosts accusing groan!   100

Like blazing comets in the sky,
  That shake the stars of light,
Which drop like fruit unto the earth,
  Thro' the fierce burning night;

Like these did Gwin and Gordred meet,
  And the first blow decides;
Down from the brow unto the breast
  Gordred his head divides!

Gwin fell; the Sons of Norway fled,
  All that remain'd alive;   110
The rest did fill the vale of death,
  For them the eagles strive.

The river Dorman roll'd their blood
  Into the northern sea;
Who mourn'd his sons, and overwhelm'd
  The pleasant south country.

AN IMITATION OF SPEN[S]ER

Golden Apollo, that thro' heaven wide
  Scatter'st the rays of light, and truth's beams!
In lucent words my darkling verses dight,
  And wash my earthy mind in thy clear streams,
  That wisdom may descend in fairy dreams:
All while the jocund hours in thy train
Scatter their fancies at thy poet's feet;
  And when thou yields to night thy wide domain,
Let rays of truth enlight his sleeping brain.

For brutish Pan in vain might thee assay   10
  With tinkling sounds to dash thy nervous verse,
Sound without sense; yet in his rude affray,

(For ignorance is Folly's leesing nurse,
    And love of Folly needs none other curse;)
Midas the praise hath gain'd of lengthen'd eares,
    For which himself might deem him ne'er the worse
    To sit in council with his modern peers,
And judge of tinkling rhimes, and elegances terse.

And thou, Mercurius, that with winged brow
    Dost mount aloft into the yielding sky,   20
And thro' Heav'n's halls thy airy flight dost throw,
Entering with holy feet to where on high
Jove weighs the counsel of futurity;
    Then, laden with eternal fate, dost go
Down, like a falling star, from autumn sky,
And o'er the surface of the silent deep dost fly.

If thou arrivest at the sandy shore,
Where nought but envious hissing adders dwell,
    Thy golden rod, thrown on the dusty floor,
Can charm to harmony with potent spell;   30
Such is sweet Eloquence, that does dispel
    Envy and Hate, that thirst for human gore:
And cause in sweet society to dwell
Vile savage minds that lurk in lonely cell.

O Mercury, assist my lab'ring sense,
That round the circle of the world wou'd fly!
    As the wing'd eagle scorns the tow'ry fence
Of Alpine hills round his high aery,
And searches thro' the corners of the sky,
    Sports in the clouds to hear the thunder's sound,   40
And see the winged lightnings as they fly,
    Then, bosom'd in an amber cloud, around
Plumes his wide wings, and seeks Sol's palace high.

And thou, O warrior maid, invincible,
Arm'd with the terrors of Almighty Jove!
    Pallas, Minerva, maiden terrible,
Lov'st thou to walk the peaceful solemn grove,

In solemn gloom of branches interwove?
Or bear'st thy Egis o'er the burning field,
    Where, like the sea, the waves of battle move?   50
Or have thy soft piteous eyes beheld
    The weary wanderer thro' the desert rove?
Or does th' afflicted man thy heav'nly bosom move?

BLIND-MAN'S BUFF

When silver Snow decks Susan's cloaths,
And jewel hangs at th' shepherd's nose,
The blushing bank is all my care,
With hearth so red, and walls so fair;
'Heap the sea-coal; come, heap it higher,
'The oaken log lay on the fire:'
The well-wash'd stools, a circling row,
With lad and lass, how fair the show!
The merry can of nut-brown ale,
The laughing jest, the love-sick tale,   10
'Till tir'd of chat, the game begins,
The lasses prick the lads with pins;
Roger from Dolly twitch'd the stool,
She falling, kiss'd the ground, poor fool!
She blush'd so red, with side-long glance
At hob-nail Dick, who griev'd the chance.
But now for Blind-man's Buff they call;
Of each incumbrance clear the hall –
Jenny her silken 'kerchief folds,
And blear-ey'd Will the black lot holds;   20
Now laughing, stops, with 'Silence! hush!'
And Peggy Pout gives Sam a push. –
The Blind-man's arms, extended wide,
Sam slips between; – 'O woe betide
Thee, clumsy Will!' – but titt'ring Kate
Is pen'd up in the corner strait!
And now Will's eyes beheld the play,
He thought his face was t'other way. –

'Now, Kitty, now; what chance hast thou,
'Roger so near thee, Trips; I vow![']
She catches him – then Roger ties   30
His own head up – but not his eyes;
For thro' the slender cloth he sees,
And runs at Sam, who slips with ease
His clumsy hold; and, dodging round,
Sukey is tumbled on the ground! –
'See what it is to play unfair!
'Where cheating is, there's mischief there.'
But Roger still pursues the chace, –
'He sees! he sees!' cries softly Grace;   40
'O Roger, thou, unskill'd in art,
'Must, surer bound, go thro' thy part!'
Now Kitty, pert, repeats the rhymes,
And Roger turns him round three times;
Then pauses ere he starts – but Dick
Was mischief bent upon a trick:
Down on his hands and knees he lay,
Directly in the Blind-man's way –
Then cries out, 'Hem!' Hodge heard, and ran
With hood-wink'd chance – sure of his man;   50
But down he came. – Alas, how frail
Our best of hopes, how soon they fail!
With crimson drops he stains the ground,
Confusion startles all around!
Poor piteous Dick supports his head,
And fain would cure the hurt he made;
But Kitty hasted with a key,
And down his back they strait convey
The cold relief – the blood is stay'd,
And Hodge again holds up his head.   60
Such are the fortunes of the game,
And those who play should stop the same
By wholesome laws; such as all those
Who on the blinded man impose,
Stand in his stead; as long a-gone
When men were first a nation grown;

Lawless they liv'd – till wantonness
And liberty began t' increase;
And one man lay in another's way,
Then laws were made to keep fair play.   70

King Edward the Third

PERSONS
King Edward   Lord Audley
The Black Prince   Lord Percy
Queen Philippa   Bishop
Duke of Clarence   William, Dagworth's Man
Sir John Chandos   Peter Blunt, a common Soldier
Sir Thomas Dagworth
Sir Walter Manny

SCENE [I]

The Coast of France, King Edward and Nobles.
The Army.

KING: O thou, to whose fury the nations are
  But as dust! maintain thy servant's right.
  Without thine aid, the twisted mail, and spear,
  And forged helm, and shield of seven times beaten
    brass,
  Are idle trophies of the vanquisher.
  When confusion rages, when the field is in a flame,
  When the cries of blood tear horror from heav'n,
  And yelling death runs up and down the ranks,
  Let Liberty, the charter'd right of Englishmen,
  Won by our fathers in many a glorious field,   10
  Enerve my soldiers; let Liberty
  Blaze in each countenance, and fire the battle.
  The enemy fight in chains, invisible chains, but
    heavy;

Their minds are fetter'd; then how can they be free,
While, like the mounting flame,
We spring to battle o'er the floods of death?
And these fair youths, the flow'r of England,
Vent'ring their lives in my most righteous cause,
O sheathe their hearts with triple steel, that they
May emulate their fathers' virtues.   20
And thou, my son, be strong; thou fightest for a
    crown
That death can never ravish from thy brow,
A crown of glory: but from thy very dust
Shall beam a radiance, to fire the breasts
Of youth unborn! Our names are written equal
In fame's wide trophied hall; 'tis ours to gild
The letters, and to make them shine with gold
That never tarnishes: whether Third Edward,
Or the Prince of Wales, or Montacute, or Mortimer,
Or ev'n the least by birth, shall gain the brightest
    fame,   30
Is in his hand to whom all men are equal.
The world of men are like the num'rous stars,
That beam and twinkle in the depth of night,
Each clad in glory according to his sphere; –
But we, that wander from our native seats,
And beam forth lustre on a darkling world,
Grow larger as we advance! and some perhaps
The most obscure at home, that scarce were seen
To twinkle in their sphere, may so advance,
That the astonish'd world, with up-turn'd eyes,   40
Regardless of the moon, and those that once were
    bright,
Stand only for to gaze upon their splendor!
He here knights the Prince, and other young Nobles.

Now let us take a just revenge for those
Brave Lords, who fell beneath the bloody axe
At Paris. Thanks, noble Harcourt, for 'twas
By your advice we landed here in Brittany –

A country not yet sown with destruction,
And where the fiery whirlwind of swift war
Has not yet swept its desolating wing. –
Into three parties we divide by day,   50
And separate march, but join again at night:
Each knows his rank, and Heav'n marshal all.
Exeunt.

SCENE [2]

English Court; Lionel, Duke of Clarence; Queen Philippa,
Lords, Bishop, &c.

CLARENCE: My Lords, I have, by the advice of her
  Whom I am doubly bound to obey, my Parent
  And my Sovereign, call'd you together.
  My task is great, my burden heavier than
  My unfledg'd years;
  Yet, with your kind assistance, Lords, I hope
  England shall dwell in peace; that while my father
  Toils in his wars, and turns his eyes on this
  His native shore, and sees commerce fly round
  With his white wings, and sees his golden London,   10
  And her silver Thames, throng'd with shining spires
  And corded ships; her merchants buzzing round
  Like summer bees, and all the golden cities
  In his land, overflowing with honey,
  Glory may not be dimm'd with clouds of care.
  Say, Lords, should not our thoughts be first to
    commerce?
  My Lord Bishop, you would recommend us
    agriculture?
BISHOP: Sweet Prince! the arts of peace are great,
  And no less glorious than those of war,
  Perhaps more glorious in the ph[i]losophic mind.   20
  When I sit at my home, a private man,
  My thoughts are on my gardens, and my fields,
  How to employ the hand that lacketh bread.
  If Industry is in my diocese,

Religion will flourish; each man's heart
Is cultivated, and will bring forth fruit:
This is my private duty and my pleasure.
But as I sit in council with my prince,
My thoughts take in the gen'ral good of the whole,
And England is the land favour'd by Commerce;   30
For Commerce, tho' the child of Agriculture,
Fosters his parent, who else must sweat and toil,
And gain but scanty fare. Then, my dear Lord,
Be England's trade our care; and we, as tradesmen,
Looking to the gain of this our native land.

CLAR: Oh my good Lord, true wisdom drops like honey
From your tongue, as from a worship'd oak!
Forgive, my Lords, my talkative youth, that speaks
Not merely what my narrow observation has
Pick'd up, but what I have concluded from your
    lessons: 40
Now, by the Queen's advice, I ask your leave
To dine to-morrow with the Mayor of London:
If I obtain your leave, I have another boon
To ask, which is, the favour of your company;
I fear Lord Percy will not give me leave.

PERCY: Dear Sir, a prince should always keep his state,
And grant his favours with a sparing hand,
Or they are never rightly valued.
These are my thoughts, yet it were best to go;
But keep a proper dignity, for now   50
You represent the sacred person of
Your father; 'tis with princes as 'tis with the sun,
If not sometimes o'er-clouded, we grow weary
Of his officious glory.

CLAR: Then you will give me leave to shine sometimes,
My Lord?

LORD: Thou hast a gallant spirit, which I fear
Will be imposed on by the closer sort! [Aside.

CLAR: Well, I'll endeavour to take
Lord Percy's advice; I have been used so much   60
To dignity, that I'm sick on't.

QUEEN PHIL: Fie, Fie, Lord Clarence; you proceed not
    to business,
  But speak of your own pleasures.
  I hope their Lordships will excuse your giddiness.
CLAR: My Lords, the French have fitted out many
  Small ships of war, that, like to ravening wolves,
  Infest our English seas, devouring all
  Our burden'd vessels, spoiling our naval flocks.
  The merchants do complain, and beg our aid.
PERCY: The merchants are rich enough;   70
  Can they not help themselves?
BISH: They can, and may; but how to gain their will,
  Requires our countenance and help.
PERCY: When that they find they must, my Lord, they
    will:
  Let them but suffer awhile, and you shall see
  They will bestir themselves.
BISH: Lord Percy cannot mean that we should suffer
  This disgrace; if so, we are not sovereigns
  Of the sea; our right, that Heaven gave
  To England, when at the birth of nature   80
  She was seated in the deep, the Ocean ceas'd
  His mighty roar; and, fawning, play'd around
  Her snowy feet, and own'd his awful Queen.
  Lord Percy, if the heart is sick, the head
  Must be aggriev'd; if but one member suffer,
  The heart doth fail. You say, my Lord, the merchants
  Can, if they will, defend themselves against
  These rovers: this is a noble scheme,
  Worthy the brave Lord Percy, and as worthy
  His generous aid to put it into practice.   90
PERCY: Lord Bishop, what was rash in me, is wise
  In you; I dare not own the plan. 'Tis not
  Mine. Yet will I, if you please,
  Quickly to the Lord Mayor, and work him onward
  To this most glorious voyage, on which cast
  I'll set my whole estate.
  But we will bring these Gallic rovers under.

QUEEN PHIL: Thanks, brave Lord Percy; you have the
 thanks
Of England's Queen, and will, ere long, of England.
      Exeunt.

SCENE [3]

At Cressey. Sir Thomas Dagworth and Lord Audley, meeting.

AUD: Good morrow, brave Sir Thomas; the bright
 morn
 Smiles on our army, and the gallant sun
 Springs from the hills like a young hero
 Into the battle, shaking his golden locks
 Exultingly; this is a promising day.
DAGW: Why, my Lord Audley, I don't know.
 Give me your hand, and now I'll tell you what
 I think you do not know – Edward's afraid of Philip.
AUD: Ha, Ha, Sir Thomas! you but joke;
 Did you eer see him fear? At Blanchetaque,   10
 When almost singly he drove six thousand
 French from the ford, did he fear then?
DAGW: Yes, fear; that made him fight so.
AUD: By the same reason I might say, 'tis fear
 That makes you fight.
DAGW: Mayhap you may; look upon Edward's face –
 No one can say he fears. But when he turns
 His back, then I will say it to his face,
 He is afraid; he makes us all afraid.
 I cannot bear the enemy at my back.   20
 Now here we are at Cressy; where, to-morrow,
 To-morrow we shall know. I say, Lord Audley,
 That Edward runs away from Philip.
AUD: Perhaps you think the Prince too is afraid?
DAGW: No; God forbid! I'm sure he is not –
 He is a young lion. O I have seen him fight,
 And give command, and lightning has flashed
 From his eyes across the field; I have seen him

Shake hands with death, and strike a bargain for
The enemy; he has danc'd in the field   30
Of battle, like the youth at morrice play.
I'm sure he's not afraid, nor Warwick, nor none,
None of us but me; and I am very much afraid.
AUD: Are you afraid too, Sir Thomas?
  I believe that as much as I believe
  The King's afraid; but what are you afraid of?
DAGW: Of having my back laid open; we turn
  Our backs to the fire, till we shall burn our skirts.
AUD: And this, Sir Thomas, you call fear? Your fear
  Is of a different kind then from the King's;   40
  He fears to turn his face, and you to turn your back. –
  I do not think, Sir Thomas, you know what fear is.
              Enter Sir John Chandos.

CHAND: Good morrow, Generals; I give you joy;
  Welcome to the fields of Cressy. Here we stop,
  And wait for Philip.
DAGW: I hope so.
AUD: There, Sir Thomas; do you call that fear?
DAGW: I don't know; perhaps he takes it by fits.
  Why, noble Chandos, look you here –
  One rotten sheep spoils the whole flock;   50
  And if the bell-weather is tainted, I wish
  The Prince may not catch the distemper too.
CHAND: Distemper, Sir Thomas! what distemper?
  I have not heard.
DAGW: Why, Chandos, you are a wise man,
  I know you understand me; a distemper
  The King caught here in France of running away.
AUD: Sir Thomas, you say, you have caught it too.
DAGW: And so will the whole army; 'tis very catching,
  For when the coward runs, the brave man totters.   60
  Perhaps the air of the country is the cause. –
  I feel it coming upon me, so I strive against it;
  You yet are whole, but after a few more
  Retreats, we all shall know how to retreat

Better than fight. – To be plain, I think retreating
Too often, takes away a soldier's courage.

CHAND: Here comes the King himself; tell him your
thoughts
Plainly, Sir Thomas.

DAGW: I've told him before, but his disorder
Makes him deaf.   70

Enter King Edward and Black Prince.

KING: Good morrow, Generals; when English courage
fails,
Down goes our right to France;
But we are conquerors every where; nothing
Can stand our soldiers; each man is worthy
Of a triumph. Such an army of heroes
Ne'er shouted to the Heav'ns, nor shook the field.
Edward, my son, thou art
Most happy, having such command; the man
Were base who were not fir'd to deeds
Above heroic, having such examples.   80

PRINCE: Sire! with respect and deference I look
Upon such noble souls, and wish myself
Worthy the high command that Heaven and you
Have given me. When I have seen the field glow,
And in each countenance the soul of war
Curb'd by the manliest reason, I have been wing'd
With certain victory; and 'tis my boast,
And shall be still my glory. I was inspir'd
By these brave troops.

DAGW: Your Grace had better make   90
Them all Generals.

KING: Sir Thomas Dagworth, you must have your joke,
And shall, while you can fight as you did at
The Ford.

DAGW: I have a small petition to your Majesty.

KING: What can Sir Thomas Dagworth ask, that Edward
Can refuse?

DAGW: I hope your Majesty cannot refuse so great

A trifle: I've gilt your cause with my best blood,
And would again, were I not forbid   100
By him whom I am bound to obey: my hands
Are tied up, my courage shrunk and wither'd,
My sinews slacken'd, and my voice scarce heard;
Therefore I beg I may return to England.

KING: I know not what you could have ask'd, Sir
    Thomas,
That I would not have sooner parted with
Than such a soldier as you have been, and such a
    friend;
Nay, I will know the most remote particulars
Of this your strange petition; that, if I can,
I still may keep you here.   110

DAGW: Here on the fields of Cressy we are settled,
'Till Philip springs the tim'rous covey again.
The Wolf is hunted down by causeless fear;
The Lion flees, and fear usurps his heart;
Startled, astonish'd at the clam'rous Cock;
The Eagle, that doth gaze upon the sun,
Fears the small fire that plays about the fen;
If, at this moment of their idle fear,
The Dog doth seize the Wolf, the Forester the Lion,
The Negro in the crevice of the rock,   120
Doth seize the soaring Eagle; undone by flight,
They tame submit; such the effect flight has
On noble souls. Now hear its opposite:
The tim'rous Stag starts from the thicket wild,
The fearful Crane springs from the splashy fen,
The shining Snake glides o'er the bending grass,
The Stag turns head! and bays the crying Hounds;
The Crane o'ertaken, sighteth with the Hawk;
The Snake doth turn, and bite the padding foot;
And, if your Majesty's afraid of Philip,   130
You are more like a Lion than a Crane:
Therefore I beg I may return to England.

KING: Sir Thomas, now I understand your mirth,
    Which often plays with Wisdom for its pastime,

And brings good counsel from the breast of laughter,
I hope you'll stay, and see us fight this battle,
And reap rich harvest in the fields of Cressy;
Then go to England, tell them how we fight,
And set all hearts on fire to be with us.
Philip is plum'd, and thinks we flee from him,   140
Else he would never dare to attack us. Now,
Now the quarry's set! and Death doth sport
In the bright sunshine of this fatal day.

DAGW: Now my heart dances, and I am as light
As the young bridegroom going to be married.
Now must I to my soldiers, get them ready,
Furbish our armours bright, new plume our helms,
And we will sing, like the young housewives busied
In the dairy; my feet are wing'd, but not
For flight, an please your grace.   150

KING: If all my soldiers are as pleas'd as you,
'Twill be a gallant thing to fight or die;
Then I can never be afraid of Philip.

DAGW: A raw-bon'd fellow t'other day pass'd by me;
I told him to put off his hungry looks –
He answer'd me, 'I hunger for another battle.'
I saw a little Welchman with a fiery face;
I told him he look'd like a candle half
Burn'd out; he answer'd, he was 'pig enough
'To light another pattle.' Last night, beneath   160
The moon I walk'd abroad, when all had pitch'd
Their tents, and all were still,
I heard a blooming youth singing a song
He had compos'd, and at each pause he wip'd
His dropping eyes. The ditty was, 'if he
'Return'd victorious, he should wed a maiden
'Fairer than snow, and rich as midsummer.'
Another wept, and wish'd health to his father.
I chid them both, but gave them noble hopes.
These are the minds that glory in the battle,   170
And leap and dance to hear the trumpet sound.

KING: Sir Thomas Dagworth, be thou near our person;

Thy heart is richer than the vales of France:
I will not part with such a man as thee.
If Philip came arm'd in the ribs of death,
And shook his mortal dart against my head,
Thoud'st laugh his fury into nerveless shame!
Go now, for thou art suited to the work,
Throughout the camp; enflame the timorous,
Blow up the sluggish into ardour, and   180
Confirm the strong with strength, the weak inspire,
And wing their brows with hope and expectation:
Then to our tent return, and meet to council.

Exit Dagworth.

CHAND: That man's a hero in his closet, and more
   A hero to the servants of his house
   Than to the gaping world; he carries windows
   In that enlarged breast of his, that all
   May see what's done within.
PRINCE: He is a genuine Englishman, my Chandos,
   And hath the spirit of Liberty within him.   190
   Forgive my prejudice, Sir John; I think
   My Englishmen the bravest people on
   The face of the earth.
CHAND: Courage, my Lord, proceeds from self-
      dependence;
   Teach man to think he's a free agent,
   Give but a slave his liberty, he'll shake
   Off sloth, and build himself a hut, and hedge
   A spot of ground; this he'll defend; 'tis his
   By right of nature: thus set in action,
   He will still move onward to plan conveniences,   200
   'Till glory fires his breast to enlarge his castle,
   While the poor slave drudges all day, in hope
   To rest at night.
KING: O Liberty, how glorious art thou!
   I see thee hov'ring o'er my army, with
   Thy wide-stretch'd plumes; I see thee
   Lead them on to battle;

I see thee blow thy golden trumpet, while
Thy sons shout the strong shout of victory!
O noble Chandos! think thyself a gardener,   210
My son a vine, which I commit unto
Thy care; prune all extravagant shoots, and guide
Th' ambitious tendrils in the paths of wisdom;
Water him with thy advice, and Heav'n
Rain fresh'ning dew upon his branches. And,
O Edward, my dear son! learn to think lowly of
Thyself, as we may all each prefer other –
'Tis the best policy, and 'tis our duty.
                Exit King Edward.

PRINCE: And may our duty, Chandos, be our pleasure –
Now we are alone, Sir John, I will unburden,   220
And breathe my hopes into the burning air,
Where thousand deaths are posting up and down,
Commission'd to this fatal field of Cressy;
Methinks I see them arm my gallant soldiers,
And gird the sword upon each thigh, and fit
Each shining helm, and string each stubborn bow,
And dance to the neighing of our steeds.
Methinks the shout begins, the battle burns;
Methinks I see them perch on English crests,
And roar the wild flame of fierce war, upon   230
The thronged enemy! In truth, I am too full;
It is my sin to love the noise of war.
Chandos, thou seest my weakness; strong nature
Will bend or break us; my blood, like a springtide,
Does rise so high, to overflow all bounds
Of moderation; while Reason, in his
Frail bark, can see no shore or bound for vast
Ambition. Come, take the helm, my Chandos,
That my full-blown sails overset me not
In the wild tempest; condemn my 'ventrous youth,   240
That plays with danger, as the innocent child,
Unthinking, plays upon the viper's den:
I am a coward, in my reason, Chandos.

CHAND: You are a man, my prince, and a brave man,
    If I can judge of actions; but your heat
    Is the effect of youth, and want of use;
    Use makes the armed field and noisy war
    Pass over as a summer cloud, unregarded,
    Or but expected as a thing of course.
    Age is contemplative; each rolling year   250
    Brings forth fruit to the mind's treasure-house;
    While vacant youth doth crave and seek about
    Within itself, and findeth discontent:
    Then, tir'd of thought, impatient takes the wing,
    Seizes the fruits of time, attacks experience,
    Roams round vast Nature's forest, where no bounds
    Are set, the swiftest may have room, the strongest
    Find prey; till tir'd at length, sated and tired
    With the changing sameness, old variety,
    We sit us down, and view our former joys   260
    With distaste and dislike.
PRINCE: Then if we must tug for experience,
    Let us not fear to beat round Nature's wilds,
    And rouze the strongest prey; then if we fall,
    We fall with glory; I know the wolf
    Is dangerous to fight, not good for food,
    Nor is the hide a comely vestment; so
    We have our battle for our pains. I know
    That youth has need of age to point fit prey,
    And oft the stander-by shall steal the fruit   270
    Of th' other's labour. This is philosophy;
    These are the tricks of the world; but the pure soul
    Shall mount on native wings, disdaining
    Little sport, and cut a path into the heaven of glory,
    Leaving a track of light for men to wonder at.
    I'm glad my father does not hear me talk;
    You can find friendly excuses for me, Chandos;
    But do you not think, Sir John, that if it please
    Th' Almighty to stretch out my span of life,
    I shall with pleasure view a glorious action,   280
    Which my youth master'd.

CHAND: Considerate age, my Lord, views motives,
 And not acts; when neither warbling voice,
 Nor trilling pipe is heard, nor pleasure sits
 With trembling age; the voice of Conscience then,
 Sweeter than music in a summer's eve,
 Shall warble round the snowy head, and keep
 Sweet symphony to feather'd angels, sitting
 As guardians round your chair; then shall the pulse
 Beat slow, and taste, and touch, and sight, and sound,
  and smell,   290
 That sing and dance round Reason's fine-wrought
  throne,
 Shall flee away, and leave him all forlorn;
 Yet not forlorn if Conscience is his friend.
       Exeunt.

SCENE [4]

In Sir Thomas Dagworth's Tent. Dagworth and William
his Man.

DAGW: Bring hither my armour, William;
 Ambition is the growth of ev'ry clime.
WILL: Does it grow in England, Sir?
DAGW: Aye, it grows most in lands most cultivated.
WILL: Then it grows most in France; the vines here
 Are finer than any we have in England.
DAGW: Aye, but the oaks are not.
WILL: What is the tree you mentioned? I don't think
 I ever saw it.
DAGW: Ambition.   10
WILL: Is it a little creeping root that grows in ditches?
DAGW: Thou dost not understand me, William.
 It is a root that grows in every breast;
 Ambition is the desire or passion that one man
 Has to get before another, in any pursuit after glory;
 But I don't think you have any of it.
WILL: Yes, I have; I have a great ambition to know
 every thing, Sir.

DAGW: But when our first ideas are wrong, what follows must all be wrong of course; 'tis best to know a little, and to know that little aright.   20

WILL: Then, Sir, I should be glad to know if it was not ambition that brought over our King to France to fight for his right?

DAGW: Tho' the knowledge of that will not profit thee much, yet I will tell you that it was ambition.

WILL: Then if ambition is a sin, we are all guilty in coming with him, and in fighting for him.

DAGW: Now, William, thou dost thrust the question home; but I must tell you, that guilt being an act of the   30
mind, none are guilty but those whose minds are prompted by that same ambition.

WILL: Now I always thought, that a man might be guilty of doing wrong, without knowing it was wrong.

DAGW: Thou art a natural philosopher, and knowest truth by instinct; while reason runs aground, as we have run our argument. Only remember, William, all have it in their power to know the motives of their own actions, and 'tis a sin to act without some reason.

WILL: And whoever acts without reason, may do a great   40
deal of harm without knowing it.

DAGW: Thou art an endless moralist.

WILL: Now there's a story come into my head, that I will tell your honour, if you'll give me leave.

DAGW: No, William, save it till another time; this is no time for storytelling; but here comes one who is as entertaining as a good story.

Enter Peter Blunt.

PETER: Yonder's a musician going to play before the King; it's a new song about the French and English, and the Prince has made the minstrel a 'squire, and given him I   50
don't know what, and I can't tell whether he don't mention us all one by one; and he is to write another about all us that are to die, that we may be remembered in Old England, for all our blood and bones are in France; and

a great deal more that we shall all hear by and by; and I
came to tell your honour, because you love to hear war-
songs.

DAGW: And who is this minstrel, Peter, do'st know?

PETER: O aye, I forgot to tell that; he has got the same
name as Sir John Chandos, that the prince is always   60
with – the wise man, that knows us all as well as your
honour, only e'nt so good natur'd.

DAGW: I thank you, Peter, for your information, but not
for your compliment, which is not true; there's as much
difference between him and me, as between glittering
sand and fruitful mold; or shining glass and a wrought
diamond, set in rich gold, and fitted to the finger of an
emperor: such is that worthy Chandos.

PETER: I know your honour does not think any thing of
yourself, but every body else does.   70

DAGW: Go, Peter, get you gone; flattery is delicious, even
from the lips of a babbler.

Exit Peter.

WILL: I never flatter your honour.

DAGW: I don't know that.

WILL: Why you know, Sir, when we were in England, at
the tournament at Windsor, and the Earl of Warwick
was tumbled over, you ask'd me if he did not look well
when he fell? and I said, No, he look'd very foolish; and
you was very angry with me for not flattering you.

DAGW: You mean that I was angry with you for not   80
flattering the Earl of Warwick.

Exeunt.

SCENE [5]

*Sir Thomas Dagworth's Tent. Sir Thomas Dagworth – to
him.*

Enter Sir Walter Manny.

SIR WALTER: Sir Thomas Dagworth, I have been
weeping
Over the men that are to die to-day.

DAGW: Why, brave Sir Walter, you or I may fall.
SIR WALTER: I know this breathing flesh must lie and
    rot,
  Cover'd with silence and forgetfulness. –
  Death wons in cities' smoke, and in still night,
  When men sleep in their beds, walketh about!
  How many in walled cities lie and groan,
  Turning themselves upon their beds,
  Talking with death, answering his hard demands!   10
  How many walk in darkness, terrors are round
  The curtains of their beds, destruction is
  Ready at the door! How many sleep
  In earth, cover'd with stones and deathy dust,
  Resting in quietness, whose spirits walk
  Upon the clouds of heaven, to die no more!
  Yet death is terrible, tho' borne on angels' wings!
  How terrible then is the field of death,
  Where he doth rend the vault of heaven,
  And shake the gates of hell!   20
  O Dagworth, France is sick! the very sky,
  Tho' sunshine light it, seems to me as pale
  As the pale fainting man on his death-bed,
  Whose face is shewn by light of sickly taper!
  It makes me sad and sick at very heart,
  Thousands must fall to-day!
DAGW: Thousands of souls must leave this prison
    house,
  To be exalted to those heavenly fields,
  Where songs of triumph, palms of victory,
  Where peace, and joy, and love, and calm content,   30
  Sit singing in the azure clouds, and strew
  Flowers of heaven's growth over the banquet-table:
  Bind ardent Hope upon your feet like shoes,
  Put on the robe of preparation,
  The table is prepar'd in shining heaven,
  The flowers of immortality are blown;
  Let those that fight, fight in good stedfastness,
  And those that fall shall rise in victory.

SIR WALTER: I've often seen the burning field of war,
  And often heard the dismal clang of arms;   40
  But never, till this fatal day of Cressy,
  Has my soul fainted with these views of death!
  I seem to be in one great charnel-house,
  And seem to scent the rotten carcases!
  I seem to hear the dismal yells of death,
  While the black gore drops from his horrid jaws:
  Yet I not fear the monster in his pride. –
  But O the souls that are to die to-day!
DAGW: Stop, brave Sir Walter; let me drop a tear,
  Then let the clarion of war begin;   50
  I'll fight and weep, 'tis in my country's cause;
  I'll weep and shout for glorious liberty.
  Grim war shall laugh and shout, decked in tears,
  And blood shall flow like streams across the
    meadows,
  That murmur down their pebbly channels, and
  Spend their sweet lives to do their country service:
  Then shall England's verdure shoot, her fields shall
    smile,
  Her ships shall sing across the foaming sea,
  Her mariners shall use the flute and viol,
  And rattling guns, and black and dreary war,   60
  Shall be no more.
SIR WALTER: Well; let the trumpet sound, and the
    drum beat;
  Let war stain the blue heavens with bloody banners,
  I'll draw my sword, nor ever sheath it up,
  'Till England blow the trump of victory,
  Or I lay stretch'd upon the field of death!
                Exeunt.

SCENE [6]

In the Camp. Several of the Warriors met at the King's Tent with a Minstrel, who sings the following Song:

O sons of Trojan Brutus, cloath'd in war,
Whose voices are the thunder of the field,
Rolling dark clouds o'er France, muffling the sun
In sickly darkness like a dim eclipse,
Threatening as the red brow of storms, as fire
Burning up nations in your wrath and fury!

Your ancestors came from the fires of Troy,
(Like lions rouz'd by light'ning from their dens,
Whose eyes do glare against the stormy fires)
Heated with war, fill'd with the blood of Greeks,   10
With helmets hewn, and shields covered with gore,
In navies black, broken with wind and tide!

They landed in firm array upon the rocks
Of Albion; they kiss'd the rocky shore;
'Be thou our mother, and our nurse,' they said;
'Our children's mother, and thou shalt be our grave;
'The sepulchre of ancient Troy, from whence
'Shall rise cities, and thrones, and arms, and awful
pow'rs.'

Our fathers swarm from the ships. Giant voices
Are heard from the hills, the enormous sons   20
Of Ocean run from rocks and caves: wild men,
Naked and roaring like lions, hurling rocks,
And wielding knotty clubs, like oaks entangled
Thick as a forest, ready for the axe.

Our fathers move in firm array to battle,
The savage monsters rush like roaring fire;
Like as a forest roars with crackling flames,
When the red lightning, borne by furious storms,
Lights on some woody shore; the parched heavens
Rain fire into the molten raging sea!   30

The smoaking trees are strewn upon the shore,
Spoil'd of their verdure! O how oft have they
Defy'd the storm that howled o'er their heads!
Our fathers, sweating, lean on their spears, and view
The mighty dead: giant bodies, streaming blood,
Dread visages, frowning in silent death!

Then Brutus spoke, inspir'd; our fathers sit
Attentive on the melancholy shore: –
Hear ye the voice of Brutus – 'The flowing waves
'Of time come rolling o'er my breast,' he said;   40
'And my heart labours with futurity:
'Our sons shall rule the empire of the sea.

'Their mighty wings shall stretch from east to west,
'Their nest is in the sea; but they shall roam
'Like eagles for the prey; nor shall the young
'Crave or be heard; for plenty shall bring forth,
'Cities shall sing, and vales in rich array
'Shall laugh, whose fruitful laps bend down with
     fulness.

'Our sons shall rise from thrones in joy,
'Each one buckling on his armour; Morning   50
'Shall be prevented by their swords gleaming,
'And Evening hear their song of victory!
'Their towers shall be built upon the rocks,
'Their daughters shall sing, surrounded with shining
     spears!

'Liberty shall stand upon the cliffs of Albion,
'Casting her blue eyes over the green ocean;
'Or, tow'ring, stand upon the roaring waves,
'Stretching her mighty spear o'er distant lands;
'While, with her eagle wings, she covereth
'Fair Albion's shore, and all her families '

Dramatic Fragments

PROLOGUE, INTENDED FOR A DRAMATIC
PIECE OF KING EDWARD THE FOURTH

O For a voice like thunder, and a tongue
To drown the throat of war! – When the senses
Are shaken, and the soul is driven to madness,
Who can stand? When the souls of the oppressed
Fight in the troubled air that rages, who can stand?
When the whirlwind of fury comes from the
Throne of God, when the frowns of his countenance
Drive the nations together, who can stand?
When Sin claps his broad wings over the battle,
And sails rejoicing in the flood of Death;   10
When souls are torn to everlasting fire,
And fiends of Hell rejoice upon the slain,
O who can stand? O who hath caused this?
O who can answer at the throne of God?
The Kings and Nobles of the Land have done it!
Hear it not, Heaven, thy Ministers have done it!

PROLOGUE TO KING JOHN

Justice hath heaved a sword to plunge in Albion's breast;
for Albion's sins are crimson dy'd, and the red scourge
follows her desolate sons! Then Patriot rose; full oft did
Patriot rise, when Tyranny hath stain'd fair Albion's
breast with her own children's gore. Round his majestic
feet deep thunders roll; each heart does tremble, and each
knee grows slack. The stars of heaven tremble: the roaring
voice of war, the trumpet, calls to battle! Brother in
brother's blood must bathe, rivers of death! O land, most
hapless! O beauteous island, how forsaken! Weep from thy   10
silver fountains; weep from thy gentle rivers! The angel of
the island weeps! Thy widowed virgins weep beneath thy

shades! Thy aged fathers gird themselves for war! The
sucking infant lives to die in battle; the weeping mother
feeds him for the slaughter! The husbandman doth leave
his bending harvest! Blood cries afar! The land doth sow
itself! The glittering youth of courts must gleam in arms!
The aged senators their ancient swords assume! The
trembling sinews of old age must work the work of death
against their progeny; for Tyranny hath stretch'd his   20
purple arm, and 'blood,' he cries; 'the chariots and the
horses, the noise of shout, and dreadful thunder of the
battle heard afar!' – Beware, O Proud! thou shalt be
humbled; thy cruel brow, thine iron heart is smitten,
though lingering Fate is slow. O yet may Albion smile
again, and stretch her peaceful arms, and raise her
golden head, exultingly! Her citizens shall throng about
her gates, her mariners shall sing upon the sea, and
myriads shall to her temples crowd! Her sons shall joy as
in the morning! Her daughters sing as to the rising year!   30

A WAR SONG TO ENGLISHMEN

Prepare, prepare, the iron helm of war,
Bring forth the lots, cast in the spacious orb;
Th' Angel of Fate turns them with mighty hands,
And casts them out upon the darken'd earth!
      Prepare, prepare.

Prepare your hearts for Death's cold hand! prepare
Your souls for flight, your bodies for the earth!
Prepare your arms for glorious victory!
Prepare your eyes to meet a holy God!
      Prepare, prepare.   10

Whose fatal scroll is that? Methinks 'tis mine!
Why sinks my heart, why faultereth my tongue?
Had I three lives, I'd die in such a cause,
And rise, with ghosts, over the well-fought field.
      Prepare, prepare.

The arrows of Almighty God are drawn!
Angels of Death stand in the low'ring heavens!
Thousands of souls must seek the realms of light,
And walk together on the clouds of heaven!
                    Prepare, prepare.   20

Soldiers, prepare! Our cause is Heaven's cause;
Soldiers, prepare! Be worthy of our cause:
Prepare to meet our fathers in the sky:
Prepare, O troops, that are to fall to-day!
                    Prepare, prepare.

Alfred shall smile, and make his harp rejoice;
The Norman William, and the learned Clerk,
And Lion Heart, and black-brow'd Edward, with
His loyal queen shall rise, and welcome us!
                    Prepare, prepare.   30

Poems Written in a Copy of Poetical Sketches

SONG 1ST BY A SHEPHERD

Welcome stranger to this place,
Where joy doth sit on every bough,
Paleness flies from every face,
We reap not what we do not sow.

Innocence doth like a Rose,
Bloom on every Maidens cheek;
Honor twines around her brows,
The jewel Health adorns her neck.

SONG 2ND BY A YOUNG SHEPHERD

When the trees do laugh with our merry wit,
And the green hill laughs with the noise of it,
When the meadow laughs with lively green,
And the grasshopper laughs in the merry scene;

When the greenwood laughs with the voice of joy,
And the dimpling stream runs laughing by,
When Edessa, and Lyca, and Emilie,
With their sweet round mouths sing Ha, Ha, He.

When the painted birds laugh in the shade
Where our table with cherries and nuts is spread,   10
Come live and be merry and join with me,
To sing the sweet chorus of Ha, Ha, He.

SONG 3RD BY AN OLD SHEPHERD

When silver snow decks Sylvio's cloaths
And jewel hangs at shepherd's nose,
We can abide life's pelting storm
That makes our limbs quake, if our hearts be warm.

Whilst Virtue is our walking staff,
And Truth a lantern to our path;
We can abide life's pelting storm
That makes our limbs quake, if our hearts be warm.

Blow boisterous Wind, stern Winter frown,
Innocence is a Winter's gown;   10
So clad, we'll abide life's pelting storm
That makes our limbs quake, if our hearts be warm.

SONGS FROM
'AN ISLAND IN THE MOON'

From CHAP 3^d

In the Moon as Phebus stood over his oriental Garden-
ing O ay come Ill sing you a song said the Cynic. the
trumpeter shit in his hat said the Epicurean & clapt it on
his head said the Pythagorean
    Ill begin again said the Cynic
Little Phebus came strutting in
With his fat belly & his round chin
What is it you would please to have
Ho Ho
I wont let it go at only so & so   10

*

Then the Cynic sung
Honour & Genius is all I ask
And I ask the Gods no more
   No more   No more⎤ the three Philosophers
   No more   No more⎦ bear Chorus
Here Aradobo suckd his under lip

From CHAP 6

Ah said Sipsop, I only wish Jack [*Hunter*] Tearguts had
had the cutting of Plutarch he understands anatomy
better than any of the Ancients hell plunge his knife up to
the hilt in a single drive and thrust his fist in, and all in the
space of a Quarter of an hour. he does not mind their
crying – tho they cry ever so hell Swear at them & keep

them down with his fist & tell them that hell scrape their
bones if they dont lay still & be quiet – What the devil
should the people in the hospital that have it done for
nothing, make such a piece of work for   10

    Hang that said Suction let us have a Song

    Then [*Sipsop sang*] the Cynic sang

When old corruption first begun
Adornd in yellow vest
He committed on flesh a whoredom
O what a wicked beast

2

From them a callow babe did spring
And old corruption smild
To think his race should never end
For now he had a child   20

3

He calld him Surgery & fed
The babe with his own milk
For flesh & he could neer agree
She would not let him suck

4

And this he always kept in mind
And formd a crooked knife
And ran about with bloody hands
To seek his mothers life

5

And as he ran to seek his mother
He met with a dead woman
He fell in love & married her   30
A deed which is not common

6

She soon grew pregnant & brought forth
Scurvy & spotted fever
The father grind & skipt about
And said I'm made for ever

7

For now I have procurd these imps
Ill try experiments
With that he tied poor scurvy down
& stopt up all its vents   40

8

And when the child began to swell
He shouted out aloud
Ive found the dropsy out & soon
Shall do the world more good

9

He took up fever by the neck
And cut out all its spots
And thro the holes which he had made
He first discovered guts

From CHAP 8

Hear then the pride & knowledge of a Sailor
His sprit sail fore sail main sail & his mizen
A poor frail man god wot I know none frailer
I know no greater sinner than John Taylor

                              *

Phebe drest like beauties Queen
Jellicoe in faint peagreen
Sitting all beneath a grot
Where the little [*lambs do*] lambkins trot

Maidens dancing loves a sporting
All the country folks a courting   10
Susan Johnny Bet & Joe
Lightly tripping on a row

Happy people who can be
In happiness compard with ye
The Pilgrim with his crook & hat
Sees your happiness compleat

CHAP 9

I say this evening [*we'd*] we'll all get drunk. I say dash,
an Anthem an Anthem, said Suction

        Lo the Bat with Leathern wing
        Winking & blinking
        Winking & blinking
        Winking & blinking
        Like Doctor Johnson

Quid----O ho Said Doctor Johnson
        To Scipio Africanus
        If you dont own me a Philosopher   10
        Ill kick your Roman Anus

Suction – A ha To Doctor Johnson
        Said Scipio Africanus
        Lift up my Roman Petticoatt
        And kiss my Roman Anus

        And the Cellar goes down with a Step (Grand
        Chorus

Ho Ho Ho Ho Ho Ho Ho Hooooo my **pooooor** siiides
I I should die if I was to live here said Scopprell Ho Ho Ho
Ho Ho

   1st Vo Want Matches
   2^d Vo Yes Yes Yes   20
   1st Vo Want Matches
   2^d Vo No---------

1st Vo   Want Matches
2^d Vo   Yes Yes Yes
1st Vo   Want Matches
2^d Vo   No----------

Here was Great confusion & disorder Aradobo said that
the boys in the street sing something very pritty & funny
[*about London O no*] about Matches Then Mrs Nanni-
cantipot sung

I cry my matches as far as Guild hall   30
God bless the duke & his aldermen all

    Then sung Scopprell

I ask the Gods no more
    no more no more

    Then Said Suction   come Mr Lawgiver your song and
the Lawgiver sung

As I walkd forth one may morning
To see the fields so pleasant & so gay
O there did I spy a young maiden sweet

Among the Violets that smell so sweet   40
    Smell so sweet
    Smell so sweet
Among the Violets that smell so sweet

    Hang your Violets heres your Rum & water [*sweeter*] O
ay said Tilly Lally. Joe Bradley & I was going along one
day in the Sugar house   Joe Bradley saw   for he had but
one eye   saw a treacle Jar   So he goes of his blind side &
dips his hand up to the shoulder in treacle. here lick lick
lick said he   Ha Ha Ha Ha Ha   For he had but one eye
Ha Ha Ha Ho   then sung Scopprell   50

And I ask the Gods no more
    no more no more
    no more no more

Miss Gittipin said he you sing like a harpsichord. let
your bounty descend to our fair ears and favour us with a
fine song
   then she sung

This frog he would a wooing ride
   Kitty alone   Kitty alone
This frog he would a wooing ride   60
Kitty alone & I
[*This frog*] Sing cock I cary Kitty alone
Kitty alone   Kitty alone
Cock I cary Kitty alone
Kitty alone & I

   Charming truly elegant said Scopprell

And I ask the gods no more

   Hang your Serious Songs, said Sipsop   & he sung as
follows

Fa ra so bo ro   70
   Fa ra bo ra
Sa ba ra ra ba rare roro
Sa ra ra ra bo ro ro ro
Radara
Sarapodo no flo ro

   Hang Italian songs   lets have English said Quid [*Sing a
Mathematical Song Obtuse Angle then he sung*] English
Genius for ever   here I go

Hail Matrimony made of Love
To thy wide gates how great a drove   80
On purpose to be yok'd do come
Widows & maids & Youths also
That lightly trip on beauty's toe
Or sit on beauty's bum

Hail fingerfooted lovely Creatures
The females of our human Natures

Formed to suckle all Mankind
Tis you that come in time of need
Without you we shoud never Breed
Or any Comfort find   90

For if a Damsel's blind or lame
Or Nature's hand has crooked her frame
Or if she's deaf or is wall eyed
Yet if her heart is well inclined
Some tender lover she shall find
That panteth for a Bride

The universal Poultice this
To cure whatever is amiss
In damsel or in Widow gay
It makes them smile it makes them skip   100
Like Birds just cured of the pip
They chirp & hop away

Then come ye Maidens come ye Swains
Come & be eased of all your pains
In Matrimony's Golden cage –

I [*None of*] Go & be hanged said Scopprel how can you
have the face to make game of Matrimony [*What you
skipping flea how dare ye? Ill dash you through your chair
says the Cynic   This Quid* (*cries out Miss Gittipin*) *always
spoils good company in this manner & its a shame*]   110
      Then Quid calld upon Obtuse Angle for a Song & he
wiping his face & looking on the corner of the cieling Sang

To be or not to be
Of great capacity
Like Sir Isaac Newton
Or Locke or Doctor South
Or Sherlock upon death
Id rather be Sutton

For he did build a house
For aged men & youth   120
With walls of brick & stone
He furnished it within
With whatever he could win
And all his own

He drew out of the Stocks
His money in a box
And sent his servant
To Green the Bricklayer
And to the Carpenter
He was so fervent   130

The chimneys were three score
The windows many more
And for convenience
He sinks & gutters made
And all the way he pavd
To hinder pestilence

Was not this a good man
Whose life was but a span
Whose name was Sutton
As Locke or Doctor South   140
Or Sherlock upon Death
Or Sir Isaac Newton

    The Lawgiver was very attentive & begd to have it sung
over again & again till the company were tired & insisted
on the Lawgiver singing a song himself which he readily
complied with

This city & this country has brought forth many mayors
To sit in state & give forth laws out of their old oak
      chairs
With face as brown as any nut with drinking of strong
      ale
Good English hospitality O then it did not fail   150

With scarlet gowns & broad gold lace would make a
    yeoman sweat
With stockings rolld above their knees & shoes as black
    as jet
With eating beef & drinking beer O they were stout and
    hale
Good English hospitality O then it did not fail

Thus sitting at the table wide the Mayor & Aldermen
Were fit to give law to the city each eat as much as ten
The hungry poor enterd the hall to eat good beef & ale
Good English hospitality O then it did not fail

Here they gave a shout & the company broke up

From CHAP 11

Upon a holy thursday their innocent faces clean
The children walking two & two in grey & blue & green
Grey headed beadles walkd before with wands as white
    as snow
Till into the high dome of Pauls they like thames water
    flow

O what a multitude they seemd, these flowers of
    London town
Seated in companies they sit with radiance all their own
The hum of multitudes were there but multitudes of
    lambs
[*And all in order sit waiting the chief chanters commands*]
Thousands of little girls & boys raising their innocent
    hands

[*When the whole multitude of innocents their voices raise*   10
Like angels on the throne of heaven raising the voice of
    praise]
[*Let Cherubim & Seraphim now raise their voices high*]

Then like a mighty wind they raise to heavn the voice of song
Or like harmonious thunderings the seats of heavn among

Beneath them sit the revrend men the guardians of the poor
Then cherish pity lest you drive an angel from your door

    After this they all sat silent for a quarter of an hour [*&
Mrs Sigtagatist*] & Mrs Nannicantipot said it puts me in
Mind of my [*grand*] mothers song

[*The voice/The tongues*] When the tongues of children are
    heard on the green   20
And laughing [*upon*] is heard on the hill
My heart is at rest within my breast
And every thing else is still

Then come home [*children the sun is down*] my children
    the sun is gone down
And the dews of night arise
Come Come leave off play & let us away
Till the morning appears in the skies

No No let us play for it is yet day
And we cannot [*sleep till its dark*] go to sleep
[*The flocks are at play & we cant go away*]   30
Besides in the Sky the little birds fly
And the meadows are coverd with Sheep

Well Well go & play till the light fades away
And then go home to bed
The little ones leaped & shouted & laughd
And all the hills ecchoed

Then [*Miss Gittipin*] [*Tilly Lally sung*] [*Quid*] sung
Quid

O father father where are you going
O do not walk so fast
O speak father speak to your little boy   40
Or else I shall be lost

The night it was dark & no father was there
And the child was wet with dew
The mire was deep & the child did weep
And away the vapour flew

Here nobody could sing any longer, till Tilly Lally
pluckd up a spirit & he sung.

O I say you Joe
Throw us the ball
Ive a good mind to go   50
And leave you all
I never saw saw such a bowler
To bowl the ball in a [*turd*] tansey
And to clean it with my handkercher
Without saying a word

That Bills a foolish fellow
[*To hit me with the bat*]
He has given me a black eye
He does not know how to handle a bat
Any more than a dog or a cat   60
He has knockd down the wicket
And broke the stumps
And runs without shoes to save his pumps

    Here a laugh began and Miss Gittipin sung

Leave O leave [me] to my sorrows
Here Ill sit & fade away
Till Im nothing but a spirit
And I lose this form of clay
Then if chance along this forest
Any walk in pathless ways   70
Thro the gloom he'll see my shadow
Hear my voice upon the Breeze

The Lawgiver all the while sat delighted to see them in
such a serious humour Mr Scopprell said he you must be
acquainted with a great many songs. O dear sir Ho Ho Ho
I am no singer I must beg of one of these tender hearted
ladies to sing for me – they all declined & he was forced to
sing himself

Theres Doctor Clash
And Signior Falalasole   80
O they sweep in the cash
Into their purse hole
Fa me la sol   La me fa Sol

[(*If*) *How many Blackamoors*
Could sing with their thick lips]

Great A little A
Bouncing B
Play away   Play away
Your out of the key
Fa me la sol   La me fa sol   90

Musicians should have
A pair of very good ears
And Long fingers & thumbs
And not like clumsy bears
Fa me la sol   La me fa sol

Gentlemen Gentlemen
Rap Rap Rap
Fiddle Fiddle Fiddle
Clap Clap Clap
Fa me la sol   La me fa sol   100

    Hm said the Lawgiver, funny enough lets have handels
waterpiece then Sipsop sung

A crowned king,
On a white horse sitting
With his trumpets sounding
And Banners flying
Thro the clouds of smoke he makes his way
And the shout of his thousands fills his heart with
    rejoicing & victory
And the shout of his thousands fills his heart with
    rejoicing & victory
Victory Victory – twas William the prince of Orange   110

THERE IS NO NATURAL RELIGION

[a]

The Argument. Man has no notion of moral fitness but from Education. Naturally he is only a natural organ subject to Sense.

I   Man cannot naturally Percieve. but through his natural or bodily organs.

II   Man by his reasoning power. can only compare & judge of what he has already perciev'd.

III   From a perception of only 3 senses or 3 elements none could deduce a fourth or fifth

IV   None could have other than natural or organic thoughts if he had none but organic perceptions

V   Mans desires are limited by his perceptions. none can desire what he has not perciev'd

VI   The desires & perceptions of man untaught by any thing but organs of sense, must be limited to objects of sense.

Conclusion. If it were not for the Poetic or Prophetic character the Philosophic & Experimental would soon be at the ratio of all things, & stand still unable to do other than repeat the same dull round over again

[b]

I   Mans perceptions are not bounded by organs of perception. he percieves more than sense (tho' ever so acute) can discover.

II   Reason or the ratio of all we have already known. is not the same that it shall be when we know more.

[III lacking]

IV   The bounded is loathed by its possessor. The same dull round even of a univer[s]e would soon become a mill with complicated wheels

V   If the many become the same as the few when possess'd, More! More! is the cry of a mistaken soul, less than All cannot satisfy Man.

VI   If any could desire what he is incapable of possessing, despair must be his eternal lot.

VII   The desire of Man being Infinite the possession is Infinite & himself Infinite

Application.   He who sees the Infinite in all things sees God. He who sees the Ratio only sees himself only.

Therefore God becomes as we are, that we may be as he is

ALL RELIGIONS ARE ONE

The Voice of one crying in the Wilderness

The Argument. As the true method of knowledge is experiment the true faculty of knowing must be the faculty which experiences. This faculty I treat of.

PRINCIPLE 1ˢᵗ That the Poetic Genius is the true Man. and that the body or outward form of Man is derived from the Poetic Genius. Likewise that the forms of all things are derived from their Genius, which by the Ancients was call'd an Angel & Spirit & Demon.

PRINCIPLE 2ᵈ As all men are alike in outward form, So (and with the same infinite variety) all are alike in the Poetic Genius

PRINCIPLE 3ᵈ No man can think write or speak from his heart, but he must intend truth. Thus all sects of Philosophy are from the Poetic Genius adapted to the weaknesses of every individual

PRINCIPLE 4 As none by travelling over known lands can find out the unknown. So from already acquired knowledge Man could not acquire more. therefore an universal Poetic Genius exists

PRINCIPLE 5 The Religeons of all Nations are derived from each Nation's different reception of the Poetic Genius which is every where call'd the Spirit of Prophecy.

PRINCIPLE 6 The Jewish & Christian Testaments are An original derivation from the Poetic Genius. this is necessary from the confined nature of bodily sensation

PRINCIPLE 7ᵗʰ As all men are alike (tho' infinitely various) So all Religions & as all similars have one source.

The true Man is the source he being the Poetic Genius

THE BOOK OF THEL

PLATE i

THEL'S MOTTO

Does the Eagle know what is in the pit?
Or wilt thou go ask the Mole:
Can Wisdom be put in a silver rod?
Or Love in a golden bowl?

PLATE I

THEL

I

The daughters of Mne Seraphim led round their sunny
    flocks,
All but the youngest. she in paleness sought the secret
    air.
To fade away like morning beauty from her mortal day:
Down by the river of Adona her soft voice is heard:
And thus her gentle lamentation falls like morning dew.

O life of this our spring! why fades the lotus of the
    water?
Why fade these children of the spring? born but to smile
    & fall.
Ah! Thel is like a watry bow, and like a parting cloud,
Like a reflection in a glass. like shadows in the water.
Like dreams of infants. like a smile upon an infants face,   10
Like the doves voice, like transient day, like music in
    the air;
Ah! gentle may I lay me down, and gentle rest my head.

And gentle sleep the sleep of death. and gentle hear the
    voice
Of him that walketh in the garden in the evening time.

The Lilly of the valley breathing in the humble grass
Answer'd the lovely maid and said: I am a watry weed,
And I am very small, and love to dwell in lowly vales;
So weak, the gilded butterfly scarce perches on my head
Yet I am visited from heaven. and he that smiles on all.
Walks in the valley. and each morn over me spreads his
    hand   20
Saying, rejoice thou humble grass, thou new-born lilly
    flower,
Thou gentle maid of silent valleys. and of modest
    brooks;
For thou shalt be clothed in light, and fed with morning
    manna:
Till summers heat melts thee beside the fountains and
    the springs
To flourish in eternal vales: then why should Thel
    complain,

PLATE 2

Why should the mistress of the vales of Har, utter a sigh.

She ceasd & smild in tears, then sat down in her silver
    shrine.

Thel answerd. O thou little virgin of the peaceful valley.
Giving to those that cannot crave, the voiceless, the
    o'ertired.
Thy breath doth nourish the innocent lamb, he smells
    thy milky garments,
He crops thy flowers. while thou sittest smiling in his
    face,
Wiping his mild and meekin mouth from all contagious
    taints.
Thy wine doth purify the golden honey, thy perfume,

Which thou dost scatter on every little blade of grass
that springs
Revives the milked cow, & tames the fire-breathing steed.   10
But Thel is like a faint cloud kindled at the rising sun:
I vanish from my pearly throne, and who shall find my
place.

Queen of the vales the Lilly answerd, ask the tender
cloud,
And it shall tell thee why it glitters in the morning sky,
And why it scatters its bright beauty thro' the humid air.
Descend O little cloud & hover before the eyes of Thel.

The Cloud descended, and the Lilly bowd her modest
head:
And went to mind her numerous charge among the
verdant grass.

PLATE 3

II

O little Cloud the virgin said, I charge thee tell to me,
Why thou complainest not when in one hour thou fade
away:
Then we shall seek thee but not find; ah Thel is like to
Thee.
I pass away. yet I complain, and no one hears my voice.

The Cloud then shew'd his golden head & his bright
form emerg'd,
Hovering and glittering on the air before the face of
Thel.

O virgin know'st thou not. our steeds drink of the golden
springs
Where Luvah doth renew his horses: look'st thou on my
youth,
And fearest thou because I vanish and am seen no more.
Nothing remains; O maid I tell thee, when I pass away,   10

It is to tenfold life, to love, to peace, and raptures holy:
Unseen descending, weigh my light wings upon balmy
    flowers;
And court the fair eyed dew. to take me to her shining
    tent;
The weeping virgin, trembling kneels before the risen
    sun,
Till we arise link'd in a golden band, and never part;
But walk united, bearing food to all our tender flowers
Dost thou O little Cloud? I fear that I am not like thee;
For I walk through the vales of Har. and smell the
    sweetest flowers:
But I feed not the little flowers: I hear the warbling
    birds.
But I feed not the warbling birds. they fly and seek their
    food;   20
But Thel delights in these no more because I fade away.
And all shall say. without a use this shining woman liv'd
Or did she only live. to be at death the food of worms.

The Cloud reclind upon his airy throne and answer'd
    thus.

Then if thou art the food of worms, O virgin of the
    skies,
How great thy use. how great thy blessing; every thing
    that lives,
Lives not alone. nor for itself: fear not and I will call
The weak worm from its lowly bed, and thou shalt hear
    its voice.
Come forth worm of the silent valley, to thy pensive
    queen.

The helpless worm arose, and sat upon the Lillys leaf,   30
And the bright Cloud saild on, to find his partner in the
    vale.

PLATE 4

III

Then Thel astonish'd view'd the Worm upon its dewy
   bed.

Art thou a Worm? image of weakness. art thou but a
   Worm?
I see thee like an infant wrapped in the Lillys leaf:
Ah weep not little voice, thou can'st not speak. but thou
   can'st weep;
Is this a Worm? I see thee lay helpless & naked:
   weeping,
And none to answer, none to cherish thee with mothers
   smiles.

The Clod of Clay heard the Worms voice, & raisd her
   pitying head;
She bow'd over the weeping infant. and her life exhal'd
In milky fondness. then on Thel she fix'd her humble
   eyes.

O beauty of the vales of Har. we live not for ourselves,   10
Thou seest me the meanest thing, and so I am indeed;
My bosom of itself is cold. and of itself is dark,

PLATE 5

But he that loves the lowly. pours his oil upon my head.
And kisses me, and binds his nuptial bands around my
   breast.
And says; Thou mother of my children, I have loved
   thee.
And I have given thee a crown that none can take away
But how this is sweet maid, I know not. and I cannot
   know,
I ponder. and I cannot ponder; yet I live and love.

The daughter of beauty wip'd her pitying tears with her
   white veil,

And said. Alas! I knew not this, and therefore did I
   weep:
That God would love a Worm I knew. and punish the
   evil foot
That wilful, bruis'd its helpless form: but that he
   cherish'd it   10
With milk and oil, I never knew; and therefore did I
   weep.
And I complaind in the mild air, because I fade away.
And lay me down in thy cold bed, and leave my shining
   lot.

Queen of the vales, the matron Clay answerd; I heard
   thy sighs,
And all thy moans flew o'er my roof. but I have call'd
   them down:
Wilt thou O Queen enter my house. 'tis given thee to
   enter,
And to return; fear nothing. enter with thy virgin feet.

PLATE 6

IV

The eternal gates terrific porter lifted the northern bar:
Thel enter'd in & saw the secrets of the land unknown;
She saw the couches of the dead, & where the fibrous
   roots
Of every heart on earth infixes deep its restless twists:
A land of sorrows & of tears where never smile was seen.

She wanderd in the land of clouds thro' valleys dark,
   listning
Dolours & lamentations: waiting oft beside a dewy
   grave
She stood in silence. listning to the voices of the ground,
Till to her own grave plot she came. & there she sat
   down.
And heard this voice of sorrow breathed from the hollow
   pit.   10

Why cannot the Ear be closed to its own destruction?
Or the glistning Eye to the poison of a smile!
Why are Eyelids stord with arrows ready drawn,
Where a thousand fighting men in ambush lie?
Or an Eye of gifts & graces, show'ring fruits & coined
   gold!
Why a Tongue impress'd with honey from every wind?
Why an Ear, a whirlpool fierce to draw creations in?
Why a Nostril wide inhaling terror trembling & affright
Why a tender curb upon the youthful burning boy!
Why a little curtain of flesh on the bed of our desire?   20

The Virgin started from her seat, & with a shriek.
Fled back unhinderd till she came into the vales of Har

The End

TIRIEL

I

And Aged Tiriel. stood before the Gates of his beautiful
    palace
[*But dark were his once piercing eyes*]
With Myratana. once the Queen of all the western plains
But now his eyes were darkned. & his wife fading in
    death
They stood before their once delightful palace. & thus
    the Voice
Of aged Tiriel. arose. that his sons might hear in their
    gates

Accursed race of Tiriel. behold your [*aged*] father
Come forth & look on her that bore you. come you
    accursed sons.
In my weak [*aged*] arms. I here have borne your dying
    mother
Come forth sons of the Curse come forth. see the death
    of Myratana   10

His sons ran from their gates. & saw their aged parents
    stand
And thus the eldest son of Tiriel raisd his mighty voice

Old man unworthy to be calld. the father of Tiriels race
For evry one of those thy wrinkles. each of those grey
    hairs
Are cruel as death. & as obdurate as the devouring pit
Why should thy sons care for thy curses thou accursed
    man
Were we not slaves till we rebeld. Who cares for Tiriels
    curse

His blessing was a cruel curse. His curse may be a
   blessing

He ceast the aged man raisd up his right hand to the
   heavens
His left supported Myratana [*living*/ *?shriecking*]
   shrinking in pangs of death   20
The orbs of his large eyes he opend. & thus his voice
   went forth

Serpents not sons. wreathing around the bones of Tiriel
Ye worms of death feasting upon your aged parents flesh
Listen & hear your mothers groans. No more accursed
   Sons
She bears. she groans not at the birth of Heuxos or
   Yuva
These are the groans of death ye serpents. These are the
   groans of death

Nourished with milk ye serpents. nourishd with
   mothers tears & cares
Look at my eyes blind as the orbless scull among the
   stones
Look at my bald head. Hark listen ye serpents [*all*] listen
What Myratana. What my wife. O Soul O Spirit O fire   30
What Myratana. art thou dead. Look here ye serpents
   look
The serpents sprung from her own bowels have draind
   her dry as this
Curse on your ruthless heads. for I will bury her even
   here

So saying he began to dig a grave with his aged hands
But Heuxos calld a son of Zazel. to dig their mother a
   grave

Old cruelty desist & let us dig a grave for thee
Thou hast refusd our charity thou hast refusd our food
Thou hast refusd our clothes our beds our houses for
   thy dwelling

Chusing to wander like a Son of Zazel in the rocks
Why dost thou curse. is not the curse now come upon
    your head   40
Was it not you enslavd the sons of Zazel. & they have
    cursd
And now you feel it. Dig a grave & let us bury our
    mother

There take the body. cursed sons. & may the heavens
    rain wrath
As thick as northern fogs. around your gates. to choke
    you up
That you may lie as now your mother lies. like dogs.
    cast out
The stink. of your dead carcases. annoying man & beast
Till your white bones are bleachd with age for a
    memorial.
No your remembrance shall perish. for when your
    carcases
Lie stinking on the earth. the buriers shall arise from the
    east
And. not a bone of all the sons of Tiriel remain   50
Bury your mother but you cannot bury the curse of
    Tiriel

He ceast & darkling oer the mountains sought his
    pathless way

2

He wanderd day & night to him both day & night were
    dark
The sun he felt but the bright moon was now a useless
    globe
Oer mountains & thro vales of woe. the blind & aged
    man
Wanderd till he that leadeth all. led him to the vales of
    Har

And Har & Heva like two children sat beneath the Oak
Mnetha now aged waited on them. & brought them food
  & clothing
But they were as the shadow of Har. & as the years
  forgotten
Playing with flowers. & running after birds they spent
  the day
And in the night like infants slept delighted with infant
  dreams

Soon as the blind wanderer enterd the pleasant gardens
  of Har   10
[*The aged father & mother saw him as they sat at play*]
They ran weeping like frighted infants for refuge in
  Mnethas arms
The blind man felt his way & cried peace to these open
  doors
Let no one fear for poor blind Tiriel hurts none but
  himself
Tell me O friends where am I now. & in what pleasant
  place

This is the valley of Har said Mnetha & this the tent of
  Har
Who art thou poor blind man. that takest the name of
  Tiriel on thee
Tiriel is king of all the west. who art thou I am Mnetha
And this is Har & Heva. trembling like infants by my
  side

I know Tiriel is king of the west & there he lives in joy   20
No matter who I am O Mnetha. if thou hast any food
Give it me. for I cannot stay my journey is far from
  hence

Then Har said O my mother Mnetha venture not so
  near him
For he is the king of rotten wood & of the bones of
  death

He wanders. without eyes. & passes thro thick walls &
doors
Thou shalt not smite my mother Mnetha O thou eyeless
man

[*O venerable O most piteous O most woeful day*]
A wanderer. I beg for food. you see I cannot weep
[*But I can kneel down at your door. I am a harmless man*]
I cast away my staff the kind companion of my travel   30
And I kneel down that you may see I am a harmless
man

He kneeled down & Mnetha said Come Har & Heva rise
He is an innocent old man & hungry with his travel

Then Har arose & laid his hand upon old Tiriels head

God bless thy poor bald pate. God bless. thy hollow
winking eyes
God bless thy shriveld beard. God. bless. thy many
wrinkled forehead
Thou hast no teeth old man & thus I kiss thy sleek bald
head
Heva come kiss his bald head for he will not hurt us
Heva

Then Heva came & took old Tiriel in her mothers arms

Bless thy poor eyes old man. & bless the old father of
Tiriel   40
Thou art my Tiriels old father. I know thee thro thy
wrinkles
Because thou smellest. like the figtree. thou smellest like
ripe figs
How didst thou lose thy eyes old Tiriel. bless thy
wrinkled face

[*The aged Tiriel could not speak his heart was full of grief
He strove against his rising passions. but still he could not
speak*]

Mnetha said come in aged wanderer tell us of thy name
Why shouldest thou conceal thyself from those of thine
   own flesh

I am not of this region. said Tiriel dissemblingly
[*Fearing to tell him who he was. because of the weakness of
   Har*]
I am an aged wanderer once father of a race   50
Far in the north. but they were wicked & were all
   destroyd
And I their father sent an outcast. I have told you all
Ask me no more I pray for grief hath seald my precious
   sight

O Lord said Mnetha how I tremble are there then more
   people
More human creatures on this earth beside the sons of
   Har

No more said Tiriel but I remain on all this globe
And I remain an outcast. hast thou any thing to drink

Then Mnetha gave him milk & fruits. & they sat down
   together

3

They sat & eat & Har & Heva smild on Tiriel

Thou art a very old old man but I am older than thou
How came thine hair to leave thy forehead how came thy
   face so brown
My hair is very long my beard. doth cover all my breast
God bless thy piteous face. to count the wrinkles in thy
   face
Would puzzle Mnetha. bless thy face for thou art Tiriel

[*Tiriel could scarce dissemble more & his tongue could
   scarce refrain
But still he feard that Har & Heva would die of joy &
   grief.*]

Tiriel I never saw but once I sat with him & eat
He was as chearful as a prince & gave me entertainment   10
But long I staid not at his palace for I am forcd to
    wander

What wilt thou leave us too said Heva thou shalt not
    leave us too
For we have many sports to shew thee & many songs to
    sing
And after dinner we will walk into the cage of Har
And thou shalt help us to catch birds. & gather them
    ripe cherries
Then let thy name be Tiriel & never leave us more

If thou dost go said Har I wish thine eyes may see thy
    folly
My sons have left me did thine leave thee O twas very
    cruel

No venerable man said Tiriel ask me not such things
For thou dost make my heart to bleed my sons were not
    like thine   20
But worse O never ask me more or I must flee away

Thou shalt not go said Heva till thou hast seen our
    singing birds
And heard Har sing in the great cage & slept upon our
    fleeces
Go not for thou art so like Tiriel. that I love thine head
Tho it is wrinkled like the earth parchd with the summer
    heat

Then Tiriel rose up from the seat & said god bless these
    tents
[*God bless my benefactors. for I cannot tarry longer*]
My Journey is oer rocks & mountains. not in pleasant
    vales
I must not sleep nor rest because of madness & dismay

[Then Mnetha led him to the door & gave to him his staff   30
*And Har & Heva stood & watchd him till he enterd the
   wood*
*And then they went & wept to Mnetha but they soon
   forgot their tears]*

And Mnetha said Thou must not go to wander dark.
   alone
But dwell with us & let us be to thee instead of eyes
And I will bring thee food old man. till death shall call
   thee hence

Then Tiriel frownd & answerd. Did I not command you
   saying
Madness & deep dismay posses[s] the heart of the blind
   man
The wanderer who [*runs*] seeks the woods leaning upon
   his staff

Then Mnetha trembling at his frowns led him to the
   tent door
And gave to him his staff & blest him. he went on his
   way   40

But Har & Heva stood & watchd him till he enterd the
   wood
And then they went & wept to Mnetha. but they soon
   forgot their tears

4

Over the weary hills the blind man took his lonely way
To him the day & night alike was dark & desolate
But far he had not gone when Ijim from his woods
   come down
Met him at entrance of the forest in a dark & lonely way

Who art thou Eyeless wretch that thus obstructst the
   lions path

Ijim shall rend thy feeble joints thou tempter of dark
    Ijim
Thou hast the form of Tiriel but I know thee well
    enough
Stand from my path foul fiend is this the last of thy
    deceits
To be a hypocrite & stand in shape of a blind beggar

The blind man heard his brothers voice & kneeld down
    on his knee   10

O brother Ijim if it is thy voice that speaks to me
Smite not thy brother Tiriel tho weary of his life
My sons have smitten me already. and if thou smitest me
The curse that rolls over their heads will rest itself on
    thine
Tis now seven years Since in my palace I beheld thy
    face
[*Seven years of sorrow then the curse of Zazel*]

Come thou dark fiend I dare thy cunning know that
    Ijim scorns
To smite the[e] in the form of helpless age & eyeless
    policy
Rise up for I discern thee & I dare thy eloquent
    tongue
Come I will lead thee on thy way & use thee as a scoff   20

O Brother Ijim thou beholdest wretched Tiriel
Kiss me my brother & then leave me to wander desolate

No artful fiend. but I will lead thee dost thou want to go
Reply not lest I bind thee with the green flags of the
    brook
Ay now thou art discoverd I will use thee like a slave

When Tiriel heard the words of Ijim he sought not to
    reply
He knew twas vain for Ijims words were as the voice of
    Fate

And they went on together over hills thro woody dales
Blind to the pleasures of the sight & deaf to warbling
   birds
All day they walkd & all the night beneath the pleasant
   Moon
Westwardly journeying till Tiriel grew weary with his
   travel

    30

O Ijim I am faint & weary for my knees forbid
To bear me further. urge me not lest I should die with
   travel
A little rest I crave a little water from a brook
Or I shall soon discover that I am a mortal man
And you will lose your once lovd Tiriel alas how faint
   I am

Impudent fiend said Ijim hold thy glib & eloquent
   tongue
Tiriel is a king. & thou the tempter of dark Ijim
Drink of this running brook. & I will bear thee on my
   shoulders

He drank & Ijim raisd him up & bore him on his
   shoulders
All day he bore him & when evening drew her solemn
   curtain
Enterd the gates of Tiriels palace. & stood & calld aloud

    40

Heuxos come forth I here have brought the fiend that
   troubles Ijim
Look knowst thou aught of this grey beard. or of these
   blinded eyes

Heuxos & Lotho ran forth at the sound of Ijims voice
And saw their aged father borne upon his mighty
   shoulders
Their eloquent tongues were dumb & sweat stood on
   their trembling limbs
They knew twas vain to strive with Ijim they bowd &
   silent stood

What Heuxos call thy father for I [*must*] mean to sport
  to night
This is the hypocrite that sometimes roars a dreadful lion   50
Then I have rent his limbs & left him rotting in the
  forest
For birds to eat but I have scarce departed from the
  place
But like a tyger he would come & so I rent him too
Then like a river he would seek to drown me in his ·
  waves
But soon I buffetted the torrent anon like to a cloud
Fraught with the swords of lightning. but I bravd the
  vengeance too
Then he would creep like a bright serpent till around my
  neck
While I was Sleeping he would twine I squeezd his
  poisnous soul
Then like a toad or like a newt. would whisper in my
  ears
Or like a rock stood in my way. or like a poisnous shrub   60
At iast I caught him in the form of Tiriel blind & old
And so Ill keep him fetch your father forth Myratana

They stood confounded. and Thus Tiriel raisd his silver
  voice

Serpents not sons [*you see and know your father*] why do
  you stand fetch hither Tiriel
Fetch hither Myratana & delight yourselves with scoffs
For poor blind Tiriel is returnd & this much injurd head
Is ready for your bitter taunts. come forth sons of the
  curse

Mean time the other sons of Tiriel ran around their
  father
Confounded at the terrible strength of Ijim they knew
  twas vain
Both spear & shield were useless & the coat of iron mail   70

When Ijim stretchd his mighty arm. the arrow from his
    limbs
Rebounded & the piercing sword broke on his naked
    [*limbs*] flesh

[*Then Ijim said Lotho. Clithyma. Makuth fetch your*
    father
Why do you stand confounded thus. Heuxos why art thou
    silent
O noble Ijim thou hast brought our father to (th e gates)
    our eyes
That we may tremble & repent before thy mighty knees
O we are but the slaves of Fortune. & that most cruel man
Desires our deaths. O Ijim (tis one whose aged tongue)
(Decieve the noble & xxxx) if the eloquent voice of Tiriel
Hath workd our ruin we submit nor strive against stern fate   80

He spoke & kneeld upon his knee. Then Ijim on the
    pavement
Set aged Tiriel. in deep thought whether these things were
    so]

Then is it true Heuxos that thou hast turnd thy aged
    parent
To be the sport of wintry winds. (said Ijim) is this true
It is a lie & I am [*torn*] like the tree torn by the wind
Thou eyeless fiend. & you dissemblers. Is this Tiriels
    house
It is as false [*as*] Matha. & as dark as vacant Orcus
Escape ye fiends for Ijim will not lift his hand against ye

So saying. Ijim gloomy turnd his back & silent sought
The [*gloom*] secret forests & all night wanderd in desolate
    ways   90

5

And aged Tiriel stood & said where does the thunder
    sleep

Where doth he hide his terrible head & his swift & fiery
    daughters
Where do they shroud their fiery wings & the terrors of
    their hair
Earth thus I stamp thy bosom rouse the earthquake
    from his den
[*Display thy*] To raise his dark & burning visage thro the
    cleaving [*world*] ground
To thrust these towers with his shoulders. let his fiery
    dogs
Rise from the center belching flames & roarings. dark
    smoke
Where art thou Pestilence that bathest in fogs & standing
    lakes
Rise up thy sluggish limbs. & let the loathsomest of
    poisons
Drop from thy garments as thou walkest. wrapt in yellow
    clouds   10
Here take thy seat. in this wide court. let it be strown
    with dead
And sit & smile upon these cursed sons of Tiriel
Thunder & fire & pestilence. here you not Tiriels curse

He ceast the heavy clouds confusd rolld round the lofty
    towers
Discharging their enormous voices. at the fathers curse
The earth trembled fires belched from the yawning clefts
And when the shaking ceast a fog possest the accursed
    clime
The cry was great in Tiriels palace his five daughters ran
And caught him by the garments weeping with cries of
    bitter woe

Aye now you feel the curse you cry. but may all ears be
    deaf   20
As Tiriels & all eyes as blind as Tiriels to your woes
May never stars shine on your roofs may never sun nor
    moon
Visit you but eternal fogs hover around your walls

Hela my youngest daughter you shall lead me from this
  place
And let the curse fall on the rest & wrap them up
  together

He ceast & Hela led her father from the noisom place
In haste they fled while all the sons & daughters of
  Tiriel
Chaind in thick darkness utterd cries of mourning all
  the night
And in the morning Lo an hundred men in ghastly
  death
The four daughters [*& all the children in their silent beds*]
  stretchd on the marble pavement silent all   30
[*And*] falln by the pestilence the rest moped round in
  [*ghastly*] guilty fears
And all the children in their beds were cut off in one
  night
Thirty of Tiriels sons remaind. to wither in the palace
Desolate. Loathed. Dumb Astonishd waiting for black
  death

6

And Hela led her father thro the silent of the night
Astonishd silent. till the morning beams began to spring

Now Hela I can go with pleasure & dwell with Har &
  Heva
Now that the curse shall clean devour all those guilty
  sons
This is the right & ready way I know it by the sound
That our feet make. Remember Hela I have savd thee
  from death
Then be obedient to thy father for the curse is taken off
  thee
I dwelt with Myratana five years in the desolate rock
And all that time we waited for the fire to fall from
  heaven

Or for the torrents of the sea to overwhelm you all   10
But now my wife is dead & all the time of grace is past
You see the parents curse. Now lead me where I have
   commanded

O Leagued with evil spirits thou accursed man of sin
True I was born thy [*child*] slave who askd thee to save
   me from death –
Twas for thy self thou cruel man because thou wantest
   eyes

True Hela this is the desert of all those cruel ones
Is Tiriel cruel look. his daughter & his youngest
   daughter
Laughs at affection glories in rebellion. scoffs at Love: –
I have not eat these two days lead me to Har & Hevas
   tent
Or I will wrap the[e] up in such a terrible fathers curse   20
That thou shalt feel worms in thy marrow creeping thro
   thy bones
Yet thou shalt lead me. Lead me I command to Har &
   Heva

O cruel O destroyer O consumer. O avenger
To Har & Heva I will lead thee then would that they
   would curse
Then would they curse as thou hast cursed but they are
   not like thee
O they are holy. & forgiving filld with loving mercy
Forgetting the offences of their most rebellious children
Or else thou wouldest not have livd to curse thy helpless
   children

Look on my eyes Hela & see for thou hast eyes to see
The tears swell from my stony fountains. wherefore do I
   weep   30
Wherefore from my blind orbs art thou not siezd with
   poisnous stings
Laugh serpent youngest venomous reptile of the flesh of
   Tiriel

Laugh. for thy father Tiriel shall give the[e] cause to
    laugh
Unless thou lead me to the tent of Har child of the
    curse

Silence thy evil tongue thou murderer of thy helpless
    children
I lead thee to the tent of Har not that I mind thy curse
But that I feel they will curse thee & hang upon thy
    bones
Fell shaking agonies. & in each wrinkle of that face
Plant worms of death to feast upon the tongue of
    terrible curses

Hela my daughter listen. thou [*child*] art the daughter of
    Tiriel   40
Thy father calls. Thy father lifts his hand unto the [*air*]
    heavens
For thou hast laughed at my tears. & curst thy aged
    father
Let snakes rise from thy bedded locks & laugh among
    thy curls

He ceast her dark hair upright stood while snakes
    infolded round
Her madding brows. her shrieks appalld the soul of Tiriel

What have I done Hela my daughter fearst thou now
    the curse
Or wherefore dost thou cry Ah wretch to curse thy aged
    father
Lead me to Har & Heva & the curse of Tiriel
Shall (*fall*) fail. If thou refuse howl in the desolate
    mountains

7

She howling led him over mountains & thro frighted
    vales
Till to the caves of Zazel they approachd at even tide

Forth from their caves [*the sons of Zazel*] old Zazel &
  his sons ran. [*&*] when they saw
Their tyrant prince blind & his daughter howling &
  leading him

They laughd & mocked some threw dirt & stones as they
  passd by
But when Tiriel turnd around & raisd his awful voice
[*They fled away (& hid themselves) but some stood still &
  thus scoffing began*]
Some fled away but Zazel stood still & thus began

Bald tyrant, wrinkled cunning [*wretch*] listen to Zazels
  chains
Twas thou that chaind thy brother Zazel where are now
  thine eyes   10
Shout beautiful daughter of Tiriel. thou singest a sweet
  song
Where are you going. come & eat some roots & drink
  some water
Thy crown is bald old man. the sun will dry thy brains
  away
And thou wilt be as foolish as thy foolish brother Zazel

The blind man heard. & smote his breast & trembling
  passed on
They threw dirt after them. till to the covert of a wood
[*They*] The howling maiden led her father where wild
  beasts resort
Hoping to end her [*life*] woes. but from her cries the
  tygers fled
All night they wanderd thro the wood & when the sun
  arose
They enterd on the mountains of Har at Noon the
  happy tents   20
Were frighted by the dismal cries of Hela on the
  mountains

But Har & Heva slept fearless as babes. on loving breasts
Mnetha awoke she ran & stood at the tent door [*in*] & saw

The aged wanderer led towards the tents she took her
  bow
And chose her arrows then advancd to meet the terrible
  pair

8

And Mnetha hasted & met them at the gate of the
  lower garden

Stand still or from my bow recieve a sharp & winged
  death

Then Tiriel stood. saying what soft voice threatens such
  bitter things
Lead me to Har & Heva I am Tiriel King of the west

And Mnetha led them to the tent of Har. and Har &
  Heva
Ran to the door. when Tiriel felt the ankles of aged Har
He said. O weak mistaken father of a lawless race
Thy laws O Har & Tiriels wisdom end together in a curse

[*Thy God of love thy heaven of joy*]
Why is one law given to the lion & the [*Ox*] patient Ox   10
[*Dost thou not see that men cannot be formed all alike*
Some nostrild wide breathing out blood. Some close shut up
In silent deceit. poisons inhaling from the morning rose
With daggers hid beneath their lips & poison in their
  tongue
Or eyed with little sparks of Hell or with infernal brands
Flinging flames of discontent & plagues of dark despair
Or those whose mouths are graves whose teeth the gates of
  eternal death
Can wisdom be put in a silver rod or love in a golden bowl
Is the son of a king warmed without wool or does he cry
  with a voice
Of thunder does he look upon the sun & laugh or stretch   20
His little hands into the depths of the sea, to bring forth

The deadly cunning of the (scaly tribe) flatterer & spread
  it to the morning]

And why men bound beneath the heavens in a reptile
  form
A worm of sixty winters creeping on the dusky ground
The child springs from the womb. the father ready
  stands to form
The infant head while the mother idle plays with her
  dog on her couch
The young bosom is cold for lack of mothers
  nourishment & milk
Is cut off from the weeping mouth with difficulty & pain
The little lids are lifted & the little nostrils opend
The father forms a whip to rouze the sluggish senses to
  act
And scourges off all youthful fancies from the new-born   30
  man
Then walks the weak infant in sorrow compelld to
  number footsteps
Upon the sand. &c
And when the [*foolish crawling*] drone has reachd his
  crawling length
Black berries appear that poison all around him. Such
  [*is*] was Tiriel
[*Hypocrisy the idiots wisdom & the wise mans folly*]
Compelld to pray repugnant & to humble the immortal
  spirit
Till I am subtil as a serpent in a paradise
Consuming all both flowers & fruits insects & warbling
  birds
And now my paradise is falln & a drear sandy plain
Returns my thirsty hissings in a curse on thee O Har   40
Mistaken father of a lawless race my voice is past

He ceast outstretchd at Har & Hevas feet in awful death

SONGS OF INNOCENCE AND OF EXPERIENCE
Shewing the Two Contrary States of the Human Soul

Songs of Innocence

INTRODUCTION

Piping down the valleys wild
Piping songs of pleasant glee
On a cloud I saw a child.
And he laughing said to me.

Pipe a song about a Lamb;
So I piped with merry chear,
Piper pipe that song again –
So I piped, he wept to hear.

Drop thy pipe thy happy pipe
Sing thy songs of happy chear,
So I sung the same again
While he wept with joy to hear

Piper sit thee down and write
In a book that all may read –
So he vanish'd from my sight.
And I pluck'd a hollow reed.

And I made a rural pen,
And I stain'd the water clear,
And I wrote my happy songs
Every child may joy to hear

THE SHEPHERD

How sweet is the Shepherds sweet lot,
From the morn to the evening he strays:
He shall follow his sheep all the day
And his tongue shall be filled with praise.

For he hears the lambs innocent call.
And he hears the ewes tender reply.
He is watchful while they are in peace.
For they know when their Shepherd is nigh.

THE ECCHOING GREEN

The Sun does arise,
And make happy the skies.
The merry bells ring
To welcome the Spring.
The sky-lark and thrush,
The birds of the bush,
Sing louder around.
To the bells chearful sound.
While our sports shall be seen
On the Ecchoing Green.   10

Old John with white hair
Does laugh away care,
Sitting under the oak,
Among the old folk,
They laugh at our play,
And soon they all say.
Such such were the joys.
When we all girls & boys,
In our youth-time were seen,
On the Ecchoing Green.   20

Till the little ones weary
No more can be merry
The sun does descend.

And our sports have an end:
Round the laps of their mothers,
Many sisters and brothers,
Like birds in their nest,
Are ready for rest;
And sport no more seen,
On the darkening Green.   30

THE LAMB

   Little Lamb who made thee
   Dost thou know who made thee
Gave thee life & bid thee feed.
By the stream & o'er the mead;
Gave thee clothing of delight,
Softest clothing wooly bright;
Gave thee such a tender voice,
Making all the vales rejoice:
   Little Lamb who made thee
   Dost thou know who made thee   10

   Little Lamb I'll tell thee,
   Little Lamb I'll tell thee:
He is called by thy name,
For he calls himself a Lamb:
He is meek & he is mild,
He became a little child:
I a child & thou a lamb,
We are called by his name.
   Little Lamb God bless thee.
   Little Lamb God bless thee.   20

THE LITTLE BLACK BOY

My mother bore me in the southern wild,
And I am black, but O! my soul is white;
White as an angel is the English child:
But I am black as if bereav'd of light.

My mother taught me underneath a tree
And sitting down before the heat of day,
She took me on her lap and kissed me,
And pointing to the east began to say.

Look on the rising sun: there God does live
And gives his light, and gives his heat away.   10
And flowers and trees and beasts and men recieve
Comfort in morning joy in the noon day.

And we are put on earth a little space,
That we may learn to bear the beams of love,
And these black bodies and this sun-burnt face
Is but a cloud, and like a shady grove.

For when our souls have learn'd the heat to bear
The cloud will vanish we shall hear his voice.
Saying: come out from the grove my love & care,
And round my golden tent like lambs rejoice.   20

Thus did my mother say and kissed me,
And thus I say to little English boy.
When I from black and he from white cloud free,
And round the tent of God like lambs we joy:

Ill shade him from the heat till he can bear,
To lean in joy upon our fathers knee.
And then I'll stand and stroke his silver hair,
And be like him and he will then love me.

THE BLOSSOM

Merry Merry Sparrow
Under leaves so green
A happy Blossom
Sees you swift as arrow
Seek your cradle narrow
Near my Bosom.

Pretty Pretty Robin
Under leaves so green
A happy Blossom
Hears you sobbing sobbing   10
Pretty Pretty Robin
Near my Bosom.

THE CHIMNEY SWEEPER

When my mother died I was very young,
And my father sold me while yet my tongue,
Could scarcely cry weep weep weep weep.
So your chimneys I sweep & in soot I sleep.

Theres little Tom Dacre, who cried when his head
That curl'd like a lambs back, was shav'd, so I said.
Hush Tom never mind it, for when your head's bare,
You know that the soot cannot spoil your white hair.

And so he was quiet, & that very night,
As Tom was a sleeping he had such a sight,   10
That thousands of sweepers Dick, Joe Ned & Jack
Were all of them lock'd up in coffins of black

And by came an Angel who had a bright key,
And he open'd the coffins & set them all free.
Then down a green plain leaping laughing they run
And wash in a river and shine in the Sun.

Then naked & white, all their bags left behind,
They rise upon clouds, and sport in the wind.
And the Angel told Tom if he'd be a good boy,
He'd have God for his father & never want joy.   20

And so Tom awoke and we rose in the dark
And got with our bags & our brushes to work.
Tho' the morning was cold, Tom was happy & warm,
So if all do their duty, they need not fear harm.

THE LITTLE BOY LOST

Father, father, where are you going
O do not walk so fast.
Speak father, speak to your little boy
Or else I shall be lost,

The night was dark no father was there
The child was wet with dew.
The mire was deep, & the child did weep
And away the vapour flew.

THE LITTLE BOY FOUND

The little boy lost in the lonely fen,
Led by the wand'ring light,
Began to cry, but God ever nigh,
Appeard like his father in white.

He kissed the child & by the hand led
And to his mother brought,
Who in sorrow pale, thro' the lonely dale
Her little boy weeping sought.

LAUGHING SONG

When the green woods laugh, with the voice of joy
And the dimpling stream runs laughing by,
When the air does laugh with our merry wit,
And the green hill laughs with the noise of it.

When the meadows laugh with lively green
And the grasshopper laughs in the merry scene,
When Mary and Susan and Emily,
With their sweet round mouths sing Ha, Ha, He.

When the painted birds laugh in the shade
Where our table with cherries and nuts is spread
Come live & be merry and join with me,
To sing the sweet chorus of Ha, Ha, He.

10

A CRADLE SONG

Sweet dreams form a shade,
O'er my lovely infants head.
Sweet dreams of pleasant streams.
By happy silent moony beams.

Sweet sleep with soft down,
Weave thy brows an infant crown.
Sweet sleep Angel mild,
Hover o'er my happy child.

Sweet smiles in the night,
Hover over my delight.
Sweet smiles Mothers smiles   10
All the livelong night beguiles.

Sweet moans, dovelike sighs,
Chase not slumber from thy eyes.
Sweet moans, sweeter smiles.
All the dovelike moans beguiles.

Sleep sleep happy child.
All creation slept and smil'd.
Sleep sleep. happy sleep.
While o'er thee thy mother weep   20

Sweet babe in thy face,
Holy image I can trace.
Sweet babe once like thee,
Thy maker lay and wept for me

Wept for me for thee for all.
When he was an infant small.
Thou his image ever see.
Heavenly face that smiles on thee.

Smiles on thee on me on all,
Who became an infant small,
Infant smiles are his own smiles.   30
Heaven & earth to peace beguiles.

THE DIVINE IMAGE

To Mercy Pity Peace and Love,
All pray in their distress:
And to these virtues of delight
Return their thankfulness.

For Mercy Pity Peace and Love,
Is God our father dear:
And Mercy Pity Peace and Love,
Is Man his child and care.

For Mercy has a human heart
Pity, a human face: 10
And Love, the human form divine,
And Peace, the human dress.

Then every man of every clime,
That prays in his distress,
Prays to the human form divine
Love Mercy Pity Peace.

And all must love the human form,
In heathen, turk or jew.
Where Mercy, Love & Pity dwell
There God is dwelling too.   20

HOLY THURSDAY

Twas on a Holy Thursday their innocent faces clean
The children walking two & two in red & blue & green
Grey headed beadles walkd before with wands as white
     as snow
Till into the high dome of Pauls they like Thames
     waters flow

O what a multitude they seemd these flowers of
     London town
Seated in companies they sit with radiance all their own

The hum of multitudes was there but multitudes of
    lambs
Thousands of little boys & girls raising their innocent
    hands

Now like a mighty wind they raise to heaven the voice
    of song
Or like harmonious thunderings the seats of heaven
    among   10
Beneath them sit the aged men wise guardians of the
    poor
Then cherish pity, lest you drive an angel from your
    door

NIGHT

The sun descending in the west
The evening star does shine.
The birds are silent in their nest,
And I must seek for mine,
The moon like a flower,
In heavens high bower;
With silent delight,
Sits and smiles on the night.

Farewell green fields and happy groves,
Where flocks have took delight;   10
Where lambs have nibbled, silent moves
The feet of angels bright;
Unseen they pour blessing,
And joy without ceasing,
On each bud and blossom,
And each sleeping bosom.

They look in every thoughtless nest,
Where birds are coverd warm;
They visit caves of every beast,
To keep them all from harm;   20
If they see any weeping,
That should have been sleeping

They pour sleep on their head
And sit down by their bed.

When wolves and tygers howl for prey
They pitying stand and weep;
Seeking to drive their thirst away,
And keep them from the sheep.
But if they rush dreadful;
The angels most heedful,   30
Recieve each mild spirit,
New worlds to inherit.

And there the lions ruddy eyes,
Shall flow with tears of gold:
And pitying the tender cries,
And walking round the fold:
Saying: wrath by his meekness
And by his health, sickness,
Is driven away,
From our immortal day.   40

And now beside thee bleating lamb,
I can lie down and sleep;
Or think on him who bore thy name,
Grase after thee and weep.
For wash'd in lifes river,
My bright mane for ever.
Shall shine like the gold.
As I guard o'er the fold.

SPRING

Sound the Flute!
Now it's mute.
Birds delight
Day and Night.
Nightingale
In the dale
Lark in Sky
Merrily
Merrily Merrily to welcome in the Year

Little Boy   10
Full of joy.
Little Girl
Sweet and small,
Cock does crow
So do you.
Merry voice
Infant noise
Merrily Merrily to welcome in the Year

Little Lamb
Here I am,   20
Come and lick
My white neck.
Let me pull
Your soft Wool.
Let me kiss
Your soft face.
Merrily Merrily we welcome in the Year

NURSE'S SONG

When the voices of children are heard on the green
And laughing is heard on the hill,
My heart is at rest within my breast
And every thing else is still

Then come home my children, the sun is gone down
And the dews of night arise
Come come leave off play, and let us away
Till the morning appears in the skies

No no let us play, for it is yet day
And we cannot go to sleep   10
Besides in the sky, the little birds fly
And the hills are all covered with sheep

Well well go & play till the light fades away
And then go home to bed
The little ones leaped & shouted & laugh'd
And all the hills ecchoed

INFANT JOY

I have no name
I am but two days old. –
What shall I call thee?
I happy am
Joy is my name, –
Sweet joy befall thee!

Pretty joy!
Sweet joy but two days old.
Sweet joy I call thee:
Thou dost smile.   10
I sing the while
Sweet joy befall thee.

A DREAM

Once a dream did weave a shade,
O'er my Angel-guarded bed,
That an Emmet lost it's way
Where on grass methought I lay.

Troubled wilderd and folorn
Dark benighted travel-worn,
Over many a tangled spray
All heart-broke I heard her say.

O my children! do they cry
Do they hear their father sigh.   10
Now they look abroad to see,
Now return and weep for me.

Pitying I drop'd a tear:
But I saw a glow-worm near:
Who replied. What wailing wight
Calls the watchman of the night.

I am set to light the ground,
While the beetle goes his round:
Follow now the beetles hum,
Little wanderer hie thee home.   20

ON ANOTHERS SORROW

Can I see anothers woe,
And not be in sorrow too.
Can I see anothers grief,
And not seek for kind relief.

Can I see a falling tear,
And not feel my sorrows share,
Can a father see his child,
Weep, nor be with sorrow fill'd.

Can a mother sit and hear,
An infant groan an infant fear –   10
No no never can it be.
Never never can it be.

And can he who smiles on all
Hear the wren with sorrows small,
Hear the small birds grief & care
Hear the woes that infants bear –

And not sit beside the nest
Pouring pity in their breast,
And not sit the cradle near
Weeping tear on infants tear.   20

And not sit both night & day,
Wiping all our tears away.
O! no never can it be.
Never never can it be.

He doth give his joy to all.
He becomes an infant small.
He becomes a man of woe
He doth feel the sorrow too.

Think not, thou canst sigh a sigh,
And thy maker is not by.   30
Think not, thou canst weep a tear,
And thy maker is not near.

O! he gives to us his joy,
That our grief he may destroy
Till our grief is fled & gone
He doth sit by us and moan

Songs of Experience

INTRODUCTION

Hear the voice of the Bard!
Who Present, Past, & Future sees
Whose ears have heard,
The Holy Word,
That walk'd among the ancient trees.

Calling the lapsed Soul
And weeping in the evening dew:
That might controll,
The starry pole;
And fallen fallen light renew!   10

O Earth O Earth return!
Arise from out the dewy grass;
Night is worn,
And the morn
Rises from the slumberous mass.

Turn away no more:
Why wilt thou turn away
The starry floor
The watry shore
Is giv'n thee till the break of day.   20

EARTH'S ANSWER

Earth rais'd up her head,
From the darkness dread & drear.
Her light fled:
Stony dread!
And her locks cover'd with grey despair.

Prison'd on watry shore
Starry Jealousy does keep my den
Cold and hoar
Weeping o'er
I hear the Father of the ancient men   10

Selfish father of men
Cruel jealous selfish fear
Can delight
Chain'd in night
The virgins of youth and morning bear.

Does spring hide its joy
When buds and blossoms grow?
Does the sower?
Sow by night?
Or the plowman in darkness plow?   20

Break this heavy chain,
That does freeze my bones around
Selfish! vain,
Eternal bane!
That free Love with bondage bound.

THE CLOD & THE PEBBLE

Love seeketh not Itself to please,
Nor for itself hath any care;
But for another gives its ease,
And builds a Heaven in Hells despair.

So sang a little Clod of Clay,
Trodden with the cattles feet:
But a Pebble of the brook,
Warbled out these metres meet.

Love seeketh only Self to please,
To bind another to its delight;   10
Joys in anothers loss of ease,
And builds a Hell in Heavens despite.

HOLY THURSDAY

Is this a holy thing to see,
In a rich and fruitful land,
Babes reduced to misery,
Fed with cold and usurous hand?

Is that trembling cry a song?
Can it be a song of joy?
And so many children poor?
It is a land of poverty!

And their sun does never shine.
And their fields are bleak & bare.   10
And their ways are fill'd with thorns.
It is eternal winter there.

For where-e'er the sun does shine,
And where-e'er the rain does fall:
Babe can never hunger there,
Nor poverty the mind appall.

THE LITTLE GIRL LOST

In futurity
I prophetic see,
That the earth from sleep,
(Grave the sentence deep)

Shall arise and seek
For her maker meek:
And the desart wild
Become a garden mild.

In the southern clime,
Where the summers prime,   10
Never fades away;
Lovely Lyca lay.

Seven summers old
Lovely Lyca told.
She had wanderd long,
Hearing wild birds song.

Sweet sleep come to me
Underneath this tree;
Do father, mother weep. –
'Where can Lyca sleep'.   20

Lost in desart wild
Is your little child.
How can Lyca sleep,
If her mother weep.

If her heart does ake,
Then let Lyca wake;
If my mother sleep,
Lyca shall not weep.

Frowning frowning night,
O'er this desart bright,   30
Let thy moon arise,
While I close my eyes.

Sleeping Lyca lay;
While the beasts of prey,
Come from caverns deep,
View'd the maid asleep

The kingly lion stood
And the virgin view'd,
Then he gambold round
O'er the hallowd ground: 40

Leopards, tygers play,
Round her as she lay;
While the lion old,
Bow'd his mane of gold.

And her bosom lick,
And upon her neck,
From his eyes of flame,
Ruby tears there came;

While the lioness,
Loos'd her slender dress,   50
And naked they convey'd
To caves the sleeping maid.

THE LITTLE GIRL FOUND

All the night in woe
Lyca's parents go:
Over vallies deep,
While the desarts weep.

Tired and woe-begone,
Hoarse with making moan:
Arm in arm seven days,
They trac'd the desert ways.

Seven nights they sleep,
Among shadows deep: 10
And dream they see their child
Starv'd in desert wild.

Pale thro pathless ways
The fancied image strays,
Famish'd, weeping, weak
With hollow piteous shriek

Rising from unrest,
The trembling woman prest,
With feet of weary woe;
She could no further go.   20

In his arms he bore,
Her arm'd with sorrow sore;
Till before their way,
A couching lion lay.

Turning back was vain,
Soon his heavy mane,
Bore them to the ground;
Then he stalk'd around,

Smelling to his prey.
But their fears allay,   30
When he licks their hands;
And silent by them stands.

They look upon his eyes
Fill'd with deep surprise:
And wondering behold,
A spirit arm'd in gold.

On his head a crown
On his shoulders down,
Flow'd his golden hair.
Gone was all their care.   40

Follow me he said,
Weep not for the maid;
In my palace deep,
Lyca lies asleep.

Then they followed,
Where the vision led:
And saw their sleeping child,
Among tygers wild.

To this day they dwell
In a lonely dell   50
Nor fear the wolvish howl,
Nor the lions growl.

THE CHIMNEY SWEEPER

A little black thing among the snow:
Crying weep, weep. in notes of woe!
Where are thy father & mother? say?
They are both gone up to the church to piay.

Because I was happy upon the heath.
And smil'd among the winters snow:
They clothed me in the clothes of death.
And taught me to sing the notes of woe.

And because I am happy. & dance & sing.
They think they have done me no injury: 10
And are gone to praise God & his Priest & King
Who make up a heaven of our misery.

NURSES SONG

When the voices of children, are heard on the green
And whisperings are in the dale:
The days of my youth rise fresh in my mind,
My face turns green and pale.

Then come home my children, the sun is gone down
And the dews of night arise
Your spring & your day, are wasted in play
And your winter and night in disguise.

THE SICK ROSE

O Rose thou art sick.
The invisible worm,
That flies in the night
In the howling storm:

Has found out thy bed
Of crimson joy:
And his dark secret love
Does thy life destroy.

THE FLY

Little Fly
Thy summers play,
My thoughtless hand
Has brush'd away.

Am not I
A fly like thee?
Or art not thou
A man like me?

For I dance
And drink & sing;   10
Till some blind hand
Shall brush my wing.

If thought is life
And strength & breath;
And the want
Of thought is death;

Then am I
A happy fly,
If I live,
Or if I die.   20

THE ANGEL

I Dreamt a Dream! what can it mean?
And that I was a maiden Queen:
Guarded by an Angel mild;
Witless woe, was ne'er beguil'd!

And I wept both night and day
And he wip'd my tears away
And I wept both day and night
And hid from him my hearts delight

So he took his wings and fled:
Then the morn blush'd rosy red: 10
I dried my tears & armd my fears,
With ten thousand shields and spears.

Soon my Angel came again:
I was arm'd, he came in vain:
For the time of youth was fled
And grey hairs were on my head.

THE TYGER

Tyger Tyger, burning bright,
In the forests of the night:
What immortal hand or eye,
Could frame thy fearful symmetry?

In what distant deeps or skies
Burnt the fire of thine eyes!
On what wings dare he aspire?
What the hand, dare sieze the fire?

And what shoulder, & what art,
Could twist the sinews of thy heart?   10
And when thy heart began to beat,
What dread hand? & what dread feet?

What the hammer? what the chain,
In what furnace was thy brain?
What the anvil? what dread grasp,
Dare its deadly terrors clasp?

When the stars threw down their spears
And water'd heaven with their tears:
Did he smile his work to see?
Did he who made the Lamb make thee?   20

Tyger, Tyger burning bright,
In the forests of the night:
What immortal hand or eye,
Dare frame thy fearful symmetry?

MY PRETTY ROSE TREE

A flower was offerd to me;
Such a flower as May never bore.
But I said I've a Pretty Rose-tree.
And I passed the sweet flower o'er.

Then I went to my Pretty Rose-tree;
To tend her by day and by night.
But my Rose turned away with jealousy:
And her thorns were my only delight.

AH! SUN-FLOWER

Ah Sun-flower! weary of time.
Who countest the steps of the Sun:
Seeking after that sweet golden clime
Where the travellers journey is done.

Where the Youth pined away with desire,
And the pale Virgin shrouded in snow:
Arise from their graves and aspire,
Where my Sun-flower wishes to go.

THE LILLY

The modest Rose puts forth a thorn:
The humble Sheep, a threatning horn:
While the Lilly white, shall in Love delight,
Nor a thorn nor a threat stain her beauty bright

THE GARDEN OF LOVE

I went to the Garden of Love.
And saw what I never had seen:
A Chapel was built in the midst,
Where I used to play on the green.

And the gates of this Chapel were shut,
And Thou shalt not. writ over the door;
So I turn'd to the Garden of Love,
That so many sweet flowers bore.

And I saw it was filled with graves,
And tomb-stones where flowers should be: 10
And Priests in black gowns, were walking their rounds,
And binding with briars, my joys & desires.

THE LITTLE VAGABOND

Dear Mother, dear Mother, the Church is cold.
But the Ale-house is healthy & pleasant & warm;
Besides I can tell where I am use'd well,
Such usage in heaven will never do well.

But if at the Church they would give us some Ale.
And a pleasant fire, our souls to regale;
We'd sing and we'd pray, all the live-long day;
Nor ever once wish from the Church to stray,

Then the Parson might preach & drink & sing.
And we'd be as happy as birds in the spring: 10
And modest dame Lurch, who is always at Church,
Wou'd not have bandy children nor fasting nor birch.

And God like a father rejoicing to see,
His children as pleasant and happy as he:
Would have no more quarrel with the Devil or the
    Barrel
But kiss him & give him both drink and apparel.

LONDON

I wander thro' each charter'd street,
Near where the charter'd Thames does flow.
And mark in every face I meet
Marks of weakness, marks of woe.

In every cry of every Man,
In every Infants cry of fear,
In every voice: in every ban,
The mind-forg'd manacles I hear

How the Chimney-sweepers cry
Every blackning Church appalls,
And the hapless Soldiers sigh,
Runs in blood down Palace walls

But most thro' midnight streets I hear
How the youthful Harlots curse
Blasts the new-born Infants tear
And blights with plagues the Marriage hearse

10

THE HUMAN ABSTRACT

Pity would be no more,
If we did not make somebody Poor:
And Mercy no more could be,
If all were as happy as we;

And mutual fear brings peace;
Till the selfish loves increase.
Then Cruelty knits a snare,
And spreads his baits with care.

He sits down with holy fears,
And waters the ground with tears:
Then Humility takes its root
Underneath his foot.

10

Soon spreads the dismal shade
Of Mystery over his head;
And the Catterpiller and Fly,
Feed on the Mystery.

And it bears the fruit of Deceit,
Ruddy and sweet to eat;
And the Raven his nest has made
In its thickest shade.   20

The Gods of the earth and sea,
Sought thro' Nature to find this Tree
But their search was all in vain:
There grows one in the Human Brain

INFANT SORROW

My mother groand! my father wept.
Into the dangerous world I leapt:
Helpless, naked, piping loud;
Like a fiend hid in a cloud.

Struggling in my fathers hands:
Striving against my swadling bands:
Bound and weary I thought best
To sulk upon my mothers breast.

A POISON TREE

I was angry with my friend:
I told my wrath, my wrath did end.
I was angry with my foe:
I told it not, my wrath did grow.

And I watered it in fears.
Night & morning with my tears:
And I sunned it with smiles.
And with soft deceitful wiles.

And it grew both day and night.
Till it bore an apple bright.   10
And my foe beheld it shine.
And he knew that it was mine.

And into my garden stole.
When the night had veild the pole;
In the morning glad I see;
My foe outstretchd beneath the tree.

A LITTLE BOY LOST

Nought loves another as itself
Nor venerates another so.
Nor is it possible to Thought
A greater than itself to know:

And Father, how can I love you,
Or any of my brothers more?
I love you like the little bird
That picks up crumbs around the door.

The Priest sat by and heard the child.
In trembling zeal he siez'd his hair: 10
He led him by his little coat:
And all admir'd the Priestly care.

And standing on the altar high,
Lo what a fiend is here! said he:
One who sets reason up for judge
Of our most holy Mystery.

The weeping child could not be heard.
The weeping parents wept in vain:
They strip'd him to his little shirt.
And bound him in an iron chain.   20

And burn'd him in a holy place,
Where many had been burn'd before:
The weeping parents wept in vain.
Are such things done on Albions shore.

A LITTLE GIRL LOST

Children of the future Age,
Reading this indignant page:
Know that in a former time,
Love! sweet Love! was thought a crime.

In the Age of Gold,
Free from winters cold:
Youth and maiden bright,
To the holy light,
Naked in the sunny beams delight.

Once a youthful pair   10
Fill'd with softest care:
Met in garden bright,
Where the holy light,
Had just remov'd the curtains of the night.

There in rising day,
On the grass they play:
Parents were afar:
Strangers came not near:
And the maiden soon forgot her fear.

Tired with kisses sweet   20
They agree to meet,
When the silent sleep
Waves o'er heavens deep;
And the weary tired wanderers weep.

To her father white
Came the maiden bright:
But his loving look.
Like the holy book,
All her tender limbs with terror shook.

Ona! pale and weak!
To thy father speak:
O the trembling fear!
O the dismal care!
That shakes the blossoms of my hoary hair

TO TIRZAH

Whate'er is Born of Mortal Birth,
Must be consumed with the Earth
To rise from Generation free;
Then what have I to do with thee?

The Sexes sprung from Shame & Pride
Blow'd in the morn: in evening died
But Mercy changd Death into Sleep;
The Sexes rose to work & weep.

Thou Mother of my Mortal part
With cruelty didst mould my Heart,   10
And with false self-decieving tears,
Didst bind my Nostrils Eyes & Ears.

Didst close my Tongue in senseless clay
And me to Mortal Life betray:
The Death of Jesus set me free,
Then what have I to do with thee?

THE SCHOOL BOY [Classed in Songs of Innocence in same volumns → expresses the chd's feelings + not the ADTS recollection however: school is the repressive ATT hense Songs of Exp.]

I love to rise in a summer morn,
When the birds sing on every tree;
The distant huntsman winds his horn,
And the sky-lark sings with me.
O! what sweet company.

But to go to school in a summer morn
O! it drives all joy away;
Under a cruel eye outworn,
The little ones spend the day,
In sighing and dismay.   10

[handwritten margin note: Blake was a lover of Books]

[handwritten margin note: over disciplined]

Ah! then at times I drooping sit,
And spend many an anxious hour.
Nor in my book can I take delight,
Nor sit in learnings bower, *tree*
Worn thro' with the dreary shower

[handwritten margin note: not against learning but against the form this education stops you maturing in the way you should]

How can the bird that is born for joy,
Sit in a cage and sing.
How can a child when fears annoy,
But droop his tender wing,
And forget his youthful spring.   20

O! father & mother, if buds are nip'd,
And blossoms blown away,
And if the tender plants are strip'd
Of their joy in the springing day,
By sorrow and cares dismay,

How shall the summer arise in joy
Or the summer fruits appear
Or how shall we gather what griefs destroy
Or bless the mellowing year,
When the blasts of winter appear.   30

[handwritten margin note: suggesting that there will be difficult time but you could get over these with the right thoughts + soul]

THE VOICE OF THE ANCIENT BARD

Youth of delight come hither:
And see the opening morn,
Image of truth new born
Doubt is fled & clouds of reason
Dark disputes & artful teazing.
Folly is an endless maze,
Tangled roots perplex her ways,
How many have fallen there!
They stumble all night over bones of the dead;
And feel they know not what but care;   10
And wish to lead others when they should be led.

A flower was offerd to me
Such a flower as may never bore
But I said Ive a pretty rose tree
And I passed the sweet flower oer

Then I went to my pretty rose tree
[*In the silent of the night*]
To tend it by day & by night
But my rose [*was turnd from me/was filld*] turnd away
   with Jealousy
And her thorns were my only delight

*

[*Never (seek) pain to tell thy love
Love that never told can be
For the gentle wind does move
Silently invisibly*]

I told my love I told my love
I told her all my heart
Trembling cold in ghastly fears
Ah she doth depart

Soon as she was gone from me
A traveller came by
Silently invisibly
[*He took her with a sigh*]
O was no deny

*

Love seeketh not itself to please
Nor for itself hath any care
But for another gives its ease
And builds a heaven in hells despair

So sung a little clod of clay
Trodden with the cattles feet
But a pebble of the brook
Warbled out these metres meet

Love seeketh only self to please
To bind another to its delight
Joys in anothers loss of ease
And builds a hell in heavens despite

*

I laid me down upon a bank
Where love lay sleeping
I heard among the rushes dank
Weeping Weeping

Then I went to the heath & the wild
To the thistles & thorns of the waste
And they told me how they were beguild
Driven out & compeld to be chaste

*

I went to the garden of love
And I saw what I never had seen
A chapel was built in the midst
Where I used to play on the green

And the gates of the chapel were shut
And thou shalt not writ over the door
[And] So I turned to the garden of love
That so many sweet flowers bore

And I saw it was filled with graves
And tomb-stones where flowers should be   10
And priests in black gounds were walking their rounds
And binding with briars my joys & desires

*

I saw a chapel all of gold
That none did dare to enter in
And many weeping stood without
Weeping mourning worshipping

I saw a serpent rise between
The white pillars of the door
And he forcd & forcd & forcd
[*Till he broke the pearly door*]
Down the golden hinges tore

And along the pavement sweet   10
Set with pearls & rubies bright
All his slimy length he drew
Till upon the altar white

Vomiting his poison out
On the bread & on the wine
So I turned into a sty
And laid me down among the swine

*

I asked a thief [*if he'd*] to steal me a peach
[*And*] He turned up his eyes
I askd a lithe lady to lie her down
[*And*] Holy & meek she cries

As soon as I went An angel came
[*And*] He winkd at the thief
And [*he*] smild at the dame

And without one word [*spoke*] said
Had a peach from the tree   10
[*And twixt earnest & (game) joke*] And still as a maid
[*He*] Enjoy'd the [*da*] lady.

*

I heard an Angel singing
When the day was springing
Mercy Pity [*&*] Peace
Is the worlds release

Thus he sung all day
Over the new mown hay
Till the sun went down
And haycocks looked brown

I heard a Devil curse
Over the heath & the furze   10
Mercy could be no more
If there was nobody poor

And pity no more could be
If all were as happy as we
[*Thus he sang &*] At his curse the sun went down
And the heavens gave a frown

[(*And*) *Down pourd the heavy rain*
Over the new reapd grain
And Mercy & Pity & Peace descended
The Farmers were ruind & harvest was ended]   20

[*And Mercy Pity & Peace*   [*And by distress increase*
Joyd at their increase   *Mercy Pity Peace*
With Povertys Increase   *By Misery to increase*
Are]   *Mercy Pity Peace*]

And Miseries increase
Is Mercy Pity Peace

*

A CRADLE SONG

1   3 Sleep Sleep; in thy sleep
       [*Thou wilt every secret keep*]
       [*Canst*] [*Thou canst any secret keep*]
    4 Little sorrows sit & weep
    1 Sleep Sleep beauty bright
       [*Thou shalt taste the joys of night*]
    2 Dreaming oer the joys of night

[*Yet a little while the moon*
Silent]

3   As thy softest limbs I [*touch/stroke*] feel   10
    Smiles as of the morning [*broke*] steal
    Oer thy cheek & oer thy breast
    Where thy little heart does rest

4   O the cunning wiles that creep
    In thy little heart asleep
    When thy little heart does wake
    Then the dreadful lightnings break

2   Sweet Babe in thy face
    Soft desires I can trace
    Secret joys & secret smiles   20
    [*Such as burning youth beguiles*]
    Little pretty infant wiles

5   From thy cheek & from thy eye
    Oer the youthful harvests nigh
    [*Female*] Infant wiles & [*female*] infant smiles
    Heaven & Earth of peace beguiles

*

CHRISTIAN FORBEARANCE

I was angry with my friend
I told my wrath my wrath did end
I was angry with my foe
I told it not my wrath did grow

And I waterd it in fears
Night & morning with my tears
And I sunned it with smiles
And with soft deceitful wiles

And it grew by day & night
Till it bore an apple bright   10
[*And I gave it to my foe*]
And my foe beheld it shine
And he knew that it was mine

And into my garden stole
When the night had veild the pole
In the morning Glad I see
My foe outstretchd beneath the tree

*

I feard the [*roughness*] fury of my wind
Would blight all blossoms fair & true
And my sun it shind & shind
And my wind it never blew

But a blossom fair or true
Was not found on any tree
For all blossoms grew & grew
Fruitless false tho fair to see

*

[*THAMES*]

Why should I care for the men of thames
Or the cheating waves of charterd streams
Or shrink at the little blasts of fear
That the hireling blows into my ear

Tho born on the cheating banks of Thames
Tho his waters bathed my infant limbs
[*I spurnd his waters away from me*]
The Ohio shall wash his stains from me
I was born a slave but I [*long*] go to be free

*

INFANT SORROW

My mother groand my father wept
Into the dangerous world I leapt
Helpless naked piping loud
Like a fiend hid in a cloud

Struggling in my fathers hands
Striving against my swaddling bands
Bound & weary I thought best
To sulk upon my mothers breast

When I saw that rage was vain
And to sulk would nothing gain   10
[*I began to so/Seeking many an artful wile*]
Turning many a trick or wile
I began to soothe & smile

And I [*grew/smild*] soothd day after day
Till upon the ground I stray
And I [*grew*] smild night after night
Seeking only for delight

[*But upon the nettly ground*
No delight was to be found]
And I saw before me shine   20
Clusters of the wandring vine
[*And beyond a mirtle tree*]
And many a lovely flower and tree
Stretchd [*its*] their blossoms out to me

[*But a Priest/But many a*] My father then with holy look
In [*his/their*] hands a holy book
Pronouncd curses on [*his*] my head
[*Who the fruit or blossoms shed*]
And bound me in a mirtle shade

[*I beheld the (Priest) Priests by night*   30
(*He*) *They embracd (my mirtle) the blossoms bright*
Like a serpent in the] Like to holy men by day
Underneath [*my*] the vines [*he*] they lay

So I smote [*him*] them & [*his*] their gore
Staind the roots my mirtle bore
But the time of youth is fled
And grey hairs are on my head

*

Silent Silent Night
Quench the holy light
Of thy torches bright

For possessd of Day
Thousand spirits stray
That sweet joys betray

Why should joys be sweet
Used with deceit   10
Nor with sorrows meet

But an honest joy
Does itself destroy
For a harlot coy

*

O lapwing thou fliest around the heath
Nor seest the net that is spread beneath
Why dost thou not fly among the corn fields
They cannot spread nets where a harvest yields

*

Thou hast a lap full of seed
And this is a fine country
Why dost thou not cast thy seed
And live in it merrily

[*Oft Ive*] Shall I cast it on the sand
And [*turnd*] turn it into fruitful land
[*But*] For on no other ground
Can I sow my seed
Without [*pulling*] tearing up
Some stinking weed   10

*

[*THE*] EARTHS ANSWER

Earth raisd up her head
From the darkness dread & drear
Her [*eyes/orbs*] [*fled/dead*] light fled
Stony dread;
And her locks coverd with grey despair:

Prisond on watry shore
Starry Jealousy does keep my den
Cold & hoar
Weeping oer
I hear the [*father of the*] ancient [*father of*] men   10

[(*Cruel*) *Selfish father of men*
Cruel jealous (*wintry*) *selfish fear*
Can delight
(*Closd*) *Chaind in night*
The virgins of youth & morning bear]

Does spring hide its [*delight*] joy
When buds & blossoms grow
Does the sower [*sow*
His seed] Sow by night
Or the plowman in darkness plow   20

Break this heavy chain
That does [*close*] freeze my bones around
Selfish vain
[*Thou my*] Eternal bane
[*Hast my*] That free love with bondage bound

*

IN A MIRTLE SHADE

    [*To a lovely mirtle bound*
    Blossoms showring all around]
2   O how sick & weary I
    Underneath my mirtle lie

    Like to dung upon the ground
    Underneath my mirtle bound

1   Why should I be bound to thee
    O my lovely mirtle tree
    Love free love cannot be bound
    To any tree that grows on ground   10

3   Oft my mirtle sighd in vain
    To behold my heavy chain
    Oft [*the priest beheld*] my father saw us sigh
    And laughd at our simplicity

    So I smote him & his gore
    Staind the roots my mirtle bore
    But the time of youth is fled
    And grey hairs are on my head

*

LONDON

I wander thro each dirty street
Near where the dirty Thames does flow
And [*see*] mark in every face I meet
Marks of weakness marks of woe

In every cry of every man
In [*every voice of every child*] every infants cry of fear
In every voice in every ban
The [*german forged links*] mind forgd manacles I hear

[*But most*] How the chimney sweepers cry
[*Blackens oer the churches walls*]   10
Every blackning church appalls
And the hapless soldiers sigh
Runs in blood down palace walls

[*But most the midnight harlots curse
From every dismal street I hear
Weaves around the marriage hearse
And blasts the newborn infants tear*]

But most [*from every*] thro wintry streets I hear
How the midnight harlots curse
Blasts the newborn infants tear   20
And [*hangs*] smites with plagues the marriage hearse

But most the shrieks of youth I hear
But most thro midnight &c
How the youthful

*

TO NOBODADDY

Why art thou silent & invisible
[*Man*] Father of Jealousy
Why dost thou hide thyself in clouds
From every searching Eye

Why darkness & obscurity
In all thy words & laws
That none dare eat the fruit but from
The wily serpents jaws
Or is it because secresy gains [*feminine*] females loud
   applause

*

The [*rose puts envious*] [*lustful*] modest rose puts forth
   a thorn
The [*coward*] humble sheep a threatning horn
While the lilly white shall in love delight
[*And the lion increase freedom & peace*]
[*The prist loves war & the soldier peace*]
Nor a thorn nor a threat stain her beauty bright

*

When the voices of children are heard on the green
And whisprings are in the dale
The [*desires*] days of my youth rise fresh in my mind
My face turns green & pale

Then come home my children the sun is gone down
And the dews of night arise
Your spring & your day are wasted in play
And your winter & night in disguise

*

Are not the joys of morning sweeter
Than the joys of night
And are the vigrous joys of youth
Ashamed of the light

Let age & sickness silent rob
The vineyards in the night
But those who burn with vigrous youth
Pluck fruits before the light

*

THE TYGER [FIRST VERSION]

1   Tyger Tyger burning bright
     In the forests of the night
     What immortal hand [&] or eye
     [*Could/Dare*] frame thy fearful symmetry

2   [*In what/Burnt in*] distant deeps or skies
     [*Burnt the/The cruel*] fire of thine eyes
     On what wings dare he aspire
     What the hand dare sieze the fire

3   And what shoulder & what art
     Could twist the sinews of thy heart   10
     And when thy heart began to beat
     What dread hand & what dread feet

     [*Could fetch it from the furnace deep*
     And in (the) thy horrid ribs dare steep
     In the well of sanguine woe
     In what clay & in what mould
     Were thy eyes of fury rolld]

4 [*What/Where*] the hammer [*what/where*] the chain
   In what furnace was thy brain
   What the anvil what [*the arm/grasp/clasp*]
      dread grasp   20
   [*Could*] Dare its deadly terrors [*clasp/grasp*] clasp

6 Tyger Tyger burning bright
   In thee forests of the night
   What immortal hand & eye
   Dare [*form*] frame thy fearful symmetry

5 3 And [*did he laugh*] dare he [*smile/laugh*] his work
      to see
    [*What the shoulder (ankle) what the knee*]
   4 [*Did*] Dare he who made the lamb make thee
   1 When the stars threw down their spears   30
   2 And waterd heaven with their tears

[SECOND VERSION]

Tyger Tyger burning bright
In the forests of the night
What Immortal hand [*or*] & eye
Dare frame thy fearful symmetry

Burnt in distant deeps or skies
The cruel fire of thine eyes
Could heart descend or wings aspire
What the hand dare sieze the fire

And what shoulder & what art
Could twist the sinews of thy heart
And when thy heart began to beat   10
What dread hand & what dread feet

When the stars threw down their spears
And waterd heaven with their tears
Did he smile his work to see
Did he who made the lamb make thee

Tyger Tyger burning bright
In the forests of the night
What immortal hand & eye
Dare frame thy fearful symmetry   20

*

[*How came pride in Man*
From Mary it began
How Contempt & Scorn
What a world is Man
His Earth]

*

THE HUMAN IMAGE

[*Mercy*] Pity could be no more
[*If there was nobody poor*]
If we did not make somebody poor
And Mercy no more could be
If all were as happy as we

And mutual fear brings Peace
Till the selfish Loves increase
Then Cruelty knits a snare
And spreads his [*nets*] baits with care

He sits down with holy fears   10
And waters the ground with tears
Then humility takes its root
Underneath his foot

Soon spreads the dismal shade
Of Mystery over his head
And the caterpillar & fly
Feed on the Mystery

And it bears the fruit of deceit
Ruddy & sweet to eat
And the raven his nest has made
In its thickest shade   20

The Gods of the Earth & Sea
Sought thro nature to find this tree
But their search was all in vain
[*Till they sought in the human brain*]
There grows one in the human brain
They said this mystery never shall cease
The prest [*loves*] promotes war and the soldier peace

There souls of men are bought & sold
And [*cradled*] milk fed infancy [*is sold*] for gold
And youth[*s*] to slaughter houses led
And [*maidens*] beauty for a bit of bread

30

*

[*HOW TO KNOW LOVE FROM DECEIT*]

Love to faults is always blind
Always is to joy inclind
[*Always*] Lawless wingd & unconfind
And breaks all chains from every mind

Deceit to secresy [*inclind*] confind
[*Modest prudish & confind*]
Lawful cautious [*changeful and*] & refind
[*Never is to*] To every thing but interest blind
[*And chains & fetters every mind*]
And forges fetters for the mind

*

THE WILD FLOWERS SONG

As I wanderd the forest
The green leaves among
I heard a wild [*thistle*] flower
Singing a song

I [*was found*] slept in the [*dark*] Earth
In the silent night
I murmurd my fears
And I felt delight

In the morning I went
As rosy as morn
To seek for new Joy
But I met with scorn

10

*

THE SICK ROSE

O Rose thou art sick
The invisible worm
That flies in the night
In the howling storm

Hath found out thy bed
Of crimson joy
[*O dark secret love*
Doth life destroy]
And [*his*] her dark secret love
Does thy life destroy

*

SOFT SNOW

I walked abroad in a snowy day
I askd the soft snow with me to play
She playd & she melted in all her prime
[*Ah that sweet love should be thought a crime*]
And the winter calld it a dreadful crime

*

AN ANCIENT PROVERB

Remove away that blackning church
Remove away that marriage hearse
Remove away that [*place*] man of blood
[*Twill*] Youll quite remove the ancient curse

*

TO MY MIRTLE

5 Why should I be bound to thee
6 O my lovely mirtle tree
  [*Love free love cannot be bound*
  To any tree that grows on ground]

1 To a lovely mirtle bound
2 Blossoms showring all around
  [*Like to dung upon the ground*
  Underneath my mirtle bound]
3 O how sick & weary I
4 Underneath my mirtle lie   10

*

Naught loves another as itself
Nor venerates another so
Nor is it possible to Thought
A greater than itself to know

[*Then*] And father [*I cannot*] how can I love you
[*Nor*] Or any of my brothers more
I love [*myself so does the bird*] you like the little bird
That picks up crumbs around the door

The Priest sat by and heard the child
In trembling zeal he seizd his hair   10
[*The mother followed weeping loud*
O that I such a fiend should bear
Then] He led him by the little coat
[*To show his zealous priestly care*]
And all admird his priestly care

And standing on the altar high
Lo what a fiend is here said he
One who sets reason up for judge
Of our most holy mystery

The weeping child could not be heard   20
The weeping parents wept in vain
[*They bound his little ivory limbs*
In a cruel Iron chain
And] They strip'd him to his little shirt
& bound him in an iron chain

[*They*] And burnd him in a holy [*fire*] place
Where many had been burnd before
The weeping parents wept in vain
Are Such things [*are*] done on Albions shore

*

THE CHIMNEY SWEEPER

A little black thing among the snow
Crying weep weep in notes of woe
Where are thy father & mother say
They are both gone up to Church to pray

Because I was happy upon the heath
And smild among the winters [*wind*] snow
They clothd me in the clothes of death
And taught me to sing the notes of woe

And because I am happy and dance and sing
They think they have done me no injury   10
And are gone to praise God & his Priest & King
[*Who wrap themselves up in our misery*]
Who make up a heaven of our misery

*

MERLINS PROPHECY

The harvest shall flourish in wintry weather
When two virginities meet together

The King & the Priest must be tied in a tether
Before two virgins can meet together

*

DAY

The [*day*] Sun arises in the East
Clothd in robes of blood & gold
Swords & spears & wrath increast
All around his [*ancles*] bosom rolld
Crownd with warlike fires & raging desires

*

[*THE MARRIAGE RING*] THE FAIRY

Come hither my spàrrows
My little arrows
If a tear or a smile
Will a man beguile
If an amorous delay
Clouds a sunshiny day
If the [*tread*] step of a foot
Smites the heart to its root
Tis the marriage ring
Makes each fairy a king   10

So a fairy sung
From the leaves I sprung
He leapd from the spray
To flee away
[*And*] But in my hat caught
He soon shall be taught
Let him laugh let him cry
Hes my butterfly
[*And a marriage ring*
Is a foolish thing/Is a childs play thing]
For I've pulld out the Sting
Of the marriage ring

*

The sword sung on the barren heath
The sickle [*on*] in the fruitful field
The sword he sung a song of death
But could not make the sickle yield

*

Abstinence sows sand all over
The ruddy limbs &[*flourishing*] flaming hair
But Desire Gratified
Plants fruits of life & beauty there

*

In a wife I would desire
What in whores is always found
The lineaments of Gratified desire

*

If you [*catch*] trap the moment before its ripe
The tears of repentance youll certainly wipe
But if once you let the ripe moment go
You[*ll*] can never wipe off the tears of woe

*

ETERNITY

He who binds to himself [*to*] a joy
Does the winged life destroy
But he who[*just*] kisses the joy as it flies
Lives in [*an eternal*] eternity's sun rise

*

THE KID

Thou little Kid didst play
  &c

*

THE LITTLE [*A PRETTY*] VAGABOND

Dear Mother Dear Mother the church is cold
But the alehouse is healthy & pleasant & warm
Besides I can tell where I am usd well
[*Such usage in heaven makes us all go to hell*]
The poor parsons with wind like a blown bladder swell

But if at the Church they would give us some Ale
And a pleasant fire our souls to regale
We'd sing and we'd pray all the livelong day
Nor ever once wish from the Church to stray

Then the parson might preach & drink & sing   10
And wed be as happy as birds in the spring
And Modest dame Lurch who is always at Church
Would not have bandy children nor fasting nor birch

Then God like a father [*that joys for*] rejoicing to see
His children as pleasant & happy as he
Would have no more quarrel with the Devil or the Barrel
[*But shake hands & kiss him & thered be no more hell*]
But kiss him & give him both [*food*] drink & apparel

*

THE QUESTION ANSWERD

What is it men [*of*] in women do require?
The lineaments of Gratified Desire.
What is it women do [*of*] in men require?
The lineaments of Gratified Desire.

*

LACEDEMONIAN INSTRUCTION

Come hither my boy tell me what thou seest there
A fool tangled in a religious snare

*

RICHES

The [*weal*] countless gold of a merry heart
The rubies & pearls of a loving eye
The [*idle man*] indolent never can bring to the mart
Nor the [*cunning*] secret hoard up in his treasury

*

AN ANSWER TO THE PARSON

Why of the sheep do you not learn peace
Because I dont want you to shear my fleece

*

HOLY THURSDAY

Is this a holy thing to see
In a rich & fruitful land
Babes reducd to misery
Fed with cold & usurous hand

Is that trembling cry a song
Can it be a song of joy
And so great a number poor
Tis a land of poverty

And their sun does never shine
And their fields are bleak & bare   10
And their ways are filld with thorns
Tis eternal winter there

But whereeer the sun does shine
And whereeer the rain does fall
Babe can never hunger there
Nor poverty the mind appall

*

[THE ANGEL]

I dreamt a dream what can it mean
And that I was a maiden queen
Guarded by an angel mild
Witless woe was neer beguild

And I wept both night and day
And he wiped my tears away
And I wept both day & night
And hid from him my hearts delight

So he took his wings & fled
Then the morn blushd rosy red   10
I dried my tears & armd my fears
With ten thousand shields & spears

Soon my angel came again
I was armd he came in vain
[*But*] For the time of youth was fled
And grey hairs were on my head

*

The look of love alarms
Because tis filld with fire
But the look of soft deceit
Shall win the lovers hire

*

[*Which are beauties sweetest dress*]
Soft deceit & idleness
These are beauties sweetest dress

*

   [*Woe alas my guilty hand*
   Brushed across thy summer joy
   All thy gilded painted pride
   Shatterd fled]
1 Little fly
   Thy summer play
   My [*guilty hand*] thoughtless hand
   Hath brushd away

   [*The cut worm*
   Forgives the plow   10
   And dies in peace
   And so do thou]

2 Am not I
   A fly like thee
   Or art not thou
   A man like me

3 For I dance
    And drink & sing
    Till some blind hand
    Shall brush my wing   20

5 Then am I
    A happy fly
    If I live
    Or if I die

[4 *Thought is life*
    And strength & breath
    But the want (*of*)
    Of Thought is death]

4 If thought is life
    And strength & breath   30
    And the want [*of*]
    Of Thought is death

*

MOTTO TO THE SONGS OF INNOCENCE & OF EXPERIENCE

The Good are attracted by Mens perceptions
    And Think not for themselves
    Till Experience teaches them to catch
    And to cage the Fairies & Elves

And then the Knave begins to snarl
And the Hypocrite to howl
And all his good Friends shew their private ends
And the Eagle is known from the Owl

*

Her whole Life is an Epigram smack smooth & neatly pend
Platted quite neat to catch applause with a sliding
   noose at the end

*

An old maid early eer I knew
Ought but the love that on me grew
And now Im coverd oer & oer
And wish that I had been a Whore

O I cannot cannot find
The undaunted courage of a Virgin Mind
For Early I in love was crost
Before my flower of love was lost

*

SEVERAL QUESTIONS ANSWERD

He who binds to himself a joy
Doth the winged life destroy
But he who kisses the joy as it flies
Lives in Eternitys sun rise

The look of love alarms
Because tis filld with fire
But the look of soft deceit
Shall Win the lovers hire

Soft deceit & Idleness
These are Beautys sweetest dress

What is it men in women do require
The lineaments of Gratified Desire
What is it women do in men require
The lineaments of Gratified Desire

*

AN ANCIENT PROVERB

Remove away that blackning church
Remove away that marriage hearse
Remove away that – of blood
Youll quite remove the ancient curse

*

1   1 Let the Brothels of Paris be opened
    2 With many an alluring dance
    3 To awake the [*Pestilence*] Physicians thro the city
    4 Said the beautiful Queen of France

4   9 The King awoke on his couch of gold
  10 As soon as he heard these tidings told
  11 Arise & come both fife & drum
  12 And the [*Famine*] shall eat both crust & crumb

[2   *Then old Nobodaddy aloft*
     Farted & belchd & coughd
  7 *And said I love hanging & drawing & quartering*   10
  8 *Every bit as well as war & slaughtering*
    (Damn praying & singing
    Unless they will bring in
    The blood of ten thousand by fighting or swinging)
3   5 *Then he swore a great & solemn Oath*
  6 *To kill the people I am loth*
    But If they rebel they must go to hell
    They shall have a Priest & a passing bell]

The Queen of France just touchd this Globe   20
And the Pestilence darted from her robe
[*But the bloodthirsty people across the water*
Will not submit to the gibbet & halter]
But our good Queen quite grows to the ground
[*There is just such a tree at Java found*]
And a great many suckers grow all around

*

[*Fayette beside King Lewis stood*
He saw him sign his hand
And soon he saw the famine rage
About the fruitful land

Fayette beheld the Queen to smile
And wink her lovely eye
And soon he saw the pestilence
From street to street to fly]

Fayette beheld the King & Queen
In tears & iron bound   10
But mute Fayette wept tear for tear
And guarded them around

[*Fayette Fayette thourt bought & sold*
For well I see thy tears
Of Pity are exchanged for those
Of selfish slavish fears]

[*Fayette beside his banner stood*
His captains false around
Thourt bought & sold]

3 Who will exchange his own fire side   20
   For the steps of anothers door
   Who will exchange his wheaten loaf
   For the links of a dungeon floor

   [*Who will exchange his own hearts blood*
   For the drops of a harlots eye]

2 [*Will the mother exchange her new born babe*
   For the dog at the wintry door
   Yet thou dost exchange thy pitying tears
   For the links of a dungeon floor

1 *Fayette Fayette thourt bought & sold*   30
   And sold is thy happy morrow
   Thou gavest the tears of Pity away
   In exchange for the tears of sorrow]

2   Fayette beheld the King & Queen
    In [*tears*] curses & iron bound
    But mute Fayette wept tear for tear
    And guarded them around

1   Who will exchange his own fire side
    For the [*steps*] stone of anothers door
    Who will exchange his wheaten loaf   40
    For the links of a dungeon floor

3   O who would smile on the wintry seas
    [*Or*] & Pity the stormy roar
    Or who will exchange his new born child
    For the dog at the wintry door

*

When a Man has Married a Wife
    he finds out whether
Her knees & elbows are only
    glued together

THE FRENCH REVOLUTION

A Poem, in Seven Books

PAGE [iii]
ADVERTISEMENT

The remaining Books of this Poem are finished, and
will be published in their Order.

PAGE [I]

THE FRENCH REVOLUTION

BOOK THE FIRST

The dead brood over Europe, the cloud and vision
  descends over chearful France;
O cloud well appointed! Sick, sick: the Prince on his
  couch, wreath'd in dim
And appalling mist; his strong hand outstretch'd, from
  his shoulder down the bone
Runs aching cold into the scepter too heavy for mortal
  grasp. No more
To be swayed by visible hand, nor in cruelty bruise the
  mild flourishing mountains.

Sick the mountains, and all their vineyards weep, in the
  eyes of the kingly mourner;
Pale is the morning cloud in his visage. Rise, Necker: the
  ancient dawn calls us
To awake from slumbers of five thousand years. I
  awake, but my soul is in dreams;
From my window I see the old mountains of France, like
  aged men, fading away.

PAGE 2

Troubled, leaning on Necker, descends the King, to his
    chamber of council; shady mountains   10
In fear, utter voices of thunder; the woods of France em-
    bosom the sound;
Clouds of wisdom prophetic reply, and roll over the palace
    roof heavy.
Forty men: each conversing with woes in the infinite
    shadows of his soul,
Like our ancient fathers in regions of twilight, walk,
    gathering round the King;
Again the loud voice of France cries to the morning, the
    morning prophecies to its clouds.

For the Commons convene in the Hall of the Nation.
    France shakes! And the heavens of France
Perplex'd vibrate round each careful countenance!
    Darkness of old times around them
Utters loud despair, shadowing Paris; her grey towers
    groan, and the Bastile trembles.
In its terrible towers the Governor stood, in dark fogs
    list'ning the horror;
A thousand his soldiers, old veterans of France, breathing   20
    red clouds of power and dominion,
Sudden seiz'd with howlings, despair, and black night, he
    stalk'd like a lion from tower
To tower, his howlings were heard in the Louvre; from
    court to court restless he dragg'd
His strong limbs; from court to court curs'd the fierce
    torment unquell'd,
Howling and giving the dark command; in his soul stood
    the purple plague,
Tugging his iron manacles, and piercing through the
    seven towers dark and sickly,
Panting over the prisoners like a wolf gorg'd; and the den
    nam'd Horror held a man
Chain'd hand and foot, round his neck an iron band,
    bound to the impregnable wall.

In his soul was the serpent coil'd round in his heart, hid
 from the light, as in a cleft rock;
And the man was confin'd for a writing prophetic: in the
 tower nam'd Darkness, was a man
Pinion'd down to the stone floor, his strong bones scarce   30
 cover'd with sinews; the iron rings
Were forg'd smaller as the flesh decay'd, a mask of iron on
 his face hid the lineaments

PAGE 3

Of ancient Kings, and the frown of the eternal lion was hid
 from the oppressed earth.
In the tower named Bloody, a skeleton yellow remained
 in its chains on its couch
Of stone, once a man who refus'd to sign papers of ab-
 horrence; the eternal worm
Crept in the skeleton. In the den nam'd Religion, a
 loathsome sick woman, bound down
To a bed of straw; the seven diseases of earth, like birds of
 prey, stood on the couch,
And fed on the body. She refus'd to be whore to the
 Minister, and with a knife smote him.
In the tower nam'd Order, an old man, whose white beard
 cover'd the stone floor like weeds
On margin of the sea, shrivel'd up by heat of day and cold
 of night; his den was short
And narrow as a grave dug for a child, with spiders webs
 wove, and with slime   40
Of ancient horrors cover'd, for snakes and scorpions are
 his companions; harmless they breathe
His sorrowful breath: he, by conscience urg'd, in the city
 of Paris rais'd a pulpit,
And taught wonders to darken'd souls. In the den nam'd
 Destiny a strong man sat,
His feet and hands cut off, and his eyes blinded; round his
 middle a chain and a band
Fasten'd into the wall; fancy gave him to see an image of
 despair in his den,

Eternally rushing round, like a man on his hands and
    knees, day and night without rest:
He was friend to the favourite. In the seventh tower,
    nam'd the tower of God, was a man
Mad, with chains loose, which he dragg'd up and down;
    fed with hopes year by year, he pined
For liberty; vain hopes: his reason decay'd, and the world
    of attraction in his bosom
Center'd, and the rushing of chaos overwhelm'd his dark
    soul. He was confin'd   50
For a letter of advice to a King, and his ravings in winds
    are heard over Versailles.

But the dens shook and trembled, the prisoners look up
    and assay to shout; they listen,
Then laugh in the dismal den, then are silent, and a light
    walks round the dark towers.

PAGE 4
For the Commons convene in the Hall of the Nation; like
    spirits of fire in the beautiful
Porches of the Sun, to plant beauty in the desart craving
    abyss, they gleam
On the anxious city; all children new-born first behold
    them; tears are fled,
And they nestle in earth-breathing bosoms. So the city of
    Paris, their wives and children,
Look up to the morning Senate, and visions of sorrow
    leave pensive streets.

But heavy brow'd jealousies lower o'er the Louvre, and
    terrors of ancient Kings
Descend from the gloom and wander thro' the palace
    and weep round the King and his Nobles.   60
While loud thunders roll, troubling the dead, Kings are
    sick throughout all the earth,
The voice ceas'd: the Nation sat: And the triple forg'd
    fetters of times were unloos'd.
The voice ceas'd: the Nation sat: but ancient darkness
    and trembling wander thro' the palace.

As in day of havock and routed battle, among thick
shades of discontent,
On the soul-skirting mountains of sorrow cold waving:
the Nobles fold round the King,
Each stern visage lock'd up as with strong bands of iron,
each strong limb bound down as with marble,
In flames of red wrath burning, bound in astonishment a
quarter of an hour.

Then the King glow'd: his Nobles fold round, like the
sun of old time quench'd in clouds;
In their darkness the King stood, his heart flam'd, and
utter'd a with'ring heat, and these words burst forth:

'The nerves of five thousand years ancestry tremble,
shaking the heavens of France;   70
'Throbs of anguish beat on brazen war foreheads, they
descend and look into their graves.

PAGE 5

'I see thro' darkness, thro' clouds rolling round me, the
spirits of ancient Kings
'Shivering over their bleached bones; round them their
counsellors look up from the dust,
'Crying: "Hide from the living! Our b[a]nds and our
prisoners shout in the open field,
' "Hide in the nether earth! Hide in the bones! Sit
obscured in the hollow scull.
' "Our flesh is corrupted, and we [wear] away. We are not
numbered among the living. Let us hide
' "In stones, among roots of trees. The prisoners have
burst their dens,
' "Let us hide; let us hide in the dust; and plague and
wrath and tempest shall cease." '

He ceas'd, silent pond'ring, his brows folded heavy, his
forehead was in affliction,
Like the central fire: from the window he saw his vast
armies spread over the hills,   80

Breathing red fires from man to man, and from horse to
    horse; then his bosom
Expanded like starry heaven, he sat down: his Nobles
    took their ancient seats.

Then the ancientest Peer, Duke of Burgundy, rose
    from the Monarch's right hand, red as wines
From his mountains, an odor of war, like a ripe vine-
    yard, rose from his garments,
And the chamber became as a clouded sky; o'er the
    council he stretch'd his red limbs,
Cloth'd in flames of crimson, as a ripe vineyard stretches
    over sheaves of corn,
The fierce Duke hung over the council; around him
    croud, weeping in his burning robe,
A bright cloud of infant souls; his words fall like purple
    autumn on the sheaves.

'Shall this marble built heaven become a clay cottage,
    this earth an oak stool, and these mowers
'From the Atlantic mountains, mow down all this great
    starry harvest of six thousand years?   90
'And shall Necker, the hind of Geneva, stretch out his
    crook'd sickle o'er fertile France,
PAGE 6
'Till our purple and crimson is faded to russet, and the
    kingdoms of earth bound in sheaves,
'And the ancient forests of chivalry hewn, and the joys of
    the combat burnt for fuel;
'Till the power and dominion is rent from the pole,
    sword and scepter from sun and moon,
'The law and gospel from fire and air, and eternal reason
    and science
'From the deep and the solid, and man lay his faded
    head down on the rock
'Of eternity, where the eternal lion and eagle remain to
    devour?
'This to prevent, urg'd by cries in day, and prophetic
    dreams hovering in night,

'To enrich the lean earth that craves, furrow'd with
plows; whose seed is departing from her;
'Thy Nobles have gather'd thy starry hosts round this
rebellious city   100
'To rouze up the ancient forests of Europe, with clarions of
[loud] breathing war;
'To hear the horse neigh to the drum and trumpet, and
the trumpet and war shout reply;
'Stretch the hand that beckons the eagles of heaven; they
cry over Paris, and wait
'Till Fayette point his finger to Versailles; the eagles of
heaven must have their prey.'

The King lean'd on his mountains, then lifted his head and
look'd on his armies, that shone
Through heaven, tinging morning with beams of blood,
then turning to Burgundy troubled:

PAGE 7

'Burgundy, thou wast born a lion! My soul is o'ergrown
with distress
'For the Nobles of France, and dark mists roll round me
and blot the writing of God
'Written in my bosom. Necker rise, leave the kingdom, thy
life is surrounded with snares;
'We have call'd an Assembly, but not to destroy; we have
given gifts, not to the weak;   110
'I hear rushing of muskets, and bright'ning of swords,
and visages redd'ning with war,
'Frowning and looking up from brooding villages and
every dark'ning city;
'Ancient wonders frown over the kingdom, and cries of
women and babes are heard,
'And tempests of doubt roll around me, and fierce sorrows,
because of the Nobles of France;
'Depart, answer not, for the tempest must fall, as in
years that are passed away.'
He ceas'd, and burn'd silent, red clouds roll round Necker,
a weeping is heard o'er the palace;

Like a dark cloud Necker paus'd, and like thunder on
the just man's burial day he paus'd;
Silent sit the winds, silent the meadows, while the
husbandman and woman of weakness
And bright children look after him into the grave, and
water his clay with love,
Then turn towards pensive fields; so Necker paus'd, and
his visage was cover'd with clouds.   120

Dropping a tear the old man his place left, and when
he was gone out
He set his face toward Geneva to flee, and the women
and children of the city
Kneel'd round him and kissed his garments and wept; he
stood a short space in the street,
Then fled; and the whole city knew he was fled to
Geneva, and the Senate heard it.

But the Nobles burn'd wrathful at Necker's departure, and
wreath'd their clouds and waters
In dismal volumes; as risen from beneath the Archbishop
of Paris arose,
In the rushing of scales and hissing of flames and rolling
of sulphurous smoke.

'Hearken, Monarch of France, to the terrors of heaven,
and let thy soul drink of my counsel;
'Sleeping at midnight in my golden tower, the repose of
the labours of men
'Wav'd its solemn cloud over my head. I awoke; a cold
hand passed over my limbs, and behold   130
'An aged form, white as snow, hov'ring in mist, weeping in
the uncertain light,
PAGE 8
'Dim the form almost faded, tears fell down the shady
cheeks; at his feet many cloth'd
'In white robes, strewn in air censers and harps, silent
they lay prostrated;

'Beneath, in the awful void, myriads descending and
    weeping thro' dismal winds,
'Endless the shady train shiv'ring descended, from the
    gloom where the aged form wept.
'At length, trembling, the vision sighing, in a low voice,
    like the voice of the grasshopper whisper'd:
' "My groaning is heard in the abbeys, and God, so long
    worshipp'd, departs as a lamp
' "Without oil; for a curse is heard hoarse thro' the land,
    from a godless race
' "Descending to beasts; they look downward and labour
    and forget my holy law;
' "The sound of prayer fails from lips of flesh, and the
    holy hymn from thicken'd tongues: 140
' "For the bars of Chaos are burst; her millions prepare
    their fiery way
' "Thro' the orbed abode of the holy dead, to root up and
    pull down and remove,
' "And Nobles and Clergy shall fail from before me, and
    my cloud and vision be no more;
' "The mitre become black, the crown vanish, and the
    scepter and ivory staff
' "Of the ruler wither among bones of death; they shall
    consume from the thistly field,
' "And the sound of the bell, and voice of the sabbath,
    and singing of the holy choir,
' "Is turn'd into songs of the harlot in day, and cries of the
    virgin in night.
' "They shall drop at the plow and faint at the harrow,
    unredeem'd, unconfess'd, unpardon'd;
' "The priest rot in his surplice by the lawless lover, the
    holy beside the accursed,
' "The King, frowning in purple, beside the grey plow-
    man, and their worms embrace together."   150
'The voice ceas'd, a groan shook my chamber; I slept,
    for the cloud of repose returned,
'But morning dawn'd heavy upon me. I rose to bring
    my Prince heaven utter'd counsel.

'Hear my counsel, O King, and send forth thy Generals,
the command of Heaven is upon thee;
'Then do thou command, O King, to shut up this
Assembly in their final home;

PAGE 9
'Let thy soldiers possess this city of rebels, that threaten
to bathe their feet
'In the blood of Nobility; trampling the heart and the
head; let the Bastile devour
'These rebellious seditious; seal them up, O Anointed,
in everlasting chains.'
He sat down, a damp cold pervaded the Nobles, and
monsters of worlds unknown
Swam round them, watching to be delivered; When
Aumont, whose chaos-born soul
Eternally wand'ring a Comet and swift-falling fire, pale
enter'd the chamber;   160
Before the red Council he stood, like a man that returns
from hollow graves.
'Awe surrounded, alone thro' the army a fear and a
with'ring blight blown by the north;
'The Abbe de S[i]eyes from the Nation's Assembly.
O Princes and Generals of France,
'Unquestioned, unhindered, awe-struck are the soldiers;
a dark shadowy man in the form
'Of King Henry the Fourth walks before him in fires, the
captains like men bound in chains
'Stood still as he pass'd, he is come to the Louvre, O
King, with a message to thee;
'The strong soldiers tremble, the horses their manes bow,
and the guards of thy palace are fled.'

Up rose awful in his majestic beams Bourbon's strong
Duke; his proud sword from his thigh
Drawn, he threw on the Earth! the Duke of Bretagne and
the Earl of Borgogne
Rose inflam'd, to and fro in the chamber, like thunder-
clouds ready to burst.   170

'What, damp all our fires, O spectre of Henry,' said
  Bourbon; 'and rend the flames
'From the head of our King! Rise, Monarch of France;
  command me, and I will lead
'This army of superstition at large, that the ardor of
  noble souls quenchless,
'May yet burn in France, nor our shoulders be plow'd
  with the furrows of poverty.'

PAGE 10

Then Orleans generous as mountains arose, and un-
  folded his robe, and put forth
His benevolent hand, looking on the Archbishop, who
  changed as pale as lead;
Would have risen but could not, his voice issued harsh
  grating; instead of words harsh hissings
Shook the chamber; he ceas'd abash'd. Then Orleans
  spoke, all was silent,
He breath'd on them, and said, 'O princes of fire, whose
  flames are for growth not consuming,
'Fear not dreams, fear not visions, nor be you dismay'd
  with sorrows which flee at the morning;   180
'Can the fires of Nobility ever be quench'd, or the stars by
  a stormy night?
'Is the body diseas'd when the members are healthful?
  can the man be bound in sorrow
'Whose ev'ry function is fill'd with its fiery desire? can
  the soul whose brain and heart
'Cast their rivers in equal tides thro' the great Paradise,
  languish because the feet
'Hands, head, bosom, and parts of love, follow their high
  breathing joy?
'And can Nobles be bound when the people are free,
  or God weep when his children are happy?
'Have you never seen Fayette's forehead, or Mirabeau's
  eyes, or the shoulders of Target,
'Or Bailly the strong foot of France, or Clermont the
  terrible voice, and your robes

'Still retain their own crimson? mine never yet faded, for
  fire delights in its form.
'But go, merciless man! enter into the infinite labyrinth
  of another's brain   190
'Ere thou measure the circle that he shall run. Go, thou
  cold recluse, into the fires
'Of another's high flaming rich bosom, and return un-
  consum'd, and write laws.
'If thou can'st not do this, doubt thy theories, learn to
  consider all men as thy equals,
'Thy brethern, and not as thy foot or thy hand, unless
  thou first fearest to hurt them.'

The Monarch stood up, the strong Duke his sword to its
  golden scabbard return'd,
The Nobles sat round like clouds on the mountains,
  when the storm is passing away.
PAGE 11
'Let the Nation's Ambassador come among Nobles, like
  incense of the valley.'

Aumont went out and stood in the hollow porch, his
  ivory wand in his hand;
A cold orb of disdain revolv'd round him, and covered
  his soul with snows eternal.
Great Henry's soul shuddered, a whirlwind and fire tore
  furious from his angry bosom;   200
He indignant departed on horses of heav'n. Then the
  Abbe de S[i]eyes rais'd his feet
On the steps of the Louvre, like a voice of God following
  a storm, the Abbe follow'd
The pale fires of Aumont into the chamber, as a father
  that bows to his son;
Whose rich fields inheriting spread their old glory, so the
  voice of the people bowed
Before the ancient seat of the kingdom and mountains to
  be renewed.
'Hear, O Heavens of France, the voice of the people,
  arising from valley and hill,

'O'erclouded with power. Hear the voice of vallies, the
  voice of meek cities,
'Mourning oppressed on village and field, till the village
  and field is a waste.
'For the husbandman weeps at blights of the fife, and
  blasting of trumpets consume
'The souls of mild France; the pale mother nourishes her
  child to the deadly slaughter.   210
'When the heavens were seal'd with a stone, and the
  terrible sun clos'd in an orb, and the moon
'Rent from the nations, and each star appointed for
  watchers of night,
'The millions of spirits immortal were bound in the ruins
  of sulphur heaven
'To wander inslav'd; black, deprest in dark ignorance,
  kept in awe with the whip,
'To worship terrors, bred from the blood of revenge
  and breath of desire,
'In beastial forms; or more terrible men, till the dawn of
  our peaceful morning,
'Till dawn, till morning, till the breaking of clouds, and
  swelling of winds, and the universal voice,

PAGE 12

'Till man raise his darken'd limbs out of the caves of night,
  his eyes and his heart
'Expand: where is space! where O Sun is thy dwelling!
  where thy tent, O faint slumb'rous Moon.
'Then the valleys of France shall cry to the soldier,
  "throw down thy sword and musket,   220
' "And run and embrace the meek peasant." Her Nobles
  shall hear and shall weep, and put off
'The red robe of terror, the crown of oppression, the
  shoes of contempt, and unbuckle
'The girdle of war from the desolate earth; then the
  Priest in his thund'rous cloud
'Shall weep, bending to earth embracing the valleys, and
  putting his hand to the plow,

'Shall say, "No more I curse thee; but now I will bless
  thee: No more in deadly black
' "Devour thy labour; nor lift up a cloud in thy heavens,
  O laborious plow,
' "That the wild raging millions, that wander in forests,
  and howl in law blasted wastes,
' "Strength madden'd with slavery, honesty, bound in
  the dens of superstition,
' "May sing in the village, and shout in the harvest, and
  woo in pleasant gardens,
' "Their once savage loves, now beaming with knowledge,
  with gentle awe adorned;   230
' "And the saw, and the hammer, the chisel, the pencil,
  the pen, and the instruments
' "Of heavenly song sound in the wilds once forbidden, to
  teach the laborious plowman
' "And shepherd deliver'd from clouds of war, from
  pestilence, from night-fear, from murder,
' "From falling, from stifling, from hunger, from cold,
  from slander, discontent and sloth;
' "That walk in beasts and birds of night, driven back
  by the sandy desert
' "Like pestilent fogs round cities of men: and the happy
  earth sing in its course,
' "The mild peaceable nations be opened to heav'n, and
  men walk with their fathers in bliss."
'Then hear the first voice of the morning: "Depart, O
  clouds of night, and no more
' "Return; be withdrawn cloudy war, troops of warriors
  depart, nor around our peaceable city
' "Breathe fires, but ten miles from Paris, let all be peace,
  nor a soldier be seen!" '   240

PAGE 13

He ended; the wind of contention arose and the clouds
  cast their shadows, the Princes
Like the mountains of France, whose aged trees utter an
  awful voice, and their branches

Are shatter'd, till gradual a murmur is heard descending
    into the valley,
Like a voice in the vineyards of Burgundy, when grapes
    are shaken on grass;
Like the low voice of the labouring man, instead of the
    shout of joy;
And the palace appear'd like a cloud driven abroad; blood
    ran down the ancient pillars,
Thro' the cloud a deep thunder, the Duke of Burgundy,
    delivers the King's command.

'Seest thou yonder dark castle, that moated around, keeps
    this city of Paris in awe.
'Go command yonder tower, saying, "Bastile depart, and
    take thy shadowy course.
' "Overstep the dark river, thou terrible tower, and get
    thee up into the country ten miles.   250
' "And thou black southern prison, move along the dusky
    road to Versailles; there
' "Frown on the gardens", and if it obey and depart, then
    the King will disband
'This war-breathing army; but if it refuse, let the Nation's
    Assembly thence learn,
'That this army of terrors, that prison of horrors, are the
    bands of the murmuring kingdom.'

Like the morning star arising above the black waves, when
    a shipwreck'd soul sighs for morning,
Thro' the ranks, silent, walk'd the Ambassador back to
    the Nation's Assembly, and told
The unwelcome message; silent they heard; then a
    thunder roll'd round loud and louder,
Like pillars of ancient halls, and ruins of times remote they
    sat.
Like a voice from the dim pillars Mirabeau rose; the
    thunders subsided away;
PAGE 14
A rushing of wings around him was heard as he brighten'd,
    and cried out aloud,   260

'Where is the General of the Nation?' the walls re-
echo'd: 'Where is the General of the Nation?'
Sudden as the bullet wrapp'd in his fire, when brazen
cannons rage in the field,
Fayette sprung from his seat saying, Ready! then bowing
like clouds, man toward man, the Assembly
Like a council of ardors seated in clouds, bending over
the cities of men,
And over the armies of strife, where their children are
marshall'd together to battle;
They murmuring divide, while the wind sleeps beneath,
and the numbers are counted in silence,
While they vote the removal of War, and the pestilence
weighs his red wings in the sky.

So Fayette stood silent among the Assembly, and the
votes were given and the numbers numb'red;
And the vote was, that Fayette should order the army to
remove ten miles from Paris.

The aged sun rises appall'd from dark mountains, and
gleams a dusky beam
On Fayette, but on the whole army a shadow, for a cloud
on the eastern hills
Hover'd, and stretch'd across the city and across the
army, and across the Louvre,
Like a flame of fire he stood before dark ranks, and before
expecting captains
On pestilent vapours around him flow frequent spectres
of religious men weeping
In winds driven out of the abbeys, their naked souls
shiver in keen open air,
Driven out by the fiery cloud of Voltaire, and thund'rous
rocks of Rousseau,
They dash like foam against the ridges of the army, utter-
ing a faint feeble cry.

PAGE 15
Gleams of fire streak the heavens, and of sulphur the
earth, from Fayette as he lifted his hand;

270

But silent he stood, till all the officers rush round him
    like waves

Round the shore of France, in day of the British flag,
    when heavy cannons   280

Affright the coasts, and the peasant looks over the sea and
    wipes a tear;

Over his head the soul of Voltaire shone fiery, and over
    the army Rousseau his white cloud

Unfolded, on souls of war-living terrors silent list'ning
    toward Fayette,

His voice loud inspir'd by liberty, and by spirits of the
    dead, thus thunder'd.

'The Nation's Assembly command, that the Army remove
    ten miles from Paris;

'Nor a soldier be seen in road or in field, till the Nation
    command return.'

Rushing along iron ranks glittering the officers each to his
    station

Depart, and the stern captain strokes his proud steed, and
    in front of his solid ranks

Waits the sound of trumpet; captains of foot stand each
    by his cloudy drum;

Then the drum beats, and the steely ranks move, and
    trumpets rejoice in the sky.   290

Dark cavalry like clouds fraught with thunder ascend
    on the hills, and bright infantry, rank

Behind rank, to the soul shaking drum and shrill fife
    along the roads glitter like fire.

The noise of trampling, the wind of trumpets, smote
    the palace walls with a blast.

Pale and cold sat the King in midst of his peers, and his
    noble heart sunk, and his pulses

Suspended their motion, a darkness crept over his eye-lids,
    and chill cold sweat

Sat round his brows faded in faint death, his peers pale
    like mountains of the dead,

Cover'd with dews of night, groaning, shaking forests and
    floods. The cold newt

PAGE 16

And snake, and damp toad, on the kingly foot crawl, or
    croak on the awful knee,

Shedding their slime, in folds of the robe the crown'd
    adder builds and hisses

From stony brows; shaken the forests of France, sick the
    kings of the nations,   300

And the bottoms of the world were open'd, and the graves
    of arch-angels unseal'd;

The enormous dead, lift up their pale fires and look over
    the rocky cliffs.

A faint heat from their fires reviv'd the cold Louvre; the
    frozen blood reflow'd.

Awful up rose the king, him the peers follow'd, they saw
    the courts of the Palace

Forsaken, and Paris without a soldier, silent, for the
    noise was gone up

And follow'd the army, and the Senate in peace, sat be-
    neath morning's beam.

END OF THE FIRST BOOK

[No further books are extant.]

THE MARRIAGE OF HEAVEN AND HELL

PLATE 2

THE ARGUMENT

Rintrah roars & shakes his fires in the burdend air;
Hungry clouds swag on the deep

Once meek, and in a perilous path,
The just man kept his course along
The vale of death.
Roses are planted where thorns grow.
And on the barren heath
Sing the honey bees.

Then the perilous path was planted:
And a river, and a spring   10
On every cliff and tomb;
And on the bleached bones
Red clay brought forth.

Till the villain left the paths of ease,
To walk in perilous paths, and drive
The just man into barren climes.

Now the sneaking serpent walks
In mild humility.
And the just man rages in the wilds
Where lions roam.   20

Rintrah roars & shakes his fires in the burdend air;
Hungry clouds swag on the deep.

PLATE 3

As a new heaven is begun, and it is now thirty-three years since its advent: the Eternal Hell revives. And lo! Swedenborg is the Angel sitting at the tomb; his writings are the linen clothes folded up. Now is the dominion of Edom, & the return of Adam into Paradise; see Isaiah XXXIV & XXXV Chap:

Without Contraries is no progression. Attraction and Repulsion, Reason and Energy, Love and Hate, are necessary to Human existence.

From these contraries spring what the religious call   10
Good & Evil. Good is the passive that obeys Reason[.] Evil is the active springing from Energy.

Good is Heaven. Evil is Hell.

PLATE 4

THE VOICE OF THE DEVIL

All Bibles or sacred codes. have been the causes of the following Errors.

1. That Man has two real existing principles Viz: a Body & a Soul.

2. That Energy. calld Evil. is alone from the Body. & that Reason. calld Good. is alone from the Soul.

3. That God will torment Man in Eternity for following his Energies.

But the following Contraries to these are True

1 Man has no Body distinct from his Soul for that   10
calld Body is a portion of Soul discernd by the five Senses, the chief inlets of Soul in this age

2 Energy is the only life and is from the Body and Reason is the bound or outward circumference of Energy.

3 Energy is Eternal Delight

———————

PLATE 5

Those who restrain desire, do so because theirs is weak enough to be restrained; and the restrainer or reason usurps its place & governs the unwilling.

And being restraind it by degrees becomes passive till it is only the shadow of desire.

The history of this is written in Paradise Lost. & the Governor or Reason is call'd Messiah.

And the original Archangel or possessor of the command of the heavenly host, is calld the Devil or Satan and his children are call'd Sin & Death

But in the Book of Job Miltons Messiah is call'd Satan. For this history has been adopted by both parties

It indeed appear'd to Reason as if Desire was cast out, but the Devils account is, that the Messi[PL.6]ah fell. & formed a heaven of what he stole from the Abyss

This is shewn in the Gospel, where he prays to the Father to send the comforter or Desire that Reason may have Ideas to build on, the Jehovah of the Bible being no other than he, who dwells in flaming fire. Know that after Christs death, he became Jehovah.

But in Milton; the Father is Destiny, the Son, a Ratio of the five senses. & the Holy-ghost, Vacuum!

Note. The reason Milton wrote in fetters when he wrote of Angels & God, and at liberty when of Devils & Hell, is because he was a true Poet and of the Devils party without knowing it

A MEMORABLE FANCY

As I was walking among the fires of hell, delighted with the enjoyments of Genius; which to Angels look like torment and insanity. I collected some of their Proverbs: thinking that as the sayings used in a nation, mark its character, so the Proverbs of Hell, shew the nature of Infernal wisdom better than any description of buildings or garments.

When I came home; on the abyss of the five senses,
where a flat sided steep frowns over the present world.
I saw a mighty Devil folded in black clouds, hovering on
the sides of the rock, with cor[PL.7]roding fires he
wrote the following sentence now percieved by the minds
of men, & read by them on earth.

How do you know but ev'ry Bird that cuts the airy way,
Is an immense world of delight, clos'd by your senses
     five?

PROVERBS OF HELL

In seed time learn, in harvest teach, in winter enjoy.
Drive your cart and your plow over the bones of the dead.
The road of excess leads to the palace of wisdom.
Prudence is a rich ugly old maid courted by Incapacity.
He who desires but acts not, breeds pestilence.   10
The cut worm forgives the plow.
Dip him in the river who loves water.
A fool sees not the same tree that a wise man sees.
He whose face gives no light, shall never become a star.
Eternity is in love with the productions of time.
The busy bee has no time for sorrow.
The hours of folly are measur'd by the clock, but of
     wisdom: no clock can measure.
All wholsom food is caught without a net or a trap.
Bring out number weight & measure in a year of dearth.
No bird soars too high. if he soars with his own wings.   20
A dead body. revenges not injuries.
The most sublime act is to set another before you.
If the fool would persist in his folly he would become wise
Folly is the cloke of knavery.
Shame is Prides cloke.

PLATE 8
Prisons are built with stones of Law, Brothels with
     bricks of Religion.
The pride of the peacock is the glory of God.

The lust of the goat is the bounty of God.

The wrath of the lion is the wisdom of God.

The nakedness of woman is the work of God.

Excess of sorrow laughs. Excess of joy weeps.

The roaring of lions, the howling of wolves, the raging
   of the stormy sea, and the destructive sword. are por-
   tions of eternity too great for the eye of man.

The fox condemns the trap, not himself.

Joys impregnate. Sorrows bring forth.

Let man wear the fell of the lion. woman the fleece of the
   sheep.

10

The bird a nest, the spider a web, man friendship.

The selfish smiling fool. & the sullen frowning fool. shall
   be both thought wise. that they may be a rod.

What is now proved was once, only imagin'd.

The rat, the mouse, the fox, the rabbet; watch the roots,
   the lion, the tyger, the horse, the elephant, watch the
   fruits.

The cistern contains: the fountain overflows

One thought. fills immensity.

Always be ready to speak your mind, and a base man will
   avoid you.

Every thing possible to be believ'd is an image of truth.

The eagle never lost so much time. as when he submitted
   to learn of the crow.

PLATE 9

The fox provides for himself. but God provides for the
   lion.

Think in the morning, Act in the noon, Eat in the even-
   ing, Sleep in the night.

He who has sufferd you to impose on him knows you.

As the plow follows words, so God rewards prayers.

The tygers of wrath are wiser than the horses of in-
   struction

Expect poison from the standing water.

You never know what is enough unless you know what
   is more than enough.

Listen to the fools reproach! it is a kingly title!
The eyes of fire, the nostrils of air, the mouth of water, the
    beard of earth.
The weak in courage is strong in cunning.   10
The apple tree never asks the beech how he shall grow,
    nor the lion, the horse, how he shall take his prey.
The thankful reciever bears a plentiful harvest.
If others had not been foolish, we should be so.
The soul of sweet delight, can never be defil'd,
When thou seest an Eagle, thou seest a portion of Genius.
    lift up thy head!
As the catterpiller chooses the fairest leaves to lay her
    eggs on, so the priest lays his curse on the fairest
    joys.
To create a little flower is the labour of ages.
Damn. braces: Bless relaxes.
The best wine is the oldest. the best water the newest.
Prayers plow not! Praises reap not!   20
Joys laugh not! Sorrows weep not!

PLATE 10
The head Sublime, the heart Pathos, the genitals Beauty,
    the hands & feet Proportion.
As the air to a bird or the sea to a fish, so is contempt to
    the contemptible.
The crow wish'd every thing was black, the owl, that
    every thing was white.
Exuberance is Beauty.
If the lion was advis'd by the fox. he would be cunning.
Improve[me]nt makes strait roads, but the crooked roads
    without Improvement, are roads of Genius.
Sooner murder an infant in its cradle than nurse unacted
    desires
Where man is not nature is barren.
Truth can never be told so as to be understood, and not
    be believ'd.
              Enough! or Too much   10

PLATE 11

The ancient Poets animated all sensible objects with
Gods or Geniuses, calling them by the names and adorn-
ing them with the properties of woods, rivers, mountains,
lakes, cities, nations, and whatever their enlarged &
numerous senses could percieve.

And particularly they studied the genius of each city
& country. placing it under its mental deity.

Till a system was formed, which some took advantage
of & enslav'd the vulgar by attempting to realize or
abstract the mental deities from their objects; thus
began Priesthood.

Choosing forms of worship from poetic tales.

And at length they pronounced that the Gods had
orderd such things.

Thus men forgot that All deities reside in the human
breast.

PLATE 12

A MEMORABLE FANCY

The Prophets Isaiah and Ezekiel dined with me, and
I asked them how they dared so roundly to assert. that
God spake to them; and whether they did not think at the
time, that they would be misunderstood, & so be the
cause of imposition.

Isaiah answer'd. I saw no God. nor heard any, in a
finite organical perception; but my senses discover'd
the infinite in every thing, and as I was then perswaded, &
remain confirm'd; that the voice of honest indignation is
the voice of God, I cared not for consequences but wrote.

Then I asked: does a firm perswasion that a thing is
so, make it so?

He replied. All poets believe that it does, & in ages of
imagination this firm perswasion removed mountains;
but many are not capable of a firm perswasion of any
thing.

Then Ezekiel said. The philosophy of the east taught the first principles of human perception some nations held one principle for the origin & some another, we of Israel taught that the Poetic Genius (as you now call it) was the first principle and all the others merely derivative, which was the cause of our despising the Priests & Philosophers of other countries, and prophecying that all Gods [PL.13] would at last be proved to originate in ours & to be the tributaries of the Poetic Genius, it was this. that our great poet King David desired so fervently & invokes so patheticly, saying by this he conquers enemies & governs kingdoms; and we so loved our God. that we cursed in his name all the deities of surrounding nations, and asserted that they had rebelled; from these opinions the vulgar came to think that all nations would at last be subject to the jews.

This said he, like all firm perswasions, is come to pass, for all nations believe the jews code and worship the jews god, and what greater subjection can be

I heard this with some wonder, & must confess my own conviction. After dinner I ask'd Isaiah to favour the world with his lost works, he said none of equal value was lost. Ezekiel said the same of his.

I also asked Isaiah what made him go naked and barefoot three years? he answered, the same that made our friend Diogenes the Grecian.

I then asked Ezekiel. why he eat dung, & lay so long on his right & left side? he answerd. the desire of raising other men into a perception of the infinite this the North American tribes practise. & is he honest who resists his genius or conscience. only for the sake of present ease or gratification?

PLATE 14
The ancient tradition that the world will be consumed in fire at the end of six thousand years is true. as I have heard from Hell.

For the cherub with his flaming sword is hereby commanded to leave his guard at tree of life, and when he does, the whole creation will be consumed, and appear infinite. and holy whereas it now appears finite & corrupt.

This will come to pass by an improvement of sensual enjoyment.

But first the notion that man has a body distinct from 10
his soul, is to be expunged; this I shall do, by printing in the infernal method. by corrosives, which in Hell are salutory and medicinal, melting apparent surfaces away, and displaying the infinite which was hid.

If the doors of perception were cleansed every thing would appear to man as it is, infinite.

For man has closed himself up, till he sees all things thro' narrow chinks of his cavern.

PLATE 15

A MEMORABLE FANCY

I was in a Printing house in Hell & saw the method in which knowledge is transmitted from generation to generation.

In the first chamber was a Dragon-Man, clearing away the rubbish from a caves mouth; within, a number of Dragons were hollowing the cave,

In the second chamber was a Viper folding round the rock & the cave, and others adorning it with gold silver and precious stones.

In the third chamber was an Eagle with wings and 10
feathers of air, he caused the inside of the cave to be infinite, around were numbers of Eagle like men, who built palaces in the immense cliffs.

In the fourth chamber were Lions of flaming fire raging around & melting the metals into living fluids.

In the fifth chamber were Unnam'd forms, which cast the metals into the expanse.

There they were reciev'd by Men who occupied the sixth chamber, and took the forms of books & were arranged in libraries.   20

PLATE 16

The Giants who formed this world into its sensual existence and now seem to live in it in chains, are in truth. the causes of its life & the sources of all activity, but the chains are, the cunning of weak and tame minds. which have power to resist energy, according to the proverb, the weak in courage is strong in cunning.

Thus one portion of being, is the Prolific. the other, the Devouring: to the devourer it seems as if the producer was in his chains, but it is not so, he only takes portions of existence and fancies that the whole.   10

But the Prolific would cease to be Prolific unless the Devourer as a sea recieved the excess of his delights.

Some will say, Is not God alone the Prolific? I answer, God only Acts & Is, in existing beings or Men.

These two classes of men are always upon earth, & they should be enemies; whoever tries [PL. 17] to reconcile them seeks to destroy existence.

Religion is an endeavour to reconcile the two.

Note. Jesus Christ did not wish to unite but to separate them, as in the Parable of sheep and goats! & he says I came not to send Peace but a Sword.

Messiah or Satan or Tempter was formerly thought to be one of the Antediluvians who are our Energies.

A MEMORABLE FANCY

An Angel came to me and said   O pitiable foolish young man! O horrible! O dreadful state! consider the   10 hot burning dungeon thou art preparing for thyself to all eternity, to which thou art going in such career.

I said. perhaps you will be willing to shew me my eternal lot & we will contemplate together upon it and see whether your lot or mine is most desirable

So he took me thro' a stable & thro' a church & down into the church vault at the end of which was a mill: thro' the mill we went, and came to a cave. down the winding cavern we groped our tedious way till a void boundless as a nether sky appeard beneath us. & we held by the roots of trees and hung over this immensity, but I said, if you please we will commit ourselves to this void, and see whether providence is here also, if you will not I will? but he answerd, do not presume O young-man but as we here remain behold thy lot which will soon appear when the darkness passes away

So I remaind with him sitting in the twisted [PL. 18] root of an oak. he was suspended in a fungus which hung with the head downward into the deep;

By degrees we beheld the infinite Abyss, fiery as the smoke of a burning city; beneath us at an immense distance was the sun, black but shining[;] round it were fiery tracks on which revolv'd vast spiders, crawling after their prey; which flew or rather swum in the infinite deep, in the most terrific shapes of animals sprung from corruption. & the air was full of them, & seemd composed of them; these are Devils. and are called Powers of the air, I now asked my companion which was my eternal lot? he said, between the black & white spiders

But now, from between the black & white spiders a cloud and fire burst and rolled thro the deep blackning all beneath, so that the nether deep grew black as a sea & rolled with a terrible noise: beneath us was nothing now to be seen but a black tempest, till looking east between the clouds & the waves. we saw a cataract of blood mixed with fire and not many stones throw from us appeard and sunk again the scaly fold of a monstrous serpent[.] at last to the east, distant about three degrees appeard a fiery crest above the waves slowly it reared like a ridge of golden rocks till we discoverd two globes of crimson fire, from which the sea fled away in clouds of smoke, and now we saw, it was the head of Leviathan, his forehead was divided into streaks of green & purple like those

on a tygers forehead: soon we saw his mouth & red gills
hang just above the raging foam tinging the black deep
with beams of blood, advancing toward [PL. 19] us with
all the fury of a spiritual existence.

My friend the Angel climb'd up from his station into
the mill; I remain'd alone, & then this appearance was no
more, but I found myself sitting on a pleasant bank be-
side a river by moon light hearing a harper who sung to
the harp, & his theme was, The man who never alters his
opinion is like standing water, & breeds reptiles of the
mind.

But I arose, and sought for the mill, & there I found   10
my Angel, who surprised asked me, how I escaped?

I answerd. All that we saw was owing to your meta-
physics: for when you ran away, I found myself on a
bank by moonlight hearing a harper, But now we have
seen my eternal lot, shall I shew you yours? he laughd at
my proposal; but I by force suddenly caught him in my
arms, & flew westerly thro' the night, till we were ele-
vated above the earths shadow: then I flung myself with
him directly into the body of the sun, here I clothed
myself in white, & taking in my hand Swedenborgs   20
volumes sunk from the glorious clime, and passed all
the planets till we came to saturn, here I staid to rest &
then leap'd into the void. between saturn & the fixed stars.

Here said I! is your lot, in this space, if space it may
be calld, Soon we saw the stable and the church, & I
took him to the altar and open'd the Bible, and lo! it was
a deep pit, into which I descended driving the Angel
before me, soon we saw seven houses of brick, one we
enterd; in it were a [PL. 20] number of monkeys, baboons,
& all of that species chaind by the middle, grinning and
snatching at one another, but witheld by the shortness of
their chains: however I saw that they sometimes grew
numerous, and then the weak were caught by the strong
and with a grinning aspect, first coupled with & then
devourd, by plucking off first one limb and then another
till the body was left a helpless trunk. this after grinning &

kissing it with seeming fondness they devour'd too; and
here & there I saw one savourily picking the flesh off his   10
own tail; as the stench terribly annoyd us both we went
into the mill, & I in my hand brought the skeleton of a
body, which in the mill was Aristotles Analytics.

So the Angel said: thy phantasy has imposed upon
me & thou oughtest to be ashamed.

I answerd: we impose on one another, & it is but lost
time to converse with you whose works are only Analytics

Opposition is true Friendship.

PLATE 21

I have always found that Angels have the vanity to
speak of themselves as the only wise; this they do with a
confident insolence sprouting from systematic reasoning:

Thus Swedenborg boasts that what he writes is new:
tho' it is only the Contents or Index of already publish'd
books

A man carried a monkey about for a shew. & because
he was a little wiser than the monkey, grew vain. and
conciev'd himself as much wiser than seven men. It is so
with Swedenborg; he shews the folly of churches &   10
exposes hypocrites, till he imagines that all are religious.
& himself the single [PL. 22] one on earth that ever broke a
net.

Now hear a plain fact: Swedenborg has not written
one new truth: Now hear another: he has written all the
old falshoods.

And now hear the reason. He conversed with Angels
who are all religious, & conversed not with Devils who
all hate religion, for he was incapable thro' his con-
ceited notions.

Thus Swedenborgs writings are a recapitulation of all   10
superficial opinions, and an analysis of the more sub-
lime. but no further.

Have now another plain fact: Any man of mechanical

talents may from the writings of Paracelsus or Jacob
Behmen, produce ten thousand volumes of equal value
with Swedenborg's. and from those of Dante or Shakes-
pear, an infinite number.

But when he has done this, let him not say that he
knows better than his master, for he only holds a candle
in sunshine.   20

A MEMORABLE FANCY

Once I saw a Devil in a flame of fire. who arose before
an Angel that sat on a cloud. and the Devil utterd these
words.

The worship of God is. Honouring his gifts in other
men each according to his genius. and loving the [PL. 23]
greatest men best, those who envy or calumniate great
men hate God, for there is no other God.

The Angel hearing this became almost blue but
mastering himself he grew yellow, & at last white pink &
smiling. and then replied,

Thou Idolater, is not God One? & is not he visible in
Jesus Christ? and has not Jesus Christ given his sanction
to the law of ten commandments and are not all other
men fools, sinners, & nothings?

The Devil answer'd; bray a fool in a morter with   10
wheat. yet shall not his folly be beaten out of him: if
Jesus Christ is the greatest man, you ought to love him
in the greatest degree; now hear how he has given his
sanction to the law of ten commandments: did he not
mock at the sabbath, and so mock the sabbaths God?
murder those who were murderd because of him? turn
away the law from the woman taken in adultery? steal
the labor of others to support him? bear false witness
when he omitted making a defence before Pilate? covet
when he pray'd for his disciples, and when he bid them   20
shake off the dust of their feet against such as refused to
lodge them? I tell you, no virtue can exist without
breaking these ten commandments ∴. Jesus was all virtue,
and acted from im[PL. 24]pulse. not from rules.

When he had so spoken: I beheld the Angel who stretched out his arms embracing the flame of fire & he was consumed and arose as Elijah.

Note. This Angel, who is now become a Devil, is my particular friend: we often read the Bible together in its infernal or diabolical sense which the world shall have if they behave well

I have also: The Bible of Hell: which the world shall have whether they will or no. 10

One Law for the Lion & Ox is Oppression

PLATE 25
A Song of Liberty

1. The Eternal Female groand! it was heard over all the Earth:
2. Albions coast is sick silent; the American meadows faint!
3. Shadows of Prophecy shiver along by the lakes and the rivers and mutter across the ocean? France rend down thy dungeon;
4. Golden Spain burst the barriers of old Rome;
5. Cast thy keys O Rome into the deep down falling, even to eternity down falling, 10
6. And weep
7. In her trembling hands she took the new born terror howling:
8. On those infinite mountains of light now barr'd out by the atlantic sea, the new born fire stood before the starry king!
9. Flag'd with grey brow'd snows and thunderous visages the jealous wings wav'd over the deep.
10. The speary hand burned aloft, unbuckled was the shield, forth went the hand of jealousy among the 20 flaming hair, and [PL. 26] hurl'd the new born wonder thro' the starry night.

11. The fire, the fire, is falling!

12. Look up! look up! O citizen of London. enlarge thy countenance; O Jew, leave counting gold! return to thy oil and wine; O African! black African! (go. winged thought widen his forehead.)

13. The fiery limbs, the flaming hair, shot like the sinking sun into the western sea.

14. Wak'd from his eternal sleep, the hoary element   10 roaring fled away:

15. Down rushd beating his wings in vain the jealous king; his grey brow'd councellors, thunderous warriors, curl'd veterans, among helms, and shields, and chariots[,] horses, elephants: banners, castles, slings and rocks,

16. Falling, rushing, ruining! buried in the ruins, on Urthona's dens.

17. All night beneath the ruins, then their sullen flames faded emerge round the gloomy king,

18. With thunder and fire: leading his starry hosts thro'   20 the waste wilderness [PL. 27] he promulgates his ten commands, glancing his beamy eyelids over the deep in dark dismay,

19. Where the son of fire in his eastern cloud, while the morning plumes her golden breast.

20. Spurning the clouds written with curses. stamps the stony law to dust, loosing the eternal horses from the dens of night, crying

Empire is no more! and now the lion & wolf shall cease.

CHORUS

Let the Priests of the Raven of dawn, no longer in   10 deadly black. with hoarse note curse the sons of joy. Nor his accepted brethren whom, tyrant, he calls free: lay the bound or build the roof. Nor pale religious letchery call that virginity, that wishes but acts not!

For every thing that lives is Holy

VISIONS OF THE DAUGHTERS OF AL

The Eye sees more than the Heart knows.

PLATE iii
THE ARGUMENT

I loved Theotormon
And I was not ashamed
I trembled in my virgin fears
And I hid in Leutha's vale!

I plucked Leutha's flower,
And I rose up from the vale;
But the terrible thunders tore
My virgin mantle in twain.

PLATE I
VISIONS

Enslav'd, the Daughters of Albion weep: a trembling
  lamentation
Upon their mountains; in their valleys, sighs toward
  America.

For the soft soul of America, Oothoon wanderd in woe,
Along the vales of Leutha seeking flowers to comfort her;
And thus she spoke to the bright Marygold of Leutha's
  vale
Art thou a flower! art thou a nymph! I see thee now a
  flower;
Now a nymph! I dare not pluck thee from thy dewy bed!

The Golden nymph replied; pluck thou my flower
  Oothoon the mild

Another flower shall spring, because the soul of sweet
    delight
Can never pass away. she ceas'd & closd her golden
    shrine.   10

Then Oothoon pluck'd the flower saying, I pluck thee
    from thy bed
Sweet flower. and put thee here to glow between my
    breasts
And thus I turn my face to where my whole soul seeks.

Over the waves she went in wing'd exulting swift delight;
And over Theotormons reign, took her impetuous course.

Bromion rent her with his thunders. on his stormy bed
Lay the faint maid, and soon her woes appalld his
    thunders hoarse

Bromion spoke. behold this harlot here on Bromions bed,
And let the jealous dolphins sport around the lovely
    maid;
Thy soft American plains are mine, and mine thy north
    & south: 20
Stampt with my signet are the swarthy children of the
    sun:
They are obedient, they resist not, they obey the
    scourge:
Their daughters worship terrors and obey the violent:
PLATE 2
Now thou maist marry Bromions harlot, and protect the
    child
Of Bromions rage, that Oothoon shall put forth in nine
    moons time

Then storms rent Theotormons limbs; he rolld his
    waves around.
And folded his black jealous waters round the adulterate
    pair
Bound back to back in Bromions caves terror &
    meekness dwell

At entrance Theotormon sits wearing the threshold hard
With secret tears; beneath him sound like waves on a
   desert shore
The voice of slaves beneath the sun, and children bought
   with money.
That shiver in religious caves beneath the burning fires
Of lust, that belch incessant from the summits of the
   earth   10

Oothoon weeps not: she cannot weep! her tears are
   locked up;
But she can howl incessant writhing her soft snowy
   limbs.
And calling Theotormons Eagles to prey upon her flesh.

I call with holy voice! kings of the sounding air,
Rend away this defiled bosom that I may reflect.
The image of Theotormon on my pure transparent
   breast.

The Eagles at her call descend & rend their bleeding
   prey;
Theotormon severely smiles. her soul reflects the smile;
As the clear spring mudded with feet of beasts grows
   pure & smiles.

The Daughters of Albion hear her woes. & eccho back
   her sighs.   20
Why does my Theotormon sit weeping upon the
   threshold;
And Oothoon hovers by his side, perswading him in
   vain:
I cry arise O Theotormon for the village dog
Barks at the breaking day. the nightingale has done
   lamenting.
The lark does rustle in the ripe corn, and the Eagle
   returns
From nightly prey, and lifts his golden beak to the pure
   east;
Shaking the dust from his immortal pinions to awake

The sun that sleeps too long. Arise my Theotormon I
  am pure.
Because the night is gone that clos'd me in its deadly
  black.
They told me that the night & day were all that I could
  see;   30
They told me that I had five senses to inclose me up.
And they inclos'd my infinite brain into a narrow circle.
And sunk my heart into the Abyss, a red round globe hot
  burning
Till all from life I was obliterated and erased.
Instead of morn arises a bright shadow, like an eye
In the eastern cloud: instead of night a sickly charnel
  house;
That Theotormon hears me not! to him the night and
  morn
Are both alike: a night of sighs, a morning of fresh tears;
PLATE 3
And none but Bromion can hear my lamentations.

With what sense is it that the chicken shuns the
  ravenous hawk?
With what sense does the tame pigeon measure out the
  expanse?
With what sense does the bee form cells? have not the
  mouse & frog
Eyes and ears and sense of touch? yet are their
  habitations.
And their pursuits, as different as their forms and as
  their joys:
Ask the wild ass why he refuses burdens: and the meek
  camel
Why he loves man: is it because of eye ear mouth or
  skin
Or breathing nostrils? No. for these the wolf and tyger
  have.
Ask the blind worm the secrets of the grave, and why
  her spires   10

Love to curl round the bones of death; and ask the
rav'nous snake

Where she gets poison: & the wing'd eagle why he loves
the sun

And then tell me the thoughts of man, that have been
hid of old.

Silent I hover all the night, and all day could be silent.
If Theotormon once would turn his loved eyes upon me;
How can I be defild when I reflect thy image pure?
Sweetest the fruit that the worm feeds on. & the soul
prey'd on by woe

The new wash'd lamb ting'd with the village smoke &
the bright swan

By the red earth of our immortal river: I bathe my
wings.

And I am white and pure to hover round Theotormons
breast.   20

Then Theotormon broke his silence. and he answered.

Tell me what is the night or day to one o'erflowd with
woe?

Tell me what is a thought? & of what substance is it
made?

Tell me what is a joy? & in what gardens do joys grow?
And in what rivers swim the sorrows? and upon what
mountains

PLATE 4

Wave shadows of discontent? and in what houses dwell
the wretched

Drunken with woe forgotten. and shut up from cold
despair.

Tell me where dwell the thoughts forgotten till thou call
them forth

Tell me where dwell the joys of old? & where the
ancient loves?

And when will they renew again & the night of
  oblivion past?
That I might traverse times & spaces far remote and
  bring
Comforts into a present sorrow and a night of pain
Where goest thou O thought! to what remote land is thy
  flight?
If thou returnest to the present moment of affliction
Wilt thou bring comforts on thy wings. and dews and
  honey and balm;   10
Or poison from the desart wilds, from the eyes of the
  envier.

Then Bromion said: and shook the cavern with his
  lamentation

Thou knowest that the ancient trees seen by thine eyes
  have fruit;
But knowest thou that trees and fruits flourish upon the
  earth
To gratify senses unknown? trees beasts and birds
  unknown:
Unknown, not unpercievd, spread in the infinite
  microscope,
In places yet unvisited by the voyager, and in worlds
Over another kind of seas, and in atmospheres
  unknown:
Ah! are there other wars, beside the wars of sword and
  fire!
And are there other sorrows, beside the sorrows of
  poverty!   20
And are there other joys, beside the joys of riches and
  ease?
And is there not one law for both the lion and the ox?
And is there not eternal fire, and eternal chains?
To bind the phantoms of existence from eternal life?

Then Oothoon waited silent all the day. and all the
  night,

PLATE 5

But when the morn arose, her lamentation renewd,
The Daughters of Albion hear her woes, & eccho back her
  sighs.

O Urizen! Creator of men! mistaken Demon of heaven:
Thy joys are tears! thy labour vain, to form men to
  thine image.
How can one joy absorb another? are not different joys
Holy, eternal, infinite! and each joy is a Love.

Does not the great mouth laugh at a gift? & the narrow
  eyelids mock
At the labour that is above payment, and wilt thou take
  the ape
For thy councellor? or the dog, for a schoolmaster to
  thy children?
Does he who contemns poverty, and he who turns with
  abhorrence   10
From usury: feel the same passion or are they moved
  alike?
How can the giver of gifts experience the delights of the
  merchant?
How the industrious citizen the pains of the
  husbandman.
How different far the fat fed hireling with hollow drum;
Who buys whole corn fields into wastes, and sings upon
  the heath:
How different their eye and ear! how different the
  world to them!
With what sense does the parson claim the labour of the
  farmer?
What are his nets & gins & traps. & how does he
  surround him
With cold floods of abstraction, and with forests of
  solitude,
To build him castles and high spires. where kings &
  priests may dwell.   20

Till she who burns with youth. and knows no fixed lot;
   is bound
In spells of law to one she loaths: and must she drag the
   chain
Of life, in weary lust: must chilling murderous thoughts,
   obscure
The clear heaven of her eternal spring? to bear the
   wintry rage
Of a harsh terror driv'n to madness, bound to hold a rod
Over her shrinking shoulders all the day; & all the night
To turn the wheel of false desire: and longings that
   wake her womb
To the abhorred birth of cherubs in the human form
That live a pestilence & die a meteor & are no more.
Till the child dwell with one he hates. and do the deed
   he loaths   30
And the impure scourge force his seed into its unripe
   birth
E'er yet his eyelids can behold the arrows of the day.

Does the whale worship at thy footsteps as the hungry
   dog?
Or does he scent the mountain prey, because his nostrils
   wide
Draw in the ocean? does his eye discern the flying cloud
As the ravens eye? or does he measure the expanse like
   the vulture?
Does the still spider view the cliffs where eagles hide
   their young?
Or does the fly rejoice, because the harvest is brought in?
Does not the eagle scorn the earth & despise the treasures
   beneath?
But the mole knoweth what is there, & the worm shall
   tell it thee.   40
Does not the worm erect a pillar in the mouldering
   church yard?

PLATE 6

And a palace of eternity in the jaws of the hungry grave
Over his porch these words are written. Take thy bliss
   O Man!
And sweet shall be thy taste & sweet thy infant joys
   renew!

Infancy, fearless, lustful, happy! nestling for delight
In laps of pleasure; Innocence! honest, open, seeking
The vigorous joys of morning light; open to virgin bliss,
Who taught thee modesty, subtil modesty! child of night
   & sleep
When thou awakest. wilt thou dissemble all thy secret
   joys
Or wert thou not, awake when all this mystery was
   disclos'd!
Then com'st thou forth a modest virgin knowing to
   dissemble   10
With nets found under thy night pillow, to catch virgin
   joy,
And brand it with the name of whore; & sell it in the
   night,
In silence. ev'n without a whisper, and in seeming sleep:
Religious dreams and holy vespers, light thy smoky fires:
Once were thy fires lighted by the eyes of honest morn
And does my Theotormon seek this hypocrite modesty!
This knowing, artful, secret, fearful, cautious, trembling
   hypocrite.
Then is Oothoon a whore indeed! and all the virgin joys
Of life are harlots: and Theotormon is a sick mans
   dream
And Oothoon is the crafty slave of selfish holiness.   20
But Oothoon is not so, a virgin fill'd with virgin fancies
Open to joy and to delight where ever beauty appears
If in the morning sun I find it: there my eyes are fix'd
PLATE 7
In happy copulation; if in evening mild. wearied with
   work;

Sit on a bank and draw the pleasures of this free born
   joy.

The moment of desire! the moment of desire! The
   virgin
That pines for man; shall awaken her womb to
   enormous joys
In the secret shadows of her chamber; the youth shut up
   from
The lustful joy. shall forget to generate. & create an
   amorous image
In the shadows of his curtains and in the folds of his
   silent pillow.
Are not these the places of religion? the rewards of
   continence?
The self enjoyings of self denial? Why dost thou seek
   religion?
Is it because acts are not lovely, that thou seekest
   solitude,   10
Where the horrible darkness is impressed with
   reflections of desire.

Father of Jealousy. be thou accursed from the earth!
Why hast thou taught my Theotormon this accursed
   thing?
Till beauty fades from off my shoulders darken'd and
   cast out,
A solitary shadow wailing on the margin of non-entity.

I cry, Love! Love! Love! happy happy Love! free as the
   mountain wind!
Can that be Love, that drinks another as a sponge drinks
   water?
That clouds with jealousy his nights, with weepings all
   the day:
To spin a web of age around him. grey and hoary! dark!
Till his eyes sicken at the fruit that hangs. before his
   sight.   20

Such is self-love that envies all! a creeping skeleton
With lamplike eyes watching around the frozen marriage
  bed.

But silken nets and traps of adamant will Oothoon
  spread,
And catch for thee girls of mild silver, or of furious
  gold;
I'll lie beside thee on a bank & view their wanton play
In lovely copulation bliss on bliss with Theotormon:
Red as the rosy morning, lustful as the first born beam,
Oothoon shall view his dear delight, nor e'er with jealous
  cloud
Come in the heaven of generous love; nor selfish
  blightings bring.

Does the sun walk in glorious raiment. on the secret
  floor   30
PLATE 8
Where the cold miser spreads his gold? or does the
  bright cloud drop
On his stone threshold? does his eye behold the beam
  that brings
Expansion to the eye of pity? or will he bind himself
Beside the ox to thy hard furrow? does not that mild
  beam blot
The bat, the owl, the glowing tyger, and the king of
  night.
The sea fowl takes the wintry blast. for a cov'ring to her
  limbs:
And the wild snake, the pestilence to adorn him with
  gems & gold.
And trees. & birds. & beasts. & men. behold their
  eternal joy.
Arise you little glancing wings, and sing your infant
  joy!
Arise and drink your bliss, for every thing that lives is
  holy!   10

Thus every morning wails Oothoon. but Theotormon
  sits
Upon the margind ocean conversing with shadows dire.

The Daughters of Albion hear her woes, & eccho back
  her sighs.

The End

AMERICA

A PROPHECY

PLATE 1

PRELUDIUM

The shadowy daughter of Urthona stood before red Orc.
When fourteen suns had faintly journey'd o'er his dark
    abode;
His food she brought in iron baskets, his drink in cups
    of iron;
Crown'd with a helmet & dark hair the nameless female
    stood;
A quiver with its burning stores, a bow like that of
    night,
When pestilence is shot from heaven; no other arms she
    need:
Invulnerable tho' naked, save where clouds roll round
    her loins,
Their awful folds in the dark air; silent she stood as
    night;
For never from her iron tongue could voice or sound
    arise;
But dumb till that dread day when Orc assay'd his fierce
    embrace. 10

Dark virgin; said the hairy youth, thy father stern
    abhorr'd;
Rivets my tenfold chains while still on high my spirit
    soars;

Sometimes an eagle screaming in the sky, sometimes a
   lion,
Stalking upon the mountains, & sometimes a whale I
   lash
The raging fathomless abyss, anon a serpent folding
Around the pillars of Urthona, and round thy dark
   limbs,
On the Canadian wilds I fold, feeble my spirit folds.
For chaind beneath I rend these caverns; when thou
   bringest food
I howl my joy! and my red eyes seek to behold thy face
In vain! these clouds roll to & fro, & hide thee from my
   sight.   20

PLATE 2
Silent as despairing love, and strong as jealousy,
The hairy shoulders rend the links, free are the wrists of
   fire;
Round the terrific loins he siez'd the panting struggling
   womb;
It joy'd: she put aside her clouds & smiled her first-born
   smile;
As when a black cloud shews its light'nings to the silent
   deep.

Soon as she saw the terrible boy then burst the virgin
   cry.

I know thee, I have found thee, & I will not let thee go;
Thou art the image of God who dwells in darkness of
   Africa;
And thou art fall'n to give me life in regions of dark
   death.
On my American plains I feel the struggling afflictions   10
Endur'd by roots that writhe their arms into the nether
   deep:
I see a serpent in Canada, who courts me to his love;
In Mexico an Eagle, and a Lion in Peru;
I see a Whale in the South-sea, drinking my soul away.
O what limb rending pains I feel, thy fire & my frost

Mingle in howling pains, in furrows by thy lightnings
    rent;
This is eternal death; and this the torment long foretold.

The stern Bard ceas'd, asham'd of his own song;
    enrag'd he swung
His harp aloft sounding, then dash'd its shining frame
    against
A ruin'd pillar in glittring fragments; silent he turn'd
    away,   20
And wander'd down the vales of Kent in sick & drear
    lamentings.

PLATE 3

A PROPHECY

The Guardian Prince of Albion burns in his nightly tent,
Sullen fires across the Atlantic glow to America's shore:
Piercing the souls of warlike men, who rise in silent
    night,
Washington, Franklin, Paine & Warren, Gates,
    Hancock & Green;
Meet on the coast glowing with blood from Albions fiery
    Prince.

Washington spoke; Friends of America look over the
    Atlantic sea;
A bended bow is lifted in heaven, & a heavy iron chain
Descends link by link from Albions cliffs across the sea
    to bind
Brothers & sons of America, till our faces pale and
    yellow;
Heads deprest, voices weak, eyes downcast, hands
    work-bruis'd,   10
Feet bleeding on the sultry sands, and the furrows of the
    whip
Descend to generations that in future times forget. –

The strong voice ceas'd; for a terrible blast swept over
    the heaving sea;
The eastern cloud rent; on his cliffs stood Albions
    wrathful Prince
A dragon form clashing his scales at midnight he arose,
And flam'd red meteors round the land of Albion
    beneath[.]
His voice, his locks, his awful shoulders, and his glowing
    eyes,
PLATE 4
Appear to the Americans upon the cloudy night.

Solemn heave the Atlantic waves between the gloomy
    nations,
Swelling, belching from its deeps red clouds & raging
    Fires!
Albion is sick! America faints! enrag'd the Zenith grew.
As human blood shooting its veins all round the orbed
    heaven
Red rose the clouds from the Atlantic in vast wheels of
    blood
And in the red clouds rose a Wonder o'er the Atlantic
    sea;
Intense! naked! a Human fire fierce glowing, as the
    wedge
Of iron heated in the furnace; his terrible limbs were fire
With myriads of cloudy terrors banners dark & towers   10
Surrounded; heat but not light went thro' the murky
    atmosphere

The King of England looking westward trembles at the
    vision

PLATE 5
Albions Angel stood beside the Stone of night, and saw
The terror like a comet, or more like the planet red
That once inclos'd the terrible wandering comets in its
    sphere.

Then Mars thou wast our center, & the planets three
    flew round
Thy crimson disk; so e'er the Sun was rent from thy red
    sphere;
The Spectre glowd his horrid length staining the temple
    long
With beams of blood; & thus a voice came forth, and
    shook the temple

PLATE 6

The morning comes, the night decays, the watchmen
    leave their stations;
The grave is burst, the spices shed, the linen wrapped
    up;
The bones of death, the cov'ring clay, the sinews shrunk
    & dry'd.
Reviving shake, inspiring move, breathing! awakening!
Spring like redeemed captives when their bonds & bars
    are burst;
Let the slave grinding at the mill, run out into the field:
Let him look up into the heavens & laugh in the bright
    air;
Let the inchained soul shut up in darkness and in
    sighing,
Whose face has never seen a smile in thirty weary years;
Rise and look out, his chains are loose, his dungeon doors
    are open.   10
And let his wife and children return from the opressors
    scourge;
They look behind at every step & believe it is a dream.
Singing. The Sun has left his blackness, & has found a
    fresher morning
And the fair Moon rejoices in the clear & cloudless
    night;
For Empire is no more, and now the Lion & Wolf shall
    cease.

PLATE 7

In thunders ends the voice. Then Albions Angel wrathful
   burnt
Beside the Stone of Night; and like the Eternal Lions
   howl
In famine & war, reply'd. Art thou not Orc; who
   serpent-form'd
Stands at the gate of Enitharmon to devour her children;
Blasphemous Demon, Antichrist, hater of Dignities;
Lover of wild rebellion, and transgresser of Gods Law;
Why dost thou come to Angels eyes in this terrific form?

PLATE 8

The terror answerd: I am Orc, wreath'd round the
   accursed tree:
The times are ended; shadows pass the morning gins to
   break;
The fiery joy, that Urizen perverted to ten commands,
What night he led the starry hosts thro' the wide
   wilderness:
That stony law I stamp to dust: and scatter religion
   abroad
To the four winds as a torn book, & none shall gather
   the leaves;
But they shall rot on desart sands, & consume in
   bottomless deeps;
To make the desarts blossom, & the deeps shrink to their
   fountains,
And to renew the fiery joy, and burst the stony roof.
That pale religious letchery, seeking Virginity,   10
May find it in a harlot, and in coarse-clad honesty
The undefil'd tho' ravish'd in her cradle night and
   morn:
For every thing that lives is holy, life delights in life;
Because the soul of sweet delight can never be defil'd.
Fires inwrap the earthly globe, yet man is not consumd;
Amidst the lustful fires he walks: his feet become like
   brass,

His knees and thighs like silver, & his breast and head
  like gold.

PLATE 9

Sound! sound! my loud war-trumpets & alarm my
  Thirteen Angels!
Loud howls the eternal Wolf! the eternal Lion lashes his
  tail!
America is darkned; and my punishing Demons
  terrified
Crouch howling before their caverns deep like skins
  dry'd in the wind.
They cannot smite the wheat, nor quench the fatness of
  the earth.
They cannot smite with sorrows, nor subdue the plow
  and spade.
They cannot wall the city, nor moat round the castle of
  princes.
They cannot bring the stubbed oak to overgrow the
  hills.
For terrible men stand on the shores, & in their robes I
  see
Children take shelter from the lightnings, there stands
  Washington
And Paine and Warren with their foreheads reard
  toward the east
But clouds obscure my aged sight. A vision from afar!
Sound! sound! my loud war-trumpets & alarm my
  thirteen Angels:
Ah vision from afar! Ah rebel form that rent the ancient
Heavens; Eternal Viper self-renew'd, rolling in clouds
I see thee in thick clouds and darkness on America's
  shore.
Writhing in pangs of abhorred birth; red flames the crest
  rebellious
And eyes of death; the harlot womb oft opened in vain
Heaves in enormous circles, now the times are
  return'd upon thee,

10

Devourer of thy parent, now thy unutterable torment
   renews.   20
Sound! sound! my loud war trumpets & alarm my
   thirteen Angels!
Ah terrible birth! a young one bursting! where is the
   weeping mouth?
And where the mothers milk? instead those ever-hissing
   jaws
And parched lips drop with fresh gore; now roll thou in
   the clouds
Thy mother lays her length outstretch'd upon the shore
   beneath.
Sound! sound! my loud war-trumpets & alarm my
   thirteen Angels!
Loud howls the eternal Wolf: the eternal Lion lashes his
   tail!

PLATE 10
Thus wept the Angel voice & as he wept the terrible
   blasts
Of trumpets, blew a loud alarm across the Atlantic deep.
No trumpets answer; no reply of clarions or of fifes,
Silent the Colonies remain and refuse the loud alarm.

On those vast shady hills between America & Albions
   shore;
Now barr'd out by the Atlantic sea: call'd Atlantean
   hills:
Because from their bright summits you may pass to the
   Golden world
An ancient palace, archetype of mighty Emperies,
Rears its immortal pinnacles, built in the forest of God
By Ariston the king of beauty for his stolen bride,   10

Here on their magic seats the thirteen Angels sat
   perturb'd
For clouds from the Atlantic hover o'er the solemn roof.

PLATE 11

Fiery the Angels rose, & as they rose deep thunder
  roll'd
Around their shores: indignant burning with the fires of
  Orc
And Bostons Angel cried aloud as they flew thro' the
  dark night.

He cried: Why trembles honesty and like a murderer,
Why seeks he refuge from the frowns of his immortal
  station!
Must the generous tremble & leave his joy, to the idle:
  to the pestilence!
That mock him? who commanded this? what God?
  what Angel!
To keep the gen'rous from experience till the
  ungenerous
Are unrestraind performers of the energies of nature;
Till pity is become a trade, and generosity a science,   10
That men get rich by, & the sandy desert is giv'n to the
  strong
What God is he, writes laws of peace, & clothes him in a
  tempest
What pitying Angel lusts for tears, and fans himself
  with sighs
What crawling villain preaches abstinence & wraps
  himself
In fat of lambs? no more I follow, no more obedience
  pay.

PLATE 12

So cried he, rending off his robe & throwing down his
  scepter.
In sight of Albions Guardian, and all the thirteen Angels
Rent off their robes to the hungry wind, & threw their
  golden scepters
Down on the land of America, indignant they descended

Headlong from out their heav'nly heights, descending
   swift as fires
Over the land; naked & flaming are their lineaments seen
In the deep gloom, by Washington & Paine & Warren
   they stood
And the flame folded roaring fierce within the pitchy
   night
Before the Demon red, who burnt towards America,
In black smoke thunders and loud winds rejoicing in its
   terror   .   10
Breaking in smoky wreaths from the wild deep, &
   gath'ring thick
In flames as of a furnace on the land from North to
   South

PLATE 13

What time the thirteen Governors that England sent
   convene
In Bernards house; the flames coverd the land, they
   rouze they cry
Shaking their mental chains they rush in fury to the sea
To quench their anguish; at the feet of Washington
   down fall'n
They grovel on the sand and writhing lie, while all
The British soldiers thro' the thirteen states sent up a
   howl
Of anguish: threw their swords & muskets to the earth
   & ran
From their encampments and dark castles seeking where
   to hide
From the grim flames; and from the visions of Orc: in
   sight
Of Albions Angel; who enrag'd his secret clouds open'd   10
From north to south, and burnt outstretchd on wings of
   wrath cov'ring
The eastern sky, spreading his awful wings across the
   heavens;
Beneath him roll'd his num'rous hosts, all Albions
   Angels camp'd

Darkend the Atlantic mountains & their trumpets shook
the valleys
Arm'd with diseases of the earth to cast upon the Abyss,
Their numbers forty millions, must'ring in the eastern
sky.

PLATE 14
In the flames stood & view'd the armies drawn out in the
sky
Washington Franklin Paine & Warren Allen Gates &
Lee:
And heard the voice of Albions Angel give the
thunderous command:
His plagues obedient to his voice flew forth out of their
clouds
Falling upon America, as a storm to cut them off
As a blight cuts the tender corn when it begins to appear.
Dark is the heaven above, & cold & hard the earth
beneath;
And as a plague wind fill'd with insects cuts off man &
beast;
And as a sea o'erwhelms a land in the day of an
earthquake:

Fury! rage! madness! in a wind swept through America   10
And the red flames of Orc that folded roaring fierce
around
The angry shores, and the fierce rushing of
th'inhabitants together:
The citizens of New-York close their books & lock their
chests;
The mariners of Boston drop their anchors and unlade;
The scribe of Pensylvania casts his pen upon the earth;
The builder of Virginia throws his hammer down in fear.

Then had America been lost, o'erwhelm'd by the
Atlantic,
And Earth had lost another portion of the infinite,

But all rush together in the night in wrath and raging
    fire
The red fires rag'd! the plagues recoil'd! then rolld they
    back with fury   20
PLATE 15
On Albions Angels; then the Pestilence began in streaks
    of red
Across the limbs of Albions Guardian, the spotted
    plague smote Bristols
And the Leprosy Londons Spirit, sickening all their
    bands:
The millions sent up a howl of anguish and threw off
    their hammerd mail,
And cast their swords & spears to earth, & stood a
    naked multitude.
Albions Guardian writhed in torment on the eastern sky
Pale quivring toward the brain his glimmering eyes, teeth
    chattering
Howling & shuddering his legs quivering; convuls'd each
    muscle & sinew
Sick'ning lay Londons Guardian, and the ancient miter'd
    York
Their heads on snowy hills, their ensigns sick'ning in the
    sky   10
The plagues creep on the burning winds driven by flames
    of Orc,
And by the fierce Americans rushing together in the
    night
Driven o'er the Guardians of Ireland and Scotland and
    Wales
They spotted with plagues forsook the frontiers & their
    banners seard
With fires of hell, deform their ancient heavens with
    shame & woe.
Hid in his caves the Bard of Albion felt the enormous
    plagues.
And a cowl of flesh grew o'er his head & scales on his
    back & ribs;

And rough with black scales all his Angels fright their
   ancient heavens
The doors of marriage are open, and the Priests in
   rustling scales
Rush into reptile coverts, hiding from the fires of Orc,   20
That play around the golden roofs in wreaths of fierce
   desire,
Leaving the females naked and glowing with the lusts of
   youth

For the female spirits of the dead pining in bonds of
   religion;
Run from their fetters reddening, & in long drawn arches
   sitting:
They feel the nerves of youth renew, and desires of
   ancient times,
Over their pale limbs as a vine when the tender grape
   appears

PLATE 16
Over the hills, the vales, the cities, rage the red flames
   fierce;
The Heavens melted from north to south; and Urizen
   who sat
Above all heavens in thunders wrap'd, emerg'd his
   leprous head
From out his holy shrine, his tears in deluge piteous
Falling into the deep sublime! flag'd with grey-brow'd
   snows
And thunderous visages, his jealous wings wav'd over
   the deep;
Weeping in dismal howling woe he dark descended
   howling
Around the smitten bands, clothed in tears & trembling
   shudd'ring cold.
His stored snows he poured forth, and his icy magazines
He open'd on the deep, and on the Atlantic sea white
   shiv'ring.   10

Leprous his limbs, all over white, and hoary was his
 visage.
Weeping in dismal howlings before the stern Americans
Hiding the Demon red with clouds & cold mists from the
 earth;
Till Angels & weak men twelve years should govern o'er
 the strong:
And then their end should come, when France reciev'd
 the Demons light.

Stiff shudderings shook the heav'nly thrones! France
 Spain & Italy,
In terror view'd the bands of Albion, and the ancient
 Guardians
Fainting upon the elements, smitten with their own
 plagues
They slow advance to shut the five gates of their law-
 built heaven
Filled with blasting fancies and with mildews of despair   20
With fierce disease and lust, unable to stem the fires of
 Orc;
But the five gates were consum'd, & their bolts and
 hinges melted
And the fierce flames burnt round the heavens, & round
 the abodes of men

FINIS

[CANCELLED PLATES]

PLATE [b]
Reveal the dragon thro' the human; coursing swift as fire
To the close hall of counsel, where his Angel form
 renews.

In a sweet vale shelter'd with cedars, that eternal stretch
Their unmov'd branches, stood the hall; built when the
 moon shot forth,
In that dread night when Urizen call'd the stars round
 his feet;

Then burst the center from its orb, and found a place
  beneath;
And Earth conglob'd, in narrow room, roll'd round its
  sulphur Sun.

To this deep valley situated by the flowing Thames;
Where George the third holds council. & his Lords &
  Commons meet:
Shut out from mortal sight the Angel came; the vale was
  dark
With clouds of smoke from the Atlantic, that in volumes
  roll'd
Between the mountains, dismal visions mope around the
  house.

On chairs of iron, canopied with mystic ornaments
Of life by magic power condens'd; infernal forms
  art-bound
The council sat; all rose before the aged apparition;
His snowy beard that streams like lambent flames down
  his wide breast
Wetting with tears, & his white garments cast a wintry
  light.

Then as arm'd clouds arise terrific round the northern
  drum;
The world is silent at the flapping of the folding
  banners;
So still terrors rent the house: as when the solemn globe
Launch'd to the unknown shore, while Sotha held the
  northern helm,
Till to that void it came & fell; so the dark house was
  rent,
The valley mov'd beneath; its shining pillars split in
  twain,
And its roofs crack across down falling on th'Angelic
  seats.

10

20

PLATE [c]

[*Then Albions Angel rose*] resolv'd to the cove of
    armoury:
His shield that bound twelve demons & their cities in its
    orb,
He took down from its trembling pillar; from its cavern
    deep,
His helm was brought by Londons Guardian, & his
    thirsty spear
By the wise spirit of Londons river: silent stood the
    King breathing [*with flames/hoar frosts*] damp mists:
And on his [*shining*] aged limbs they clasp'd the armour
    of terrible gold.
Infinite Londons awful spires cast a dreadful [*gleam*]
    cold
Even on rational things beneath, and from the palace
    walls
Around Saint James's [*glow the fires/till by the freeze*]
    chill & heavy, even to the city gate.

On the vast stone whose name is Truth he stood, his
    cloudy shield   10
Smote with his scepter, the scale bound orb loud howld;
    th' [*eternal*] ancie[nt] pillar
Trembling sunk, an earthquake roll'd along the mossy
    pile.
In glittring armour, swift as winds; intelligent as
    [*flames*] clouds;
Four winged heralds mount the furious blasts & blow
    their trumps
Gold, silver, brass & iron [*ardors*] clangors clamoring
    rend the shores.
Like white clouds rising from the deeps, his fifty-two
    armies
From the four cliffs of Albion rise, [*glowing*] mustering
    around their Prince;
Angels of cities and of parishes and villages and families,
In armour as the nerves of wisdom, each his station holds.

In opposition dire, a warlike cloud the myriads stood 20
In the red air before the Demon; [*seen even by mortal men:*
Who call it Fancy, or shut the gates of sense & in their chambers,
Sleep like the dead.] But like a constellation ris'n and blazing
Over the rugged ocean; so the Angels of Albion hung
[*Over the frowning shadow, like a King*]
a frowning shadow, like an aged King in arms of gold,
Who wept over a den, in which his only son outstretch'd
By rebels hands was slain; his white beard wav'd in the wild wind.

On mountains & cliffs of snow the awful apparition hover'd;
And like the voices of religious dead, heard in the mountains:
When holy zeal scents the sweet valleys of ripe virgin bliss;
Such was the hollow voice that o'er [*the red demon*] America lamented.

[FRAGMENT]

As when a dream of Thiralatha flies the midnight hour:
In vain the dreamer grasps the joyful images, they fly
Seen in obscured traces in the Vale of Leutha, So
The British Colonies beneath the woful Princes fade.

And so the Princes fade from earth, scarce seen by souls of men
But tho' obscur'd, this is the form of the Angelic land.

EUROPE

A PROPHECY

PLATE iii

Five windows light the cavern'd Man; thro' one he
   breathes the air;
Thro' one, hears music of the spheres; thro' one, the
   eternal vine
Flourishes, that he may recieve the grapes; thro' one can
   look.
And see small portions of the eternal world that ever
   groweth;
Thro' one, himself pass out what time he please, but he
   will not;
For stolen joys are sweet, & bread eaten in secret
   pleasant.

So sang a Fairy mocking as he sat on a streak'd Tulip,
Thinking none saw him: when he ceas'd I started from
   the trees!
And caught him in my hat as boys knock down a
   butterfly
How know you this said I small Sir? where did you
   learn this song   10
Seeing himself in my possession thus he answered me:
My master, I am yours. command me, for I must obey.

Then tell me, what is the material world, and is it dead?
He laughing answer'd: I will write a book on leaves of
   flowers,
If you will feed me on love-thoughts, & give me now and
   then
A cup of sparkling poetic fancies; so when I am tipsie,

I'll sing to you to this soft lute; and shew you all alive
The world, when every particle of dust breathes forth its
    joy.

I took him home in my warm bosom: as we went along
Wild flowers I gatherd; & he shew'd me each eternal
    flower: 20
He laugh'd aloud to see them whimper because they
    were pluck'd.
They hover'd round me like a cloud of incense: when I
    came
Into my parlour and sat down, and took my pen to
    write:
My Fairy sat upon the table, and dictated EUROPE.

PLATE I

PRELUDIUM
The nameless shadowy female rose from out the breast
    of Orc:
Her snaky hair brandishing in the winds of Enitharmon;
And thus her voice arose.

O mother Enitharmon wilt thou bring forth other sons?
To cause my name to vanish, that my place may not be
    found.
For I am faint with travel!
Like the dark cloud disburdend in the day of dismal
    thunder.

My roots are brandish'd in the heavens. my fruits in
    earth beneath
Surge, foam, and labour into life, first born & first
    consum'd!
Consumed and consuming!   10
Then why shouldst thou accursed mother bring me into
    life?

I wrap my turban of thick clouds around my lab'ring
    head;

And fold the sheety waters as a mantle round my limbs.
Yet the red sun and moon,
And all the overflowing stars rain down prolific pains.

PLATE 2
Unwilling I look up to heaven! unwilling count the stars!
Sitting in fathomless abyss of my immortal shrine.
I sieze their burning power
And bring forth howling terrors, all devouring fiery
    kings.

Devouring & devoured roaming on dark and desolate
    mountains
In forests of eternal death, shrieking in hollow trees.
Ah mother Enitharmon!
Stamp not with solid form this vig'rous progeny of fires.

I bring forth from my teeming bosom myriads of
    flames.
And thou dost stamp them with a signet, then they
    roam abroad   10
And leave me void as death:
Ah! I am drown'd in shady woe, and visionary joy.

And who shall bind the infinite with an eternal band?
To compass it with swaddling bands? and who shall
    cherish it
With milk and honey?
I see it smile & I roll inward & my voice is past.

   She ceast & rolld her shady clouds
     Into the secret place.

PLATE 3

A PROPHECY
            The deep of winter came;
            What time the secret child,
Descended thro' the orient gates of the eternal day:
War ceas'd, & all the troops like shadows fled to their
    abodes.

Then Enitharmon saw her sons & daughters rise around.
Like pearly clouds they meet together in the crystal
  house:
And Los, possessor of the moon, joy'd in the peaceful
  night:
Thus speaking while his num'rous sons shook their
  bright fiery wings

Again the night is come
That strong Urthona takes his rest,   10
And Urizen unloos'd from chains
Glows like a meteor in the distant north
Stretch forth your hands and strike the elemental strings!
Awake the thunders of the deep,
PLATE 4
The shrill winds wake!
Till all the sons of Urizen look out and envy Los:
Sieze all the spirits of life and bind
Their warbling joys to our loud strings
Bind all the nourishing sweets of earth
To give us bliss, that we may drink the sparkling wine of
  Los
And let us laugh at war,
Despising toil and care,
Because the days and nights of joy, in lucky hours
  renew.

Arise O Orc from thy deep den,   10
First born of Enitharmon rise!
And we will crown thy head with garlands of the
  ruddy vine;
For now thou art bound;
And I may see thee in the hour of bliss, my eldest born.

The horrent Demon rose, surrounded with red stars of
  fire,
Whirling about in furious circles round the immortal
  fiend.

Then Enitharmon down descended into his red light,
And thus her voice rose to her children, the distant
  heavens reply:

PLATE 6
Now comes the night of Enitharmons joy!
Who shall I call? Who shall I send?
That Woman, lovely Woman! may have dominion?
Arise O Rintrah thee I call! & Palamabron thee!
Go! tell the Human race that Womans love is Sin!
That an Eternal life awaits the worms of sixty winters
In an allegorical abode where existence hath never come:
Forbid all Joy, & from her childhood shall the little
  female
Spread nets in every secret path.

My weary eyelids draw towards the evening, my bliss is
  yet but new.   10

PLATE 8
Arise O Rintrah eldest born: second to none but Orc:
O lion Rintrah raise thy fury from thy forests black:
Bring Palamabron horned priest, skipping upon the
  mountains:
And silent Elynittria the silver bowed queen:
Rintrah where hast thou hid thy bride:
Weeps she in desart shades?
Alas my Rintrah! bring the lovely jealous Ocalythron.

Arise my son: bring all thy brethren O thou king of fire.
Prince of the sun I see thee with thy innumerable race:
Thick as the summer stars: 10
But each ramping his golden mane shakes,
And thine eyes rejoice because of strength O Rintrah
  furious king

PLATE 9
Enitharmon slept,
Eighteen hundred years: Man was a Dream!
The night of Nature and their harps unstrung:

She slept in middle of her nightly song,
Eighteen hundred years, a female dream!

Shadows of men in fleeting bands upon the winds:
Divide the heavens of Europe:
Till Albions Angel smitten with his own plagues fled
    with his bands
The cloud bears hard on Albions shore:
Fill'd with immortal demons of futurity: 10
In council gather the smitten Angels of Albion
The cloud bears hard upon the council house; down
    rushing
On the heads of Albions Angels.

One hour they lay buried beneath the ruins of that hall;
But as the stars rise from the salt lake they arise in pain,
In troubled mists o'erclouded by the terrors of
    strugling times.
PLATE 10
In thoughts perturb'd. they rose from the bright ruins
    silent following
The fiery King, who sought his ancient temple
    serpent-form'd
That stretches out its shady length along the Island
    white.
Round him roll'd his clouds of war; silent the Angel
    went,
Along the infinite shores of Thames to golden Verulam.
There stand the venerable porches that high-towering
    rear
Their oak-surrounded pillars, form'd of massy stones,
    uncut
With tool; stones precious; such eternal in the heavens,
Of colours twelve. few known on earth, give light in the
    opake,
Plac'd in the order of the stars, when the five senses
    whelm'd   10

In deluge o'er the earth-born man; then turn'd the
    fluxile eyes
Into two stationary orbs, concentrating all things.
The ever-varying spiral ascents to the heavens of
    heavens
Were bended downward; and the nostrils golden gates
    shut
Turn'd outward, barr'd and petrify'd against the infinite.

Thought chang'd the infinite. to a serpent; that which
    pitieth:
To a devouring flame; and man fled from its face and
    hid
In forests of night; then all the eternal forests were
    divided
Into earths rolling in circles of space, that like an ocean
    rush'd
And overwhelmed all except this finite wall of flesh.   20
Then was the serpent temple form'd, image of infinite
Shut up in finite revolutions, and man became an Angel;
Heaven a mighty circle turning; God a tyrant crown'd.

Now arriv'd the ancient Guardian at the southern porch,
That planted thick with trees of blackest leaf, & in a vale
Obscure, enclos'd the Stone of Night; oblique it stood,
    o'erhung
With purple flowers and berries red; image of that
    sweet south,
Once open to the heavens and elevated on the human
    neck,
Now overgrown with hair and covered with a stony
    roof,
Downward 'tis sunk beneath th' attractive north, that
    round the feet   30
A raging whirlpool draws the dizzy enquirer to his grave:
PLATE 11
        Albions Angel rose upon the Stone of Night.
        He saw Urizen on the Atlantic;

And his brazen Book,
That Kings & Priests had copied on Earth
Expanded from North to South.

PLATE 12

And the clouds & fires pale rolld round in the night of
Enitharmon
Round Albions cliffs & Londons walls; still Enitharmon
slept!
Rolling volumes of grey mist involve Churches, Palaces,
Towers:
For Urizen unclaspd his Book! feeding his soul with pity
The youth of England hid in gloom curse the paind
heavens; compell'd
Into the deadly night to see the form of Albions Angel
Their parents brought them forth & aged ignorance
preaches canting,
On a vast rock, percievd by those senses that are clos'd
from thought:
Bleak, dark, abrupt, it stands & overshadows London
city
They saw his boney feet on the rock, the flesh consum'd
in flames: 10
They saw the Serpent temple lifted above, shadowing the
Island white:
· They heard the voice of Albions Angel howling in flames
of Orc,
Seeking the trump of the last doom

Above the rest the howl was heard from Westminster
louder & louder:
The Guardian of the secret codes forsook his ancient
mansion,
Driven out by the flames of Orc; his furr'd robes &
false locks
Adhered and grew one with his flesh, and nerves & veins
shot thro' them
With dismal torment sick, hanging upon the wind: he
fled

Groveling along Great George Street thro' the Park
    gate; all the soldiers
Fled from his sight: he drag'd his torments to the
    wilderness.   20

Thus was the howl thro Europe!
For Orc rejoic'd to hear the howling shadows
But Palamabron shot his lightnings trenching down his
    wide back
And Rintrah hung with all his legions in the nether deep

Enitharmon laugh'd in her sleep to see (O womans
    triumph)
Every house a den, every man bound; the shadows are
    filld
With spectres, and the windows wove over with curses
    of iron:
Over the doors Thou shalt not; & over the chimneys
    Fear is written:
With bands of iron round their necks fasten'd into the
    walls
The citizens: in leaden gyves the inhabitants of suburbs   30
Walk heavy: soft and bent are the bones of villagers

Between the clouds of Urizen the flames of Orc roll
    heavy
Around the limbs of Albions Guardian, his flesh
    consuming.
Howlings & hissings, shrieks & groans, & voices of
    despair
Arise around him in the cloudy
Heavens of Albion, Furious
PLATE 13
The red limb'd Angel siez'd, in horror and torment;
The Trump of the last doom; but he could not blow the
    iron tube!
Thrice he assay'd presumptuous to awake the dead to
    Judgment.

A mighty Spirit leap'd from the land of Albion,
Nam'd Newton; he siez'd the Trump. & blow'd the
    enormous blast!
Yellow as leaves of Autumn the myriads of Angelic
    hosts,
Fell thro' the wintry skies seeking their graves;
Rattling their hollow bones in howling and lamentation.

    Then Enitharmon woke, nor knew that she had slept
And eighteen hundred years were fled   10
As if they had not been
She calld her sons & daughters
To the sports of night,
Within her crystal house;
And thus her song proceeds.

Arise Ethinthus! tho' the earth-worm call;
Let him call in vain;
Till the night of holy shadows
And human solitude is past!
PLATE 14
Ethinthus queen of waters, how thou shinest in the sky:
My daughter how do I rejoice! for thy children flock
    around
Like the gay fishes on the wave, when the cold moon
    drinks the dew.
Ethinthus! thou art sweet as comforts to my fainting
    soul:
For now thy waters warble round the feet of Enitharmon.

Manathu-Vorcyon! I behold thee flaming in my halls,
Light of thy mothers soul! I see thy lovely eagles
    round;
Thy golden wings are my delight, & thy flames of soft
    delusion.

Where is my lureing bird of Eden! Leutha silent love!
Leutha, the many colourd bow delights upon thy wings: 10

Soft soul of flowers Leutha!
Sweet smiling pestilence! I see thy blushing light:
Thy daughters many changing,
Revolve like sweet perfumes ascending O Leutha silken
    queen!

Where is the youthful Antamon. prince of the pearly
    dew.
O Antamon. why wilt thou leave thy mother
    Enitharmon?
Alone I see thee crystal form.
Floting upon the bosomd air:
With lineaments of gratified desire.
My Antamon the seven churches of Leutha seek thy love.   20

I hear the soft Oothoon in Enitharmons tents:
Why wilt thou give up womans secrecy my melancholy
    child?
Between two moments bliss is ripe:
O Theotormon robb'd of joy, I see thy salt tears flow
Down the steps of my crystal house.

Sotha & Thiralatha, secret dwellers of dreamful caves,
Arise and please the horrent fiend with your
    melodious songs.
Still all your thunders golden hoofd, & bind your
    horses black.
Orc! smile upon my children!
Smile son of my afflictions.   30
Arise O Orc and give our mountains joy of thy red
    light.

She ceas'd, for All were forth at sport beneath the
    solemn moon
Waking the stars of Urizen with their immortal songs,
That nature felt thro' all her pores the enormous
    revelry,
Till morning ope'd the eastern gate.
Then every one fled to his station. & Enitharmon wept.

But terrible Orc, when he beheld the morning in the
east,
PLATE 15
Shot from the heights of Enitharmon;
And in the vineyards of red France appear'd the light of
his fury

The sun glow'd fiery red!
The furious terrors flew around!
On golden chariots raging, with red wheels dropping
with blood;
The Lions lash their wrathful tails!
The Tigers couch upon the prey & suck the ruddy tide:
And Enitharmon groans & cries in anguish and dismay.

Then Los arose his head he reard in snaky thunders
clad:
And with a cry that shook all nature to the utmost pole,   10
Call'd all his sons to the strife of blood.

FINIS

THE SONG OF LOS

PLATE 3

AFRICA

> *I will sing you a song of Los. the Eternal Prophet:*
> *He sung it to four harps at the tables of Eternity.*
> *In heart-formed Africa.*
> *Urizen faded! Ariston shudderd!*
> *And thus the Song began*

Adam stood in the garden of Eden:
And Noah on the mountains of Ararat;
They saw Urizen give his Laws to the Nations
By the hands of the children of Los.

Adam shudderd! Noah faded! black grew the sunny
  African   10
When Rintrah gave Abstract Philosophy to Brama in the
  East:
(Night spoke to the Cloud!
Lo these Human form'd spirits in smiling hipocrisy
  War
Against one another; so let them War on; slaves to the
  eternal Elements)
Noah shrunk, beneath the waters;
Abram fled in fires from Chaldea;
Moses beheld upon Mount Sinai forms of dark delusion:

To Trismegistus. Palamabron gave an abstract Law:
To Pythagoras Socrates & Plato.

Times rolled on o'er all the sons of Har, time after time   20
Orc on Mount Atlas howld, chain'd down with the
   Chain of Jealousy
Then Oothoon hoverd over Judah & Jerusalem
And Jesus heard her voice (a man of sorrows) he
   recievd
A Gospel from wretched Theotormon.

The human race began to wither, for the healthy built
Secluded places, fearing the joys of Love
And the disease'd only propagated:
So Antamon call'd up Leutha from her valleys of
   delight:
And to Mahomet a loose Bible gave.
But in the North, to Odin, Sotha gave a Code of War,   30
Because of Diralada thinking to reclaim his joy.

PLATE 4
These were the Churches: Hospitals: Castles: Palaces:
Like nets & gins & traps to catch the joys of Eternity
   And all the rest a desart;
Till like a dream Eternity was obliterated & erased.

Since that dread day when Har and Heva fled.
Because their brethren & sisters liv'd in War & Lust;
And as they fled they shrunk
Into two narrow doleful forms:
Creeping in reptile flesh upon
The bosom of the ground: 10
And all the vast of Nature shrunk
Before their shrunken eyes.

Thus the terrible race of Los & Enitharmon gave
Laws & Religions to the sons of Har binding them more
And more to Earth: closing and restraining:
Till a Philosophy of Five Senses was complete
Urizen wept & gave it into the hands of Newton &
   Locke
Clouds roll heavy upon the Alps round Rousseau &
   Voltaire:

And on the mountains of Lebanon round the deceased
  Gods
Of Asia; & on the desarts of Africa round the Fallen
  Angels   20
The Guardian Prince of Albion burns in his nightly tent

PLATE 6

ASIA

The Kings of Asia heard
The howl rise up from Europe!
And each ran out from his Web;
From his ancient woven Den;
For the darkness of Asia was startled
At the thick-flaming, thought-creating fires of Orc.

And the Kings of Asia stood
And cried in bitterness of soul.

Shall not the King call for Famine from the heath?
Nor the Priest, for Pestilence from the fen?   10
To restrain! to dismay! to thin!
The inhabitants of mountain and plain;
In the day, of full-feeding prosperity;
And the night of delicious songs.

Shall not the Councellor throw his curb
Of Poverty on the laborious?
To fix the price of labour;
To invent allegoric riches:

And the privy admonishers of men
Call for fires in the City   20
For heaps of smoking ruins,
In the night of prosperity & wantonness

To turn man from his path,
To restrain the child from the womb,

PLATE 7

To cut off the bread from the city,
That the remnant may learn to obey,

That the pride of the heart may fail;
That the lust of the eyes, may be quench'd:
That the delicate ear in its infancy
May be dull'd; and the nostrils clos'd up;

To teach mortal worms the path
That leads from the gates of the Grave.

Urizen heard them cry!
And his shudd'ring waving wings   10
Went enormous above the red flames
Drawing clouds of despair thro' the heavens
Of Europe as he went:
And his Books of brass iron & gold
Melted over the land as he flew,
Heavy-waving, howling, weeping.

And he stood over Judea:
And stay'd in his ancient place:
And stretch'd his clouds over Jerusalem;

For Adam, a mouldering skeleton   20
Lay bleach'd on the garden of Eden;
And Noah as white as snow
On the mountains of Ararat.

Then the thunders of Urizen bellow'd aloud
From his woven darkness above.

Orc, raging in European darkness
Arose like a pillar of fire above the Alps
Like a serpent of fiery flame!
  The sullen Earth
  Shrunk!   30

Forth from the dead dust rattling bones to bones
Join: shaking convuls'd the shivring clay breathes

And all flesh naked stands: Fathers and Friends;
Mothers & Infants; Kings & Warriors:

The Grave shrieks with delight, & shakes
Her hollow womb, & clasps the solid stem:
Her bosom swells with wild desire:
And milk & blood & glandous wine
In rivers rush & shout & dance,
On mountain, dale and plain. 40

The SONG of LOS is Ended.
Urizen Wept.

THE [*FIRST*] BOOK OF URIZEN

PLATE 2

PRELUDIUM TO THE [*FIRST*] BOOK OF URIZEN

Of the primeval Priests assum'd power,
When Eternals spurn'd back his religion;
And gave him place in the north,
Obscure, shadowy, void, solitary.

Eternals I hear your call gladly,
Dictate swift winged words, & fear not
To unfold your dark visions of torment.

PLATE 3

CHAP: I
1. Lo, a shadow of horror is risen
In Eternity! Unknown, unprolific!
Self-closed, all-repelling: what Demon
Hath form'd this abominable void
This soul-shudd'ring vacuum? – Some said
'It is Urizen', But unknown, abstracted
Brooding secret, the dark power hid.

2. Times on times he divided, & measur'd
Space by space in his ninefold darkness
Unseen, unknown! changes appeard
In his desolate mountains rifted furious
By the black winds of perturbation

10

3. For he strove in battles dire
In unseen conflictions with shapes
Bred from his forsaken wilderness,
Of beast, bird, fish, serpent & element
Combustion, blast, vapour and cloud.

4. Dark revolving in silent activity:
Unseen in tormenting passions;
An activity unknown and horrible;   20
A self-contemplating shadow,
In enormous labours occupied

5. But Eternals beheld his vast forests
Age on ages he lay, clos'd, unknown,
Brooding shut in the deep; all avoid
The petrific abominable chaos

6. His cold horrors silent, dark Urizen
Prepar'd: his ten thousands of thunders
Rang'd in gloom'd array stretch out across
The dread world, & the rolling of wheels   30
As of swelling seas, sound in his clouds
In his hills of stor'd snows, in his mountains
Of hail & ice; voices of terror,
Are heard, like thunders of autumn,
When the cloud blazes over the harvests

CHAP: II

1. Earth was not: nor globes of attraction
The will of the Immortal expanded
Or contracted his all flexible senses.
Death was not, but eternal life sprung

2. The sound of a trumpet the heavens   40
Awoke & vast clouds of blood roll'd
Round the dim rocks of Urizen, so nam'd
That solitary one in Immensity

3. Shrill the trumpet: & myriads of Eternity,
PLATE 4
Muster around the bleak desarts
Now fill'd with clouds, darkness & waters
That roll'd perplex'd labring & utter'd
Words articulate, bursting in thunders
That roll'd on the tops of his mountains

4: From the depths of dark solitude, From
The eternal abode in my holiness,
Hidden set apart in my stern counsels
Reserv'd for the days of futurity,
I have sought for a joy without pain,   10
For a solid without fluctuation
Why will you die O Eternals?
Why live in unquenchable burnings?

5 First I fought with the fire; consum'd
Inwards, into a deep world within:
A void immense, wild dark & deep,
Where nothing was; Natures wide womb
And self balanc'd stretch'd o'er the void
I alone, even I! the winds merciless
Bound; but condensing, in torrents   20
They fall & fall; strong I repell'd
The vast waves, & arose on the waters
A wide world of solid obstruction

6. Here alone I in books formd of metals
Have written the secrets of wisdom
The secrets of dark contemplation
By fightings and conflicts dire,
With terrible monsters Sin-bred:
Which the bosoms of all inhabit;
Seven deadly Sins of the soul.   30

7. Lo! I unfold my darkness: and on
This rock, place with strong hand the Book
Of eternal brass, written in my solitude.

8. Laws of peace, of love, of unity:
Of pity, compassion, forgiveness.
Let each chuse one habitation:
His ancient infinite mansion:
One command, one joy, one desire,
One curse, one weight, one measure
One King, one God, one Law.   40

CHAP: III

1. The voice ended, they saw his pale visage
Emerge from the darkness; his hand
On the rock of eternity unclasping
The Book of brass. Rage siez'd the strong

2. Rage, fury, intense indignation
In cataracts of fire blood & gall
In whirlwinds of sulphurous smoke:
And enormous forms of energy;
All the seven deadly sins of the soul
PLATE 5
In living creations appear'd
In the flames of eternal fury.

3. Sund'ring, dark'ning, thund'ring!
Rent away with a terrible crash
Eternity roll'd wide apart
Wide asunder rolling
Mountainous all around
Departing; departing; departing:
Leaving ruinous fragments of life
Hanging frowning cliffs & all between   10
An ocean of voidness unfathomable.

4. The roaring fires ran o'er the heav'ns
In whirlwinds & cataracts of blood
And o'er the dark desarts of Urizen
Fires pour thro' the void on all sides
On Urizens self-begotten armies.

5. But no light from the fires. all was darkness
In the flames of Eternal fury

6. In fierce anguish & quenchless flames
To the desarts and rocks he ran raging   20
To hide, but he could not: combining
He dug mountains & hills in vast strength,
He piled them in incessant labour,
In howlings & pangs & fierce madness
Long periods in burning fires labouring
Till hoary, and age-broke, and aged,
In despair and the shadows of death.

7. And a roof, vast petrific around,
On all sides he fram'd: like a womb;
Where thousands of rivers in veins   30
Of blood pour down the mountains to cool
The eternal fires beating without
From Eternals; & like a black globe
View'd by sons of Eternity, standing
On the shore of the infinite ocean
Like a human heart strugling & beating
The vast world of Urizen appear'd.

8. And Los round the dark globe of Urizen,
Kept watch for Eternals to confine,
The obscure separation alone;   40
For Eternity stood wide apart,
PLATE 6
As the stars are apart from the earth

9. Los wept howling around the dark Demon:
And cursing his lot; for in anguish,
Urizen was rent from his side;
And a fathomless void for his feet;
And intense fires for his dwelling.

10. But Urizen laid in a stony sleep
Unorganiz'd, rent from Eternity

11. The Eternals said: What is this? Death[.]
Urizen is a clod of clay.   10

PLATE 7
12: Los howld in a dismal stupor,
Groaning! gnashing! groaning!
Till the wrenching apart was healed

13: But the wrenching of Urizen heal'd not
Cold, featureless, flesh or clay,
Rifted with direful changes
He lay in a dreamless night

14: Till Los rouz'd his fires, affrighted
At the formless unmeasurable death.

PLATE 8
CHAP: IV[a]
1: Los smitten with astonishment
Frightend at the hurtling bones

2: And at the surging sulphureous
Perturbed Immortal mad raging

3: In whirlwinds & pitch & nitre
Round the furious limbs of Los

4: And Los formed nets & gins
And threw the nets round about

5: He watch'd in shuddring fear
The dark changes & bound every change   10
With rivets of iron & brass;

6. And these were the changes of Urizen.

PLATE 10
CHAP: IV[b]
1. Ages on ages roll'd over him!
In stony sleep ages roll'd over him!
Like a dark waste stretching chang'able

By earthquakes riv'n, belching sullen fires
On ages roll'd ages in ghastly
Sick torment; around him in whirlwinds
Of darkness the eternal Prophet howl'd
Beating still on his rivets of iron
Pouring sodor of iron; dividing
The horrible night into watches.   10

2. And Urizen (so his eternal name)
His prolific delight obscurd more & more
In dark secresy hiding in surgeing ·
Sulphureous fluid his phantasies.
The Eternal Prophet heavd the dark bellows,
And turn'd restless the tongs; and the hammer
Incessant beat; forging chains new & new
Numb'ring with links. hours, days & years

3 The eternal mind bounded began to roll
Eddies of wrath ceaseless round & round,   20
And the sulphureous foam surgeing thick
Settled, a lake, bright, & shining clear:
White as the snow on the mountains cold.

4. Forgetfulness, dumbness, necessity!
In chains of the mind locked up,
Like fetters of ice shrinking together
Disorganiz'd, rent from Eternity,
Los beat on his fetters of iron;
And heated his furnaces & pour'd
Iron sodor and sodor of brass   30

5. Restless turnd the immortal inchain'd
Heaving dolorous! anguish'd! unbearable
Till a roof shaggy wild inclos'd
In an orb, his fountain of thought.

6. In a horrible dreamful slumber;
Like the linked infernal chain;
A vast Spine writh'd in torment
Upon the winds; shooting pain'd

Ribs, like a bending cavern
And bones of solidness, froze   40
Over all his nerves of joy.
And a first Age passed over,
And a state of dismal woe.

PLATE 11
7. From the caverns of his jointed Spine,
Down sunk with fright a red
Round globe hot burning deep
Deep down into the Abyss:
Panting: Conglobing, Trembling
Shooting out ten thousand branches
Around his solid bones.
And a second Age passed over,
And a state of dismal woe.

8. In harrowing fear rolling round;   10
His nervous brain shot branches
Round the branches of his heart.
On high into two little orbs
And fixed in two little caves
Hiding carefully from the wind,
His Eyes beheld the deep,
And a third Age passed over:
And a state of dismal woe.

9. The pangs of hope began,
In heavy pain striving, struggling.   20
Two Ears in close volutions.
From beneath his orbs of vision
Shot spiring out and petrified
As they grew. And a fourth Age passed
And a state of dismal woe.

10. In ghastly torment sick;
Hanging upon the wind;
PLATE 13
Two Nostrils bent down to the deep.
And a fifth Age passed over;
And a state of dismal woe.

11. In ghastly torment sick;
Within his ribs bloated round,
A craving Hungry Cavern;
Thence arose his channeld Throat,
And like a red flame a Tongue
Of thirst & of hunger appeard.
And a sixth Age passed over: 10
And a state of dismal woe.

12. Enraged & stifled with torment
He threw his right Arm to the north
His left Arm to the south
Shooting out in anguish deep,
And his Feet stampd the nether Abyss
In trembling & howling & dismay.
And a seventh Age passed over:
And a state of dismal woe.

CHAP: V

1. In terrors Los shrunk from his task: 20
His great hammer fell from his hand:
His fires beheld, and sickening,
Hid their strong limbs in smoke.
For with noises ruinous loud;
With hurtlings & clashings & groans
The Immortal endur'd his chains,
Tho' bound in a deadly sleep.

2. All the myriads of Eternity:
All the wisdom & joy of life:
Roll like a sea around him,   30
Except what his little orbs
Of sight by degrees unfold.

3. And now his eternal life
Like a dream was obliterated

4. Shudd'ring, the Eternal Prophet smote
With a stroke, from his north to south region
The bellows & hammer are silent now

A nerveless silence, his prophetic voice
Siez'd; a cold solitude & dark void
The Eternal Prophet & Urizen clos'd   40

5. Ages on ages rolld over them
Cut off from life & light frozen
Into horrible forms of deformity
Los suffer'd his fires to decay
Then he look'd back with anxious desire
But the space undivided by existence
Struck horror into his soul.

6. Los wept obscur'd with mourning:
His bosom earthquak'd with sighs;
He saw Urizen deadly black,   50
In his chains bound, & Pity began,

7. In anguish dividing & dividing
For pity divides the soul
In pangs eternity on eternity
Life in cataracts pourd down his cliffs
The void shrunk the lymph into Nerves
Wand'ring wide on the bosom of night
And left a round globe of blood
Trembling upon the Void

PLATE 15
Thus the Eternal Prophet was divided
Before the death-image of Urizen
For in changeable clouds and darkness
In a winterly night beneath,
The Abyss of Los stretch'd immense:
And now seen now obscur'd to the eyes
Of Eternals, the visions remote
Of the dark seperation appear'd.
As glasses discover Worlds
In the endless Abyss of space,   10
So the expanding eyes of Immortals
Beheld the dark visions of Los,
And the globe of life blood trembling.

PLATE 18
8. The globe of life blood trembled
Branching out into roots;
Fibrous, writhing upon the winds;
Fibres of blood, milk and tears;
In pangs, eternity on eternity.
At length in tears & cries imbodied
A female form trembling and pale
Waves before his deathly face

9. All Eternity shudderd at sight
Of the first female now separate
Pale as a cloud of snow
Waving before the face of Los

10

10. Wonder, awe, fear, astonishment,
Petrify the eternal myriads;
At the first female form now separate
PLATE 19
They call'd her Pity, and fled

11. 'Spread a Tent, with strong curtains around them
'Let cords & stakes bind in the Void
That Eternals may no more behold them'

12. They began to weave curtains of darkness
They erected large pillars round the Void
With golden hooks fastend in the pillars
With infinite labour the Eternals
A woof wove, and called it Science

CHAP: VI

1. But Los saw the Female & pitied
He embrac'd her, she wept, she refus'd
In perverse and cruel delight
She fled from his arms, yet he followd

10

2. Eternity shudder'd when they saw,
Man begetting his likeness,
On his own divided image.

3. A time passed over, the Eternals
Began to erect a tent;
When Enitharmon, sick,
Felt a Worm within her womb.   20

4. Yet helpless it lay like a Worm
In the trembling womb
To be moulded into existence

5. All day the worm lay on her bosom
All night within her womb
The worm lay till it grew to a serpent
With dolorous hissings & poisons
Round Enitharmons loins folding,

6. Coild within Enitharmons womb
The serpent grew casting its scales,   30
With sharp pangs the hissings began
To change to a grating cry,
Many sorrows and dismal throes
Many forms of fish, bird & beast,
Brought forth an Infant form
Where was a worm before.

7. The Eternals their tent finished
Alarm'd with these gloomy visions
When Enitharmon groaning
Produc'd a man Child to the light.   40

8. A shriek ran thro' Eternity:
And a paralytic stroke;
At the birth of the Human shadow.

9. Delving earth in his resistless way;
Howling, the Child with fierce flames
Issu'd from Enitharmon.

10. The Eternals, closed the tent:
They beat down the stakes the cords

PLATE 20
Stretch'd for a work of eternity;
No more Los beheld Eternity.

11. In his hands he siez'd the infant
He bathed him in springs of sorrow
He gave him to Enitharmon.

CHAP: VII

1. They named the child Orc, he grew
Fed with milk of Enitharmon

2. Los awoke her; O sorrow & pain!
A tight'ning girdle grew,
Around his bosom. In sobbings   10
He burst the girdle in twain,
But still another girdle
Oppressd his bosom, In sobbings
Again he burst it. Again
Another girdle succeeds
The girdle was form'd by day;
By night was burst in twain.

3. These falling down on the rock
Into an iron Chain
In each other link by link lock'd   20

4. They took Orc to the top of a mountain.
O how Enitharmon wept!
They chain'd his young limbs to the rock
With the Chain of Jealousy
Beneath Urizens deathful shadow

5. The dead heard the voice of the child
And began to awake from sleep
All things. heard the voice of the child
And began to awake to life.

6. And Urizen craving with hunger   30
Stung with the odours of Nature
Explor'd his dens around

7. He form'd a line & a plummet
To divide the Abyss beneath.
He form'd a dividing rule:

8. He formed scales to weigh;
He formed massy weights;
He formed a brazen quadrant;
He formed golden compasses
And began to explore the Abyss   40
And he planted a garden of fruits

9. But Los encircled Enitharmon
With fires of Prophecy
From the sight of Urizen & Orc.

10. And she bore an enormous race

CHAP: VIII

1. Urizen explor'd his dens
Mountain, moor, & wilderness,
With a globe of fire lighting his journey
A fearful journey, annoy'd
By cruel enormities: forms   50
PLATE 23
Of life on his forsaken mountains

2. And his world teemd vast enormities
Frightning; faithless; fawning
Portions of life; similitudes
Of a foot, or a hand, or a head
Or a heart, or an eye, they swam mischevous
Dread terrors! delighting in blood

3. Most Urizen sicken'd to see
His eternal creations appear
Sons & daughters of sorrow on mountains   10

Weeping! wailing! first Thiriel appear'd
Astonish'd at his own existence
Like a man from a cloud born, & Utha
From the waters emerging, laments!
Grodna rent the deep earth howling
Amaz'd! his heavens immense cracks
Like the ground parch'd with heat; then Fuzon
Flam'd out! first begotten, last born.
All his eternal sons in like manner
His daughters from green herbs & cattle   20
From monsters, & worms of the pit.

4. He in darkness clos'd, view'd all his race
And his soul sicken'd! he curs'd
Both sons & daughters; for he saw
That no flesh nor spirit could keep
His iron laws one moment,

5. For he saw that life liv'd upon death
PLATE 25
The Ox in the slaughter house moans
The Dog at the wintry door
And he wept, & he called it Pity
And his tears flowed down on the winds

6. Cold he wander'd on high, over their cities
In weeping & pain & woe!
And where-ever he wanderd in sorrows
Upon the aged heavens
A cold shadow follow'd behind him
Like a spiders web, moist, cold, & dim   10
Drawing out from his sorrowing soul
The dungeon-like heaven dividing
Where ever the footsteps of Urizen
Walk'd over the cities in sorrow.

7. Till a Web dark & cold, throughout all
The tormented element stretch'd
From the sorrows of Urizens soul
And the Web is a Female in embrio.
None could break the Web, no wings of fire.

8. So twisted the cords, & so knotted 20
The meshes: twisted like to the human brain

9. And all calld it, The Net of Religion.

CHAP: IX

1. Then the Inhabitants of those Cities:
Felt their Nerves change into Marrow
And hardening Bones began
In swift diseases and torments,
In throbbings & shootings & grindings
Thro' all the coasts; till weaken'd
The Senses inward rush'd shrinking,
Beneath the dark net of infection. 30

2. Till the shrunken eyes clouded over
Discernd not the woven hipocrisy
But the streaky slime in their heavens
Brought together by narrowing perceptions
Appeard transparent air; for their eyes
Grew small like the eyes of a man
And in reptile forms shrinking together
Of seven feet stature they remaind

3. Six days they shrunk up from existence
And on the seventh day they rested 40
And they bless'd the seventh day, in sick hope:
And forgot their eternal life

4. And their thirty cities divided
In form of a human heart
No more could they rise at will
In the infinite void, but bound down
To earth by their narrowing perceptions
PLATE 28
They lived a period of years
Then left a noisom body
To the jaws of devouring darkness

5. And their children wept, & built
Tombs in the desolate places,
And form'd laws of prudence, and call'd them
The eternal laws of God

6. And the thirty cities remain
Surrounded by salt floods, now call'd
Africa: its name was then Egypt.   10

7. The remaining sons of Urizen
Beheld their brethren shrink together
Beneath the Net of Urizen;
Perswasion was in vain;
For the ears of the inhabitants
Were wither'd, & deafen'd, & cold.
And their eyes could not discern,
Their brethren of other cities.

8. So Fuzon call'd all together
The remaining children of Urizen: 20
And they left the pendulous earth:
They called it Egypt, & left it.

9. And the salt ocean rolled englob'd

   The End of the [first] book of Urizen

THE BOOK OF AHANIA

PLATE 2

AHANIA

CHAP: Ist

1: Fuzon, on a chariot iron-wing'd
On spiked flames rose; his hot visage
Flam'd furious! sparkles in his hair & beard
Shot down his wide bosom and shoulders.
On clouds of smoke rages his chariot
And his right hand burns red in its cloud
Moulding into a vast globe, his wrath
As the thunder-stone is moulded.
Son of Urizens silent burnings

2: Shall we worship this Demon of smoke,   10
Said Fuzon, this abstract non-entity
This cloudy God seated on waters
Now seen, now obscur'd, King of sorrow?

3: So he spoke, in a fiery flame,
On Urizen frowning indignant,
The Globe of wrath shaking on high
Roaring with fury, he threw
The howling Globe: burning it flew
Lengthning into a hungry beam. Swiftly

4: Oppos'd to the exulting flam'd beam   20
The broad Disk of Urizen upheav'd
Across the Void many a mile.

5: It was forg'd in mills where the winter
Beats incessant; ten winters the disk
Unremitting endur'd the cold hammer.

6: But the strong arm that sent it, remember'd
The sounding beam; laughing it tore through
That beaten mass: keeping its direction
The cold loins of Urizen dividing.

7: Dire shriek'd his invisible Lust   30
Deep groan'd Urizen! stretching his awful hand
Ahania (so name his parted soul)
He siez'd on his mountains of Jealousy.
He groand anguishd & called her Sin,
Kissing her and weeping over her;
Then hid her in darkness in silence;
Jealous tho' she was invisible.

8: She fell down a faint shadow wandring
In chaos and circling dark Urizen,
As the moon anguishd circles the earth;   40
Hopeless! abhorrd! a death-shadow,
Unseen, unbodied, unknown,
The mother of Pestilence.

9: But the fiery beam of Fuzon
Was a pillar of fire to Egypt
Five hundred years wandring on earth
Till Los siezd it and beat in a mass
With the body of the sun.

PLATE 3

CHAP: II^d

1: But the forehead of Urizen gathering,
And his eyes pale with anguish, his lips
Blue & changing; in tears and bitter
Contrition he prepar'd his Bow,

2: Form'd of Ribs: that in his dark solitude
When obscur'd in his forests fell monsters,
Arose. For his dire Contemplations
Rush'd down like floods from his mountains
In torrents of mud settling thick
With Eggs of unnatural production   10
Forthwith hatching; some howl'd on his hills
Some in vales; some aloft flew in air

3: Of these: an enormous dread Serpent
Scaled and poisonous horned
Approach'd Urizen even to his knees
As he sat on his dark rooted Oak.

4: With his horns he push'd furious.
Great the conflict & great the jealousy
In cold poisons: but Urizen smote him

5: First he poison'd the rocks with his blood   20
Then polish'd his ribs, and his sinews
Dried; laid them apart till winter;
Then a Bow black prepar'd: on this Bow,
A poisoned rock plac'd in silence:
He utter'd these words to the Bow:

6: O Bow of the clouds of secresy!
O nerve of that lust form'd monster!
Send this rock swift, invisible thro'
The black clouds, on the bosom of Fuzon

7: So saying, In torment of his wounds,   30
He bent the enormous ribs slowly;
A circle of darkness! then fixed
The sinew in its rest: then the Rock
Poisonous source! plac'd with art, lifting difficult
Its weighty bulk: silent the rock lay.

8: While Fuzon his tygers unloosing
Thought Urizen slain by his wrath.
I am God. said he, eldest of things!

9: Sudden sings the rock, swift & invisible
On Fuzon flew, enter'd his bosom;   40
His beautiful visage, his tresses,
That gave light to the mornings of heaven
Were smitten with darkness, deform'd
And outstretch'd on the edge of the forest

10: But the rock fell upon the Earth,
Mount Sinai, in Arabia.

CHAP: III

1: The Globe shook; and Urizen seated
On black clouds his sore wound anointed
The ointment flow'd down on the void
Mix'd with blood; here the snake gets her poison   50

2: With difficulty & great pain; Urizen
Lifted on high the dead corse:
On his shoulders he bore it to where
A Tree hung over the Immensity

3: For when Urizen shrunk away
From Eternals, he sat on a rock
Barren; a rock which himself
From redounding fancies had petrified
Many tears fell on the rock,
Many sparks of vegetation;   60
Soon shot the painted root
Of Mystery, under his heel:
It grew a thick tree; he wrote
In silence his book of iron:
Till the horrid plant bending its boughs
Grew to roots when it felt the earth
And again sprung to many a tree.

4: Amaz'd started Urizen! when
He beheld himself compassed round
And high roofed over with trees   70
He arose but the stems stood so thick

He with difficulty and great pain
Brought his Books, all but the Book
PLATE 4
Of iron, from the dismal shade

5: The Tree still grows over the Void
Enrooting itself all around
An endless labyrinth of woe!

6: The corse of his first begotten
On the accursed Tree of MYSTERY:
On the topmost stem of this Tree
Urizen nail'd Fuzon's corse.

CHAP: IV

1: Forth flew the arrows of pestilence
Round the pale living Corse on the tree   10

2: For in Urizens slumbers of abstraction
In the infinite ages of Eternity:
When his Nerves of Joy melted & flow'd
A white Lake on the dark blue air
In perturb'd pain and dismal torment
Now stretching out, now swift conglobing.

3: Effluvia vapor'd above
In noxious clouds; these hover'd thick
Over the disorganiz'd Immortal,
Till petrific pain scurfd o'er the Lakes   20
As the bones of man, solid & dark

4: The clouds of disease hover'd wide
Around the Immortal in torment
Perching around the hurtling bones
Disease on disease, shape on shape,
Winged screaming in blood & torment.

5: The Eternal Prophet beat on his anvils
Enrag'd in the desolate darkness
He forg'd nets of iron around
And Los threw them around the bones   30

6: The shapes screaming flutter'd vain
Some combin'd into muscles & glands
Some organs for craving and lust
Most remain'd on the tormented void:
Urizens army of horrors.

7: Round the pale living Corse on the Tree
Forty years flew the arrows of pestilence

8: Wailing and terror and woe
Ran thro' all his dismal world:
Forty years all his sons & daughters
Felt their skulls harden; then Asia
Arose in the pendulous deep.

9: They reptilize upon the Earth.

10: Fuzon groand on the Tree.

CHAP: V

1: The lamenting voice of Ahania
Weeping upon the void.
And round the Tree of Fuzon:
Distant in solitary night
Her voice was heard, but no form
Had she: but her tears from clouds   50
Eternal fell round the Tree

2: And the voice cried: Ah Urizen! Love!
Flower of morning! I weep on the verge
Of Non-entity; how wide the Abyss
Between Ahania and thee!

3: I lie on the verge of the deep.
I see thy dark clouds ascend,
I see thy black forests and floods,
A horrible waste to my eyes!

4: Weeping I walk over rocks   60
Over dens & thro' valleys of death
Why didst thou despise Ahania
To cast me from thy bright presence
Into the World of Loneness

5: I cannot touch his hand:
Nor weep on his knees, nor hear
His voice & bow, nor see his eyes
And joy, nor hear his footsteps, and
My heart leap at the lovely sound!
I cannot kiss the place   70
Whereon his bright feet have trod,
PLATE 5
But I wander on the rocks
With hard necessity.

6: Where is my golden palace
Where my ivory bed
Where the joy of my morning hour
Where the sons of eternity, singing

7: To awake bright Urizen, my king!
To arise to the mountain sport,
To the bliss of eternal valleys:

8: To awake my king in the morn!   10
To embrace Ahanias joy
On the bredth of his open bosom:
From my soft cloud of dew to fall
In showers of life on his harvests.

9: When he gave my happy soul
To the sons of eternal joy:
When he took the daughters of life.
Into my chambers of love:

10: When I found babes of bliss on my beds.
And bosoms of milk in my chambers   20
Fill'd with eternal seed
O! eternal births sung round Ahania,
In interchange sweet of their joys.

11: Swell'd with ripeness & fat with fatness
Bursting on winds my odors,
My ripe figs and rich pomegranates
In infant joy at thy feet
O Urizen, sported and sang;

12: Then thou with thy lap full of seed
With thy hand full of generous fire   30
Walked forth from the clouds of morning
On the virgins of springing joy,
On the human soul to cast
The seed of eternal science.

13: The sweat poured down thy temples
To Ahania return'd in evening
The moisture awoke to birth
My mothers-joys, sleeping in bliss.

14: But now alone over rocks, mountains
Cast out from thy lovely bosom: 40
Cruel jealousy! selfish fear!
Self-destroying: how can delight,
Renew in these chains of darkness
Where bones of beasts are strown
On the bleak and snowy mountains
Where bones from the birth are buried
Before they see the light.

FINIS

THE BOOK OF LOS

PLATE 3
LOS

CHAP: I

1: Eno aged Mother,
Who the chariot of Leutha guides,
Since the day of thunders in old time

2: Sitting beneath the eternal Oak
Trembled and shook the stedfast Earth
And thus her speech broke forth.

3: O Times remote!
When Love & Joy were adoration:
And none impure were deem'd.
Not Eyeless Covet   10
Nor Thin-lip'd Envy
Nor Bristled Wrath
Nor Curled Wantonness

4: But Covet was poured full:
Envy fed with fat of lambs:
Wrath with lions gore:
Wantonness lulld to sleep
With the virgins lute,
Or sated with her love.

5: Till Covet broke his locks & bars,   20
And slept with open doors:
Envy sung at the rich mans feast:
Wrath was follow'd up and down

By a little ewe lamb
And Wantonness on his own true love
Begot a giant race:

6: Raging furious the flames of desire
Ran thro' heaven & earth, living flames
Intelligent, organiz'd: arm'd
With destruction & plagues. In the midst   30
The Eternal Prophet bound in a chain
Compell'd to watch Urizens shadow

7: Rag'd with curses & sparkles of fury
Round the flames roll as Los hurls his chains
Mounting up from his fury, condens'd
Rolling round & round, mounting on high
Into vacuum: into non-entity.
Where nothing was! dash'd wide apart
His feet stamp the eternal fierce-raging
Rivers of wide flame; they roll round   40
And round on all sides making their way
Into darkness and shadowy obscurity

8: Wide apart stood the fires: Los remain'd
In the void between fire and fire
In trembling and horror they beheld him
They stood wide apart, driv'n by his hands
And his feet which the nether abyss
Stamp'd in fury and hot indignation

9: But no light from the fires all was
PLATE 4
Darkness round Los: heat was not; for bound up
Into fiery spheres from his fury
The gigantic flames trembled and hid

10: Coldness, darkness, obstruction, a Solid
Without fluctuation, hard as adamant
Black as marble of Egypt; impenetrable
Bound in the fierce raging Immortal.

And the seperated fires froze in
A vast solid without fluctuation,
Bound in his expanding clear senses   10

CHAP: II

1: The Immortal stood frozen amidst
The vast rock of eternity; times
And times; a night of vast durance:
Impatient, stifled, stiffend, hardned.

2: Till impatience no longer could bear
The hard bondage, rent: rent, the vast solid
With a crash from immense to immense

3: Crack'd across into numberless fragments
The Prophetic wrath, strug'ling for vent
Hurls apart, stamping furious to dust   20
And crumbling with bursting sobs; heaves
The black marble on high into fragments

4: Hurl'd apart on all sides, as a falling
Rock: the innumerable fragments away
Fell asunder; and horrible vacuum
Beneath him & on all sides round.

5: Falling, falling! Los fell & fell
Sunk precipitant heavy down down
Times on times, night on night, day on day
Truth has bounds. Error none: falling, falling: 30
Years on years, and ages on ages
Still he fell thro' the void, still a void
Found for falling day & night without end.
For tho' day or night was not; their spaces
Were measurd by his incessant whirls
In the horrid vacuity bottomless.

6: The Immortal revolving; indignant
First in wrath threw his limbs, like the babe
New born into our world: wrath subsided

And contemplative thoughts first arose   40
Then aloft his head rear'd in the Abyss
And his downward-borne fall chang'd oblique

7: Many ages of groans: till there grew
Branchy forms: organizing the Human
Into finite inflexible organs.

8: Till in process from falling he bore
Sidelong on the purple air, wafting
The weak breeze in efforts oerwearied

9: Incessant the falling Mind labour'd
Organizing itself: till the Vacuum   50
Became element, pliant to rise,
Or to fall, or to swim, or to fly:
With ease searching the dire vacuity

CHAP: III

1: The Lungs heave incessant, dull and heavy
For as yet were all other parts formless
Shiv'ring: clinging around like a cloud
Dim & glutinous as the white Polypus
Driv'n by waves & englob'd on the tide.

2: And the unformed part crav'd repose
Sleep began: the Lungs heave on the wave   60
Weary overweigh'd, sinking beneath
In a stifling black fluid he woke

3: He arose on the waters, but soon
Heavy falling his organs like roots
Shooting out from the seed, shot beneath,
And a vast world of waters around him
In furious torrents began.

4: Then he sunk, & around his spent Lungs
Began intricate pipes that drew in
The spawn of the waters. Outbranching   70
PLATE 5
An immense Fibrous form, stretching out
Thro' the bottoms of immensity raging.

5: He rose on the floods: then he smote
The wild deep with his terrible wrath,
Seperating the heavy and thin.

6: Down the heavy sunk; cleaving around
To the fragments of solid: up rose
The thin, flowing round the fierce fires
That glow'd furious in the expanse.

CHAP: IV

1: Then Light first began; from the fires   10
Beams, conducted by fluid so pure
Flow'd around the Immense: Los beheld
Forthwith, writhing upon the dark void
The Back bone of Urizen appear
Hurtling upon the wind
Like a serpent! like an iron chain
Whirling about in the Deep.

2: Upfolding his Fibres together
To a Form of impregnable strength
Los astonish'd and terrified, built   20
Furnaces; he formed an Anvil
A Hammer of adamant then began
The binding of Urizen day and night

3: Circling round the dark Demon, with howlings
Dismay & sharp blightings; the Prophet
Of Eternity beat on his iron links.

4: And first from those infinite fires
The light that flow'd down on the winds
He siez'd; beating incessant, condensing
The subtil particles in an Orb.   30

5: Roaring indignant the bright sparks
Endur'd the vast Hammer; but unwearied
Los beat on the Anvil; till glorious
An immense Orb of fire he fram'd

6: Oft he quench'd it beneath in the Deeps
Then survey'd the all-bright mass. Again
Siezing fires from the terrific Orbs
He heated the round Globe, then beat
While roaring his Furnaces endur'd
The chaind Orb in their infinite wombs   40

7: Nine ages completed their circles
When Los heated the glowing mass, casting
It down into the Deeps: the Deeps fled
Away in redounding smoke; the Sun
Stood self-balanc'd. And Los smild with joy.
He the vast Spine of Urizen siez'd
And bound down to the glowing illusion

8: But no light, for the Deep fled away
On all sides, and left an unform'd
Dark vacuity: here Urizen lay   50
In fierce torments on his glowing bed

9: Till his Brain in a rock, & his Heart
In a fleshy slough formed four rivers
Obscuring the immense Orb of fire
Flowing down into night: till a Form
Was completed, a Human Illusion
In darkness and deep clouds involvd.

> The End of the
> Book of LOS

VALA, OR THE FOUR ZOAS

PAGE 1 [Title, first form]

VALA

or

The Death and
Judgement
of the
[*Eternal*] Ancient Man

A DREAM

of Nine Nights

[Revised Title]

THE FOUR ZOAS

The torments of Love & Jealousy in
The Death and
Judgement
of Albion the
Ancient Man

PAGE 2

Rest before Labour

PAGE 3

Οτι ουκ εοτιν ημιν η παλη προς αιμα και σαρκα, αλλα προς τας αρχας,
προς τας εξουσιας, προς τους κοσμοκρατορας του σκοτους του αιωνος τουτου,
προς τα πνευματικα της πονηριας εν τοις επουρανιοις.

Εφες: vi κεφ. 12 ver.

[For we wrestle not against flesh and blood, but against principalities,
against powers, against the rulers of the darkness of this world, against
spiritual wickedness in high places.   (King James version)]

VALA
NIGHT THE FIRST

The Song of the Aged Mother which shook the heavens
    with wrath
Hearing the march of long resounding strong heroic
    Verse
Marshalld in order for the day of Intellectual Battle
[*The heavens quake, the earth was moved & shudderd &*
    the mountains
With all their woods, the streams & valleys: waild in
    dismal fear]

Four Mighty Ones are in every Man: a Perfect Unity
Cannot Exist. but from the Universal Brotherhood of
    Eden
The Universal Man. To Whom be Glory Evermore
    Amen

            John XVII c.21 & 22 & 23 v
            John I c. 14 v
            και. εξκηνωσεν εν. ημιν

What are the Natures of those Living Creatures the
    Heavenly Father only
Knoweth [*Individual Man knoweth not*] No Individual
    Knoweth nor Can know in all Eternity   10
Los was the fourth immortal starry one, & in the Earth
Of a bright Universe, Empery attended day & night
Days & nights of revolving joy, Urthona was his name

PAGE 4
In Eden; in the Auricular Nerves of Human Life,
Which is the Earth of Eden, he his Emanations
    propagated
Fairies of Albion afterwards Gods of the Heathen
[*Like Sons & Daughters*] Daughter of Beulah Sing
His fall into Division & his Resurrection to Unity
His fall into the Generation of decay & death & his

Regeneration by the Resurrection from the dead
Begin with Tharmas Parent power. darkning in the West

Lost! Lost! Lost! are my Emanations   Enion [*come forth*]
  O Enion
[*I am*] We are become a Victim to the Living [*I*] We
  hide in secret   10
I have hidden [*thee Enion in Jealous Despair*] Jerusalem
  in Silent Contrition   O Pity Me
I will build thee a Labyrinth [*where we may remain for
  ever alone*] also O pity me   O Enion
Why hast thou taken sweet Jerusalem from my inmost
  Soul
Let her Lay secret in the Soft recess of darkness &
  silence
It is not Love I bear to Enitharmon It is Pity
She hath taken refuge in my bosom & I cannot cast her
  out.

The Men have recieved their death wounds & their
  Emanations are fled
To me for refuge & I cannot turn them out for Pitys
  sake

Enion said – [*His*] Thy fear has made me tremble thy
  terrors have surrounded me
All Love is lost Terror succeeds & Hatred instead of
  Love   20
And stern demands of Right & Duty instead of Liberty
Once thou wast to Me the loveliest son of heaven – But
  now
Why art thou Terrible and yet I love thee in thy terror
  till
I am almost Extinct & soon shall be a shadow in
  Oblivion
Unless some way can be found that I may look upon
  thee & live
Hide me some shadowy semblance. secret whispring
  in my Ear

In secret of Soft Wings. in mazes of delusive beauty
I have lookd into the secret soul of him I lovd,
And in the Dark recesses found Sin & cannot return

Trembling & pale sat Tharmas weeping in his clouds   30

Why wilt thou Examine every little fibre of my soul
Spreading them out before the Sun like Stalks of flax
   to dry
The infant joy is beautiful but its anatomy
Horrible Ghast & Deadly nought shalt thou find in it
But Death Despair & Everlasting brooding Melancholy

Thou wilt go mad with horror if thou dost Examine thus
Every moment of my secret hours Yea I know
That I have sinnd & that my Emanations are become
   harlots
I am already distracted at their deeds & if I look
Upon them more Despair will bring self murder on my
   soul   40
O Enion thou art thyself a root growing in hell
Tho thus heavenly beautiful to draw me to destruction

Sometimes I think thou art a flower expanding
Sometimes I think thou art fruit breaking from its bud
In dreadful dolor & pain & I am like an atom
A Nothing left in darkness yet I am an identity
I wish & feel & weep & groan Ah terrible terrible

PAGE 5
In [Beulah] Eden Females sleep the winter in soft silken
   veils
Woven by their own hands to hide them in the darksom
   grave
But Males immortal live renewd by female deaths. in soft
Delight they die & they revive in spring with music &
   songs
Enion said Farewell I die I hide from thy searching
   eyes

So saying – From her bosom weaving soft in Sinewy
    threads
A tabernacle [*of delight/for Enitharmon*] for Jerusalem
    She sat among the Rocks
Singing her lamentation. Tharmas groand among his
    Clouds
Weeping, [*and*] then bending from his Clouds he stoopd
    his innocent head
And stretching out his holy hand in the vast Deep
    sublime   10
Turnd round the circle of Destiny with tears & bitter
    sighs
And said. Return O Wanderer when the Day of Clouds
    is oer

So saying he sunk down into the sea a pale white corse
[*So saying*] In torment he sunk down & flowd among
    her filmy Woof
His Spectre issuing from his feet in flames of fire
In [*dismal*] gnawing pain drawn out by her lovd fingers
    every nerve

She counted. every vein & lacteal threading them among
Her woof of terror. Terrified & drinking tears of woe
Shuddring she wove. – nine days & night Sleepless her
    food was tears
Wondring she saw her woof begin to animate. & not   20
As Garments woven subservient to her hands but
    having a will
Of its own perverse & wayward Enion Lovd & wept

Nine days she labourd at her work & nine dark sleepless
    nights
But on the tenth [*?dread*] trembling morn the Circle
    of Destiny Complete
Round rolld the Sea Englobing in a watry Globe self
    balancd
A Frowning Continent appeard Where Enion in the
    desart

Terrified in her own Creation viewing her woven shadow
Sat in a [*sweet*] dread intoxication of [*false woven bliss/
   soft woven sorrow*] Repentance & Contrition

There is from Great Eternity a mild & pleasant rest
Namd Beulah a Soft Moony Universe feminine lovely   30
Pure mild & Gentle given in Mercy to those who sleep
Eternally. Created by the Lamb of God around
On all sides within & without the Universal Man
The Daughters of Beaulah follow sleepers in all their
   [*wanderings*] Dreams
Creating Spaces lest they fall into Eternal Death
The Circle of Destiny complete they gave to it a Space
And namd the Space Ulro & brooded over it in care &
   love

They said The Spectre is in every man insane & most
Deformd Thro the three heavens descending in fury &
   fire
We meet it with our Songs & loving blandishments &
   give   40
To it a form of vegetation But this Spectre of Tharmas
Is Eternal Death What shall we do O God [*help*] pity &
   help
So spoke they & closd the Gate of [*Auricular power/
   nerves*] the Tongue in trembling fear

[*He spurnd Enion with his foot he sprang aloft in Clouds
Alighting in his drunken joy in a far distant Grove*]
[*What have I done said Enion accursed wretch! What deed.
Is this a deed of Love I know what I have done. I know
Too late now to repent. Love is changd to deadly Hate,
A life is blotted out & I alone remain possessd with Fears
I see the (remembrance) shadow of the dead within my (eyes)
   soul wandering   50
In darkness & solitude forming Seas of (Trouble) Doubt &
   rocks of (sorrow) Repentance
Already are my Eyes reverted. all that I behold
Within my soul has lost its splendor & a brooding Fear*]

Shadows me oer & drives me outward to a world of woe
So waild she trembling before her own Created Phantasm]
[*But standing on the Rocks her woven shadow glowing*
    bright]
Who animating times on times by the force of her sweet
    song

PAGE 6
She drew the Spectre forth from Tharmas in [*her silken*]
    her shining loom
Of vegetation weeping in wayward infancy & sullen
    youth
Listning to her soft lamentations soon his tongue began
To Lisp out words & soon in masculine strength
    augmenting he
Reard up a form of gold & stood upon the glittering rock
A shadowy human form winged & in his depths
The dazzlings as of gems shone clear, rapturous in [*joy*]
    fury
Glorying in his own eyes Exalted in terrific Pride

[*Searching for glory wishing that the heavens had eyes to*
    See
And courting that the Earth would ope her Eyelids &
    behold   10
Such wondrous beauty repining in the midst of all his glory
That nought but Enion could be found to praise adore &
    love
Three days in self admiring raptures on the rocks he flamd
And three dark nights repind the solitude. but the third
    morn
Astonishd he found Enion hidden in the darksome Cave

She spoke What am I wherefore was I put forth on these
    rocks
Among the Clouds to tremble in the wind in solitude
Where is the voice that lately woke the desart Where the
    Face

That wept among the clouds & where the voice that shall
  reply
No other living thing is here. The Sea the Earth. the
  Heaven   20
And Enion desolate where art thou Tharmas O return

Three days she waild & three dark nights sitting among
  the Rocks
While the bright spectre hid himself among the ?trailing
  clouds
Then sleep fell on her eyelids in a Chasm of the Valley
The Sixteenth morn the Spectre stood before her manifest]

[The Spectre thus spoke. (Art thou not my slave & shalt
  thou dare
To smite me with thy tongue beware lest I sting also thee)
  Who art thou Diminutive husk & shell
Broke from my bonds I scorn my prison I scorn & yet I
  love
If thou hast sinnd & art polluted know that I am pure   30
And unpolluted & will bring to rigid strict account
All thy past deeds hear what I tell thee! mark it well!
  remember!
This world is (Mine) Thine in which thou dwellest that
  within thy soul
That dark & dismal infinite where Thought roams up &
  down
Is (thine) Mine & there thou goest when with one Sting
  of my tongue
Envenomed thou rollst inward to the place (of death &
  hell) whence I emergd

She trembling answerd Wherefore was I born & what am I
A sorrow & a fear a living torment & naked Victim
I thought to weave a Covering (from) for my Sins from
  wrath of Tharmas]

PAGE 7
[Examining the sins of Tharmas I (have) soon found my
  own

O slay me not thou art his Wrath embodied in Deceit]
[*I thought Tharmas a Sinner & murderd his Emanations*
His secret loves & Graces Ah me wretched What have I
  done
(*But*) *For now I find that all those Emanations were my*
  Childrens Souls
And I have murderd them with Cruelty above atonement
Those that remain have fled from my cruelty into the
  desarts
(*Among wild beasts to roam*) *And thou the delusive*
  tempter to these deeds sittest before me
(*But where is/Thou art not*) *And art thou Tharmas all thy*
  soft delusive beauty cannot
Tempt me to murder (*honest love*) *my own soul & wipe*
  my tears & smile   10
In this thy world (*for ah! how*) *not mine! tho dark I*
  feel my world within

The Spectre said Thou sinful Woman. was it thy Desire
That I should hide thee with my power & delight thee
  with my beauty

And now thou darknest in my presence. never from my sight
Shalt thou depart to weep in secret. In my jealous wings
I evermore will hold thee when thou goest out or comest in
Tis thou has darkend all My World O Woman lovely bane]

[*Thus they contended all the day among the Caves of*
  Tharmas
Twisting in fearful forms & howling, howling harsh
  shrieking
Howling harsh shrieking, mingling their bodies join in
  burning anguish]   20

Opening his rifted rocks mingling together they join in
  burning anguish
Mingling his [*horrible/ terrible*] horrible [*brightness*]
  darkness with her tender limbs then high she soard
Shrieking above the ocean: a bright wonder that [*Beulah*]
  nature shudderd at

Half Woman & half [*Spectre/ Serpent*] desart all his
    [*lovely changing*] darkly waving colours mix
With her fair crystal clearness in her lips & cheeks his
    [*poisons*] metals rose
In blushes like the morning & his [*scaly armour*] rocky
    features softning

A [*monster*] wonder lovely in the heavens or wandring
    on the earth
With [*Spectre*] female voice [*incessant wailing in incessant
    thirst*] warbling upon the hollow vales
Beauty all blushing with desire [*mocking her fell despair*]
    a self enjoying wonder

[*Wandering desolate, a wonder abhorr'd by Gods & men*]   30
For Enion brooded groaning loud the rough seas
    vegetate.
Golden rocks rise from the [*vortex*] vast
And thus her voice. Glory, delight: & sweet enjoyment
    born
To mild Eternity shut in a threefold shape delightful
To wander in sweet solitude enrapturd at every wind

PAGE 8
Till with fierce pain she brought forth on the rocks her
    sorrow & woe
Behold two little Infants wept upon the desolate wind.

The first state weeping they began & helpless as a wave
Beaten along its sightless way growing enormous in its
    motion to
Its utmost goal, till strength from Enion like richest
    summer shining
Raisd the [*bright/ fierce*] bright boy & girl with glories
    from their heads out beaming
Drawing forth drooping mothers pity drooping
    mothers sorrow

[*But those in Great Eternity Met in the Council of God
As One Man hovering over Gilead & Hermon*]

He is the Good Shepherd He is the Lord & Master   10
To Create Man Morning by Morning to Give gifts at
*   Noon day*]

[*Enion brooded, oer the rocks, the rough rocks groaning*
*   vegetate*
Such power was given to the Solitary wanderer.
The barked Oak, the long limbd Beech; the Ches'nut tree;
*   the Pine.*
The Pear tree mild, the frowning Walnut, the sharp Crab,
*   & Apple sweet,*
The rough bark opens; twittering peep forth little beaks &
*   wings*
The Nightingale, the Goldfinch, Robin, Lark, Linnet &
*   Thrush*
The Goat leap'd from the craggy cliff the Sheep awoke
*   from the mould*
Upon its green stalk rose the Corn, waving innumerable
Infolding the bright Infants from the desolating winds]   20

They sulk upon her breast her hair became like snow on
    mountains
Weaker & weaker, weeping woful, wearier and wearier
Faded & her bright Eyes decayd melted with pity & love

PAGE 9
And then they wander'd far away she sought for them in
    vain
In weeping blindness stumbling she followd them oer
    rocks & mountains
Rehumanizing from the Spectre in pangs of maternal
    love
Ingrate they wanderd scorning her drawing her [*life;*
    ingrate] Spectrous Life
Repelling her away & away by a dread repulsive power
Into Non Entity revolving round in dark despair.
And drawing in the Spectrous life in pride and haughty
    joy

Thus Enion gave them all her spectrous life [*in deep
    despair*]

Then [*Ona*] Eno a daughter of Beulah took a Moment of
    Time
And drew it out to [*twenty years*] Seven thousand years
    with much care & affliction   10
And many tears & in the [*twenty*] Every year [*gave
    visions toward heaven*] made windows into Eden
She also took an atom of space & opend its center
Into Infinitude & ornamented it with wondrous art
Astonishd sat her Sisters of Beulah to see her soft
    affections
To Enion & her children & they ponderd these things
    wondring
And they Alternate kept watch over the Youthful terrors
They saw not yet the Hand Divine for it was not yet
    reveald
But they went on in Silent Hope & Feminine repose

But Los & Enitharmon delighted in the Moony spaces
    of [*Ona*] Eno
Nine Times they livd among the forests, feeding on
    sweet fruits   20
And nine bright Spaces wanderd weaving mazes of
    delight
Snaring the wild Goats for their milk they eat the flesh
    of Lambs
A male & female naked & ruddy as the pride of summer

Alternate Love & Hate his breast; hers Scorn &
    Jealousy
In embryon passions. they kiss'd not nor embrac'd for
    shame & fear
His head beamd light & in his vigorous voice was
    prophecy
He could controll the times & seasons, & the days &
    years

She could controll the spaces, regions, desart, flood &
  forest
But had no power to weave a Veil of covering for her
  Sins
She drave the Females all away from Los   30
And Los drave all the Males from her away
They wanderd long, till they sat down upon the
  margind sea.
Conversing with the visions of Beulah in dark slumberous
  bliss

[*NIGHT THE SECOND*]

[*Nine years they view the ?gleaming spheres ?reading the
  Visions of Beulah*]

But the two youthful wonders wanderd in the world of
  Tharmas
Thy name is Enitharmon; said the [*bright*] fierce
  prophetic boy
While thy mild voice fills all these Caverns with sweet
  harmony
O how [*thy*] our Parents sit & [*weep*] mourn in their
  silent secret bowers

PAGE 10
But Enitharmon answerd with a dropping tear &
  [*?smiling*] frowning
[*Bright*] Dark as a dewy morning when the crimson light
  appears
To make us happy [*how they*] let them weary their
  immortal powers
While we draw in their sweet delights while we return
  them scorn
On scorn to feed our discontent; for if we grateful prove
They will withhold sweet love, whose food is thorns &
  bitter roots.
We hear the warlike clarions we view the turning spheres
Yet Thou in indolence reposest holding me in bonds

Hear! I will sing a Song of Death! it is a Song of Vala!
The Fallen Man takes his repose: Urizen sleeps in the
   porch   10
Luvah and Vala [*wake & fly*] woke & flew up from the
   Human Heart
Into the Brain; from thence upon the pillow Vala
   slumber'd.
And Luvah siez'd the Horses of Light, & rose into the
   Chariot of Day
Sweet laughter siezd me in my sleep! silent & close I
   laughd
For in the visions of Vala I walkd with the mighty
   Fallen One
I heard his voice among the branches, & among sweet
   flowers.

Why is the light of Enitharmon darken'd in [*her*] dewy
   morn
Why is the silence of Enitharmon a [*cloud*] terror & her
   smile a whirlwind
Uttering this darkness in my halls, in the pillars of my
   Holy-ones
Why dost thou weep as Vala? & wet thy veil with dewy
   tears,   20
In slumbers of my night-repose, infusing a false
   morning?
Driving the Female Emanations all away from Los
I have refused to look upon the Universal Vision
And wilt thou slay with death him who devotes himself
   to thee
[*If thou drivest all the* (Males) *Females away from* (Vala)
   Luvah I will drive all
The Males away from thee]
Once born for the sport & amusement of Man now born
   to drink up all his Powers
PAGE II
I heard the sounding sea; I heard the voice weaker and
   weaker;

The voice came & went like a dream, I awoke in my
    sweet bliss.

Then Los smote her upon the Earth twas long eer she
    revivd
[*Los*] He answer'd, darkning [*with foul*] more with
    indignation hid in smiles

I die not Enitharmon tho thou singst thy Song of
    Death
Nor shalt thou me torment   For I behold the [*Eternal*]
    Fallen Man
Seeking to comfort Vala, she will not be comforted
She rises from his throne and seeks the shadows of her
    garden
Weeping for Luvah lost, in the bloody beams of your
    false morning
Sickning lies the [*Eternal*] Fallen Man his head sick his
    heart faint   10
Mighty atchievement of your power! Beware the
    punishment

[*Refusing to behold the Divine image which all behold
And live thereby. he is sunk down into a deadly sleep
But we immortal in our own strength survive by stern
    debate
Till we have drawn the Lamb of God into a mortal form
And that he must be born is certain for One must be All
And comprehend within himself all things both small &
    great
We therefore for whose sake all things aspire to be & live
Will so recieve the Divine Image that amongst the
    Reprobate
He may be devoted to Destruction from his mothers womb*]   20

I see, invisible descend into the Gardens of Vala
Luvah walking on the winds, I see the invisible knife
I see the shower of blood: I see the swords & spears of
    futurity

Tho in the Brain of Man we live, & in his circling
   Nerves.
Tho' this bright world of all our joy is in the Human
   Brain.
Where Urizen & all his Hosts hang their immortal
   lamps
Thou neer shalt leave this cold expanse where watry
   Tharmas mourns

So spoke Los. Scorn & Indignation rose upon
   Enitharmon
Then Enitharmon reddning fierce stretchd her immortal
   hands

Descend O Urizen descend with horse & chariots   30
Threaten not me O visionary thine the punishment
The Human Nature shall no more remain nor Human
   acts
Form the [free] rebellious Spirits of Heaven. but War &
   Princedom & Victory & Blood

PAGE 12
Night darkend as she spoke! a shuddring ran from East
   to West
A Groan was heard on high. The warlike clarions ceast.
   the Spirits
Of Luvah & Vala shudderd in their Orb: an orb of
   blood!

Eternity groand & was troubled at the Image of Eternal
   Death
The Wandering Man bow'd his faint head and Urizen
   descended
And the one must have murderd the other if he had not
   descended
Indignant muttering low thunders; Urizen descended
Gloomy sounding, Now I am God from Eternity to
   Eternity

Sullen sat Los plotting Revenge. Silent he [*Urizen*]
   eye'd the Prince
Of Light. Silent the prince of Light viewd Los. at
   length a brooded   10
Smile broke from Urizen for Enitharmon brightend
   more & more
Sullen he lowerd on Enitharmon but he smild on Los

Saying Thou art the Lord of Luvah into thine hands
   I give
The prince of Love the murderer his soul is in thine
   hands
Pity not Vala for she pitied not the Eternal Man
Nor pity thou the cries of Luvah. Lo these starry hosts
They are thy servants if thou wilt obey my awful
   Law

Los answered furious art thou one of those who when
   most complacent
Mean mischief most. If you are such Lo! I am also such
One must be master. try thy Arts I also will try mine   20
For I percieve Thou hast Abundance which I claim as
   mine

Urizen startled stood but not Long soon he cried
Obey my voice young Demon I am God from Eternity
   to Eternity

Thus Urizen spoke collected in himself in awful pride

Art thou a visionary of Jesus the soft delusion of
   Eternity
Lo I am God the terrible destroyer & not the Saviour
Why should the Divine Vision compell the sons of Eden
to forego each his own delight to war against his Spectre
The Spectre is the Man the rest is only delusion &
   fancy

So spoke the Prince of Light & sat beside the Seat of
   Los
Upon the sandy shore rested his chariot of fire   30

Ten thousand thousand were his hosts of spirits on the
　wind:
Ten thousand thousand glittering Chariots shining in
　the sky:
They pour upon the golden shore beside the silent ocean.
Rejoicing in the Victory & the heavens were filld with
　blood

The Earth spread forth her table wide. the Night a
　silver cup
Fill'd with the wine of anguish waited at the golden
　feast
But the bright Sun was not as yet; he filling all the
　expanse
Slept as a bird in the blue shell that soon shall burst
　away

Los saw the wound of his blow he saw he pitied he
　wept
Los now repented that he had smitten Enitharmon he
　felt love
Arise in all his Veins he threw his arms around her
　loins
To heal the wound of his smiting

They eat the fleshly bread, they drank the nervous wine
PAGE 13
They listend to the Elemental Harps & Sphery Song
They view'd the dancing Hours, quick sporting thro'
　the sky
With winged radiance scattering joys thro the ever
　changing light

But Luvah & Vala standing in the bloody sky
On high remain alone forsaken in fierce jealousy
They stood above the heavens forsaken desolate
　suspended in blood
Descend they could not. nor from Each other avert their
　eyes
Eternity appeard above them as One Man infolded

40

In Luvah[s] robes of blood & bearing all his afflictions
As the sun shines down on the misty earth Such was
    the Vision   10

But purple night and crimson morning & golden day
    descending
Thro' the clear changing atmosphere display'd green
    fields among
The varying clouds, like paradises stretch'd in the
    expanse
With towns & villages and temples, tents sheep-folds
    and pastures
Where dwell the children of the elemental worlds in
    harmony.
Not long in harmony they dwell, their life is drawn
    away
And wintry woes succeed; successive driven into the
    Void
Where Enion craves: successive drawn into the golden
    feast

And Los & Enitharmon sat in discontent & scorn
The Nuptial Song arose from all the thousand thousand
    spirits   20
Over the joyful Earth & Sea, and ascended into the
    Heavens
For Elemental Gods their thunderous Organs blew;
    creating
Delicious Viands. Demons of Waves their watry Eccho's
    woke!
[?*Elements*] Bright Souls of vegetative life, budding and
    blossoming
PAGE 14
Stretch their immortal hands to smite the gold & silver
    Wires
And with immortal Voice soft warbling fill all Earth &
    Heaven.
With doubling Voices & loud Horns wound round
    sounding

Cavernous dwellers fill'd the enormous Revelry,
Responding!
And Spirits of Flaming fire on high, govern'd the mighty
Song.

And This the Song! sung at The Feast of Los &
Enitharmon

[*The Mountain*] Ephraim calld out to [*The Mountain*]
Zion: Awake O Brother Mountain
Let us refuse the Plow & Spade, the heavy Roller &
spiked
Harrow. burn all these Corn fields. throw down all
these fences
Fattend on Human blood & drunk with wine of life is
better far   10

Than all these labours of the harvest & the vintage. See
the river
Red with the blood of Men. swells lustful round my
rocky knees
My clouds are not the clouds of verdant fields & groves
of fruit
But Clouds of Human Souls. my nostrils drink the lives
of Men

The Villages Lament. they faint outstretchd upon the
plain
Wailing runs round the Valleys from the Mill & from
the Barn
But most the polishd Palaces [?*weak*] dark silent bow
with dread
Hiding their books & pictures. underneath the dens of
Earth

The Cities send to one another saying My sons are
Mad
With wine of cruelty. Let us plat a scourge O Sister
City   20

Children are nourishd for the Slaughter; once the Child
was fed
With Milk; but wherefore now are Children fed with
blood

PAGE 15
The Horse is of more value than the Man. The Tyger
fierce
Laughs at the Human form. the Lion mocks & thirsts
for blood
They cry O Spider spread thy web! Enlarge thy bones
& fill'd
With marrow. sinews & flesh Exalt thyself attain a voice

Call to thy dark armd hosts, for all the sons of Men
muster together
To desolate their cities! Man shall be no more!
Awake O Hosts
The bow string sang upon the hills! Luvah & Vala ride
Triumphant in the bloody sky. & the Human form is
no more
The listning Stars heard, & the first beam of the
morning started back
He cried out to his Father, depart! depart! but sudden
Siez'd,
And clad in steel. & his Horse proudly neighd; he smelt
the battle
Afar off, Rushing back, reddning with rage the [*Eternal*]
Mighty Father

Siezd his bright Sheephook studded with gems & gold,
he Swung it round
His head shrill sounding in the sky, down rushd the Sun
with noise
Of war. The Mountains fled away they sought a place
beneath
Vala remaind in desarts of dark solitude. nor Sun nor
Moon

By night nor day to comfort her, she labourd in thick
  smoke
Tharmas endurd not, he fled howling. then a barren
  waste sunk down
Conglobing in the dark confusion, Mean time Los was
  born
And Thou O Enitharmon! Hark I hear the hammers of
  Los   20

PAGE 16

They melt the bones of Vala, & the bones of Luvah
  into wedges
The innumerable sons & daughters of Luvah closd in
  furnaces
Melt into furrows. winter blows his bellows: Ice &
  Snow
Tend the dire anvils. Mountains mourn & Rivers faint
  & fail

There is no City nor Corn-field nor Orchard! all is
  Rock & Sand
There is no Sun nor Moon nor Star. but rugged wintry
  rocks
Justling together in the void suspended by inward fires
Impatience now no longer can endure. Distracted Luvah

Bursting forth from the loins of Enitharmon, Thou
  fierce Terror
Go howl in vain, Smite Smite his fetters Smite O
  wintry hammers   10
Smite Spectre of Urthona, mock the fiend who drew us
  down
From heavens of joy into this Deep. Now rage but rage
  in vain

Thus Sang the Demons of the Deep. the Clarions of
  War blew loud
The Feast redounds & Crownd with roses & the circling
  vine

The Enormous Bride & Bridegroom sat, beside them
   Urizen
With faded radiance sighd, forgetful of the flowing wine
And of Ahania his Pure Bride but She was distant far

But Los & Enitharmon sat in discontent & scorn
Craving the more the more enjoying, drawing out sweet
   bliss
From all the turning wheels of heaven & the chariots of
   the Slain   20

At distance Far in Night repelld. in direful hunger
   craving
Summers & Winters round revolving in the frightful
   deep.

PAGE 17
[*And*] Enion blind & age-bent wept upon the desolate
   wind

Why does the Raven cry aloud and no eye pities her?
Why fall the Sparrow & the Robin in the foodless
   winter?
Faint! shivering they sit on leafless bush, or frozen stone

Wearied with seeking food across the snowy waste; the
   little
Heart, cold; and the little tongue consum'd, that once
   in thoughtless joy
Gave songs of gratitude to [*the*] waving corn fields round
   their nest.

Why howl the Lion & the Wolf? why do they roam
   abroad?
Deluded by [*the*] summers heat they sport in enormous
   love
And cast their young out to the hungry wilds & sandy
   desarts

PAGE 18

Why is the Sheep given to the knife? the Lamb plays
 in the Sun
He starts! he hears the foot of Man! he says, Take thou
 my wool
But spare my life, but he knows not that [*the*] winter
 cometh fast.

The Spider sits in his labourd Web, eager watching for
 the Fly
Presently comes a famishd Bird & takes away the Spider
His Web is left all desolate, that his little anxious heart
So careful wove; & spread it out with sighs and
 weariness.

This was the Lamentation of Enion round the golden
 Feast
Eternity groand and was troubled at the image of Eternal
 Death
Without the body of Man an Exudation from his
 sickning limbs   10

Now Man was come to the Palm tree & to the Oak of
 Weeping
Which stand upon the Edge of Beulah & he sunk down
From the supporting arms of the Eternal Saviour; who
 disposd
The pale limbs of his Eternal Individuality
Upon The Rock of Ages. Watching over him with Love
 & Care
                    [*End of the First Night*]
PAGE 21

Then those in Great Eternity met in the Council of God
As one Man for contracting their Exalted Senses
They behold Multitude or Expanding they behold as
 one
As One Man all the Universal family & that one Man
They call Jesus the Christ & they in him & he in them

Live in Perfect harmony in Eden the land of life
Consulting as One Man above [*Mount Gilead*] the
    Mountain of Snowdon Sublime

For messengers from Beulah come in tears & darkning
    clouds
Saying Shiloh is in ruins our brother is sick [*Shiloh*]
    Albion He
Whom thou lovest is sick he wanders from his house of
    Eternity   10
The daughters of Beulah terrified have closd the Gate of
    the Tongue
Luvah & Urizen contend in war around the holy tent

So spoke the Ambassadors from Beulah & with solemn
    mourning
They were introducd to the divine presence & they
    kneeled down
In [*Beth Peor*] Conways Vale thus recounting the Wars
    of Death Eternal

The Eternal Man wept in the holy tent Our Brother in
    Eternity
Even [*Shiloh*] Albion whom thou lovest wept in pain his
    family
Slept round on hills & valleys in the regions of his love
But Urizen awoke & Luvah woke & thus conferrd

Thou Luvah said the Prince of Light behold our sons &
    daughters   20
Reposd on beds. let them sleep on, do thou alone depart
Into thy wished Kingdom where in Majesty & Power
We may erect a throne. deep in the North I place my
    lot
Thou in the South listen attentive. In silent of this night
I will infold the Eternal tent in clouds opake while thou
Siezing the chariots of the morning. Go outfleeting ride
Afar into the Zenith high bending thy furious course
Southward with half the tents of men inclosd in clouds

Of Tharmas & Urthona. I remaining in porches of the
  brain
Will lay my scepter on Jerusalem the Emanation   30
On all her sons & on thy sons O Luvah & on mine
Till dawn was wont to wake them then my trumpet
  sounding loud
Ravishd away in night my strong command shall be
  obeyd
For I have placd my centinels in stations each tenth
  man
Is bought & sold & in dim night my Word shall be
  their law

PAGE 22

Luvah replied Dictate to thy Equals. am not I
The Prince of all the hosts of Men nor Equal know in
  Heaven
If I arise into the Zenith leaving thee to watch
The Emanation & her Sons the Satan & the Anak
Sihon and Og. wilt thou not rebel to my laws remain
In darkness building thy strong throne & in my ancient
  night
Daring my power wilt arm my sons against me in the
  [deep] Atlantic
My deep   My night which thou assuming hast assumd
  my Crown
I will remain as well as thou & here with hands of blood
Smite this dark sleeper in his tent then try my strength
  with thee.   10

While thus he spoke his fires reddend [round] oer the
  holy tent
Urizen cast deep darkness round him silent brooding
  death
Eternal death to Luvah. raging Luvah pourd
The Lances of Urizen from chariots. round the holy
  tent
Discord began & yells & cries shook the wide firmament

Beside his anvil stood Urthona dark. a mass of iron
Glowd furious on the anvil prepard for spades &
    coulters   All
His sons fled from his side to join the conflict pale he
    heard
The Eternal voice he stood the sweat chilld on his
    mighty limbs
He dropd his hammer, dividing from his aking bosom
    fled   20
A portion of his life shrieking upon the wind she fled
And Tharmas took her in pitying Then Enion in jealous
    fear
Murderd her & hid her in her bosom embalming her for
    fear
She should arise again to life   Embalmd in Enions bosom
Enitharmon remains a corse such thing was never known
In Eden that one died a death never to be revivd
Urthona stood in terror but not long his spectre fled

To Enion & his body fell. Tharmas beheld him fall
Endlong a raging serpent rolling round the holy tent
The sons of war astonishd at the Glittring monster drove   30
Him far into the world of Tharmas into a cavernd rock

But Urizen with darkness overspreading all the armies
Sent round his heralds   secretly commanding to depart
Into the north Sudden with thunders sound his
    multitudes
Retreat from the fierce conflict all the sons of Urizen at
    once
Mustring together in thick clouds leaving the rage of
    Luvah
To pour its fury on himself & on the Eternal Man

Sudden down fell they all together into an unknown
    Space
Deep horrible without End. Separated from Beulah far
    beneath

The Mans exteriors are become indefinite opend to pain   40
In a fierce hungring void & none can visit his regions

PAGE 19

Jerusalem his Emanation [*will soon*] is become a ruin
Her little ones [*will be*] are slain on the top of every
    street
And she herself le[d] captive & scatterd into [*all nations*]
    the indefinite
Gird on thy sword O thou most mighty in glory &
    majesty
Destroy these opressors of Jerusalem & those who ruin
    Shiloh

So spoke the Messengers of Beulah. Silently removing
The Family Divine drew up the Universal tent
Above [*Mount Gilead*] High Snowdon & closd the
    Messengers in clouds around
Till the time of the End. Then they Elected Seven.
    called the Seven
Eyes of God & the Seven lamps of the Almighty   10
The Seven are one within the other the Seventh is
    named Jesus
The Lamb of God blessed for ever & he followd the
    Man
Who wanderd in mount Ephraim seeking a Sepulcher
His inward eyes closing from the Divine vision & all
His children wandering outside from his bosom fleeing
    away
           [*End of The First Night*]
PAGE 20

The Daughters of Beulah beheld the Emanation they
    pitied
They wept before the Inner gates of Enitharmons bosom
And of her fine wrought brain & of her bowels within
    her loins
Three gates within Glorious & bright open into
    [*Eternity*] Beulah

From Enitharmons inward parts but the bright female
  terror
Refusd to open the bright gates she closd and barrd
  them fast
Lest Los should enter into Beulah thro her beautiful
  gates

The Emanation stood before the Gates of Enitharmon
Weeping. the Daughters of Beulah silent in the Porches
Spread her a couch unknown to Enitharmon here
  reposd   10
Jerusalem in slumbers soft lulld into silent rest

Terrific ragd the Eternal Wheels of intellect terrific ragd
The living creatures of the wheels in the Wars of
  Eternal life
But perverse rolld the wheels of Urizen & Luvah back
  reversd
Downwards & outwards [*tending*] consuming in the wars
  of Eternal Death

PAGE 23

VALA
NIGHT THE [SECOND] [*FIRST*/*THIRD*]

Rising upon his Couch of Death Albion beheld his Sons
Turning his Eyes outward to Self. losing the Divine
  Vision
[*The Man*] Albion calld Urizen & said. Behold these
  sickning Spheres
Whence is this Voice of Enion that soundeth in my
  [*Ears*] Porches
Take thou possession! take this Scepter! go forth in
  my might
For I am weary, & must sleep in the dark sleep of
  Death
Thy brother Luvah hath smitten me but pity thou his
  youth

Tho thou hast not pitid my Age O Urizen Prince of
Light

Urizen rose from the bright Feast like a star thro' the
evening sky
Exulting at the voice that calld him from the Feast of
envy   10
First he beheld the body of Man pale, cold, the horrors
of death
Beneath his feet shot thro' him as he stood in the
Human Brain
And all its golden porches grew pale with his sickening
light
No more Exulting for he saw Eternal Death beneath
Pale he beheld futurity; pale he beheld the Abyss
Where Enion blind & age bent wept in direful hunger
craving
All rav'ning like the hungry worm, & like the silent grave
PAGE 24
Mighty was the draught of Voidness to draw Existence
in

Terrific Urizen strode above, in fear & pale dismay
He saw the indefinite space beneath & his soul shrunk
with horror
His feet upon the verge of Non Existence; his voice
went forth

Luvah & Vala trembling & shrinking, beheld the great
Work master
And heard his Word! Divide ye bands influence by
influence
Build we a Bower for heavens darling in the grizly deep
Build we the Mundane Shell around the Rock of Albion

The Bands of Heaven flew thro the air singing &
shouting to Urizen
Some fix'd the anvil, some the loom erected, some the
plow   10

And harrow formd & framd the harness of silver &
    ivory
The golden compasses, the quadrant & the rule &
    balance
They erected the furnaces, they formd the anvils of
    gold beaten in mills
Where winter beats incessant, fixing them firm on their
    base
The bellows began to blow & the Lions of Urizen stood
    round the anvil

PAGE 25

And the leopards coverd with skins of beasts tended
    the roaring fires
Sublime distinct their lineaments divine of human
    beauty
The tygers of wrath called the horses of instruction
    from their mangers
They unloos'd them & put on the harness of gold &
    silver & ivory
In human forms distinct they stood round Urizen prince
    of Light
Petrifying all the Human Imagination into rock & sand
Groans ran along Tyburns brook and along the River
    of Oxford
Among the Druid Temples. Albion groand on Tyburns
    brook
Albion gave his loud death groan The Atlantic
    Mountains trembled
Aloft the Moon fled with a cry the Sun with streams of
    blood   10
From Albions Loins fled all Peoples and Nations of the
    Earth [Fled]
Fled with the noise of Slaughter & the stars of heaven
    Fled
Jerusalem came down in a dire ruin over all the Earth
She fell cold from Lambeths Vales in groans & Dewy
    death

The dew of anxious souls the death-sweat of the dying
In every pillard hall & arched roof of Albions skies
The brother & the brother bathe in blood upon the
  Severn
The Maiden weeping by. The father & the mother with
The Maidens father & her mother fainting over the
  body
And the Young Man the Murderer fleeing over the
  mountains   20

Reuben slept on Penmaenmawr & Levi slept on
  Snowdon
Their eyes their ears nostrils & tongues roll outward
  they behold
What is within now seen without they are raw to the
  hungry wind
They become Nations far remote in a little & dark Land
The Daughters of Albion girded around their garments
  of Needlework
Stripping Jerusalems curtains from mild demons of the
  hills
Across Europe & Asia to China & Japan like
  lightenings
They go forth & return to Albion on his rocky couch
Gwendolen Ragan Sabrina Gonorill Mehetabel
  Cordella
Boadicea Conwenna Estrild Gwinefrid Ignoge Cambel   30
Binding Jerusalems Children in the dungeons of
  Babylon
They play before the Armies before the hounds of
  Nimrod
While The Prince of Light on Salisbury plain among
  the druid stones

Rattling the adamantine chains & hooks heave up the ore
In mountainous masses, plung'd in furnaces, & they shut
  & seald
The furnaces a time & times; all the while blew the
  North

His cloudy bellows & the South & East & dismal West
And all the while the plow of iron cut the dreadful
    furrows
In Ulro beneath Beulah where the Dead wail Night &
    Day

Luvah was cast into the Furnaces of affliction & sealed   40
And Vala fed in cruel delight, the furnaces with fire
Stern Urizen beheld urg'd by necessity to keep
The evil day afar, & if perchance with iron power
He might avert his own despair; in woe & fear he saw

PAGE 26
Vala incircle round the furnaces where Luvah was clos'd
In joy she heard his howlings, & forgot he was her
    Luvah
With whom she walkd in bliss, in times of innocence &
    youth

Hear ye the voice of Luvah from the furnaces of Urizen

If I indeed am Valas King & ye O sons of Men
The workmanship of Luvahs hands; in times of
    Everlasting
When I called forth the Earth-worm from the cold &
    dark obscure
I nurturd her I fed her with my rains & dews, she grew
A scaled Serpent, yet I fed her tho' she hated me
Day after day she fed upon the mountains in Luvahs
    sight   10
I brought her thro' the Wilderness, a dry & thirsty land
And I commanded springs to rise for her in the black
    desart
Till she became a Dragon winged bright & poisonous
I opend all the floodgates of the heavens to quench her
    thirst
PAGE 27
And I commanded the Great deep to hide her in his
    hand
Till she became a little weeping Infant a span long

I carried her in my bosom as a man carries a lamb
I loved her I gave her all my soul & my delight
I hid her in soft gardens & in secret bowers of Summer
Weaving mazes of delight along the sunny paradise
Inextricable labyrinths, She bore me sons & daughters
And they have taken her away & hid her from my sight
They have surrounded me with walls of iron & brass, O
    Lamb
Of God clothed in Luvahs garments little knowest thou   10
Of death Eternal that we all go to Eternal Death
To our Primeval Chaos in fortuitous concourse of
    incoherent
Discordant principles of Love & Hate I suffer affliction
Because I love. for I [*am*] was love [*&*] but hatred
    awakes in me
And Urizen who was Faith & Certainty is changd to
    Doubt
The hand of Urizen is upon me because I blotted out
That Human [*terror*] delusion to deliver all the sons of
    God
From bondage of the Human form, O first born Son of
    Light
O Urizen my enemy I weep for thy stern ambition
But weep in vain O when will you return Vala the
    Wanderer   20

PAGE 28

These were the words of Luvah patient in afflictions
Reasoning from the loins in the unreal forms of Ulros
    night

And when Luvah age after age was quite melted with
    woe
The fires of Vala faded like a shadow cold & pale
An evanescent shadow. last she fell a heap of Ashes
Beneath the furnaces a woful heap in living death

Then were the furnaces unseald with spades & pickaxes
Roaring let out the fluid, the molten metal ran in
    channels

Cut by the plow of ages held in Urizens strong hand
In many a valley, for the Bulls of Luvah dragd the Plow   10

With trembling horror pale aghast the Children of
   [*Men*] Man
Stood on the infinite Earth & saw these visions in the
   air
In waters & in Earth beneath they cried to one another
What are we terrors to one another. Come O brethren
   wherefore
Was this wide Earth spread all abroad. not for wild
   beasts to roam
But many stood silent & busied in their families
And many said We see no Visions in the darksom air
Measure the course of that sulphur orb that lights the
   [*dismal*] darksom day
Set stations on this breeding Earth & let us buy & sell
Others arose & schools Erected forming Instruments   20
To measure out the course of heaven. Stern Urizen
   beheld
In woe his brethren & his Sons in darkning woe
   lamenting
Upon the winds in clouds involvd Uttering his voice in
   thunders
Commanding all the work with care & power & severity

Then siezd the Lions of Urizen their work, & heated in
   the forge
Roar the bright masses, thund'ring beat the hammers,
   many a [*Globe*] pyramid
Is form'd & thrown down thund'ring into the deeps of
   Non Entity
Heated red hot they hizzing rend their way down many
   a league
Till resting. each his [*center/basement*] finds; suspended
   there they stand
Casting their sparkles dire abroad into the dismal deep   30
For measurd out in orderd spaces the Sons of Urizen

With compasses divide the deep; they the strong scales
    erect

PAGE 29

That Luvah rent from the faint Heart of the [*Eternal*|
    Ancient] Fallen Man

And weigh the massy [*Globes*] Cubes, then fix them in
    their awful stations

And all the time in Caverns shut, the golden Looms
    erected

First spun, then wove the Atmospheres, there the
    Spider & Worm

Plied the wingd shuttle piping shrill thro' all the
    list'ning threads

Beneath the Caverns roll the weights of lead & spindles
    of iron

The enormous warp & woof rage direful in the affrighted
    deep

While far into the vast unknown, the strong wing'd
    Eagles bend

Their venturous flight, in Human forms distinct; thro
    darkness deep

They bear the woven draperies; on golden hooks they
    hang abroad

The universal curtains & spread out from Sun to Sun

The vehicles of light, they separate the furious particles

Into mild currents as the water mingles with the wine.

While thus the Spirits of strongest wing enlighten the
    dark deep

The threads are spun & the cords twisted & drawn out;
    then the weak

Begin their work; & many a net is netted; many a net

PAGE 30

Spread & many a Spirit caught, innumerable the nets

Innumerable the gins & traps; & many a soothing flute

Is form'd & many a corded lyre, outspread over the
    immense

10

In cruel delight they trap the listeners, & in cruel
  delight
Bind them, [*together*] condensing the strong energies
  into little compass
Some became seed of every plant that shall be planted;
  some
The bulbous roots, thrown up together into barns &
  garners

Then rose the Builders; First the Architect divine his
  plan
Unfolds, The wondrous scaffold reard all round the
  infinite
Quadrangular the building rose the heavens squared by
  a line.   10
Trigons & cubes divide the elements in finite bonds
Multitudes without number work incessant: the hewn
  stone
Is placd in beds of mortar mingled with the ashes of
  Vala
Severe the labour, female slaves the mortar trod
  oppressed

Twelve halls after the names of his twelve sons composd
The [*golden*] wondrous building & three Central Domes
  after the Names
Of his three daughters were encompassed by the twelve
  bright halls
Every hall surrounded by bright Paradises of Delight
In which [*were*] are towns & Cities Nations Seas
  Mountains & Rivers
Each Dome opend toward four halls & the Three
  Domes Encompassd   20
The Golden Hall of Urizen whose western side glowd
  bright
With ever streaming fires beaming from his awful limbs

His Shadowy Feminine Semblance here reposd on a
  [*bright*] White Couch

Or hoverd oer his Starry head & when he smild she
  brightend
Like a bright Cloud in harvest. but when Urizen frownd
  she wept
In mists over his carved throne & when he turnd his
  back
Upon his Golden hall & sought the Labyrinthine porches
Of his wide heaven Trembling, cold in paling fears she
  sat
A shadow of Despair therefore toward the West Urizen
  formd
A recess in the wall for fires to glow upon the pale   30
Females limbs in his absence & her Daughters oft upon
A Golden Altar burnt perfumes with Art Celestial formd
Foursquare sculpturd & sweetly Engravd to please their
  shadowy mother
Ascending into her [*cloudy*] misty garments the blue
  smoke rolld to revive
Her cold limbs in the absence of her Lord. Also her sons
With lives of Victims sacrificed upon an altar of brass
On the East side. Revivd her Soul with lives of beasts &
  birds
Slain on the Altar up ascending into her cloudy bosom
Of terrible workmanship the Altar labour of ten
  thousand Slaves
One thousand Men of wondrous power spent their
  lives in its formation   40
It stood on twelve steps namd after the names of her
  twelve sons
And was Erected at the chief entrance of Urizens
  hall

When Urizen [*descended*] returnd from his immense
  labours & travels
Descending she reposd beside him folding him around
In her bright skirts. Astonished & Confounded he beheld
Her shadowy form now Separate he shudderd & was
  silent

Till her caresses & her tears revivd him to life & joy
Two wills they had two intellects & not as in times of
  old
This Urizen percievd & silent brooded in darkning
  Clouds
To him his Labour was but Sorrow & his Kingdom was
  Repentance   50
He drave the Male Spirits all away from Ahania
And she drave all the Females from him away

Los joyd & Enitharmon laughd, saying   Let us go down
And see this labour & sorrow; They went down to see
  the woes
Of Vala & the woes of Luvah, to draw in their delights

And Vala like a shadow oft appeard to Urizen
PAGE 31
The King of Light beheld her mourning among the
  Brick kilns compelld
To labour night & day among the fires, her lamenting
  voice
Is heard when silent night returns & the labourers take
  their rest

O Lord wilt thou not look upon our sore afflictions
Among these flames incessant labouring, our hard
  masters laugh
At all our sorrow. We are made to turn the wheel for
  water
To carry the heavy basket on our scorched shoulders,
  to sift
The sand & ashes, & to mix the clay with tears &
  repentance
I see not Luvah as of old I only see his feet
Like pillars of fire travelling thro darkness & non entity   10
The times are now returnd upon us, we have given
  ourselves
To scorn and now are scorned by the slaves of our
  enemies

Our beauty is coverd over with clay & ashes, & our
  backs
Furrowd with whips, & our flesh bruised with the heavy
  basket
Forgive us O thou piteous one whom we have offended,
  forgive
The weak remaining shadow of Vala that returns in
  sorrow to thee.

Thus she lamented day & night, compelld to labour &
  sorrow
Luvah in vain her lamentations heard; in vain his love
Brought him in various forms before her still she knew
  him not

PAGE 32

Still she despisd him, calling on his name & knowing
  him not
Still hating still professing love, still labouring in the
  smoke

And Los & Enitharmon joyd, they drank in tenfold joy
From all the sorrow of Luvah & the labour of Urizen
And Enitharmon joyd Plotting to rend the secret cloud
To plant divisions in the Soul of Urizen & Ahania

[*For*] But infinitely beautiful the wondrous work arose
In [*songs & joy*] sorrow & care. a Golden World whose
  porches round the heavens
And pillard halls & rooms recievd the eternal wandering
  stars
A wondrous golden Building; many a window many a
  door   10
And many a division let in & out into the vast unknown
[*Circled/ Cubed*] in [*infinite orb/ window square*]
  immoveable, within its [*arches all*] walls & cielings
The heavens were closd and spirits mournd their
  bondage night and day
And the Divine Vision appeard in Luvahs robes of
  blood

Thus was the Mundane shell builded by Urizens strong
power

[*Then*] Sorrowing went the Planters forth to plant, the
Sowers[*forth*] to sow
They dug the channels for the rivers & they pourd
abroad

PAGE 33

The seas & lakes, they reard the mountains & the rocks
& hills
On broad pavilions, on pillard roofs & porches & high
towers
In beauteous order, thence arose soft clouds &
exhalations
Wandering even to the sunny [*orbs*] Cubes of light &
heat
For many a window ornamented with sweet ornaments
Lookd out into the World of Tharmas, where in ceaseless
torrents
His billows roll where monsters wander in the foamy
paths

On clouds the Sons of Urizen beheld Heaven walled
round
They weighd & orderd all & Urizen comforted saw
The wondrous work flow forth like visible out of the
invisible   10
For the Divine Lamb Even Jesus who is the Divine
Vision
Permitted all lest Man should fall into Eternal Death
For when Luvah sunk down himself put on the robes
of blood
Lest the state calld Luvah should cease. & the Divine
Vision
Walked in robes of blood till he who slept should
awake

Thus were the stars of heaven created. like a golden
chain

To bind the Body of Man to heaven from falling into
  the Abyss
Each took his station, & his course began with [*songs &
  joy*] sorrow & care

In sevens & tens & fifties, hundreds, thousands,
  numberd all
According to their various powers. Subordinate to
  Urizen   20
And to his sons in their degrees & to his beauteous
  daughters

Travelling in silent majesty along their orderd ways
In right lined paths outmeasurd by proportions of
  [*weight & measure*] number weight
And measure. mathematic motion wondrous. along the
  deep
In fiery pyramid. or Cube. or unornamented pillar
  square
Of fire far shining. travelling along even to its destind
  end
Then falling down. a terrible space recovring in winter
  dire
Its wasted strength. it back returns upon a nether course
Till fired with ardour fresh recruited in its humble
  [*spring*] season
It rises up on high all summer till its wearied course   30
Turns into autumn. such the periods of many worlds
Others triangular [*their*] right angled course maintain.
  others obtuse
Acute [*& oblong*] Scalene, in simple paths. but others
  move
In intricate ways biquadrate. Trapeziums Rhombs
  Rhomboids
Paralellograms. triple & quadruple. polygonic
In their amazing [*fructifying*] hard subdued course in
  the vast deep

PAGE 34

And Los & Enitharmon were drawn down by their
    desires
Descending sweet upon the wind among soft harps &
    voices
To plant divisions in the Soul of Urizen & Ahania
To conduct the Voice of Enion to Ahanias midnight
    pillow

Urizen saw & envied & his imagination was filled
Repining he contemplated the past in his bright sphere
Terrified with his heart & spirit at the visions of
    futurity
That his dread fancy formd before him in the unformd
    void

[*Now*] For Los & Enitharmon walkd forth on the dewy
    Earth
Contracting or expanding their all flexible senses   10
At will to murmur in the flowers small as the honey bee
At will to stretch across the heavens & step from star to
    star
Or standing on the Earth erect, or on the stormy waves
Driving the storms before them or delighting in sunny
    beams
While round their heads the Elemental Gods kept
    harmony

And Los said. Lo the Lilly pale & the rose reddning
    fierce
Reproach thee & the beamy gardens sicken at thy
    beauty
I grasp thy vest in my strong hand in vain. like water
    springs
In the bright sands of Los. evading my embrace. then
    I alone
Wander among the virgins of the summer   Look they
    cry   20

The poor forsaken Los mockd by the worm the shelly
    snail
The Emmet & the beetle hark they laugh & mock at Los

Enitharmon answerd   Secure now from the smitings of
    thy Power
Demon of fury If the God enrapturd me infolds
In clouds of sweet obscurity my beauteous form dissolving
Howl thou over the body of death tis thine But if among
    the virgins
Of summer   I have seen thee sleep & turn thy cheek
    delighted
Upon the rose or lilly pale. or on a bank where sleep
The beamy daughters of the light starting they rise they
    flee
From thy fierce love for tho I am dissolvd in the bright
    God   30
My spirit still pursues thy false love over rocks &
    valleys

Los answerd Therefore fade I thus dissolvd in rapturd
    trance
Thou canst repose on clouds of secrecy while oer my
    limbs
Cold dews & hoary frost creeps tho I lie on banks of
    summer
Among the beauties of the World   Cold & repining
    Los
Still dies for Enitharmon nor a spirit springs from my
    dead corse
Then I am dead till thou revivest me with thy sweet
    song
Now taking on Ahanias form & now the form of
    Enion
I know thee not as once I knew thee in those blessed
    fields
Where memory wishes to repose among the flocks of
    Tharmas   40

Enitharmon answerd Wherefore didst thou throw thine
    arms around
Ahanias Image I decievd thee & will still decieve
Urizen saw thy sin & hid his beams in darkning Clouds
I still keep watch altho I tremble & wither across the
    heavens
In strong vibrations of fierce jealousy for thou art mine
Created for my will my slave tho strong tho I am weak
Farewell the God calls me away   I depart in my sweet
    bliss

She fled vanishing on the wind And left a dead cold
    corse
In Los's arms howlings began over the body of death
Los spoke. Thy God in vain shall call thee if by my
    strong power   50
I can infuse my dear revenge into his glowing breast
Then jealousy shall shadow all his mountains & Ahania
Curse thee thou plague of woful Los & seek revenge on
    thee

So saying in deep sobs he languishd till dead he also fell
Night passd & Enitharmon eer the dawn returnd in bliss
She sang Oer Los. reviving him to Life his groans were
    terrible
But thus she sang   I sieze the sphery harp I strike the
    strings

At the first Sound the Golden sun arises from the Deep
And shakes his awful hair
The Eccho wakes the moon to unbind her silver locks   60
The golden sun bears on my song
And nine bright spheres of harmony rise round the fiery
    King

The joy of woman is the Death of her most best
    beloved
Who dies for Love of her
In torments of fierce jealousy & pangs of adoration
The Lovers night bears on my song

And the nine Spheres rejoice beneath my powerful
   controll

They sing unceasing to the notes of my immortal hand
The solemn silent moon
Reverberates the living harmony upon my limbs   70
The birds & beasts rejoice & play
And every one seeks for his mate to prove his inmost
   joy

Furious & terrible they sport & rend the nether deeps
The deep lifts up his rugged head
And lost in infinite hum[m]ing wings vanishes with a
   cry
The fading cry is ever dying
The living voice is ever living in its inmost joy

Arise you little glancing wings & sing your infant joy
Arise & drink your bliss
For every thing that lives is holy for the source of life   80
Descends to be a weeping babe
For the Earthworm renews the moisture of the sandy
   plain

Now my left hand I stretch to earth beneath
And strike the terrible string
I wake sweet joy in dens of sorrow & I plant a smile
In forests of affliction
And wake the bubbling springs of life in regions of dark
   death

O I am weary lay thine hand upon me or I faint
I faint beneath these beams of thine
For thou hast touchd my five senses & they answerd thee   90
Now I am nothing & I sink
And on the bed of silence sleep till thou awakest me

Thus sang the Lovely one in Rapturous delusive trance
Los heard [*delighted*] reviving he siezd her in his arms
   delusive hopes

Kindling She led him into Shadows & thence fled
   outstretchd
Upon the immense like a bright rainbow weeping &
   smiling & fading

Thus livd Los driving Enion far into the deathful infinite
That he may also draw Ahania's spirit into her Vortex
Ah happy blindness [*she*] Enion sees not the terrors of
   the uncertain
Thus Enion wails from the dark deep, the golden
   heavens tremble   100

PAGE 35

I am made to sow the thistle for wheat; the nettle for a
   nourishing dainty
I have planted a false oath in the earth, it has brought
   forth a poison tree
I have chosen the serpent for a councellor & the dog
For a schoolmaster to my children
I have blotted out from light & living the dove &
   nightingale
And I have caused the earth worm to beg from door to
   door
I have taught the thief a secret path into the house of
   the just
I have taught pale artifice to spread his nets upon the
   morning
My heavens are brass my earth is iron my moon a clod
   of clay
My sun a pestilence burning at noon & a vapour of death
   in night   10

What is the price of Experience do men buy it for a
   song
Or wisdom for a dance in the street? No it is bought
   with the price
Of all that a man hath his house his wife his children
Wisdom is sold in the desolate market where none come
   to buy

And in the witherd field where the farmer plows for
    bread in vain

It is an easy thing to triumph in the summers sun
And in the vintage & to sing on the waggon loaded with
    corn
It is an easy thing to talk of patience to the afflicted
To speak the laws of prudence to the houseless
    wanderer
PAGE 36
To listen to the hungry ravens cry in wintry season
When the red blood is filld with wine & with the
    marrow of lambs

It is an easy thing to laugh at wrathful elements
To hear the dog howl at the wintry door, the ox in the
    slaughter house moan
To see a god on every wind & a blessing on every blast
To hear sounds of love in the thunder storm that
    destroys our enemies house
To rejoice in the blight that covers his field, & the
    sickness that cuts off his children
While our olive & vine sing & laugh round our door &
    our children bring fruits & flowers

Then the groan & the dolor are quite forgotten & the
    slave grinding at the mill
And the captive in chains & the poor in the prison, &
    the soldier in the field
When the shatterd bone hath laid him groaning among
    the happier dead

It is an easy thing to rejoice in the tents of prosperity
Thus could I sing & thus rejoice, but it is not so with
    me!

        [End of the Second Night]
Ahania heard the Lamentation & a swift Vibration
Spread thro her Golden frame. She rose up eer the
    dawn of day

When Urizen slept on his couch. drawn thro unbounded
   space
Onto the margin of Non Entity the bright Female came
There she beheld the [*terrible*] Spectrous form of Enion
   in the Void
And never from that moment could she rest upon her
   pillow

End of the Second Night

PAGE 37

VALA

NIGHT THE [*?First ?Third*] THIRD

Now sat the King of Light on high upon his starry
   throne
And bright Ahania bow'd herself before his splendid feet

O Urizen look on [*thy wife that*] Me. like a
   mournful stream
I Embrace[*s*] round thy knees & wet[*s her*] My bright
   hair with [*her*] My tears.
Why sighs my Lord! are not the morning stars thy
   obedient Sons
Do they not bow their bright heads at thy voice? at thy
   command
Do they not fly into their stations & return their light to
   thee
The immortal Atmospheres are thine, there thou art seen
   in glory
Surrounded by the ever changing Daughters of the
   Light
[*Thou sitst in harmony for God hath set thee over all*]   10
Why wilt thou look upon futurity darkning present joy

She ceas'd the Prince his light obscurd & the splendors
   of his crown

PAGE 38

Infolded in thick clouds, from whence his mighty voice
   burst forth

O bright [*Ahania/shadow*] a Boy is born of the dark
   Ocean

Whom Urizen doth serve, with Light replenishing his
   darkness

I am set here a King of trouble commanded here to
   serve

And do my ministry to those who eat of my wide table

All this is mine yet I must serve & that Prophetic boy

Must grow up to command his Prince [*& all my Kingly
   power*] but hear my determind Decree

[*But*] Vala shall become a Worm in Enitharmons Womb

Laying her seed upon the fibres soon to issue forth

And Luvah in the loins of Los a dark & furious death   10

Alas for me! what will become of me at that dread time?

Ahania bow'd her head & wept seven days before the
   King

And on the eighth day when his clouds unfolded from
   his throne

She rais'd her bright head sweet perfumd & thus with
   heavenly voice

O Prince the Eternal One hath set thee leader of his
   hosts

PAGE 39

[*Raise then thy radiant eyes to him raise thy obedient hands
And comforts shall descend from heaven into thy
   darkning clouds*]

Leave all futurity to him resume thy fields of Light

Why didst thou listen to the voice of Luvah that dread
   morn

To give the immortal steeds of light to his deceitful
   hands

No longer now obedient to thy will thou art compell'd

To forge the curbs of iron & brass to build the iron
   mangers

To feed them with intoxication from the wine presses of
  Luvah
Till the Divine Vision & Fruition is quite obliterated
They call thy lions to the fields of blood, they rowze thy
  tygers   10
Out of the halls of justice, till these dens thy wisdom
  framd
Golden & beautiful but O how unlike those sweet fields
  of bliss
Where liberty was justice & eternal science was mercy
Then O my dear lord listen to Ahania, listen to the
  vision
The vision of Ahania in the slumbers of Urizen
When Urizen slept in the porch & the [*Eternal*] Ancient
  Man was smitten
The [*Eternal/Fallen*] Darkning Man walkd on the steps
  of fire before his halls
And Vala walkd with him in dreams of soft deluding
  slumber
He looked up & saw [*the*] thee Prince of Light [*with*] thy
  splendor faded
[*But saw not Los nor Enitharmon for Luvah hid them in
  shadow*]   20
PAGE 40
[*of*] [*In a soft cloud Outstretch'd across, & Luvah dwelt in
  the cloud*]

Then Man ascended mourning into the splendors of his
  palace
Above him rose a Shadow from his wearied intellect
Of living gold, pure, perfect, holy; in white linen pure
  he hover'd
A sweet entrancing self delusion, a watry vision of Man
Soft exulting in existence all the Man absorbing

Man fell upon his face prostrate before the watry shadow
Saying O Lord whence is this change thou knowest I am
  nothing

And Vala trembled & coverd her face, & her locks.
 were spread on the pavement
I heard astonishd at the Vision & my heart trembled
 within me   10
I heard the voice of the Slumberous Man & thus he
 spoke
Idolatrous to his own Shadow words of Eternity uttering

O I am nothing when I enter into judgment with thee
If thou withdraw thy breath I die & vanish into Hades
If thou dost lay thine hand upon me behold I am silent
If thou withhold thine hand I perish like a fallen leaf
O I am nothing & to nothing must return again
If thou withdraw thy breath, behold I am oblivion

He ceasd: the shadowy voice was silent; but the cloud
 hoverd over their heads

PAGE 41

In golden wreathes, the sorrow of Man & the balmy
 drops fell down
And Lo that Son of Man, that shadowy Spirit of the
 [*Eternal*] Fallen One/Albion
Luvah, descended from the cloud; [*The Eternal Man
 arose*] In terror Albion rose
Indignant rose the [*Eternal/Fallen*] Awful Man &
 turnd his back on Vala

Why roll thy clouds in sick'ning mists. I can no longer
 hide
The dismal vision of mine Eyes, O love & life & light!
Prophetic dreads urge me to speak. futurity is before me
Like a dark lamp. Eternal death haunts all my
 expectation
Rent from Eternal Brotherhood we die & are no more

I heard the Voice of the [*Eternal/Falln One*] Albion
 starting from his sleep   10

Whence is this voice crying Enion that soundeth in my
 ears
O cruel pity! O dark deceit! can Love seek for dominion

And Luvah strove to gain dominion over the [*Eternal*]
    Ancient Man/Mighty Albion
They strove together above the Body where Vala was
    inclos'd
And the dark body of [*Man*] Albion left prostrate upon
    the crystal pavement
Coverd with boils from head to foot. the terrible smitings
    of Luvah

Then frownd the [*Eternal*] Fallen Man/Albion & put
    forth Luvah from his presence
(I heard him: frown not Urizen: but listen to my Vision)

PAGE 42
Saying, Go & die the Death of Man for Vala the sweet
    wanderer
I will turn the volutions of your Ears outward; & bend
    your Nostrils
Downward; & your fluxile Eyes englob'd, roll round in
    fear
Your withring Lips & Tongue shrink up into a narrow
    circle
Till into narrow forms you creep. Go take your fiery
    way
And learn what 'tis to absorb the Man you Spirits of
    Pity & Love

O Urizen why art thou pale at the visions of Ahania
Listen to her who loves thee lest we also are driven
    away.

They heard the Voice & fled swift as the winters setting
    sun
And now the Human Blood foamd high, I saw that
    Luvah & Vala   10
Went down the Human Heart where Paradise & its joys
    abounded
In jealous fears in fury & rage, & flames roll'd round
    their fervid feet

And the vast form of Nature like a Serpent play'd
before them

And as they went in folding fires & thunders of the deep
Vala shrunk in like the dark sea that leaves its slimy
banks
And from her bosom Luvah fell far as the east & west
And the vast form of Nature like a Serpent roll'd
between.
Whether this is Jerusalem or Babylon we know not.
All is Confusion All is tumult & we alone are escaped

She ended. for his wrathful throne burst forth the black
hail storm   20

Am I not God   said Urizen. Who is Equal to me
Do I not stretch the heavens abroad or fold them up
like a garment

He spoke mustering his heavy clouds around him black
opake
PAGE 43
Then thunders rolld around & lightnings darted to &
fro
His visage changd to darkness & his strong right hand
came forth
To cast Ahania to the Earth he siezd her by the hair
And threw her from the steps of ice that froze around
his throne

Saying Art thou also become like Vala. thus I cast thee
out
Shall the feminine indolent bliss. the indulgent self of
weariness
The passive idle sleep the enormous night & darkness
of Death
Set herself up to give her laws to the active masculine
virtue
Thou little diminutive portion that darst be a
counterpart

Thy passivity thy laws of obedience & insincerity   10
Are my abhorrence. Wherefore hast thou taken that fair
    form
Whence is this power given to thee! once thou wast in
    my breast
A sluggish current of dim waters. on whose verdant
    margin
A cavern shaggd with horrid shades. dark cool & deadly.
    where
I laid my head in the hot noon after the broken clods
Had wearied me. there I laid my plow & there my horses
    fed
And thou hast risen with thy moist locks into a watry
    image
Reflecting all my indolence my weakness & my death
To weigh me down beneath the grave into non Entity
Where Luvah strives scorned by Vala age after age
    wandering   20
Shrinking & shrinking from her Lord & calling him the
    Tempter
And art thou also become like Vala thus I cast thee
    out.

So loud in thunders spoke the King folded in dark
    despair
And threw Ahania from his bosom obdurate She fell like
    lightning
Then fled the sons of Urizen from his thunderous
    throne petrific
They fled to East & West & left the North & South of
    Heaven
A crash ran thro the immense The bounds of Destiny
    were broken
The bounds of Destiny crashd direful & the swelling
    Sea
Burst from its bonds in whirlpools fierce roaring with
    Human voice
Triumphing even to the Stars at bright Ahanias fall   30

Down from the dismal North the Prince in thunders &
 thick clouds

PAGE 44

As when the thunderbolt down falleth on the appointed
 place
Fell down down rushing ruining thundering [*darkning*]
 shuddering
Into the Caverns of the Grave & places of Human Seed
Where the impressions of Despair & Hope enroot
 forever
A world of Darkness. Ahania fell far into Non Entity

She Continued falling. Loud the Crash continud loud &
 Hoarse
From the Crash roared a flame of blue sulphureous fire
 from the flame
A dolorous groan that struck with dumbness all
 confusion
Swallowing up the horrible din in agony on agony
Thro the Confusion like a crack across from immense
 to immense   10
Loud strong a universal groan of death louder
Than all the wracking elements deafend & rended worse
Than Urizen & all his hosts in curst despair down
 rushing
But from the Dolorous Groan one like a shadow of
 smoke appeard
And human bones rattling together in the smoke &
 stamping
The nether Abyss & gnasshing in fierce despair. panting
 in sobs
Thick short incessant bursting sobbing. deep despairing
 stamping struggling
Struggling to utter the voice of Man struggling to take
 the features of Man. Struggling
To take the limbs of Man at length emerging from the
 smoke
Of Urizen dashed in pieces from his precipitant fall   20

Tharmas reard up his hands & stood on the affrighted
  Ocean
The dead reard up his Voice & stood on the resounding
  shore

Crying. Fury in my limbs. destruction in my bones &
  marrow
My skull riven into filaments. my eyes into sea jellies
Floating upon the tide wander bubbling & bubbling
Uttering my lamentations & begetting little monsters
Who sit mocking upon the little pebbles of the tide
In all my rivers & on dried shells that the fish

PAGE 45

Have quite forsaken. O fool fool to lose my sweetest bliss
Where art thou Enion ah too near to cunning too far off
And yet too near. Dashd down I send thee into distant
  darkness
Far as my strength can hurl thee wander there & laugh
  & play
Among the frozen arrows they will tear thy tender flesh
Fall off afar from Tharmas come not too near my strong
  fury
Scream & fall off & laugh at Tharmas lovely summer
  beauty
Till winter rends thee into Shivers as thou hast rended
  me

So Tharmas bellowd oer the ocean thundring sobbing
  bursting
The bounds of Destiny were broken & hatred now
  began   10
Instead of love to Enion. Enion blind & age bent
Plungd into the cold billows living a life in midst of
  waters
In terrors she witherd away to Entuthon Benithon
A world of deep darkness where all things in horrors are
  rooted

These are the words of Enion heard from the cold waves
  of despair

O Tharmas I had lost thee. & when I hoped I had
found thee
O Tharmas do not thou destroy me quite but let
A little shadow. but a little showery form of Enion
Be near thee loved Terror. let me still remain & then
do thou
Thy righteous doom upon me. only let me hear thy voice   20
Driven by thy rage I wander like a cloud into the deep
Where never yet Existence came, there losing all my life
I back return weaker & weaker, consume me not away
In thy great wrath. tho I have sinned. tho I have rebelld
Make me not like the things forgotten as they had not
been
Make not the thing that loveth thee. a tear wiped away

Tharmas replied riding on storms [the] his voice of
[*Tharmas*] Thunder rolld

Image of grief thy fading lineaments make my eyelids
fail
What have I done! both rage & mercy are alike to me
Looking upon thee Image of faint waters. I recoil   30
From my fierce rage into thy semblance. Enion return
Why does thy piteous face Evanish like a rainy cloud
PAGE 46
Melting. a shower of falling tears. nothing but tears!
Enion:
Substanceless. voiceless, weeping. vanishd. nothing but
tears! Enion
Art thou for ever vanishd from the watry eyes of
Tharmas
Rage Rage shall never from my bosom. winds & waters
of woe
Consuming all to the end consuming   Love and [*Joy*]
Hope are ended

For now no more remaind of Enion in the dismal air
Only a voice eternal wailing in the Elements

Where Enion, blind & age bent wanderd Ahania wanders
  now
She wanders in Eternal fear of falling into the indefinite
For her bright eyes behold the Abyss. Sometimes a little
  sleep   10
Weighs down her eyelids then she falls then starting
  wakes in fears
Sleepless to wander round repelld on the margin of Non
  Entity

             The End of the Third Night

PAGE 47

VALA

NIGHT THE FOURTH

But Tharmas rode on the dark Abyss. the voice of
  Tharmas rolld
Over the heaving deluge. he saw Los & Enitharmon
  Emerge
In strength & brightness from the Abyss his bowels
  yearnd over them
They rose in strength above the heaving deluge. in
  mighty scorn
Red as the Sun in the hot morning of the bloody day
Tharmas beheld them his bowels yearnd over them

And he said Wherefore do I feel such love & pity
Ah Enion Ah Enion Ah lovely lovely Enion
How is this All my hope is gone [*Enion*] for ever fled
Like a famishd Eagle Eyeless raging in the vast expanse   10
Incessant tears are now my food. incessant rage & tears
Deathless for ever now I wander seeking oblivion
In torrents of despair in vain. for if I plunge beneath
Stifling I live. If dashd in pieces from a rocky height
I reunite in endless torment. would I had never risen
From deaths cold sleep [*upon*] beneath the bottom of the
  raging Ocean

And cannot those who once have lovd. ever forget their
   Love?
Are love & rage the same passion? they are the same in
   me
Are those who love. like those who died. risen again
   from death
Immortal. in immortal torment. never to be deliverd   20
Is it not possible that one risen again from Death
Can die! When dark despair comes over can I not
Flow down into the sea & slumber in oblivion. Ah
   Enion

PAGE 48

Deformd I see these lineaments of ungratified Desire
The all powerful curse of an honest man be upon
   Urizen & Luvah
But thou My Son Glorious in brightness comforter of
   Tharmas
Go forth Rebuild this Universe beneath my indignant
   power
A Universe of Death & Decay. Let Enitharmons hands
Weave soft delusive forms of Man above my watry
   world
Renew these ruind souls of Men thro Earth Sea Air &
   Fire
To waste in endless corruption. renew thou I will
   destroy
Perhaps Enion may resume some little semblance
To ease my pangs of heart & to restore some peace to
   Tharmas   10

Los answerd in his furious pride sparks issuing from his
   hair
Hitherto shalt thou come. no further. here thy proud
   waves cease
We have drunk up the Eternal Man by our unbounded
   power
Beware lest we also drink up thee rough demon of the
   waters

Our God is Urizen the King. King of the Heavenly
  hosts
We have no other God but he thou father of worms &
  clay
And he is falln into the Deep rough Demon of the
  waters
And Los remains God over all. weak father of worms &
  clay
I know I was Urthona keeper of the gates of heaven
But now I am all powerful Los & Urthona is but my
  shadow   20

Doubting stood Tharmas in the [*dismal*] solemn
  darkness. his dim Eyes
Swam in red tears. he reard his waves above the head of
  Los
In wrath. but pitying back withdrew with many a sigh
Now he resolvd to destroy Los & now his tears flowd
  down

In scorn stood Los red sparks of blighting from his
  furious head
Flew over the waves of Tharmas. pitying Tharmas stayd
  his Waves

For Enitharmon shriekd amain crying O my sweet world
Built by the Architect divine whose love to Los &
  Enitharmon
Thou rash abhorred Demon in thy fury hast oerthrown

PAGE 49
What Sovereign Architect said Tharmas dare my will
  controll
For if I will urge these waters. If I will they sleep
In peace beneath my awful frown my will shall be my
  Law

So saying in a Wave he rap'd bright Enitharmon far
Apart from Los. but coverd her with softest brooding
  care

On a broad wave in the warm west. balming her
    bleeding wound

O how Los howld at the rending asunder all the fibres
    rent
Where Enitharmon joind to his left side in [*dismal*]
    griding pain
He falling on the rocks bellowd his Dolor. till the blood
Stanch'd, then in ululation waild his woes upon the
    wind   10

And Tharmas calld to the Dark Spectre who upon the
    Shores
With dislocated Limbs had falln. The Spectre rose in
    pain
A Shadow blue obscure & dismal. like a statue of lead
Bent by its fall from a high tower the dolorous shadow
    rose

Go forth said Tharmas works of joy are thine   obey &
    live
So shall the spungy marrow issuing from thy splinterd
    bones
Bonify. & thou shalt have rest when this thy labour is
    done
Go forth bear Enitharmon back to the Eternal Prophet
Build her a bower in the midst of all my dashing waves
Make first a resting place for Los & Enitharmon. then   20
Thou shalt have rest. If thou refusest dashd abroad on
    all
My waves. thy limbs shall separate in stench & rotting
    & thou
Become a prey to all my demons of despair & hope

The Spectre of Urthona [*answerd*] seeing Enitharmon
    writhd
His cloudy form in jealous fear & muttering thunders
    hoarse
And casting round thick glooms. thus utterd his fierce
    pangs of heart

Tharmas I know thee. how are we alterd our beauty
   decayd
But still I know thee tho in this horrible ruin whelmd
Thou once the mildest son of heaven art now become a
   Rage
A terror to all living things. think not that I am ignorant   30
That thou art risen from the dead or that my power
   forgot

PAGE 50

I slumber here in weak repose. I well remember the
   Day
The day of terror & abhorrence [*eternal*]
When fleeing from the battle thou fleeting like the raven
Of dawn outstretching an expanse where neer expanse
   had been
Drewst all the Sons of Beulah into thy [*great*] dread
   vortex following
Thy Eddying spirit down the hills of Beulah. All my sons
Stood round me at the anvil where new heated the
   wedge
Of iron glowd furious prepard for spades & mattocks
Hearing the symphonies of war loud sounding   All my
   sons
Fled from my side then pangs smote me unknown
   before. I saw   10
My loins begin to break forth into veiny pipes & writhe
Before me in the wind englobing trembling with strong
   vibrations
The bloody mass began to animate. I bending over
Wept bitter tears incessant. Still beholding how the
   piteous form
Dividing & dividing from my loins a weak & piteous
Soft cloud of snow a female pale & weak I soft embracd
My counter part & calld it Love   I named her
   Enitharmon
But found myself & her together issuing down the tide
Which now our rivers were become delving thro caverns
   huge

Of goary blood strugg[l]ing to be deliverd from our
    bonds   20
She strove in vain not so Urthona strove for breaking
    forth,
A shadow blue obscure & dismal from the breathing
    Nostrils
Of Enion I issued into the air divided from Enitharmon
I howld in sorrow   I beheld thee rotting upon the Rocks
I pitying hoverd over thee I protected thy ghastly corse
From Vultures of the deep then wherefore shouldst thou
    rage
Against me who thee guarded in the night of death from
    harm

Tharmas replied. Art thou Urthona My friend my old
    companion
With whom I livd in happiness before that deadly night
When Urizen gave the horses of Light into the hands of
    Luvah   30
Thou knowest not what Tharmas knows. O I could tell
    thee tales
That would enrage thee as it has Enraged me even
From Death in wrath & fury. But now come bear back
Thy loved Enitharmon. For thou hast her here before
    thine Eyes

PAGE 51

But my sweet Enion is vanishd & I never more
Shall see her unless thou O Shadow. wilt protect this
    Son
Of Enion & him assist. to bind the fallen King
Lest he should rise again from death in all his [*dismal*]
    dreary power
Bind him, take Enitharmon for thy sweet reward while I
In vain am driven on false hope. hope sister of despair

Groaning the terror rose & drave his solid rocks before
Upon the tide till underneath the feet of Los a World
Dark dreadful rose & Enitharmon lay at Los's feet

The dolorous shadow joyd. weak hope appeard around
    his head   10

Tharmas before Los stood & thus the Voice of
    Tharmas rolld

Now all comes into the power of Tharmas. Urizen is
    falln
And Luvah hidden in the Elemental forms of Life &
    Death
Urthona is My Son   O Los thou art Urthona & Tharmas
Is God. The Eternal Man is seald never to be deliverd
I roll my floods over his body my billows & waves pass
    over him
The Sea encompasses him & monsters of the deep are
    his companions
Dreamer of furious oceans cold sleeper of weeds & shells
Thy Eternal form shall never renew my uncertain prevails
    against thee
Yet tho I rage God over all. A portion of my Life   20
That in Eternal fields in comfort wanderd with my flocks
At noon & laid her head upon my wearied bosom at
    night
She is divided   She is vanishd even like Luvah & Vala
O why did foul ambition sieze thee Urizen Prince of
    Light
And thee O Luvah prince of Love till Tharmas was
    divided
And I what can I now behold but an Eternal Death
Before my Eyes & an Eternal weary work to strive
Against the monstrous forms that breed among my silent
    waves
Is this to be A God far rather would I be a Man
To know sweet Science & to do with simple companions   30
Sitting beneath a tent & viewing sheepfolds & soft
    pastures
Take thou the hammer of Urthona rebuild these
    furnaces

Dost thou refuse   mind I the sparks that issue from thy
  hair
PAGE 52
I will compell thee to rebuild by these my furious waves
Death choose or life thou strugglest in my waters, now
  choose life
And all the Elements shall serve thee to their soothing
  flutes
Their sweet inspiriting lyres thy labours shall administer
And they to thee only remit not faint not thou my son
Now thou dost know what tis to strive against the God
  of waters

So saying Tharmas on his furious chariots of the Deep
Departed far into the Unknown & left a wondrous void
Round Los. afar his waters bore on all sides round. with
  noise
Of wheels & horses hoofs & Trumpets Horns &
  Clarions   10

Terrified Los beheld the ruins of Urizen beneath
A horrible Chaos to his eyes. a formless unmeasurable
  Death
Whirling up broken rocks on high into the dismal air
And fluctuating all beneath in Eddies of molten fluid

Then Los with terrible hands siezd on the Ruind
  Furnaces
Of Urizen. Enormous work: he builded them anew
Labour of Ages in the Darkness & the war of Tharmas
And Los formd Anvils of Iron petrific. for his blows
Petrify with incessant beating many a rock. many a
  planet

But Urizen slept in a stoned stupor in the nether Abyss   20
A dreamful horrible State in tossings on his icy bed
Freezing to solid all beneath, his grey oblivious form
Stretchd over the immense heaves in strong shudders.
  silent his voice

In brooding contemplation stretching out from North
    to South
In mighty power. Round him Los rolld furious
His thunderous wheels from furnace to furnace. tending
    diligent
The contemplative terror. frightend in his scornful
    sphere
Frightend with cold infectious madness. in his hand the
    thundering
Hammer of Urthona. forming under his heavy hand the
    hours

PAGE 53
The days & years. in chains of iron round the limbs of
    Urizen
Linkd hour to hour & day to night & night to day &
    year to year
In periods of pulsative furor. mills he formd & works
Of many wheels resistless in the power of dark Urthona

But Enitharmon wrapd in clouds waild loud. for as Los
    beat
The anvils of Urthona link by link the chains of sorrow
Warping upon the winds & whirling round in the dark
    deep
Lashd on the limbs of Enitharmon & the sulphur fires
Belchd from the furnaces wreathd round her. chaind in
    ceaseless fire
The lovely female howld & Urizen beneath deep
    groand   10
Deadly between the hammers beating grateful to the
    Ears
Of Los. absorbd in dire revenge he drank with joy the
    cries
Of Enitharmon & the groans of Urizen fuel for his wrath
And for his pity secret feeding on thoughts of cruelty

The Spectre wept at his dire labours when from Ladles
    huge

He pourd the molten iron round the limbs of
  Enitharmon
But when he pourd it round the bones of Urizen he
  laughd
Hollow upon the hollow wind. his shadowy form
  obeying
The voice of Los compelld he labourd round the
  Furnaces

And thus began the binding of Urizen day & night in
  fear   20
Circling round the dark Demon with howlings dismay &
  sharp blightings
The Prophet of Eternity beat on his iron links & links of
  brass
And as he beat round the hurtling Demon. terrified at
  the Shapes
Enslavd humanity put on he became what he beheld
Raging against Tharmas his God & uttering
Ambiguous words blasphemous filld with envy firm
  resolvd
On hate Eternal in his vast disdain he labourd beating
The Links of fate link after link an endless chain of
  sorrows

PAGE 54
The Eternal Mind bounded began to roll eddies of wrath
  ceaseless
Round & round & the sulphureous foam surgeing thick
Settled a Lake bright & shining clear. White as the snow

Forgetfulness dumbness necessity in chains of the mind
  lockd up
In fetters of ice shrinking. disorganizd rent from Eternity
Los beat on his fetters & [pourd] heated his furnaces
And pourd iron sodor & sodor of brass

Restless the immortal inchaind heaving dolorous
Anguished unbearable till a roof shaggy wild inclosd
In an orb his fountain of thought   10

In a horrible dreamful slumber like the linked chain
A vast spine writhd in torment upon the wind
Shooting paind. ribbs like a bending Cavern
And bones of solidness froze over all his nerves of joy
A first age passed. a State of dismal woe

From the Caverns of his jointed spine down sunk with
   fright
A red round globe. hot burning. deep deep down into
   the Abyss
Panting Conglobing trembling Shooting out ten
   thousand branches
Around his solid bones & a Second age passed over

In harrowing fear rolling his nervous brain shot
   branches   20
[*Round the branches of his heart*]
On high into two little orbs hiding in two little caves
Hiding carefully from the wind his eyes beheld the deep
And a third age passed   a State of dismal woe

The pangs of hope began in heavy pain striving
   struggling
Two Ears in close volutions from beneath his orbs of
   vision
Shot spiring out & petrified as they grew. And a Fourth
Age passed over & a State of dismal woe

In ghastly torment sick hanging upon the wind
Two nostrils bent down to the deeps –
PAGE 55 (FIRST PORTION)
And a fifth age passed & a state of dismal woe

In ghastly torment sick. within his ribs bloated round
A craving hungry cavern. Thence arose his channeld
Throat. then like a red flame a tongue of hunger
And thirst appeard and a sixth age passed of dismal woe

Enraged & stifled with torment he threw his right arm
   to the north
His left arm to the south shooting out in anguish deep

And his feet stamped the nether abyss in trembling
   howling & dismay
And a seventh age passed over & a state of dismal woe

The Council of God on high watching over the Body   10
Of Man clothd in Luvahs robes of blood saw & wept
Descending over Beulahs mild moon coverd regions
The daughters of Beulah saw the Divine Vision they
   were comforted
And as a Double female form loveliness & perfection of
   beauty
They bowd the head & worshippd & with mild voice
   spoke these words

PAGE 56

Lord. Saviour if thou hadst been here our brother had
   not died
And now we know that whatsoever thou wilt ask of
   God
He will give it thee for we are weak women & dare not
   lift
Our eyes to the Divine pavilions. therefore in mercy
   thou
Appearest clothd in Luvahs garments that we may
   behold thee
And live. Behold Eternal Death is in Beulah Behold

We perish & shall not be found unless thou grant a
   place
In which we may be hidden under the Shadow of wings
For if we who are but for a time & who pass away in
   winter
Behold these wonders of Eternity we shall consume   10

Such were the words of Beulah of the Feminine
   Emanation
The Empyrean groand throughout All Eden was
   darkend
The Corse of [Man] Albion lay on the Rock the sea of
   Time & Space

Beat round the Rock in mighty waves & as a Polypus
That vegetates beneath the Sea the limbs of Man
  vegetated
In monstrous forms of Death a Human polypus of
  Death

The Saviour mild & gentle bent over the corse of Death
Saying If ye will Believe your Brother shall rise again
And first he found the Limit of Opacity & namd it
  Satan
In Albions bosom for in every human bosom these
  limits stand   20
And next he found the Limit of Contraction & namd it
  Adam
While yet those beings were not born nor knew of good
  or Evil

Then wondrously the [*Deep beneath*] Starry Wheels felt
  the divine hand. Limit
Was put to Eternal Death Los felt the Limit & saw
The Finger of God touch the Seventh furnace in terror
And Los beheld the hand of God over his furnaces
Beneath the Deeps in dismal Darkness beneath
  immensity

PAGE 55 (SECOND PORTION)
In terrors Los shrunk from his task. his great hammer
Fell from his hand his fires hid their strong limbs in
  smoke
For with noises ruinous   hurtlings & clashings &
  groans
The immortal endur'd. tho bound in a deadly sleep
Pale terror siezd the Eyes of Los as he beat round
The hurtling Demon. terrifid at the shapes
Enslavd humanity put on he became what he beheld
He became what he was doing he was himself
  transformd

Bring in here the Globe of Blood as in the B of Urizen

Spasms siezd his muscular fibres writhing to & fro his
  pallid lips   10
Unwilling movd as Urizen howld his loins wavd like the
  sea
At Enitharmons shrieks his knees each other smote &
  then he lookd
With stony Eyes on Urizen & then swift writhd his neck
Involuntary to the Couch where Enitharmon lay
The bones of Urizen hurtle on the wind the bones of
  Los
Twinge & his iron sinews bend like lead & fold
Into unusual forms dancing & howling stamping the
  Abyss

PAGE 56 (SECOND PORTION)

> End of the Fourth Night

PAGE 57

VALA
[BOOK] NIGHT THE FIFTH

Infected Mad he dancd on his mountains high & dark
  as heaven
Now fixd into one stedfast bulk his features stonify
From his mouth curses & from his eyes sparks of
  blighting
Beside the anvil cold he dancd with the hammer of
  Urthona
Terrific pale. Enitharmon stretchd on the [dismal] dreary
  Earth
Felt her immortal limbs freeze stiffning pale inflexible
His feet shr[u]nk withring from the deep shrinking &
  withering
And Enitharmon shrunk up all their fibres withring
  beneath
As plants witherd by winter leaves & stems & roots
  decaying

Melt into thin air while the seed drivn by the furious
 wind   10
Rests on the distant Mountains top. So Los &
 Enitharmon
Shrunk into fixed space stood trembling on a Rocky
 cliff
Yet mighty bulk & majesty & beauty remaind but
 unexpansive
As far as highest Zenith from the lowest Nadir. so far
 shrunk
Los from the furnaces a Space immense & left the cold
Prince of Light bound in chains of intellect among the
 furnaces
But all the furnaces were out & the bellows had ceast to
 blow

He stood trembling & Enitharmon clung around his
 knees
Their senses unexpansive in one stedfast bulk remain
The night blew cold & Enitharmon shriekd on the
 dismal wind   20

PAGE 58

Her pale hands cling around her husband & over her
 weak head
Shadows of Eternal Death sit in the leaden air

But the soft pipe the flute the viol organ harp & cymbal
And the sweet sound of silver voices calm the weary
 couch
Of Enitharmon but her groans drown the immortal
 harps
Loud & more loud the living music floats upon the air
Faint & more faint the daylight wanes. The wheels of
 turning darkness
Began in solemn revolutions. Earth convulsd with
 rending pangs
Rockd to & fro & cried sore at the groans of Enitharmon
Still the faint harps & silver voices calm the weary
 couch   10

But from the caves of deepest night ascending in clouds
    of mist
The winter spread his wide black wings across from pole
    to pole
Grim frost beneath & terrible snow linkd in a marriage
    chain
Began a dismal dance. The winds around on pointed
    rocks
Settled like bats innumerable ready to fly abroad
The groans of Enitharmon shake the skies the labring
    Earth
Till from her heart rending his way a terrible Child
    sprang forth
In thunder smoke & sullen flames & howlings & fury
    & blood

Soon as his burning Eyes were opend on the Abyss
The horrid trumpets of the deep bellowd with bitter
    blasts
The Enormous Demons woke & howld around the
    [*youthful*] new born king
Crying Luvah King of Love thou art the King of rage
    & death
Urizen cast deep darkness round him raging Luvah
    pourd
The spears of Urizen from Chariots round the Eternal
    tent
Discord began then yells & cries shook the wide
    firma[m]ent

20

PAGE 59
Where is Sweet Vala gloomy prophet where the lovely
    form
That drew the body of Man from heaven into this
    dark Abyss
Soft tears & sighs where are you come forth shout on
    bloody fields
Shew thy soul Vala shew thy bow & quiver of secret
    fires

Draw thy bow Vala from the depths of hell thy black
  bow draw
And twang the bow string to our howlings let thine
  arrows black
Sing in the Sky as once they sang upon the hills of
  Light
When dark Urthona wept in torment of the secret pain

He wept & he divided & he laid his gloomy head
Down on the Rock of Eternity on darkness of the deep   10
Torn by black storms & ceaseless torrents of consuming
  fire
Within his breast his fiery sons chaind down & filld with
  cursings

And breathing terrible blood & vengeance gnashing his
  teeth with pain
Let loose the Enormous Spirit in the darkness of the
  deep
And his dark wife that once fair crystal form divinely
  clear
Within his ribs producing serpents whose souls are
  flames of fire

But now the times return upon thee Enitharmons womb
Now holds thee soon to issue forth. Sound Clarions of
  war
Call Vala from her close recess in all her dark deceit
Then rage on rage shall fierce redound out of her crystal
  quiver   20

So sung the Demons [*of the deep*] round red Orc &
  round faint Enitharmon
Sweat & blood stood on the limbs of Los in globes. his
  fiery Eyelids
Faded. he rouzd he siezd the wonder in his hands &
  went
Shuddring & weeping thro the Gloom & down into the
  deeps

Enitharmon nursd her fiery child in the dark deeps
Sitting in darkness. over her Los mournd in anguish
   fierce
Coverd with gloom. the fiery boy grew fed by the milk
Of Enitharmon. Los around her builded pillars of iron
PAGE 60
And brass & silver & gold fourfold in dark prophetic
   fear
For now he feard Eternal Death & uttermost Extinction
He builded Golgonooza on the Lake of Udan Adan
Upon the Limit of Translucence then he builded Luban
Tharmas laid the Foundations & Los finishd it in
   howling woe

But when fourteen summers & winters had revolved
   over
Their solemn habitation Los beheld the ruddy boy
Embracing his bright mother & beheld malignant fires
In his young eyes discerning plain that Orc plotted his
   death
Grief rose upon his ruddy brows. a tightening girdle
   grew   10
Around his bosom like a bloody cord. in secret sobs
He burst it, but next morn another girdle succeeds
Around his bosom. Every day he viewd the fiery youth
With silent fear & his immortal cheeks grew deadly pale
Till many a morn & many a night passd over in dire
   woe
Forming a girdle in the day & bursting it at night
The girdle was formd by day by night was burst in twain
Falling down on the rock an iron chain link by link
   lockd

Enitharmon beheld the bloody chain of nights & days
Depending from the bosom of Los & how with
   [*dismal*] griding pain   20
He went each morning to his labours with the spectre
   dark
Calld it the chain of Jealousy. Now Los began to speak

His woes aloud to Enitharmon. since he could not hide
His uncouth plague. He siezd the boy in his immortal
 hands
While Enitharmon followd him weeping in dismal woe
Up to the iron mountains top & there the Jealous chain
Fell from his bosom on the mountain. The Spectre dark
Held the fierce boy Los naild him down binding
 around his limbs
The [*dismal*] accursed chain O how bright Enitharmon
 howld & cried
Over her son. Obdurate Los bound down her loved Joy   30

PAGE 61

The hammer of Urthona smote the rivets in terror. of
 brass
Tenfold. the Demons rage flamd tenfold forth rending
Roaring redounding. Loud Loud Louder & Louder &
 fird
The darkness warring with the waves of Tharmas &
 Snows of Urizen
Crackling the flames went up with fury from the
 immortal demon
Surrounded with flames the Demon grew loud howling in
 his fires
Los folded Enitharmon in a cold white cloud in fear
Then led her down into the deeps & into his labyrinth
Giving the Spectre sternest charge over the howling
 fiend

Concenterd into Love of Parent Storgous Appetite
 Craving   10
His limbs bound down mock at his chains for over them
 a flame
Of circling fire unceasing plays to feed them with life &
 bring
The virtues of the Eternal worlds ten thousand
 thousand spirits
Of life [*rejoice*] lament around the Demon going forth &
 returning

At his enormous call they flee into the heavens of
    heavens
And back return with wine & food. Or dive into the
    deeps
To bring the thrilling joys of sense to quell his
    ceaseless rage
His eyes the lights of his large soul contract or else
    expand
Contracted they behold the secrets of the infinite
    mountains

The veins of gold & silver & the hidden things of Vala   20
Whatever grows from its pure bud or breathes a fragrant
    soul
Expanded they behold the terrors of the Sun & Moon
The Elemental Planets & the orbs of eccentric fire
His nostrils breathe [*with*] a fiery flame. his locks are
    like the forests
Of wild beasts there the lion glares the tyger & wolf
    howl there
And there the Eagle hides her young in cliffs &
    precipices
His bosom is like starry heaven expanded all the stars
Sing round. there waves the harvest & the vintage
    rejoices. the Springs
Flow into rivers of delight. there the spontaneous flowers
Drink laugh & sing. the grasshopper the Emmet & the
    Fly   30
The golden Moth builds there a house & spreads her
    silken bed

PAGE 62

His loins inwove with silken fires are like a furnace fierce
As the strong Bull in summer time when bees sing round
    the heath
Where the herds low after the shadow & after the water
    spring
The numrous flocks cover the mountain & shine along
    the valley

His knees are rocks of adamant & rubie & emerald
Spirits of strength in Palaces rejoice in golden armour
Armed with spear & shield they drink & rejoice over
    the slain
Such is the Demon such his terror in the nether deep

But when returnd to Golgonooza Los & Enitharmon
Felt all the sorrow Parents feel. they wept toward one
    another   10
And Los repented that he had chaind Orc upon the
    mountain
And Enitharmons tears prevaild   parental love returnd
Tho terrible his dread of that infernal chain   They rose
At midnight hasting to their much beloved care
Nine days they traveld thro the Gloom of Entuthon
    Benithon
Los taking Enitharmon by the hand led her along
The dismal vales & up to the iron mountains top where
    Orc
Howld in the furious wind he thought to give to
    Enitharmon
Her son in tenfold joy & to compensate for her tears
Even if his own death resulted so much pity him paind   20

But when they came to the dark rock & to the spectrous
    cave
Lo the young limbs had strucken root into the rock &
    strong
Fibres had from the Chain of Jealousy inwove
    themselves
In a swift vegetation round the rock & round the Cave
And over the immortal limbs of the terrible fiery boy
In vain they strove now to unchain. In vain with bitter
    tears
To melt the chain of Jealousy. not Enitharmons death
Nor the Consummation of Los could ever melt the chain
Nor unroot the infernal fibres from their rocky bed
Nor all Urthonas strength nor all the power of Luvahs
    Bulls   30

Tho they each morning drag the unwilling Sun out of
  the deep
Could uproot the infernal chain. for it had taken root
PAGE 63
Into the iron rock & grew a chain beneath the Earth
Even to the Center wrapping round the Center & the
  limbs
Of Orc entering with fibres. became one with him a
  living Chain
Sustained by the Demons life. Despair & Terror & Woe
  & Rage
Inwrap the Parents in cold clouds as they bend howling
  over
The terrible boy till fainting by his side the Parents fell

Not long they lay Urthonas spectre found herbs of the
  pit
Rubbing their temples he reviv'd them. all their
  lamentations
I write not here but all their after life was lamentation

When satiated with grief they returnd back to
  Golgonooza   10
Enitharmon on the road of Dranthon felt the inmost
  gate
Of her bright heart burst open & again close with a
  [dismal] deadly pain
Within her heart Vala began to reanimate in bursting
  sobs
And when the Gate was open she beheld that [dismal]
  dreary Deep
Where bright Ahania wept. She also saw the infernal
  roots
Of the chain of Jealousy & felt the rendings of fierce
  howling Orc

Rending the Caverns like a mighty wind pent in the
  Earth

Tho wide apart as furthest north is from the furthest
   south
Urizen trembled where he lay to hear the howling terror
The rocks shook the Eternal bars tuggd to & fro were
   rifted   20
Outstretchd upon the stones of ice the ruins of his
   throne
Urizen shuddring heard his trembling limbs shook the
   strong caves

The Woes of Urizen shut up in the deep dens of
   Urthona

Ah how shall Urizen the King submit to this dark
   mansion
Ah how is this! Once on the heights I stretchd my
   throne sublime
The mountains of Urizen once of silver where the sons
   of wisdom dwelt
And on whose tops the Virgins sang are rocks of
   Desolation

My fountains once the haunt of Swans now breed the
   scaly tortoise
The houses of my harpers are become a haunt of crows
The gardens of wisdom are become a field of horrid
   graves   30
And on the bones I drop my tears & water them in vain

PAGE 64
Once how I walked from my palace in gardens of delight
The sons of wisdom stood around the harpers followd
   with harps
Nine virgins clothd in light composd the song to their
   immortal voices
And at my banquets of new wine my head was crownd
   with joy

Then in my ivory pavilions I slumberd [*with*] in the
   noon

And walked in the silent night among sweet smelling
   flowers
Till on my silver bed I slept & sweet dreams round me
   hoverd
But now my land is darkend & my wise men are
   departed

My songs are turned into cries of Lamentation
Heard on my Mountains & deep sighs under my palace
   roofs   10
Because the Steeds of Urizen once swifter than the light
Were kept back from my Lord & from his chariot of
   mercies

O did I keep the horses of the day in silver pastures
O I refusd the Lord of day the horses of his prince
O did I close my treasuries with roofs of solid stone
And darken all my Palace walls with envyings & hate

O Fool to think that I could hide from his all piercing
   eyes
The gold & silver & costly stones his holy workmanship
O Fool could I forget the light that filled my bright
   spheres
Was a reflection of his face who calld me from the deep   20

I well remember for I heard the mild & holy voice
Saying O light spring up & shine & I sprang up from
   the deep
He gave to me a silver scepter & crownd me with a
   golden crown
[Saying] & said Go forth & guide my Son who wanders
   on the ocean

I went not forth. I hid myself in black clouds of my
   wrath
I calld the stars around my feet in the night of councils
   dark
The stars threw down their spears & fled naked away
We fell. I siezd thee dark Urthona In my left hand
   falling

I siezd thee beauteous Luvah thou art faded like a flower
And like a lilly is thy wife Vala witherd by winds   30
When thou didst bear the golden cup at the immortal
    tables
Thy children smote their fiery wings crownd with the
    gold of heaven

PAGE 65

Thy pure feet stepd on the steps divine. too pure for
    other feet
And thy fair locks shadowd thine eyes from the divine
    effulgence
Then thou didst keep with Strong Urthona the living
    gates of heaven
But now thou art bound down with him even to the
    gates of hell

Because thou gavest Urizen the wine of the Almighty
For steeds of Light that they might run in thy golden
    chariot of pride
I gave to thee the Steeds   I pourd the stolen wine
And drunken with the immortal draught fell from my
    throne sublime

I will arise Explore these dens & find that deep pulsation
That shakes my caverns with strong shudders. perhaps
    this is the night   10
Of Prophecy & Luvah hath burst his way from
    Enitharmon
When Thought is closd in Caves. Then love shall shew
    its root in deepest Hell
                End of the Fifth [*Book*] Night

PAGE 67

VALA
NIGHT THE SIXTH

So Urizen arose & leaning on his Spear explord his dens
He threw his flight thro the dark air to where a river flowd

And taking off his silver helmet filled it & drank
But when unsatiated his thirst he assayd to gather
    more
Lo three terrific women at the verge of the bright flood
Who would not suffer him to approach. but drove him
    back with storms

Urizen knew them not & thus addressd the spirits of
    darkness

Who art thou Eldest Woman sitting in thy clouds
What is that name written on thy forehead? what art
    thou?
And wherefore dost thou pour this water forth in sighs
    & care   10

She answerd not but filld her urn & pourd it forth
    abroad

Answerest thou not said Urizen. then thou maist answer
    me
Thou terrible woman clad in blue whose strong attractive
    power
Draws all into a fountain   at the rock of thy attraction
With frowning brow thou sittest mistress of these
    mighty waters

She answerd not but stretchd her arms & threw her
    limbs abroad

Or wilt thou answer youngest Woman clad in shining
    green
With labour & care thou dost divide the [river] current
    into four
Queen of these dreadful rivers speak & let me hear thy
    voice

PAGE 68
[but] They reard up a wall of rocks [then] and Urizen
    raisd his spear.
They gave a scream, they knew their father Urizen knew
    his daughters

They shrunk into their channels. dry the rocky strand
    beneath his feet
Hiding themselves in rocky forms from the Eyes of
    Urizen

Then Urizen wept & thus his lamentation poured forth

O horrible O dreadful state! those whom I loved best
On whom I pourd the beauties of my light adorning
    them
With jewels & precious ornament labourd with art
    divine
Vests of the radiant colours of heaven & crowns of
    golden fire
I gave sweet lillies to their breasts & roses to their hair   10
I taught them songs of sweet delight. I gave their
    tender voices
Into the blue expanse & I invented with laborious art
Sweet instruments of sound. in pride encompassing
    my Knees
They pourd their radiance above all. the daughters of
    Luvah Envied
At their exceeding brightness & the sons of eternity
    sent them gifts
Now will I pour my fury on them & I will reverse
The precious benediction. for their colours of loveliness
I will give blackness for jewels hoary frost for ornament
    deformity
For crowns wreathd Serpents for sweet odors stinking
    corruptibility
For voices of delight hoarse croakings inarticulate thro
    frost   20
For labourd fatherly care & sweet instruction. I will
    give
Chains of dark ignorance & cords of twisted self conceit
And whips of stern repentance & food of stubborn
    obstinacy
That they may curse Tharmas their God & Los his
    adopted son

That they may curse & worship the obscure Demon of
    destruction
That they may worship terrors & obey the violent
Go forth sons of my curse Go forth daughters of my
    abhorrence

Tharmas heard the deadly scream across his watry
    world
And Urizens loud sounding voice lamenting on the wind
And he came riding in his fury. froze to solid were his
    waves   30
PAGE 69
Silent in ridges he beheld them stand round Urizen
A dreary waste of solid waters for the King of Light
Darkend his brows with his cold helmet & his gloomy
    spear
Darkend before him. Silent on the ridgy waves he took
His gloomy way before him Tharmas fled & flying
    fought

Crying. What & who art thou Cold Demon. art thou
    Urizen
Art thou like me risen again from death or art thou
    deathless
If thou art he my desperate purpose hear & give me
    death
For death to me is better far than life. death my desire
That I in vain in various paths have sought but still I
    live   10
The Body of Man is given to me I seek in vain to
    destroy
For still it surges forth in fish & monsters of the deeps
And in these monstrous forms I Live in an Eternal woe
And thou O Urizen art falln never to be deliverd
Withhold thy light from me for ever & I will withhold
From thee thy food so shall we cease to be & all our
    sorrows
[Cease] End & the Eternal Man no more renew beneath
    our power

If thou refusest in eternal flight thy beams in vain
Shall pursue Tharmas & in vain shalt crave for food I
   will
Pour down my flight thro dark immensity Eternal
   falling   20
Thou shalt pursue me but in vain till starvd upon the
   void
Thou hangst a dried skin shrunk up weak wailing in
   the wind

So Tharmas spoke but Urizen replied not. On his way
He took. high bounding over hills & desarts floods &
   horrible chasms
Infinite was his labour without end his travel   he strove
In vain for hideous monsters of the deeps annoyd him
   sore
Scaled & finnd with iron & brass they devourd the path
   before him
Incessant was the conflict. On he bent his weary steps
Making a path toward the dark world of Urthona. he
   rose
With pain upon the [*dismal*] dreary mountains & with
   pain descended   30
And saw their grizly fears & his eyes sickend at the
   sight

The howlings gnashings groanings shriekings
   shudderings sobbings burstings
Mingle together to create a world for Los. In cruel
   delight
PAGE 70 (FIRST PORTION)
Los brooded on the darkness. nor saw Urizen with a
   Globe of fire
Lighting his dismal journey thro the pathless world of
   death
Writing in bitter tears & groans in books of iron &
   brass
The enormous wonders of the Abysses once his
   brightest joy

For Urizen beheld the terrors of the Abyss wandring
   among
The ruind spirits once his children & the children of
   Luvah
Scard at the sound of their own sigh that seems to
   shake the immense
They wander Moping in their heart a Sun a Dreary
   moon
A Universe of fiery constellations in their brain
An Earth of wintry woe beneath their feet & round
   their loins   10
Waters or winds or clouds or brooding lightnings &
   pestilential plagues
Beyond the bounds of their own self their senses cannot
   penetrate
As the tree knows not what is outside of its leaves &
   bark
And yet it drinks the summer joy & fears the winter
   sorrow
So in the regions of the grave none knows his dark
   compeer
Tho he partakes of his dire woes & mutual returns the
   pang
The throb the dolor the convulsion in soul sickening
   woes

[*Not so closd up the Prince of Light now darkend
   wandring among*
*For Urizen beheld the terrors of the Abyss wandring
   among*
*The Ruind Spirits once his Children & the Children of
   Luvah*]   20

The horrid shapes & sights of torment in burning
   dungeons & in
Fetters of red hot iron some with crowns of serpents &
   some
With monsters girding round their bosoms. Some lying
   on beds of sulphur

On racks & wheels he beheld women marching oer
    burning wastes
Of Sand in bands of hundreds & of fifties & of
    thousands strucken with
Lightnings which blazed after them upon their shoulders
    in their march
In successive vollies with loud thunders swift flew the
    King of Light
Over the burning desarts   Then the desarts passd.
    involvd in clouds
Of smoke with myriads moping in the stifling vapours.
    Swift
Flew the King tho flagd his powers labring. till over
    rocks   30
And Mountains faint weary he wanderd. where multitudes
    were shut
Up in the solid mountains & in rocks which heaved
    with their torments
Then came he among fiery cities & castles built of
    burning steel
Then he beheld the forms of tygers & of Lions
    dishumanizd men
Many in serpents & in worms stretchd out enormous
    length
Over the sullen mould & slimy tracks obstruct his way
Drawn out from deep to deep woven by ribbd
And scaled monsters or armd in iron shell or shell of
    brass
Or gold a glittering torment shining & hissing in eternal
    pain
Some [as] columns of fire or of water sometimes stretchd
    out in [length] heighth   40
Sometimes in [breadth] length sometimes englobing
    wandering in vain seeking for ease
His voice to them was but an inarticulate thunder for
    their Ears
Were heavy & dull & their eyes & nostrils closed up
Oft he stood by a howling victim Questioning in words

Soothing or Furious no one answerd every one wrapd
    up
In his own sorrow howld regardless of his words, nor
    voice
Of sweet response could he obtain tho oft assayd with
    tears
He knew they were his Children ruind in his ruind
    world

PAGE 71 (FIRST PORTION)

Oft would he stand & question a fierce scorpion glowing
    with gold
In vain the terror heard not. then a lion he would Sieze
By the fierce mane staying [*their*] his howling course in
    vain the voice
Of Urizen in vain the Eloquent tongue. A Rock a
    Cloud a Mountain
Were now not Vocal as in Climes of happy Eternity
Where the lamb replies to the infant voice & the lion to
    the man of years
Giving them sweet instructions Where the Cloud the
    River & the Field
Talk with the husbandman & shepherd. But these
    attackd him sore
Siezing upon his feet & rending the Sinews that in
    Caves
He hid to recure his obstructed powers with rest &
    oblivion   10

PAGE 70 (SECOND PORTION)

Here he had time enough to repent of his rashly
    threatend curse
He saw them cursd beyond his Curse his soul melted
    with fear

PAGE 71 (SECOND PORTION)

He could not take their fetters off for they grew from
    the soul
Nor could he quench the fires for they flamd out from
    the heart

Nor could he calm the Elements because himself was
  Subject
So he threw his flight in terror & pain & in repentant
  tears

When he had passd these southern terrors he approachd
  the East
Void pathless beaten with [*eternal*] iron sleet & eternal
  hail & [*snow*] rain
No form was there no living thing & yet his way lay thro
This dismal world. he stood a while & lookd back oer
  his former
Terrific voyage. Hills & Vales of torment & despair
Sighing & wiping a fresh tear. then turning round he
  threw   20
Himself into the dismal void. falling he fell & fell
Whirling in unresistible revolutions down & down
In the horrid bottomless vacuity falling falling falling
Into the Eastern vacuity the empty world of Luvah

The ever pitying one who seeth all things saw his fall
And in the dark vacuity created a bosom of [*slime*] clay
When wearied dead he fell his limbs reposd in the
  bosom of slime
As the seed falls from the sowers hand so Urizen fell &
  death
Shut up his powers in oblivion. then as the seed shoots
  forth
In pain & sorrow. So the slimy bed his limbs renewd   30
At first an infant weakness. periods passd he gatherd
  strength
But still in solitude he sat then rising threw his flight
Onward tho falling thro the waste of night & ending in
  death
And in another resurrection to sorrow & weary travel
But still his books he bore in his strong hands & his iron
  pen
For when he died they lay beside his grave & when he
  rose

He siezd them with a [*dismal*] gloomy smile for wrapd in
    his death clothes
He hid them when he slept in death when he revivd the
    clothes
Were rotted by the winds the books remaind still
    unconsumd
Still to be written & interleavd with brass & iron &
    gold   40
Time after time for such a journey none but iron pens
Can write And adamantine leaves recieve nor can the
    man who goes

PAGE 72

The journey obstinate refuse to write time after time

Endless had been his travel but the Divine hand him
    led
For infinite the distance & obscurd by Combustions
    dire
By rocky masses frowning in the abysses revolving
    erratic
Round Lakes of fire in the dark deep the ruins of
    Urizens world
Oft would he sit in a dark rift & regulate his books
Or sleep such sleep as spirits eternal wearied in his
    dark
Tearful & sorrowful state. then rise look out & ponder
His dismal voyage eyeing the next sphere tho far
    remote
Then darting into the Abyss of night his venturous
    limbs   10
Thro lightnings thunders earthquakes & concussions
    fires & floods
Stemming his downward fall labouring up against
    futurity
Creating many a Vortex fixing many a Science in the
    deep
And thence throwing his venturous limbs into the Vast
    unknown

Swift swift from Chaos to chaos from void to void a
   road immense

For when he came to where a Vortex ceasd to operate
Nor down nor up remaind then if he turnd &
   lookd back
From whence he came twas upward all. & if he turnd
   and viewd
The unpassd void upward was still his mighty
   wandring
The midst between an Equilibrium grey of air serene   20
Where he might live in peace & where his life might
   meet repose

But Urizen said Can I not leave this world of Cumbrous
   wheels
Circle oer Circle nor on high attain a void
Where self sustaining I may view all things beneath my
   feet
Or sinking thro these Elemental wonders swift to fall
I thought perhaps to find an End a world beneath of
   voidness
Whence I might travel round the outside of this Dark
   confusion
When I bend downward bending my head downward
   into the deep
Tis upward all which way soever I my course begin
But when A Vortex formd on high by labour & sorrow
   & care   30
And weariness begins on all my limbs then sleep
   revives
My wearied spirits waking then tis downward all which
   way
So ever I my spirits turn no end I find of all
O what a world is here unlike those climes of bliss
Where my sons gatherd round my knees   O thou poor
   ruind world
Thou horrible ruin once like me thou wast all glorious

And now like me partaking desolate thy masters lot
Art thou O ruin the once glorious heaven are these thy
    rocks
Where joy sang in the trees & pleasure sported on the
    rivers
PAGE 73
And laughter sat beneath the Oaks & innocence sported
    round
Upon the green plains & sweet friendship met in palaces
And books & instruments of song & pictures of delight
Where are they whelmd beneath these ruins in horrible
    [*confusion*] destruction
And if Eternal falling I repose on the dark bosom
Of winds & waters or thence fall into a Void where air
Is not down falling thro immensity ever & ever
I lose my powers weakend every revolution till a death
Shuts up my powers then a seed in the vast womb of
    darkness
I dwell in dim oblivion. brooding over me the Enormous
    worlds   10
Reorganize me shooting forth in bones & flesh & blood
I am regenerated to fall or rise at will or to remain
A labourer of ages a dire discontent a living woe
Wandring in vain. Here will I fix my foot & here rebuild
Here Mountains of Brass promise much riches in their
    dreadful [*bowels*] bosoms

So [*saying*] he began to form/dig of gold silver &
    [*brass*] iron
And brass vast instruments to measure out the immense
    & fix
The whole into another world better suited to obey
His will where none should dare oppose his will himself
    being King
Of All & all futurity be bound in his vast chain   20

And the Sciences were fixd & the Vortexes began to operate
On all the suns of men & every human soul terrified

At the turning wheels of heaven shrunk away inward
    withring away
Gaining a New Dominion over all his Sons &
    Daughters
& over the sons & daughters of Luvah in the horrible
    Abyss
For Urizen lamented over them in a selfish lamentation
Till a white woof coverd his cold limbs from head to
    [*foot*] feet
Hair white as snow coverd him in flaky locks terrific
Overspreading his limbs. in pride he wanderd weeping
Clothed in aged venerableness obstinately resolvd   30
Travelling thro darkness & whereever he traveld a dire
    Web
Followd behind him as the Web of a Spider dusky &
    cold
Shivering across from Vortex to Vortex drawn out from
    his mantle of years
A living Mantle adjoind to his life & growing from his
    Soul

And the Web of Urizen stre[t]chd direful shivring in
    clouds
And uttering such woes such [*burstings*] bursts such
    thunderings
The eyelids expansive as morning & the Ears
As a golden ascent winding round to the heavens of
    heavens
Within the dark horrors of the Abysses lion or tyger or
    scorpion

PAGE 74
For every one opend within into Eternity at will
But they refusd because their outward forms were in the
    Abyss
And the wing like tent of the Universe beautiful
    surrounding all
Or drawn up or let down at the will of the immortal man

Vibrated in such anguish the eyelids quiverd
Weak & Weaker their expansive orbs began shrinking
Pangs smote thro the brain & a universal shriek
Ran thro the Abysses rending the web torment on
    torment

Thus Urizen in sorrows wanderd many a dreary way
Warring with monsters of the Deeps in his most
    hideous pilgrimage   10
Till his bright hair scatterd in snows his skin barkd oer
    with wrinkles
Four Caverns rooting downwards their foundations
    thrusting forth
The metal rock & stone in ever painful throes of
    vegetation
The Cave of Orc stood to the South a furnace of dire
    flames
Quenchless unceasing. In the west the Cave of Urizen
For Urizen fell as the Midday sun falls down into the
    West
North stood Urthonas stedfast throne a World of Solid
    darkness
Shut up in stifling obstruction rooted in dumb
    despair
The East was Void. But Tharmas rolld his billows in
    ceaseless eddies
Void pathless beat with Snows eternal & iron hail &
    rain   20
All thro the caverns of fire & air & Earth. Seeking
For Enions limbs nought finding but the black sea weed
    & sickning slime
Flying away from Urizen that he might not give him
    food
Above beneath on all sides round in the vast deep of
    immensity
That he might starve the sons & daughters of Urizen on
    the winds
Making between horrible chasms into the vast unknown

All these around the world of Los cast forth their
    monstrous births
But in Eternal times the Seat of Urizen is in the South
Urthona in the North Luvah in East Tharmas in West

And now he came into the Abhorred world of Dark
    Urthona   30
By Providence divine conducted not bent from his own
    will
Lest death Eternal should be the result for the Will
    cannot be violated
Into the doleful vales where no tree grew nor river
    flowd
Nor man nor beast nor creeping thing nor sun nor
    cloud nor star
Still he with his globe of fire immense in his venturous
    hand
Bore on thro the Affrighted vales ascending &
    descending
Oerwearied or in cumbrous flight he venturd oer dark
    rifts
Or down dark precipices or climbd with pain and
    labour huge
Till he beheld the world of Los from the Peaked rock
    of Urthona
And heard the howling of red Orc distincter &
    distincter   40

PAGE 75
Redoubling his immortal efforts thro the narrow vales
With difficulty down descending guided by his Ear
And [*with*] by his globe of fire he went down the Vale
    of Urthona
Between the enormous iron walls built by the Spectre
    dark
Dark grew his globe reddning with mists & full before
    his path
Striding across the narrow vale the [*Shade*] Shadow of
    Urthona

A spectre Vast appeard whose feet & legs with iron
   scaled
Stampd the hard rocks expectant of the unknown
   wanderer
Whom he had seen wandring his nether world when
   distant far
And watchd his swift approach collected dark the
   Spectre stood
Beside hi[m] Tharmas stayd his flight & stood in stern
   defiance
Communing with the Spectre who rejoicd along the vale
Round his loins a girdle glowd with many colourd fires
In his hand a knotted Club whose knots like mountains
   frownd
Desart among the Stars them withering with its ridges
   cold
Black scales of iron arm the dread visage iron spikes
   instead
Of hair shoot from his orbed scull. his glowing eyes
Burn like two furnaces. he calld with Voice of Thunder

Four winged heralds mount the furious blasts & blow
   their trumps
Gold Silver Brass & iron clangors clamoring rend the
   [*deeps*] shores   20
Like white clouds rising from the Vales his fifty two
   armies
From the four Cliffs of Urthona rise glowing around
   the Spectre
Four sons of Urizen the Squadrons of Urthona led in
   arms
Of gold & silver brass & iron he knew his mighty sons

Then Urizen arose upon the wind back many a mile
Retiring into his dire Web scattering fleecy snows
As he ascended howling loud the Web vibrated strong
From heaven to heaven from globe to globe. In vast
   excentric paths

Compulsive rolld the Comets at his dread command the
    dreary way
Falling with wheel impetuous down among Urthonas
    vales   30
And round red Orc returning back to Urizen gorgd with
    blood
Slow roll the massy Globes at his command & slow
    oerwheel
The dismal squadrons of Urthona. weaving the dire
    Web
In their progressions & preparing Urizens path before
    him
                    End of The Sixth Night

PAGE 77

VALA

NIGHT THE SEVENTH [a]

Then Urizen arose The Spectre fled & Tharmas fled
The darkening Spectre of Urthona hid beneath a rock
Tharmas threw his impetuous flight thro the deeps of
    immensity
Revolving round in whirlpools fierce all round the
    cavernd worlds

But Urizen silent descended to the Caves of Orc & saw
A Cavernd Universe of flaming fire the horses of Urizen
Here bound to fiery mangers furious dash their golden
    hoofs
Striking fierce sparkles from their brazen fetters. fierce
    his lions
Howl in the burning dens his tygers roam in the
    redounding smoke
In forests of affliction. the adamantine scales of justice   10
Consuming in the raging lamps of mercy pourd in
    rivers
The holy oil rages thro all the cavernd rocks   fierce
    flames

Dance on the rivers & the rocks howling & drunk with
    fury
The plow of ages & the golden harrow wade thro fields
Of goary blood the immortal seed is nourishd for the
    slaughter
The bulls of Luvah breathing fire bellow on burning
    pastures
Round howling Orc whose awful limbs cast forth red
    smoke & fire
That Urizen approachd not near but took his seat on a
    rock
And rangd his books around him brooding Envious
    over Orc

Howling & rending his dark caves the awful Demon lay   20
Pulse after pulse beat on his fetters pulse after pulse his
    spirit
Darted & darted higher & higher to the shrine of
    Enitharmon
As when the thunder folds himself in thickest clouds
The watry nations couch & hide in the profoundest
    deeps
Then bursting from his troubled head with terrible
    visages & flaming hair
His swift wingd daughters sweep across the vast black
    ocean

Los felt the Envy in his limbs like to a blighted tree
PAGE 78
For Urizen fixd in Envy sat brooding & coverd with
    snow
His book of iron on his knees he tracd the dreadful
    letters
While his snows fell & his storms beat to cool the flames
    of Orc
Age after Age till underneath his heel a deadly root
Struck thro the rock the root of Mystery accursed
    shooting up

Branches into the heaven of Los they pipe formd
    bending down
Take root again whereever they touch again branching
    forth
In intricate labyrinths oerspreading many a grizly deep

Amazd started Urizen when he found himself compassd
    round
And high roofed over with trees. he arose but the stems   10
Stood so thick he with difficulty & great pain brought
His books out of the dismal shade. all but the book of
    iron
Again he took his seat & rangd his Books around
On a rock of iron frowning over the foaming fires of
    Orc

And Urizen hung over Orc & viewd his terrible wrath
Sitting upon [*his*] an iron Crag at length his words
    broke forth

Image of dread whence art thou whence is this most
    woful place
Whence these fierce fires but from thyself No other
    living thing
In all this Chasm I behold. No other living thing
Dare thy most terrible wrath abide Bound here to waste
    in pain   20
Thy vital substance in these fires that issue new & new
Around thee sometimes like a flood & sometimes
    like a rock
Of living pangs thy horrible bed glowing with ceaseless
    fires
Beneath thee & around Above a Shower of fire now
    beats
Moulded to globes & arrowy wedges rending thy
    bleeding limbs
And now a whirling pillar of burning sands to
    overwhelm thee

Steeping thy wounds in salts infernal & in bitter
  anguish
And now a rock moves on the surface of this lake of
  fire
To bear thee down beneath the waves in stifling despair
Pity for thee movd me to break my dark & long repose   30
And to reveal myself before thee in a form of wisdom
Yet thou dost laugh at all these tortures & this horrible
  place
Yet throw thy limbs these fires abroad that back return
  upon thee
While thou reposest throwing rage on rage feeding
  thyself
With visions of sweet bliss far other than this burning
  clime
Sure thou art bathd in rivers of delight on verdant
  fields
Walking in joy in bright Expanses sleeping on bright
  clouds
With visions of delight so lovely that they urge thy rage
Tenfold with fierce desire to rend thy chain & howl in
  fury
And dim oblivion of all woe & desperate repose   40
Or is thy joy founded on torment which others bear for
  thee

Orc answerd curse thy hoary brows. What dost thou in
  this deep
Thy Pity I contemn scatter thy snows elsewhere
PAGE 79
I rage in the deep for Lo my feet & hands are naild to
  the burning rock
Yet my fierce fires are better than thy snows   Shuddring
  thou sittest
Thou art not chaind Why shouldst thou sit cold
  grovelling demon of woe
In tortures of dire coldness now a Lake of waters deep
Sweeps over thee freezing to solid still thou sitst closd up

In that transparent rock as if in joy of thy bright prison
Till overburdend with its own weight drawn out thro
    immensity
With a crash breaking across the horrible mass comes
    down
Thundring & hail & frozen iron haild from the Element
Rends thy white hair   yet thou dost fixd obdurate
    brooding sit   10
Writing thy books. Anon a cloud filld with a waste of
    snows
Covers thee still obdurate still resolvd & writing still
Tho rocks roll oer thee tho floods pour tho winds black
    as the Sea
Cut thee in gashes tho the blood pours down around
    thy ankles
Freezing thy feet to the hard rock still thy pen obdurate
Traces the wonders of Futurity in horrible fear of the
    future
I rage furious in the deep for lo my feet & hands are
    naild
To the hard rock or thou shouldst feel my enmity &
    hate
In all the diseases of man falling upon thy grey
    accursed front

Urizen answerd Read my books explore my
    Constellations   20
Enquire of my Sons & they shall teach thee how to War
Enquire of my Daughters who accursd in the dark
    depths
Knead bread of Sorrow by my stern command for I am
    God
Of all this dreadful ruin   Rise O daughters at my Stern
    command

Rending the Rocks Eleth & Uveth rose & Ona rose
Terrific with their iron vessels driving them across
In the dim air they took the book of iron & placd
    above

On clouds of death & sang their songs kneading the
    bread of Orc
Orc listend to the song compelld hungring on the cold
    wind
That swaggd heavy with the accursed dough. the hoar
    frost ragd   30
Thro Onas sieve   the torrent rain pourd from the iron
    pail
Of Eleth & the icy hands of Uveth kneaded the bread
The heavens bow with terror underneath their iron
    hands
Singing at their dire work the words of Urizens book of
    iron
While the enormous scrolls rolld dreadful in the heavens
    above
And still the burden of their song in tears was poured
    forth
The bread is Kneaded let us rest O cruel father of
    children

But Urizen remitted not their labours upon his rock
PAGE 80
And Urizen Read in his book of brass in sounding
    tones

Listen O Daughters to my voice Listen to the Words of
    Wisdom
So shall [you] govern over all let Moral Duty tune your
    tongue
But be your hearts harder than the nether millstone
To bring the shadow of Enitharmon beneath our
    wondrous tree
That Los may Evaporate like smoke & be no more
Draw down Enitharmon to the Spectre of Urthona
And let him have dominion over Los the terrible shade

Compell the poor to live upon a Crust of bread by soft
    mild arts
Smile when they frown frown when they smile & when
    a man looks pale   10

With labour & abstinence say he looks healthy & happy
And when his children sicken let them die there are
    enough
Born even too many & our Earth will be overrun
Without these arts   If you would make the poor live with
    temper
With pomp give every crust of bread you give with
    gracious cunning
Magnify small gifts reduce the man to want a gift &
    then give with pomp
Say he smiles if you hear him sigh If pale say he is
    ruddy
Preach temperance   say he is overgorgd & drowns his
    wit
In strong drink tho you know that bread & water are
    all
He can afford   Flatter his wife pity his children till we
    can   20
Reduce all to our will as spaniels are taught with art
Lo how the heart & brain are formed in the breeding
    womb
Of Enitharmon how it buds with life & forms the bones
The little heart the liver & the red blood in its labyrinths
By gratified desire by strong devouring appetite she fills
Los with ambitious fury that his race shall all devour

Then Orc [*answerd*] cried Curse thy Cold hypocrisy.
    already round thy Tree
In scales that shine with gold & rubies thou beginnest to
    weaken
My divided Spirit Like a worm I rise in peace unbound
From wrath Now When I rage my fetters bind me more   30
O torment O torment A Worm compelld. Am I a worm
Is it in strong deceit that man is born. In strong deceit
Thou dost refrain my fury that the worm may fold the
    tree
Avaunt Cold hypocrite   I am chaind or thou couldst
    not use me thus

The Man shall rage bound with this Chain the worm in
    silence creep
Thou wilt not cease from rage Grey Demon silence all
    thy storms
Give me example of thy mildness King of furious hail
    storms
Art thou the cold attractive power that holds me in this
    chain
I well remember how I stole thy light & it became fire
Consuming. Thou Knowst me now O Urizen Prince of
    Light
And I know thee is this the triumph this the Godlike
    State
That lies beyond the bounds of Science in the Grey
    obscure

40

Terrified Urizen heard Orc now certain that he was
    Luvah
And Orc [*So saying*] he began to Organize a Serpent
    body
Despising Urizens light & turning it into flaming fire
Recieving as a poisond Cup Recieves the heavenly
    wine
And turning [*wisdom*] affection into fury & thought into
    abstraction
A Self consuming dark devourer rising into the heavens

Urizen envious brooding sat & saw the secret terror
Flame high in pride & laugh to scorn the source of his
    deceit
Nor knew the source of his own but thought himself the
    Sole author

50

PAGE 81

Of all his wandering Experiments in the horrible Abyss
He knew that weakness stretches out in breadth & length
    he knew
That wisdom reaches high & deep & therefore he made
    Orc

In Serpent form compelld stretch out & up the
    mysterious tree
He sufferd him to Climb that he might draw all human
    forms
Into submission to his will nor knew the dread result

Los sat in showers of Urizen [*cold*] watching cold
    Enitharmon
His broodings rush down to his feet producing Eggs that
    hatching
Burst forth upon the winds above the tree of Mystery
Enitharmon lay on his knees. Urizen tracd his Verses   10
In the dark deep the dark tree grew. her shadow was
    drawn down
Down to the roots it wept over Orc. the Shadow of
    Enitharmon

Los saw her stretchd the image of death upon his
    witherd valleys
Her Shadow went forth & returnd Now she was pale
    as snow
When the mountains & hills are coverd over & the paths
    of Men shut up
But when her spirit returnd as ruddy as a morning when
The ripe fruit blushes into joy in heavens eternal halls
[*She Secret joyd to see She fed herself on his Despair*
She said I am avengd for all my sufferings of old]
Sorrow shot thro him from his feet it shot up to his
    head   20
Like a cold night that nips the roots & shatters off the
    leaves
Silent he stood oer Enitharmon watching her pale face
He spoke not he was Silent till he felt the cold disease
Then Los mournd on the dismal wind in his jealous
    lamentation

Why can I not Enjoy thy beauty   Lovely Enitharmon
When I return from clouds of Grief in the wandring
    Elements

Where thou in thrilling joy in beaming summer
    loveliness
Delectable reposest ruddy in my absence flaming with
    beauty
Cold pale in sorrow at my approach trembling at my
    terrific
Forehead & eyes thy lips decay like roses in [*early*] the
    spring   30
How art thou Shrunk thy grapes that burst in summers
    vast Excess
Shut up in little purple covering faintly bud & die
Thy olive trees that pourd down oil upon a thousand
    hills
Sickly look forth & scarcely stretch their branches to the
    plain
Thy roses that expanded in the face of glowing morn
PAGE 82
Hid in a little silken veil scarce breathe & faintly shine
Thy lilies that gave light what time the morning looked
    forth
Hid in the Vales faintly lament & no one hears their
    voice
All things beside the woful Los enjoy the delights of
    beauty
Once how I sang & calld the beasts & birds to their
    delights
Nor knew that I alone exempted from the joys of love
Must war with secret monsters of the animating worlds
O that I had not seen the day then should I be at rest
Nor felt the stingings of desire nor longings after life
For life is Sweet to Los the wretched to his winged
    woes   10
Is given a craving cry that they may sit at night on
    barren rocks
And whet their beaks & snuff the air & watch the
    opening dawn
And Shriek till at the smells of blood they stretch their
    boney wings

And cut the winds like arrows shot by troops of
   Destiny

Thus Los lamented in the night unheard by Enitharmon
For the Shadow of Enitharmon descended down the tree
   of Mystery
The Spectre saw the Shade Shivering over his gloomy
   rocks
Beneath the tree of Mystery which in the dismal Abyss
Began to blossom in fierce pain shooting its writhing
   buds
In throes of birth & now the blossoms falling shining
   fruit   20
Appeard of many colours & of various poisonous
   qualities
Of Plagues hidden in shining globes that grew on the
   living tree

The Spectre of Urthona saw the Shadow of Enitharmon
Beneath the Tree of Mystery among the leaves & fruit
Reddning the Demon strong prepard the poison of
   sweet Love
He turnd from side to side in [vain] tears he wept &
   he embracd
The fleeting image & in whispers mild wood the faint
   shade

Loveliest delight of Men. Enitharmon shady hiding
In secret places where no eye can trace thy watry way
Have I found thee have I found thee tremblest thou in
   fear   30
Because of Orc because he rent his discordant way
From thy sweet loins of bliss. red flowd thy blood
Pale grew thy face [thy/& his] lightnings playd around
   thee thunders hoverd
Over thee, & the terrible Orc rent his discordant way
But the next joy of thine shall be in sweet delusion
And its birth in fainting & sleep & [woe] Sweet delusions
   of Vala

The Shadow of Enitharmon answerd Art thou terrible
  Shade
Set over this sweet boy of mine to guard him lest he
  rend
PAGE 83
His mother to the winds of heaven Intoxicated with
The fruit of this delightful tree. I cannot flee away
From thy embrace else be assurd so horrible a form
Should never in my arms repose. now listen I will tell
Thee Secrets of Eternity which neer before unlockd
My golden lips nor took the bar from Enitharmons
  breast
Among the Flowers of Beulah walkd the Eternal Man &
  Saw
Vala the lilly of the desert. melting in high noon
Upon her bosom in sweet bliss he fainted   Wonder siezd
All heaven they saw him dark. they built a golden wall   10
Round Beulah   There he reveld in delight among the
  Flowers
Vala was pregnant & brought forth Urizen Prince of
  Light
First born of Generation. Then behold a wonder to
  the Eyes
Of the now fallen Man a double form Vala appeard. A
  Male
And female shuddring pale the Fallen Man recoild
From the Enormity & calld them Luvah & Vala.
  turning down
The vales to find his way back into Heaven but found
  none
For his frail eyes were faded & his ears heavy & dull

Urizen grew up in the plains of Beulah   Many Sons
And many daughters flourishd round the holy Tent of
  Man   20
Till he forgot Eternity delighted in his sweet joy
Among his family his flocks & herds & tents & pastures

But Luvah close conferrd with Urizen in darksom night

To bind the father & enslave the brethren Nought he
   knew
Of sweet Eternity the blood flowd round the holy tent
   & rivn
From its hinges uttering its final groan all Beulah fell
In dark confusion mean time Los was born &
   Enitharmon
But how I know not then forgetfulness quite wrapd me
   up
A period nor do I more remember till I stood
Beside Los in the Cavern dark enslavd to vegetative
   forms   30
According to the Will of Luvah who assumd the Place
Of the Eternal Man & smote him. But thou Spectre dark
Maist find a way to punish Vala in thy fiery South
To bring her down subjected to the rage of my fierce
   boy

PAGE 84
The Spectre said. Thou lovely Vision this delightful
   Tree
Is given us for a Shelter from the tempests of Void &
   Solid
Till once again the morn of ages shall renew upon us
To reunite in those mild fields of happy Eternity
Where thou & I in undivided Essence walkd about
Imbodied. thou my garden of delight & I the spirit in
   the garden
Mutual there we dwelt in one anothers joy revolving
Days of Eternity with Tharmas mild & Luvah sweet
   melodious
Upon our waters. This thou well rememberest listen I
   will tell
What thou forgettest. They in us & we in them
   alternate Livd   10
Drinking the oys of Universal Manhood. One dread
   morn

Listen O vision of Delight One dread morn of goary
   blood
The manhood was divided for the gentle passions
   making way
Thro the infinite labyrinths of the heart & thro the
   nostrils issuing
In odorous stupefaction stood before the Eyes of Man
A female bright. I stood beside my anvil dark a mass
Of iron glowd bright prepard for spades & plowshares.
   sudden down
I sunk with cries of blood issuing downward in the veins
Which now my rivers were become rolling in tubelike
   forms
Shut up within themselves descending down I sunk
   along   20
The goary tide even to the place of seed & there
   dividing
I was divided in darkness & oblivion thou an infant
   woe
And I an infant terror in the womb of Enion
My masculine spirit scorning the frail body issud forth
From Enions brain In this deformed form leaving thee
   there
Till times passd over thee but still my spirit returning
   hoverd
And formd a Male to be a counterpart to thee O Love
Darkend & Lost In due time issuing forth from Enions
   womb
Thou & that demon Los wert born Ah jealousy & woe
Ah poor divided dark Urthona now a Spectre wandering   30
The deeps of Los the Slave of that Creation I created
I labour night & day for Los but listen thou my vision
I view futurity in thee I will bring down soft Vala
To the embraces of this terror & I will destroy
That body I created then shall we unite again in bliss

Thou knowest that the Spectre is in Every Man insane
   brutish

Deformd that I am thus a ravening devouring lust
    continually
Craving & devouring but my Eyes are always upon thee
    O lovely
Delusion & I cannot crave for any thing but thee [& *till*
I have thee in my arms & am again united to Los   40
To be one body & One spirit with him] not so
The spectres of the Dead for I am as the Spectre of the
    Living
For till these terrors planted round the Gates of Eternal
    life
Are driven away & annihilated we never can repass the
    Gates

PAGE 85
Astonishd filld with tears the spirit of Enitharmon
    beheld
And heard the Spectre bitterly she wept Embracing
    fervent
Her once lovd Lord now but a Shade herself also a
    shade
Conferring times on times among the branches of that
    Tree

Thus they conferrd among the intoxicating fumes of
    Mystery
Till Enitharmons shadow pregnant in the deeps beneath
Brought forth a wonder horrible. While Enitharmon
    shriekd
And trembled thro the Worlds above Los wept his fierce
    soul was terrifid
At the shrieks of Enitharmon at her tossings nor could
    his eyes percieve
The cause of her dire anguish for she lay the image of
    Death   10
Movd by strong shudders till her shadow was deliverd
    then she ran
Raving about the upper Elements in maddning fury

She burst the Gates of Enitharmons heart with direful
    Crash
Nor could they ever be closd again the golden hinges
    were broken
And the gates [*burst*] broke in sunder & their ornaments
    defacd
Beneath the tree of Mystery for the immortal shadow
    shuddering
Brought forth this wonder horrible a Cloud she grew &
    grew
Till many of the dead burst forth from the bottoms of
    their tombs
In male forms without female counterparts or
    Emanations
Cruel and ravening with Enmity & Hatred & War   20
In dreams of Ulro [*sweet*] dark delusive drawn by the
    lovely shadow

The Spectre [*smild*] terrified gave her Charge over the
    howling Orc
Then took the tree of Mystery root in the World of Los
Its topmost [*branches*] boughs shooting a [*stem*] fibre
    beneath Enitharmons couch
The double rooted Labyrinth soon wavd around their
    heads
          [*End of the Seventh Night*]

But then the Spectre enterd Los's bosom Every sigh &
    groan
Of Enitharmon bore Urthonas Spectre on its wings
Obdurate Los felt Pity Enitharmon told the tale
Of Urthona. Los embracd the Spectre first as a brother
Then as another Self; astonishd humanizing & in tears   30
In Self abasement Giving up his Domineering lust
          [*The End of the Seventh Night*]

Thou never canst embrace sweet Enitharmon terrible
    Demon. Till
Thou art united with thy Spectre Consummating by
    pains & labours

[*Thy*] That mortal body & by Self annihilation back
    returning
To Life Eternal be assurd I am thy real Self
Tho thus divided from thee & the Slave of Every passion
Of thy fierce Soul Unbar the Gates of Memory look
    upon me
Not as another but as thy real Self I am thy Spectre
Tho horrible & Ghastly to thine Eyes tho buried beneath
The ruins of the Universe. hear what inspird I speak &
    be silent   40
Thou didst subdue me in old times by thy Immortal
    Strength
When I was a ravning hungring & thirsting cruel lust &
    murder
If [*once*] we unite in one another better world will be
Opend within your heart & loins & wondrous brain
Threefold as it was in Eternity & this the fourth
    Universe
Will be Renewd by the three & consummated in Mental
    fires
But if thou dost refuse Another body will be prepared
PAGE 86
For me & thou annihilate evaporate & be no more
For thou art but a form & organ of life & of thyself
Art nothing being Created Continually by Mercy & Love
    divine

Los furious answerd. Spectre horrible thy words astound
    my Ear
With irresistible conviction I feel I am not one of those
Who when convincd can still persist tho furious
    controllable
By Reasons power. Even I already feel a World within
Opening its gates & in it all the real substances
Of which these in the outward World are shadows which
    pass away
Come then into my Bosom & in thy shadowy arms
    bring with thee   10

My lovely Enitharmon. I will quell my fury & teach
Peace to the Soul of dark revenge & repentance to
   Cruelty

So spoke Los & Embracing Enitharmon & the Spectre
Clouds would have folded round in Extacy & Love
   uniting
PAGE 87
But Enitharmon trembling fled & hid beneath Urizens
   tree
[Then] But mingling together with his Spectre the Spectre
   of Urthona
Wondering beheld the Center opend by Divine Mercy
   inspired
He in his turn Gave Tasks to Los Enormous to destroy
That body he created but in vain for Los performd
Wonders of labour
They Builded Golgonooza Los labouring [inspird]
   builded pillars high
And Domes terrific in the nether heavens for beneath
Was opend new heavens & a new Earth beneath &
   within
Threefold within the brain within the heart within the
   loins   10
A Threefold Atmosphere Sublime continuous from
   Urthonas world
But yet having a Limit Twofold named Satan & Adam

But Los stood on the Limit of Translucence weeping &
   trembling
Filled with doubts in self accusation [gatherd] beheld the
   fruit
Of Urizens Mysterious tree For Enitharmon thus spake

When In the Deeps beneath I gatherd of this ruddy fruit
It was by that I knew that I had Sinnd & then I knew
That without a ransom I could not be savd from Eternal
   death
That Life lives upon Death & by devouring appetite

All things subsist on one another thenceforth in despair   20
I spend my glowing time but thou art strong & mighty
To bear this Self conviction take then Eat thou also of
The fruit & give me proof of life Eternal or I die

Then Los plucked the fruit & Eat & sat down in
    Despair
And must have given himself to death Eternal But
Urthonas spectre in part mingling with him comforted
    him
Being a medium between him & Enitharmon   But This
    Union
Was not to be Effected without Cares & Sorrows &
    Troubles
Of six thousand Years of self denial and [*many Tears.*]
    of bitter Contrition

Urthonas Spectre terrified beheld the Spectres of the
    Dead   30
Each Male formd without a counterpart without a
    concentering vision
The Spectre of Urthona wept before Los Saying I am
    the cause
That this dire state commences I began the dreadful
    state
Of Separation & on my dark head the curse &
    punishment
Must fall unless a way be found to Ransom & Redeem

But I have thee my [*Counterpart/Vegetative*]
    miraculous
These Spectres have no [*Counterparts*] therefore they
    ravin
Without the food of life Let us Create them
    Coun[terparts]
For without a Created body the Spectre is Eternal Death

Los trembling answerd Now I feel the weight of stern
    repentance   40
Tremble not so my Enitharmon at the awful gates

Of thy poor broken Heart I see thee like a shadow
    withering
As on the outside of Existence but look! behold! take
    comfort!
Turn inwardly thine Eyes & there behold the Lamb of
    God
Clothed in Luvahs robes of blood descending to redeem

O Spectre of Urthona take comfort O Enitharmon
Couldst thou but cease from terror & trembling &
    affright
When I appear before thee in forgiveness of [*former
    injuries*] ancient injuries
Why shouldst thou remember & be afraid. I surely
    have died in pain
Often enough to convince thy jealousy & fear & terror   50
Come hither be patient let us converse together because
I also tremble at myself & at all my former life

Enitharmon answerd I behold the Lamb of God
    descending
To Meet these Spectres of the Dead I therefore fear that
    he
Will give us to Eternal Death fit punishment for such
Hideous offenders Uttermost extinction in eternal pain
An ever dying life of stifling & obstruction shut out
Of existence to be a sign of terror to all who behold
Lest any should in futurity do as we have done in heaven
Such is our state nor will the Son of God redeem us
    but destroy   60

PAGE 90
So Enitharmon spoke trembling & in torrents of tears

Los sat in Golgonooza in the Gate of Luban where
He had erected many porches [*which*] where branchd the
    Mysterious Tree
Where the Spectrous dead wail & sighing thus he spoke
    to Enitharmon

Lovely delight of Men Enitharmon [*sweet*] shady
    refuge from furious war
Thy bosom translucent is a soft repose for the weeping
    souls
Of those piteous victims of battle there they sleep in
    happy obscurity
They feed upon our life we are their victims. Stern
    desire
I feel to fabricate embodied semblances in which the
    dead
May live before us in our palaces & in our gardens of
    [*pleasure*] labour   10
Which now opend within the Center we behold spread
    abroad
To form a world of [*life & love*] Sacrifice of brothers &
    sons & daughters
To comfort Orc in his dire sufferings look my fires
    enlume afresh
Before my face ascending with delight as in ancient
    times

Enitharmon spread her beaming locks upon the wind &
    said
O Lovely terrible Los wonder of Eternity O Los my
    defence & guide
Thy works are all my joy. & in thy fires my soul delights
If mild they burn in just proportion & in secret night
And silence build their day in shadow of soft clouds &
    dews
Then I can sigh forth on the winds of Golgonooza
    piteous forms   20
That vanish again into my bosom   but if thou my Los
Wilt in sweet moderated fury. fabricate [*sweet*] forms
    sublime
Such as the piteous spectres may assimilate themselves
    into
They shall be ransoms for our Souls that we may
    live

So Enitharmon spoke & Los his hands divine inspired
  began
[*To hew the cavernd rocks of Dranthon into forms of
  beauty*]
To modulate his fires studious the loud roaring flames
He vanquishd with the strength of Art bending their
  iron points
And drawing them forth delighted upon the winds of
  Golgonooza
From out the ranks of Urizens war & from the fiery lake   30
Of Orc bending down as the binder of the Sheaves
  follows
The reaper in both arms embracing the furious raging
  flames
Los drew them forth out of the deeps planting his right
  foot firm
Upon the Iron crag of Urizen thence springing up
  aloft
Into the heavens of Enitharmon in a mighty circle

And first he drew a line upon the walls of shining
  heaven
And Enitharmon tincturd it with beams of blushing
  love
It remaind permanent a lovely form inspird divinely
  human
Dividing into just proportions Los unwearied labourd
The immortal lines upon the heavens till with sighs
  of love   40
Sweet Enitharmon mild Entrancd breathd forth upon
  the wind
The spectrous dead Weeping the Spectres viewd the
  immortal works
Of Los Assimilating to those forms Embodied & Lovely
In youth & beauty in the arms of Enitharmon mild
  reposing

First Rintrah & then Palamabron drawn from out the
  ranks of war

In infant innocence reposd on Enitharmons bosom
Orc was comforted in the deeps his Soul revivd in
    them
As the Eldest brother is the [*second*] fathers image So
    Orc became
As Los a father to his brethren & he joyd in the dark
    lake
Tho bound with chains of Jealousy & in scales of iron
    & brass   50
But Los loved them & refusd to Sacrifice their infant
    limbs
And Enitharmons smiles & tears prevaild over self
    protection
They rather chose to meet Eternal death than to destroy
The offspring of their Care & Pity Urthonas spectre
    was comforted
But Tharmas most rejoicd in hope of Enions return
For he beheld new Female forms born forth upon the
    air
Who wove soft silken veils of covering in sweet rapturd
    trance
Mortal & not as Enitharmon without a covering veil

First his immortal spirit drew Urizen[s] [*Spectre*]
    Shadow away
From out the ranks of war separating him in sunder   60
Leaving his Spectrous form which could not be drawn
    away
Then he divided Thiriel the Eldest of Urizens sons
Urizen became Rintrah Thiriel became Palamabron
Thus dividing the powers of Every Warrior
Startled was Los he found his Enemy Urizen now
In his hands. he wonderd that he felt love & not hate
His whole soul loved him he beheld him an infant
Lovely breathd from Enitharmon he trembled within
    himself

PAGE 91 (FIRST PORTION)

VALA

NIGHT THE SEVENTH [b]

PAGE 95 (SECOND PORTION)

But in the deeps beneath the [*tree*] roots of Mystery in
    darkest night
Where Urizen sat on his rock the Shadow brooded
    [*dismal*]
Urizen saw & triumphd & he cried to [*the Shadowy
    Female*] his warriors

The time of Prophecy is now revolvd & all
This Universal Ornament is mine & in my hands
The ends of heaven like a Garment will I fold them
    round me   20
Consuming what must be consumd then in power &
    majesty
I will walk forth thro those wide fields of endless
    Eternity
A God & not a Man a Conqueror in triumphant glory
And all the Sons of Everlasting shall bow down at my
    feet

[*The shadowy voice answerd O urizen Prince of Light*]
First Trades & Commerce ships & armed vessels he
    builded laborious
To swim the deep & on the Land children are sold to
    trades
Of dire necessity still laboring day & night till all
Their life extinct they took the spectre form in dark
    despair
And slaves in myriads in ship loads burden the hoarse
    sounding deep   30
Rattling with clanking chains the Universal Empire
    groans

And he commanded his Sons found a Center in the
    Deep
And Urizen laid the first Stone & all his myriads
Builded a temple in the image of the human heart
PAGE 96
And in the inner part of the Temple wondrous
    workmanship
They formd the Secret place reversing all the order of
    delight
That whosoever enterd into the temple might not
    behold
The hidden wonders allegoric of the Generations
Of secret lust when hid in chambers dark the nightly
    harlot
Plays in Disguise in whisperd hymn & mumbling prayer
    The priests
He ordaind & Priestesses clothd in disguises beastial
Inspiring secrecy & lamps they bore intoxicating fumes
Roll round the Temple & they took the Sun that glowd
    oer Los
And with immense machines down rolling. the terrific
    orb   10
Compell'd. The Sun reddning like a fierce lion in his
    chains
Descended to the sound of instruments that drownd the
    noise
Of the hoarse wheels & the terrific howlings of wild
    beasts
That dragd the wheels of the Suns chariot & they put
    the Sun
Into the temple of Urizen to give light to the Abyss
To light the War by day to hide his secret beams by
    night
For he divided day & night in different orderd
    portions
The day for war the night for secret religion in his
    temple
[*Urizen namd it Pande*]

Los reard his mighty [*forehead*] stature on Earth stood   20
   his feet. Above
The moon his furious forehead circled with black
   bursting thunders
His naked limbs glittring upon the dark blue sky his
   knees
Bathed in bloody clouds. his loins in fires of war where
   spears
And swords rage where the Eagles cry & the Vultures
   laugh saying
Now comes the night of Carnage now the flesh of
   Kings & Princes
Pamperd in palaces for our food the blood of Captains
   nurturd
With lust & murder for our drink the drunken Raven
   shall wander
All night among the slain & mock the wounded that
   groan in the field

Tharmas laughd. furious among the Banners clothd in
   blood

Crying As I will rend the Nations all asunder rending   30
The People, vain their combinations I will scatter them
But thou O Son whom I have crowned and inthrond
   thee Strong
I will preserve tho Enemies arise around thee numberless
I will command my winds & they shall scatter them or
   call
PAGE 97
My Waters like a flood around thee fear not trust in me
And I will give thee all the ends of heaven for thy
   possession
In war shalt thou bear rule in blood shalt thou triumph
   for me
Because in times of Everlasting I was rent in sunder
And what I loved best was divided among my Enemies
My little daughters were made captives & I saw them
   beaten

With whips along the sultry [*roads*] sands. I heard those
  whom I lovd
Crying in secret tents at night & in the morn compelld
To labour & behold my heart sunk down beneath
In sighs & sobbings all dividing till I was divided   10
In twain & lo my Crystal form that lived in my bosom
Followd her daughters to the fields of blood they left me
  naked
Alone & they refusd to return from the fields of the
  mighty
Therefore I will reward them as they have rewarded me
I will divide them in my anger & thou O my King
Shalt gather them from out their graves & put thy fetter
  on them
And bind them to thee that my crystal form may come
  to me

So cried the Demon of the Waters in the Clouds of Los
Outstretchd upon the hills lay Enitharmon clouds &
  tempests
Beat round her head all night all day she riots in Excess   20
But [*day by*] night or day Los follows War & the
  dismal moon rolls over her
That when Los warrd upon the South reflected the fierce
  fires
Of his immortal head into the North upon faint
  Enitharmon
Red rage the furies of fierce Orc black thunders roll
  round Los
Flaming his head like the bright sun seen thro a mist
  that magnifies
His disk into a terrible vision to the Eyes of trembling
  mortals

And Enitharmon trembling & in fear utterd these
  words

I put not any trust in thee nor in thy glittering scales
Thy eyelids are a terror to me & the flaming of thy crest

The rushing of thy Scales confound me thy hoarse
   rushing scales   30
And if that Los had not built me a tower upon a rock
I must have died in the dark desart among noxious
   worms
How shall I flee how shall I flee into the tower of Los
My feet are turned backward & my footsteps slide in
   clay
And clouds are closd around my tower my arms labour
   in vain
Does not the God of waters in the wracking Elements
Love those who hate rewarding with hate the Loving
   Soul

PAGE 98

And must not I obey the God thou Shadow of Jealousy
I cry the watchman heareth not I pour my voice in
   roarings
Watchman the night is thick & darkness cheats my rayie
   sight
Lift up Lift up O Los awake my watchman for he
   sleepeth
Lift up Lift up Shine forth O Light watchman thy
   light is out
O Los unless thou keep my tower the Watchman will
   be slain

So Enitharmon cried upon her terrible Earthy bed
While the broad Oak wreathd his roots round her forcing
   his dark way
Thro caves of death into Existence The Beech long
   limbd advancd
Terrific into the paind heavens The fruit trees
   humanizing   10
Shewd their immortal energies in warlike desperation
Rending the heavens & earths & drinking blood in the
   hot battle
To feed their fruit to gratify their hidden sons &
   daughters

That far within the close recesses of their secret
  palaces
Viewd the vast war & joyd wishing to vegetate
Into the Worlds of Enitharmon   Loud the roaring winds
Burdend with clouds howl round the Couch sullen the
  wooly sheep
Walks thro the battle Dark & fierce the Bull his rage
Propagates thro the warring Earth The Lion raging in
  flames
The Tyger in redounding smoke The Serpent of the
  woods   20
And of the waters & the scorpion of the desart irritate
With harsh songs every living soul. The Prester
  Serpent runs
Along the ranks crying Listen to the Priest of God ye
  warriors
This Cowl upon my head he placd in times of
  Everlasting
And said Go forth & guide my battles. like the jointed
  spine
Of Man I made thee when I blotted Man from life &
  light
Take thou the seven Diseases of Man store them for
  times to come
In store houses in secret places that I will tell the[e] of
To be my great & awful curses at the time appointed

The Prester Serpent ceasd the War song sounded loud &
  strong   30
Thro all the heavens Urizens Web vibrated torment on
  torment
Then I heard the earthquake &c.

PAGE 91 (SECOND PORTION)
Now in the Caverns of the Grave & Places of human
  seed
The nameless shadowy Vortex stood before the face of
  Orc

The Shadow reard her dismal head over the flaming
    youth
With sighs & howling & deep sobs that he might lose
    his rage
And with it lose himself in meekness she embracd his
    fire
As when the Earthquake rouzes from his den his
    shoulders huge
Appear above the crumb[l]ing Mountain. Silence waits
    around him
A moment then astounding horror belches from the
    Center
The fiery dogs arise the shoulders huge appear
So Orc rolld round his clouds upon the deeps of dark
    Urthona   10
Knowing the arts of Urizen were Pity & Meek [*love*]
    affection
And that by these arts the Serpent form exuded from
    his limbs

Silent as despairing love & strong as Jealousy
Jealous that she was Vala now become Urizens harlot
And the Harlot of Los & the deluded harlot of the
    Kings of Earth
His soul was gnawn in sunder
The hairy shoulders rend the links free are the wrists of
    fire
Red rage redounds he rouzd his lions from his forests
    black
They howl around the flaming youth rending the
    nameless shadow
And running their immortal course thro solid darkness
    borne   20

Loud Sounds the war song round red Orc in his
    [*?triumphant*] fury
And round the nameless shadowy Female in her howling
    terror

When all the Elemental Gods joind in the wondrous
  Song

Sound the War trumpet terrific Souls clad in attractive
  steel
Sound the shrill fife serpents of war. I hear the northern
  drum
Awake, I hear the flappings of the folding banners

The dragons of the North put on their armour
Upon the Eastern sea direct they take their course
The glittring of their horses trappings stains the vault
  of night

Stop we the rising of the glorious King. spur spur your
  [*steeds*] clouds   30
PAGE 92
Of death O northern drum awake O hand of iron sound
The northern drum. Now give the charge! bravely
  obscurd!
With darts of wintry hail. Again the black bow draw
Again the Elemental Strings to your right breasts draw
And let the thundring drum speed on the arrows black

The arrows flew from cloudy bow all day. till blood
From east to west flowd like the human veins in rivers
Of life upon the plains of death & valleys of despair

Now sound the clarions of Victory now strip the slain
[*Now*] clothe yourselves in golden arms brothers of war   10
They sound the clarions strong they chain the howling
  captives
they give the Oath of blood They cast the lots into the
  helmet,
They vote the death of Luvah & they naild him to the
  tree
They piercd him with a spear & laid him in a
  sepulcher
To die a death of Six thousand years bound round with
  desolation

The sun was black & the moon rolld a useless globe thro
    heaven

Then left the Sons of Urizen the plow & harrow the
    loom
The hammer & the Chisel & the rule & compasses
They forgd the sword the chariot of war the battle ax
The trumpet fitted to the battle & the flute of summer   20
And all the arts of life they changd into the arts of death
The hour glass contemnd because its simple
    workmanship
Was as the workmanship of the plowman & the water
    wheel
That raises water into Cisterns broken & burnd in fire
Because its workmanship was like the workmanship of
    the Shepherd
And in their stead intricate wheels invented Wheel
    without wheel
To perplex youth in their outgoings & to bind to
    labours
Of day & night the myriads of Eternity. that they might
    file
And polish brass & iron hour after hour laborious
    workmanship
Kept ignorant of the use that they might spend the
    days of wisdom   30
In sorrowful drudgery to obtain a scanty pittance of
    bread
In ignorance to view a small portion & think that All
And call it Demonstration blind to all the simple rules
    of life

Now now the Battle rages round thy tender limbs O
    Vala
Now smile among thy bitter tears now put on all thy
    beauty
Is not the wound of the sword Sweet & the broken
    bone delightful

Wilt thou now smile among the slain when the wounded
   groan in the field

PAGE 93
Lift up thy blue eyes Vala & put on thy sapphire shoes
O Melancholy Magdalen behold the morning breaks
Gird on thy flaming Zone. descend into the Sepulcher
Scatter the blood from thy golden brow the tears from
   thy silver locks
Shake off the waters from thy wings & the dust from thy
   white garments

Remember all thy feigned terrors on the secret Couch
When the sun rose in glowing morn with arms of mighty
   hosts
Marching to battle who was wont to rise with Urizens
   harps
Gift as a Sower with his seed to scatter life abroad

Arise O Vala bring the bow of Urizen bring the swift
   arrows of light   10
How ragd the golden horses of Urizen bound to the
   chariot of Love
Compelld to leave the plow to the Ox to snuff up the
   winds of desolation
To trample the corn fields in boastful neighings. this is
   no gentle harp
This is no warbling brook nor Shadow of a Myrtle tree

But blood & wounds & dismal cries & clarions of war
And hearts laid open to the light by the broad grizly
   sword
And bowels hidden [*in darkness are*] in hammerd steel
   rippd forth upon the ground
Call forth thy smiles of soft deceit call forth thy cloudy
   tears
We hear thy sighs in trumpets shrill when Morn shall
   blood renew

So sung the demons of the deep the Clarions of war
   blew loud   20

Orc rent her & his human form consumd in his own fires
Mingled with her dolorous members strewn thro the
Abyss
She joyd in all the Conflict Gratified & ?dropping tears
of woe
No more remaind of Orc but the Serpent round the tree
of Mystery
The form of Orc was gone he reard his serpent bulk
among
The stars of Urizen in Power rending the form of life
Into a formless indefinite & strewing her on the Abyss
Like clouds upon the winter sky broken with winds &
thunders

This was to her Supreme delight The Warriors mournd
disappointed
They go out to war with Strong Shouts & loud Clarions
O Pity   30
They return with lamentations mourning & weeping

Invisible or visible drawn out in length or stretchd in
breadth
The Shadowy Female Varied in the War in her delight
Howling in discontent black & heavy uttering brute
sounds
Wading thro fens among the slimy weeds making
Lamentations
To decieve Tharmas in his rage to soothe his furious
soul
To stay him in his flight that Urizen might live tho in
pain
He said Art thou bright Enion is the Shadow of hope
returnd

And She said Tharmas I am Vala bless thy innocent
face
Doth Enion avoid the sight of thy blue watry eyes   40
Be not perswaded that the air knows this or the falling
dew

Tharmas replid O Vala once I livd in a garden of
  delight

PAGE 94

I wakend Enion in the Morning & she turnd away
Among the apple trees & all the gardens of delight
Swam like a dream before my eyes I went to seek the
  steps
Of Enion in the gardens & the shadows compassd me
And closd me in a watry world of woe where Enion
  stood
Trembling before me like a shadow like a mist like air
And she is gone & here alone I war with darkness &
  death
I hear thy voice but not thy form see. thou & all
  delight
And life appear & vanish mocking me with shadows of
  false hope
Hast thou forgot that the air listens thro all its districts
  telling   10
The subtlest thoughts shut up from light in chambers
  of the Moon

Tharmas. The Moon has chambers where the babes of
  love lie hid
And whence they never can be brought in all Eternity
Unless exposd by their vain parents. Lo him whom I
  love
Is hidden from me & I never in all Eternity
Shall see him   Enitharmon & Ahania combind with
  Enion
Hid him in that Outrageous form of Orc which torments
  me for Sin
For all my Secret faults which he brings forth upon the
  light
Of day in jealousy & blood my Children are led to
  Urizens war
Before my eyes & for every one of these I am
  condemnd   20

To Eternal torment in these flames for tho I have the
    power
To rise on high Yet love here binds me down & never
    never
Will I arise till him I love is loosd from this dark chain

Tharmas replied Vala thy Sins have lost us heaven &
    bliss
Thou art our Curse and till I can bring love into the
    light
I never will depart from my great wrath

So Tharmas waild [*then furious*] wrathful then rode upon
    the Stormy Deep
Cursing the Voice that mockd him with false hope in
    furious mood
Then She returns swift as a blight upon the infant bud
Howling in all the notes of woe to stay his furious rage   30
Stamping the hills wading or swimming flying furious or
    falling
Or like an Earthquake rumbling in the bowels of the
    earth
Or like a cloud beneath & like a fire flaming on high
Walking in pleasure of the hills or murmuring in the
    dales
Like to a rushing torrent beneath & a falling rock above
A thunder cloud in the south & a lulling voice heard in
    the north

And she went forth & saw the forms of life & of delight
Walking on Mountains or flying in the open expanse of
    heaven
She heard sweet voices in the winds & in the voices of
    birds
That rose from waters for the waters were as the voice
    of Luvah   40
Not seen to her like waters or like this dark world of
    death

Tho all those fair perfections which men know only by
    name
In beautiful substantial forms appeard & served her
As food or drink or ornament or in delightful works
To build her bowers for the Elements brought forth
    abundantly
The living soul in glorious forms & every one came
    forth
Walking before her Shadowy face & bowing at her feet
But in vain delights were poured forth on the howling
    melancholy
For her delight the horse his proud neck bowd & his
    white mane
And the Strong Lion deignd in his mouth to wear the
    golden bit   50
While the far beaming Peacock waited on the fragrant
    wind
To bring her fruits of sweet delight from trees of
    richest wonders
And the strong piniond Eagle bore the fire of heaven in
    the night season
Wood & subdud into Eternal Death the Demon Lay
In [*anguish for*] rage against the dark despair, the
    howling Melancholy
PAGE 95 (FIRST PORTION)
For far & wide she stretchd thro all the worlds of
    Urizens journey
And was Ajoind to Beulah as the Polypus to the Rock
Mo[u]rning the daughters of Beulah saw nor could they
    have sustaind
The horrid sight of death & torment   But the Eternal
    Promise
They wrote on all their tombs & pillars & on every Urn
These words   If ye will believe your B[r]other shall rise
    again
In golden letters ornamented with sweet labours of Love
Waiting with Patience [*of*] for the fulfilment of the
    Promise Divine

And all the Songs of Beulah sounded comfortable notes
Not suffring doubt to rise up from the Clouds of the
    Shadowy Female   10
Then myriads of the Dead burst thro the bottoms of
    their tombs
Descending on the shadowy females clouds in Spectrous
    terror
Beyond the Limit of Translucence on the Lake of Udan
    Adan
These they namd Satans & in the Aggregate they namd
    Them Satan

End of the Seventh Night [b]

PAGE 99

VALA
NIGHT THE EIGHTH

Then All in Great Eternity [*which is called*] Met in the
    Council of God
[*Met*] as one Man Even Jesus upon Gilead & Hermon
Upon the Limit of Contraction to create the fallen Man
The [*Eternal*] Fallen Man stretchd like a Corse upon the
    oozy Rock
Washd with the tides Pale overgrown with weeds
That movd with horrible dreams hovring high over his
    head
Two winged immortal shapes one standing at his feet
Toward the East one standing at his head toward the
    west
Their wings joind in the Zenith over head [*but other
    wings*
*They had which clothd their bodies like a garment of soft
    down*
Silvery white shining upon the dark blue sky in silence   10
Their wings touchd the heavens their fair feet hoverd above
The swelling tides they bent over the dead corse like an arch

Pointed at top in highest heavens of precious stones &
   pearl]

Such is a Vision of All Beulah hovring over the Sleeper

The limit of Contraction now was fixd & Man began
To wake upon the Couch of Death he sneezed seven
   times
A tear of blood dropped from either eye again he reposd
In the saviours arms, in the arms of tender mercy &
   loving kindness

Then [*first*] Los [*beheld*] said I behold the Divine Vision
   thro the broken Gates   20
Of [*Enitharmons*] thy poor broken heart astonishd melted
   into Compassion & Love
And Enitharmon [*saw*] said I see the Lamb of God upon
   Mount Zion
Wondring with love & Awe they felt the divine hand
   upon them

For nothing could restrain the dead in Beulah from
   descending
Unto Ulros night tempted by the Shadowy females sweet
Delusive cruelty they descend away from the Daughters
   of Beulah
And Enter Urizens temple Enitharmon pitying & her
   heart
Gates broken down, they descend thro the Gate of Pity
The broken heart Gate of Enitharmon She sighs them
   forth upon the wind
Of Golgonooza Los stood recieving them   30
For Los could enter into Enitharmons bosom & explore
Its intricate Labyrinths now the Obdurate heart was
   broken
PAGE 100 (FIRST PORTION)
From out the War of Urizen & Tharmas recieving them
Into his hands. Then Enitharmon erected Looms in
   Lubans Gate

And calld the Looms Cathedron in these Looms She
  wove the Spectres
Bodies of Vegetation Singing lulling Cadences to drive
  away
Despair from the poor wandering spectres and Los loved
  them
With a parental love for the Divine hand was upon him
And upon Enitharmon & the Divine Countenance shone
In Golgonooza Looking down the Daughters of Beulah
  saw
With joy the bright Light & in it a Human form
And knew he was the Saviour Even Jesus & they
  worshipped   10

[*Astonishd Comforted Delighted the Daughters of Beulah*
  saw]
Astonishd Comforted Delighted in notes of Rapturous
  Extacy
All Beulah stood astonishd Looking down to Eternal
  Death
They saw the Saviour beyond the Pit of death &
  destruction
For whether they lookd upward they saw the Divine
  Vision
Or whether they lookd downward still they saw the
  Divine Vision
Surrounding them on all sides beyond sin & death & hell

Enitharmon wove in tears singing Songs of Lamentation
And pitying comfort as she sighd forth on the wind the
  Spectres
Also the Vegetated bodies which Enitharmon wove   20
Opend within their hearts & in their loins & in their
  brain
To Beulah & the Dead in Ulro descended from the War
Of Urizen & Tharmas & from the Shadowy females
  clouds
And some were woven [*One fold*] single & some two fold
  & some three fold

In Head or Heart or Reins according to the fittest order
Of most merciful pity & compassion to the Spectrous
    dead

PAGE 101 (FIRST PORTION)
When Urizen saw the Lamb of God clothed in Luvahs
    robes
Perplexd & terrifid he Stood tho well he knew that Orc
Was Luvah But he now beheld a new Luvah. Or One
Who assumd Luvahs form & stood before him opposite
But he saw Orc a Serpent form augmenting times on
    times
In the fierce battle & he saw the Lamb of God & the
    World of Los
Surrounded by his dark machines for Orc augmented
    swift
In fury a Serpent wondrous among the Constellations of
    Urizen
A crest of fire rose on his forehead red as the carbuncle
Beneath down to his eyelids scales of pearl then gold
    & silver   10
Immingled with the ruby overspread his Visage down
His furious neck writ[h]ing contortive in dire budding
    pains
The scaly armour shot out. Stubborn down his back &
    bosom
The Emerald Onyx Sapphire jasper beryl amethyst
Strove in terrific emulation which should gain a place
[*On the immortal fiend*] Upon the mighty Fiend the fruit
    of the mysterious tree
Kneaded in Uveths kneading trough. Still Orc devourd
    the food
In raging hunger Still the pestilential food in gems &
    gold
Exuded round his awful limbs Stretching to serpent
    length
His human bulk While the dark shadowy female
    brooding over   20

Measurd his food morning & evening in cups & baskets
of iron

With tears of sorrow incessant she labourd the food of
Orc

Compelld by the iron hearted sisters Daughters of
Urizen

Gathring the fruit of that mysterious tree circling its
root

She spread herself thro all the branches in the power of
Orc

Thus Urizen in self deceit his warlike preparations
fabricated

And when all things were finishd sudden wavd [*his
hurtling hand*] among the Stars

[*Among the stars*] His hurtling hand gave the dire signal
thunderous Clarions blow

And all the hollow deep rebellowd with the
wonderous war

PAGE 100 (SECOND PORTION)

[*But thus*] But Urizen his mighty rage let loose in the
mid deep

Sparkles of Dire affliction issud [*from*] round his frozen
limbs

Horrible hooks & nets he formd twisting the cords of iron

And brass & molten metals cast in hollow globes & bor'd   30

Tubes in petrific steel & rammd combustibles & wheels

And chains & pullies fabricated all round the heavens of
Los

Communing with the Serpent of Orc in dark
dissimulation

And with the Synagogue of Satan in dark Sanhedrim

To undermine the World of Los & tear bright
Enitharmon

PAGE 101 (SECOND PORTION)

To the four winds hopeless of future. All futurity   30

Seems teeming with Endless destruction never to be
repelld

Desperate remorse swallows the present in a quenchless
    rage

Terrified & astonishd Urizen beheld the battle take a
    form
Which he intended not a Shadowy [*male*] hermaphrodite
    black & opake
The Soldiers namd it Satan but he was yet unformd &
    vast
Hermaphroditic it at length became hiding the Male
Within as in a Tabernacle Abominable Deadly

The battle howls the terrors fird rage in the work of
    death
Enormous Works Los Contemplated inspird by the holy
    Spirit
Los builds the Walls of Golgonooza against the stirring
    battle   40
That only thro the Gates of Death they can enter to
    Enitharmon
Raging they take the human visage & the human form

Feeling the hand of Los in Golgonooza & the force
Attractive of his hammers beating & the Silver looms
Of Enitharmon singing lulling cadences on the wind
They humanize in the fierce battle where in direful pain
Troop by troop the beastial droves rend one another
    sounding loud
The instruments of sound & troop by troop in human
    forms they urge

PAGE 102
The dire confusion till the battle faints those that remain
Return in pangs & horrible convulsions to their beastial
    state
For the monsters of the Elements Lions or Tygers or
    Wolves
Sound loud the howling music Inspird by Los &
    Enitharmon Sounding loud terrific men

They seem to one another laughing terrible among the
    banners
And when the revolution of their day of battles over
Relapsing in dire torment they return to forms of woe
To moping visages returning inanimate tho furious
No more erect tho strong drawn out in length they ravin
For senseless gratification & their visages thrust forth   10
Flatten above & beneath & stretch out into beastial length
Weakend they stretch beyond their power in dire droves
    till war begins
Or Secret religion in their temples before secret shrines

And Urizen gave life & sense by his immortal power
To all his Engines of deceit that linked chains might run
Thro ranks of war spontaneous & that hooks & boring
    screws
Might act according to their forms by innate cruelty
He formed also harsh instruments of sound
To grate the soul into destruction or to inflame with fury
The spirits of life to pervert all the faculties of sense   20
Into their own destruction if perhaps he might avert
His own despair even at the cost of every thing that
    breathes

Thus in the temple of the Sun his books of iron & brass
And silver & gold he consecrated reading incessantly
To myriads of perturbed spirits thro the universe
They propagated the deadly words the Shadowy Female
    absorbing
The enormous Sciences of Urizen ages after ages
    exploring
The fell destruction. And she said O Urizen Prince of
    Light
What words of Dread pierce my faint Ear what fal[l]ing
    snows around
My feeble limbs infold my destind misery   30
I alone dare the lash abide to sit beneath the blast
Unhurt & dare the inclement forehead of the King of
    Light

From dark abysses of the times remote fated to be
PAGE 103
The sorrower of Eternity in love with tears Submiss I
    rear
My Eyes to thy Pavilions hear my prayer for Luvahs Sake
I see the murderer of my Luvah clothd in robes of blood
He who assumd my Luvahs throne in times of
    Everlasting
Where hast thou hid him whom I love in what remote
    Abyss
Resides that God of my delight O might my eyes
    behold
My Luvah then could I deliver all the sons of God
From Bondage of [*the human form*] these terrors & with
    influences sweet
As once in those eternal fields in brotherhood & Love
United we should live in bliss as those who sinned not   10
The Eternal Man is seald by thee never to be deliverd
We are all servants to thy will O King of Light relent
Thy furious power be our father & our loved King
But if my Luvah is no more If [*that*] thou hast smitten
    him
And laid him in the Sepulcher Or if [*that*] thou wilt
    revenge
His murder on another Silent I bow with dread
But happiness can never [come] to thee O King nor me
For he was source of every joy that this mysterious tree
Unfolds in Allegoric fruit. When shall the dead revive
Can that which has existed cease or can love & life
    Expire   20

Urizen heard the Voice & saw the Shadow. underneath
His woven darkness & in laws & deceitful religions
Beginning at the tree of Mystery circling its root
She spread herself thro all the branches in the power of
    Orc
A shapeless & indefinite cloud in tears of sorrow
    incessant

Steeping the Direful Web of Religion swagging heavy it
    fell
From heaven to heavn thro all its meshes altering the
    Vortexes
Misplacing every Center hungry desire & lust began
Gathering the fruit of that Mysterious tree till Urizen
Sitting within his temple furious felt the num[m]ing
    stupor   30
Himself tangled in his own net in sorrow lust repentance

Enitharmon wove in tears Singing Songs of Lamentations
And pitying comfort as she sighd forth on the wind the
    spectres
And wove them bodies calling them her belovd sons &
    daughters
Employing the daughters in her looms & Los employd
    the Sons
In Golgonoozas Furnaces among the Anvils of time &
    space
Thus forming a Vast family wondrous in beauty & love
And they appeard a Universal female form created
From those who were dead in Ulro from the Spectres of
    the dead

PAGE 104 (FIRST PORTION)
And Enitharmon namd the Female Jerusa[le]m the holy
Wondring she saw the Lamb of God within Jerusalems
    Veil
The divine Vision seen within the inmost deep recess
Of fair Jerusalems bosom in a gently beaming fire

Then sang the Sons of Eden round the Lamb of God &
    said
Glory Glory Glory to the holy Lamb of God
Who now beginneth to put off the dark Satanic body
Now we behold redemption Now we know that life
    Eternal
Depends alone upon the Universal hand & not in us
Is aught but death In individual weakness sorrow & pain   10

PAGE 113 (FIRST PORTION)

[*Daughters of Beulah describe*] We behold with wonder
    Enitharmons Looms & Los's Forges
And the Spindles of Tirzah & Rahab and the Mills of
    Satan & Beelzeboul
In Golgonooza Los's anvils stand & his Furnaces rage
[*The hard dentant hammers are lulld by the flute lula lula*
The bellowing furnaces blare by the long sounding Clarion]
Ten thousand demons labour at the forges Creating
    Continually
The times & spaces of Mortal Life the Sun the Moon the
    Stars
In periods of Pulsative furor beating into [*bars*] wedges
    & bars
Then drawing into wires the terrific Passions & Affections
Of Spectrous dead. Thence to the Looms of Cathedron
    conveyd   10
The Daughters of Enitharmon weave the ovarium & the
    integument
In soft silk drawn from their own bowels in lascivious
    delight
With songs of sweetest cadence to the turning spindle &
    reel
Lulling the weeping spectres of the dead. Clothing their
    limbs
With gifts & gold of Eden. Astonishd stupified with
    delight
The terrors put on their sweet clothing on the banks of
    [*the Moon*] Arnon
Whence they plunge into the river of space for a period till
The dread Sleep of Ulro is past. But Satan [*receives*] Og
    & Sihon
Build Mills of resistless wheels to unwind the soft
    threads & reveal
Naked of their clothing the poor spectres before the
    accusing heavens   20
While Rahab & Tirzah far different mantles prepare
    webs of torture

Mantles of despair girdles of bitter compunction shoes of
    indolence
Veils of ignorance covering from head to feet with a cold
    web

We look down into Ulro we behold the Wonders of the
    Grave
Eastward of Golgonooza stands the Lake of Udan Adan
    In
Entuthon Benithon [*it is*] a Lake not of Waters but of
    Spaces
Perturbd black & deadly on [*the*] its Islands & [*the*] its
    Margins [*of this Lake*]
The Mills of Satan and Beelzeboul stand round the
    roots of Urizens tree
For this Lake is formd from the tears & sighs & death
    sweat of the Victims
Of Urizens laws. to irrigate the roots of the tree of
    Mystery   30
They unweave the soft threads then they weave them
    anew in the forms
Of dark death & despair & none from Eternity to
    Eternity could Escape
But [*All*] thou O Universal Humanity who is One Man
    blessed for Ever
Recievest the Integuments woven Rahab beholds the
    Lamb of God
She smites with her knife of flint She destroys her own
    work
Times upon times thinking to destroy the Lamb blessed
    for Ever
He puts off the clothing of blood he redeems the spectres
    from their bonds
He awakes the sleepers in Ulro the Daughters of Beulah
    praise him
They anoint his feet with ointment they wipe them
    with the hair of their head

PAGE 104 (SECOND PORTION)

We now behold the Ends of Beulah & we now behold
Where Death Eternal is put off Eternally
Assume the dark Satanic body in the Virgins womb
O Lamb divin[e] it cannot thee annoy O pitying one
Thy pity is from the foundation of the World & thy
    Redemption
Begun Already in Eternity   Come then O Lamb of God
Come Lord Jesus come quickly

So sang they in Eternity looking down into Beulah.

The war roard round Jerusalems Gates it took a hideous
    form
Seen in the aggregate a Vast Hermaphroditic form   20
[*Heaving ?tw*] Heavd like an Earthquake labring with
    convulsive groans
Intolerable at length an awful wonder burst
From the Hermaphroditic bosom Satan he was namd
Son of Perdition terrible his form dishumanizd
    monstrous
A male without a female counterpart a howling fiend
Fo[r]lorn of Eden & repugnant to the forms of life
Yet hiding the shadowy female Vala as in an ark &
    Curtains
Abhorrd accursed ever dying an Eternal death

Being multitudes of tyrant Men in union blasphemous
Against the divine image. Congregated Assemblies of
    wicked men   30

Los said to Enitharmon Pitying I saw
Pitying the Lamb of God Descended thro Jerusalems
    gates
To put off Mystery time after time & as a Man
Is born on Earth so was he born of Fair Jerusalem
In mysterys woven mantle & in the Robes of Luvah

He stood in fair Jerusalem to awake up into Eden
The fallen Man but first to [*rend the Veil of Mystery*]
    Give his vegetated body

[*And then call Urizen & Luvah & Tharmas & Urthona*]
To be cut off & separated that the Spiritual body may
    be Reveald

PAGE 105
The Lamb of God stood before [*Urizen*] Satan opposite
In Entuthon Benithon in the shadows of torments & woe
Upon the heights of [*Entuthon that*] Amalek taking
    refuge in his arms
The Victims fled from punishment [*that*] for all his
    words were peace

[*He*] Urizen calld together the Synagogue of Satan in
    dire Sanhedrim
To Judge the Lamb of God to Death as a murderer &
    robber
As it is written he was numberd among the transgressors

Cold dark opake the Assembly met twelvefold in
    Amalek
Twelve rocky unshapd forms terrific forms of torture &
    woe
Such seemd the Synagogue to distant view [*around*]
    amidst them [*stood*] beamd   10
A False Feminine Counterpart of Lovely Delusive
    Beauty

Dividing & Uniting at will in the Cruelties of Holiness
Vala drawn down into a Vegetated body now
    triumphant
The Synagogue of Satan Clothed her with Scarlet robes
    & Gems
And on her forehead was her name written in blood
    Mystery
When viewd remote She is One when viewd near she
    divides
To multitude as it is in Eden so permitted because
It was the best possible in the State called Satan to Save
From Death Eternal & to put off Satan Eternally

The Synagogue Created her from Fruit of Urizens tree   20
By devilish arts abominable unlawful unutterable
Perpetually vegetating in detestable births
Of Female forms beautiful thro poisons hidden in secret
Which give a tincture to false beauty [*therefore they were
   calld*
The daughters &] there was hidden within
The bosom of Satan The false Female as in an ark & veil
Which christ must rend & her reveal Her Daughters are
   Calld
Tirzah She is namd Rahab their various divisions are
   [*namd*] calld
The Daughters of Amalek Canaan & Moab binding on
   the [*Stems*] Stones
Their victims & with [*songs*] knives tormenting them
   singing with tears
Over their victims Hear ye the song of the Females of
   Amalek   30

O thou poor human form O thou poor child of woe
Why dost thou wander away from Tirzah why me
   compell to bind thee
If thou dost go away from me I shall consume upon the
   rocks
These fibres of thine eyes that used to wander in distant
   heavens
Away from me I have bound down with a hot iron
These nostrils that Expanded with delight in morning
   skies
I have bent downward with lead molten in my roaring
   furnaces
My soul is seven furnaces incessant roars the bellows
Upon my terribly flaming heart the molten metal runs
In channels thro my fiery limbs O love O pity O pain   40
O the pangs the bitter pangs of love forsaken

Ephraim was a wilderness of joy where all my wild
   beasts ran
The river Kanah wanderd by my sweet Manassehs side

[To see the boy spring into heaven sounding from my sight]
Go Noah fetch the girdle of strong brass heat it red hot
Press it around the loins of this expanding cruelty
Shriek not so my only love
Bind him down Sisters bind him down on Ebal mount of
    Cursing
Malah come forth from Lebanon & Hoglah from Mount
    sinai
Come circumscribe this tongue of sweets & with a
    Screw of iron
Fasten this Ear into the Rock Milcah the task is thine
Weep not so sisters weep not so our life depends on this
Or mercy & truth are fled away from Shechem & Mount
    Gilead
Unless my beloved is bound upon the Stems of
    Vegetation

Such are the songs of Tirzah such the loves of Amalek
The Lamb of God descended thro the twelve portions of
    Luvah
Bearing his sorrows & rec[iev]ing all his cruel wounds

PAGE 106 (FIRST PORTION)
Thus was the Lamb of God condemnd to Death
They naild him upon the tree of Mystery weeping over
    him
And then mocking & then worshipping calling him
    Lord & King
Sometimes as twelve daughters lovely & sometimes as
    five
They stood in beaming beauty & sometimes as one even
    Rahab
[In which is Tirzah untranslucent an opake covering]
Who is Mystery Babylon the Great the Mother of
    Harlots

[And Rahab stripd off Luvahs robes from off the lamb of
    God
Then first she saw his glory & her harlot form appeard

50

In all its turpitude beneath the divine light & of Luvahs
*   robes*   10
She made herself a Mantle
Also the Vegetated bodies which Enitharmon wove in her
*   looms*
Opend within the heart & in the loins & in the brain
To Beulah & the dead in Beulah descended thro their
*   gates*
And some were woven one fold some two fold & some
*   threefold*
In head or heart or reins according to the fittest order
Of most mournful pity & compassion to the spectrous dead]

[*She*] Jerusalem saw the Body dead upon the Cross She
    fled away
Saying Is this Eternal Death   Where shall I hide from
    Death
Pity me Los pity me Urizen & [*build*] let us build   20
A Sepulcher & worship Death in fear while yet we live
Death! God of All from whom we rise to whom we all
    return
And Let all Nations [*in*] of the Earth worship at the
    Sepulcher
With Gifts & Spices with lamps rich embossd jewels &
    gold

Los took the Body from the Cross Jerusalem weeping
    over
They bore it to the Sepulcher which Los had hewn in
    the rock
Of Eternity for himself he hewd it despairing of Life
    Eternal
PAGE 113 (SECOND PORTION)
[*And*] But when Rahab had cut off the Mantle of Luvah
    from   40
The Lamb of God it rolld apart, revealing to all in
    heaven
And all on Earth the Temple & the Synagogue of Satan
    & Mystery

Even Rahab in all her turpitude Rahab divided herself
She stood before Los in her Pride [*above*] among the
　Furnaces
Dividing & uniting in Delusive feminine pomp
　questioning him

He answerd her with tenderness & love not uninspird
Los sat upon his anvil stock they sat beside the forge
Los wipd the sweat from his red brow & thus began
To the delusive female forms shining among his furnaces

I am that shadowy Prophet who six thousand years ago　　50
Fell from my station in the Eternal bosom. I divided
To multitude & my multitudes are children of Care &
　Labour
O Rahab I behold thee I was once like thee a Son
Of Pride and I also have piercd the Lamb of God in
　pride & wrath
Hear me repeat my Generations that thou mayst also
　repent

PAGE 115

And these [*were*] are the Sons of Los & Enitharmon.
　Rintrah Palamabron
Theotormon Bromion Antamon Ananton Ozoth Ohana
Sotha Mydon Ellayol Natho Gon Harhath Satan
Har Ochim Ijim Adam Reuben Simeon Levi Judah Dan
　Naphtali
Gad Asher Issachar Zebulun Joseph Benjamin David
　Solomon
Paul Constantine Charlemaine Luther Milton
These [*were their*] are our daughters Ocalythron
　Elynittria Oothoon Leutha
Elythiria Enanto Manathu Vorcyon Ethinthus Moab
　Midian
Adah Zillah Caina Naamah Tamar Rahab Tirzah Mary
And myriads more of Sons & Daughters to whom [*their*]
　our love increasd　　10

To each according to the multiplication of their
　multitudes

But Satan accusd Palamabron before [*Los*] his brethren
  also he maddend
The horses of palambrons harrow wherefor Rintrah &
  Palamabron
Cut him off from Golgonooza. But Enitharmon in tears
Wept over him Created him a Space closd with a tender
  moon
And he rolld down beneath the fires of Orc a Globe
  immense
Crusted with snow in a dim void. here by the Arts of
  Urizen
He tempted many of the Sons & Daughters of Los to flee
Away from [*Los*] Me first Reuben fled then Simeon then
  Levi then Judah
Then Dan then Naphtali then Gad then Asher then
  Issachar   20
Then Zebulun then Joseph then Benjamin twelve sons of
  Los
And this is the manner in which Satan became the
  Tempter

There is a State namd Satan learn distinct to know O
  [*Mortals*] Rahab
The Difference between States & Individuals of those
  States
The State namd Satan never can be redeemd in all
  Eternity
But when Luvah in Orc became a Serpent he
  des[c]ended into
That State calld Satan Enitharmon breathd forth on the
  Winds
Of Golgonooza her well beloved knowing he was Orc's
  human remains
She tenderly lovd him above all his brethren he grew up
In mothers tenderness The Enormous worlds rolling in
  Urizens power   30
Must have given Satan by these mild arts Dominion over
  all

Wherefore [*Rintrah &*] Palamabron being accusd by
    Satan to Los
Calld down a Great Solemn assembly Rintrah in fury &
    fire
Defended Palamabron & rage filld the Universal Tent

Because Palamabron was good naturd Satan supposd he
    feard him
And Satan not having the Science of Wrath but only of
    Pity
Was soon condemnd & wrath was left to wrath & Pity
    to Pity
Rintrah & Palamabron Cut sheer off from Golgonooza
Enitharmons Moony space & in it Satan & his
    companions
They rolld down a dim world Crusted with Snow deadly
    & dark   40

Jerusalem pitying them wove them mantles of life &
    death
Times after times And those in Eden sent Lucifer for
    their Guard
Lucifer refusd to die for Satan & in pride he forsook his
    charge
Then they sent Molech Molech was impatient They sent
Molech impatient They Sent Elohim who created Adam
To die for Satan Adam refusd but was compelld to die
By Satans arts. Then the Eternals Sent Shaddai
Shaddai was angry Pachad descended Pachad was
    terrified
And then they Sent Jehovah who leprous stretchd his
    hand to Eternity
Then Jesus Came & Died willing beneath Tirzah &
    Rahab   50
Thou art that Rahab Lo the Tomb what can we purpose
    more

PAGE 116

Lo Enitharmon terrible & beautiful in Eternal youth
Bow down before her you children & set Jerusalem free

Rahab burning with pride & revenge departed from Los
Los dropd a tear at her departure but he wipd it away
    in hope
She went to Urizen in pride the Prince of Light beheld
Reveald before the face of heaven his secret holiness

PAGE 106 (SECOND PORTION)
Darkness & sorrow coverd all flesh Eternity was
    darkend

Urizen sitting in his web of dece[i]tful Religion [*was
    ?darkend*]
[*He*] felt the female death a dull & numming stupor such
    as neer   30
Before assaulted the bright human form he felt his pores
Drink in the deadly dull delusion horrors of Eternal
    death
Shot thro him Urizen sat Stonied upon his rock
Forgetful of his own Laws pitying he began to Embrace
The Shadowy Female since life cannot be quenchd Life
    exuded
His eyes shot outwards then his breathing nostrils drawn
    forth
Scales coverd over a cold forehead & a neck outstretchd
Into the deep to sieze the shadow scales his neck &
    bosom
Coverd & scales his hands & feet upon his belly falling
Outstretchd [*over*] thro the immense his mouth wide
    opening tongueless   40
His teeth a triple row he strove to sieze the shadow in
    vain
And his immense tail lashd the Abyss his human form a
    Stone
A form of Senseless Stone remaind in terrors on the rock
Abominable to the eyes of mortals who explore his books
His wisdom still remaind & all his memory stord with woe

And still his stony form remaind in the Abyss immense
Like the pale visage in its sheet of lead that cannot follow

Incessant stern disdain his scaly form gnaws inwardly
With deep repentance for the loss of that fair form of
    Man
With Envy he saw Los with Envy Tharmas &
    [*Urthona*] the Spectre   50
With Envy & in vain he swam around his stony form

No longer now Erect the King of Light outstretchd in
    fury
Lashes his tail in the [*wide*] wild deep his Eyelids like the
    Sun
Arising in his pride enlighten all the Grizly deeps
His scales transparent give forth light like windows of the
    morning
His neck flames with wrath & majesty he lashes the
    Abyss
Beating the Desarts & the rocks the desarts feel his
    power
They shake their slumbers off. They wave in awful fear
Calling the Lion & the Tyger the horse & the wild Stag
PAGE 107
The Elephant the wolf the Bear the Lamia the Satyr
His Eyelids give their light around his folding tail aspires
Among the stars the Earth & all the Abysses feel h[i]s
    fury
When as the snow covers the mountains oft petrific
    hardness
Covers the deeps at his vast fury mo[a]ning in his rock
Hardens the Lion & the Bear trembling in the Solid
    mountain
They view the light & wonder crying out in terrible
    existence
Up bound the wild stag & the horse behold the King of
    Pride

Oft doth his Eye emerge from the Abyss into the realms
Of his Eternal day & memory strives to augment his
    ruthfulness   10

Then weeping he descends in wrath drawing all things
    in his fury
Into obedience to his will & now he finds in vain
That not of his own power he bore the human form
    erect
Nor of his own will gave his Laws in times of Everlasting
For now fierce Orc in wrath & fury rises into the heavens
A King of wrath & fury a dark enraged horror
And Urizen repentant forgets his wisdom in the abyss
In forms of priesthood in the dark delusions of repentance
Repining in his heart & spirit that Orc reignd over all
And that his wisdom servd but to augment the
    indefinite lust   20

Then Tharmas & Urthona felt the stony stupor rise
Into their limbs Urthona shot forth a Vast Fibrous form
Tharmas like a pillar of sand rolld round by the
    whirlwind
An animated Pillar rolling round & round in incessant
    rage

Los felt the stony stupor & his head rolld down beneath
Into the Abysses of his bosom the vessels of his blood
Dart forth upon the wind in pipes writhing about in the
    Abyss
And Enitharmon pale & cold in milky juices flowd
Into a form of Vegetation living having a voice
Moving in rootlike fibres trembling in fear upon the
    Earth   30

And Tharmas gave his Power to Los Urthona gave his
    strength
Into the youthful prophet for the Love of Enitharmon
And of the nameless Shadowy female in the nether deep
And for the dread of the dark terrors of Orc & Urizen

Thus in a living Death the nameless shadow all things
    bound
All mortal things made permanent that they may be put
    off

Time after time by the Divine Lamb who died for all
And all in him died. & he put off all mortality

PAGE 108
Tharmas [*above*] on high rode furious thro the afflicted
    worlds
Pursuing the Vain Shadow of Hope fleeing from identity
In abstract false Expanses that he may not hear the
    Voice
Of Ahania wailing on the winds in vain he flies for still
The voice incessant calls on all the children of Men
For she spoke of all in heaven & all upon the Earth
Saw not as yet the Divine vision her Eyes are Toward
    Urizen
And thus Ahania cries aloud to the Caverns of the
    Grave

Will you keep a flock of wolves & lead them will you take
    the wintry blast
For a covering to your limbs or the summer pestilence
    for a tent to abide in   10
Will you erect a lasting habitation in the mouldering
    Church yard
Or a pillar & palace of Eternity in the jaws of the
    hungry grave
Will you seek pleasure from the festering wound or
    marry for a Wife
The ancient Leprosy that the King & Priest may still
    feast on your decay
And the grave mock & laugh at the plowd field saying

I am the nourisher thou the destroyer in my bosom is
    milk & wine
And a fountain from my breasts to me come all
    multitudes
To my breath they obey they worship me I am a
    goddess & queen
But listen to Ahania O ye sons of the Murderd one
Listen to her whose memory beholds your ancient days   20

Listen to her whose eyes behold the dark body of
  corruptible death
Looking for Urizen in vain. in vain I seek for morning
The Eternal Man sleeps in the Earth nor feels the
  vigrous sun
Nor silent moon nor all the hosts of heaven move in his
  body
His fiery halls are dark & round his limbs the Serpent
  Orc
Fold without fold encompasses him And his corrupting
  members
Vomit out the Scaly monsters of the restless deep

They come up in the rivers & annoy the nether parts
Of Man who lays upon the shores leaning his faded head
Upon the Oozy rock inwrapped with the weeds of death   30
His eyes sink hollow in his head his flesh coverd with
  slime
And shrunk up to the bones alas that Man should come
  to this
His strong bones beat with snows & hid within the caves
  of night
Marrowless bloodless falling into dust driven by the
  winds
O how the horrors of Eternal Death take hold on Man
His faint groans shake the caves & issue thro the
  desolate rocks
PAGE 109
And the Strong Eagle now with num[m]ing cold
  blighted of feathers
Once like the pride of the sun now flagging in cold night
Hovers with blasted wings aloft watching with Eager
  Eye
Till Man shall leave a corruptible body he famishd hears
  him groan
And now he fixes his strong talons in the pointed rock
And now he beats the heavy air with his enormous wings
Beside him lies the Lion dead & in his belly worms

Feast on his death till universal death devours all
And the pale horse seeks for the pool to lie him down &
     die
But finds the pools filled with serpents devouring one
     another   10
He droops his head & trembling stands & his bright eyes
     decay
These are the Visions of My Eyes the Visions of Ahania

Thus cries ahania Enion replies from the Caverns of the
     Grave

Fear not O poor forsaken one O land of briars & thorns
Where once the Olive flourishd & the Cedar spread his
     wings
Once I waild desolate like thee my fallow fields in fear
Cried to the Churchyards & the Earthworm came in
     dismal state
I found him in my bosom & I said the time of Love
Appears upon the rocks & hills in silent shades but   soon
A voice came in the night a midnight cry upon the
     mountains   20
Awake the bridegroom cometh I awoke to sleep no more
But an Eternal Consummation is dark Enion
The watry Grave. O thou Corn field O thou Vegetater
     happy
More happy is the dark consumer hope drowns all my
     torment
For I am now surrounded by a shadowy vortex drawing
The Spectre quite away from Enion that I die a death
Of better hope altho I consume in these raging waters
The furrowd field replies to the grave I hear her reply to
     me
Behold the time approaches fast that thou shalt be as a
     thing
Forgotten when one speaks of thee he will not be
     believd   30
When the man gently fades away in his immortality

When the mortal disappears in improved knowledge cast
away
The former things so shall the Mortal gently fade away
And so become invisible to those who still remain
Listen I will tell thee what is done in the caverns of the
grave
PAGE 110 (FIRST PORTION)
The Lamb of God has rent the Veil of Mystery soon to
return
In Clouds & Fires around the rock & the Mysterious tree
As the seed waits Eagerly watching for its flower & fruit
Anxious its little soul looks out into the clear expanse
To see if hungry winds are abroad with their invisible
army
So Man looks out in tree & herb & fish & bird & beast
Collecting up the scatterd portions of his immortal body
Into the Elemental forms of every thing that grows
He tries the sullen north wind riding on its angry
furrows
The sultry south when the sun rises & the angry east   10
When the sun sets when the clods harden & the cattle
stand
Drooping & the birds hide in their silent nests. he stores
his thoughts
As in a store house in his memory he regulates the forms
Of all beneath & all above   & in the gentle West
Reposes where the Suns heat dwells   he rises to the Sun
And to the Planets of the Night & to the stars that gild
The Zodiac & the stars that sullen stand to north &
south
He touches the remotest pole & in the Center weeps
That Man should Labour & sorrow & learn & forget &
return
To the dark valley whence he came to begin his labours
anew   20
In pain he sighs in pain he labours in his universe
Screaming in birds over the deep & howling in the Wolf
Over the slain & moaning in the cattle & in the winds

And weeping over Orc & Urizen in clouds & [*dismal*]
  flaming fires
And in the cries of birth & in the groans of death his
  voice
Is heard throughout the Universe whereever a grass
  grows
Or a leaf buds   The Eternal Man is seen is heard   is
  felt
And all his Sorrows till he reassumes his ancient bliss
Such are the words of Ahania & Enion. Los hears &
  weeps

[The End of the Eighth Night]

[But Rahab (built) hewd a Sepulcher in the Rock of
  Eternity   30
And placing in the Sepulcher the body which she had taken
From the divine Lamb wept over the Sepulcher weaving
Her web of Religion around the Sepulcher times after times
  beside Jerusalems Gate
But as she wove behold the bottom of the Sepulcher
Rent & a door was opend thro the bottom of the
  Sepulcher
Into Eternity And as she wove she heard a Voice behind her
  calling her
She turnd & saw the Divine Vision & her]
And Los & Enitharmon took the Body of the Lamb
Down from the Cross & placd it in a Sepulcher which
  Los had hewn
For himself in the Rock of Eternity trembling & in
  despair   40
Jerusalem wept over the Sepulcher two thousand Years

[End of the Eighth Night]

PAGE 111
Rahab triumphs over all she took Jerusalem
Captive A Willing Captive by delusive arts impelld
To worship Urizens Dragon form to offer her own
  Children

Upon the bloody Altar. John Saw these things Reveald
in Heaven
On Patmos Isle & heard the Souls cry out to be
deliverd
He saw the Harlot of the Kings of Earth & saw her Cup
Of fornication food of Orc & Satan pressd from the fruit
of Mystery
But when she saw the form of Ahania weeping on the
Void
And heard Enions voice sound from the caverns of the
Grave
No more spirit remain in her She secretly left the
Synagogue of Satan   10
She commund with Orc in secret She hid him with the
flax
That Enitharmon had numberd away from the Heavens
She gatherd it together to consume her Harlot Robes
In bitterest Contrition sometimes Self condemning
repentant
And Sometimes kissing her Robes & Jewels & weeping
over them
Sometimes returning to the Synagogue of Satan in Pride
And Sometimes weeping before Orc in humility &
trembling
The Synagogue of Satan therefore uniting against
Mystery
Satan divided against Satan resolvd in open Sanhedrim
To burn Mystery with fire & form another from her
ashes   20
For God put it into their heart to fulfill all his will

The Ashes of Mystery began to animate they calld it
Deism
And Natural Religion as of old so now anew began
Babylon again in Infancy Calld Natural Religion

PAGE 117

VALA

NIGHT THE NINTH
BEING THE LAST JUDGMENT

And Los & Enitharmon builded Jerusalem weeping
Over the Sepulcher & over the Crucified body
Which to their Phantom Eyes appear'd Still in the
  Sepulcher
But Jesus stood beside them in the Spirit Separating
Their Spirit from their body. Terrified at Non
  Existence
For such they deemd the death of the body. Los his
  vegetable hands
Outstretchd his right hand branching out in fibrous
  strength
Siezd the Sun. His left hand like dark roots coverd the
  Moon
And tore them down cracking the heavens across from
  immense to immense
Then fell the fires of Eternity with loud & shrill   10
Sound of Loud Trumpet thundering along from heaven
  to heaven
A mighty sound articulate Awake ye dead & come
To Judgment from the four winds Awake & Come
  away
Folding like scrolls of the Enormous volume of Heaven
  & Earth
With thunderous noise & dreadful shakings rocking to &
  fro
The heavens are shaken & the Earth removed from its
  place
The foundations of the Eternal hills discoverd
The thrones of Kings are shaken they have lost their
  robes & crowns

The poor smite their opressors they awake up to the
  harvest
The naked warriors rush together down to the sea shore   20
Trembling before the multitudes of slaves now set at
  liberty
They are become like wintry flocks like forests stripd of
  leaves
The opressed pursue like the wind there is no room for
  escape
The Spectre of Enitharmon let loose on the troubled
  deep
Waild shrill in the confusion & the Spectre of Urthona
PAGE 118
Recievd her in the darkning South their bodies lost they
  stood
Trembling & weak a faint embrace a fierce desire as
  when
Two shadows mingle on a wall they wail & shadowy
  tears
Fell down & shadowy forms of joy mixd with despair &
  grief
Their bodies buried in the ruins of the Universe
Mingled with the confusion. Who shall call them from
  the Grave

Rahab & Tirzah wail aloud in the wild flames they give
  up themselves to Consummation

The books of Urizen unroll with dreadful noise the
  folding Serpent
Of Orc began to Consume in fierce raving fire his fierce
  flames
Issud on all sides gathring strength in animating
  volumes   10
Roaming abroad on all the winds raging intense
  reddening
Into resistless pillars of fire rolling round & round
  gathering

Strength from the Earths consumd & heavens & all
hidden abysses
Wherever the Eagle has Explord or Lion or Tyger trod
Or where the Comets of the night or stars of [*eternal*]
asterial day
Have shot their arrows or long beamed spears in wrath
& fury

And all the while the trumpet sounds [*Awake ye dead &
come
To Judgment.*] from the clotted gore & from the hollow
den
Start forth the trembling millions into flames of mental
fire
Bathing their limbs in the bright visions of Eternity

Then like the doves from pillars of Smoke the trembling
families   20
Of women & children throughout every nation under
heaven
Cling round the men in bands of twenties & of fifties
pale
As snow that falls around a leafless tree upon the green
Their opressors are falln they have Stricken them they
awake to life
Yet pale the just man stands erect & looking up to
heavn
Trembling & strucken by the Universal stroke the trees
unroot
The rocks groan horrible & run about. The mountains &
Their rivers cry with a dismal cry   the cattle gather
together
Lowing they kneel before the heavens. the wild beasts of
the forests
Tremble the Lion shuddering asks the Leopard. Feelest
thou   30
The dread I feel unknown before My voice refuses to
roar
And in weak moans I speak to thee This night

Before the mornings dawn the Eagle calld the Vulture
The Raven calld the hawk I heard them from my forests
    black
Saying Let us go up far for soon I smell upon the wind
A terror coming from the South. The Eagle & Hawk
    fled away
At dawn & Eer the sun arose the raven & Vulture
    followd
Let us flee also to the north. They fled. The Sons oɪ
    Men
Saw them depart in dismal droves. The trumpet sounded
    loud
And all the Sons of Eternity Descended into Beulah   40

PAGE 119
[*Vala*
Night the Ninth
Being The Last Judgment]
In the fierce flames the limbs of Mystery lay consuming
    with howling
And deep despair. Rattling go up the flames around the
    Synagogue
Of Satan   Loud the Serpent Orc ragd thro his twenty
    Seven
Folds. The tree of Mystery went up in folding flames
Blood issud out in mighty volumes pouring in whirlpools
    fierce
From out the flood gates of the Sky The Gates are
    burst down pour
The torrents black upon the Earth the blood pours down
    incessant
Kings in their palaces lie drownd Shepherds their flocks
    their tents
Roll down the mountains in black torrents Cities
    Villages
High spires & Castles drownd in the black deluge Shoal
    on Shoal   10

Float the dead carcases of Men & Beasts driven to & fro
  on waves
Of foaming blood beneath the black incessant Sky till all
Mysterys tyrants are cut off & not one left on Earth

And when all Tyranny was cut off from the face of
  Earth
Around the Dragon form of Urizen & round his stony
  form
The flames rolling intense thro the wide Universe
[*Began to draw near to the Earth*] Began to Enter the
  Holy City   Entring the dismal clouds
In furrowd lightnings break their way the wild flames
  ?whirling up
The Bloody Deluge living flames winged with intellect
And Reason round the Earth they march in order flame
  by flame   20
From the clotted gore & from the hollow den
Start forth the trembling millions into flames of mental
  fire
Bathing their Limbs in the bright visions of Eternity

[*without*] Beyond this Universal Confusion beyond the
  remotest Pole
Where their vortexes begin to operate there stands
A Horrible rock far in the South   it was forsaken when
Urizen gave the horses of Light into the hands of Luvah
On this rock lay the faded head of the Eternal Man
Enwrapped round with weeds of death pale cold in
  sorrow & woe
He lifts the blue lamps of his Eyes & cries with heavenly
  voice   30
Bowing his head over the consuming Universe he cried

O weakness & O weariness   O war within my members
My sons exiled from my breast pass to & fro before me
My birds are silent on my hills flocks die beneath my
  branches
My tents are fallen my trumpets & the sweet sounds of
  my harp

Is silent on my clouded hills that belch forth storms &
    fires
My milk of cows & honey of bees & fruit of golden
    harvest
Are gatherd in the scorching heat & in the driving rain
My robe is turned to confusion & my bright gold to
    stones
Where once I sat   I weary walk in misery & pain   40
For from within my [*narrow*] witherd breast grown
    narrow with my woes
The Corn is turnd to thistles & the apples into poison
The birds of song to murderous crows My joys to bitter
    groans
PAGE 120
The voices of children in my tents to cries of helpless
    infants
And all exiled from the face of light & shine of morning
In this dark world a narrow house I wander up & down
I hear Mystery howling in these flames of Consummation
When shall the Man of future times become as in days of
    old
O weary life why sit I here & give up all my powers
To indolence to the night of death when indolence &
    mourning
Sit hovring over my dark threshold. tho I arise look out
And scorn the war within my members yet my heart is
    weak
And my head faint Yet will I look again unto the
    morning   10
Whence is this sound of rage of Men drinking each
    others blood
Drunk with the smoking gore & red but not with
    nourishing wine

The Eternal Man sat on the Rocks & cried with awful
    voice

O Prince of Light where art thou I behold thee not as
    once

In those Eternal fields in clouds of morning stepping
    forth
With harps & songs where bright Ahania sang before thy
    face
And all thy sons & daughters gatherd round my ample
    table
See you not all this wracking furious confusion
Come forth from slumbers of thy cold abstraction come
    forth
Arise to Eternal births shake off thy cold repose   20
Schoolmaster of souls great opposer of change arise
That the Eternal worlds may see thy face in peace & joy
That thou dread form of Certainty maist sit in town &
    village
While little children play around thy feet in gentle awe
Fearing thy frown loving thy smile O Urizen Prince of
    light

He calld the deep buried his voice & answer none
    returnd
Then wrath burst round the Eternal Man was wrath
    again he cried

Arise O stony form of death O dragon of the Deeps
Lie down before my feet O Dragon let Urizen arise
O how couldst thou deform those beautiful proportions   30
Of life & person for as the Person so is his life
    proportiond
Let Luvah rage in the dark deep even to Consummation
For if thou feedest not his rage it will subside in peace
But if thou darest obstinate refuse my stern behest
Thy crown & scepter I will sieze & regulate all my
    members
In stern severity & cast thee out into the indefinite
Where nothing lives, there to wander. & if thou returnst
    weary
Weeping at the threshold of Existence I will steel my
    heart
Against thee to Eternity & never recieve thee more

Thy self destroying beast formd Science shall be thy
    eternal lot   40
My anger against thee is greater than against this Luvah
For war is [*honest*] energy Enslavd but thy religion
The first author of this war & the distracting of honest
    minds
Into confused perturbation & strife & honour & pride
Is a deceit so detestable that I will cast thee out
If thou repentest not & leave thee as a rotten branch to
    be burnd
With Mystery the Harlot & with Satan for Ever & Ever
Error can never be redeemd in all Eternity
But Sin Even Rahab is redeemd in blood & fury &
    jealousy
That line of blood that stretchd across the windows of
    the morning   50
Redeemd from Errors power. Wake thou dragon of the
    Deeps

PAGE 121
Urizen wept in the dark deep anxious his Scaly form
To reassume the human & he wept in the dark deep

Saying O that I had never drank the wine nor eat the
    bread
Of dark mortality nor cast my view into the [*past*]
    futurity nor turnd
My back darkning the present clouding with a cloud
And building arches high & cities turrets & [*high*]
    towers & domes
Whose smoke destroyd the pleasant garden & whose
    running Kennels
Chokd the bright rivers burdning with my Ships the
    angry deep
Thro Chaos seeking for delight & in spaces remote
Seeking the Eternal which is always present to the wise   10
Seeking for pleasure which unsought falls round the
    infants path

And on the fleeces of mild flocks who neither care nor
   labour
But I the labourer of ages whose unwearied hands
Are thus deformd with hardness with the [*?plow*] sword
   & with the spear
And with the Chisel & the mallet I whose labours vast
Order the nations separating family by family
Alone enjoy not   I alone in misery supreme
Ungratified give all my joy unto this Luvah & Vala
Then Go O dark [*remembrance*] futurity I will cast thee
   forth from these
Heavens of my brain nor will I look upon
   [*remembrance*] futurity more   20
I cast [*remembrance*] futurity away & turn my back upon
   that void
Which I have made for lo futurity is in this moment
Let Orc consume let Tharmas rage let dark Urthona give
All strength to Los & Enitharmon & let Los self cursd
Rend down this fabric as a wall ruind & family extinct
Rage Orc Rage Tharmas Urizen no longer curbs your
   rage

So Urizen spoke he shook his snows from off his
   Shoulders & arose
As on a Pyramid of mist his white robes scattering
The fleecy white renewd he shook his aged mantles off
Into the fires Then glorious bright Exulting in his joy   30
He sounding rose into the heavens in naked majesty
In radiant Youth. when Lo like garlands in the Eastern
   sky
When vocal may comes dancing from the East Ahania
   came
Exulting in her flight as when a bubble rises up
On to the surface of a lake. Ahania rose in joy
Excess of Joy is worse than grief – her heart beat high
   her blood
Burst its bright Vessels She fell down dead at the feet
   of Urizen

Outstretchd a Smiling corse they buried her in a silent
  cave
Urizen dropt a tear the Eternal Man Darkend with
  sorrow

The three daughters of Urizen guard Ahanias Death
  couch   40
Rising from the confusion in tears & howlings & despair
Calling upon their fathers Name upon their Rivers dark

And the Eternal Man Said Hear my [*voice*] words O
  Prince of Light

PAGE 122

Behold Jerusalem in whose bosom the Lamb of God
Is seen tho slain before her Gates he self renewd
  remains
Eternal & I thro him awake from deaths dark vale
The times revolve the time is coming when all these
  delights
Shall be renewd & all these Elements that now consume
Shall reflourish. Then bright Ahania shall awake from
  death
A glorious Vision [*of*] to thine Eyes a Self renewing
  Vision
The spring. the summer to be thine then sleep the
  wintry days
In silken garments spun by her own hands against her
  funeral
The winter thou shalt plow & lay thy stores into thy
  barns   10
Expecting to recieve Ahania in the spring with joy
Immortal thou. Regenerate She & all the lovely Sex
From her shall learn obedience & prepare for a wintry
  grave
That spring may see them rise in tenfold joy & sweet
  delight
Thus shall the male & female live the life of Eternity
Because the Lamb of God Creates himself a bride &
  wife

That we his Children evermore may live in Jerusalem
Which now descendeth out of heaven a City yet a
    Woman
Mother of myriads redeemd & born in her spiritual
    palaces
By a New Spiritual birth Regenerated from Death   20

Urizen said. I have Erred & my Error remains with me
What Chain encompasses in what Lock is the river of
    light confind
That issues forth in the morning by measure & the
    evening by carefulness
Where shall we take our stand to view the infinite &
    unbounded
Or where are human feet for Lo our eyes are in the
    heavens

He ceasd for rivn link from link the bursting Universe
    explodes
All things reversd flew from their centers rattling bones
    [*to bones*]
To bones Join, shaking convulsd the shivering clay
    breathes
Each speck of dust to the Earths center nestles round &
    round
In pangs of an Eternal Birth in torment & awe & fear   30
All spirits deceasd let loose from reptile prisons come in
    shoals
Wild furies from the tygers brain & from the lions Eyes
And from the ox & ass come moping terrors. from the
    Eagle
And raven numerous as the leaves of autumn   every
    species
Flock to the trumpet muttring over the sides of the grave
    & crying
In the fierce wind round heaving rocks & mountains filld
    with groans
On rifted rocks suspended in the air by inward fires
Many a woful company & many on clouds & waters

Fathers & friends Mothers & Infants Kings & Warriors
Priests & chaind Captives met together in a horrible fear   40
And every one of the dead appears as he had livd before
PAGE 123
And all the marks remain of the slaves scourge & tyrants
   Crown
And of the Priests oergorged Abdomen & of the
   merchants thin
Sinewy deception & of the warriors ou[t]braving &
   thoughtlessness
In lineaments too extended & in bones too strait & long

They shew their wounds they accuse they sieze the
   opressor howlings began
On the golden palace Songs & joy on the desart the Cold
   babe
Stands in the furious air he cries the children of six
   thousand years
Who died in infancy rage furious a mighty multitude rage
   furious
Naked & pale standing on the expecting air to be
   deliverd
Rend limb from limb the Warrior & the tyrant reuniting
   in pain   10
The furious wind still rends around they flee in sluggish
   effort

They beg they intreat in vain now they Listend not to
   intreaty
They view the flames red rolling on thro the wide
   universe
From the [*black*] dark jaws of death beneath & desolate
   shores remote
These covering Vaults of heaven & these trembling
   globes of Earth
One Planet [*cries*] calls to another & one star enquires of
   another
What flames are these coming from the South what
   noise what dreadful rout

As of a battle in the heavens hark heard you not the
 'trumpet
As of fierce battle While they spoke the flames come on
  intense roaring

They see him whom they have piercd they wail because
  of him   20
They magnify themselves no more against Jerusalem Nor
Against her little ones the innocent accused before the
  Judges
Shines with immortal Glory trembling the Judge springs
  from his throne
Hiding his face in the dust beneath the prisoners feet &
  saying
Brother of Jesus what have I done intreat thy lord for me
Perhaps I may be forgiven While he speaks the flames
  roll on

And after the flames appears the Cloud of the Son of
  Man
Descending from Jerusalem with power and great Glory
All nations look up to the Cloud & behold him who was
  Crucified

The Prisoner answers you scourgd my father to death
  before my face   30
While I stood bound with cords & heavy chains. your
  hipocrisy
Shall now avail you nought. So speaking he dashd him
  with his foot

The Cloud is Blood dazling upon the heavens & in the
  cloud
Above upon its volumes is beheld [as] a throne & [as] a
  pavement
Of precious stones. surrounded by twenty four venerable
  patriarchs
And these again surrounded [of] by four Wonders of the
  Almighty
Incomprehensible. pervading all amidst & round about

Fourfold each in the other reflected they are named
    Life's in Eternity
Four Starry Universes going forward from Eternity to
    Eternity
And the Falln Man who was arisen upon the Rock of
    Ages   40
PAGE 124
Beheld the Vision of God & he arose up from the Rock
And Urizen arose up with him walking thro the flames
To meet the Lord coming to Judgment but the flames
    repelld them
Still to the Rock in vain they strove to Enter the
    Consummation
Together for the [*Fallen*] Redeemd Man could not enter
    the Consummation

Then siezd the Sons of Urizen the Plow they polishd it
From rust of ages all its ornaments of Gold & silver &
    ivory
Reshone across the field immense where all the nations
Darkend like Mould in the divided fallows where the
    weed
Triumphs in its own destruction they took down the
    harness   10
From the blue walls of heaven starry jingling ornamented
With beautiful art the study of angels the workmanship
    of Demons
When Heaven & Hell in Emulation strove in sports of
    Glory

The noise of rural work resounded thro the heavens of
    heavens
The horse[s] neigh from the battle the wild bulls from
    the sultry waste
The tygers from the forests & the lions [*of*] from the
    sandy desarts
They Sing they sieze the instruments of harmony they
    throw away

The spear the bow the gun the mortar they level the
    fortifications
They beat the iron engines of destruction into wedges
They give them to Urthonas Sons ringing the hammers
    sound   20
In dens of death to forge the spade the mattock & the ax
The heavy roller to break the clods to pass over the
    nations

The Sons of Urizen Shout Their father rose The
    Eternal horses
Harnessd They calld to Urizen the heavens moved at
    their call
The limbs of Urizen shone with ardor. [*he rose up from
the Rock.*

The Fallen Man wondring beheld] He laid his ha[n]d on
    the Plow
Thro dismal darkness drave the Plow of ages over Cities
And all their Villages over Mountains & all their Vallies
Over the graves & caverns of the dead   Over the Planets
And over the void Spaces over Sun & moon & star &
    constellation

Then Urizen commanded & they brought the Seed of
    Men   30
The trembling souls of All the Dead stood before
    Urizen
Weak wailing in the troubled air East west & north &
    south
PAGE 125
He turnd the horses loose & laid his Plow in the
    northern corner
Of the wide Universal field. then Stepd [*out*] forth into
    the immense

Then he began to sow the seed he girded round his
    loins
With a bright girdle & his skirt filld with immortal souls

Howling & Wailing fly the souls from Urizens strong
  hand

For from the hand of Urizen the myriads fall like stars
Into their own appointed places driven back by the
  winds
The naked warriors rush together down to the sea shores
They are become like wintry flocks like forests stripd of
  leaves
The Kings & Princes of the Earth cry with a feeble cry   10
Driven on the unproducing sands & on the hardend
  rocks
And all the while the flames of Orc follow the ventrous
  feet
Of Urizen & all the while the Trump of Tharmas sounds
Weeping & wailing fly the souls from Urizens strong
  hand
The daughters of Urizen stand with Cups & measures of
  foaming wine
Immense upon the heavens with bread & delicate repasts

Then follows the golden harrow in the midst of Mental
  fires
To ravishing melody of flutes & harps & softest voice
The seed is harrowd in while flames heat the black
  mould & cause
The human harvest to begin Towards the south first
  sprang   20
The myriads & in silent fear they look out from their
  graves

Then Urizen sits down to rest & all his wearied Sons
Take their repose on beds they drink they sing they view
  the flames
Of Orc in joy they view the human harvest springing up
A time they give to sweet repose till all the harvest is ripe

And Lo like the harvest Moon Ahania cast off her death
  clothes

She folded them up in care in silence & her brightning
  limbs
Bathd in the clear spring of the rock then from her
  darksom cave
Issud in majesty divine   Urizen rose up from his couch
On wings of tenfold joy clapping his hands his feet his
  radiant wings
In the immense as when the Sun dances upon the
  mountains
A shout of jubilee in lovely notes responding from
  daughter to daughter
From son to Son as if the Stars beaming innumerable
Thro night should sing soft warbling filling Earth &
  heaven
And bright Ahania took her seat by Urizen in songs & joy

The Eternal Man also sat down upon the Couches of
  Beulah
Sorrowful that he could not put off his new risen body
In mental flames the flames refusd they drove him back
  to Beulah
His body was redeemd to be permanent thro Mercy
  Divine

PAGE 126
And now fierce Orc had quite consumd himself in
  Mental flames
Expending all his energy against the fuel of fire
The [*Ancient Man*] Regenerate Man stoopd his head
  over the Universe & in
His holy hands recievd the flaming Demon & Demoness
  of Smoke
And gave them to Urizens hands the Immortal frownd
  Saying

Luvah & Vala henceforth you are Servants obey & live
You shall forget your former state return O Love in peace
Into your place the place of seed not in the brain or
  heart

30

If Gods combine against Man Setting their Dominion
   above
The Human form Divine. Thrown down from their high
   Station   10
In the Eternal heavens of Human [*Thought*] Imagination:
   buried beneath
In dark oblivion with incessant pangs ages on ages
In Enmity & war first weakend then in stern repentance
They must renew their brightness & their disorganizd
   functions
Again reorganize till they resume the image of the
   human
Cooperating in the bliss of Man obeying his Will
Servants to the infinite & Eternal of the Human form

Luvah & Vala descended & enterd the Gates of Dark
   Urthona
And walkd from the hands of Urizen in the shadows of
   Valas Garden
Where the impressions of Despair & Hope for ever
   vegetate   20
In flowers in fruits in fishes birds & beasts & clouds &
   waters
The land of doubts & shadows sweet delusions unformd
   hopes
They saw no more the terrible confusion of the wracking
   universe
They heard not saw not felt not all the terrible confusion
For in their orbed senses within closd up they wanderd
   at will
And those upon the Couches viewd them in the dreams
   of Beulah
As they reposd from the terrible wide universal harvest
Invisible Luvah in bright clouds hoverd over Valas head
And thus their ancient golden age renewd for Luvah
   spoke
With voice mild from his golden Cloud upon the breath
   of morning   30

Come forth O Vala from the grass & from the silent Dew
Rise from the dews of death for the Eternal Man is
    Risen

She rises among flowers & looks toward the Eastern
    clearness
She walks yea runs her feet are wingd on the tops of the
    bending grass
Her garments rejoice in the vocal wind & her hair
    glistens with dew

She answerd thus Whose voice is this in the voice of the
    nourishing air
In the spirit of the morning awaking the Soul from its
    grassy bed
PAGE 127
Where dost thou dwell for it is thee I seek & but for
    thee
I must have slept Eternally nor have felt the dew of thy
    morning
Look how the opening dawn advances with vocal
    harmony
Look how the beams foreshew the rising of some
    glorious power
The sun is thine [*when*] he goeth forth in his majestic
    brightness
O thou creating voice that callest & who shall answer
    thee

Where dost thou flee O fair one where dost thou seek thy
    happy place

To yonder brightness there I haste for sure I came from
    thence
Or I must have slept eternally nor have felt the dew of
    morning

Eternally thou must have slept nor have felt the
    morning dew
But for yon nourishing sun tis that by which thou art
    arisen

10

The birds adore the sun the beasts rise up & play in his
    beams
And every flower & every leaf rejoices in his light
Then O thou fair one sit thee down for thou art as the
    grass
Thou risest in the dew of morning & at night art folded
    up

Alas am I but as a flower then will I sit me down
Then will I weep then Ill complain & sigh for
    immortality
And chide my maker thee O Sun that raisedst me to fall

So saying she sat down & wept beneath the apple trees

O be thou blotted out thou Sun that raisedst me to
    trouble   20
That gavest me a heart to crave & raisedst me thy
    phantom
To feel thy heat & see thy light & wander here alone
Hopeless if I am like the grass & so shall pass away

Rise sluggish Soul why sitst thou here why dost thou sit
    & weep
Yon Sun shall wax old & decay but thou shalt ever
    flourish
The fruit shall ripen & fall down & the flowers consume
    away
But thou shalt still survive arise O dry thy dewy tears

Hah! Shall I still survive whence came that sweet &
    comforting voice
And whence that voice of sorrow O sun thou art nothing
    now to me
Go on thy course rejoicing & let us both rejoice together   30
I walk among his flocks & hear the bleating of his lambs
O that I could behold his face & follow his pure feet
I walk by the footsteps of his flocks come hither tender
    flocks
Can you converse with a pure Soul that seeketh for her
    maker

You answer not then am I set your mistress in this
    garden
Ill watch you & attend your footsteps you are not like
    the birds

PAGE 128

That sing & fly in the bright air but you do lick my feet
And let me touch your wooly backs   follow me as I sing
For in my bosom a new song arises to my Lord

Rise up O Sun most glorious minister & light of day
Flow on ye gentle airs & bear the voice of my rejoicing
Wave freshly clear waters flowing around the tender grass
And thou sweet smelling ground put forth thy life
    in fruits & flowers
Follow me O my flocks & hear me sing my rapturous
    Song
I will cause my voice to be heard on the clouds that
    glitter in the sun
I will call & who shall answer me   I will sing   who
    shall reply   10
For from my pleasant hills behold the living living
    springs
Running among my green pastures delighting among my
    trees
I am not here alone my flocks you are my brethren
And you birds that sing & adorn the sky you are my
    sisters
I sing & you reply to my Song   I rejoice & you are glad
Follow me O my flocks we will now descend into the
    valley
O how delicious are the grapes flourishing in the Sun
How clear the spring of the rock running among the
    golden sand
How cool the breezes of the vally & the arms of the
    branching trees
Cover us from the sun come & let us sit in the Shade   20
My Luvah here hath placd me in a Sweet & pleasant
    Land

And given me fruits & pleasant waters & warm hills &
   cool valleys
Here will I build myself a house & here Ill call on his
   name
Here Ill return when I am weary & take my pleasant rest

So spoke the Sinless Soul & laid her head on the downy
   fleece
Of a curld Ram who stretchd himself in sleep beside his
   mistress
And soft sleep fell upon her eyelids in the silent noon of
   day

Then Luvah passed by & saw the sinless Soul
And said   Let a pleasant house arise to be the dwelling
   place
Of this immortal Spirit growing in lower Paradise   30
He spoke & pillars were builded & walls as white as ivory
The grass she slept upon was pavd with pavement as of
   pearl
Beneath her rose a downy bed & a cieling coverd all

Vala awoke. When in the pleasant gates of sleep I
   enterd
I saw my Luvah like a spirit stand in the bright air
Round him stood spirits like me who reard me a bright
   house
And here I see thee house remain in my most pleasant
   world
PAGE 129
My Luvah smild I kneeled down he laid his hand on my
   head
And when he laid his hand upon me from the gates of
   sleep I came
Into this bodily house to tend my flocks in my pleasant
   garden

So saying she arose & walked round her beautiful house
And then from her white door she lookd to see her
   bleating lambs

But her flocks were gone up from beneath the trees into
    the hills

I see the hand that leadeth me doth also lead my flocks
She went up to her flocks & turned oft to see her shining
    house
She stopd to drink of the clear spring & eat the grapes
    & apples
She bore the fruits in her lap she gatherd flowers for her
    bosom
She called to her flocks saying follow me o my flocks

They followd her to the silent vally beneath the
    spreading trees
And on the rivers margin she ungirded her golden girdle
She stood in the river & viewd herself within the watry
    glass
And her bright hair was wet with the waters She rose up
    from the river
And as she rose her Eyes were opend to the world of
    waters
She saw Tharmas sitting upon the rocks beside the wavy
    sea
He strokd the water from his beard & mournd faint thro
    the summer vales

And Vala stood on the rocks of Tharmas & heard his
    mournful voice

O Enion my weary head is in the bed of death
For weeds of death have wrapd around my limbs in the
    hoary deeps
I sit in the place of shells & mourn & thou art closd in
    clouds
When will the time of Clouds be past & the dismal night
    of Tharmas
Arise O Enion Arise & smile upon my head
As thou dost smile upon the barren mountains and they
    rejoice

10

20

When wilt thou smile on Tharmas O thou bringer of
    golden day
Arise O Enion arise for Lo I have calmd my seas

So saying his faint head he laid upon the Oozy rock
And darkness coverd all the deep the light of Enion
    faded
Like a fa[i]nt flame quivering upon the surface of the
    darkness   30

Then Vala lifted up her hands to heaven to call on Enion
She calld but none could answer her & the Eccho of her
    voice returnd

Where is the voice of God that calld me from the silent
    dew
Where is the Lord of Vala dost thou hide in clefts of the
    rock
Why shouldst thou hide thyself from Vala from the soul
    that wanders desolate

She ceas'd & light beamd round her like the glory of the
    morning
PAGE 130
And She arose out of the river & girded her golden
    girdle

And now her feet step on the grassy bosom of the
    ground
Among her flocks & she turnd her eyes toward her
    pleasant house
And saw in the door way beneath the trees two little
    children playing
She drew near to her house & her flocks followd her
    footsteps
The Children clung around her knees she embracd them
    & wept over them

Thou little Boy art Tharmas & thou bright Girl Enion
How are ye thus renewd & brought into the Gardens of
    Vala

She embracd them in tears. till the sun descended the
   western hills
And then she enterd her bright house leading her mighty
   children   10
And when night came the flocks laid round the house
   beneath the trees
She laid the Children on the beds which she saw prepard
   in the house
Then last herself laid down & closd her Eyelids in soft
   slumbers

And in the morning when the Sun arose in the crystal
   sky
Vala awoke & calld the children from their gentle
   slumbers

Awake O Enion awake & let thine innocent Eyes
Enlighten all the Crystal house of Vala awake awake
Awake Tharmas awake awake thou child of dewy tears
Open the orbs of thy blue eyes & smile upon my gardens

The Children woke & smild on Vala. she kneeld by the
   golden couch   20
She presd them to her bosom & her pearly tears dropd
   down
O my sweet Children Enion let Tharmas kiss thy Cheek
Why dost thou turn thyself away from his sweet watry
   eyes
Tharmas henceforth in Valas bosom thou shalt find
   sweet peace
O bless the lovely eyes of Tharmas & the Eyes of Enion

They rose they went out wandring sometimes together
   sometimes alone
Why weepest thou Tharmas Child of tears in the bright
   house of joy
Doth Enion avoid the sight of thy blue heavenly Eyes
And dost thou wander with my lambs & [with] wet their
   innocent faces

With thy bright tears because the steps of Enion are in
    the gardens   30
Arise sweet boy & let us follow the path of Enion

So saying they went down into the garden among the
    fruits
And Enion sang among the flowers that grew among the
    trees
And Vala said Go Tharmas weep not Go to Enion

PAGE 131
He said O Vala I am sick & all this garden of Pleasure
Swims like a dream before my eyes but the sweet
    smelling fruit
Revives me to new deaths I fade even like a water lilly
In the suns heat till in the night on the couch of Enion
I drink new life & feel the breath of sleeping Enion
But in the morning she arises to avoid my Eyes
Then my loins fade & in the house I sit me down & weep

Chear up thy Countenance bright boy & go to Enion
Tell her that Vala waits her in the shadows of her garden

He went with timid steps & Enion like the ruddy morn   10
When infant spring appears in swelling buds & opening
    flowers
Behind her Veil withdraws so Enion turnd her modest
    head

But Tharmas spoke Vala seeks thee sweet Enion in the
    shades
Follow the steps of Tharmas, O thou brightness of the
    gardens
He took her hand reluctant she followd in infant doubts

Thus in Eternal Childhood straying among Valas flocks
In infant sorrow & joy alternate Enion & Tharmas playd
Round Vala in the Gardens of Vala & by her rivers
    margin
They are the shadows of Tharmas & of Enion in Valas
    world

And the sleepers who rested from their harvest work
   beheld these visions   20
Thus were the sleepers entertaind upon the Couches of
   Beulah

When Luvah & Vala were closd up in their world of
   shadowy forms
Darkness was all beneath the heavens only a little light
Such as glows out from sleeping spirits appeard in the
   deeps beneath
As when the wind sweeps over a Corn field the noise of
   souls
Thro all the immense borne down by Clouds swagging
   in autumnal heat
Muttering along from heaven to heaven hoarse roll the
   human forms
Beneath thick clouds dreadful lightnings burst & thunders
   roll
Down pour the torrent Floods of heaven on all the human
   harvest
Then Urizen sitting at his repose on beds in the bright
   South   30
Cried Times are Ended he Exulted he arose in joy he
   exulted
He pourd his light & all his Sons & daughters pourd their
   light
To exhale the spirits of Luvah & Vala thro the
   atmosphere
And Luvah & Vala saw the Light their spirits were
   Exhald
In all their ancient innocence the floods depart the clouds
Dissipate or sink into the Seas of Tharmas   Luvah sat
Above on the bright heavens in peace. the Spirits of
   Men beneath
Cried out to be deliverd & the Spirit of Luvah wept
Over the human harvest & over Vala the sweet wanderer
In pain the human harvest wavd in horrible groans of
   woe   40

PAGE 132

The Universal Groan went up the Eternal Man was
   Darkend

Then Urizen arose & took his Sickle in his hand
There is a brazen sickle & a scythe of iron hid
Deep in the South guarded by a few solitary stars
This sickle Urizen took the scythe his sons embracd
And went forth & began to reap & all his joyful sons
Reapd the wide Universe & bound in Sheaves a
   wondrous harvest
They took them into the wide barns with loud rejoicings
   & triumph
Of flute & harp & drum & trumpet horn & clarion

The feast was spread in the bright South & the
   Regenerate Man   10
Sat at the feast rejoicing & the wine of Eternity
Was servd round by the flames of Luvah all Day & all
   the Night
And when Morning began to dawn upon the distant
   hills
[*Then*] a whirlwind rose up in the Center & in the
   Whirlwind a Shriek
And in the Shriek a rattling of bones & in the rattling of
   bones
A dolorous groan & from the dolorous groan in tears
Rose Enion like a gentle light & Enion spoke saying

O Dreams of Death the human form dissolving
   companied
[*With*] By beasts & worms & creeping things & darkness
   & despair
The clouds fall off from my wet brow the dust from my
   cold limbs   20
Into the Sea of Tharmas Soon renewd a Golden Moth
I shall cast off my death clothes & Embrace Tharmas
   again
For Lo the winter melted away upon the distant hills

And all the black mould sings. She speaks to her infant
   race her milk
Descends [*of*] down on the sand. the thirsty sand drinks
   & rejoices
Wondering to behold the Emmet the Grasshopper the
   jointed worm
The roots shoot thick thro the solid rocks bursting their
   way
They cry out in joys of existence. the broad stems
Rear on the mountains stem after stem the scaly newt
   creeps
From the stone & the armed fly springs from the rocky
   crevice
The spider. The bat burst from the hardend slime
   crying
To one another What are we & whence is our joy &
   delight
Lo the little moss begins to spring & the tender weed
Creeps round our secret nest. Flocks brighten the
   Mountains
Herds throng up the Valley wild beasts fill the forests

Joy thrilld thro all the Furious form of Tharmas
   humanizing
Mild he Embracd her whom he sought he raisd her thro
   the heavens
Sounding his trumpet to awake the dead on high he
   soard
Over the ruind worlds the smoking tomb of the Eternal
   Prophet

PAGE 133
The Eternal Man arose He welcomd them to the Feast
The feast was spread in the bright South & the Eternal
   Man
Sat at the feast rejoicing & the wine of Eternity
Was servd round by the flames of Luvah all day & all
   the night

And Many Eternal Men sat at the golden feast to see
The female form now separate They shudderd at the
   horrible thing
Not born for the sport and amusement of Man but born
   to drink up all his powers
[*And*] They wept to see their shadows they said to one
   another this is Sin
This is the [*vegetative*] Generative world they
   rememberd the Days of old

And One of the Eternals spoke All was silent at the feast   10

Man is a Worm wearied with joy he seeks the caves of
   sleep
Among the Flowers of Beulah in his selfish cold repose
Forsaking Brotherhood & Universal love in selfish clay
Folding the pure wings of his mind seeking the places
   dark
Abstracted from the roots of [*Nature*] Science then
   inclosd around
In walls of Gold we cast him like a Seed into the Earth
Till times & spaces have passd over him duly every
   morn
We visit him covering with a Veil the immortal seed
With windows from the inclement sky we cover him &
   with walls
And hearths protect the Selfish terror till divided all   20
In families we see our shadows born. & thence we know ⎫ Ephesi-
That Man subsists by Brotherhood & Universal Love ⎬ ans iii
We fall on one anothers necks more closely we embrace ⎭ c. 10 v

Not for ourselves but for the Eternal family we live
Man liveth not by Self alone but in his brothers face
Each shall behold the Eternal Father & love & joy
   abound

So spoke the Eternal at the Feast they embracd the New
   born Man
Calling him Brother image of the Eternal Father. they
   sat down

At the immortal tables sounding loud their instruments
   of joy
Calling the Morning into Beulah the Eternal Man
   rejoicd   30

When Morning dawnd The Eternals rose to labour at the
   Vintage
Beneath they saw their sons & daughters wondering
   inconceivable
At the dark myriads in Shadows in the worlds beneath

The morning dawnd Urizen rose & in his hand the Flail
Sounds on the Floor heard terrible by all beneath the
   heavens
Dismal loud redounding the nether floor shakes with the
   sound
PAGE 134
And all Nations were threshed out & the stars threshd
   from their husks

Then Tharmas took the Winnowing fan the winnowing
   wind furious
Above veerd round by the violent whirlwind driven west
   & south
Tossed the Nations like Chaff into the seas of Tharmas

O Mystery Fierce Tharmas cries Behold thy end is come
Art thou she that made the nations drunk with the cup of
   Religion
Go down ye Kings & Councillors & Giant Warriors
Go down into the depths go down & hide yourselves
   beneath
Go down with horse & Chariots & Trumpets of hoarse
   war

Lo how the Pomp of Mystery goes down into the Caves   10
Her great men howl & throw the dust & rend their
   hoary hair
Her delicate women & children shriek upon the bitter
   wind

Spoild of their beauty their hair rent & their skin
    shriveld up
Lo darkness covers the long pomp of banners on the
    wind
And black horses & armed men & miserable bound
    captives
Where shall the graves recieve them all & where shall be
    their place
And who shall mourn for Mystery who never loosd her
    Captives
Let the slave grinding at the mill run out into the field
Let him look up into the heavens & laugh in the bright
    air
Let the inchaind soul shut up in darkness & in sighing   20
Whose face has never seen a smile in thirty weary years
Rise & look out his chains are loose his dungeon doors
    are open
And let his wife & children return from the opressors
    scourge
They look behind at every step & believe it is a dream
Are these the Slaves that groand along the streets of
    Mystery
Where are your bonds & task masters are these the
    prisoners
Where are your chains where are your tears why do you
    look around
If you are thirsty there is the river go bathe your parched
    limbs
The good of all the Land is before you for Mystery is no
    more

Then All the Slaves from every Earth in the wide
    Universe   30
Sing a New Song drowning confusion in its happy notes
While the flail of Urizen sounded long & the winnowing
    wind of Tharmas
So loud so clear in the wide heavens & the song that they
    sung was this

Composed by an African Black from the little Earth of
    Sotha

Aha Aha how came I here so soon in my sweet native
    land
How came I here Methinks I am as I was in my youth
PAGE 135
When in my fathers house I sat & heard his chearing
    voice
Methinks I see his flocks & herds & feel my limbs
    renewd
And Lo my Brethren in their tents & their little ones
    around them

The song arose to the Golden feast the Eternal Man
    rejoicd
Then the Eternal Man said Luvah the Vintage is ripe
    arise
The sons of Urizen shall gather the vintage with sharp
    hooks
And all thy sons O Luvah bear away the families of
    Earth
I hear the flail of Urizen his barns are full no roo[m]
Remains & in the Vineyards stand the abounding
    sheaves beneath
The falling Grapes that odorous burst upon the winds.
    Arise   10
My flocks & herds trample the Corn my cattle browze
    upon
The ripe Clusters The shepherds shout for Luvah prince
    of Love
Let the Bulls of Luvah tread the Corn & draw the loaded
    waggon
Into the Barn while children glean the Ears around the
    door
Then shall they lift their innocent hands & stroke his
    furious nose
And he shall lick the little girls white neck & on her head

Scatter the perfume of his breath while from his
    mountains high
The lion of terror shall come down & bending his bright
    mane
And couching at their side shall eat from the curld boys
    white lap
His golden food and in the evening sleep before the door   20

Attempting to be more than Man We become less said
    Luvah
As he arose from the bright feast drunk with the wine of
    ages
His crown of thorns fell from his head he hung his living
    Lyre
Behind the seat of the Eternal Man & took his way
Sounding the Song of Los descending to the Vineyards
    bright
His sons arising from the feast with golden baskets follow
A fiery train as when the Sun sings in the ripe vineyards
Then Luvah stood before the wine press all his fiery
    sons
Brought up the loaded Waggons with shoutings ramping
    tygers play
In the jingling traces furious lions sound the song of joy   30
To the golden wheels circling upon the pavement of
    heaven & all
The Villages of Luvah ring the golden tiles of the
    villages
Reply to violins & tabors to the pipe flute lyre & cymbal
Then fell the Legions of Mystery in maddning confusion
Down Down thro the immense with outcry fury &
    despair
Into the wine presses of Luvah howling fell the Clusters
Of human families thro the deep. the wine presses were
    filld
The blood of life flowd plentiful Odors of life arose
All round the heavenly arches & the Odors rose singing
    this song

PAGE 136

O terrible wine presses of Luvah O caverns of the Grave
How lovely the delights of those risen again from death
O trembling joy excess of joy is like Excess of grief

So sang the Human Odors round the wine presses of
    Luvah

But in the Wine presses is wailing terror & despair
Forsaken of their Elements they vanish & are no more
No more but a desire of Being a distracted ravening
    desire
Desiring like the hungry worm & like the [*silent*]
    gaping grave
They plunge into the Elements the Elements cast them
    forth
Or else consume their shadowy semblance Yet they
    obstinate   10
Tho pained to distraction Cry O let us Exist for
This dreadful Non Existence is worse than pains of
    Eternal [*death*] Birth
Eternal Death who can Endure. let us consume in fires
In waters stifling or in air corroding or in earth shut up
The Pangs of Eternal birth are better than the Pangs of
    Eternal Death

How red the Sons & daughters of Luvah how they tread
    the Grapes
Laughing & shouting drunk with odors many fall
    oerwearied
Drownd in the wine is many a youth & maiden those
    around
Lay them on skins of tygers or the spotted Leopard or
    wild Ass
Till they revive or bury them in cool Grots making
    lamentation   20

But in the Wine Presses the Human Grapes Sing not nor
    dance

They howl & writhe in shoals of torment in fierce flames
   consuming
In chains of iron & in dungeons circled with ceaseless
   fires
In pits & dens & shades of death in shapes of torment &
   woe
The Plates the Screws [*the nets*] and Racks & Saws &
   cords & fires & floods
The cruel joy of Luvahs daughters lacerating with
   knives
And whip[s] their Victims & the deadly sports of Luvahs
   sons

Timbrels & Violins sport round the Wine Presses The
   little Seed
The Sportive root the Earthworm the small beetle the
   wise Emmet
Dance round the Wine Presses of Luvah. the Centipede
   is there   30
The ground Spider with many Eyes the Mole clothed in
   Velvet
The Earwig armd the tender maggot emblem of
   Immortality
The Slow Slug the grasshopper that sings & laughs &
   drinks
The winter comes he folds his slender bones without a
   murmur
There is the Nettle that stings with soft down & there
The indignant Thistle whose bitterness is bred in his
   milk
And who lives on the contempt of his neighbour there all
   the idle weeds
That creep about the obscure places shew their various
   limbs
Naked in all their beauty dancing round the Wine
   Presses
They Dance around the Dying & they Drink the howl
   & groan   40

PAGE 137

They catch the Shrieks in cups of gold they hand them
    to one another

These are the sports of love & these the sweet delights of
    amorous play

Tears of the grapes the death sweat of the Cluster the
    last sigh

Of the mild youth who listens to the luring songs of
    Luvah

The Eternal Man darkend with Sorrow & a wintry
    mantle

Coverd the Hills   He said O Tharmas rise & O Urthona

Then Tharmas & Urthona rose from the Golden feast
    satiated

With Mirth & Joy Urthona limping from his fall on
    Tharmas leand

In his right hand his hammer Tharmas held his
    Shepherds crook

Beset with gold gold were the ornaments formd by sons
    of Urizen   10

Then Enion & Ahania & Vala & the wife of Dark
    Urthona

Rose from the feast in joy ascending to their Golden
    Looms

There the wingd shuttle Sang the spindle & the distaff
    & the Reel

Rang sweet the praise of industry. Thro all the golden
    rooms

Heaven rang with winged Exultation   All beneath
    howld loud

With tenfold rout & desolation roard the Chasms beneath

Where the wide woof flowd down & where the Nations
    are gatherd together

Tharmas went down to the Wine presses & beheld the
    sons & daughters

Of Luvah quite exhausted with the Labour & quite filld

With new wine. that they began to torment one another
    and to tread   20
The weak. Luvah & Vala slept on the floor o'erwearied
Urthona calld his Sons around him Tharmas calld his
    sons
Numrous. they took the wine they separated the Lees
And Luvah was put for dung on the ground by the Sons
    of Tharmas & Urthona
They formed heavens of sweetest wo[o]d[s] of gold &
    silver & ivory
Of glass & precious stones They loaded all the waggons
    of heaven
And took away the wine of ages with solemn songs &
    joy

Luvah & Vala woke & all the sons & daughters of Luvah
Awoke they wept to one another & they reascended
To the Eternal Man in woe he cast them wailing into   30
The world of shadows thro the air till winter is over &
    gone

But the Human Wine stood wondering in all their
    delightful Expanses
The Elements subside the heavens rolld on with vocal
    harmony

Then Los who is Urthona rose in all his regenerate
    power
The Sea that rolld & foamd with darkness & the
    shadows of death
Vomited out & gave up all the floods lift up their hands
Singing & shouting to the Man they bow their hoary
    heads
And murmuring in their channels flow & circle round his
    feet
PAGE 138
Then Dark Urthona took the Corn out of the Stores of
    Urizen
He ground it in his rumbling Mills Terrible the distress

Of all the Nations of Earth ground in the Mills of
   Urthona
In his hand Tharmas takes the Storms. he turns the
   whirlwind Loose
Upon the wheels the stormy seas howl at his dread
   command
And Eddying fierce rejoice in the fierce agitation of the
   wheels
Of Dark Urthona Thunders Earthquakes Fires Water
   floods
Rejoice to one another loud their voices shake the Abyss
Their dread forms tending the dire mills The grey hoar
   frost was there
And his pale wife the aged Snow they watch over the
   fires   10
They build the Ovens of Urthona Nature in darkness
   groans
And Men are bound to sullen contemplations in the
   night
Restless they turn on beds of sorrow. in their inmost
   brain
Feeling the crushing Wheels they rise they write the
   bitter words
Of Stern Philosophy & knead the bread of knowledge
   with tears & groans

Such are the works of Dark Urthona Tharmas sifted the
   corn
Urthona made the Bread of Ages & he placed it
In golden & in silver baskets in heavens of precious stone
And then took his repose in Winter in the night of Time

The Sun has left his blackness & has found a fresher
   morning   20
[*Then*] And the mild moon rejoices in the clear &
   cloudless night
And Man walks forth from midst of the fires the evil is
   all consumd
His eyes behold the Angelic spheres arising night & day

The stars consumd like a lamp blown out & in their
    stead behold
The Expanding Eyes of Man behold the depths of
    wondrous worlds
One Earth one sea beneath nor Erring Globes wander
    but Stars
Of fire rise up nightly from the Ocean & one Sun
Each morning like a New born Man issues with songs &
    Joy
Calling the Plowman to his Labour & the Shepherd to
    his rest
He walks upon the Eternal Mountains raising his
    heavenly voice   30
Conversing with the Animal forms of wisdom night &
    day
That risen from the Sea of fire renewd walk oer the
    Earth

For Tharmas brought his flocks upon the hills & in the
    Vales
Around the Eternal Mans bright tent the little Children
    play
Among the wooly flocks The hammer of Urthona
    sounds
In the deep caves beneath his limbs renewd his Lions
    roar
Around the Furnaces & in the Evening sport upon the
    plains
They raise their faces from the Earth conversing with the
    Man

How is it we have walkd thro fires & yet are not
    consumd
How is it that all things are changd even as in ancient
    times   40
PAGE 139
The Sun arises from his dewy bed & the fresh airs
Play in his smiling beams giving the seeds of life to
    grow

And the fresh Earth beams forth ten thousand thousand
  springs of life
Urthona is arisen in his strength no longer now
Divided from Enitharmon no longer the Spectre Los
Where is the Spectre of Prophecy where the delusive
  Phantom

Departed & Urthona rises from the ruinous walls
In all his ancient strength to form the golden armour of
  science
For intellectual War The war of swords departed now
The dark Religions are departed & sweet Science reigns   10

              End of The Dream

Notes Written on the Pages of The Four Zoas

PAGE 56
Christs Crucifix shall be made an excuse for Executing
Criminals

PAGE 70
Till thou dost injure the distrest
Thou shalt never have peace within thy breast

PAGE 88
  The Christian Religion teaches that No Man is
Indifferent to you but that every one is Either your friend
or your enemy. he must necessarily be either the one or the
other   And that he will be equally profitable both ways if
you treat him as he deserves

PAGE 93
Unorganizd Innocence, An Impossibility
Innocence dwells with Wisdom but never with Ignorance

Additional Fragments

PAGE 141
Beneath the veil of Vala rose Tharmas from dewy tears
The [*ancient*] eternal man bowd his bright head &
 Urizen prince of light
[*Astonishd lookd from his bright Portals calling thus to*
 Luvah
O Luvah in the]
Astonishd lookd from his bright portals. Luvah king of
 Love
Awakend Vala. Ariston ran forth with bright ?Onana
And dark Urthona rouzd his shady bride from her deep
 den
[*Awaking from his stony slumber*]
Pitying they viewd the new born demon. for they could
 not love
[*?After their sin*]   10
Male formd the demon mild athletic force his shoulders
 spread
And his bright feet firm as a brazen altar. but. the parts
To love devoted. female, all astonishd stood the hosts
Of heaven, while Tharmas with wingd speed flew to the
 sandy [*ocean*] shore
He rested on the desart wild & on the raging sea
He stood & stretchd his wings &^c ----

With printless feet scorning the concave of the joyful sky
Female her form bright as the summer but the parts of
 love
Male & her brow radiant as day. darted a lovely scorn
Tharmas beheld from his high rocks & --- ---
PAGE 142
The ocean calm the clouds fold round & fiery flames of
 love

Inwrap the immortal limbs struggling in terrific joy
Not long thunders lightnings swift rendings & blasting
   winds
Sweep oer. the struggling copulation. in fell writhing
   pangs
They lie in twisting agonies beneath the covring heavens

The womb impressd Enion fled & hid in verdant
   mountains
Yet here his heavenly orbs &c

From Enion pours the seed of life & death in all her
   limbs
Frozen in the womb of Tharmas rush the rivers of
   Enions pain
Trembling he lay swelld with the deluge stifling in the
   anguish

10

THREE POEMS,? *c.* 1800

A fairy [*leapt*] skipd upon my knee
Singing & dancing merrily
I said Thou thing of patches rings
Pins Necklaces & such like things
Disguiser of the Female Form
Thou paltry gilded poisnous worm
Weeping he fell upon my thigh
And thus in tears did soft reply
Knowest thou not O Fairies Lord
How much by us Contemnd Abhorrd
Whatever hides the Female form
That cannot bear the Mental storm
Therefore in Pity still we give
Our lives to make the Female live
And what would turn into disease
We turn to what will joy & please

*

Around the Springs of Gray my wild root weaves
Traveller repose & Dream among my leaves.

TO M^rs ANN FLAXMAN

A little Flower grew in a lonely Vale
Its form was lovely but its colours. pale
One standing in the Porches of the Sun
When his Meridian Glories were begun
Leapd from the steps of fire & on the grass

Alighted where this little flower was
With hands divine he movd the gentle Sod
And took the Flower up in its native Clod
Then planting it upon a Mountains brow
'Tis your own fault if you dont flourish now

POEMS FROM LETTERS

TO JOHN FLAXMAN, 12 SEPTEMBER 1800 [POSTMARK]

To My Dearest Friend, John Flaxman, these lines:

I bless thee, O Father of Heaven & Earth, that ever I
    saw Flaxman's face.
Angels stand round my Spirit in Heaven, the blessed of
    Heaven are my friends upon Earth.
When Flaxman was taken to Italy, Fuseli was given to
    me for a season,
And now Flaxman hath given me Hayley his friend to
    be mine, such my lot upon Earth.
Now my lot in the Heavens is this, Milton lov'd me in
    childhood & shew'd me his face.
Ezra came with Isaiah the Prophet, but Shakespeare in
    riper years gave me his hand;
Paracelsus & Behmen appear'd to me, terrors appear'd
    in the Heavens above
And in Hell beneath, & a mighty & awful change
    threatened the Earth.
The American War began. All its dark horrors passed
    before my face
Across the Atlantic to France. Then the French
    Revolution commenc'd in thick clouds,   10
And My Angels have told me that seeing such visions I
    could not subsist on the Earth,
But by my conjunction with Flaxman, who knows to
    forgive Nervous Fear.

TO MRS FLAXMAN, 14 SEPTEMBER 1800

To my dear Friend Mrs Anna Flaxman
H[ercules] B[uildings] Lambeth, 14 Sepr 1800

This Song to the flower of Flaxmans joy
To the blossom of hope for a sweet decoy
Do all that you can or all that you may
To entice him to Felpham & far away

Away to Sweet Felpham for Heaven is there
The Ladder of Angels descends thro the air
On the Turret its spiral does softly descend
Thro' the village then winds at My Cot i[t] does end

You stand in the village & look up to heaven
The precious stones glitter on flights seventy seven   10
And My Brother is there & My Friend & Thine
Descend & Ascend with the Bread & the Wine

The Bread of sweet Thought & the Wine of Delight
Feeds the Village of Felpham by day & by night
And at his own door the blessd Hermit does stand
Dispensing Unceasing to all the whole Land

TO THOMAS BUTTS, 2 OCTOBER 1800

To my Friend Butts I write
My first Vision of Light
On the yellow sands sitting
The Sun was Emitting
His Glorious beams
From Heavens high Streams
Over Sea over Land
My Eyes did Expand
Into regions of air
Away from all Care   10
Into regions of fire
Remote from Desire
The Light of the Morning
Heavens Mountains adorning

In particles bright
The jewels of Light
Distinct shone & clear –
Amazd & in fear
I each particle gazed,
Astonishd Amazed   20
For each was a Man
Human formd. Swift I ran
For they beckond to me
Remote by the Sea
Saying. Each grain of Sand
Every Stone on the Land
Each rock & each hill
Each fountain & rill
Each herb & each tree
Mountain hill Earth & Sea   30
Cloud Meteor & Star
Are Men Seen Afar
I stood in the Streams
Of Heavens bright beams
And Saw Felpham sweet
Beneath my bright feet
In soft Female charms
And in her fair arms
My Shadow I knew
And my wifes shadow too   40
And My Sister & Friend.
We like Infants descend
In our Shadows on Earth
Like a weak mortal birth
My Eyes more & more
Like a Sea without shore
Continue Expanding
The Heavens commanding
Till the Jewels of Light
Heavenly Men beaming bright   50
Appeard as One Man
Who Complacent began

My limbs to infold
In his beams of bright gold
Like dross purgd away
All my mire & my clay
Soft consumd in delight
In his bosom Sun bright
I remaind. Soft he smild
And I heard his voice Mild   60
Saying This is My Fold
O thou Ram hornd with gold
Who awakest from Sleep
On the Sides of the Deep
On the Mountains around
The roarings resound
Of the lion & wolf
The loud Sea & deep gulf.
These are guards of My Fold
O thou Ram hornd with gold   70
And the voice faded mild
I remaind as a Child
All I ever had known
Before me bright Shone
I saw you & your wife
By the fountains of Life
Such the Vision to me
Appeard on the Sea

TO MRS BUTTS

Wife of the Friend of those I most revere.
Recieve this tribute from a Harp sincere
Go on in Virtuous Seed sowing on Mold
Of Human Vegetation & Behold
Your Harvest Springing to Eternal life
Parent of Youthful Minds & happy Wife

TO THOMAS BUTTS, 22 NOVEMBER 1802

With happiness stretchd across the hills
In a cloud that dewy sweetness distills
With a blue sky spread over with wings
And a mild sun that mounts & sings
With trees & fields full of Fairy elves
And little devils who fight for themselves
Remembring the Verses that Hayley sung
When my heart knockd against the root of my tongue
With Angels planted in Hawthorn bowers
And God himself in the passing hours   10
With Silver Angels across my way
And Golden Demons that none can stay
With my Father hovering upon the wind
And my Brother Robert just behind
And my Brother John the evil one
In a black cloud making his mone
Tho dead they appear upon my path
Notwithstanding my terrible wrath
They beg they intreat they drop their tears
Filld full of hopes filld full of fears   20
With a thousand Angels upon the Wind
Pouring disconsolate from behind
To drive them off & before my way
A frowning Thistle implores my stay
What to others a trifle appears
Fills me full of smiles or tears
For double the vision my Eyes do see
And a double vision is always with me
With my inward Eye 'tis an old Man grey
With my outward a Thistle across my way   30
'If thou goest back the thistle said
Thou art to endless woe betrayd
For here does Theotormon lower
And here is Enitharmons bower
And Los the terrible thus hath sworn
Because thou backward dost return

Poverty Envy old age & fear
Shall bring thy Wife upon a bier
And Butts shall give what Fuseli gave
A dark black Rock & a gloomy Cave.'   40

I struck the Thistle with my foot
And broke him up from his delving root
'Must the duties of life each other cross'
'Must every joy be dung & dross'
'Must my dear Butts feel cold neglect'
'Because I give Hayley his due respect'
'Must Flaxman look upon me as wild'
'And all my friends be with doubts beguild'
'Must my Wife live in my Sisters bane'
'Or my sister survive on my Loves pain'   50
'The curses of Los the terrible shade'
'And his dismal terrors make me afraid'

So I spoke & struck in my wrath
The old man weltering upon my path
Then Los appeard in all his power
In the Sun he appeard descending before
My face in fierce flames in my double sight
Twas outward a Sun: inward Los in his might

'My hands are labourd day & night'
'And Ease comes never in my sight'   60
'My Wife has no indulgence given'
'Except what comes to her from heaven'
'We eat little we drink less'
'This Earth breeds not our happiness'
'Another Sun feeds our lifes streams'
'We are not warmed with thy beams'
'Thou measurest not the Time to me'
'Nor yet the Space that I do see'
'My Mind is not with thy light arrayd'
'Thy terrors shall not make me afraid'   70

When I had my Defiance given
The Sun stood trembling in heaven

The Moon that glowd remote below
Became leprous & white as snow
And every Soul of men on the Earth
Felt affliction & sorrow & sickness & dearth
Los flamd in my path & the Sun was hot
With the bows of my Mind & the Arrows of Thought
My bowstring fierce with Ardour breathes
My arrows glow in their golden sheaves   80
My brothers & father march before
The heavens drop with human gore

Now I a fourfold vision see
And a fourfold vision is given to me
Tis fourfold in my supreme delight
And three fold in soft Beulahs night
And twofold Always. May God us keep
From Single vision & Newtons sleep

TO THOMAS BUTTS, 16 AUGUST 1803

O why was I born with a different face
Why was I not born like the rest of my race
When I look each one starts! when I speak I offend
Then I'm silent & passive & lose every Friend

Then my verse I dishonour. My pictures despise
My person degrade & my temper chastise
And the pen is my terror. the pencil my shame
All my Talents I bury, and dead is my Fame

I am either too low or too highly prizd
When Elate I am Envy'd, When Meek I'm despis'd   10

When Klopstock England defied
Uprose terrible Blake in his pride
For old Nobodaddy aloft
Farted & Belchd & coughd
Then swore a great oath that made heavn quake
And calld aloud to English Blake
Blake was giving his body ease
At Lambeth beneath the poplar trees
From his seat then started he
And turnd himself round three times three   10
The Moon at that sight blushd scarlet red
The stars threw down their cups & fled
And all the devils that were in hell
Answered with a ninefold yell
Klopstock felt the [*ninefold*] intripled turn
And all his bowels began to [*burn*] churn
[*They/And*] And his bowels turned round three times
    three
And lockd in his soul with a ninefold key
That from his body it neer could be parted
Till to the last trumpet it was farted   20
Then again old nobodaddy swore
He neer had seen such a thing before
Since Noah was shut in the ark
Since Eve first chose her hell fire spark
Since twas the fashion to go naked
Since the old anything was created
And so feeling he begd him to turn again
And ease poor Klopstocks nine fold pain

[*Then after*] From pity then he redend round
And the Spell removed unwound
[*If thus Blake could Shite what Klopstock did write*]
If Blake could do this when he [*sat down to*] rose up
   from shite   30
What might he not do if he sat down to write

ON THE VIRGINITY OF THE VIRGIN
MARY & JOHANNA SOUTHCOTT

Whateer is done to her she cannot know
And if youll ask her she will swear it so
Whether tis good or evil none's to blame
No one can take the pride no one the shame

*

Beneath the white thorn lovely May
[*Three Virgins at the Break of day*
Whither Young Man whither away]
Alas for wo alas for wo alas for wo
They cry & tears for ever flow
The one was clothd in flames of fire
The other clothd in [*sweet desire*] Iron wire
The other clothd in [*sighs*] & tears & sighs
Dazzling bright before my Eyes
They bore a Net of Golden twine   10
To hang upon the branches fine
[*Pitying I wept to see the woe*
That Love & Beauty undergo
To be consumd in burning fires
And in ungratified desires]
[*Wings they had (& when they chose) that soft inclose*
Round their body when they chose
They would let them down at will
Or make translucent]
And in tears clothd night & day   20
Melted all my soul away

When they saw my tears a smile
That did heaven itself beguile
Bore the Golden net aloft
As by downy pinions soft
Oer the morning of my day
Underneath the net I stray
Now intreating flaming fire
Now intreating [*sweet desire*] iron wire
Now intreating tears & sighs   30
[*When*] O when will the Morning rise

THE BIRDS

He. Where thou dwellest in what Grove
    Tell me Fair one tell me love
    Where thou thy charming Nest dost build
    O thou pride of every field

She. Yonder stands a lonely tree
    There I live & mourn for thee
    Morning drinks my silent tear
    And evening winds my sorrows bear

He. O thou Summers harmony
    I have livd & mournd for thee   10
    Each day I mourn along the wood
    And night hath heard my sorrows loud

She. Dost thou truly long for me
    And am I thus sweet to thee
    Sorrow now is at an End
    O my Lover & my Friend

He. Come on wings of joy well fly
    To where my Bower hangs on high
    Come & make thy calm retreat
    Among green leaves & blossoms sweet   20

*

I saw a Monk of [*Constantine*] Charlemaine
Arise before my sight
I talkd to the Grey Monk where he stood
In beams of infernal light

Gibbon arose with a lash of steel
And Voltaire with a wracking wheel
[*Charlemaine and his barons bold*]
The Schools in Clouds of Learning rolld
Arose with War in iron and gold

[*Seditious*] Thou Lazy Monk [*said Charlemaine*] they
   sound afar   10
[*The Glory of War thou condemnst in vain*]
In vain condemning Glorious War
And in thy Cell thou shall ever dwell
Rise War & bind him in his Cell

The blood red ran from the Grey monks side
His hands & feet were wounded wide
His body bent his arms & knees
Like to the roots of ancient trees

I die I die the Mother said
My Children will die for lack of bread   20
What more has the merciless tyrant said
The Monk sat down on her stony bed

His Eye was dry no tear coud flow
A hollow groan first spoke his woe
[*From his dry tongue these accents flow*]
He trembled & shudderd upon the bed
At length with a feeble cry he said

When God commanded this hand to write
In the studious hours of deep midnight
He told me that All I wrote should prove   30
The bane of all that on Earth I love

My brother starvd between two walls
His childrens cry my soul appalls
[*But*] I mockd at the wrack & griding chain
My bent body mocks at their torturing pain

Thy father drew his sword in the north
With his thousands strong he is marched forth
Thy brother has armd himself in steel
To revenge the wrongs thy Children feel

But vain the sword & vain the bow
They never can work wars overthrow
The Hermits prayer & the widows tear
Alone can free the world from fear

The hand of vengeance sought the bed
To which the purple tyrant fled
The iron hand crushd the tyrants head
[*And usurpd the tyrants throne and bed*]
And became a tyrant in his stead

Untill the Tyrant himself relent
The Tyrant who first the black bow bent   50
Slaughter shall heap the bloody plain
Resistance & war is the Tyrants gain

But the Tear of Love & forgiveness sweet
And submission to death beneath his feet
The Tear shall melt the sword of steel
And every wound it has made shall heal

[*For the tear is an intellectual thing*]
And a sigh is the Sword of an Angel King
And the bitter groan [*for anothers*] of the Martyrs woe
Is an arrow from the Almighties bow.   60

[Additional Stanzas]

When Satan first the black bow bent
And the Moral Law from the Gospel rent
He forg'd the Law into a Sword
And spilld the blood of Mercys Lord

[*O Charlemaine O Charlemaine*]
Titus. Constantine Charlemaine
O Voltaire Rousseau Gibbon vain
Your [*mocks & scorn*] Grecian mocks & Roman Sword
Against this image of his Lord

A tear is an &c   70

Gibbon plied his lash of steel
Voltaire turnd his wracking wheel
Charlemaine & his barons bold
Stood by & mockd in iron & gold

The Wheel of Voltaire whirld on high
Gibbon aloud his lash does ply
Charlemaine & his clouds of War
Muster around the Polar Bar

A Grecian Scoff is a wracking wheel
The Roman pride is a sword of steel   80
[*Vict*] Glory & Victory a [*plaited*] Phallic Whip

*

MORNING

To find the Western path
Right thro the Gates of Wrath
I urge my way
Sweet Mercy leads me on
With soft repentant moan
I see the break of day

The war of swords & spears
Melted by dewy tears
Exhales on high
The Sun is freed from fears   10
And with soft grateful tears
Ascends the sky

*

Terror in the house does roar
But Pity stands before the door

*

[*This world*] Each Man is in [*the*] His Spectres power
Untill the arrival of that hour
[*Untill the*] When his Humanity awake
And Cast [*the*] his own Spectre into the Lake

And there to Eternity aspire
The selfhood in a flame of fire
Till then the Lamb of God

*

Mock on Mock on Voltaire Rousseau
Mock on Mock on tis all in vain
You throw the sand against the wind
And the wind blows it back again

And every sand becomes a Gem
Reflected in the beams divine
Blown back they blind the mocking Eye
But still in Israels paths they shine

The Atoms of Democritus
And Newtons Particles of light   10
Are sands upon the Red sea shore
Where Israels tents do shine so bright

*

My Spectre around me night & day
Like a Wild beast guards my way
My Emanation far within
Weeps incessantly for my Sin

[(*Her*) *Thy weeping* (*She*) *thou shall neer give oer*
I Sin against (*her*) *thee more & more*
And never will from sin be free
Till she forgives & comes to me

Thou hast parted from my side
Once thou wast a virgin bride
Never shalt thou a (lover) true love find
My Spectre follows thee Behind]

[*In a dark cold winter night*]
[*A deep winter (night) dark & cold*
Within my (loves) Heart thou didst unfold
A Fathomless & boundless Deep
There we wander there we weep

When my Love did first begin
Thou didst call that Love a Sin
Secret trembling night & day   20
Driving all my Loves away]

A Fathomless & boundless deep
There we wander there we weep
On the hungry craving wind
My Spectre follows thee behind

He scents thy footsteps in the snow
Wheresoever thou dost go
Thro the wintry hail & rain
When wilt thou return again

[*Didst*] Dost thou not in Pride & Scorn   30
Fill with tempests all my morn
And with jealousies & fears
Fill my pleasant nights with tears

Seven of my sweet loves thy knife
Has bereaved of their life
Their marble tombs I built with tears
And with cold & shuddering fears

Seven more loves weep night & day
Round the tombs where my loves lay
And seven more loves attend each night   40
Around my couch with torches bright

And seven more Loves in my bed
Crown with wine my mournful head
Pitying & forgiving all
Thy transgressions great & small

When wilt thou return & view
My loves & them to life renew
When wilt thou return & live
When wilt thou pity [&] as I forgive

Never Never I return   50
Still for Victory I burn
Living thee alone Ill have
And when dead Ill be thy Grave

Thro the Heaven & Earth & Hell
Thou shalt never never quell
I will fly & thou pursue
Night & Morn the flight renew

Till [*thou*] I turn from Female Love
And [*dig*] root up the Infernal Grove
[*Thou shalt*] I shall never worthy be   60
To Step into Eternity

And [*I*] to end thy cruel mocks
Annihilate [*them*] thee on the rocks
And another form create
To be subservient to my Fate

Let us agree to give up Love
And root up the infernal grove
Then shall we return & see
The worlds of happy Eternity

& Throughout all Eternity   70
I forgive you you forgive me
As our Dear Redeemer said
This the Wine & this the Bread

[Additional Stanzas]

Oer [*thy*] my Sins Thou sit & moan
[*Have I*] Hast thou no sins of [*my*] thy own
Oer [*thy*] my Sins [*I*] thou sit & weep
And lull [*my*] thy own Sins fast asleep

What transgressions I commit
Are for thy Transgressions fit
They thy Harlots thou their Slave   80
And my Bed becomes their Grave

Poor pale pitiable form
That I follow in a Storm
Iron tears & groans of lead
Bind around my akeing head

And let us go to the highest downs
With many pleasing wiles
The Woman that does not love your Frowns
Will never embrace your smiles

*

The Hebrew Nation did not write it
Avarice & Chastity did shite it

*

Grown old in Love from Seven till Seven times Seven
I oft have wishd for Hell for Ease from Heaven

*

A Woman Scaly & a Man all Hairy
Is such a Match as he who dares
Will find the Womans Scales scrape off the Mans Hairs

POEMS FROM THE
PICKERING MANUSCRIPT

THE SMILE

There is a Smile of Love
And there is a Smile of Deceit
And there is a Smile of Smiles
In which these two Smiles meet

And there is a Frown of Hate
And there is a Frown of disdain
And there is a Frown of Frowns
Which you strive to forget in vain

For it sticks in the Hearts deep Core
And it sticks in the deep Back bone
And no Smile that ever was smild
But only one Smile alone

That betwixt the Cradle & Grave
It only once Smild can be
But when it once is Smild
Theres an end to all Misery

THE GOLDEN NET

Three Virgins at the break of day
Whither young Man whither away
Alas for woe! alas for woe!
They cry & tears for ever flow
The one was Clothd in flames of fire
The other Clothd in iron wire
The other Clothd in tears & sighs
Dazling bright before my Eyes

They bore a Net of Golden twine
To hang upon the Branches fine   10
Pitying I wept to see the woe
That Love & Beauty undergo
To be consumd in burning Fires
And in ungratified desires
And in tears clothd Night & day
Melted all my Soul away
When they saw my Tears a Smile
That did Heaven itself beguile
Bore the Golden Net aloft
As on downy Pinions soft   20
Over the Morning of my day
Underneath the Net I stray
Now intreating Burning Fire
Now intreating Iron Wire
Now intreating Tears & Sighs
O when will the morning rise

THE MENTAL TRAVELLER

I traveld thro' a Land of Men
A Land of Men & Women too
And heard & saw such dreadful things
As cold Earth wanderers never knew

For there the Babe is born in joy
That was begotten in dire woe
Just as we Reap in joy the fruit
Which we in bitter tears did sow

And if the Babe is born a Boy
He's given to a Woman Old   10
Who nails him down upon a rock
Catches his shrieks in cups of gold

She binds iron thorns around his head
She pierces both his hands & feet
She cuts his heart out at his side
To make it feel both cold & heat

Her fingers number every Nerve
Just as a Miser counts his gold
She lives upon his shrieks & cries
And she grows young as he grows old   20

Till he becomes a bleeding youth
And she becomes a Virgin bright
Then he rends up his Manacles
And binds her down for his delight

He plants himself in all her Nerves
Just as a Husbandman his mould
And she becomes his dwelling place
And Garden fruitful seventy fold

An aged Shadow soon he fades
Wandring round an Earthly Cot   30
Full filled all with gems & gold
Which he by industry had got

And these are the gems of the Human Soul
The rubies & pearls of a lovesick eye
The countless gold of the akeing heart
The martyrs groan & the lovers sigh

They are his meat they are his drink
He feeds the Beggar & the Poor
And the wayfaring Traveller
For ever open is his door   40

His grief is their eternal joy
They make the roofs & walls to ring
Till from the fire on the hearth
A little Female Babe does spring

And she is all of solid fire
And gems & gold that none his hand
Dares stretch to touch her Baby form
Or wrap her in his swaddling-band

But She comes to the Man she loves
If young or old or rich or poor   50
They soon drive out the aged Host
A Beggar at anothers door

He wanders weeping far away
Untill some other take him in
Oft blind & age-bent sore distrest
Untill he can a Maiden win

And to allay his freezing Age
The Poor Man takes her in his arms
The Cottage fades before his sight
The Garden & its lovely Charms   60

The Guests are scatterd thro' the land
For the Eye altering alters all
The Senses roll themselves in fear
And the flat Earth becomes a Ball

The Stars Sun Moon all shrink away
A desart vast without a bound
And nothing left to eat or drink
And a dark desart all around

The honey of her Infant lips
The bread & wine of her sweet smile   70
The wild game of her roving Eye
Does him to Infancy beguile

For as he eats & drinks he grows
Younger & younger every day
And on the desart wild they both
Wander in terror & dismay

Like the wild Stag she flees away
Her fear plants many a thicket wild
While he pursues her night & day
By various arts of Love beguild   80

By various arts of Love & Hate
Till the wide desart planted oer
With Labyrinths of wayward Love
Where roams the Lion Wolf & Boar

Till he becomes a wayward Babe
And she a weeping Woman Old
Then many a Lover wanders here
The Sun & Stars are nearer rolld

The trees bring forth sweet Extacy
To all who in the desert roam   90
Till many a City there is Built
And many a pleasant Shepherds home

But when they find the frowning Babe
Terror strikes thro the region wide
They cry the Babe the Babe is Born
And flee away on Every side

For who dare touch the frowning form
His arm is witherd to its root
Lions Boars Wolves all howling flee
And every Tree does shed its fruit   100

And none can touch that frowning form
Except it be a Woman Old
She nails him down upon the Rock
And all is done as I have told

THE LAND OF DREAMS

Awake awake my little Boy
Thou wast thy Mothers only joy
Why dost thou weep in thy gentle sleep
Awake thy Father does thee keep

O what Land is the Land of Dreams
What are its Mountains & what are its Streams
O Father I saw my Mother there
Among the Lillies by waters fair

Among the Lambs clothed in white
She walkd with her Thomas in sweet delight   10
I wept for joy like a dove I mourn
O when shall I again return

Dear Child I also by pleasant Streams
Have wanderd all Night in the Land of Dreams
But tho calm & warm the waters wide
I could not get to the other side

Father O Father what do we here
In this Land of unbelief & fear
The Land of Dreams is better far
Above the light of the Morning Star   20

MARY

Sweet Mary the first time she ever was there
Came into the Ball room among the Fair
The young Men & Maidens around her throng
And these are the words upon every tongue

An Angel is here from the heavenly Climes
Or again does return the Golden times
Her eyes outshine every brilliant ray
She opens her lips tis the Month of May

Mary moves in soft beauty & conscious delight
To augment with sweet smiles all the joys of the Night   10
Nor once blushes to own to the rest of the Fair
That sweet Love & Beauty are worthy our care

In the Morning the Villagers rose with delight
And repeated with pleasure the joys of the night
And Mary arose among Friends to be free
But no Friend from henceforward thou Mary shalt see

Some said she was proud some calld her a whore
And some when she passed by shut to the door
A damp cold came oer her her blushes all fled
Her lillies & roses are blighted & shed   20

O why was I born with a different Face
Why was I not born like this Envious Race
Why did Heaven adorn me with bountiful hand
And then set me down in an envious Land

To be weak as a Lamb & smooth as a dove
And not to raise Envy is calld Christian Love
But if you raise Envy your Merits to blame
For planting such spite in the weak & the tame

I will humble my Beauty I will not dress fine
I will keep from the Ball & my Eyes shall not shine   30
And if any Girls Lover forsakes her for me
I'll refuse him my hand & from Envy be free

She went out in Morning attird plain & neat
Proud Marys gone Mad said the Child in the Street
She went out in Morning in plain neat attire
And came home in Evening bespatterd with mire

She trembled & wept sitting on the Bed side
She forgot it was Night & she trembled & cried
She forgot it was Night she forgot it was Morn
Her soft Memory imprinted with Faces of Scorn   40

With Faces of Scorn & with Eyes of disdain
Like foul Fiends inhabiting Marys mild Brain
She remembers no Face like the Human Divine
All Faces have Envy sweet Mary but thine

And thine is a Face of sweet Love in Despair
And thine is a Face of mild sorrow & care
And thine is a Face of wild terror & fear
That shall never be quiet till laid on its bier

THE CRYSTAL CABINET

The Maiden caught me in the Wild
Where I was dancing merrily
She put me into her Cabinet
And Lockd me up with a golden Key

This Cabinet is formd of Gold
And Pearl & Crystal shining bright
And within it opens into a World
And a little lovely Moony Night

Another England there I saw
Another London with its Tower   10
Another Thames & other Hills
And another pleasant Surrey Bower

Another Maiden like herself
Translucent lovely shining clear
Threefold each in the other closd
O what a pleasant trembling fear

O what a smile a threefold Smile
Filld me that like a flame I burnd
I bent to Kiss the lovely Maid
And found a Threefold Kiss returnd   20

I strove to sieze the inmost Form
With ardor fierce & hands of flame
But burst the Crystal Cabinet
And like a Weeping Babe became

A weeping Babe upon the wild
And Weeping Woman pale reclind
And in the outward air again
I filld with woes the passing Wind

THE GREY MONK

I die I die the Mother said
My Children die for lack of Bread
What more has the merciless Tyrant said
The Monk sat down on the Stony Bed

The blood red ran from the Grey Monks side
His hands & feet were wounded wide
His Body bent his arms & knees
Like to the roots of ancient trees

His eye was dry no tear could flow
A hollow groan first spoke his woe   10
He trembled & shudderd upon the Bed
At length with a feeble cry he said

When God commanded this hand to write
In the studious hours of deep midnight
He told me the writing I wrote should prove
The Bane of all that on Earth I lovd

My Brother starvd between two Walls
His Childrens Cry my Soul appalls
I mockd at the wrack & griding chain
My bent body mocks their torturing pain   20

Thy Father drew his sword in the North
With his thousands strong he marched forth
Thy Brother has armd himself in Steel
To avenge the wrongs thy Children feel

But vain the Sword & vain the Bow
They never can work Wars overthrow
The Hermits Prayer & the Widows tear
Alone can free the World from fear

For a Tear is an Intellectual Thing
And a Sigh is the Sword of an Angel King   30
And the bitter groan of the Martyrs woe
Is an Arrow from the Almighties Bow

The hand of Vengeance found the Bed
To which the Purple Tyrant fled
The iron hand crushd the Tyrants head
And became a Tyrant in his stead

AUGURIES OF INNOCENCE

To see a World in a Grain of Sand
And a Heaven in a Wild Flower
Hold Infinity in the palm of your hand
And Eternity in an hour

A Robin Red breast in a Cage
Puts all Heaven in a Rage
A dove house filld with doves & Pigeons
Shudders Hell thro all its regions
A dog starvd at his Masters Gate
Predicts the ruin of the State   10
A Horse misusd upon the Road
Calls to Heaven for Human blood
Each outcry of the hunted Hare
A fibre from the Brain does tear
A Skylark wounded in the wing
A Cherubim does cease to sing
The Game Cock clipd & armd for fight
Does the Rising Sun affright
Every Wolfs & Lions howl
Raises from Hell a Human Soul   20
The wild deer wandring here & there
Keeps the Human Soul from Care
The Lamb misusd breeds Public strife
And yet forgives the Butchers Knife
The Bat that flits at close of Eve
Has left the Brain that wont Believe
The Owl that calls upon the Night
Speaks the Unbelievers fright
He who shall hurt the little Wren
Shall never be belovd by Men   30
He who the Ox to wrath has movd
Shall never be by Woman lovd
The wanton Boy that kills the Fly
Shall feel the Spiders enmity
He who torments the Chafers sprite
Weaves a Bower in endless Night
The Catterpiller on the Leaf
Repeats to thee thy Mothers grief
Kill not the Moth nor Butterfly
For the Last Judgment draweth nigh   40
He who shall train the Horse to War
Shall never pass the Polar Bar

The Beggers Dog & Widows Cat
Feed them & thou wilt grow fat
The Gnat that sings his Summers song
Poison gets from Slanders tongue
The poison of the Snake & Newt
Is the sweat of Envys Foot
The Poison of the Honey Bee
Is the Artists Jealousy   50
The Princes Robes & Beggars Rags
Are Toadstools on the Misers Bags
A truth thats told with bad intent
Beats all the Lies you can invent
It is right it should be so
Man was made for Joy & Woe
And when this we rightly know
Thro the World we safely go
Joy & Woe are woven fine
A Clothing for the Soul divine   60
Under every grief & pine
Runs a joy with silken twine
The Babe is more than swadling Bands
Throughout all these Human Lands
Tools were made & Born were hands
Every Farmer Understands
Every Tear from Every Eye
Becomes a Babe in Eternity
This is caught by Females bright
And returnd to its own delight   70
The Bleat the Bark Bellow & Roar
Are Waves that Beat on Heavens Shore
The Babe that weeps the Rod beneath
Writes Revenge in realms of death
The Beggars Rags fluttering in Air
Does to Rags the Heavens tear
The Soldier armd with Sword & Gun
Palsied strikes the Summers Sun
The poor Mans Farthing is worth more
Than all the Gold on Africs Shore   80

One Mite wrung from the Labrers hands
Shall buy & sell the Misers Lands
Or if protected from on high
Does that whole Nation sell & buy
He who mocks the Infants Faith
Shall be mock'd in Age & Death
He who shall teach the Child to Doubt
The rotting Grave shall neer get out
He who respects the Infants faith
Triumphs over Hell & Death   90
The Childs Toys & the Old Mans Reasons
Are the Fruits of the Two seasons
The Questioner who sits so sly
Shall never know how to Reply
He who replies to words of Doubt
Doth put the Light of Knowledge out
The Strongest Poison ever known
Came from Caesars Laurel Crown
Nought can deform the Human Race
Like to the Armours iron brace   100
When Gold & Gems adorn the Plow
To peaceful Arts shall Envy Bow
A Riddle or the Crickets Cry
Is to Doubt a fit Reply
The Emmets Inch & Eagles Mile
Make Lame Philosophy to smile
He who Doubts from what he sees
Will neer Believe do what you Please
If the Sun & Moon should doubt
Theyd immediately Go out   110
To be in a Passion you Good may do
But no Good if a Passion is in you
The Whore & Gambler by the State
Licencd build that Nations Fate
The Harlots cry from Street to Street
Shall weave Old Englands winding Sheet
The Winners Shout the Losers Curse
Dance before dead Englands Hearse

Every Night & every Morn
Some to Misery are Born   120
Every Morn & every Night
Some are Born to sweet delight
Some are Born to sweet delight
Some are Born to Endless Night
We are led to Believe a Lie
When we see [*with*] not Thro the Eye
Which was Born in a Night to perish in a Night
When the Soul Slept in Beams of Light
God Appears & God is Light
To those poor Souls who dwell in Night   130
But does a Human Form Display
To those who Dwell in Realms of day

LONG JOHN BROWN & LITTLE MARY BELL

[*Pretty*] Little Mary Bell had a Fairy in a Nut
[*Young*] Long John Brown had the Devil in his Gut
[*Young*] Long John Brown lovd [*Pretty*] Little Mary Bell
And the Fairy drew the Devil into the Nut-shell

Her Fairy skipd out & her Fairy skipd in
He laughd at the devil saying Love is a Sin
The devil he raged & the devil he was wroth
And the devil enterd into the Young Mans broth

He was soon in the Gut of the loving Young Swain
For John eat & drank to drive away Loves pain   10
But all he could do he grew thinner & thinner
Tho he eat & drank as much as ten Men for his dinner

Some said he had a Wolf in his stomach day & night
Some said he had the devil & they guessd right
The fairy skipd about in his glory Joy & Pride
And he laughd at the devil till poor John Brown died

Then the Fairy skipd out of the old Nut shell
And woe & alack for Pretty Mary Bell
For the Devil crept in when the Fairy skipd out
And there goes Miss Bell with her fusty old Nut   20

WILLIAM BOND

I wonder whether the Girls are mad
And I wonder whether they mean to kill
And I wonder if William Bond will die
For assuredly he is very ill

He went to Church in a May morning
Attended by Fairies one two & three
But the Angels of Providence drove them away
And he returnd home in Misery

He went not out to the Field nor Fold
He went not out to the Village nor Town   10
But he came home in a black black cloud
And took to his Bed & there lay down

And an Angel of Providence at his Feet
And an Angel of Providence at his Head
And in the midst a Black Black Cloud
And in the midst the Sick Man on his Bed

And on his Right hand was Mary Green
And on his Left hand was his Sister Jane
And their tears fell thro the black black Cloud
To drive away the sick mans pain   20

O William if thou dost another Love
Dost another Love better than poor Mary
Go & take that other to be thy Wife
And Mary Green shall her Servant be

Yes Mary I do another Love
Another I Love far better than thee
And Another I will have for my Wife
Then what have I to do with thee

For thou art Melancholy Pale
And on thy Head is the cold Moons shine   30
But she is ruddy & bright as day
And the sun beams dazzle from her eyne

Mary trembled & Mary chilld
And Mary fell down on the right hand floor
That William Bond & his Sister Jane
Scarce could recover Mary more

When Mary woke & found her Laid
On the Right hand of her William dear
On the Right hand of his loved Bed
And saw her William Bond so near 40

The Fairies that fled from William Bond
Danced around her Shining Head
They danced over the Pillow white
And the Angels of Providence left the Bed

I thought Love livd in the hot sun shine
But O he lives in the Moony light
I thought to find Love in the heat of day
But sweet Love is the Comforter of Night

Seek Love in the Pity of others Woe
In the gentle relief of anothers care
In the darkness of night & the winters snow 50
In the naked & outcast Seek Love there

MILTON

a Poem in 2 Books
To Justify the Ways of God to Men

PLATE I

PREFACE

The Stolen and Perverted Writings of Homer & Ovid: of
Plato & Cicero. which all Men ought to contemn: are set
up by artifice against the Sublime of the Bible. but when
the New Age is at leisure to Pronounce: all will be set
right: & those Grand Works of the more ancient &
consciously & professedly Inspired Men, will hold their
proper rank, & the Daughters of Memory shall become
the Daughters of Inspiration. Shakspeare & Milton were
both curbd by the general malady & infection from the
silly Greek & Latin slaves of the Sword.   10
      Rouze up O Young Men of the New Age! set your
foreheads against the ignorant Hirelings! For we have
Hirelings in the Camp, the Court & the University:
who would if they could, for ever depress Mental &
prolong Corporeal War. Painters! on you I call! Sculptors!
Architects! Suffer not the fash[i]onable Fools to depress
your powers by the prices they pretend to give for con-
temptible works or the expensive advertizing boasts that
they make of such works; believe Christ & his Apostles that
there is a Class of Men whose whole delight is in Destroy-   20
ing. We do not want either Greek or Roman Models if we
are but just & true to our own Imaginations, those
Worlds of Eternity in which we shall live for ever; in
Jesus our Lord.

And did those feet in ancient time.
Walk upon Englands mountains green:
And was the holy Lamb of God,
On Englands pleasant pastures seen!

And did the Countenance Divine,
Shine forth upon our clouded hills?
And was Jerusalem builded here,
Among these dark Satanic Mills?

Bring me my Bow of burning gold:
Bring me my Arrows of desire:
Bring me my Spear: O clouds unfold!
Bring me my Chariot of fire!

10

I will not cease from Mental Fight,
Nor shall my Sword sleep in my hand:
Till we have built Jerusalem,
In Englands green & pleasant Land.

Would to God that all the Lords people were Prophets.
Numbers XI. ch 29 v.

PLATE 2

MILTON
BOOK THE FIRST

Daughters of Beulah! Muses who inspire the Poets Song
Record the journey of immortal Milton thro' your
     Realms
Of terror & mild moony lustre, in soft sexual delusions
Of varied beauty, to delight the wanderer and repose
His burning thirst & freezing hunger! Come into my
     hand
By your mild power; descending down the Nerves of my
     right arm
From out the Portals of my Brain, where by your
     ministry
The Eternal Great Humanity Divine, planted his
     Paradise,

And in it caus'd the Spectres of the Dead to take sweet
forms
In likeness of himself. Tell also of the False Tongue!
vegetated   10
Beneath your land of shadows: of its sacrifices. and
Its offerings; even till Jesus, the image of the Invisible
God
Became its prey; a curse, an offering. and an atonement,
For Death Eternal in the heavens of Albion, & before
the Gates
Of Jerusalem his Emanation, in the heavens beneath
Beulah

Say first! what mov'd Milton, who walkd about in
Eternity
One hundred years, pondring the intricate mazes of
Providence
Unhappy tho in heav'n, he obey'd, he murmur'd not.
he was silent
Viewing his Sixfold Emanation scatter'd thro' the deep
In torment! To go into the deep her to redeem &
himself perish?   20
What cause at length mov'd Milton to this unexampled
deed?
A Bards prophetic Song! for sitting at eternal tables,
Terrific among the Sons of Albion in chorus solemn &
loud
A Bard broke forth! all sat attentive to the awful man.

Mark well my words! they are of your eternal salvation:

Three Classes are Created by the Hammer of Los, &
Woven
PLATE 3
By Enitharmons Looms when Albion was slain upon
his Mountains
And in his Tent, thro envy of Living Form, even of the
Divine Vision
And of the sports of Wisdom in the Human Imagination

Which is the Divine Body of the Lord Jesus. blessed
   for ever.
Mark well my words. they are of your eternal salvation:

Urizen lay in darkness & solitude, in chains of the mind
   lock'd up
Los siezd his Hammer & Tongs; he labourd at his
   resolute Anvil
Among indefinite Druid rocks & snows of doubt &
   reasoning.

Refusing all Definite Form, the Abstract Horror roofd.
   stony hard
And a first Age passed over & a State of dismal woe: 10

Down sunk with fright a red round Globe hot burning.
   deep
Deep down into the Abyss. panting: conglobing:
   trembling
And a second Age passed over & a State of dismal woe.

Rolling round into two little Orbs & closed in two little
   Caves
The Eyes beheld the Abyss: lest bones of solidness
   freeze over all
And a third Age passed over & a State of dismal woe.

From beneath his Orbs of Vision, Two Ears in close
   volutions
Shot spiring out in the deep darkness & petrified as
   they grew
And a fourth Age passed over & a State of dismal woe.

Hanging upon the wind, Two Nostrils bent down into
   the Deep   20
And a fifth Age passed over & a State of dismal woe.

In ghastly torment sick, a Tongue of hunger & thirst
   flamed out
And a sixth Age passed over & a State of dismal woe.

Enraged & stifled without & within: in terror & woe,
 he threw his
Right Arm to the north, his left Arm to the south, &
 his Feet
Stampd the nether Abyss in trembling & howling &
 dismay
And a seventh Age passed over & a State of dismal woe

Terrified Los stood in the Abyss & his immortal limbs
Grew deadly pale; he became what he beheld: for a red
Round Globe sunk down from his Bosom into the Deep
 in pangs   30
He hoverd over it trembling & weeping. suspended it
 shook
The nether Abyss in tremblings. he wept over it, he
 cherish'd it
In deadly sickening pain: till separated into a Female
 pale
As the cloud that brings the snow: all the while from
 his Back
A blue fluid exuded in Sinews hardening in the Abyss
Till it separated into a Male Form howling in Jealousy

Within labouring. beholding Without: from Particulars
 to Generals
Subduing his Spectre, they Builded the Looms of
 Generation
They Builded Great Golgonooza Times on Times Ages
 on Ages
First Orc was Born then the Shadowy Female: then All
 Los's Family   40
At last Enitharmon brought forth Satan Refusing Form,
 in vain
The Miller of Eternity made subservient to the Great
 Harvest
That he may go to his own Place Prince of the Starry
 Wheels

PLATE 4

Beneath the Plow of Rintrah & the Harrow of the
    Almighty
In the hands of Palamabron. Where the Starry Mills of
    Satan
Are built beneath the Earth & Waters of the Mundane
    Shell
Here the Three Classes of Men take their Sexual
    texture Woven
The Sexual is Threefold: the Human is Fourfold.

If you account it Wisdom when you are angry to be
    silent, and
Not to shew it: I do not account that Wisdom but Folly.
Every Mans Wisdom is peculiar to his own
    Individ[u]ality
O Satan my youngest born, art thou not Prince of the
    Starry Hosts
And of the Wheels of Heaven, to turn the Mills day &
    night?   10
Art thou not Newtons Pantocrator weaving the Woof
    of Locke
To Mortals thy Mills seem every thing & the Harrow
    of Shaddai
A scheme of Human conduct invisible &
    incomprehensible
Get to thy Labours at the Mills & leave me to my
    wrath.

Satan was going to reply, but Los roll'd his loud
    thunders.

Anger me not! thou canst not drive the Harrow in pitys
    paths.
Thy Work is Eternal Death, with Mills & Ovens &
    Cauldrons.
Trouble me no more. thou canst not have Eternal Life

So Los spoke! Satan trembling obeyd weeping along the
    way.
Mark well my words, they are of your eternal Salvation   20

Between South Molton Street & Stratford Place:
    Calvarys foot
Where the Victims were preparing for Sacrifice their
    Cherubim
Around their loins pourd forth their arrows & their
    bosoms beam
With all colours of precious stones, & their inmost
    palaces
Resounded with preparation of animals wild & tame
(Mark well my words! Corporeal Friends are Spiritual
    Enemies)
Mocking Druidical Mathematical Proportion of Length
    Bredth Highth
Displaying Naked Beauty! with Flute & Harp & Song

PLATE 5
Palamabron with the fiery Harrow in morning returning
From breathing fields. Satan fainted beneath the
    artillery
Christ took on Sin in the Virgins Womb, & put it off
    on the Cross

All pitied the piteous & was wrath with the wrathful
    & Los heard it.

And this is the manner of the Daughters of Albion in
    their beauty
Every one is threefold in Head & Heart & Reins, &
    every one
Has three Gates into the Three Heavens of Beulah
    which shine
Translucent in their Foreheads & their Bosoms & their
    Loins
Surrounded with fires unapproachable: but whom they
    please
They take up into their Heavens in intoxicating delight   10
For the Elect cannot be Redeemd, but Created
    continually

By Offering & Atonement in the crue[l]ties of Moral
    Law
Hence the three Classes of Men take their fix'd
    destinations
They are the Two Contraries & the Reasoning
    Negative.

While the Females prepare the Victims, the Males at
    Furnaces
And Anvils dance the dance of tears & pain: loud
    lightnings
Lash on their limbs as they turn the whirlwinds loose
    upon
The Furnaces, lamenting around the Anvils & this
    their Song

Ah weak & wide astray: Ah shut in narrow doleful form
Creeping in reptile flesh upon the bosom of the ground   20
The Eye of Man a little narrow orb closd up & dark
Scarcely beholding the great light conversing with the
    Void
The Ear, a little shell in small volutions shutting out
All melodies & comprehending only Discord and
    Harmony
The Tongue a little moisture fills, a little food it cloys
A little sound it utters & its cries are faintly heard
Then brings forth Moral Virtue the cruel Virgin
    Babylon

Can such an Eye judge of the stars? & looking thro its
    tubes
Measure the sunny rays that point their spears on
    Udanadan
Can such an Ear filld with the vapours of the yawning
    pit.   30
Judge of the pure melodious harp struck by a hand
    divine?
Can such closed Nostrils feel a joy? or tell of autumn
    fruits

When grapes & figs burst their covering to the joyful
   air
Can such a Tongue boast of the living waters? or take
   in
Ought but the Vegetable Ratio & loathe the faint
   delight
Can such gross Lips percieve? alas! folded within
   themselves
They touch not ought but pallid turn & tremble at
   every wind

Thus they sing Creating the Three Classes among
   Druid Rocks
Charles calls on Milton for Atonement. Cromwell is
   ready
James calls for fires in Golgonooza. for heaps of smoking
   ruins   40
In the night of prosperity and wantonness which he
   himself Created
Among the Daughters of Albion among the Rocks of the
   Druids
When Satan fainted beneath the arrows of Elynittria
And Mathematic Proportion was subdued by Living
   Proportion

PLATE 6
From Golgonooza the spiritual Four-fold London
   eternal
In immense labours & sorrows, ever building, ever
   falling,
Thro Albions four Forests which overspread all the
   Earth,
From London Stone to Blackheath east: to
   Hounslow west:
To Finchley north: to Norwood south: and the
   weights
Of Enitharmons Loom play lulling cadences on the
   winds of Albion

From Caithness in the north, to Lizard-point & Dover
  in the south

Loud sounds the Hammer of Los, & loud his Bellows
  is heard
Before London to Hampsteads breadths & Highgates
  heights To
Stratford & old Bow: & across to the Gardens of
  Kensington   10
On Tyburns Brook: loud groans Thames beneath the
  iron Forge
Of Rintrah & Palamabron of Theotorm[on] &
  Bromion, to forge the instruments
Of Harvest: the Plow & Harrow to pass over the
  Nations

The Surrey hills glow like the clinkers of the furnace:
  Lambeths Vale
Where Jerusalems foundations began; where they were
  laid in ruins
Where they were laid in ruins from every Nation & Oak
  Groves rooted
Dark gleams before the Furnace-mouth a heap of
  burning ashes
When shall Jerusalem return & overspread all the
  Nations
Return: return to Lambeths Vale O building of human
  souls
Thence stony Druid Temples overspread the Island
  white   20
And thence from Jerusalem ruins. from her walls of
  salvation
And praise: thro the whole Earth were reard from
  Ireland
To Mexico & Peru west, & east to China & Japan; till
  Babel
The Spectre of Albion frownd over the Nations in
  glory & war

All things begin & end in Albions ancient Druid rocky
shore
But now the Starry Heavens are fled from the mighty
limbs of Albion

Loud sounds the Hammer of Los, loud turn the
Wheels of Enitharmon
Her Looms vibrate with soft affections, weaving the Web
of Life
Out from the ashes of the Dead; Los lifts his iron
Ladles
With molten ore: he heaves the iron cliffs in his
rattling chains
From Hyde Park to the Alms-houses of Mile-end & old
Bow
Here the Three Classes of Mortal Men take their fixd
destinations
And hence they overspread the Nations of the whole
Earth & hence
The Web of Life is woven: & the tender sinews of life
created
And the Three Classes of Men regulated by Los's
Hammer.
PLATE 7
The first, The Elect from before the foundation of the
World:
The second, The Redeem'd. The Third, The Reprobate
& form'd
To destruction from the mothers womb: follow with me
my plow:

Of the first class was Satan: with incomparable
mildness;
His primitive tyrannical attempts on Los: with most
endearing love
He soft intreated Los to give to him Palamabrons
station;
For Palamabron returnd with labour wearied every
evening

30

Palamabron oft refus'd; and as often Satan offer'd
His service till by repeated offers and repeated intreaties
Los gave to him the Harrow of the Almighty; alas
    blamable
Palamabron fear'd to be angry lest Satan should accuse
    him of
Ingratitude, & Los believe the accusation thro Satans
    extreme
Mildness. Satan labour'd all day. it was a thousand
    years
In the evening returning terrified overlabourd &
    astonish'd
Embrac'd soft with a brothers tears Palamabron, who
    also wept

Mark well my words! they are of your eternal
    salvation

Next morning Palamabron rose: the horses of the
    Harrow
Were maddend with tormenting fury, & the servants of
    the Harrow
The Gnomes, accus'd Satan, with indignation fury and
    fire.
Then Palamabron reddening like the Moon in an eclipse,
Spoke saying, You know Satans mildness and his self-
    imposition,
Seeming a brother, being a tyrant, even thinking himself
    a brother
While he is murdering the just; prophetic I behold
His future course thro' darkness and despair to eternal
    death
But we must not be tyrants also: he hath assum'd my
    place
For one whole day, under pretence of pity and love to
    me:
My horses hath he maddend: and my fellow servants
    injur'd:

How should he[,] he[,] know the duties of another? O
   foolish forbearance
Would I had told Los, all my heart! but patience O my
   friends,
All may be well: silent remain, while I call Los and
   Satan.   30

Loud as the wind of Beulah that unroots the rocks &
   hills
Palamabron call'd: and Los & Satan came before him
And Palamabron shew'd the horses & the servants.
   Satan wept,
And mildly cursing Palamabron, him accus'd of crimes
Himself had wrought. Los trembled; Satans
   blandishments almost
Perswaded the Prophet of Eternity that Palamabron
Was Satans enemy, & that the Gnomes being
   Palamabron's friends
Were leagued together against Satan thro' ancient
   enmity.
What could Los do? how could he judge, when Satans
   self, believ'd
That he had not oppres'd the horses of the Harrow, nor
   the servants.   40

So Los said, Henceforth Palamabron, let each his own
   station
Keep: nor in pity false, nor in officious brotherhood,
   where
None needs, be active. Mean time Palamabrons horses.
Rag'd with thick flames redundant, & the Harrow
   maddend with fury.
Trembling Palamabron stood, the strongest of Demons
   trembled:
Curbing his living creatures; many of the strongest
   Gnomes,
They bit in their wild fury, who also madden'd like
   wildest beasts
Mark well my words; they are of your eternal salvation

PLATE 8

Mean while wept Satan before Los, accusing
  Palamabron;
Himself exculpating with mildest speech. for himself
  believ'd
That he had not opress'd nor injur'd the refractory
  servants.
But Satan returning to his Mills (for Palamabron had
  serv'd
The Mills of Satan as the easier task) found all
  confusion
And back return'd to Los, not fill'd with vengeance but
  with tears,
Himself convinc'd of Palamabrons turpitude. Los beheld
The servants of the Mills drunken with wine and
  dancing wild
With shouts and Palamabrons songs, rending the forests
  green
With ecchoing confusion, tho' the Sun was risen on
  high.   10

Then Los took off his left sandal placing it on his head,
Signal of solemn mourning: when the servants of the
  Mills
Beheld the signal they in silence stood, tho' drunk with
  wine.
Los wept! But Rintrah also came, and Enitharmon on
His arm lean'd tremblingly observing all these things

And Los said. Ye Genii of the Mills! the Sun is on high
Your labours call you! Palamabron is also in sad
  dilemma.
His horses are mad! his Harrow confounded! his
  companions enrag'd.
Mine is the fault! I should have remember'd that pity
  divides the soul
And man, unmans: follow with me my Plow. this
  mournful day   20

Must be a blank in Nature: follow with me, and
  tomorrow again
Resume your labours, & this day shall be a mournful
  day

Wildly they follow'd Los and Rintrah, & the Mills were
  silent
They mourn'd all day, this mournful day of Satan &
  Palamabron:
And all the Elect & all the Redeem'd mourn'd one
  toward another
Upon the mountains of Albion among the cliffs of the
  Dead.

They Plow'd in tears! incessant pourd Jehovahs rain, &
  Molechs
Thick fires contending with the rain, thunder'd above
  rolling
Terrible over their heads; Satan wept over Palamabron
Theotormon & Bromion contended on the side of Satan   30
Pitying his youth and beauty; trembling at eternal
  death:
Michael contended against Satan in the rolling thunder
Thulloh the friend of Satan also reprovd him; faint
  their reproof.

But Rintrah who is of the reprobate: of those form'd to
  destruction
In indignation. for Satans soft dissimulation of
  friendship!
Flam'd above all the plowed furrows, angry red and
  furious,
Till Michael sat down in the furrow weary dissolv'd in
  tears[.]
Satan who drave the team beside him, stood angry &
  red
He smote Thulloh & slew him, & he stood terrible over
  Michael
Urging him to arise: he wept! Enitharmon saw his tears   40

But Los hid Thulloh from her sight, lest she should die
of grief
She wept: she trembled! she kissed Satan; she wept
over Michael
She form'd a Space for Satan & Michael & for the
poor infected[.]
Trembling she wept over the Space, & clos'd it with a
tender Moon

Los secret buried Thulloh, weeping disconsolate over
the moony Space
But Palamabron called down a Great Solemn Assembly,
That he who will not defend Truth, may be compelled
to
Defend a Lie, that he may be snared & caught & taken

PLATE 9
And all Eden descended into Palamabrons tent
Among Albions Druids & Bards, in the caves beneath
Albions
Death Couch, in the caverns of death, in the corner of
the Atlantic.
And in the midst of the Great Assembly Palamabron
pray'd:
O God, protect me from my friends, that they have not
power over me
Thou hast giv'n me power to protect myself from my
bitterest enemies.

Mark well my words, they are of your eternal salvation

Then rose the Two Witnesses, Rintrah & Palamabron:
And Palamabron appeal'd to all Eden, and recievd
Judgment: and Lo! it fell on Rintrah and his rage: 10
Which now flam'd high & furious in Satan against
Palamabron
Till it became a proverb in Eden. Satan is among the
Reprobate.

Los in his wrath curs'd heaven & earth, he rent up
Nations,

Standing on Albions rocks among high-reard Druid
temples
Which reach the stars of heaven & stretch from pole to
pole.
He displacd continents, the oceans fled before his face
He alter'd the poles of the world, east, west & north &
south
But he clos'd up Enitharmon from the sight of all these
things

For Satan flaming with Rintrahs fury hidden beneath
his own mildness
Accus'd Palamabron before the Assembly of ingratitude!
of malice: 20
He created Seven deadly Sins drawing out his infernal
scroll,
Of Moral laws and cruel punishments upon the clouds
of Jehovah
To pervert the Divine voice in its entrance to the earth
With thunder of war & trumpets sound, with armies of
disease
Punishments & deaths musterd & number'd; Saying I
am God alone
There is no other! let all obey my principles of moral
individuality
I have brought them from the uppermost innermost
recesses
Of my Eternal Mind, transgressors I will rend off for
ever,
As now I rend this accursed Family from my covering.

Thus Satan rag'd amidst the Assembly! and his bosom
grew   30
Opake against the Divine Vision: the paved terraces of
His bosom inwards shone with fires, but the stones
becoming opake:
Hid him from sight, in an extreme blackness and
darkness,

And there a World of deeper Ulro was open'd, in the
  midst
Of the Assembly. In Satans bosom a vast unfathomable
  Abyss.

Astonishment held the Assembly in an awful silence:
  and tears
Fell down as dews of night, & a loud solemn universal
  groan
Was utter'd from the east & from the west & from the
  south
And from the north; and Satan stood opake
  immeasurable
Covering the east with solid blackness, round his hidden
  heart,   40
With thunders utterd from his hidden wheels: accusing
  loud
The Divine Mercy, for protecting Palamabron in his
  tent.

Rintrah rear'd up walls of rocks and pourd rivers &
  moats
Of fire round the walls: columns of fire guard around
Between Satan and Palamabron in the terrible darkness.

And Satan not having the Science of Wrath, but only of
  Pity:
Rent them asunder, and wrath was left to wrath, & pity
  to pity.
He sunk down a dreadful Death, unlike the slumbers
  of Beulah

The Separation was terrible: the Dead was repos'd on
  his Couch
Beneath the Couch of Albion, on the seven mou[n]tains
  of Rome   50
In the whole place of the Covering Cherub, Rome
  Babylon & Tyre.
His Spectre raging furious descended into its Space

PLATE 10

Then Los & Enitharmon knew that Satan is Urizen
Drawn down by Orc & the Shadowy Female into
    Generation
Oft Enitharmon enterd weeping into the Space, there
    appearing
An aged Woman raving along the Streets (the Space is
    named
Canaan) then she returnd to Los weary frighted as
    from dreams

The nature of a Female Space is this: it shrinks the
    Organs
Of Life till they become Finite & Itself seems Infinite

And Satan vibrated in the immensity of the Space!
    Limited
To those without but Infinite to those within: it fell
    down and
Became Canaan: closing Los from Eternity in Albions
    Cliffs   10
A mighty Fiend against the Divine Humanity mustring
    to War

Satan! Ah me! is gone to his own place, said Los! their
    God
I will not worship in their Churches, nor King in their
    Theatres
Elynittria! whence is this Jealousy running along the
    mountains
British Women were not Jealous when Greek & Roman
    were Jealous
Every thing in Eternity shines by its own Internal light:
    but thou
Darkenest every Internal light with the arrows of thy
    quiver
Bound up in the horns of Jealousy to a deadly fading
    Moon

And Ocalythron binds the Sun into a Jealous Globe
That every thing is fixd Opake without Internal light   20

So Los lamented over Satan, who triumphant divided
   the Nations

PLATE 11

He set his face against Jerusalem to destroy the Eon of
   Albion

But Los hid Enitharmon from the sight of all these
   things,
Upon the Thames whose lulling harmony repos'd her
   soul:
Where Beulah lovely terminates in rocky Albion:
Terminating in Hyde Park, on Tyburns awful brook.
And the Mills of Satan were separated into a moony
   Space
Among the rocks of Albions Temples, and Satans Druid
   sons
Offer the Human Victims throughout all the Earth, and
   Albions
Dread Tomb immortal on his Rock, overshadowd the
   whole Earth:
Where Satan making to himself Laws from his own
   identity,   10
Compell'd others to serve him in moral gratitude &
   submission
Being call'd God: setting himself above all that is called
   God.
And all the Spectres of the Dead calling themselves
   Sons of God
In his Synagogues worship Satan under the Unutterable
   Name

And it was enquir'd: Why in a Great Solemn Assembly
The Innocent should be condemn'd for the Guilty?
   Then an Eternal rose

Saying. If the Guilty should be condemn'd, he must be
   an Eternal Death

And one must die for another throughout all Eternity.
Satan is fall'n from his station & never can be redeem'd
But must be new Created continually moment by
   moment 20
And therefore the Class of Satan shall be calld the
   Elect, & those
Of Rintrah, the Reprobate, & those of Palamabron the
   Redeem'd
For he is redeem'd from Satans Law, the wrath falling
   on Rintrah,
And therefore Palamabron dared not to call a solemn
   Assembly
Till Satan had assum'd Rintrahs wrath in the day of
   mourning
In a feminine delusion of false pride self-deciev'd.

So spake the Eternal and confirm'd it with a thunderous
   oath.

But when Leutha (a Daughter of Beulah) beheld Satans
   condemnation
She down descended into the midst of the Great Solemn
   Assembly
Offering herself a Ransom for Satan, taking on her, his
   Sin. 30

Mark well my words, they are of your eternal
   salvation!

And Leutha stood glowing with varying colours
   immortal, heart-piercing
And lovely: & her moth-like elegance shone over the
   Assembly

At length standing upon the golden floor of Palamabron
She spake: I am the Author of this Sin! by my
   suggestion
My Parent power Satan has committed this
   transgression.

I loved Palamabron & I sought to approach his Tent,
But beautiful Elynittria with her silver arrows repelld
   me.

PLATE 12

For her light is terrible to me. I fade before her
   immortal beauty.

O wherefore doth a Dragon-form forth issue from my
   limbs

To sieze her new born son? Ah me! the wretched
   Leutha!

This to prevent, entering the doors of Satans brain night
   after night

Like sweet perfumes I stupified the masculine
   perceptions

And kept only the feminine awake. hence rose his soft

Delusory love to Palamabron: admiration join'd with
   envy

Cupidity unconquerable! my fault, when at noon of day

The Horses of Palamabron call'd for rest and pleasant
   death:

I sprang out of the breast of Satan, over the Harrow
   beaming   10

In all my beauty: that I might unloose the flaming steeds

As Elynittria use'd to do; but too well those living
   creatures

Knew that I was not Elynittria, and they brake the
   traces

But me, the servants of the Harrow saw not: but as a
   bow

Of varying colours on the hills; terribly rag'd the horses.

Satan astonishd, and with power above his own controll

Compell'd the Gnomes to curb the horses, & to throw
   banks of sand

Around the fiery flaming Harrow in labyrinthine forms.

And brooks between to intersect the meadows in their
   course.

The Harrow cast thick flames: Jehovah thunderd
   above: 20

Chaos & ancient night fled from beneath the fiery
    Harrow:
The Harrow cast thick flames & orb'd us round in
    concave fires
A Hell of our own making. see, its flames still gird me
    round[.]
Jehovah thunder'd above: Satan in pride of heart
Drove the fierce Harrow among the constellations of
    Jehovah
Drawing a third part in the fires as stubble north &
    south
To devour Albion and Jerusalem the Emanation of
    Albion
Driving the Harrow in Pitys paths. 'twas then, with our
    dark fires
Which now gird round us (O eternal torment) I form'd
    the Serpent
Of precious stones & gold turn'd poisons on the sultry
    wastes   30
The Gnomes in all that day spar'd not; they curs'd Satan
    bitterly.
To do unkind things in kindness! with power armd, to say
The most irritating things in the midst of tears and
    love
These are the stings of the Serpent! thus did we by
    them; till thus
They in return retaliated, and the Living Creatures
    maddend.
The Gnomes labourd. I weeping hid in Satans inmost
    brain;
But when the Gnomes refus'd to labour more, with
    blandishments
I came forth from the head of Satan: back the Gnomes
    recoil'd.
And call'd me Sin, and for a sign portentous held me.
    Soon
Day sunk and Palamabron return'd, trembling I hid
    myself   40

In Satans inmost Palace of his nervous fine wrought
  Brain:
For Elynittria met Satan with all her singing women.
Terrific in their joy & pouring wine of wildest power
They gave Satan their wine: indignant at the burning
  wrath.
Wild with prophetic fury his former life became like a
  dream
Cloth'd in the Serpents folds, in selfish holiness
  demanding purity
Being most impure, self-condemn'd to eternal tears, he
  drove
Me from his inmost Brain & the doors clos'd with
  thunders sound
O Divine Vision who didst create the Female: to repose
The Sleepers of Beulah: pity the repentant Leutha. My
PLATE 13
Sick Couch bears the dark shades of Eternal Death
  infolding
The Spectre of Satan. he furious refuses to repose in
  sleep.
I humbly bow in all my Sin before the Throne Divine.
Not so the Sick-one; Alas what shall be done him to
  restore?
Who calls the Individual Law, Holy: and despises the
  Saviour
Glorying to involve Albions Body in fires of eternal
  War –

Now Leutha ceas'd: tears flow'd: but the Divine Pity
  supported her.

All is my fault! We are the Spectre of Luvah the
  murderer
Of Albion: O Vala! O Luvah! O Albion! O lovely
  Jerusalem
The Sin was begun in Eternity, and will not rest to
  Eternity   10

Till two Eternitys meet together, Ah! lost! lost! lost!
    for ever!

So Leutha spoke. But when she saw that Enitharmon had
Created a New Space to protect Satan from punishment;
She fled to Enitharmons Tent & hid herself. Loud
    raging
Thunderd the Assembly dark & clouded, and they
    ratify'd
The kind decision of Enitharmon & gave a Time to the
    Space,
Even Six Thousand years; and sent Lucifer for its
    Guard.
But Lucifer refus'd to die & in pride he forsook his
    charge
And they elected Molech, and when Molech was
    impatient
The Divine hand found the Two Limits: first of
    Opacity, then of Contraction   20
Opacity was named Satan, Contraction was named
    Adam.
Triple Elohim came: Elohim wearied fainted: they
    elected Shaddai.
Shaddai angry, Pahad descended: Pahad terrified, they
    sent Jehovah
And Jehovah was leprous; loud he call'd, stretching his
    hand to Eternity
For then the Body of Death was perfected in hypocritic
    holiness,
Around the Lamb, a Female Tabernacle woven in
    Cathedrons Looms
He died as a Reprobate. he was Punish'd as a
    Transgressor!
Glory! Glory! Glory! to the Holy Lamb of God
I touch the heavens as an instrument to glorify the
    Lord!

The Elect shall meet the Redeem'd. on Albions rocks
    they shall meet   30

Astonish'd at the Transgressor, in him beholding the
   Saviour.
And the Elect shall say to the Redeemd. We behold it is
   of Divine
Mercy alone! of Free Gift and Election that we live.
Our Virtues & Cruel Goodnesses, have deserv'd
   Eternal Death.
Thus they weep upon the fatal Brook of Albions
   River.

But Elynittria met Leutha in the place where she was
   hidden.
And threw aside her arrows, and laid down her sounding
   Bow;
She sooth'd her with soft words & brought her to
   Palamabrons bed
In moments new created for delusion, interwoven round
   about,
In dreams she bore the shadowy Spectre of Sleep, &
   namd him Death.
In dreams she bore Rahab the mother of Tirzah &
   her sisters
In Lambeths vales; in Cambridge & in Oxford, places
   of Thought
Intricate labyrinths of Times and Spaces unknown, that
   Leutha lived
In Palamabrons Tent, and Oothoon was her charming
   guard.
The Bard ceas'd. All consider'd and a loud resounding
   murmur
Continu'd round the Halls; and much they questiond
   the immortal
Loud voicd Bard. and many condemn'd the high tone'd
   Song
Saying Pity and Love are too venerable for the
   imputation
Of Guilt. Others said. If it is true! if the acts have been
   perform'd

40

Let the Bard himself witness. Where hadst thou this
    terrible Song   50

The Bard replied. I am Inspired! I know it is Truth!
    for I Sing

PLATE 14

According to the inspiration of the Poetic Genius
Who is the eternal all-protecting Divine Humanity
To whom be Glory & Power & Dominion Evermore
    Amen

Then there was great murmuring in the Heavens of
    Albion
Concerning Generation & the Vegetative power &
    concerning
The Lamb the Saviour: Albion trembled to Italy
    Greece & Egypt
To Tartary & Hindostan & China & to Great
    America
Shaking the roots & fast foundations of the Earth in
    doubtfulness
The loud voic'd Bard terrify'd took refuge in Miltons
    bosom

Then Milton rose up from the heavens of Albion
    ardorous!   10
The whole Assembly wept prophetic, seeing in Miltons
    face
And in his lineaments divine the shades of Death &
    Ulro
He took off the robe of the promise, & ungirded himself
    from the oath of God

And Milton said, I go to Eternal Death! The Nations
    still
Follow after the detestable Gods of Priam; in pomp
Of warlike selfhood, contradicting and blaspheming.
When will the Resurrection come; to deliver the
    sleeping body

From corruptibility: O when Lord Jesus wilt thou
    come?

Tarry no longer; for my soul lies at the gates of death.

I will arise and look forth for the morning of the grave.   20

I will go down to the sepulcher to see if morning
    breaks!

I will go down to self annihilation and eternal death,

Lest the Last Judgment come & find me unannihilate

And I be siez'd & giv'n into the hands of my own
    Selfhood.

The Lamb of God is seen thro' mists & shadows,
    hov'ring

Over the sepulchers in clouds of Jehovah & winds of
    Elohim

A disk of blood, distant; & heav'ns & earth's roll dark
    between

What do I here before the Judgment? without my
    Emanation?

With the daughters of memory, & not with the
    daughters of inspiration[?]

I in my Selfhood am that Satan: I am that Evil One!   30

He is my Spectre! in my obedience to loose him from
    my Hells

To claim the Hells, my Furnaces, I go to Eternal
    Death.

And Milton said. I go to Eternal Death! Eternity
    shudder'd

For he took the outside course, among the graves of the
    dead

A mournful shade. Eternity shudderd at the image of
    eternal death

Then on the verge of Beulah he beheld his own Shadow;

A mournful form double; hermaphroditic: male &
    female

In one wonderful body. and he enterd into it

In direful pain for the dread shadow, twenty-seven-fold

Reachd to the depths of direst Hell, & thence to Albions
   land: 40
Which is this earth of vegetation on which now I write.

The Seven Angels of the Presence wept over Miltons
   Shadow!

PLATE 15

As when a man dreams, he reflects not that his body
   sleeps,
Else he would wake; so seem'd he entering his Shadow:
   but
With him the Spirits of the Seven Angels of the
   Presence
Entering; they gave him still perceptions of his Sleeping
   Body;
Which now arose and walk'd with them in Eden, as an
   Eighth
Image Divine tho' darken'd; and tho walking as one
   walks
In sleep; and the Seven comforted and supported him.

Like as a Polypus that vegetates beneath the deep!
They saw his Shadow vegetated underneath the Couch
Of death: for when he enterd into his Shadow: Himself: 10
His real and immortal Self: was as appeard to those
Who dwell in immortality, as One sleeping on a couch
Of gold; and those in immortality gave forth their
   Emanations
Like Females of sweet beauty, to guard round him & to
   feed
His lips with food of Eden in his cold and dim
   repose:
But to himself he seemd a wanderer lost in dreary
   night.

Onwards his Shadow kept its course among the
   Spectres; call'd
Satan, but swift as lightning passing them, startled the
   shades

Of Hell beheld him in a trail of light as of a comet
That travels into Chaos: so Milton went guarded
    within.   20

The nature of infinity is this! That every thing has its
Own Vortex; and when once a traveller thro' Eternity
Has passd that Vortex, he percieves it roll backward
    behind
His path, into a globe itself infolding; like a sun:
Or like a moon, or like a universe of starry majesty,
While he keeps onwards in his wondrous journey on the
    earth
Or like a human form, a friend with whom he livd
    benevolent.
As the eye of man views both the east & west
    encompassing
Its vortex; and the north & south, with all their starry
    host;
Also the rising sun & setting moon he views surrounding   30
His corn-fields and his valleys of five hundred acres
    square.
Thus is the earth one infinite plane, and not as apparent
To the weak traveller confin'd beneath the moony shade.
Thus is the heaven a vortex passd already, and the
    earth
A vortex not yet pass'd by the traveller thro' Eternity.

First Milton saw Albion upon the Rock of Ages,
Deadly pale outstretchd and snowy cold, storm coverd;
A Giant form of perfect beauty outstretchd on the rock
In solemn death: the Sea of Time & Space thunderd
    aloud
Against the rock, which was inwrapped with the weeds
    of death   40
Hovering over the cold bosom, in its vortex Milton bent
    down
To the bosom of death, what was underneath soon seemd
    above.

A cloudy heaven mingled with stormy seas in loudest
    ruin;
But as a wintry globe descends precipitant thro' Beulah
    bursting,
With thunders loud, and terrible: so Miltons shadow
    fell,
Precipitant loud thundring into the Sea of Time &
    Space.

Then first I saw him in the Zenith as a falling star,
Descending perpendicular, swift as the swallow or swift;
And on my left foot falling on the tarsus, enterd there;
But from my left foot a black cloud redounding spread
    over Europe.   50

Then Milton knew that the Three Heavens of Beulah
    were beheld
By him on earth in his bright pilgrimage of sixty years

PLATE 16

[Full-page design. For caption see Textual Note.]

PLATE 17

In those three females whom his Wives, & those three
    whom his Daughters
Had represented and contain, that they might be
    resum'd
By giving up of Selfhood: & they distant view'd his
    journey
In their eternal spheres, now Human, tho' their Bodies
    remain clos'd
In the dark Ulro till the Judgment: also Milton knew:
    they and
Himself was Human, tho' now wandering thro Death's
    Vale
In conflict with those Female forms, which in blood &
    jealousy
Surrounded him, dividing & uniting without end or
    number.

He saw the Cruelties of Ulro, and he wrote them down
In iron tablets: and his Wives & Daughters names were
    these   10
Rahab and Tirzah, & Milcah & Malah & Noah &
    Hoglah.
They sat rang'd round him as the rocks of Horeb round
    the land
Of Canaan: and they wrote in thunder smoke and fire
His dictate; and his body was the Rock Sinai; that body,
Which was on earth born to corruption: & the six
    Females
Are Hor & Peor & Bashan & Abarim & Lebanon &
    Hermon
Seven rocky masses terrible in the Desarts of Midian.

But Miltons Human Shadow continu'd journeying
    above
The rocky masses of The Mundane Shell; in the Lands
Of Edom & Aram & Moab & Midian & Amalek.   20
The Mundane Shell, is a vast Concave Earth: an
    immense
Hardend shadow of all things upon our Vegetated Earth
Enlarg'd into dimension & deform'd into indefinite space
In Twenty-seven Heavens and all their Hells; with
    Chaos
And Ancient Night; & Purgatory. It is a cavernous
    Earth
Of labyrinthine intricacy, twenty-seven folds of
    opakeness
And finishes where the lark mounts; here Milton
    journeyed
In that Region call'd Midian, among the Rocks of
    Horeb[.]
For travellers from Eternity. pass outward to Satan's
    seat,
But travellers to Eternity. pass inward to Golgonooza.   30

Los the Vehicular terror beheld him, & divine
    Enitharmon

Call'd all her daughters, Saying. Surely to unloose my
bond
Is this Man come! Satan shall be unloosd upon Albion

Los heard in terror Enitharmons words: in fibrous
strength
His limbs shot forth like roots of trees against the
forward path
Of Miltons journey. Urizen beheld the immortal Man,
PLATE 18
And Tharmas Demon of the Waters, & Orc, who is
Luvah

The Shadowy Female seeing Milton, howl'd in her
lamentation
Over the Deeps outstretching her Twenty seven
Heavens over Albion

And thus the Shadowy Female howls in articulate
howlings

I will lament over Milton in the lamentations of the
afflicted
My Garments shall be woven of sighs & heart broken
lamentations
The misery of unhappy Families shall be drawn out into
its border
Wrought with the needle with dire sufferings poverty pain
& woe
Along the rocky Island & thence throughout the whole
Earth
There shall be the sick Father & his starving Family!
there
The Prisoner in the stone Dungeon & the Slave at the
Mill
I will have Writings written all over it in Human Words
That every Infant that is born upon the Earth shall
read
And get by rote as a hard task of a life of sixty years

I will have Kings inwoven upon it & Councellors &
    Mighty Men

The Famine shall clasp it together with buckles &
    Clasps

And the Pestilence shall be its fringe & the War its
    girdle

To divide into Rahab & Tirzah that Milton may come
    to our tents

For I will put on the Human Form & take the Image of
    God

Even Pity & Humanity but my Clothing shall be
    Cruelty   20

And I will put on Holiness as a breastplate & as a
    helmet

And all my ornaments shall be of the gold of broken
    hearts

And the precious stones of anxiety & care & desperation
    & death

And repentance for sin & sorrow & punishment & fear

To defend me from thy terrors O Orc! my only
    beloved!

Orc answerd. Take not the Human Form O loveliest.
    Take not

Terror upon thee! Behold how I am & tremble lest thou
    also

Consume in my Consummation; but thou maist take a
    Form

Female & lovely, that cannot consume in Mans
    consummation

Wherefore dost thou Create & Weave this Satan for a
    Covering[?]   30

When thou attemptest to put on the Human Form, my
    wrath

Burns to the top of heaven against thee in Jealousy &
    Fear.

Then I rend thee asunder, then I howl over thy clay &
    ashes

When wilt thou put on the Female Form as in times of
   old
With a Garment of Pity & Compassion like the Garment
   of God
His garments are long sufferings for the Children of
   Men
Jerusalem is his Garment & not thy Covering Cherub
   O lovely
Shadow of my delight who wanderest seeking for the
   prey.

So spoke Orc when Oothoon & Leutha hoverd over his
   Couch
Of fire in interchange of Beauty & Perfection in the
   darkness   40
Opening interiorly into Jerusalem & Babylon shining
   glorious
In the Shadowy Females bosom. Jealous her darkness
   grew:
Howlings filld all the desolate places in accusations of
   Sin
In Female beauty shining in the unformd void & Orc
   in vain
Stretch'd out his hands of fire, & wooed: they triumph
   in his pain

Thus darkend the Shadowy Female tenfold & Orc
   tenfold
Glowd on his rocky Couch against the darkness: loud
   thunders
Told of the enormous conflict[.] Earthquake beneath:
   around;
Rent the Immortal Females, limb from limb & joint
   from joint
And moved the fast foundations of the Earth to wake
   the Dead   50

Urizen emerged from his Rocky Form & from his
   Snows,

PLATE 19

And he also darkend his brows: freezing dark rocks
    between
The footsteps. and infixing deep the feet in marble beds:
That Milton labourd with his journey, & his feet bled
    sore
Upon the clay now changd to marble; also Urizen rose,
And met him on the shores of Arnon; & by the streams
    of the brooks

Silent they met, and silent strove among the streams, of
    Arnon
Even to Mahanaim, when with cold hand Urizen
    stoop'd down
And took up water from the river Jordan: pouring on
To Miltons brain the icy fluid from his broad cold
    palm.
But Milton took of the red clay of Succoth, moulding it
    with care   10
Between his palms; and filling up the furrows of many
    years
Beginning at the feet of Urizen, and on the bones
Creating new flesh on the Demon cold, and building
    him,
As with new clay a Human form in the Valley of Beth
    Peor.

Four Universes round the Mundane Egg remain
    Chaotic
One to the North, named Urthona: One to the South,
    named Urizen:
One to the East, named Luvah: One to the West,
    named Tharmas
They are the Four Zoa's that stood around the Throne
    Divine!
But when Luvah assum'd the World of Urizen to the
    South:
And Albion was slain upon his mountains, & in his
    tent;   20

All fell towards the Center in dire ruin, sinking down.
And in the South remains a burning fire; in the East a
    void.
In the West, a world of raging waters; in the North a
    solid,
Unfathomable! without end. But in the midst of these,
Is built eternally the Universe of Los and Enitharmon:
Towards which Milton went, but Urizen oppos'd his
    path.

The Man and Demon strove many periods. Rahab
    beheld
Standing on Carmel; Rahab and Tirzah trembled to
    behold
The enormous strife. one giving life, the other giving
    death
To his adversary. and they sent forth all their sons &
    daughters   30
In all their beauty to entice Milton across the river,

The Twofold form Hermaphroditic: and the Double-
    sexed;
The Female-male & the Male-female, self-dividing stood
Before him in their beauty, & in cruelties of holiness!
Shining in darkness, glorious upon the deeps of
    Entuthon.

Saying. Come thou to Ephraim! behold the Kings of
    Canaan!
The beautiful Amalekites, behold the fires of youth
Bound with the Chain of Jealousy by Los & Enitharmon;
The banks of Cam: cold learnings streams: Londons
    dark-frowning towers,
Lament upon the winds of Europe in Rephaims Vale.   40
Because Ahania rent apart into a desolate night,
Laments! & Enion wanders like a weeping inarticulate
    voice

And Vala labours for her bread & water among the
    Furnaces

Therefore bright Tirzah triumphs: putting on all
    beauty,

And all perfection, in her cruel sports among the
    Victims.

Come bring with thee Jerusalem with songs on the
    Grecian Lyre!

In Natural Religion: in experiments on Men,

Let her be Offerd up to Holiness! Tirzah numbers her;

She numbers with her fingers every fibre ere it grow;

Where is the Lamb of God? where is the promise of
    his coming?   50

Her shadowy Sisters form the bones, even the bones of
    Horeb:

Around the marrow: and the orbed scull around the
    brain:

His Images are born for War! for Sacrifice to Tirzah!

To Natural Religion! to Tirzah the Daughter of Rahab
    the Holy!

She ties the knot of nervous fibres, into a white brain!

She ties the knot of bloody veins, into a red hot heart!

Within her bosom Albion lies embalmd, never to awake

Hand is become a rock! Sinai & Horeb, is Hyle &
    Coban:

Scofield is bound in iron armour before Reubens Gate!

She ties the knot of milky seed into two lovely Heavens   60

PLATE 20

Two yet but one: each in the other sweet reflected!
    these

Are our Three Heavens beneath the shades of Beulah,
    land of rest!

Come then to Ephraim & Manasseh O beloved-one!

Come to my ivory palaces O beloved of thy mother!

And let us bind thee in the bands of War & be thou
    King

Of Canaan and reign in Hazor where the Twelve Tribes
    meet.

So spoke they as in one voice: Silent Milton stood
    before
The darkend Urizen; as the sculptor silent stands before
His forming image; he walks round it patient labouring.
Thus Milton stood forming bright Urizen, while his
    Mortal part   10
Sat frozen in the rock of Horeb: and his Redeemed
    portion,
Thus form'd the Clay of Urizen; but within that
    portion
His real Human walkd above in power and majesty
Tho darkend; and the Seven Angels of the Presence
    attended him.

O how can I with my gross tongue that cleaveth to the
    dust,
Tell of the Four-fold Man, in starry numbers fitly
    orderd
Or how can I with my cold hand of clay! But thou O
    Lord
Do with me as thou wilt! for I am nothing, and vanity.
If thou chuse to elect a worm, it shall remove the
    mountains.
For that portion namd the Elect: the Spectrous body
    of Milton: 20
Redounding from my left foot into Los's Mundane
    space,
Brooded over his Body in Horeb against the
    Resurrection
Preparing it for the Great Consummation; red the
    Cherub on Sinai
Glow'd; but in terrors folded round his clouds of
    blood.

Now Albions sleeping Humanity began to turn upon his
    Couch;
Feeling the electric flame of Miltons awful precipitate
    descent.

Seest thou the little winged fly, smaller than a grain of
   sand?
It has a heart like thee; a brain open to heaven & hell,
Withinside wondrous & expansive; its gates are not
   clos'd,
I hope thine are not: hence it clothes itself in rich array;   30
Hence thou art cloth'd with human beauty O thou
   mortal man.
Seek not thy heavenly father then beyond the skies:
There Chaos dwells & ancient Night & Og & Anak old:
For every human heart has gates of brass & bars of
   adamant,
Which few dare unbar because dread Og & Anak guard
   the gates
Terrific! and each mortal brain is walld and moated
   round
Within: and Og & Anak watch here; here is the Seat
Of Satan in its Webs, for in brain and heart and loins
Gates open behind Satans Seat to the City of
   Golgonooza
Which is the spiritual fourfold London, in the loins of
   Albion   40

Thus Milton fell thro Albions heart, travelling outside
   of Humanity
Beyond the Stars in Chaos in Caverns of the Mundane
   Shell.
But many of the Eternals rose up from eternal tables
Drunk with the Spirit, burning round the Couch of
   death they stood
Looking down into Beulah: wrathful, fill'd with rage!
They rend the heavens round the Watchers in a fiery
   circle:
And round the Shadowy Eighth: the Eight close up the
   Couch
Into a tabernacle, and flee with cries down to the Deeps:
Where Los opens his three wide gates, surrounded by
   raging fires!

They soon find their own place & join the Watchers of
   the Ulro.   50

Los saw them and a cold pale horror coverd o'er his
   limbs
Pondering he knew that Rintrah & Palamabron might
  depart:
Even as Reuben & as Gad; gave up himself to tears.
He sat down on his anvil-stock; and leand upon the
   trough.
Looking into the black water, mingling it with tears.

At last when desperation almost tore his heart in twain
He recollected an old Prophecy in Eden recorded,
And often sung to the loud harp at the immortal feasts
That Milton of the Land of Albion should up ascend
Forwards from Ulro from the Vale of Felpham; and set
   free   60
Orc from his Chain of Jealousy, he started at the thought
PLATE 21
And down descended into Udan-Adan; it was night:
And Satan sat sleeping upon his Couch in Udan-Adan:
His Spectre slept, his Shadow woke; when one sleeps
   th'other wakes.

But Milton entering my Foot; I saw in the nether
Regions of the Imagination; also all men on Earth,
And all in Heaven, saw in the nether regions of the
   Imagination
In Ulro beneath Beulah, the vast breach of Miltons
   descent.
But I knew not that it was Milton, for man cannot
   know
What passes in his members till periods of Space &
   Time
Reveal the secrets of Eternity: for more extensive   10
Than any other earthly things, are Mans earthly
   lineaments.

And all this Vegetable World appeard on my left Foot,
As a bright sandal formd immortal of precious stones &
    gold:
I stooped down & bound it on to walk forward thro'
    Eternity.

There is in Eden a sweet River, of milk & liquid pearl.
Named Ololon; on whose mild banks dwelt those who
    Milton drove
Down into Ulro: and they wept in long resounding song
For seven days of eternity, and the rivers living banks
The mountains wail'd! & every plant that grew, in
    solemn sighs lamented.

When Luvahs bulls each morning drag the sulphur Sun
    out of the Deep   20
Harnessd with starry harness black & shining kept by
    black slaves
That work all night at the starry harness, Strong and
    vigorous
They drag the unwilling Orb: at this time all the
    Family
Of Eden heard the lamentation, and Providence began.
But when the clarions of day sounded they drownd the
    lamentations
And when night came all was silent in Ololon: & all
    refusd to lament
In the still night fearing lest they should others molest.

Seven mornings Los heard them, as the poor bird within
    the shell
Hears its impatient parent bird; and Enitharmon heard
    them:
But saw them not, for the blue Mundane Shell inclos'd
    them in.   30

And they lamented that they had in wrath & fury & fire
Driven Milton into the Ulro; for now they knew too late
That it was Milton the Awakener: they had not heard
    the Bard,

Whose song calld Milton to the attempt; and Los heard
   these laments.
He heard them call in prayer all the Divine Family;
And he beheld the Cloud of Milton stretching over
   Europe.

But all the Family Divine collected as Four Suns
In the Four Points of heaven East, West & North &
   South,
Enlarging and enlarging till their Disks approachd each
   other;
And when they touch'd closed together Southward in
   One Sun   40
Over Ololon: and as One Man, who weeps over his
   brother,
In a dark tomb, so all the Family Divine. wept over
   Ololon.

Saying. Milton goes to Eternal Death! so saying, they
   groan'd in spirit
And were troubled! and again the Divine Family
   groaned in spirit!

And Ololon said, Let us descend also, and let us give
Ourselves to death in Ulro among the Transgressors.
Is Virtue a Punisher? O no! how is this wondrous
   thing?
This World beneath, unseen before: this refuge from the
   wars
Of Great Eternity! unnatural refuge! unknown by us
   till now!
Or are these the pangs of repentance? let us enter into
   them   50

Then the Divine Family said. Six Thousand Years are
   now
Accomplish'd in this World of Sorrow; Miltons Angel
   knew
The Universal Dictate; and you also feel this Dictate.

And now you know this World of Sorrow, and feel Pity.
  Obey
The Dictate! Watch over this World, and with your
  brooding wings,
Renew it to Eternal Life: Lo! I am with you alway
But you cannot renew Milton he goes to Eternal
  Death

So spake the Family Divine as One Man even Jesus
Uniting in One with Ololon & the appearance of One
  Man
Jesus the Saviour appeard coming in the Clouds of
  Ololon: 60

PLATE 22

Tho driven away with the Seven Starry Ones into the
  Ulro
Yet the Divine Vision remains Every-where For-ever.
  Amen.
And Ololon lamented for Milton with a great
  lamentation.
While Los heard indistinct in fear, what time I bound
  my sandals
On; to walk forward thro' Eternity, Los descended to
  me:
And Los behind me stood; a terrible flaming Sun: just
  close
Behind my back; I turned round in terror, and behold.
Los stood in that fierce glowing fire; & he also stoop'd
  down
And bound my sandals on in Udan-Adan; trembling I
  stood
Exceedingly with fear & terror, standing in the Vale   10
Of Lambeth: but he kissed me, and wishd me
  health.
And I became One Man with him arising in my
  strength:
Twas too late now to recede. Los had enterd into my
  soul:

His terrors now posses'd me whole! I arose in fury &
 strength.

I am that Shadowy Prophet who Six Thousand Years
 ago
Fell from my station in the Eternal bosom. Six
 Thousand Years
Are finishd. I return! both Time & Space obey my will.
I in Six Thousand Years walk up and down: for not one
 Moment
Of Time is lost, nor one Event of Space unpermanent.
But all remain: every fabric of Six Thousand Years   20
Remains permanent: tho' on the Earth where Satan
Fell, and was cut off all things vanish & are seen no
 more
They vanish not from me & mine, we guard them first
 & last[.]
The generations of men run on in the tide of Time
But leave their destind lineaments permanent for ever
 & ever.

So spoke Los as we went along to his supreme abode

Rintrah and Palamabron met us at the Gate of
 Golgonooza
Clouded with discontent. & brooding in their minds
 terrible things

They said. O Father most beloved! O merciful Parent!
Pitying and permitting evil, tho strong & mighty to
 destroy.   30
Whence is this Shadow terrible? wherefore dost thou
 refuse
To throw him into the Furnaces! knowest thou not that
 he
Will unchain Orc? & let loose Satan, Og, Sihon &
 Anak,
Upon the Body of Albion? for this he is come! behold it
 written

Upon his fibrous left Foot black! most dismal to our
    eyes
The Shadowy Female shudders thro' heaven in torment
    inexpressible!
And all the Daughters of Los prophetic wail: yet in
    deceit,
They weave a new Religion from new Jealousy of
    Theotormon!
Miltons Religion is the cause: there is no end to
    destruction!
Seeing the Churches at their Period in terror & despair: 40
Rahab created Voltaire; Tirzah created Rousseau;
Asserting the Self-righteousness against the Universal
    Saviour,
Mocking the Confessors & Martyrs, claiming Self-
    righteousness;
With cruel Virtue: making War upon the Lambs
    Redeemed;
To perpetuate War & Glory. to perpetuate the Laws of
    Sin:
They perverted Swedenborgs Visions in Beulah & in
    Ulro;
To destroy Jerusalem as a Harlot & her Sons as
    Reprobates;
To raise up Mystery the Virgin Harlot Mother of War,
Babylon the Great, the Abomination of Desolation!
O Swedenborg! strongest of men, the Samson shorn
    by the Churches!   50
Shewing the Transgressors in Hell, the proud Warriors
    in Heaven:
Heaven as a Punisher & Hell as One under Punishment:
With Laws from Plato & his Greeks to renew the
    Trojan Gods,
In Albion; & to deny the value of the Saviours blood.
But then I rais'd up Whitefield, Palamabron raisd up
    Westley,
And these are the cries of the Churches before the
    two Witnesses[']

Faith in God the dear Saviour who took on the likeness
  of men:
Becoming obedient to death, even the death of the
  Cross
The Witnesses lie dead in the Street of the Great City
No Faith is in all the Earth: the Book of God is trodden
  under Foot: 60
He sent his two Servants Whitefield & Westley; were
  they Prophets
Or were they Idiots or Madmen? shew us Miracles!

PLATE 23

Can you have greater Miracles than these? Men who
  devote
Their lifes whole comfort to intire scorn & injury &
  death
Awake thou sleeper on the Rock of Eternity Albion
  awake
The trumpet of Judgment hath twice sounded: all
  Nations are awake
But thou art still heavy and dull: Awake Albion awake!
Lo Orc arises on the Atlantic. Lo his blood and fire
Glow on Americas shore: Albion turns upon his Couch
He listens to the sounds of War, astonishd and
  confounded:
He weeps into the Atlantic deep, yet still in dismal
  dreams
Unwakend! and the Covering Cherub advances from the
  East: 10
How long shall we lay dead in the Street of the great
  City
How long beneath the Covering Cherub give our
  Emanations
Milton will utterly consume us & thee our beloved
  Father[.]
He hath enterd into the Covering Cherub, becoming
  one with
Albions dread Sons, Hand, Hyle & Coban surround him as
A girdle; Gwendolen & Conwenna as a garment woven

Of War & Religion; let us descend & bring him chained
To Bowlahoola O father most beloved! O mild Parent!
Cruel in thy mildness, pitying and permitting evil
Tho strong and mighty to destroy, O Los our beloved
    Father! 20

Like the black storm, coming out of Chaos, beyond the
    stars:
It issues thro the dark & intricate caves of the Mundane
    Shell
Passing the planetary visions, & the well adorned
    Firmament
The Sun rolls into Chaos & the stars into the Desarts;
And then the storms become visible, audible & terrible,
Covering the light of day, & rolling down upon the
    mountains,
Deluge all the country round. Such is a vision of Los;
When Rintrah & Palamabron spoke; and such his stormy
    face
Appeard, as does the face of heaven, when coverd with
    thick storms
Pitying and loving tho in frowns of terrible perturbation 30
But Los dispersd the clouds even as the strong winds of
    Jehovah.
And Los thus spoke. O noble Sons, be patient yet a
    little[.]
I have embracd the falling Death, he is become One with
    me
O Sons we live not by wrath. by mercy alone we live!
I recollect an old Prophecy in Eden recorded in gold;
    and oft
Sung to the harp: That Milton of the land of Albion
Should up ascend forward from Felphams Vale & break
    the Chain
Of Jealousy from all its roots; be patient therefore O
    my Sons
These lovely Females form sweet night and silence and
    secret

Obscurities to hide from Satans Watch-Fiends. Human
    loves   40
And graces; lest they write them in their Books, & in the
    Scroll
Of mortal life, to condemn the accused: who at
    Satans Bar
Tremble in Spectrous Bodies continually day and night
While on the Earth they live in sorrowful Vegetations
O when shall we tread our Wine-presses in heaven; and
    Reap
Our wheat with shoutings of joy, and leave the Earth in
    peace
Remember how Calvin and Luther in fury premature
Sow'd War and stern division between Papists &
    Protestants
Let it not be so now: O go not forth in Martyrdoms &
    Wars
We were plac'd here by the Universal Brotherhood &
    Mercy   50
With powers fitted to circumscribe this dark Satanic
    death
And that the Seven Eyes of God may have space for
    Redemption.
But how this is as yet we know not, and we cannot
    know;
Till Albion is arisen; then patient wait a little while.
Six Thousand years are passd away the end approaches
    fast;
This mighty one is come from Eden, he is of the
    Elect,
Who died from Earth & he is returnd before the
    Judgment. This thing
Was never known that one of the holy dead should
    willing return
Then patient wait a little while till the Last Vintage
    is over:
Till we have quenched the Sun of Salah in the Lake of
    Udan Adan   60

O my dear Sons! leave not your Father, as your brethren
    left me[.]
Twelve Sons successive fled away in that thousand
    years of sorrow

PLATE 24

Of Palamabrons Harrow, & of Rintrahs wrath & fury:
Reuben & Manazzoth & Gad & Simeon & Levi,
And Ephraim & Judah were Generated, because
They left me, wandering with Tirzah: Enitharmon wept
One thousand years, and all the Earth was in a watry
    deluge
We calld him Menassheh because of the Generations of
    Tirzah
Because of Satan: & the Seven Eyes of God continually
Guard round them, but I the Fourth Zoa am also set
The Watchman of Eternity, the Three are not! & I am
    preserved
Still my four mighty ones are left to me in Golgonooza   10
Still Rintrah fierce, and Palamabron mild & piteous
Theotormon filld with care, Bromion loving Science
You O my Sons still guard round Los. O wander not &
    leave me
Rintrah, thou well rememberest when Amalek & Canaan
Fled with their Sister Moab into that abhorred Void
They became Nations in our sight beneath the hands of
    Tirzah.
And Palamabron thou rememberest when Joseph an
    infant;
Stolen from his nurses cradle wrapd in needle-work
Of emblematic texture, was sold to the Amalekite,
Who carried him down into Egypt where Ephraim &
    Menassheh   20
Gatherd my Sons together in the Sands of Midian
And if you also flee away and leave your Fathers side,
Following Milton into Ulro, altho your power is great
Surely you also shall become poor mortal vegetations
Beneath the Moon of Ulro: pity then your Fathers tears
When Jesus raisd Lazarus from the Grave I stood & saw

Lazarus who is the Vehicular Body of Albion the
  Redeemd
Arise into the Covering Cherub who is the Spectre of
  Albion
By Martyrdoms to suffer: to watch over the Sleeping
  Body.
Upon his Rock beneath his Tomb. I saw the Covering
  Cherub   30
Divide Four-fold into Four Churches when Lazarus
  arose
Paul, Constantine, Charlemaine, Luther; behold they
  stand before us
Stretchd over Europe & Asia. come O Sons, come, come
  away
Arise O Sons give all your strength against Eternal
  Death
Lest we are vegetated, for Cathedrons Looms weave only
  Death
A Web of Death: & were it not for Bowlahoola &
  Allamanda
No Human Form but only a Fibrous Vegetation
A Polypus of soft affections without Thought or Vision
Must tremble in the Heavens & Earths thro all the Ulro
  space
Throw all the Vegetated Mortals into Bowlahoola   40
But as to this Elected Form who is returnd again
He is the Signal that the Last Vintage now approaches
Nor Vegetation may go on till all the Earth is reapd

So Los spoke. Furious they descended to Bowlahoola &
  Allamanda
Indignant, unconvincd by Los's arguments & thun[d]ers
  rolling
They saw that wrath now swayd and now pity absorbd
  him
As it was, so it remaind & no hope of an end.

Bowlahoola is namd Law. by mortals, Tharmas founded
  it:

Because of Satan, before Luban in the City of
    Golgonooza.
But Golgonooza is namd Art & Manufacture by mortal
    men.   50

In Bowlahoola Los's Anvils stand & his Furnaces rage;
Thundering the Hammers beat & the Bellows blow loud
Living self moving mourning lamenting & howling
    incessantly
Bowlahoola thro all its porches feels tho' too fast
    founded
Its pillars & porticoes to tremble at the force
Of mortal or immortal arm: and softly lilling flutes
Accordant with the horrid labours make sweet melody

The Bellows are the Animal Lungs: the Hammers the
    Animal Heart
The Furnaces the Stomach for digestion, terrible their
    fury
Thousands & thousands labour. thousands play on
    instruments   60
Stringed or fluted to ameliorate the sorrows of slavery
Loud sport the dancers in the dance of death, rejoicing
    in carnage
The hard dentant Hammers are lulld by the flutes lula
    lula
The bellowing Furnaces['] blare by the long sounding
    clarion
The double drum drowns howls & groans, the shrill
    fife. shrieks & cries:
The crooked horn mellows the hoarse raving serpent,
    terrible but harmonious
Bowlahoola is the Stomach in every individual man.

Los is by mortals nam'd Time Enitharmon is nam'd
    Space
But they depict him bald & aged who is in eternal youth
All powerful and his locks flourish like the brows of
    morning   70

He is the Spirit of Prophecy the ever apparent Elias
Time is the mercy of Eternity; without Times swiftness
Which is the swiftest of all things: all were eternal
    torment:
All the Gods of the Kingdoms of Earth labour in Los's
    Halls.
Every one is a fallen Son of the Spirit of Prophecy
He is the Fourth Zoa, that stood arou[n]d the Throne
    Divine.

PLATE 25
Loud shout the Sons of Luvah, at the Wine-presses as
    Los descended
With Rintrah & Palamabron in his fires of resistless
    fury.

The Wine-press on the Rhine groans loud, but all its
    central beams
Act more terrific in the central Cities of the Nations
Where Human Thought is crushd beneath the iron
    hand of Power.
There Los puts all into the Press, the Opressor & the
    Opressed
Together, ripe for the Harvest & Vintage & ready for
    the Loom.

They sang at the Vintage. This is the Last Vintage! &
    Seed
Shall no more be sown upon Earth, till all the Vintage
    is over
And all gatherd in, till the Plow has passd over the
    Nations   10
And the Harrow & heavy thundering Roller upon the
    mountains

And loud the Souls howl round the Porches of
    Golgonooza
Crying O God deliver us to the Heavens or to the
    Earths,

That we may preach righteousness & punish the sinner
   with death.
But Los refused, till all the Vintage of Earth was
   gatherd in.

And Los stood & cried to the Labourers of the Vintage
   in voice of awe.

Fellow Labourers! The Great Vintage & Harvest is now
   upon Earth
The whole extent of the Globe is explored: Every
   scatterd Atom
Of Human Intellect now is flocking to the sound of the
   Trumpet
All the Wisdom which was hidden in caves & dens, from
   ancient   20
Time; is now sought out from Animal & Vegetable &
   Mineral
The Awakener is come. outstretchd over Europe! the
   Vision of God is fulfilled
The Ancient Man upon the Rock of Albion Awakes,
He listens to the sounds of War astonishd & ashamed;
He sees his Children mock at Faith and deny Providence
Therefore you must bind the Sheaves not by Nations
   or Families
You shall bind them in Three Classes; according to
   their Classes
So you shall bind them. Separating What has been
   Mixed
Since Men began to be Wove into Nations by Rahab &
   Tirzah
Since Albions Death & Satans Cutting-off from our
   awful Fields;   30
When under pretence to benevolence the Elect Subdud
   All
From the Foundation of the World. The Elect is one
   Class: You
Shall bind them separate: they cannot Believe in Eternal
   Life

Except by Miracle & a New Birth. The other two
    Classes;
The Reprobate who never cease to Believe, and the
    Redeemd,
Who live in doubts & fears perpetually tormented by the
    Elect
These you shall bind in a twin-bundle for the
    Consummation
But the Elect must be saved [from] fires of Eternal
    Death,
To be formed into the Churches of Beulah that they
    destroy not the Earth
For in every Nation & every Family the Three Classes
    are born   40
And in every Species of Earth, Metal, Tree, Fish, Bird
    & Beast,
We form the Mundane Egg, that Spectres coming by
    fury or amity,
All is the same, & every one remains in his own energy[.]
Go forth Reapers with rejoicing. you sowed in tears
But the time of your refreshing cometh, only a little
    moment
Still abstain from pleasure & rest in the labours of
    eternity
And you shall Reap the whole Earth from Pole to Pole:
    from Sea to Sea
Begin[n]ing at Jerusalems Inner Court, Lambeth ruin'd
    and given
To the detestable Gods of Priam, to Apollo: and at the
    Asylum
Given to Hercules, who labour in Tirzahs Looms for
    bread   50
Who set Pleasure against Duty: who Create Olympic
    crowns
To make Learning a burden & the Work of the Holy
    Spirit: Strife.
The Thor & cruel Odin who first reard the Polar
    Caves

Lambeth mourns calling Jerusalem. she weeps & looks
   abroad

For the Lords coming, that Jerusalem may overspread
   all Nations[.]

Crave not for the mortal & perishing delights, but leave
   them

To the weak, and pity the weak as your infant care;
   Break not

Forth in your wrath lest you also are vegetated by
   Tirzah

Wait till the Judgement is past, till the Creation is
   consumed

And then rush forward with me into the glorious
   spiritual   60

Vegetation; the Supper of the Lamb & his Bride; and
   the

Awaking of Albion our friend and ancient companion.

So Los spoke. But lightnings of discontent broke on all
   sides round

And murmurs of thunder rolling heavy long & loud over
   the mountains

While Los calld his Sons around him to the Harvest &
   the Vintage.

Thou seest the Constellations in the deep & wondrous
   Night

They rise in order and continue their immortal courses

Upon the mountains & in vales with harp & heavenly
   song

With flute & clarion; with cups & measures filld with
   foaming wine

Glittering the streams reflect the Vision of beatitude,   70

And the calm Ocean joys beneath & smooths his awful
   waves!

PLATE 26

These are the Sons of Los, & these the Labourers of the
   Vintage

Thou seest the gorgeous clothed Flies that dance & sport
   in summer
Upon the sunny brooks & meadows: every one the
   dance,
Knows in its intricate mazes of delight artful to weave:
Each one to sound his instruments of music in the dance,
To touch each other & recede; to cross & change &
   return
These are the Children of Los; thou seest the Trees on
   mountains
The wind blows heavy, loud they thunder thro' the
   darksom sky
Uttering prophecies & speaking instructive words to the
   sons
Of men: These are the Sons of Los! These the Visions
   of Eternity   10
But we see only as it were the hem of their garments
When with our vegetable eyes we view these wond'rous
   Visions

There are Two Gates thro which all Souls descend. One
   Southward
From Dover Cliff to Lizard Point. the other toward
   the North
Caithness & rocky Durness, Pentland & John Groats
   House.

The Souls descending to the Body, wail on the right
   hand
Of Los; & those deliverd from the Body, on the left
   hand
For Los against the east his force continually bends
Along the Valleys of Middlesex from Hounslow to
   Blackheath
Lest those Three Heavens of Beulah should the Creation
   destroy   20
And lest they should descend before the north & south
   Gates
Groaning with pity, he among the wailing Souls laments.

And these the Labours of the Sons of Los in
    Allamanda:
And in the City of Golgonooza: & in Luban: & around
The Lake of Udan-Adan, in the Forests of Entuthon
    Benython
Where Souls incessant wail, being piteous Passions &
    Desires
With neither lineament nor form but like to watry
    clouds
The Passions & Desires descend upon the hungry
    winds
For such alone Sleepers remain meer passion & appetite;
The Sons of Los clothe them & feed & provide houses
    & fields   30

And every Generated Body in its inward form,
Is a garden of delight & a building of magnificence,
Built by the Sons of Los in Bowlahoola & Allamanda
And the herbs & flowers & furniture & beds & chambers
Continually woven in the Looms of Enitharmons
    Daughters
In bright Cathedrons golden Dome with care & love &
    tears[.]
For the various Classes of Men are all markd out
    determinate
In Bowlahoola; & as the Spectres choose their affinities
So they are born on Earth, & every Class is determinate
But not by Natural but by Spiritual power alone.
    Because   40
The Natural power continually seeks & tends to
    Destruction
Ending in Death: which would of itself be Eternal Death
And all are Class'd by Spiritual, & not by Natural
    power.

And every Natural Effect has a Spiritual Cause, and Not
A Natural: for a Natural Cause only seems, it is a
    Delusion
Of Ulro: & a ratio of the perishing Vegetable Memory.

PLATE 27

But the Wine-press of Los is eastward of Golgonooza,
  before the Seat
Of Satan. Luvah laid the foundation & Urizen finish'd it
  in howling woe.
How red the sons & daughters of Luvah: here they
  tread the grapes.
Laughing & shouting drunk with odours many fall
  oerwearied
Drownd in the wine is many a youth & maiden: those
  around
Lay them on skins of Tygers & of the spotted Leopard
  & the Wild Ass
Till they revive, or bury them in cool grots, making
  lamentation.

This Wine-press is call'd War on Earth, it is the
  Printing-Press
Of Los; and here he lays his words in order above the
  mortal brain
As cogs are formd in a wheel to turn the cogs of the
  adverse wheel.   10

Timbrels & violins sport round the Wine-presses; the
  little Seed;
The sportive Root, the Earth-worm, the gold Beetle;
  the wise Emmet;
Dance round the Wine-presses of Luvah: the Centipede
  is there:
The ground Spider with many eyes: the Mole clothed in
  velvet
The ambitious Spider in his sullen web; the lucky
  golden Spinner;
The Earwig armd: the tender Maggot emblem of
  immortality:
The Flea: Louse: Bug: the Tape-Worm: all the Armies
  of Disease:
Visible or invisible to the slothful vegetating Man.

The slow Slug: the Grasshopper that sings & laughs &
    drinks:
Winter comes, he folds his slender bones without a
    murmur.   20
The cruel Scorpion is there: the Gnat: Wasp: Hornet
    & the Honey Bee:
The Toad & venomous Newt; the Serpent clothd in
    gems & gold:
They throw off their gorgeous raiment: they rejoice with
    loud jubilee
Around the Wine-presses of Luvah, naked & drunk
    with wine.

There is the Nettle that stings with soft down; and
    there
The indignant Thistle: whose bitterness is bred in his
    milk:
Who feeds on contempt of his neighbour: there all the
    idle Weeds
That creep around the obscure places, shew their various
    limbs.
Naked in all their beauty dancing round the Wine-presses.

But in the Wine-presses the Human grapes sing not, nor
    dance   30
They howl & writhe in shoals of torment; in fierce
    flames consuming,
In chains of iron & in dungeons circled with ceaseless
    fires.
In pits & dens & shades of death: in shapes of torment
    & woe.
The plates & screws & wracks & saws & cords & fires &
    cisterns
The cruel joys of Luvahs Daughters lacerating with knives
And whips their Victims & the deadly sport of Luvahs
    Sons.
They dance around the dying, & they drink the howl &
    groan

They catch the shrieks in cups of gold, they hand them
   to one another:
These are the sports of love, & these the sweet delights
   of amorous play
Tears of the grape, the death sweat of the cluster the last
   sigh   40
Of the mild youth who listens to the lureing songs of
   Luvah

But Allamanda calld on Earth Commerce, is the
   Cultivated land
Around the City of Golgonooza in the Forests of
   Entuthon:
Here the Sons of Los labour against Death Eternal;
   through all
The Twenty-seven Heavens of Beulah in Ulro, Seat of
   Satan,
Which is the False Tongue beneath Beulah: it is the
   Sense of Touch:
The Plow goes forth in tempests & lightnings & the
   Harrow cruel
In blights of the east; the heavy Roller follows in
   howlings of woe.

Urizens sons here labour also; & here are seen the Mills
Of Theotormon, on the verge of the Lake of Udan-
   Adan: 50
These are the starry voids of night & the depths &
   caverns of earth
These Mills are oceans, clouds & waters ungovernable
   in their fury
Here are the stars created & the seeds of all things
   planted
And here the Sun & Moon recieve their fixed destinations

But in Eternity the Four Arts: Poetry, Painting, Music,
And Architecture which is Science: are the Four Faces
   of Man.

Not so in Time & Space: there Three are shut out, and only
Science remains thro Mercy: & by means of Science, the Three
Become apparent in Time & Space, in the Three Professions
Poetry in Religion: Music, Law: Painting, in Physic & Surgery: 60
That Man may live upon Earth till the time of his awaking,
And from these Three, Science derives every Occupation of Men.
And Science is divided into Bowlahoola & Allamanda.

PLATE 28

Some Sons of Los surround the Passions with porches of iron & silver
Creating form & beauty around the dark regions of sorrow,
Giving to airy nothing a name and a habitation
Delightful: with bounds to the Infinite putting off the Indefinite
Into most holy forms of Thought: (such is the power of inspiration)
They labour incessant; with many tears & afflictions:
Creating the beautiful House for the piteous sufferer.

Others: Cabinets richly fabricate of gold & ivory;
For Doubts & fears unform'd & wretched & melancholy
The little weeping Spectre stands on the threshold of Death   10
Eternal; and sometimes two Spectres like lamps quivering
And often malignant they combat (heart-breaking sorrowful & piteous)
Antamon takes them into his beautiful flexible hands,
As the Sower takes the seed, or as the Artist his clay
Or fine wax, to mould artful a model for golden ornaments.

The soft hands of Antamon draw the indelible line:
Form immortal with golden pen; such as the Spectre
  admiring
Puts on the sweet form; then smiles Antamon bright
  thro his windows
The Daughters of beauty look up from their Loom &
  prepare.
The integument soft for its clothing with joy & delight.   20

But Theotormon & Sotha stand in the Gate of Luban
  anxious
Their numbers are seven million & seven thousand &
  seven hundred
They contend with the weak Spectres, they fabricate
  soothing forms
The Spectre refuses. he seeks cruelty. they create the
  crested Cock
Terrified the Spectre screams & rushes in fear into their
  Net
Of kindness & compassion & is born a weeping terror.
Or they create the Lion & Tyger in compassionate
  thunderings
Howling the Spectres flee: they take refuge in Human
  lineaments.

The Sons of Ozoth within the Optic Nerve stand fiery
  glowing
And the number of his Sons is eight millions & eight.   30
They give delights to the man unknown; artificial riches
They give to scorn, & their posessors to trouble & sorrow
  & care,
Shutting the sun, & moon, & stars, & trees, & clouds, &
  waters,
And hills, out from the Optic Nerve & hardening it into
  a bone
Opake, and like the black pebble on the enraged beach.
While the poor indigent is like the diamond which tho
  cloth'd
In rugged covering in the mine, is open all within

And in his hallowd center holds the heavens of bright
    eternity
Ozoth here builds walls of rocks against the surging sea
And timbers crampt with iron cramps bar in the joys of
    life   40
From fell destruction in the Spectrous cunning or rage.
    He Creates
The speckled Newt, the Spider & Beetle, the Rat &
    Mouse,
The Badger & Fox: they worship before his feet in
    trembling fear.

But others of the Sons of Los build Moments & Minutes
    & Hours
And Days & Months & Years & Ages & Periods;
    wondrous buildings
And every Moment has a Couch of gold for soft repose,
(A Moment equals a pulsation of the artery)
And between every two Moments stands a Daughter of
    Beulah
To feed the Sleepers on their Couches with maternal
    care.
And every Minute has an azure Tent with silken Veils.   50
And every Hour has a bright golden Gate carved with
    skill.
And every Day & Night, has Walls of brass & Gates of
    adamant,
Shining like precious stones & ornamented with
    appropriate signs:
And every Month, a silver paved Terrace builded high:
And every Year, invulnerable Barriers with high Towers.
And every Age is Moated deep with Bridges of silver &
    gold:
And every Seven Ages is Incircled with a Flaming Fire.
Now Seven Ages is amounting to Two Hundred Years
Each has its Guard. each Moment Minute Hour Day
    Month & Year.
All are the work of Fairy hands of the Four Elements   60

The Guard are Angels of Providence on duty evermore
Every Time less than a pulsation of the artery
Is equal in its period & value to Six Thousand Years.
PLATE 29
For in this Period the Poets Work is Done: and all the
    Great
Events of Time start forth & are concievd in such a
    Period
Within a Moment: a Pulsation of the Artery.

The Sky is an immortal Tent built by the Sons of Los
And every Space that a Man views around his dwelling-
    place:
Standing on his own roof, or in his garden on a mount
Of twenty-five cubits in height, such space is his
    Universe;
And on its verge the Sun rises & sets. the Clouds bow
To meet the flat Earth & the Sea in such an orderd
    Space:
The Starry heavens reach no further but here bend and
    set   10
On all sides & the two Poles turn on their valves of gold:
And if he move his dwelling-place, his heavens also
    move,
Wher'eer he goes & all his neighbourhood bewail his
    loss:
Such are the Spaces called Earth & such its dimension:
As to that false appearance which appears to the
    reasoner,
As of a Globe rolling thro Voidness, it is a delusion of
    Ulro
The Microscope knows not of this nor the Telescope.
    they alter
The ratio of the Spectators Organs but leave Objects
    untouchd
For every Space larger than a red Globule of Mans
    blood,
Is visionary: and is created by the Hammer of Los   20

And every Space smaller than a Globule of Mans blood,
opens
Into Eternity of which this vegetable Earth is but a
shadow:
The red Globule is the unwearied Sun by Los created
To measure Time and Space to mortal Men. every
morning.
Bowlahoola & Allamanda are placed on each side
Of that Pulsation & that Globule, terrible their power.

But Rintrah & Palamabron govern over Day & Night
In Allamanda & Entuthon Benython where Souls wail:
Where Orc incessant howls burning in fires of Eternal
Youth,
Within the vegetated mortal Nerves; for every Man born
is joined
Within into One mighty Polypus, and this Polypus is   30
Orc.

But in the Optic vegetative Nerves Sleep was
transformed
To Death in old time by Satan the father of Sin &
Death
And Satan is the Spectre of Orc & Orc is the generate
Luvah

But in the Nerves of the Nostrils, Accident being
Formed
Into Substance & Principle, by the cruelties of
Demonstration
It became Opake & Indefinite; but the Divine Saviour,
Formed it into a Solid by Los's Mathematic power.
He named the Opake Satan: he named the Solid Adam

And in the Nerves of the Ear, (for the Nerves of the
Tongue are closed)
On Albions Rock Los stands creating the glorious Sun   40
each morning
And when unwearied in the evening he creates the
Moon

Death to delude, who all in terror at their splendor
  leaves
His prey while Los appoints, & Rintrah & Palamabron
  guide
The Souls clear from the Rock of Death, that Death
  himself may wake
In his appointed season when the ends of heaven meet.

Then Los conducts the Spirits to be Vegetated, into
Great Golgonooza, free from the four iron pillars of
  Satans Throne
(Temperance, Prudence, Justice, Fortitude, the four
  pillars of tyranny)
That Satans Watch-Fiends touch them not before they
  Vegetate.   50

But Enitharmon and her Daughters take the pleasant
  charge.
To give them to their lovely heavens till the Great
  Judgment Day
Such is their lovely charge. But Rahab & Tirzah pervert
Their mild influences, therefore the Seven Eyes of God
  walk round
The Three Heavens of Ulro, where Tirzah & her
  Sisters
Weave the black Woof of Death upon Entuthon
  Benython
In the Vale of Surrey where Horeb terminates in
  Rephaim
The stamping feet of Zelophehads Daughters are coverd
  with Human gore
Upon the treddles of the Loom, they sing to the winged
  shuttle:
The River rises above his banks to wash the Woof: 60
He takes it in his arms: he passes it in strength thro his
  current
The veil of human miseries is woven over the Ocean
From the Atlantic to the Great South Sea, the
  Erythrean.

Such is the World of Los the labour of six thousand
  years.
Thus Nature is a Vision of the Science of the Elohim.

End of the First Book.

PLATE 30

MILTON

BOOK THE SECOND

There is a place where Contrarieties are equally True
This place is called Beulah, It is a pleasant lovely
  Shadow
Where no dispute can come, Because of those who
  Sleep.
Into this place the Sons & Daughters of Ololon
  descended
With solemn mourning, into Beulahs moony shades &
  hills
Weeping for Milton: mute wonder held the Daughters of
  Beulah
Enrapturd with affection sweet and mild benevolence

Beulah is evermore Created around Eternity; appearing
To the inhabitants of Eden, around them on all sides.
But Beulah to its Inhabitants appears within each
  district   10
As the beloved infant in his mothers bosom round
  incircled
With arms of love & pity & sweet compassion. But to
The Sons of Eden the moony habitations of Beulah,
Are from Great Eternity a mild & pleasant Rest.

And it is thus Created. Lo the Eternal Great Humanity
To whom be Glory & Dominion Evermore Amen
Walks among all his awful Family seen in every face
As the breath of the Almighty. such are the words of
  man to man

In the great Wars of Eternity, in fury of Poetic
    Inspiration,
To build the Universe stupendous: Mental forms
    Creating   20

But the Emanations trembled exceedingly, nor could
    they
Live, because the life of Man was too exceeding
    unbounded
His joy became terrible to them, they trembled & wept
Crying with one voice. Give us a habitation & a place
In which we may be hidden under the shadow of wings
For if we who are but for a time, & who pass away in
    winter
Behold these wonders of Eternity we shall consume

But you O our Fathers & Brothers, remain in Eternity
But grant us a Temporal Habitation. do you speak
To us; we will obey your words as you obey Jesus   30
The Eternal who is blessed for ever & ever. Amen

So spake the lovely Emanations; & there appeard a
    pleasant
Mild Shadow above: beneath: & on all sides round,
PLATE 31
Into this pleasant Shadow all the weak & weary
Like Women & Children were taken away as on wings
Of dovelike softness, & shadowy habitations prepared
    for them
But every Man returnd & went still going forward thro'
The Bosom of the Father in Eternity on Eternity
Neither did any lack or fall into Error without
A Shadow to repose in all the Days of happy Eternity

Into this pleasant Shadow Beulah, all Ololon descended
And when the Daughters of Beulah heard the
    lamentation
All Beulah wept, for they saw the Lord coming in the
    Clouds   10
And the Shadows of Beulah terminate in rocky Albion.

And all Nations wept in affliction Family by Family
Germany wept towards France & Italy: England wept &
   trembled
Towards America: India rose up from his golden bed:
As one awakend in the night: they saw the Lord
   coming
In the Clouds of Ololon with Power & Great Glory!

And all the Living Creatures of the Four Elements,
   wail'd
With bitter wailing: these in the aggregate are named
   Satan
And Rahab: they know not of Regeneration, but only of
   Generation
The Fairies, Nymphs, Gnomes & Genii of the Four
   Elements   20
Unforgiving & unalterable: these cannot be Regenerated
But must be Created, for they know only of Generation
These are the Gods of the Kingdoms of the Earth: in
   contrarious
And cruel opposition: Element against Element, opposed
   in War
Not Mental, as the Wars of Eternity, but a Corporeal
   Strife
In Los's Halls continual labouring in the Furnaces of
   Golgonooza
Orc howls on the Atlantic: Enitharmon trembles: All
   Beulah weeps

Thou hearest the Nightingale begin the Song of Spring;
The Lark sitting upon his earthy bed: just as the morn
Appears; listens silent; then springing from the waving
   Corn-field! loud   30
He leads the Choir of the Day: trill, trill, trill, trill,
Mounting upon the wings of light into the Great
   Expanse:
Reecchoing against the lovely blue & shining heavenly
   Shell:
His little throat labours with inspiration; every feather

On throat & breast & wings vibrates with the effluence
    Divine
All Nature listens silent to him & the awful Sun
Stands still upon the Mountain looking on this little Bird
With eyes of soft humility, & wonder love & awe.
Then loud from their green covert all the Birds begin
    their Song
The Thrush, the Linnet & the Goldfinch, Robin & the
    Wren   40
Awake the Sun from his sweet reverie upon the
    Mountain:
The Nightingale again assays his song & thro the day,
And thro the night warbles luxuriant; every Bird of
    Song
Attending his loud harmony with admiration & love.
This is a Vision of the lamentation of Beulah over
    Ololon!

Thou percievest the Flowers put forth their precious
    Odours!
And none can tell how from so small a center comes
    such sweets
Forgetting that within that Center Eternity expands
Its ever during doors, that Og & Anak fiercely guard[.]
First eer the morning breaks joy opens in the flowery
    bosoms   50
Joy even to tears, which the Sun rising dries; first the
    Wild Thyme
And Meadow-sweet downy & soft waving among the
    reeds.
Light springing on the air lead the sweet Dance: they
    wake
The Honeysuckle sleeping on the Oak: the flaunting
    beauty
Revels along upon the wind; the White-thorn lovely
    May
Opens her many lovely eyes: listening the Rose still
    sleeps

None dare to wake her. soon she bursts her crimson
    curtaind bed
And comes forth in the majesty of beauty; every Flower:
The Pink, the Jessamine, the Wall-flower, the Carnation
The Jonquil, the mild Lilly opes her heavens: every Tree,   60
And Flower & Herb soon fill the air with an innumerable
    Dance
Yet all in order sweet & lovely, Men are sick with Love!
Such is a Vision of the lamentation of Beulah over
    Ololon

PLATE 32

And Milton oft sat up on the Couch of Death & oft
    conversed
In vision & dream beatific with the Seven Angels of the
    Presence

I have turned my back upon these Heavens builded on
    cruelty
My Spectre still wandering thro' them follows my
    Emanation
He hunts her footsteps thro' the snow & the wintry hail
    & rain
The idiot Reasoner laughs at the Man of Imagination
And from laughter proceeds to murder by undervaluing
    calumny

Then Hillel who is Lucifer replied over the Couch of
    Death
And thus the Seven Angels instructed him & thus they
    converse.

We are not Individuals but States: Combinations of
    Individuals   10
We were Angels of the Divine Presence: & were
    Druids in Annandale
Compelld to combine into Form by Satan, the Spectre
    of Albion,

Who made himself a God &, destroyed the Human Form
    Divine.

But the Divine Humanity & Mercy gave us a   כרכים
    Human Form   as multitudes

Because we were combined in Freedom &   Vox Populi
    holy Brotherhood

While those combind by Satans Tyranny first in the
    blood of War

And Sacrifice &, next, in Chains of imprisonment: are
    Shapeless Rocks

Retaining only Satans Mathematic Holiness, Length:
    Bredth & Highth

Calling the Human Imagination: which is the Divine
    Vision & Fruition

In which Man liveth eternally: madness & blasphemy,
    against   20

Its own Qualities, which are Servants of Humanity, not
    Gods or Lords[.]

Distinguish therefore States from Individuals in those
    States.

States Change: but Individual Identities never change
    nor cease:

You cannot go to Eternal Death in that which can
    never Die.

Satan & Adam are States Created into Twenty-seven
    Churches

And thou O Milton art a State about to be Created

Called Eternal Annihilation that none but the Living
    shall

Dare to enter: & they shall enter triumphant over
    Death

And Hell & the Grave: States that are not, but ah!
    Seem to be.

Judge then of thy Own Self: thy Eternal Lineaments
    explore   30

What is Eternal & what Changeable? & what
    Annihilable:

The Imagination is not a State: it is the Human
    Existence itself
Affection or Love becomes a State, when divided from
    Imagination
The Memory is a State always, & the Reason is a State
Created to be Annihilated & a new Ratio Created
Whatever can be Created can be Annihilated Forms
    cannot
The Oak is cut down by the Ax, the Lamb falls by the
    Knife
But their Forms Eternal Exist, For-ever. Amen
    Halle[l]ujah

Thus they converse with the Dead watching round the
    Couch of Death.
For God himself enters Death's Door always with those
    that enter
And lays down in the Grave with them, in Visions of
    Eternity
Till they awake & see Jesus & the Linen Clothes lying
That the Females had Woven for them, & the Gates of
    their Fathers House

40

PLATE 33

And the Divine Voice was heard in the Songs of Beulah
    Saying

When I first Married you, I gave you all my whole Soul
I thought that you would love my loves & joy in my
    delights
Seeking for pleasures in my pleasures O Daughter of
    Babylon
Then thou wast lovely, mild & gentle. now thou art
    terrible
In jealousy & unlovely in my sight, because thou hast
    cruelly
Cut off my loves in fury till I have no love left for thee
Thy love depends on him thou lovest & on his dear
    loves

Depend thy pleasures which thou hast cut off by
    jealousy
Therefore I shew my Jealousy & set before you Death.   10
Behold Milton descended to Redeem the Female Shade
From Death Eternal; such your lot, to be continually
    Redeem'd
By death & misery of those you love & by Annihilation

When the Sixfold Female percieves that Milton
    annihilates
Himself: that seeing all his loves by her cut off: he leaves
Her also: intirely abstracting himself from Female loves
She shall relent in fear of death: She shall begin to give
Her maidens to her husband: delighting in his delight
And then & then alone begins the happy Female joy
As it is done in Beulah, & thou O Virgin Babylon
    Mother of Whoredoms   20
Shalt bring Jerusalem in thine arms in the night
    watches; and
No longer turning her a wandering Harlot in the streets
Shalt give her into the arms of God your Lord &
    Husband.

Such are the Songs of Beulah in the Lamentations of
    Ololon

PLATE 34

And all the Songs of Beulah sounded comfortable notes
To comfort Ololons lamentation, for they said
Are you the Fiery Circle that late drove in fury & fire
The Eight Immortal Starry-Ones down into Ulro dark
Rending the Heavens of Beulah with your thunders &
    lightnings
And can you thus lament & can you pity & forgive?
Is terror changd to pity O wonder of Eternity:
And the Four States of Humanity in its Repose,
Were shewed them. First of Beulah a most pleasant
    Sleep
On Couches soft, with mild music, tended by Flowers of
    Beulah   10

Sweet Female forms, winged or floating in the air
　spontaneous
The Second State is Alla & the third State Al-Ulro;
But the Fourth State is dreadful; it is named Or-Ulro:
The First State is in the Head, the Second is in the
　Heart:
The Third in the Loins & Seminal Vessels & the Fourth
In the Stomach & Intestines terrible, deadly, unutterable
And he whose Gates are opend in those Regions of his
　Body
Can from those Gates view all these wondrous
　Imaginations

But Ololon sought the Or-Ulro & its fiery Gates
And the Couches of the Martyrs: & many Daughters of
　Beulah　　　　　　　　　　　　　　　　　　　　　　　20
Accompany them down to the Ulro with soft melodious
　tears
A long journey & dark thro Chaos in the track of
　Miltons course
To where the Contraries of Beulah War beneath
　Negations Banner

Then view'd from Miltons Track they see the Ulro: a
　vast Polypus
Of living fibres down into the Sea of Time & Space
　growing
A self-devouring monstrous Human Death Twenty-seven
　fold[.]
Within it sit Five Females & the nameless Shadowy
　Mother
Spinning it from their bowels with songs of amorous
　delight
And melting cadences that lure the Sleepers of Beulah
　down
The River Storge (which is Arnon) into the Dead Sea:　30
Around this Polypus Los continual builds the Mundane
　Shell .

Four Universes round the Universe of Los remain
    Chaotic
Four intersecting Globes, & the Egg form'd World of
    Los
In midst; stretching from Zenith to Nadir, in midst of
    Chaos[.]
One of these Ruind Universes is to the North named
    Urthona
One to the South this was the glorious World of Urizen
One to the East, of Luvah: One to the West; of
    Tharmas.
But when Luvah assumed the World of Urizen in the
    South
All fell towards the Center sinking downward in dire
    Ruin

Here in these Chaoses the Sons of Ololon took their
    abode   40
In Chasms of the Mundane Shell which open on all
    sides round
Southward & by the East within the Breach of Miltons
    descent
To watch the time, pitying & gentle to awaken Urizen
They stood in a dark land of death of fiery corroding
    waters
Where lie in evil death the Four Immortals pale and
    cold
And the Eternal Man, even Albion, upon the Rock of
    Ages[.]
Seeing Miltons Shadow, some Daughters of Beulah
    trembling
Returnd, but Ololon remaind before the Gates of the
    Dead

And Ololon looked down into the Heavens of Ulro in
    fear
They said. How are the Wars of man which in Great
    Eternity   50

Appear around, in the External Spheres of Visionary
Life

Here renderd Deadly within the Life & Interior Vision

How are the Beasts & Birds & Fishes, & Plants &
Minerals

Here fixd into a frozen bulk subject to decay & death

Those Visions of Human Life & Shadows of Wisdom &
Knowledge

PLATE 35

Are here frozen to unexpansive deadly destroying terrors

And War & Hunting: the Two Fountains of the River of
Life

Are become Fountains of bitter Death & of corroding
Hell

Till Brotherhood is changd into a Curse & a Flattery

By Differences between Ideas, that Ideas themselves,
(which are

The Divine Members) may be slain in offerings for
sin

O dreadful Loom of Death! O piteous Female forms
compelld

To weave the Woof of Death. On Camberwell Tirzahs
Courts

Malahs on Blackheath, Rahab & Noah, dwell on
Windsors heights

Where once the Cherubs of Jerusalem spread to
Lambeths Vale   10

Milcahs Pillars shine from Harrow to Hampstead where
Hoglah

On Highgates heights magnificent Weaves over trembling
Thames

To Shooters Hill and thence to Blackheath the dark
Woof! Loud

Loud roll the Weights & Spindles over the whole Earth
let down

On all sides round to the Four Quarters of the World,
eastward on

Europe to Euphrates & Hindu, to Nile & back in Clouds

Of Death across the Atlantic to America North &
   South

So spake Ololon in reminiscence astonishd, but they
Could not behold Golgonooza without passing the
   Polypus
A wondrous journey not passable by Immortal feet, &
   none   20
But the Divine Saviour can pass it without annihilation.
For Golgonooza cannot be seen till having passd the
   Polypus
It is viewed on all sides round by a Four-fold Vision
Or till you become Mortal & Vegetable in Sexuality
Then you behold its mighty Spires & Domes of ivory &
   gold

And Ololon examined all the Couches of the Dead.
Even of Los & Enitharmon & all the Sons of Albion
And his Four Zoas terrified & on the verge of Death
In midst of these was Miltons Couch, & when they saw
   Eight
Immortal Starry-Ones, guarding the Couch in flaming
   fires   30
They thunderous utterd all a universal groan falling
   down
Prostrate before the Starry Eight asking with tears
   forgiveness
Confessing their crime with humiliation and sorrow.

O how the Starry Eight rejoic'd to see Ololon
   descended!
And now that a wide road was open to Eternity,
By Ololons descent thro Beulah to Los & Enitharmon.

For mighty were the multitudes of Ololon, vast the
   extent
Of their great sway, reaching from Ulro to Eternity
Surrounding the Mundane Shell outside in its
   Caverns
And through Beulah. and all silent forbore to contend   40

With Ololon for they saw the Lord in the Clouds of
    Ololon

There is a Moment in each Day that Satan cannot find
Nor can his Watch Fiends find it, but the Industrious
    find
This Moment & it multiply. & when it once is found
It renovates every Moment of the Day if rightly placed
In this Moment Ololon descended to Los & Enitharmon
Unseen beyond the Mundane Shell Southward in
    Miltons track

Just in this Moment when the morning odours rise
    abroad
And first from the Wild Thyme, stands a Fountain in
    a rock
Of crystal flowing into two Streams, one flows thro
    Golgonooza   50
And thro Beulah to Eden beneath Los's western Wall
The other flows thro the Aerial Void & all the Churches
Meeting again in Golgonooza beyond Satans Seat

The Wild Thyme is Los's Messenger to Eden, a mighty
    Demon
Terrible deadly & poisonous his presence in Ulro dark
Therefore he appears only a small Root creeping in grass
Covering over the Rock of Odours his bright purple
    mantle
Beside the Fount above the Larks nest in Golgonooza
Luvah slept here in death & here is Luvahs empty
    Tomb
Ololon sat beside this Fountain on the Rock of Odours.   60

Just at the place to where the Lark mounts, is a Crystal
    Gate
It is the enterance of the First Heaven named Luther:
    for
The Lark is Los's Messenger thro the Twenty-seven
    Churches

That the Seven Eyes of God who walk even to Satans
  Seat
Thro all the Twenty-seven Heavens may not slumber
  nor sleep
But the Larks Nest is at the Gate of Los, at the eastern
Gate of wide Golgonooza & the Lark is Los's
  Messenger
PLATE 36
When on the highest lift of his light pinions he arrives
At that bright Gate, another Lark meets him & back to
  back
They touch their pinions tip tip: and each descend
To their respective Earths & there all night consult with
  Angels
Of Providence & with the Eyes of God all night in
  slumbers
Inspired: & at the dawn of day send out another Lark
Into another Heaven to carry news upon his wings
Thus are the Messengers dispatchd till they reach the
  Earth again
In the East Gate of Golgonooza, & the Twenty-eighth
  bright
Lark, met the Female Ololon descending into my
  Garden   10
Thus it appears to Mortal eyes & those of the Ulro
  Heavens
But not thus to Immortals. the Lark is a mighty
  Angel

For Ololon step'd into the Polypus within the Mundane
  Shell
They could not step into Vegetable Worlds without
  becoming
The enemies of Humanity except in a Female Form
And as One Female, Ololon and all its mighty Hosts
Appear'd: a Virgin of twelve years nor time nor space
  was
To the perception of the Virgin Ololon but as the

Flash of lightning but more quick the Virgin in my
    Garden
Before my Cottage stood, for the Satanic Space is delusion   20

For when Los joind with me he took me in his firy
    whirlwind
My Vegetated portion was hurried from Lambeths
    shades
He set me down in Felphams Vale & prepard a beautiful
Cottage for me that in three years I might write all these
    Visions
To display Natures cruel holiness: the deceits of
    Natural Religion[.]
Walking in my Cottage Garden, sudden I beheld
The Virgin Ololon & address'd her as a Daughter of
    Beulah

Virgin of Providence fear not to enter into my Cottage
What is thy message to thy friend? What am I now to
    do
Is it again to plunge into deeper affliction? behold me   30
Ready to obey, but pity thou my Shadow of Delight
Enter my Cottage, comfort her, for she is sick with
    fatigue

PLATE 37
The Virgin answerd. Knowest thou of Milton who
    descended
Driven from Eternity; him I seek! terrified at my Act
In Great Eternity which thou knowest! I come him to
    seek

So Ololon utterd in words distinct the anxious thought
Mild was the voice, but more distinct than any earthly
That Miltons Shadow heard & condensing all his Fibres
Into a strength impregnable of majesty & beauty infinite
I saw he was the Covering Cherub and within him
    Satan
And Raha[b], in an outside which is fallacious! within

Beyond the outline of Identity, in the Selfhood deadly   10
And he appeard the Wicker Man of Scandinavia in
   whom
Jerusalems children consume in flames among the Stars

Descending down into my Garden, a Human Wonder of
   God
Reaching from heaven to earth a Cloud & Human Form
I beheld Milton with astonishment & in him beheld
The Monstrous Churches of Beulah, the Gods of Ulro
   dark
Twelve monstrous dishumanizd terrors Synagogues of
   Satan.
A Double Twelve & Thrice Nine: such their divisions.

And these their Names & their Places within the
   Mundane Shell

In Tyre & Sidon I saw Baal & Ashtaroth. In Moab
   Chemosh   20
In Ammon, Molech: loud his Furnaces rage among the
   Wheels
Of Og, & pealing loud the cries of the Victims of Fire:
And pale his Priestesses infolded in Veils of Pestilence,
   border'd
With War; Woven in Looms of Tyre & Sidon by
   beautiful Ashtaroth.
In Palestine Dagon, Sea Monster! worshipd o'er the Sea.
Thammuz in Lebanon & Rimmon in Damascus
   curtaind
Osiris: Isis: Orus: in Egypt: dark their Tabernacles on
   Nile
Floating with solemn songs, & on the Lakes of Egypt
   nightly
With pomp, even till morning break & Osiris appear in
   the sky
But Belial of Sodom & Gomorrha, obscure Demon of
   Bribes   30
And secret Assasinations, not worshipd nor adord; but

With the finger on the lips & the back turnd to the
light
And Saturn Jove & Rhea of the Isles of the Sea remote
These Twelve Gods, are the Twelve Spectre Sons of the
Druid Albion

And these the names of the Twenty-seven Heavens &
their Churches
Adam, Seth, Enos, Cainan, Mahalaleel, Jared, Enoch,
Methuselah, Lamech: these are Giants mighty
Hermaphroditic
Noah, Shem, Arphaxad, Cainan the second, Salah,
Heber,
Peleg, Reu, Serug, Nahor, Terah, these are the Female-
Males
A Male within a Female hid as in an Ark & Curtains,   40
Abraham, Moses, Solomon, Paul, Constantine,
Charlemaine
Luther, these seven are the Male-Females, the Dragon
Forms
Religion hid in War, a Dragon red & hidden Harlot

All these are seen in Miltons Shadow who is the
Covering Cherub
The Spectre of Albion in which the Spectre of Luvah
inhabits
In the Newtonian Voids between the Substances of
Creation

For the Chaotic Voids outside of the Stars are measured
by
The Stars, which are the boundaries of Kingdoms,
Provinces
And Empires of Chaos invisible in the Vegetable Man
The Kingdom of Og, is in Orion: Sihon is in Ophiucus   50
Og has Twenty-seven Districts; Sihons Districts
Twenty-one
From Star to Star, Mountains & Valleys, terrible
dimension

Stretchd out, compose the Mundane Shell, a mighty
Incrustation
Of Forty-eight deformed Human Wonders of the
Almighty
With Caverns whose remotest bottoms meet again
beyond
The Mundane Shell in Golgonooza, but the Fires of
Los, rage
In the remotest bottoms of the Caves, that none can pass
Into Eternity that way, but all descend to Los
To Bowlahoola & Allamanda & to Entuthon Benython

The Heavens are the Cherub, the Twelve Gods are   60
Satan

PLATE 38

And the Forty-eight Starry Regions are Cities of the
Levites
The Heads of the Great Polypus, Four-fold twelve
enormity
In mighty & mysterious comingling enemy with enemy
Woven by Urizen into Sexes from his mantle of years
And Milton collecting all his fibres into impregnable
strength
Descended down a Paved work of all kinds of precious
stones
Out from the eastern sky; descending down into my
Cottage
Garden: clothed in black, severe & silent he descended.

The Spectre of Satan stood upon the roaring sea &
beheld
Milton within his sleeping Humanity: trembling &
shuddring   10
He stood upon the waves a Twenty-seven-fold mighty
Demon
Gorgeous & beautiful: loud roll his thunders against
Milton
Loud Satan thunderd, loud & dark upon mild Felpham
shore

Not daring to touch one fibre he howld round upon the
  Sea.

I also stood in Satans bosom & beheld its desolations!
A ruind Man: a ruind building of God not made with
  hands;
Its plains of burning sand, its mountains of marble
  terrible:
Its pits & declivities flowing with molten ore &
  fountains
Of pitch & nitre: its ruind palaces & cities & mighty
  works;
Its furnaces of affliction in which his Angels &
  Emanations   20
Labour with blackend visages among its stupendous
  ruins
Arches & pyramids & porches colonades & domes:
In which dwells Mystery Babylon, here is her secret
  place
From hence she comes forth on the Churches in delight
Here is her Cup filld with its poisons, in these horrid
  vales
And here her scarlet Veil woven in pestilence & war:
Here is Jerusalem bound in chains, in the Dens of
  Babylon

In the Eastern porch of Satans Universe Milton stood
  & said

Satan! my Spectre! I know my power thee to annihilate
And be a greater in thy place, & be thy Tabernacle   30
A covering for thee to do thy will, till one greater comes
And smites me as I smote thee & becomes my covering.
Such are the Laws of thy false Heavns! but Laws of
  Eternity
Are not such: know thou: I come to Self Annihilation
Such are the Laws of Eternity that each shall mutually
Annihilate himself for others good, as I for thee[.]

Thy purpose & the purpose of thy Priests & of thy
   Churches
Is to impress on men the fear of death; to teach
Trembling & fear, terror, constriction; abject selfishness
Mine is to teach Men to despise death & to go on   40
In fearless majesty annihilating Self, laughing to scorn
Thy Laws & terrors, shaking down thy Synagogues as
   webs
I come to discover before Heavn & Hell the Self
   righteousness
In all its Hypocritic turpitude, opening to every eye
These wonders of Satans holiness shewing to the Earth
The Idol Virtues of the Natural Heart, & Satans Seat
Explore in all its Selfish Natural Virtue & put off
In Self annihilation all that is not of God alone:
To put off Self & all I have ever & ever Amen

Satan heard! Coming in a cloud, with trumpets &
   flaming fire,   50
Saying I am God the judge of all, the living & the dead
Fall therefore down & worship me. submit thy supreme
Dictate, to my eternal Will & to my dictate bow
I hold the Balances of Right & Just & mine the Sword
Seven Angels bear my Name & in those Seven I appear
But I alone am God & I alone in Heavn & Earth
Of all that live dare utter this, others tremble & bow
PLATE 39
Till All Things become One Great Satan, in Holiness
Oppos'd to Mercy, and the Divine Delusion Jesus be no
   more

Suddenly around Milton on my Path, the Starry Seven
Burnd terrible! my Path became a solid fire, as bright
As the clear Sun & Milton silent came down on my Path.
And there went forth from the Starry limbs of the
   Seven: Forms
Human; with Trumpets innumerable, sounding articulate
As the Seven spake; and they stood in a mighty Column
   of Fire

Surrounding Felphams Vale, reaching to the Mundane
    Shell, Saying

Awake Albion awake! reclaim thy Reasoning Spectre.
    Subdue   10
Him to the Divine Mercy, Cast him down into the Lake
Of Los, that ever burneth with fire, ever & ever Amen!
Let the Four Zoa's awake from Slumbers of Six
    Thousand Years

Then loud the Furnaces of Los were heard! & seen as
    Seven Heavens
Stretching from south to north over the mountains of
    Albion

Satan heard; trembling round his Body, he incircled it
He trembled with exceeding great trembling &
    astonishment
Howling in his Spectre round his Body hungring to
    devour
But fearing for the pain for if he touches a Vital,
His torment is unendurable: therefore he cannot devour: 20
But howls round it as a lion round his prey continually.
Loud Satan thunderd, loud & dark upon mild
    Felphams Shore
Coming in a Cloud with Trumpets & with Fiery Flame
An awful Form eastward from midst of a bright Paved-
    work
Of precious stones by Cherubim surrounded: so
    permitted
(Lest he should fall apart in his Eternal Death) to imitate
The Eternal Great Humanity Divine surrounded by
His Cherubim & Seraphim in every happy Eternity
Beneath sat Chaos: Sin on his right hand Death on his
    left
And Ancient Night spread over all the heavn his Mantle
    of Laws   30
He trembled with exceeding great trembling &
    astonishment

Then Albion rose up in the Night of Beulah on his
    Couch
Of dread repose seen by the visionary eye; his face is
    toward
The east, toward Jerusalems Gates: groaning he sat
    above
His rocks. London & Bath & Legions & Edinburgh
Are the four pillars of his Throne; his left foot near
    London
Covers the shades of Tyburn: his instep from Windsor
To Primrose Hill stretching to Highgate & Holloway
London is between his knees: its basements fourfold
His right foot stretches to the sea on Dover cliffs, his
    heel
On Canterburys ruins; his right hand covers lofty Wales
His left Scotland; his bosom girt with gold involves
York, Edinburgh, Durham & Carlisle & on the front
Bath, Oxford, Cambridge, Norwich; his right elbow
Leans on the Rocks of Erins Land, Ireland ancient
    nation[.]
His head bends over London: he sees his embodied
    Spectre
Trembling before him with exceeding great trembling &
    fear
He views Jerusalem & Babylon, his tears flow down
He movd his right foot to Cornwall, his left to the Rocks
    of Bognor
He strove to rise to walk into the Deep. but strength
    failing
Forbad & down with dreadful groans he sunk upon his
    Couch
In moony Beulah. Los his strong Guard walks round
    beneath the Moon

Urizen faints in terror striving among the Brooks of
    Arnon
With Miltons Spirit: as the Plowman or Artificer or
    Shepherd

40

50

While in the labours of his Calling sends his Thought
   abroad
To labour in the ocean or in the starry heaven, So Milton
Labourd in Chasms of the Mundane Shell, tho here
   before
My Cottage midst the Starry Seven, where the Virgin
   Ololon
Stood trembling in the Porch: loud Satan thunder'd on
   the stormy Sea
Circling Albions Cliffs in which the Four-fold World
   resides   60
Tho seen in fallacy outside: a fallacy of Satans Churches

PLATE 40

Before Ololon Milton stood & percievd the Eternal
   Form
Of that mild Vision; wondrous were their acts by me
   unknown
Except remotely; and I heard Ololon say to Milton

I see thee strive upon the Brooks of Arnon. there a
   dread
And awful Man I see, oercoverd with the mantle of
   years.
I behold Los & Urizen. I behold Orc & Tharmas!
The Four Zoa's of Albion & thy Spirit with them
   striving
In Self annihilation giving thy life to thy enemies
Are those who contemn Religion & seek to annihilate it
Become in their Femin[in]e portions the causes &
   promoters   10
Of these Religions, how is this thing? this Newtonian
   Phantasm
This Voltaire & Rousseau: this Hume & Gibbon &
   Bolingbroke
This Natural Religion! this impossible absurdity
Is Ololon the cause of this? O where shall I hide my
   face

These tears fall for the little-ones: the Children of
  Jerusalem
Lest they be annihilated in thy annihilation.

No sooner she had spoke but Rahab Babylon appeard
Eastward upon the Paved work across Europe & Asia
Glorious as the midday Sun in Satans bosom glowing
A Female hidden in a Male, Religion hidden in War   20
Namd Moral Virtue; cruel two-fold Monster shining
  bright
A Dragon red & hidden Harlot which John in Patmos
  saw

And all beneath the Nations innumerable of Ulro
Appeard, the Seven Kingdoms of Canaan & Five
  Baalim
Of Philistea, into Twelve divided, calld after the Names
Of Israel: as they are in Eden, Mountain, River &
  Plain
City & sandy Desert intermingled beyond mortal ken

But turning toward Ololon in terrible majesty Milton
Replied. Obey thou the Words of the Inspired Man
All that can be annihilated must be annihilated   30
That the Children of Jerusalem may be saved from
  slavery
There is a Negation, & there is a Contrary
The Negation must be destroyd to redeem the Contraries
The Negation is the Spectre; the Reasoning Power in
  Man
This is a false Body: an Incrustation over my Immortal
Spirit; a Selfhood, which must be put off & annihilated
  alway
To cleanse the Face of my Spirit by Self-examination.
PLATE 41
To bathe in the Waters of Life; to wash off the Not
  Human
I come in Self-annihilation & the grandeur of Inspiration
To cast off Rational Demonstration by Faith in the Saviour

To cast off the rotten rags of Memory by Inspiration
To cast off Bacon, Locke & Newton from Albions
    covering
To take off his filthy garments, & clothe him with
    Imagination
To cast aside from Poetry, all that is not Inspiration
That it no longer shall dare to mock with the aspersion
    of Madness
Cast on the Inspired, by the tame high finisher of
    paltry Blots,
Indefinite, or paltry Rhymes; or paltry Harmonies,   10
Who creeps into State Government like a catterpiller to
    destroy
To cast off the idiot Questioner who is always
    questioning,
But never capable of answering; who sits with a sly
    grin
Silent plotting when to question, like a thief in a cave;
Who publishes doubt & calls it knowledge; whose
    Science is Despair,
Whose pretence to knowledge is Envy, whose whole
    Science is
To destroy the wisdom of ages to gratify ravenous Envy
That rages round him like a Wolf day & night without
    rest
He smiles with condescension; he talks of Benevolence &
    Virtue
And those who act with Benevolence & Virtue, they
    murder time on time   20
These are the destroyers of Jerusalem, these are the
    murderers
Of Jesus, who deny the Faith & mock at Eternal Life:
Who pretend to Poetry that they may destroy
    Imagination;
By imitation of Natures Images drawn from
    Remembrance
These are the Sexual Garments, the Abomination of
    Desolation

Hiding the Human Lineaments as with an Ark &
    Curtains
Which Jesus rent: & now shall wholly purge away with
    Fire
Till Generation is swallowd up in Regeneration.

Then trembled the Virgin Ololon & replyd in clouds of
    despair

Is this our Femin[in]e Portion the Six-fold Miltonic
    Female   30
Terribly this Portion trembles before thee O awful Man
Altho' our Human Power can sustain the severe
    contentions
Of Friendship, our Sexual cannot: but flies into the
    Ulro.
Hence arose all our terrors in Eternity! & now
    remembrance
Returns upon us! are we Contraries O Milton, Thou &
    I
O Immortal: how were we led to War the Wars of
    Death
Is this the Void Outside of Existence, which if enter'd
    into
PLATE 42
Becomes a Womb? & is this the Death Couch of Albion
Thou goest to Eternal Death & all must go with thee

So saying, the Virgin divided Six-fold & with a shriek
Dolorous that ran thro all Creation a Double Six-fold
    Wonder:
Away from Ololon she divided & fled into the depths
Of Miltons Shadow as a Dove upon the stormy Sea.

Then as a Moony Ark Ololon descended to Felphams
    Vale
In clouds of blood, in streams of gore, with dreadful
    thunderings
Into the Fires of Intellect that rejoic'd in Felphams Vale

Around the Starry Eight: with one accord the Starry
    Eight became   10
One Man Jesus the Saviour. wonderful! round his
    limbs
The Clouds of Ololon folded as a Garment dipped in
    blood
Written within & without in woven letters: & the
    Writing
Is the Divine Revelation in the Litteral expression:
A Garment of War, I heard it namd the Woof of Six
    Thousand Years

And I beheld the Twenty-four Cities of Albion
Arise upon their Thrones to Judge the Nations of the
    Earth
And the Immortal Four in whom the Twenty-four
    appear Four-fold
Arose around Albions body: Jesus wept & walked forth
From Felphams Vale clothed in Clouds of blood, to
    enter into   20
Albions Bosom, the bosom of death & the Four
    surrounded him
In the Column of Fire in Felphams Vale; then to their
    mouths the Four
Applied their Four Trumpets & them sounded to the
    Four winds

Terror struck in the Vale I stood at that immortal
    sound
My bones trembled. I fell outstretchd upon the path
A moment, & my Soul returnd into its mortal state
To Resurrection & Judgment in the Vegetable Body
And my sweet Shadow of Delight stood trembling by
    my side

Immediately the Lark mounted with a loud trill from
    Felphams Vale
And the Wild Thyme from Wimbletons green &
    impurpled Hills   30

And Los & Enitharmon rose over the Hills of Surrey
Their clouds roll over London with a south wind, soft
  Oothoon
Pants in the Vales of Lambeth weeping oer her Human
  Harvest
Los listens to the Cry of the Poor Man: his Cloud
Over London in volume terrific, low bended in anger.

Rintrah & Palamabron view the Human Harvest
  beneath
Their Wine-presses & Barns stand open; the Ovens are
  prepar'd
The Waggons ready: terrific Lions & Tygers sport &
  play
All Animals upon the Earth, are prepard in all their
  strength
PLATE 43
To go forth to the Great Harvest & Vintage of the
  Nations

Finis

DEDICATION TO BLAKE'S ILLUSTRATIONS TO BLAIR'S *GRAVE*

TO THE QUEEN

The Door of Death is made of Gold,
That Mortal Eyes cannot behold;
But, when the Mortal Eyes are clos'd,
And cold and pale the Limbs repos'd,
The Soul awakes; and, wond'ring, sees
In her mild Hand the golden Key
The Grave is Heaven's golden Gate,
And rich and poor around it wait;
O Shepherdess of England's Fold,
Behold this Gate of Pearl and Gold!   10

   To dedicate to England's Queen
The Visions that my Soul has seen,
And, by Her kind permission, bring
What I have borne on solemn Wing
From the vast regions of the Grave,
Before Her Throne my Wings I wave;
Bowing before my Sov'reign's Feet,
'The Grave produc'd these Blossoms sweet
'In mild repose from Earthly strife;
'The Blossoms of Eternal Life!'   20

NOTEBOOK EPIGRAMS AND SATIRIC VERSES,
c. 1808–12

You dont believe I wont attempt to make ye
You are asleep I wont attempt to wake ye
Sleep on Sleep on while in your pleasant dreams
Of Reason you may drink of Lifes clear streams
Reason and Newton they are quite two things
For so the Swallow & the Sparrow sings
Reason says Miracle. Newton says Doubt
Aye thats the way to make all Nature out
Doubt Doubt & dont believe without experiment
That is the very thing that Jesus meant   10
When he said Only Believe Believe & try
Try Try & never mind the Reason why

*

No real Style of Colouring ever appears
But advertising in the News Papers
Look there youll see Sr Joshuas Colouring
Look at his Pictures [*tis quite another Thing*] All has
    taken Wing

*

And his legs carried it like a long fork
Reachd all the way from Chichester to York
From York all across Scotland to the Sea
This was a Man of Men as seems to me
Not only in his Mouth his own Soul lay
But my Soul also would he bear away

Like as a Pedlar bears his weary Pack
[*He would bear my Soul*] So Stewhards Soul he buckld to
  his Back
But once alas committing a Mistake
He bore the wretched Soul of William Blake   10
That he might turn it into Eggs of Gold
But neither Back nor mouth those Eggs could hold
His under jaw dropd as those Eggs he laid
And [*all my*] Stewhards Eggs are addled & decayd
The Examiner whose very name is Hunt
Calld Death a Madman [*Deadly the affront*] trembling
  for the affront
Like trembling Hare sits on his weakly paper
On which he usd to dance & sport & caper
Yorkshire Jack Hemp & gentle blushing daw
Clapd Death into the corner of their jaw   20
And Felpham Billy rode out every morn
Horseback with Death over the fields of corn
[*And*] Who with iron hand cuffd in the afternoon
The Ears of Billys Lawyer & Dragoon
And Cur my Lawyer & Dady Jack Hemps Parson
Both went to Law with Death to keep our Ears on
For how to starve Death we had laid a plot
Against his Price but Death was in the Pot
He made them pay his Price alack a day
He knew both Law & Gospel better than they   30
O that I neer ha[d] seen that William Blake
Or could from death Assassinetti wake
We thought Alas that such a thought should be
That Blake would Etch for him & draw for me
For twas a kind of Bargain Screwmuch made
That Blakes designs should be by us displayed
Because he makes designs so very cheap
Then Screwmuch at Blakes soul took a long leap
Twas not a Mouse twas Death in a disguise
And I alas live to weep out mine Eyes   40
And Death sits [*mocking*] laughing on their Monuments
On which hes written Recievd the Contents

But I have writ so sorrowful my thought is
His Epitaph [*with tears of*] for my tears are aqua fortis

[*Ye*] Come Artists knock your heads against This stone
For Sorrow that [*your*] our friend Bob Screwmuchs gone
And now the Men upon me smile & Laugh
Ill also write my own dear Epitaph
And Ill be buried near a Dike
That my friends may weep as much as they like   50
Here lies Stewhard the Friend of All &c

*

Was I angry with Hayley who usd me so ill
Or can I be angry with Felphams old Mill
[*Or angry with Boydell or Bowyer or Ba*]
Or angry with Flaxman or Cromek or Stothard
Or poor Schiavonetti whom they to death botherd
Or angry with Macklin or Boydel or Bowyer
Because they did not say O what a Beau ye are
At a Friends Errors Anger shew
Mirth at the Errors of a Foe

*

Anger & Wrath my bosom rends
I thought them the Errors of friends
But all my limbs with warmth glow
I find them the Errors of the foe

*

The Sussex Men are Noted Fools
And weak is their brain pan
I wonder if H[aines] the painter
Is not a Sussex Man

*

[*Look Flaxman & Stothard do*] old acquaintance well
   renew
Prospero had One Caliban & I have Two

*

Madman I have been calld Fool they call thee
I wonder which they Envy Thee or Me

TO H[UNT]

You think Fuseli is not a Great Painter Im Glad
This is one of the best compliments he ever had

TO F[LAXMAN]

I mock thee not tho I by thee am Mocked
Thou callst me Madman but I call thee Blockhead

*

Can there be any thing more mean
More Malice in disguise
Than Praise a Man for doing [*that*] what
[*Which he*] That Man does most despise
[*This*] Reynolds Lectures [*plainly shew*] Exactly so
When he praises Michael Angelo

*

S[tothard] in Childhood on the Nursery floor
Was extreme Old & most extremely poor
He is grown old & rich & what he will
He is extreme old & extreme poor still

TO NANCY F[LAXMAN]

How can I help thy Husbands copying Me
Should that make difference twixt me & Thee

*

Of H[ayley]s birth this was the happy lot
His Mother on his Father him begot

*

Sir Joshua Praises Michael Angelo
[(*And counts it courage*) *Is it Politeness thus to praise his foe*]

Tis Christian Mildness when [*fools*] Knaves Praise a Foe
But Twould be Madness [*that we all must*] all the
   World would say
[*If All*] Should Michael Angelo [*praising*] praise Sir
   Joshua
Christ usd the Pharisees in a rougher way

*

Hes a Blockhead who wants a proof of what he Cant
   Percieve
And he's a Fool who [*seeks*] tries to make such a
   Blockhead believe

*

Cr[omek] loves artists as he loves his Meat
[*Cr* –] He loves the Art but tis the Art to Cheat

*

A Petty sneaking Knave I knew
O M^r Cr[omek] how do ye do

*

Sir Jo[s]hua praised Rubens with a Smile
By Calling his the ornamental Style
[*Because*] And yet his praise of Flaxman was the smartest
When he calld him the Ornamental Artist
But sure such ornaments we well may spare
[*Like a filthy infectious head of hair*]
[*A Crooked stick & louzy head of hair*]
As Crooked limbs & louzy heads of hair

*

He is a Cock [*wont*] would
And would be a [*crow*] Cock if he could

*

He has observd the Golden Rule
Till hes become the Golden Fool

TO S[TOTHAR]D

[*He*] You all [*his*] your Youth observd the Golden Rule
Till [*hes*] youre at last become the [*old*] golden fool
I sport with Fortune Merry Blithe & Gay
Like to the Lion Sporting with his Prey
[*He has*] Take [*thou*] you the hide & horns which [*he
    may/thou maist*] you may wear
Mine is the flesh the bones may be [*his/thy*] your Share

[*Mr CROMEK TO*] Mr STOTHARD TO
Mr CROMEK

For Fortunes favours you your riches bring
But Fortune says she gave you no such thing
Why should you be ungrateful to your friends
Sneaking & [*Calumny*] Backbiting & Odds & Ends

Mr CROMEK TO Mr STOTHARD

Fortune favours the Brave old Proverbs say
But not with Money. that is not the way
Turn back turn back you travel all in vain
Turn thro the iron gate down Sneaking lane

*

I am no Homers Hero you all know
I profess not Generosity to a Foe
My Generosity is to my Friends
That for their Friendship I may make amends.
The Generous to Enemies promotes their Ends
And becomes the Enemy & Betrayer of his Friends

*

The Angel that presided oer my birth
Said Little creature [*thou art formd for*] formd of Joy &
    Mirth
Go love without the help of any [*Thing*] King on Earth

FLORENTINE INGRATITUDE

Sir Joshua sent his own Portrait to
The birth Place of Michael Angelo
And in the hand of the simpering fool
He put a Dirty paper scroll
And on the paper to be polite
Did Sketches by Michael Angelo write

[*They said Thus Learning & Politeness from England we
    fetch*
(*We thought Michael Angelo did never sketch*)
For no good Artist Will or Can sketch
And tis English Politeness as fair as my Aunt   10
*To (say) speak Michael Angelo & (mean) Act
    Rembrand*
To Say Write Michael Angelo & mean Rembrandt]

The Florentines said Tis a Dutch English bore
Michael Angelos Name writ on Rembrandts door
The Florentines call it an English Fetch
For Michael Angelo did never Sketch
Every line of his has Meaning
And needs neither Suckling nor Weaning

[*Is this Politeness or is it Cant*]

Tis the trading English Venetian Cant   20
To speak Michael Angelo & Act Rembrandt
It will set his Dutch friends all in a roar
To write Mch Ang on Rembrandts Door
But You must not bring in your hand a Lie
If you mean [*the Florentines to*] that the Florentines
    should buy

Ghiottos Circle or Apelles Line
Were not the Work of Sketchers drunk with Wine
Nor of the City Clarks merry hearted Fashion
Nor of Sir Isaac Newtons Calculation   30
Nor of the City Clarks Idle Facilities
Which sprang from Sir Isaac Newtons great Abilities

These Verses were written by a very Envious Man
Who whatever likeness he may have to Michael Angelo
Never can have any to Sir Jehoshuan

A [*PITIABLE*] PITIFUL CASE

The Villain at the Gallows tree
When he is doomd to die
To assuage his misery
In Virtues praise does cry

So Reynolds when he came to die
To assuage his bitter woe:
Thus aloud [*was heard to*] did howl & cry
Michael Angelo Michael Angelo

TO THE ROYAL ACADEMY

A strange Erratum in all the Editions
Of Sir Joshua Reynoldss Lectures
Shou[l]d be corrected by the Young Gentlemen
And the Royal Academys Directors

Instead of Michael Angelo
Read Rembrandt [*& you will know*] for it is fit
[*That Sir Joshua never wishd to speak
Of Michael Angelo*]
To make [*either sense or*] meer common honesty   10
In all that he has writ

*

If it is True What the Prophets write
That the heathen Gods are all stocks & stones
Shall we for the sake of being Polite
Feed them with the juice of our marrow bones

And if Bezaleel & Aholiab drew
What the Finger of God pointed to their View
Shall we suffer the Roman & Grecian Rods
To compell us to worship them as Gods

They stole them from the Temple of the Lord
And Worshippd them [*to*] that they might make Inspired
   Art Abhorrd   10

The Wood & Stone were calld The Holy Things
And their Sublime Intent given to their Kings
All the Atonements of Jehovah spurnd
And Criminals to Sacrifices Turnd

[*TO*] ON F[LAXMAN] & S[TOTHARD]

I found [*thee*] them blind I taught [*thee*] how to see
And now [*thou knowst*] they know neither [*thyself*]
   themselves nor me
Tis Excellent to turn a thorn to a pin
A[*Knave*] Fool to a bolt a [*Fool*] Knave to a glass of gin

*

P[hillips] loved me, not as he lovd his Friends
For he lovd them for gain to serve his Ends
[*But*] He lovd me [*but*] and for no Gain at all
But to rejoice & triumph in my fall

*

To forgive Enemies H[ayley] does pretend
Who never in his Life forgave a friend

TO F[LAXMAN]

You call me Mad tis Folly to do so
To seek to turn a Madman to a Foe
If you think as you speak you are an Ass
If you do not you are [*just*] but what you was

ON H[AYLE]YS FRIENDSHIP

When H—y finds out what you cannot do
That is the very thing hell set you to

If you break not your Neck tis not his fault
[*A peck of poisons*] But pecks of poison are not pecks
   of salt
And when he could not act upon my wife
Hired a Villain to bereave my Life

*

Some Men created for destruction come
Into the World & make the World their home
[*Friend Caiaphas is one do what he can*]
Be they as Vile & Base as Eer they can
[*Hell*] Theyll still be called 'The Worlds' honest man

ON S[TOTHARD]

You say reserve & modesty he has
[*His*] Whose heart is iron his head wood & his face brass
The Fox the Owl the Beetle & the Bat
[*On*] By sweet reserve & modesty [*feed Fat*] get Fat

IMITATION OF POPE   A COMPLIMENT TO
THE LADIES

Wondrous the Gods more wondrous are the Men
More Wondrous Wondrous still the Cock & Hen
More Wondrous still the Table Stool & Chair
But Ah! More wondrous still the Charming Fair

TO H[AYLEY]

Thy Friendship oft has made my heart to ake
Do be my Enemy for Friendships sake

*

Cosway Frazer & Baldwin of Egypts Lake
Fear to associate with Blake
This Life is a Warfare against Evils
They heal the sick he casts out devils
Hayley Flaxman & Stothard are also in doubt
Lest their Virtue should be put to the rout

One grins[*one*] tother spits & in corners hides
And all the [*Righteous*] Virtuous have shewn their
    backsides

AN EPITAPH

Come knock your heads against this stone
For sorrow that poor John Thompsons gone

ANOTHER

I was buried near this Dike
That my Friends may weep as much as they like

ANOTHER

Here lies John Trot the Friend of all mankind
He has not left one Enemy behind
Friends were quite hard to find old authors say
But now they stand in every bodies way

*

My title as an [*Artist*] Genius thus is provd
Not Praisd by Hayley nor by Flaxman lovd

*

[*Rubens had been a Statesman or a Saint*]
I Rubens am a Statesman & a Saint
[*He mixd them both & so he Learnd to Paint*]
Deceptions? O no – so Ill learn to Paint

TO ENGLISH CONNOISSEURS

You must agree that Rubens was a Fool
And yet you make him master of your School
And give more money for his slobberings
Than you will give for Rafaels finest Things
I understood Christ was a Carpenter
And not a Brewers Servant my good Sir

*

Swelld limbs with no outline that you can descry
That Stink in the Nose of a Stander by
But all the Pulp washd painted finishd with labour
Of an hundred Journeymens how dye do Neighbour

[*MAJOR TESTAMENT OF*]
[*A PRETTY EPIGRAM FOR THOSE WHO HAVE
GIVEN HIGH PRICES FOR BAD PICTURES
AND NEVER*]

A PRETTY EPIGRAM FOR [*THOSE*] THE
ENTERTAINMENT OF THOSE WHO [*PAY*]
HAVE PAID GREAT SUMS IN THE VENETIAN &
FLEMISH OOZE

Nature & Art in this together Suit
What is Most Grand is always most Minute
Rubens thinks Tables Chairs & Stools are Grand
But Rafael thinks A Head a foot a hand

*

These are the Idiots chiefest arts
To blend & not define the Parts
[*Let it be told*] The Swallow sings in Courts of Kings
That Fools have their high finishings
And this the Princes golden rule
The Laborious stumble of a Fool
To make out the parts is the wise mans aim
But to lose them the Fool makes his foolish Game

*

Rafael Sublime Majestic Graceful Wise
His Executive Power must I despise
Rubens Low Vulgar Stupid Ignorant
His power of Execution I must grant
Learn the Laborious stumble of a Fool
And from an Idiots Actions form my rule
Go send your Children to the Slobbering School

*

If I eer Grow to Mans Estate
O Give to me a Womans fate
May I govern all both great & small
Have the last word & take the wall

*

The Cripple every step Drudges & labours
And says come learn to walk of me Good Neighbours
Sir Joshua in astonishment cries out
[*His pains are more than others theres no Doubt*]
See what Great Labour Pain him & Modest Doubt
Newton & Bacon cry being badly Nurst.
He is all Experiments from last to first
He walks & stumbles as if he crep
And how high labourd is every step

ON THE GREAT ENCOURAGEMENT
GIVEN BY ENGLISH NOBILITY & GENTRY
TO CORREGGIO RUBENS REMBRANDT
REYNOLDS GAINSBOROUGH CATALANI
DUCROWE & DILBURY DOODLE

As the Ignorant Savage will sell his own Wife
For a [*Button a (Bauble) Buckle a Bead or*] Sword or a
    Cutlass a dagger or Knife
So the [*wise/Learned*] Taught Savage Englishman [*gives*]
    spends his whole Fortune
[*For*] On a smear or a squall [*that is not*] to destroy
    Picture [*nor*] or Tune
And I call upon Colonel Wardle
To give these Rascals a dose of Cawdle

*

Give pensions to the Learned Pig
Or the Hare playing on a Tabor
Anglus can never see Perfection
But in the Journeymans Labour

*

The Cunning sures & the Aim at yours

*

All Pictures thats Panted with Sense & with Thought
Are Painted by Madmen as sure as a Groat
For the Greater the Fool in the Pencil more blest
And when they are drunk they always pant best
Thy never can Rafael it Fuseli it nor Blake it
If they cant see an outline pray how can they make it
When Men will draw outlines begin you to jaw them
Madmen see outlines & therefore they draw them

ON H[AYLEY] THE PICK THANK

I write the Rascal Thanks till he & I
With Thanks & Compliments are quite drawn dry

CROMEK SPEAKS

I always take my judgment from a Fool
Because [*I know he always judges*] his judgment is so very
   Cool
Not prejudicd by feelings great or small
[*Because we know*] Amiable state he cannot feel at all

ENGLISH ENCOURAGEMENT OF ART
CROMEKS OPINIONS PUT INTO RHYME

[First reading]

If you mean to Please Every body you will
Set to work both Ignorance & skill
For a great [*multitud*] Madjority are Ignorant
And skill to them [*seems*] looks raving & rant
Like putting oil & water into a lamp
Twill make a great splutter with smoke & damp
For there is no use as it seems to me
Of lighting a Lamp when you dont wish to see

[Final reading]

If you mean to Please Every body you will
Menny wouver both Bunglishness & skill
For a great Conquest are Bunglery
And Jenous looks to ham like mad Rantery
Like displaying oil & water into a lamp
Twill hold forth a huge splutter with smoke & damp
For its all sheer loss as it seems to me
Of displaying up a light when we want not to see

And when it smells of the Lamp we can
Say all was owing to the Skilful Man   10
For the smell of water is but small
So een let Ignorance do it all

*

When you look at a picture you always can see
If a Man of Sense has Painted he
Then never flinch but keep up a Jaw
About freedom & Jenny suck awa'

*

You say their Pictures well Painted be
And yet they are Blockheads you all agree
Thank God I never was sent to school
[*To learn to admire the works of a Fool*]
To be Flogd into following the Style of a Fool

*

The Errors of a Wise Man make your Rule
Rather than the Perfections of a Fool

THE WASHER WOMANS SONG

I washd them out & washd them in
And they told me it was a great Sin

*

When I see a Rubens Rembrant [or] Correggio
I think of the Crippled Harry & Slobbering Joe
And then I [say to myself] question thus are artists rules
To be drawn from the works of two manifest fools
Then God defend us from the Arts I say
Send Battle Murder Sudden Death [we] O pray
Rather than [let] be such a blind Human Fool
Id be an Ass a Hog a Worm a Chair a Stool

*

Great things are done when Men & Mountains meet
This is not done by Jostling in the Street

*

I [have givn] give you the end of a golden string
Only wind it into a ball
It will lead you in at Heavens Gate
Built in Jerusalems wall

*

If you play a Game of Chance know before you begin
If you are benevolent you will never win

[*Epitaph for*] WILLIAM COWPER ESQ^re

The only Man that eer I knew
Who did not make me almost spew
Was Fuseli he was both Turk & Jew
And so [sweet] dear Christian Friends how do you do

———————

For this is being a Friend just in the nick
Not when hes well but waiting till hes sick
He calls you to his help be you not movd
Untill by being Sick his wants are provd

You see him spend his Soul in Prophecy
Do you believe it a confounded lie
Till some Bookseller & the Public Fame
Proves there is truth in his extravagant claim

10

For tis [*most wicked*] atrocious in a Friend you love
To tell you any thing that he cant prove
And tis most wicked in a Christian Nation
For any Man to pretend to Inspiration

*

I will tell you what Joseph of Arimathea
Said to my Fairy was not it very queer
Pliny & Trajan what are You here
Come listen to Joseph of Arimathea
Listen patient & when Joseph has done
Twill make a fool laugh & a Fairy Fun

*

Why was Cupid a Boy
And why a boy was he
He should have been a Girl
For ought that I can see

For he shoots with his bow
And the Girl shoots with her Eye
And they both are merry & glad
And laugh when we do cry

[*Then*] And to make Cupid a Boy
Was [*surely a womans plan*] the Cupid Girls mocking plan   10
For a boy [*never learns so much*] cant interpret the thing
Till he is become a man

And then hes so piercd with care
And wounded with arrowy smarts
That the whole business of his life
Is to pick out the heads of the darts

Twas the Greeks love of war
Turnd Love into a Boy
And Woman into a Statue of Stone
And away fled every Joy   20

*

I askd my Dear Friend Orator Prigg
Whats the first part of Oratory he said a great wig
And what is the second then dancing a jig

And bowing profoundly he said a great wig
And what is the third then he snord like a pig
And [*smild like a Cherub & said*] puffing his cheeks he
    replied a Great wig

So if a Great Panter with Questions you push
Whats the first Part of Panting hell say a Paint Brush
And what is the second with modest blush
Hell [*nod wink & smile & reply*] smile like a Cherub &
    say a pant Brush   10
And what is the third hell bow like a rush
With a lear in his Eye hell reply a Pant Brush

Perhaps this is all a Painter can want
But look yonder that house is the house of Rembrant
                                      &c.
                   to come in Barry a Poem

                *

[*Then Reynolds said O woman most sage*]
O dear Mother outline [*be not in a Rage*] of knowledge most
    sage
Whats the First Part of Painting she said Patronage
And what is the second to Please & Engage
She frownd like a Fury & said Patronage
And what is the Third she put off Old Age
And smild like a Syren & said Patronage

TO VENETIAN ARTISTS

That God is colouring Newton does shew
And the devil is a Black outline all of us know
Perhaps this little Fable may make us merry
A dog went over the water without a wherry
A bone which he had stolen he had in his mouth
He cared not whether the wind was north or south

As he swam he saw the reflection of the bone
This is quite Perfection, [*heres two for one/what a
   brilliant tone*] one Generalizing Tone
Outline Theres no outline Theres no such thing   10
All is Chiaro Scuro Poco Pen [*&*] its all colouring
[*Then He snapd &*] Snap. Snap! he has lost shadow &
   substance too
He had them both before now how do ye do
A great deal better than I was before
[*Ive tasted shadow &*] Those who taste colouring love it
   more & more

*

[BLAKES APOLOGY FOR HIS CATALOGUE]

[*who cries all art is a fraud & Genius a trick
And Blake is an unfortunate Lunatic*]
Having given great offence by writing in Prose
Ill write in [*Rhyme*] Verse as soft as [*feather Pillows*]
   Bartolloze
Some blush at what others can see no crime in
But nobody [*at all*] sees any harm in Rhyming
Dryden in Rhyme cries Milton only plannd
Every Fool shook his bells throughout the land
Tom Cooke cut Hogarth down with his clean graving
[*How many*] Thousands of Connoisseurs with joy ran
   raving   10
Thus Hayley on his Toilette seeing the sope
[*says*] Cries Homer is very much improvd by Pope
Some say Ive given great Provision to my foes
And that now I lead my false friends by the nose
Flaxman & Stothard smelling a sweet savour
Cry Blakified drawing spoils painter & Engraver
While I looking up to my Umbrella
Resolvd to be a very contrary fellow
Cry [*Tom Cooke proves*] looking quite from
   [*Circumference*] Skumference to Center
No one can finish so high as the original Inventor   20

Thus Poor Schiavonetti died of the Cromek
A thing thats tied [*about*] around the Examiners neck
This is my sweet apology to my friends
That I may put them in mind of their latter Ends

*

Great Men & Fools do often me Inspire
But the Greater Fool the Greater Liar

FROM CRATETOS

Me Time has Crook'd. no good Workman
Is he. Infirm is all that he does

*

If Men will act like a maid smiling over a Churn
They ought not, when it comes to anothers turn
To grow sower at what a friend may utter
Knowing & feeling that we all have need of Butter

False Friends [*O no*] fie fie our Friendship [*neer shall*]
    you shant sever
[*For now*] In spite we will be greater friends than ever

*

Some people admire the work of a Fool
For its sure to keep your judgment cool
It does not reproach you with want of wit
It is not like a lawyer serving a writ

TO GOD

If you have formd a Circle to go into
Go into it yourself & see how you would do

*

Since all the Riches of this World
May be gifts from the Devil & Earthly Kings
I should suspect that I worshipd the Devil
If I thankd my God for Worldly things

*

To Chloes breast young Cupid slily stole
But he crept in at Myras pocket hole

*

[*when*] Now Art has lost its mental Charms
France shall subdue the World in Arms
So spoke an Angel at my birth
Then said Descend thou upon Earth
Renew the Arts on Britains Shore
And France shall fall down & adore
With works of Art their Armies meet
And [*Armies*] War shall sink beneath thy feet
But if thy Nation Arts refuse
And if they scorn the immortal Muse
France shall the arts of Peace restore
And save [*thy works*] thee from [*Britains*] the Ungrateful
    shore

Spirit who lovst Brittannias [*Shore*] Isle
Round which the Fiends of Commerce [*roar*] smile

[unfinished]

*

Nail his neck to the Cross nail it with a nail
Nail his neck to the Cross ye all have power over his tail

*

I rose up at the dawn of day
Get thee away get thee away
Prayst thou for Riches away away
This is the Throne of Mammon grey

Said I this sure is very odd
I took it to be the Throne of God
For every Thing besides I have
It is only for Riches that I can crave

I have Mental Joy & Mental Health
And Mental [*Friendship*] Friends & Mental wealth   10
Ive a Wife I love & that loves me
Ive all But Riches Bodily

I am in Gods presence night & day
And he never turns his face away
The accuser of sins by my side does stand
And he holds my money bag in his hand

For [*all that*] my worldly things God makes him pay
And hed pay for more if to him I would pray
And so you may do the worst you can do
Be assurd Mr Devil I wont pray to you   20

Then If for Riches I must not Pray
God knows I little of Prayers need say
So [*as sure*] as a Church is known by its Steeple
If I pray it must be for other People

He says if I do not worship him for a God
I shall eat coarser food & go worse shod
So as I dont value such things as these
You must do Mr Devil just as God please

*

The [*visions*] Caverns of the Grave Ive seen
And these I shewd to Englands Queen
[*And*] But now the Caves of Hell I view
Who shall I dare to shew them to
What mighty Soul in Beautys form
Shall [*dare to*] dauntless View the Infernal Storm
Egremonts Countess [*dare*] can controll
The [*waves*] flames of Hell that round me roll

If she refuse I still go on
Till the Heavens & Earth are gone   10
Still admird by [*worthy*] Noble minds
Followd by Envy on the winds
Reengravd Time after Time
Ever in their youthful prime
My Designs [*shall still*] unchangd remain
Time may rage but rage in vain
For above Times troubled Fountains
On the Great Atlantic Mountains
In my Golden House on high
There they Shine Eternally   20

Verse from the Marginalia to Reynolds's Discourses

ADVICE OF THE POPES WHO SUCCEEDED
THE AGE OF RAFAEL

Degrade first the Arts if you'd Mankind degrade,
Hire Idiots to Paint with cold light & hot shade:
Give high Price for the worst, leave the best in disgrace,
And with Labours of Ignorance fill every place.

*

Some look. to see the sweet Outlines
And beauteous Forms that Love does wear
Some look. to find out Patches. Paint.
Bracelets & Stays & Powderd Hair

*

When France got free Europe 'twixt Fools & Knaves
Were Savage first to France, & after; Slaves

*

When Sr Joshua Reynolds died
All Nature was degraded;
The King dropd a tear into the Queens Ear;
And all his Pictures Faded.

*

When Nations grow Old. The Arts grow Cold
And Commerce settles on every Tree
And the Poor & the Old can live upon Gold
For all are Born Poor. Aged Sixty three

ON THE VENETIAN PAINTER

He makes the Lame to walk we all agree
But then he strives to blind those who can see.

*

A Pair of Stays to mend the Shape
Of crooked Humpy Woman:
Put on O Venus! now thou art,
Quite a Venetian Roman.

*

Venetian; all thy Colouring is no more
Than Boulsterd Plasters on a Crooked Whore

*

O Reader behold the Philosophers Grave.
He was born quite a Fool: but he died quite a Knave

*Verse from the Advertisement to Blake's
Exhibition of Paintings, 1809*

In the last Battle that Arthur fought, the most Beautiful
  was one
That return'd, and the most Strong another: with them
  also return'd
The most Ugly, and no other beside return'd from the
  bloody Field.

The most Beautiful, the Roman Warriors trembled before
  and worshipped:

The most Strong, they melted before him and dissolved
in his presence:
The most Ugly they fled with outcries and contortion of
their Limbs.

Epigrams from A Descriptive Catalogue

'The fox, the owl, the spider, and the mole,
By sweet reserve and modesty get fat.'

*

I found them blind, I taught them how to see;
And, now, they know me not, nor yet themselves.

Epigrams from 'Public Address'

Call that the Public Voice which is their Error
Like as a Monkey peeping in a Mirror
Admires all his colours brown & warm
And never once percieves his ugly form

*

And in Melodious Accents I
Will sit me down & Cry. I. I.

JERUSALEM (opposite is Babylon)

THE EMANATION OF THE GIANT ALBION

Los: Artists/Reformer who is attempting to rise Albion from
└England   Sleep

PLATE I

[Frontispiece]

[Above the archway:]

There is a Void, outside of Existence, which if enterd
  into
Englobes itself & becomes a Womb, such was Albions
  Couch
A pleasant Shadow of Repose calld Albions lovely Land

His Sublime & Pathos become Two Rocks fixd in the
  Earth
His Reason, his Spectrous Power, covers them above[.]
Jerusalem his Emanation is a Stone laying beneath[.]
O [*Albion behold Pitying*] behold the Vision of Albion

[On right side of archway:]

Half Friendship is the bitterest Enmity said Los
As he enterd the Door of Death for Albions sake
  Inspired
The long sufferings of God are not for ever there is a
  Judgment   10

[On left side, in reversed writing:]

Every Thing has its Vermin O Spectre of the Sleeping
  Dead!

PLATE 3

TO THE PUBLIC

SHEEP   GOATS

After my three years slumber on the banks of the
Ocean, I again display my Giant forms to the Public: My
former Giants & Fairies having reciev'd the highest
reward possible: the [*love*] and [*friendship*] of those with
whom to be connected, is to be [*blessed:*] I cannot doubt
that this more consolidated & extended Work, will be as
kindly recieved

The Enthusiasm of the following Poem, the Author
hopes [*no Reader will think presumptuousness or arroganc[e]*]   10
when he is reminded that the Ancients entrusted their love to
their Writing, to the full as Enthusiastically as I have who
Acknowledge mine for my Saviour and Lord, for they were
wholly absorb'd in their Gods.] I also hope the Reader will
be with me, wholly One in Jesus our Lord, who is the God
[*of Fire*] and Lord [*of Love*] to whom the Ancients look'd
and saw his day afar off, with trembling & amazement.

The Spirit of Jesus is continual forgiveness of Sin: he
who waits to be righteous before he enters into the Saviours
kingdom, the Divine Body; will never enter there. I am
perhaps the most sinful of men! I pretend not to   20
holiness! yet I pretend to love, to see, to converse with
daily, as man with man, & the more to have an interest in
the Friend of Sinners. Therefore [*Dear*] Reader, [*forgive*]
what you do not approve, & [*love*] me for this energetic
exertion of my talent.

Reader! [*lover*] of books! [*lover*] of heaven,
And of that God from whom [*all books are given,*]
Who in mysterious Sinais awful cave
To Man the wond'rous art of writing gave,
Again he speaks in thunder and in fire!   30
Thunder of Thought, & flames of fierce desire:
Even from the depths of Hell his voice I hear,
Within the unfathomd caverns of my Ear.

Therefore I print; nor vain my types shall be:
Heaven, Earth & Hell, henceforth shall live in harmony

Of the Measure, in which
the following Poem is written

We who dwell on Earth can do nothing of ourselves,
every thing is conducted by Spirits, no less than Digestion
or Sleep. [*to Note the last words of Jesus*, Εδοθη μοι παϛα 40
εξουσια εν ουρανω και επι γης]
When this Verse was first dictated to me I consider'd a
Monotonous Cadence like that used by Milton & Shake-
speare & all writers of English Blank Verse, derived from
the modern bondage of Rhyming; to be a necessary and
indispensable part of Verse. But I soon found that in the
mouth of a true Orator such monotony was not only
awkward, but as much a bondage as rhyme itself. I
therefore have produced a variety in every line, both of
cadences & number of syllables. Every word and every 50
letter is studied and put into its fit place: the terrific
numbers are reserved for the terrific parts – the mild &
gentle, for the mild & gentle parts, and the prosaic, for
inferior parts: all are necessary to each other. Poetry
Fetter'd, Fetters the Human Race! Nations are Des-
troy'd, or Flourish, in proportion as Their Poetry Painting
and Music, are Destroy'd or Flourish! The Primeval State
of Man, was Wisdom, Art, and Science.

PLATE 4

Μονος ὁ Ιεϛους

JERUSALEM

CHAP: I

Of the Sleep of Ulro! and of the passage through
Eternal Death! and of the awaking to Eternal Life.

This theme calls me in sleep night after night, & ev'ry
morn

Awakes me at sun-rise, then I see the Saviour over me
Spreading his beams of love, & dictating the words of
    this mild song.

Awake! awake O sleeper of the land of shadows, wake!
    expand!
I am in you and you in me, mutual in love divine:
Fibres of love from man to man thro Albions pleasant
    land.
In all the dark Atlantic vale down from the hills of
    Surrey
A black water accumulates, return Albion! return!   10
Thy brethren call thee, and thy fathers, and thy sons,
Thy nurses and thy mothers, thy sisters and thy
    daughters
Weep at thy souls disease, and the Divine Vision is
    darkend:
Thy Emanation that was wont to play before thy face,
Beaming forth with her daughters into the Divine bosom
    [*Where!!*]
Where hast thou hidden thy Emanation lovely Jerusalem
From the vision and fruition of the Holy-one?
I am not a God afar off, I am a brother and friend;
Within your bosoms I reside, and you reside in me:
Lo! we are One; forgiving all Evil; Not seeking
    recompense!   20
Ye are my members O ye sleepers of Beulah, land of
    shades!

But the perturbed Man away turns down the valleys
    dark;
[*Saying. We are not One: we are Many, thou most
    simulative*]
Phantom of the over heated brain! shadow of
    immortality!
Seeking to keep my soul a victim to thy Love! which
    binds
Man the enemy of man into deceitful friendships:
Jerusalem is not! her daughters are indefinite:

By demonstration, man alone can live, and not by faith.
My mountains are my own, and I will keep them to
   myself:
The Malvern and the Cheviot, the Wolds Plinlimmon
   & Snowdon   30
Are mine, here will I build my Laws of Moral Virtue:
Humanity shall be no more: but war & princedom &
   victory!

So spoke Albion in jealous fears, hiding his Emanation
Upon the Thames and Medway, rivers of Beulah:
   dissembling
His jealousy before the throne divine, darkening, cold!

PLATE 5

The banks of the Thames are clouded: the ancient
   porches of Albion are
Darken'd! they are drawn thro' unbounded space,
   scatter'd upon
The Void in incoherent despair! Cambridge & Oxford &
   London,
Are driven among the starry Wheels, rent away and
   dissipated,
In Chasms & Abysses of sorrow, enlarg'd without
   dimension, terrible
Albions mountains run with blood, the cries of war & of
   tumult
Resound into the unbounded night, every Human
   perfection
Of mountain & river & city, are small & wither'd &
   darken'd
Cam is a little stream! Ely is almost swallowd up!
Lincoln & Norwich stand trembling on the brink of
   Udan-Adan!   10
Wales and Scotland shrink themselves to the west and to
   the north!
Mourning for fear of the warriors in the Vale of
   Entuthon-Benython

Jerusalem is scatterd abroad like a cloud of smoke thro'
    non-entity:
Moab & Ammon & Amalek & Canaan & Egypt & Aram
Recieve her little-ones for sacrifices and the delights of
    cruelty

Trembling I sit day and night, my friends are
    astonish'd at me.
Yet they forgive my wanderings, I rest not from my
    great task!
To open the Eternal Worlds, to open the immortal Eyes
Of Man inwards into the Worlds of Thought: into
    Eternity
Ever expanding in the Bosom of God, the Human
    Imagination   20
O Saviour pour upon me thy Spirit of meekness & love:
Annihilate the Selfhood in me, be thou all my life!
Guide thou my hand which trembles exceedingly upon
    the rock of ages,
While I write of the building of Golgonooza, & of the
    terrors of Entuthon:
Of Hand & Hyle & Coban, of Kwantok, Peachey,
    Brereton, Slayd & Hutton:
Of the terrible sons & daughters of Albion, and their
    Generations.

Scofield! Kox, Kotope and Bowen, revolve most mightily
    upon
The Furnace of Los: before the eastern gate bending
    their fury.
They war, to destroy the Furnaces, to desolate
    Golgonooza:
And to devour the Sleeping Humanity of Albion in rage
    & hunger.   30
They revolve into the Furnaces Southward & are driven
    forth Northward
Divided into Male and Female forms time after time.
From these Twelve all the Families of England spread
    abroad.

The Male is a Furnace of beryll; the Female is a golden
  Loom;
I behold them and their rushing fires overwhelm my
  Soul,
In Londons darkness; and my tears fall day and night,
Upon the Emanations of Albions Sons! the Daughters of
  Albion
Names anciently rememberd, but now contemn'd as
  fictions:
Although in every bosom they controll our Vegetative
  powers.
These are united into Tirzah and her Sisters, on Mount
  Gilead,   40
Cambel & Gwendolen & Conwenna & Cordella & Ignoge.
And these united into Rahab in the Covering Cherub on
  Euphrates
Gwiniverra & Gwinefred, & Gonorill & Sabrina
  beautiful,
Estrild, Mehetabel & Ragan, lovely Daughters of Albion,
They are the beautiful Emanations of the Twelve Sons
  of Albion

The Starry Wheels revolv'd heavily over the Furnaces;
Drawing Jerusalem in anguish of maternal love,
Eastward a pillar of a cloud with Vala upon the
  mountains
Howling in pain, redounding from the arms of Beulahs
  Daughters,
Out from the Furnaces of Los above the head of Los.   50
A pillar of smoke writhing afar into Non-Entity,
  redounding
Till the cloud reaches afar outstretch'd among the
  Starry Wheels
Which revolve heavily in the mighty Void above the
  Furnaces

O what avail the loves & tears of Beulahs lovely
  Daughters

They hold the Immortal Form in gentle bands & tender
    tears
But all within is open'd into the deeps of Entuthon
    Benython
A dark and unknown night, indefinite, unmeasurable,
    without end.
Abstract Philosophy warring in enmity against
    Imagination
(Which is the Divine Body of the Lord Jesus. blessed for
    ever).
And there Jerusalem wanders with Vala upon the
    mountains,   60
Attracted by the revolutions of those Wheels the Cloud
    of smoke
Immense, and Jerusalem & Vala weeping in the Cloud
Wander away into the Chaotic Void, lamenting with her
    Shadow
Among the Daughters of Albion, among the Starry
    Wheels;
Lamenting for her children, for the sons & daughters of
    Albion

Los heard her lamentations in the deeps afar! his tears
    fall
Incessant before the Furnaces, and his Emanation
    divided in pain,
Eastward towards the Starry Wheels. But Westward, a
    black Horror,
PLATE 6
His spectre driv'n by the Starry Wheels of Albions sons,
    black and
Opake divided from his back; he labours and he mourns!

For as his Emanation divided, his Spectre also divided
In terror of those starry wheels: and the Spectre stood
    over Los
Howling in pain: a blackning Shadow, blackning dark &
    opake

Cursing the terrible Los: bitterly cursing him for his
  friendship
To Albion, suggesting murderous thoughts against
  Albion.

Los rag'd and stamp'd the earth in his might & terrible
  wrath!
He stood and stampd the earth! then he threw down his
  hammer in rage &
In fury: then he sat down and wept, terrified! Then arose   10
And chaunted his song, labouring with the tongs and
  hammer:
But still the Spectre divided, and still his pain increas'd!
In pain the Spectre divided: in pain of hunger and thirst:
To devour Los's Human Perfection, but when he saw
  that Los

PLATE 7

Was living: panting like a frighted wolf, and howling
He stood over the Immortal, in the solitude and darkness:
Upon the darkning Thames, across the whole Island
  westward,
A horrible Shadow of Death, among the Furnaces:
  beneath
The pillar of folding smoke; and he sought by other
  means,
To lure Los: by tears, by arguments of science & by
  terrors:
Terrors in every Nerve, by spasms & extended pains:
While Los answer'd unterrified to the opake blackening
  Fiend

And thus the Spectre spoke: Wilt thou still go on to
  destruction?
Till thy life is all taken away by this deceitful
  Friendship?   10
He drinks thee up like water! like wine he pours thee
Into his tuns: thy Daughters are trodden in his vintage
He makes thy Sons the trampling of his bulls, they are
  plow'd

And harrowd for his profit, lo! thy stolen Emanation
Is his garden of pleasure! all the Spectres of his Sons
   mock thee
Look how they scorn thy once admired palaces! now in
   ruins
Because of Albion! because of deceit and friendship!
   For Lo!
Hand has peopled Babel & Nineveh: Hyle, Ashur &
   Aram:
Cobans son is Nimrod: his son Cush is adjoind to
   Aram,
By the Daughter of Babel, in a woven mantle of
   pestilence & war.   20
They put forth their spectrous cloudy sails; which drive
   their immense
Constellations over the deadly deeps of indefinite
   Udan-Adan[.]
Kox is the Father of Shem & Ham & Japheth, he is the
   Noah
Of the Flood of Udan-Adan. Hut'n is the Father of the
   Seven
From Enoch to Adam; Schofield is Adam who was New-
Created in Edom. I saw it indignant, & thou art not
   moved!
This has divided thee in sunder: and wilt thou still
   forgive?
O! thou seest not what I see! what is done in the
   Furnaces.
Listen, I will tell thee what is done in moments to thee
   unknown:
Luvah was cast into the Furnaces of affliction and sealed,   30
And Vala fed in cruel delight, the Furnaces with fire:
Stern Urizen beheld; urgd by necessity to keep
The evil day afar, and if perchance with iron power
He might avert his own despair: in woe & fear he saw
Vala incircle round the Furnaces where Luvah was clos'd:
With joy she heard his howlings, & forgot he was her
   Luvah,

With whom she liv'd in bliss in times of innocence &
    youth!
Vala comes from the Furnace in a cloud, but wretched
    Luvah
Is howling in the Furnaces, in flames among Albions
    Spectres,
To prepare the Spectre of Albion to reign over thee O
    Los,   40
Forming the Spectres of Albion according to his rage:
To prepare the Spectre of Adam, who is Scofield: the
    Ninth
Of Albions sons, & the father of all his brethren in the
    Shadowy
Generation. Cambel & Gwendolen wove webs of war &
    of
Religion, to involve all Albions sons, and when they had
Involv'd Eight; their webs roll'd outwards into darkness
And Scofield the Ninth remain on the outside of the
    Eight
And Kox, Kotope, & Bowen, One in him, a Fourfold
    Wonder
Involv'd the Eight: Such are the Generations of the
    Giant Albion,
To separate a Law of Sin, to punish thee in thy members.   50

Los answer'd. Altho' I know not this! I know far worse
    than this:
I know that Albion hath divided me, and that thou O
    my Spectre,
Hast just cause to be irritated: but look stedfastly upon me:
Comfort thyself in my strength the time will arrive,
When all Albions injuries shall cease, and when we shall
Embrace him tenfold bright, rising from his tomb in
    immortality.
They have divided themselves by Wrath, they must be
    united by
Pity: let us therefore take example & warning O my
    Spectre,

O that I could abstain from wrath! O that the Lamb
Of God would look upon me and pity me in my fury.   60
In anguish of regeneration: in terrors of self annihilation:
Pity must join together those whom wrath has torn in
    sunder,
And the Religion of Generation which was meant for the
    destruction
Of Jerusalem, become her covering, till the time of the
    End.
O holy Generation [*Image*] of regeneration!
O point of mutual forgiveness between Enemies!
Birthplace of the Lamb of God incomprehensible!
The Dead despise & scorn thee, & cast thee out as
    accursed:
Seeing the Lamb of God in thy gardens & thy palaces:
Where they desire to place the Abomination of
    Desolation.   70
Hand sits before his furnace: scorn of others & furious
    pride:
Freeze round him to bars of steel & to iron rocks
    beneath
His feet: indignant self-righteousness like whirlwinds of
    the north:

PLATE 8

Rose up against me thundering from the Brook of
    Albions River
From Ranelagh & Strumbolo, from Cromwells gardens
    & Chelsea
The place of wounded Soldiers, but when he saw my Mace
Whirld round from heaven to earth, trembling he sat:
    his cold
Poisons rose up: & his sweet deceits coverd them all over
With a tender cloud. As thou art now; such was he O
    Spectre
I know thy deceit & thy revenges, and unless thou desist
I will certainly create an eternal Hell for thee. Listen!
Be attentive! be obedient! Lo the Furnaces are ready to
    recieve thee.

I will break thee into shivers! & melt thee in the
    furnaces of death;   10
I will cast thee into forms of abhorrence & torment if
    thou
Desist not from thine own will, & obey not my stern
    command!
I am closd up from my children: my Emanation is
    dividing
And thou my Spectre art divided against me. But mark
I will compell thee to assist me in my terrible labours.
    To beat
These hypocritic Selfhoods on the Anvils of bitter
    Death
I am inspired: I act not for myself: for Albions sake
I now am what I am: a horror and an astonishment
Shuddring the heavens to look upon me: Behold what
    cruelties
Are practised in Babel & Shinar, & have approachd to
    Zions Hill   20

While Los spoke, the terrible Spectre fell shuddring
    before him
Watching his time with glowing eyes to leap upon his
    prey[.]
Los opend the Furnaces in fear, the Spectre saw to
    Babel & Shinar
Across all Europe & Asia, he saw the tortures of the
    Victims.
He saw now from the ou[t]side what he before saw & felt
    from within
He saw that Los was the sole, uncontrolld Lord of the
    Furnaces
Groaning he kneeld before Los's iron-shod feet on
    London Stone,
Hungring & thirsting for Los's life yet pretending
    obedience.
While Los pursud his speech in threat'nings loud &
    fierce.

Thou art my Pride & Self-righteousness: I have found
    thee out: 30
Thou art reveald before me in all thy magnitude &
    power
The Uncircumcised pretences to Chastity must be cut
    in sunder!
Thy holy wrath & deep deceit cannot avail against me
Nor shalt thou ever assume the triple-form of Albions
    Spectre
For I am one of the living: dare not to mock my inspired
    fury
If thou wast cast forth from my life! if I was dead upon
    the mountains
Thou mightest be pitied & lovd: but now I am living;
    unless
Thou abstain ravening I will create an eternal Hell for
    thee.
Take thou this Hammer & in patience heave the
    thundering Bellows
Take thou these Tongs: strike thou alternate with me:
    labour obedient[.]   40
Hand & Hyle & Koban: Skofeld, Kox & Kotope, labour
    mightily[.]
In the Wars of Babel & Shinar, all their Emanations
    were
Condensd. Hand has absorbd all his Brethen in his
    might
All the infant Loves & Graces were lost, for the mighty
    Hand

PLATE 9

Condens'd his Emanations into hard opake substances;
And his infant thoughts & desires, into cold, dark, cliffs
    of death.
His hammer of gold he siezd; and his anvil of adamant.
He siez'd the bars of condens'd thoughts, to forge them:
Into the sword of war: into the bow and arrow:
Into the thundering cannon and into the murdering
    gun[.]

I saw the limbs form'd for exercise, contemn'd: & the
  beauty of
Eternity, look'd upon as deformity & loveliness as a dry
  tree:
I saw disease forming a Body of Death around the Lamb
Of God, to destroy Jerusalem, & to devour the body of
  Albion   10
By war and stratagem to win the labour of the
  husbandman:
Awkwardness arm'd in steel: folly in a helmet of gold:
Weakness with horns & talons: ignorance with a rav'ning
  beak!
Every Emanative joy forbidden as a Crime:
And the Emanations buried alive in the earth with pomp
  of religion:
Inspiration deny'd; Genius forbidden by laws of
  punishment:
I saw terrified; I took the sighs & tears, & bitter groans:
I lifted them into my Furnaces; to form the spiritual
  sword,
That lays open the hidden heart: I drew forth the
  pang
Of sorrow red hot: I workd it on my resolute anvil: 20
I heated it in the flames of Hand, & Hyle, & Coban
Nine times; Gwendolen & Cambel & Gwineverra
Are melted into the gold, the silver, the liquid ruby,
The crysolite, the topaz, the jacinth, & every precious
  stone.
Loud roar my Furnaces and loud my hammer is heard:
I labour day and night, I behold the soft affections
Condense beneath my hammer into forms of cruelty
But still I labour in hope, tho' still my tears flow down,
That he who will not defend Truth, may be compelld to
  defend
A Lie: that he may be snared and caught and snared and
  taken   30
That Enthusiasm and Life may not cease: arise Spectre
  arise!

Thus they contended among the Furnaces with groans
& tears;
Groaning the Spectre heavd the bellows, obeying Los's
frowns;
Till the Spaces of Erin were perfected in the furnaces
Of affliction, and Los drew them forth, compelling the
harsh Spectre.

PLATE 10

Into the Furnaces & into the valleys of the Anvils of
Death
And into the mountains of the Anvils & of the heavy
Hammers
Till he should bring the Sons & Daughters of Jerusalem
to be
The Sons & Daughters of Los that he might protect
them from
Albions dread Spectres; storming, loud, thunderous &
mighty
The Bellows & the Hammers move compell'd by Los's
hand.

And this is the manner of the Sons of Albion in their
strength
They take the Two Contraries which are calld Qualities,
with which
Every Substance is clothed, they name them Good &
Evil
From them they make an Abstract, which is a Negation   10
Not only of the Substance from which it is derived
A murderer of its own Body: but also a murderer
Of every Divine Member: it is the Reasoning Power
An Abstract objecting power, that Negatives every thing
This is the Spectre of Man: the Holy Reasoning Power
And in its Holiness is closed the Abomination of
Desolation

Therefore Los stands in London building Golgonooza
Compelling his Spectre to labours mighty; trembling in
fear

The Spectre weeps, but Los unmovd by tears or threats
  remains

I must Create a System, or be enslav'd by another Mans   20
I will not Reason & Compare: my business is to Create

So Los, in fury & strength: in indignation & burning
  wrath
Shuddring the Spectre howls, his howlings terrify the
  night
He stamps around the Anvil, beating blows of stern
  despair
He curses Heaven & Earth, Day & Night & Sun &
  Moon
He curses Forest Spring & River, Desart & sandy Waste
Cities & Nations, Families & Peoples, Tongues & Laws
Driven to desperation by Los's terrors & threatning fears

Los cries, Obey my voice & never deviate from my will
And I will be merciful to thee: be thou invisible to all   30
To whom I make thee invisible, but chief to my own
  Children
O Spectre of Urthona: Reason not against their dear
  approach
Nor them obstruct with thy temptations of doubt &
  despair[.]
O Shame O strong & mighty Shame I break thy brazen
  fetters
If thou refuse, thy present torments will seem southern
  breezes
To what thou shalt endure if thou obey not my great will.

The Spectre answer'd. Art thou not ashamd of those thy
  Sins
That thou callest thy Children? lo the Law of God
  commands
That they be offered upon his Altar: O cruelty &
  torment
For thine are also mine! I have kept silent hitherto,   40

Concerning my chief delight: but thou hast broken
   silence
Now I will speak my mind! Where is my lovely
   Enitharmon
O thou my enemy, where is my Great Sin? She is also
   thine
I said: now is my grief at worst: incapable of being
Surpassed: but every moment it accumulates more &
   more
It continues accumulating to eternity! the joys of God
   advance
For he is Righteous: he is not a Being of Pity &
   Compassion
He cannot feel Distress: he feeds on Sacrifice & Offering:
Delighting in cries & tears & clothd in holiness & solitude
But my griefs advance also, for ever & ever without end   50
O that I could cease to be! Despair! I am Despair
Created to be the great example of horror & agony: also
   my
Prayer is vain I called for compassion: compassion mockd
Mercy & pity threw the grave stone over me & with lead
And iron, bound it over me for ever: Life lives on my
Consuming: & the Almighty hath made me his Contrary
To be all evil, all reversed & for ever dead: knowing
And seeing life, yet living not; how can I then behold
And not tremble; how can I be beheld & not abhorrd

So spoke the Spectre shuddring, & dark tears ran down
   his shadowy face   60
Which Los wipd off, but comfort none could give! or
   beam of hope
Yet ceasd he not from labouring at the roarings of his
   Forge
With iron & brass Building Golgonooza in great
   contendings
Till his Sons & Daughters came forth from the Furnaces
At the sublime Labours for Los, compelld the invisible
   Spectre

PLATE II

To labours mighty, with vast strength, with his mighty
chains.
In pulsations of time, & extensions of space, like Urns of
Beulah
With great labour upon his anvils   & in his ladles the
Ore
He lifted, pouring it into the clay ground prepar'd with
art;
Striving with Systems to deliver Individuals from those
Systems;
That whenever any Spectre began to devour the Dead,
He might feel the pain as if a man gnawd his own tender
nerves.

Then Erin came forth from the Furnaces, & all the
Daughters of Beulah
Came from the Furnaces, by Los's mighty power for
Jerusalems
Sake: walking up and down among the Spaces of Erin: 10
And the Sons and Daughters of Los came forth in
perfection lovely!
And the Spaces of Erin reach'd from the starry heighth,
to the starry depth.

Los wept with exceeding joy & all wept with joy
together!
They feard they never more should see their Father, who
Was built in from Eternity, in the Cliffs of Albion.

But when the joy of meeting was exhausted in loving
embrace;
Again they lament. O what shall we do for lovely
Jerusalem?
To protect the Emanations of Albions mighty ones from
cruelty?
Sabrina & Ignoge begin to sharpen their beamy spears
Of light and love: their little children stand with arrows
of gold: 20

Ragan is wholly cruel Scofield is bound in iron armour!
He is like a mandrake in the earth before Reubens gate:
He shoots beneath Jerusalems walls to undermine her
    foundations:
Vala is but thy Shadow, O thou loveliest among women!
A shadow animated by thy tears O mournful Jerusalem!
PLATE 12
Why wilt thou give to her a Body whose life is but a
    Shade?
Her joy and love, a shade: a shade of sweet repose:
But animated and vegetated, she is a devouring worm:
What shall we do for thee O lovely mild Jerusalem?

And Los said. I behold the finger of God in terrors!
Albion is dead! his Emanation is divided from him!
But I am living! yet I feel my Emanation also dividing
Such thing was never known! O pity me, thou all-
    piteous-one!
What shall I do! or how exist, divided from Enitharmon?
Yet why despair! I saw the finger of God go forth   10
Upon my Furnaces, from within the Wheels of Albions
    Sons:
Fixing their Systems, permanent: by mathematic power
Giving a body to Falshood that it may be cast off for ever.
With Demonstrative Science piercing Apollyon with his
    own bow!
God is within, & without! he is even in the depths of
    Hell!

Such were the lamentations of the Labourers in the
    Furnaces!
And they appeard within & without incircling on both
    sides
The Starry Wheels of Albions Sons, with Spaces for
    Jerusalem:
And for Vala the shadow of Jerusalem: the ever mourning
    shade:
On both sides, within & without beaming gloriously!   20

Terrified at the sublime Wonder, Los stood before his
    Furnaces.
And they stood around, terrified with admiration at Erins
    Spaces
For the Spaces reachd from the starry heighth, to the
    starry depth;
And they builded Golgonooza: terrible eternal labour!

What are those golden builders doing? where was the
    burying-place
Of soft Ethinthus? near Tyburns fatal Tree? is that
Mild Zions hills most ancient promontory; near
    mournful
Ever weeping Paddington? is that Calvary and
    Golgotha?
Becoming a building of pity and compassion? Lo!
The stones are pity and the bricks, well wrought
    affections: 30
Enameld with love & kindness, & the tiles engraven gold
Labour of merciful hands: the beams & rafters are
    forgiveness:
The mortar & cement of the work, tears of honesty: the
    nails,
And the screws & iron braces, are well wrought
    blandishments,
And well contrived words, firm fixing, never forgotten,
Always comforting the remembrance: the floors,
    humility,
The cielings, devotion: the hearths, thanksgiving:
Prepare the furniture O Lambeth in thy pitying looms!
The curtains, woven tears & sighs, wrought into lovely
    forms
For comfort. there the secret furniture of Jerusalems
    chamber   40
Is wrought: Lambeth! the Bride the Lambs Wife loveth
    thee:
Thou art one with her & knowest not of self in thy
    supreme joy.

Go on, builders in hope: tho Jerusalem wanders far
    away,
Without the gate of Los: among the dark Satanic wheels.

Fourfold the Sons of Los in their divisions: and fourfold,
The great City of Golgonooza: fourfold toward the north
And toward the south fourfold, & fourfold toward the
    east & west
Each within other toward the four points: that toward
Eden, and that toward the World of Generation,
And that toward Beulah, and that toward Ulro: 50
Ulro is the space of the terrible starry wheels of Albions
    sons:
But that toward Eden is walled up, till time of
    renovation:
Yet it is perfect in its building, ornaments & perfection.

And the Four Points are thus beheld in Great Eternity
West, the Circumference: South, the Zenith: North,
The Nadir: East, the Center, unapproachable for ever.
These are the four Faces towards the Four Worlds of
    Humanity
In every Man. Ezekiel saw them by Chebars flood.
And the Eyes are the South, and the Nostrils are the
    East.
And the Tongue is the West, and the Ear is the North.   60
And the North Gate of Golgonooza toward Generation
Has four sculpturd Bulls terrible before the Gate of iron.
And iron, the Bulls: and that which looks toward Ulro,
Clay bak'd & enamel'd, eternal glowing as four furnaces:
Turning upon the Wheels of Albions sons with enormous
    power.
And that toward Beulah four, gold, silver, brass, & iron:
PLATE 13
And that toward Eden, four, form'd of gold, silver, brass,
    & iron.

The South, a golden Gate, has four Lions terrible,
    living!

That toward Generation, four, of iron carv'd wondrous:
That toward Ulro, four, clay bak'd, laborious
    workmanship
That toward Eden, four; immortal gold, silver, brass &
    iron.

The Western Gate fourfold, is closd: having four
    Cherubim
Its guards, living, the work of elemental hands,
    laborious task!
Like Men, hermaphroditic, each winged with eight wings
That towards Generation, iron; that toward Beulah,
    stone;
That toward Ulro, clay: that toward Eden, metals.   10
But all clos'd up till the last day, when the graves shall
    yield their dead

The Eastern Gate, fourfold: terrible & deadly its
    ornaments:
Taking their forms from the Wheels of Albions sons; as
    cogs
Are formd in a wheel, to fit the cogs of the adverse
    wheel.

That toward Eden, eternal ice, frozen in seven folds
Of forms of death: and that toward Beulah, stone:
The seven diseases of the earth are carved terrible.
And that toward Ulro, forms of war: seven enormities:
And that toward Generation, seven generative forms.

And every part of the City is fourfold; & every
    inhabitant, fourfold.   20
And every pot & vessel & garment & utensil of the
    houses,
And every house, fourfold; but the third Gate in every
    one
Is closd as with a threefold curtain of ivory & fine linen
    & ermine.
And Luban stands in middle of the City, a moat of fire,

Surrounds Luban, Los's Palace & the golden Looms of
  Cathedron.

And sixty-four thousand Genii, guard the Eastern Gate:
And sixty-four thousand Gnomes, guard the Northern
  Gate:
And sixty-four thousand Nymphs, guard the Western
  Gate:
And sixty-four thousand Fairies, guard the Southern
  Gate:

Around Golgonooza lies the land of death eternal; a
  Land   30
Of pain and misery and despair and ever brooding
  melancholy:
In all the Twenty-seven Heavens, numberd from Adam
  to Luther;
From the blue Mundane Shell, reaching to the
  Vegetative Earth.

The Vegetative Universe, opens like a flower from the
  Earths center:
In which is Eternity. It expands in Stars to the Mundane
  Shell
And there it meets Eternity again, both within and
  without,
And the abstract Voids between the Stars are the
  Satanic Wheels.

There is the Cave; the Rock; the Tree; the Lake of
  Udan Adan;
The Forest, and the Marsh, and the Pits of bitumen
  deadly:
The Rocks of solid fire: the Ice valleys: the Plains   40
Of burning sand: the rivers, cataract & Lakes of Fire:
The Islands of the fiery Lakes: the Trees of Malice:
  Revenge:
And black Anxiety; and the Cities of the Salamandrine
  men:
(But whatever is visible to the Generated Man,

Is a Creation of mercy & love, from the Satanic Void.)
The land of darkness flamed but no light, & no repose:
The land of snows of trembling, & of iron hail incessant:
The land of earthquakes: and the land of woven
   labyrinths:
The land of snares & traps & wheels & pit-falls & dire
   mills:
The Voids, the Solids, & the land of clouds & regions of
   waters: 50
With their inhabitants: in the Twenty-seven Heavens
   beneath Beulah:
Self-righteousnesses conglomerating against the Divine
   Vision:
A Concave Earth wondrous, Chasmal, Abyssal,
   Incoherent:
Forming the Mundane Shell: above; beneath: on all
   sides surrounding
Golgonooza: Los walks round the walls night and day.

He views the City of Golgonooza, & its smaller Cities:
The Looms & Mills & Prisons & Work-houses of Og &
   Anak:
The Amalekite: the Canaanite: the Moabite: the
   Egyptian:
And all that has existed in the space of six thousand
   years:
Permanent, & not lost not lost nor vanishd, & every
   little act,   60
Word, work, & wish, that has existed, all remaining still
In those Churches ever consuming & ever building by
   the Spectres
Of all the inhabitants of Earth wailing to be Created:
Shadowy to those who dwell not in them, meer
   possibilities:
But to those who enter into them they seem the only
   substances
For every thing exists & not one sigh nor smile nor
   tear,

PLATE 14

One hair nor particle of dust, not one can pass away.

He views the Cherub at the Tree of Life, also the
    Serpent,
Orc the first born coild in the south: the Dragon
    Urizen:
Tharmas the Vegetated Tongue even the Devouring
    Tongue:
A threefold region, a false brain: a false heart:
And false bowels: altogether composing the False
    Tongue,
Beneath Beulah: as a watry flame revolving every way
And as dark roots and stems: a Forest of affliction,
    growing
In seas of sorrow. Los also views the Four Females:
Ahania, and Enion, and Vala, and Enitharmon lovely.   10
And from them all the lovely beaming Daughters of
    Albion,
Ahania & Enion & Vala, are three evanescent shades:
Enitharmon is a vegetated mortal Wife of Los:
His Emanation, yet his Wife till the sleep of Death is
    past.

Such are the Buildings of Los: & such are the Woofs of
    Enitharmon:

And Los beheld his Sons, and he beheld his Daughters:
Every one a translucent Wonder: a Universe within,
Increasing inwards, into length and breadth, and heighth:
Starry & glorious: and they every one in their bright
    loins:
Have a beautiful golden gate which opens into the
    vegetative world: 20
And every one a gate of rubies & all sorts of precious
    stones
In their translucent hearts, which opens into the
    vegetative world:
And every one a gate of iron dreadful and wonderful,

In their translucent heads, which opens into the
   vegetative world
And every one has the three regions Childhood:
   Manhood: & Age:
But the gate of the tongue: the western gate in them is
   clos'd,
Having a wall builded against it: and thereby the gates
Eastward & Southward & Northward, are incircled with
   flaming fires.
And the North is Breadth, the South is Heighth & Depth:
The East is Inwards: & the West is Outwards every way.   30

And Los beheld the mild Emanation Jerusalem
   eastward bending
Her revolutions toward the Starry Wheels in maternal
   anguish
Like a pale cloud arising from the arms of Beulahs
   Daughters:
In Entuthon Benythons deep Vales beneath Golgonooza.

PLATE 15
And Hand & Hyle rooted into Jerusalem by a fibre
Of strong revenge & Skofeld Vegetated by Reubens Gate
In every Nation of the Earth till the Twelve Sons of
   Albion
Enrooted into every Nation: a mighty Polypus growing
From Albion over the whole Earth: such is my awful
   Vision.

I see the Four-fold Man. The Humanity in deadly sleep
And its fallen Emanation. The Spectre & its cruel
   Shadow.
I see the Past, Present & Future, existing all at once
Before me; O Divine Spirit sustain me on thy wings!
That I may awake Albion from his long & cold repose.   10
For Bacon & Newton sheathed in dismal steel, their
   terrors hang
Like iron scourges over Albion. Reasonings like vast
   Serpents

Infold around my limbs, bruising my minute
  articulations

I turn my eyes to the Schools & Universities of Europe
And there behold the Loom of Locke whose Woof rages
  dire
Washd by the Water-wheels of Newton, black the cloth
In heavy wreathes folds over every Nation; cruel Works
Of many Wheels I view, wheel without wheel, with cogs
  tyrannic
Moving by compulsion each other: not as those in Eden:
  which
Wheel within Wheel in freedom revolve in harmony &
  peace.   20

I see in deadly fear in London Los raging round his
  Anvil
Of death: forming an Ax of gold: the Four Sons of Los
Stand round him cutting the Fibres from Albions hills
That Albions Sons may roll apart over the Nations
While Reuben enroots his brethren in the narrow
  Canaanite
From the Limit Noah to the Limit Abram in whose
  Loins
Reuben in his Twelve-fold majesty & beauty shall take
  refuge
As Abraham flees from Chaldea shaking his goary locks
But first Albion must sleep, divided from the Nations

I see Albion sitting upon his Rock in the first Winter   30
And thence I see the Chaos of Satan & the World of
  Adam
When the Divine Hand went forth on Albion in the mid
  Winter
And at the place of Death when Albion sat in Eternal
  Death
Among the Furnaces of Los in the Valley of the Son of
  Hinnom

PLATE 16

Hampstead Highgate Finchley Hendon Muswell hill:
   rage loud
Before Bromions iron Tongs & glowing Poker reddening
   fierce
Hertfordshire glows with fierce Vegetation! in the
   Forests
The Oak frowns terrible, the Beech & Ash & Elm enroot
Among the Spiritual fires; loud the Corn fields thunder
   along
The Soldiers fife; the Harlots shriek; the Virgins dismal
   groan
The Parents fear: the Brothers jealousy: the Sisters curse
Beneath the Storms of Theotormon & the thundring
   Bellows
Heaves in the hand of Palamabron who in Londons
   darkness
Before the Anvil, watches the bellowing flames:
   thundering   10
The Hammer loud rages in Rintrahs strong grasp
   swinging loud
Round from heaven to earth down falling with heavy
   blow
Dead on the Anvil, where the red hot wedge groans in
   pain
He quenches it in the black trough of his Forge:
   Londons River
Feeds the dread Forge, trembling & shuddering along
   the Valleys

Humber & Trent roll dreadful before the Seventh
   Furnace
And Tweed & Tyne anxious to give up their Souls for
   Albions sake
Lincolnshire Derbyshire Nottinghamshire Leicestershire
From Oxfordshire to Norfolk on the Lake of Udan Adan
Labour within the Furnaces, walking among the Fires   20
With Ladles huge & iron Pokers over the Island white.

Scotland pours out his Sons to labour at the Furnaces
Wales gives his Daughters to the Looms; England:
  nursing Mothers
Gives to the Children of Albion & to the Children of
  Jerusalem.
From the blue Mundane Shell even to the Earth of
  Vegetation
Throughout the whole Creation which groans to be
  deliverd
Albion groans in the deep slumbers of Death upon his
  Rock.

Here Los fixd down the Fifty-two Counties of England
  & Wales
The Thirty-six of Scotland, & the Thirty-four of Ireland
With mighty power, when they fled out at Jerusalems
  Gates   30
Away from the Conflict of Luvah & Urizen, fixing the
  Gates
In the Twelve Counties of Wales & thence Gates
  looking every way
To the Four Points: conduct to England & Scotland &
  Ireland
And thence to all the Kingdoms & Nations & Families
  of the Earth[.]
The Gate of Reuben in Carmarthenshire: the Gate of
  Simeon in
Cardiganshire: & the Gate of Levi in Montgomeryshire
The Gate of Judah Merionethshire: the Gate of Dan
  Flintshire
The Gate of Napthali, Radnorshire: the Gate of Gad
  Pembrokeshire
The Gate of Asher, Carnarvonshire the Gate of Issachar
  Brecknokshire
The Gate of Zebulun, in Anglesea & Sodor. so is
  Wales divided.   40
The Gate of Joseph, Denbighshire: the Gate of
  Benjamin Glamorganshire

For the protection of the Twelve Emanations of Albions
   Sons

And the Forty Counties of England are thus divided in
   the Gates
Of Reuben Norfolk, Suffolk, Essex. Simeon Lincoln,
   York Lancashire
Levi. Middlesex Kent Surrey. Judah Somerset
   Glouster Wiltshire.
Dan. Cornwall Devon Dorset, Napthali., Warwick
   Leicester Worcester
Gad. Oxford Bucks Harford. Asher, Sussex Hampshire
   Berkshire
Issachar, Northampton Rutland Nottgham. Zebulun
   Bedford Huntgn Camb
Joseph Stafford Shrops Heref. Benjamin, Derby
   Cheshire Monmouth;
And Cumberland Northumberland Westmoreland &
   Durham are   50
Divided in the Gates of Reuben, Judah Dan & Joseph

And the Thirty-six Counties of Scotland, divided in the
   Gates
Of Reuben Kincard Haddntn Forfar, Simeon Ayr
   Argyll Banff
Levi Edinburh Roxbro Ross. Judah, Abrdeen Berwik
   Dumfries
Dan Bute Caitnes Clakmanan. Napthali Nairn
   Invernes Linlithgo
Gad Peebles Perth Renfru. Asher Sutherlan Sterling
   Wigtoun
Issachar Selkirk Dumbartn Glasgo. Zebulun Orkney
   Shetland Skye
Joseph Elgin Lanerk Kinros. Benjamin Kromarty Murra
   Kirkubriht
Governing all by the sweet delights of secret amorous
   glances
In Enitharmons Halls builded by Los & his mighty
   Children   60

All things acted on Earth are seen in the bright
Sculptures of
Los's Halls & every Age renews its powers from these
Works
With every pathetic story possible to happen from Hate
or
Wayward Love & every sorrow & distress is carved
here
Every Affinity of Parents Marriages & Friendships are
here
In all their various combinations wrought with wondrous
Art
All that can happen to Man in his pilgrimage of seventy
years
Such is the Divine Written Law of Horeb & Sinai:
And such the Holy Gospel of Mount Olivet & Calvary:

PLATE 17

His Spectre divides & Los in fury compells it to divide:
To labour in the fire, in the water, in the earth, in the
air,
To follow the Daughters of Albion as the hound follows
the scent
Of the wild inhabitant of the forest, to drive them from
his own:
To make a way for the Children of Los to come from the
Furnaces
But Los himself against Albions Sons his fury bends, for
he
Dare not approach the Daughters openly lest he be
consumed
In the fires of their beauty & perfection & be Vegetated
beneath
Their Looms, in a Generation of death & resurrection to
forgetfulness
They wooe Los continually to subdue his strength: he
continually
Shews them his Spectre: sending him abroad over the
four points of heaven

10

In the fierce desires of beauty & in the tortures of
　　repulse! He is
The Spectre of the Living pursuing the Emanations of
　　the Dead.
Shuddring they flee: they hide in the Druid Temples in
　　cold chastity:
Subdued by the Spectre of the Living & terrified by
　　undisguisd desire.

For Los said: Tho my Spectre is divided: as I am a
　　Living Man
I must compell him to obey me wholly: that Enitharmon
　　may not
Be lost: & lest he should devour Enitharmon: Ah me!
Piteous image of my soft desires & loves: O
　　Enitharmon!
I will compell my Spectre to obey: I will restore to thee
　　thy Children.　　　　　　　　　　　　　　　　　20
No one bruises or starves himself to make himself fit for
　　labour!

Tormented with sweet desire for these beauties of Albion
They would never love my power if they did not seek to
　　destroy
Enitharmon: Vala would never have sought & loved
　　Albion
If she had not sought to destroy Jerusalem; such is that
　　false
And Generating Love: a pretence of love to destroy love:
Cruel hipocrisy unlike the lovely delusions of Beulah:
And cruel forms, unlike the merciful forms of Beulahs
　　Night

They know not why they love nor wherefore they
　　sicken & die
Calling that Holy Love: which is Envy Revenge &
　　Cruelty　　　　　　　　　　　　　　　　　　30
Which separated the stars from the mountains: the
　　mountains from Man

And left Man, a little grovelling Root, outside of
   Himself.
Negations are not Contraries: Contraries mutually
   Exist:
But Negations Exist Not: Exceptions & Objections &
   Unbeliefs
Exist not: nor shall they ever be Organized for ever &
   ever:
If thou separate from me, thou art a Negation: a meer
Reasoning & Derogation from me, an Objecting & cruel
   Spite
And Malice & Envy: but my Emanation, Alas! will
   become
My Contrary: O thou Negation, I will continually
   compell
Thee to be invisible to any but whom I please, & when   40
And where & how I please, and never! never! shalt thou
   be Organized
But as a distorted & reversed Reflexion in the Darkness
And in the Non Entity: nor shall that which is above
Ever descend into thee: but thou shalt be a Non Entity
   for ever
And if any enter into thee, thou shalt be an
   Unquenchable Fire
And he shall be a never dying Worm, mutually
   tormented by
Those that thou tormentest, a Hell & Despair for ever &
   ever.

So Los in secret with himself communed & Enitharmon
   heard
In her darkness & was comforted: yet still she divided
   away
In gnawing pain from Los's bosom in the deadly Night;   50
First as a red Globe of blood trembling beneath his
   bosom[.]
Suspended over her he hung: he infolded her in his
   garments

Of wool: he hid her from the Spectre, in shame &
  confusion of
Face; in terrors & pains of Hell & Eternal Death, the
Trembling Globe shot forth Self-living & Los howld
  over it:
Feeding it with his groans & tears day & night without
  ceasing:
And the Spectrous Darkness from his back divided in
  temptations,
And in grinding agonies in threats: stiflings: & direful
  strugglings.

Go thou to Skofield: ask him if he is Bath or if he is
  Canterbury
Tell him to be no more dubious: demand explicit words   60
Tell him: I will dash him into shivers, where & at what
  time
I please: tell Hand & Skofield they are my ministers of
  evil
To those I hate: for I can hate also as well as they!

PLATE 18
From every-one of the Four Regions of Human Majesty,
There is an Outside spread Without, & an Outside
  spread Within
Beyond the Outline of Identity both ways, which meet
  in One:
An orbed Void of doubt, despair, hunger, & thirst &
  sorrow.
Here the Twelve Sons of Albion, join'd in dark Assembly,
Jealous of Jerusalems children, asham'd of her little-ones
(For Vala produc'd the Bodies. Jerusalem gave the Souls)
Became as Three Immense Wheels, turning upon
  one-another
Into Non-Entity, and their thunders hoarse appall the
  Dead
To murder their own Souls, to build a Kingdom among
  the Dead   10

Cast! Cast ye Jerusalem forth! The Shadow ot
    delusions!
The Harlot daughter! Mother of pity and dishonourable
    forgiveness
Our Father Albions sin and shame! But father now no
    more!
Nor sons. nor hateful peace & love, nor soft
    complacencies
With transgressors meeting in brotherhood around the
    table,
Or in the porch or garden. No more the sinful delights
Of age and youth and boy and girl and animal and herb,
And river and mountain, and city & village, and house &
    family,
Beneath the Oak & Palm, beneath the Vine and Fig-tree,
In self-denial! – But War and deadly contention,
    Between   20
Father and Son, and light and love! All bold asperities
Of Haters met in deadly strife, rending the house &
    garden
The unforgiving porches, the tables of enmity, and beds
And chambers of trembling & suspition, hatreds of age
    & youth
And boy & girl, & animal & herb, & river & mountain
And city & village, and house & family. That the
    Perfect,
May live in glory, redeem'd by Sacrifice of the Lamb
And of his children, before sinful Jerusalem. To build
Babylon the City of Vala, the Goddess Virgin-Mother.
She is our Mother! Nature! Jerusalem is our
    Harlot-Sister   30
Return'd with Children of pollution, to defile our House,
With Sin and Shame. Cast! Cast her into the Potters
    field.
Her little-ones, She must slay upon our Altars: and her
    aged
Parents must be carried into captivity, to redeem her
    Soul

To be for a Shame & a Curse, and to be our Slaves for
    ever

So cry Hand & Hyle the eldest of the fathers of Albions
Little-ones; to destroy the Divine Saviour; the Friend of
    Sinners,
Building Castles in desolated places, and strong
    Fortifications.
Soon Hand mightily devour'd & absorb'd Albions
    Twelve Sons.
Out from his bosom a mighty Polypus, vegetating in
    darkness,   40
And Hyle & Coban were his two chosen ones, for
    Emissaries
In War: forth from his bosom they went and return'd,
Like Wheels from a great Wheel reflected in the Deep.
Hoarse turn'd the Starry Wheels, rending a way in
    Albions Loins
Beyond the Night of Beulah. In a dark & unknown
    Night,
Outstretch'd his Giant beauty on the ground in pain &
    tears:

PLATE 19
His Children exil'd from his breast pass to and fro before
    him
His birds are silent on his hills, flocks die beneath his
    branches
His tents are fall'n! his trumpets, and the sweet sound of
    his harp
Are silent on his clouded hills, that belch forth storms &
    fire.
His milk of Cows, & honey of Bees, & fruit of golden
    harvest,
Is gather'd in the scorching heat, & in the driving rain:
Where once he sat he weary walks in misery and pain:
His Giant beauty and perfection fallen into dust:
Till from within his witherd breast grown narrow with
    his woes:

The corn is turn'd to thistles & the apples into poison: 10
The birds of song to murderous crows, his joys to bitter
    groans!
The voices of children in his tents, to cries of helpless
    infants!
And self-exiled from the face of light & shine of
    morning,
In the dark world a narrow house! he wanders up and
    down,
Seeking for rest and finding none! and hidden far
    within,
His Eon weeping in the cold and desolated Earth.

All his Affections now appear withoutside: all his
    Sons,
Hand, Hyle & Coban, Guantok, Peachey, Brereton,
    Slayd & Hutton,
Scofeld, Kox, Kotope & Bowen; his Twelve Sons:
    Satanic Mill!
Who are the Spectres of the Twentyfour, each
    Double-form'd: 20
Revolve upon his mountains groaning in pain: beneath
The dark incessant sky, seeking for rest and finding none:
Raging against their Human natures, ravning to
    gormandize
The Human majesty and beauty of the Twentyfour,
Condensing them into solid rocks with cruelty and
    abhorrence
Suspition & revenge, & the seven diseases of the Soul
Settled around Albion and around Luvah in his secret
    cloud[.]
Willing the Friends endur'd, for Albions sake, and for
Jerusalem his Emanation shut within his bosom;
Which hardend against them more and more; as he
    builded onwards   30
On the Gulph of Death in self-righteousness, that roll'd
Before his awful feet, in pride of virtue for victory:
And Los was roofd in from Eternity in Albions Cliffs

Which stand upon the ends of Beulah, and withoutside,
   all
Appear'd a rocky form against the Divine Humanity.

Albions Circumference was clos'd: his Center began
   darkning
Into the Night of Beulah, and the Moon of Beulah rose
Clouded with storms: Los his strong Guard walkd round
   beneath the Moon
And Albion fled inward among the currents of his rivers.

He found Jerusalem upon the River of his City soft
   repos'd   40
In the arms of Vala, assimilating in one with Vala
The Lilly of Havilah: and they sang soft thro'
   Lambeths vales,
In a sweet moony night & silence that they had created
With a blue sky spread over with wings and a mild
   moon,
Dividing & uniting into many female forms: Jerusalem
Trembling! then in one comingling in eternal tears,
Sighing to melt his Giant beauty, on the moony river.

PLATE 20
But when they saw Albion fall'n upon mild Lambeths
   vale:
Astonish'd! Terrified! they hover'd over his Giant limbs.
Then thus Jerusalem spoke, while Vala wove the veil of
   tears:
Weeping in pleadings of Love, in the web of despair.

Wherefore hast thou shut me into the winter of human
   life
And clos'd up the sweet regions of youth and virgin
   innocence:
Where we live, forgetting error, not pondering on evil:
Among my lambs & brooks of water, among my warbling
   birds:

Where we delight in innocence before the face of the
    Lamb:
Going in and out before him in his love and sweet
    affection.   10

Vala replied weeping & trembling, hiding in her veil.

When winter rends the hungry family and the snow falls:
Upon the ways of men hiding the paths of man and
    beast,
Then mourns the wanderer: then he repents his
    wanderings & eyes
The distant forest; then the slave groans in the dungeon
    of stone.
The captive in the mill of the stranger, sold for scanty
    hire.
They view their former life: they number moments over
    and over;
Stringing them on their remembrance as on a thread of
    sorrow.
Thou art my sister and my daughter! thy shame is mine
    also!
Ask me not of my griefs! thou knowest all my griefs.   20

Jerusalem answer'd with soft tears over the valleys.

O Vala what is Sin? that thou shudderest and weepest
At sight of thy once lov'd Jerusalem! What is Sin but a
    little
Error & fault that is soon forgiven; but mercy is not a
    Sin
Nor pity nor love nor kind forgiveness! O! if I have
    Sinned
Forgive & pity me! O! unfold thy Veil in mercy & love!
Slay not my little ones, beloved Virgin daughter of
    Babylon
Slay not my infant loves & graces, beautiful daughter of
    Moab
I cannot put off the human form I strive but strive in
    vain

When Albion rent thy beautiful net of gold and silver
    twine;   30
Thou hadst woven it with art, thou hadst caught me in
    the bands
Of love; thou refusedst to let me go: Albion beheld thy
    beauty
Beautiful thro' our Love's comeliness, beautiful thro'
    pity.
The Veil shone with thy brightness in the eyes of Albion,
Because it inclosd pity & love; because we lov'd
    one-another!
Albion lov'd thee! he rent thy Veil! he embrac'd thee!
    he lov'd thee!
Astonish'd at his beauty & perfection, thou forgavest his
    furious love:
I redounded from Albions bosom in my virgin
    loveliness.
The Lamb of God reciev'd me in his arms he smil'd
    upon us:
He made me his Bride & Wife: he gave thee to Albion.   40
Then was a time of love: O why is it passed away!

Then Albion broke silence and with groans reply'd

PLATE 21
O Vala! O Jerusalem! do you delight in my groans
You O lovely forms, you have prepared my death-cup:
The disease of Shame covers me from head to feet: I
    have no hope
Every boil upon my body is a separate & deadly Sin.
Doubt first assaild me, then Shame took possession of
    me
Shame divides Families. Shame hath divided Albion in
    sunder!
First fled my Sons, & then my Daughters, then my Wild
    Animations
My Cattle next, last ev'n the Dog of my Gate. the
    Forests fled

The Corn-fields, & the breathing Gardens outside
  separated
The Sea; the Stars: the Sun: the Moon: drivn forth by
  my disease   10
All is Eternal Death unless you can weave a chaste
Body over an unchaste Mind! Vala! O that thou wert
  pure!
That the deep wound of Sin might be clos'd up with the
  Needle,
And with the Loom: to cover Gwendolen & Ragan with
  costly Robes
Of Natural Virtue[,] for their Spiritual forms without a
  Veil
Wither in Luvahs Sepulcher. I thrust him from my
  presence
And all my Children followd his loud howlings into the
  Deep.
Jerusalem! dissembler Jerusalem! I look into thy bosom:
I discover thy secret places: Cordella! I behold
Thee whom I thought pure as the heavens in innocence
  & fear: 20
Thy Tabernacle taken down, thy secret Cherubim
  disclosed
Art thou broken? Ah me Sabrina, running by my side:
In childhood what wert thou? unutterable anguish!
  Conwenna
Thy cradled infancy is most piteous. O hide, O hide!
Their secret gardens were made paths to the traveller:
I knew not of their secret loves with those I hated most,
Nor that their every thought was Sin & secret appetite[.]
Hyle sees in fear, he howls in fury over them, Hand sees
In jealous fear: in stern accusation with cruel stripes
He drives them thro' the Streets of Babylon before my
  face: 30
Because they taught Luvah to rise into my clouded
  heavens
Battersea and Chelsea mourn for Cambel & Gwendolen!
Hackney and Holloway sicken for Estrild & Ignoge!

Because the Peak, Malvern & Cheviot Reason in Cruelty
Penmaenmawr & Dhinas-bran Demonstrate in Unbelief
Manchester & Liverpool are in tortures of Doubt &
    Despair
Malden & Colchester Demonstrate: I hear my Childrens
    voices
I see their piteous faces gleam out upon the cruel winds
From Lincoln & Norwich, from Edinburgh &
    Monmouth:
I see them distant from my bosom scourgd along the
    roads   40
Then lost in clouds; I hear their tender voices! clouds
    divide
I see them die beneath the whips of the Captains! they
    are taken
In solemn pomp into Chaldea across the bredths of
    Europe
Six months they lie embalmd in silent death: worshipped
Carried in Arks of Oak before the armies in the spring
Bursting their Arks they rise again to life: they play
    before
The Armies: I hear their loud cymbals & their deadly
    cries
Are the Dead cruel? are those who are infolded in moral
    Law
Revengeful? O that Death & Annihilation were the
    same!

Then Vala answerd spreading her scarlet Veil over Albion   50

PLATE 22
Albion thy fear has made me tremble; thy terrors have
    surrounded me
Thy Sons have naild me on the Gates piercing my
    hands & feet:
Till Skofields Nimrod the mighty Huntsman [of]
    Jehovah came,
With Cush his Son & took me down. He in a golden
    Ark,

Bears me before his Armies tho my shadow hovers here
The flesh of multitudes fed & nourisd me in my
  childhood
My morn & evening food were prepard in Battles of
  Men
Great is the cry of the Hounds of Nimrod along the
  Valley
Of Vision, they scent the odor of War in the Valley of
  Vision.
All Love is lost! terror succeeds & Hatred instead of
  Love   10
And stern demands of Right & Duty instead of Liberty
Once thou wast to me the loveliest Son of heaven; but
  now
Where shall I hide from thy dread countenance &
  searching eyes

I have looked into the secret Soul of him I loved
And in the dark recesses found Sin & can never return.

Albion again utterd his voice beneath the silent Moon

I brought Love into light of day to pride in chaste
  beauty
I brought Love into light & fancied Innocence is no
  more

Then spoke Jerusalem O Albion! my Father Albion
Why wilt thou number every little fibre of my Soul   20
Spreading them out before the Sun like stalks of flax to
  dry?
The Infant Joy is beautiful, but its anatomy
Horrible ghast & deadly! nought shalt thou find in it
But dark despair & everlasting brooding melancholy!

Then Albion turnd his face toward Jerusalem & spoke

Hide thou Jerusalem in impalpable voidness, not to be
Touchd by the hand nor seen with the eye: O Jerusalem
Would thou wert not & that thy place might never be
  found

But come O Vala with knife & cup: drain my blood
To the last drop! then hide me in thy Scarlet Tabernacle   30
For I see Luvah whom I slew. I behold him in my
    Spectre
As I behold Jerusalem in thee O Vala dark and cold

Jerusalem then stretchd her hand toward the Moon &
    spoke

Why should Punishment Weave the Veil with Iron
    Wheels of War
When Forgiveness might it Weave with Wings of
    Cherubim

Loud groand Albion from mountain to mountain &
    replied

PLATE 23
Jerusalem! Jerusalem! deluding shadow of Albion!
Daughter of my phantasy! unlawful pleasure! Albions
    curse!
I came here with intention to annihilate thee! But
My soul is melted away, inwoven within the Veil
Hast thou again knitted the Veil of Vala, which I for thee
Pitying rent in ancient times. I see it whole and more
Perfect, and shining with beauty! But thou! O wretched
    Father!

Jerusalem reply'd, like a voice heard from a sepulcher:
Father! once piteous! Is Pity a Sin? Embalm'd in Vala's
    bosom
In an Eternal Death for Albions sake, our best beloved.   10
Thou art my Father & my Brother: Why hast thou
    hidden me,
Remote from the divine Vision: my Lord and Saviour.

Trembling stood Albion at her words in jealous dark
    despair:
He felt that Love and Pity are the same; a soft repose!
Inward complacency of Soul: a Self-annihilation!

I have erred! I am ashamed! and will never return more:
I have taught my children sacrifices of cruelty: what shall
  I answer?
I will hide it from Eternals! I will give myself for my
  Children!
Which way soever I turn, I behold Humanity and Pity!

He recoil'd: he rush'd outwards; he bore the Veil whole
  away   20
His fires redound from his Dragon Altars in Errors
  returning.
He drew the Veil of Moral Virtue, woven for Cruel
  Laws,
And cast it into the Atlantic Deep, to catch the Souls of
  the Dead.
He stood between the Palm tree & the Oak of weeping
Which stand upon the edge of Beulah; and there Albion
  sunk
Down in sick pallid languor! These were his last words,
  relapsing!
Hoarse from his rocks, from caverns of Derbyshire &
  Wales
And Scotland, utter'd from the Circumference into
  Eternity.

Blasphemous Sons of Feminine delusion! God in the
  dreary Void
Dwells from Eternity, wide separated from the Human
  Soul   30
But thou deluding Image by whom imbu'd the Veil I
  rent
Lo here is Valas Veil whole, for a Law, a Terror & a
  Curse!
And therefore God takes vengeance on me: from my
  clay-cold bosom
My children wander trembling victims of his Moral
  Justice.
His snows fall on me and cover me, while in the Veil I
  fold

My dying limbs. Therefore O Manhood, if thou art aught
But a meer Phantasy, hear dying Albions Curse!
May God who dwells in this dark Ulro & voidness,
     vengeance take,
And draw thee down into this Abyss of sorrow and
     torture,
Like me thy Victim. O that Death & Annihilation were
     the same!   40

PLATE 24

What have I said? What have I done? O all-powerful
     Human Words:
You recoil back upon me in the blood of the Lamb slain
     in his Children.
Two bleeding Contraries equally true, are his
     Witnesses against me
We reared mighty Stones: we danced naked around
     them:
Thinking to bring Love into light of day, to Jerusalems
     shame:
Displaying our Giant limbs to all the winds of heaven!
     Sudden
Shame siezd us, we could not look on one-another for
     abhorrence: the Blue
Of our immortal Veins & all their Hosts fled from our
     Limbs,
And wanderd distant in a dismal Night clouded & dark:
The Sun fled from the Britons forehead: the Moon from
     his mighty loins: 10
Scandinavia fled with all his mountains filld with groans.

O what is Life & what is Man. O what is Death!
     Wherefore
Are you my Children, natives in the Grave to where I go
Or are you born to feed the hungry ravenings of
     Destruction
To be the sport of Accident! to waste in Wrath & Love,
     a weary

Life, in brooding cares & anxious labours, that prove but
    chaff.
O Jerusalem Jerusalem I have forsaken thy Courts
Thy Pillars of ivory & gold: thy Curtains of silk & fine
Linen: thy Pavements of precious stones: thy Walls of
    pearl
And gold, thy Gates of Thanksgiving thy Windows of
    Praise: 20
Thy Clouds of Blessing; thy Cherubims of
    Tender-mercy
Stretching their Wings sublime over the Little-ones of
    Albion[.]
O Human Imagination O Divine Body I have
    Crucified
I have turned my back upon thee into the Wastes of
    Moral Law:
There Babylon is builded in the Waste, founded in
    Human desolation.
O Babylon thy Watchman stands over thee in the night
Thy severe Judge all the day long proves thee O
    Babylon
With provings of destruction, with giving thee thy hearts
    desire.
But Albion is cast forth to the Potter his Children to the
    Builders
To build Babylon because they have forsaken Jerusalem   30
The Walls of Babylon are Souls of Men: her Gates the
    Groans
Of Nations: her Towers are the Miseries of once happy
    Families.
Her Streets are paved with Destruction, her Houses built
    with Death
Her Palaces with Hell & the Grave; her Synagogues
    with Torments
Of ever-hardening Despair squard & polishd with cruel
    skill
Yet thou wast lovely as the summer cloud upon my
    hills

When Jerusalem was thy hearts desire in times of youth
& love.

Thy Sons came to Jerusalem with gifts, she sent them
away

With blessings on their hands & on their feet, blessings
of gold,

And pearl & diamond: thy Daughters sang in her
Courts: 40

They came up to Jerusalem; they walked before Albion

In the Exchanges of London every Nation walkd

And London walkd in every Nation mutual in love &
harmony

Albion coverd the whole Earth, England encompassd the
Nations,

Mutual each within others bosom in Visions of
Regeneration;

Jerusalem coverd the Atlantic Mountains & the
Erythrean,

From bright Japan & China to Hesperia France &
England.

Mount Zion lifted his head in every Nation under
heaven:

And the Mount of Olives was beheld over the whole
Earth:

The footsteps of the Lamb of God were there: but now
no more   50

No more shall I behold him, he is closd in Luvahs
Sepulcher.

Yet why these smitings of Luvah, the gentlest mildest
Zoa?

If God was Merciful this could not be: O Lamb of
God

Thou art a delusion and Jerusalem is my Sin! O my
Children

I have educated you in the crucifying cruelties of
Demonstration

Till you have assum'd the Providence of God & slain
your Father

Dost thou appear before me who liest dead in Luvahs
   Sepulcher
Dost thou forgive me! thou who wast Dead & art Alive?
Look not so merciful upon me O thou Slain Lamb of
   God
I die! I die in thy arms tho Hope is banishd from me.   60

Thundring the Veil rushes from his hand Vegetating
   Knot by
Knot, Day by Day, Night by Night; loud roll the
   indignant Atlantic
Waves & the Erythrean, turning up the bottoms of the
   Deeps
PLATE 25
And there was heard a great lamenting in Beulah: all the
   Regions
Of Beulah were moved as the tender bowels are moved:
   & they said:

Why did you take Vengeance O ye Sons of the mighty
   Albion?
Planting these Oaken Groves: Erecting these Dragon
   Temples
Injury the Lord heals but Vengeance cannot be healed:
As the Sons of Albion have done to Luvah: so they have
   in him
Done to the Divine Lord & Saviour, who suffers with
   those that suffer:
For not one sparrow can suffer, & the whole Universe
   not suffer also,
In all its Regions, & its Father & Saviour not pity and
   weep.
But Vengeance is the destroyer of Grace & Repentance in
   the bosom   10
Of the Injurer: in which the Divine Lamb is cruelly
   slain:
Descend O Lamb of God & take away the imputation of
   Sin

By the Creation of States & the deliverance of
  Individuals Evermore Amen

Thus wept they in Beulah over the Four Regions of
  Albion
But many doubted & despaird & imputed Sin &
  Righteousness
To Individuals & not to States, and these Slept in Ulro.

PLATE 26

> SUCH VISIONS HAVE APPEARD TO ME
> AS I MY ORDERD RACE HAVE RUN
> JERUSALEM IS NAMED LIBERTY
> AMONG THE SONS OF ALBION

PLATE 27

TO THE JEWS

Jerusalem the Emanation of the Giant Albion! Can it
be? Is it a Truth that the Learned have explored? Was
Britain the Primitive Seat of the Patriarchal Religion? If it
is true: my title-page is also True, that Jerusalem was & is
the Emanation of the Giant Albion. It is True, and cannot
be controverted. Ye are united O ye inhabitants of Earth
in One Religion. The Religion of Jesus: the most Ancient,
the Eternal: & the Everlasting Gospel – The Wicked will
turn it to Wickedness, the Righteous to Righteousness,
Amen! Huzza! Selah!   10
  'All things Begin & End in Albions Ancient Druid
Rocky Shore.'

Your Ancestors derived their origin from Abraham,
Heber, Shem, and Noah, who were Druids: as the Druid
Temples (which are the Patriarchal Pillars & Oak Groves)
over the whole Earth witness to this day.

You have a tradition, that Man anciently containd in his
mighty limbs all things in Heaven & Earth: this you
recieved from the Druids

'But now the Starry Heavens are fled from the mighty 20
limbs of Albion'

Albion was the Parent of the Druids; & in his Chaotic
State of Sleep
Satan & Adam & the whole World was Created by
the Elohim.

The fields from Islington to Marybone,
To Primrose Hill and Saint Johns Wood:
  Were builded over with pillars of gold,
And there Jerusalems pillars stood.

Her Little-ones ran on the fields
The Lamb of God among them seen
  And fair Jerusalem his Bride:
Among the little meadows green.

Pancrass & Kentish-town repose
Among her golden pillars high: 10
  Among her golden arches which
Shine upon the starry sky.

The Jews-harp-house & the Green Man;
The Ponds where Boys to bathe delight:
  The fields of Cows by Willans farm:
Shine in Jerusalems pleasant sight.

She walks upon our meadows green:
The Lamb of God walks by her side:
  And every English Child is seen,
Children of Jesus & his Bride,   20

Forgiving trespasses and sins
Lest Babylon with cruel Og,
  With Moral & Self-righteous Law
Should Crucify in Satans Synagogue!

What are those golden Builders doing
Near mournful ever-weeping Paddington
  Standing above that mighty Ruin
Where Satan the first victory won.

Satan seen as opposite to LOS

Where Albion slept beneath the Fatal Tree
And the Druids golden Knife,   30
   Rioted in human gore,
In Offerings of Human Life

   They groan'd aloud on London Stone   — Edgware road /Execution
They groan'd aloud on Tyburns Brook
   Albion gave his deadly groan,
And all the Atlantic Mountains shook   American revolution ??

   Albions Spectre from his Loins   BAD PART/SHADOW
Tore forth in all the pomp of War!
BAD SIDE — Satan his name: in flames of fire
He stretch'd his Druid Pillars far.   40

   Jerusalem fell from Lambeth's Vale,
Down thro Poplar & Old Bow;
   Thro Malden & acros the Sea,   The end of Jerusalem
In War & howling death & woe.

   The Rhine was red with human blood: wars in his aimage
The Danube rolld a purple tide:
   On the Euphrates Satan stood:
And over Asia stretch'd his pride.

   He witherd up sweet Zions Hill,
From every Nation of the Earth: 50
   He witherd up Jerusalems Gates,
And in a dark Land gave her birth.

   He witherd up the Human Form,
By laws of sacrifice for sin: Inside there is still something
   Till it became a Mortal Worm:
But O! translucent all within.

   The Divine Vision still was seen
Still was the Human Form, Divine
   Weeping in weak & mortal clay
O Jesus still the Form was thine.   60

And thine the Human Face & thine
The Human Hands & Feet & Breath
    Entering thro' the Gates of Birth
And passing thro' the Gates of Death

And O thou Lamb of God, whom I
Slew in my dark self-righteous pride:
    Art thou return'd to Albions Land!
And is Jerusalem thy Bride?

Come to my arms & never more
Depart; but dwell for ever here:
    Create my Spirit to thy Love:
Subdue my Spectre to thy Fear.

70

Spectre of Albion! warlike Fiend!
In clouds of blood & ruin roll'd:
    I here reclaim thee as my own
My Selfhood! Satan! armd in gold.

Is this thy soft Family-Love
Thy cruel Patriarchal pride
    Planting thy Family alone,
Destroying all the World beside.

80

A mans worst enemies are those
Of his own house & family;
    And he who makes his law a curse,
By his own law shall surely die.

In my Exchanges every Land
Shall walk, & mine in every Land,
    Mutual shall build Jerusalem:
Both heart in heart & hand in hand.

If Humility is Christianity; you O Jews are the true
Christians; If your tradition that Man contained in his
Limbs, all Animals, is True & they were separated from
him by cruel Sacrifices: and when compulsory cruel
Sacrifices had brought Humanity into a Feminine Taber-
nacle, in the loins of Abraham & David: the Lamb of

90

God, the Saviour became apparent on Earth as the Prophets had foretold? The Return of Israel is a Return to Mental Sacrifice & War. Take up the Cross O Israel & follow Jesus.

PLATE 28

JERUSALEM

CHAP: 2

Every ornament of perfection, and every labour of love,
In all the Garden of Eden, & in all the golden
    mountains
Was become an envied horror, and a remembrance of
    jealousy:
And every Act a Crime, and Albion the punisher &
    judge.

And Albion spoke from his secret seat and said

All these ornaments are crimes, they are made by the
    labours
Of loves: of unnatural consanguinities and friendships
Horrid to think of when enquired deeply into; and all
These hills & valleys are accursed witnesses of Sin
I therefore condense them into solid rocks, stedfast!   10
A foundation and certainty and demonstrative truth:
That Man be separate from Man, & here I plant my seat.

Cold snows drifted around him: ice coverd his loins
    around
He sat by Tyburns brook, and underneath his heel,
    shot up!
A deadly Tree, he nam'd it Moral Virtue, and the Law
Of God who dwells in Chaos hidden from the human
    sight.
The Tree spread over him its cold shadows, (Albion
    groand)
They bent down, they felt the earth and again enrooting
Shot into many a Tree! an endless labyrinth of woe!

From willing sacrifice of Self, to sacrifice of (miscall'd)
  Enemies   20
For Atonement: Albion began to erect twelve Altars,
Of rough unhewn rocks, before the Potters Furnace
He nam'd them Justice, and Truth. And Albions Sons
Must have become the first Victims, being the first
  transgressors
But they fled to the mountains to seek ransom: building
  A Strong
Fortification against the Divine Humanity and Mercy,
In Shame & Jealousy to annihilate Jerusalem!

PLATE 29 [33]
Turning his back to the Divine Vision, his Spectrous
Chaos before his face appeard: an Unformed Memory.

Then spoke the Spectrous Chaos to Albion darkning cold
From the back & loins where dwell the Spectrous Dead

I am your Rational Power O Albion & that Human Form
You call Divine, is but a Worm seventy inches long
That creeps forth in a night & is dried in the morning
  sun
In fortuitous concourse of memorys accumulated & lost
It plows the Earth in its own conceit, it overwhelms the
  Hills
Beneath its winding labyrinths, till a stone of the brook   10
Stops it in midst of its pride among its hills & rivers[.]
Battersea & Chelsea mourn, London & Canterbury
  tremble
Their place shall not be found as the wind passes over.
The ancient Cities of the Earth remove as a traveller
And shall Albions Cities remain when I pass over them
With my deluge of forgotten remembrances over the
  tablet

So spoke the Spectre to Albion, he is the Great Selfhood
Satan: Worshipd as God by the Mighty Ones of the
  Earth

Having a white Dot calld a Center from which branches
    out
A Circle in continual gyrations, this became a Heart   20
From which sprang numerous branches varying their
    motions
Producing many Heads three or seven or ten, & hands &
    feet
Innumerable at will of the unfortunate contemplator
Who becomes his food[:] such is the way of the
    Devouring Power

And this is the cause of the appearance in the frowning
    Chaos[.]
Albions Emanation which he had hidden in Jealousy
Appeard now in the frowning Chaos prolific upon the
    Chaos
Reflecting back to Albion in Sexual Reasoning
    Hermaphroditic

Albion spoke. Who art thou that appearest in gloomy
    pomp
Involving the Divine Vision in colours of autumn
    ripeness   30
I never saw thee till this time, nor beheld life abstracted
Nor darkness immingled with light on my furrowd field
Whence camest thou! who art thou O loveliest? the
    Divine Vision
Is as nothing before thee, faded is all life and joy

Vala replied in clouds of tears Albions garment
    embracing

I was a City & a Temple built by Albions Children.
I was a Garden planted with beauty I allured on hill &
    valley
The River of Life to flow against my walls & among my
    trees
Vala was Albions Bride & Wife in great Eternity
The loveliest of the daughters of Eternity when in
    day-break   40

I emanated from Luvah over the Towers of Jerusalem
And in her Courts among her little Children offering up
The Sacrifice of fanatic love! why loved I Jerusalem:
Why was I one with her embracing in the Vision of
    Jesus
Wherefore did I loving create love, which never yet
Immingled God & Man, when thou & I, hid the Divine
    Vision
In cloud of secret gloom which behold involve me round
    about
Know me now Albion: look upon me I alone am Beauty
The Imaginative Human Form is but a breathing of Vala
I breathe him forth into the Heaven from my secret
    Cave   50
Born of the Woman to obey the Woman O Albion the
    mighty
For the Divine appearance is Brotherhood, but I am
    Love

PLATE 30[34]
Elevate into the Region of Brotherhood with my red
    fires

Art thou Vala? replied Albion, image of my repose
O how I tremble! how my members pour down milky
    fear!
A dewy garment covers me all over, all manhood is gone:
At thy word & at thy look death enrobes me about
From head to feet, a garment of death & eternal fear
Is not that Sun thy husband & that Moon thy glimmering
    Veil?
Are not the Stars of heaven thy Children! art thou not
    Babylon?
Art thou Nature Mother of all! is Jerusalem thy
    Daughter
Why have thou elevate inward: O dweller of outward
    chambers   10
From grot & cave beneath the Moon dim region of
    death

Where I laid my Plow in the hot noon, where my hot
    team fed
Where implements of War are forged, the Plow to go
    over the Nations
In pain girding me round like a rib of iron in heaven: O
    Vala
In Eternity they neither marry nor are given in marriage
Albion the high Cliff of the Atlantic is become a barren
    Land

Los stood at his Anvil: he heard the contentions of Vala –
He heavd his thundring Bellows upon the valleys of
    Middlesex
He opend his Furnaces before Vala, then Albion frownd
    in anger
On his Rock: ere yet the Starry Heavens were fled away   20
From his awful Members, and thus Los cried aloud
To the Sons of Albion & to Hand the eldest Son of
    Albion

I hear the screech of Childbirth loud pealing, & the
    groans
Of Death, in Albions clouds dreadful utterd over all the
    Earth
What may Man be? who can tell! but what may
    Woman be?
To have power over Man from Cradle to corruptible
    Grave.
There is a Throne in every Man, it is the Throne of God
This Woman has claimd as her own & Man is no more!
Albion is the Tabernacle of Vala & her Temple
And not the Tabernacle & Temple of the Most High   30
O Albion why wilt thou Create a Female Will?
To hide the most evident God in a hidden covert, even
In the shadows of a Woman & a secluded Holy Place
That we may pry after him as after a stolen treasure
Hidden among the Dead & mured up from the paths of
    life

Hand! art thou not Reuben enrooting thyself into Bashan
Till thou remainest a vaporous Shadow in a Void! O
  Merlin!
Unknown among the Dead where never before Existence
  came
Is this the Female Will O ye lovely Daughters of Albion.
  To
Converse concerning Weight & Distance in the Wilds of   40
  Newton & Locke

So Los spoke standing on Mam-Tor looking over
  Europe & Asia
The Graves thunder beneath his feet from Ireland to
  Japan

Reuben slept in Bashan like one dead in the valley
Cut off from Albions mountains & from all the Earths
  summits
Between Succoth & Zaretan beside the Stone of Bohan
While the Daughters of Albion divided Luvah into three
  Bodies
Los bended his Nostrils down to the Earth, then sent
  him over
Jordan to the Land of the Hittite: every-one that saw him
Fled! they fled at his horrible Form: they hid in caves
And dens, they looked to one-another & became what
  they beheld   50

Reuben return'd to Bashan, in despair he slept on the
  Stone.
Then Gwendolen divided into Rahab & Tirza in Twelve
  Portions[.]
Los rolled, his Eyes into two narrow circles, then sent him
Over Jordan; all terrified fled: they became what they
  beheld.

If Perceptive Organs vary: Objects of Perception seem to
  vary:
If the Perceptive Organs close: their Objects seem to
  close also:

Consider this O mortal Man: O worm of sixty winters
   said Los
Consider Sexual Organization & hide thee in the dust.

PLATE 31 [35]
Then the Divine hand found the Two Limits, Satan
   and Adam,
In Albions bosom: for in every Human bosom those
   Limits stand.
And the Divine voice came from the Furnaces, as
   multitudes without
Number: the voices of the innumerable multitudes of
   Eternity.
And the appearance of a Man was seen in the Furnaces;
Saving those who have sinned from the punishment of
   the Law,
(In pity of the punisher whose state is eternal death,)
And keeping them from Sin by the mild counsels of his
   love.

Albion goes to Eternal Death: In Me all Eternity,
Must pass thro' condemnation, and awake beyond the
   Grave: 10
No individual can keep these Laws, for they are death
To every energy of man, and forbid the springs of life;
Albion hath enterd the State Satan! Be permanent O
   State!
And be thou for ever accursed! that Albion may arise
   again:
And be thou created into a State! I go forth to Create
States: to deliver Individuals evermore! Amen.

So spoke the voice from the Furnaces, descending into
   Non-Entity
[*To Govern the Evil by Good: and States abolish Systems.*]

PLATE 32 [36]
Reuben return'd to his place, in vain he sought beautiful
   Tirzah

For his Eyelids were narrowd, & his Nostrils scented the
    ground
And Sixty Winters Los raged in the Divisions of Reuben:
Building the Moon of Ulro, plank by plank & rib by rib
Reuben slept in the Cave of Adam, and Los folded his
    Tongue
Between Lips of mire & clay, then sent him forth over
    Jordan
In the love of Tirzah he said Doubt is my food day &
    night –
All that beheld him fled howling and gnawed their
    tongues
For pain: they became what they beheld. In reasonings
    Reuben returned
To Heshbon, disconsolate he walkd thro Moab & he
    stood   10
Before the Furnaces of Los in a horrible dreamful
    slumber,
On Mount Gilead looking toward Gilgal: and Los
    bended
His Ear in a spiral circle outward; then sent him over
    Jordan.

The Seven Nations fled before him they became what
    they beheld
Hand, Hyle & Coban fled: they became what they beheld
Gwantock & Peachy hid in Damascus beneath Mount
    Lebanon
Brereton & Slade in Egypt. Hutton & Skofeld & Kox
Fled over Chaldea in terror in pains in every nerve
Kotope & Bowen became what they beheld, fleeing over
    the Earth
And the Twelve Female Emanations fled with them
    agonizing.   20

Jerusalem trembled seeing her Children drivn by Los's
    Hammer
In the visions of the dreams of Beulah on the edge of
    Non-Entity

Hand stood between Reuben & Merlin, as the Reasoning
  Spectre
Stands between the Vegetative Man & his Immortal
  Imagination

And the Four Zoa's clouded rage East & West & North
  & South
They change their situations, in the Universal Man.
Albion groans, he sees the Elements divide before his
  face.
And England who is Brittannia divided into Jerusalem &
  Vala
And Urizen assumes the East, Luvah assumes the South
In his dark Spectre ravening from his open Sepulcher   30
And the Four Zoa's who are the Four Eternal Senses of
  Man
Became Four Elements separating from the Limbs of
  Albion
These are their names in the Vegetative Generation
[*West Weighing East & North dividing Generation South*
  [   ]*ing*]
And Accident & Chance were found hidden in Length
  Bredth & Highth
And they divided into Four ravening deathlike Forms
Fairies & Genii & Nymphs & Gnomes of the Elements.
These are States Permanently Fixed by the Divine
  Power[.]
The Atlantic Continent sunk round Albions cliffy shore
And the Sea poured in amain upon the Giants of Albion   40
As Los bended the Senses of Reuben Reuben is Merlin
Exploring the Three States of Ulro; Creation;
  Redemption, & Judgment

And many of the Eternal Ones laughed after their
  manner

Have you known the Judgment that is arisen among the
Zoa's of Albion? where a Man dare hardly to embrace
His own Wife, for the terrors of Chastity that they call

By the name of Morality, their Daughters govern all
In hidden deceit! they are Vegetable only fit for burning:
Art & Science cannot exist but by Naked Beauty displayd

Then those in Great Eternity who contemplate on Death   50
Said thus. What seems to Be: Is: To those to whom
It seems to Be, & is productive of the most dreadful
Consequences to those to whom it seems to Be: even of
Torments, Despair, Eternal Death; but the Divine
   Mercy
Steps beyond and Redeems Man in the Body of Jesus
   Amen
And Length Bredth Highth again Obey the Divine Vision
   Hallelujah

PLATE 33 [37]
And One stood forth from the Divine family & said

I feel my Spectre rising upon me! Albion! arouze thyself!
Why dost thou thunder with frozen Spectrous wrath
   against us?
The Spectre is, in Giant Man; insane, and most
   deform'd.
Thou wilt certainly provoke my Spectre against thine in
   fury!
He has a Sepulcher hewn out of a Rock ready for thee:
And a Death of Eight thousand years, forg'd by thyself,
   upon
The point of his Spear! if thou persistest to forbid with
   Laws
Our Emanations, and to attack our secret supreme
   delights

So Los spoke: But when he saw blue death in Albions
   feet,   10
Again he join'd the Divine Body, following merciful;
While Albion fled more indignant: revengeful covering
PLATE 34 [38]
His face and bosom with petrific hardness, and his hands
And feet, lest any should enter his bosom & embrace

His hidden heart; his Emanation wept & trembled
  within him:
Uttering not his jealousy, but hiding it as with
Iron and steel, dark and opake, with clouds & tempests
  brooding:
His strong limbs shudderd upon his mountains high and
  dark.

Turning from Universal Love petrific as he went,
His cold against the warmth of Eden rag'd with loud
Thunders of deadly war (the fever of the human soul)
Fires and clouds of rolling smoke! but mild the Saviour
  follow'd him,   10
Displaying the Eternal Vision! the Divine Similitude!
In loves and tears of brothers, sisters, sons, fathers, and
  friends
Which if Man ceases to behold, he ceases to exist:

Saying. Albion! Our wars are wars of life, & wounds of
  love,
With intellectual spears, & long winged arrows of
  thought:
Mutual in one anothers love and wrath all renewing
We live as One Man; for contracting our infinite senses
We behold multitude; or expanding: we behold as one,
As One Man all the Universal Family; and that One Man
We call Jesus the Christ: and he in us, and we in him,   20
Live in perfect harmony in Eden the land of life,
Giving, recieving, and forgiving each others trespasses.
He is the Good shepherd, he is the Lord and master:
He is the Shepherd of Albion, he is all in all,
In Eden: in the garden of God: and in heavenly
  Jerusalem.
If we have offended, forgive us, take not vengeance
  against us.

Thus speaking; the Divine Family follow Albion:
I see them in the Vision of God upon my pleasant
  valleys.

I behold London; a Human awful wonder of God!
He says: Return, Albion, return! I give myself for thee: 30
My Streets are my, Ideas of Imagination.
Awake Albion, awake! and let us awake up together.
My Houses are Thoughts: my Inhabitants: Affections,
The children of my thoughts, walking within my
    blood-vessels,
Shut from my nervous form which sleeps upon the verge
    of Beulah
In dreams of darkness, while my vegetating blood in
    veiny pipes,
Rolls dreadful thro' the Furnaces of Los, and the Mills
    of Satan.
For Albions sake, and for Jerusalem thy Emanation
I give myself, and these my brethren give themselves for
    Albion.

So spoke London, immortal Guardian! I heard in
    Lambeths shades: 40
In Felpham I heard and saw the Visions of Albion
I write in South Molton Street, what I both see and hear
In regions of Humanity, in Londons opening streets.

I see thee awful Parent Land in light, behold I see!
Verulam! Canterbury! venerable parent of men,
Generous immortal Guardian golden clad! for Cities
Are Men, fathers of multitudes, and Rivers & Mountains
Are also Men; every thing is Human, mighty! sublime!
In every bosom a Universe expands, as wings
Let down at will around, and call'd the Universal Tent. 50
York, crown'd with loving kindness. Edinburgh, cloth'd
With fortitude as with a garment of immortal texture
Woven in looms of Eden, in spiritual deaths of mighty
    men
Who give themselves, in Golgotha, Victims to Justice;
    where
There is in Albion a Gate of Precious stones and gold
Seen only by Emanations, by vegetations viewless,

Bending across the road of Oxford Street; it from Hyde
  Park
To Tyburns deathful shades, admits the wandering souls
Of multitudes who die from Earth: this Gate cannot be
  found
PLATE 35 [39]
By Satans Watch-fiends tho' they search numbering
  every grain
Of sand on Earth every night, they never find this Gate.
It is the Gate of Los. Withoutside is the Mill, intricate,
  dreadful
And fill'd with cruel tortures; but no mortal man can find
  the Mill
Of Satan, in his mortal pilgrimage of seventy years

For Human beauty knows it not: nor can Mercy find it!
  But
In the Fourth region of Humanity, Urthona namd[,]
Mortality begins to roll the billows of Eternal Death
Before the Gate of Los. Urthona here is named Los.
And here begins the System of Moral Virtue, named
  Rahab.   10

Albion fled thro' the Gate of Los, and he stood in the
  Gate.

Los was the friend of Albion who most lov'd him. In
  Cambridgeshire
His eternal station, he is the twenty-eighth, & is
  four-fold.
Seeing Albion had turn'd his back against the Divine
  Vision,
Los said to Albion. Whither fleest thou? Albion reply'd.

I die! I go to Eternal Death! the shades of death
Hover within me & beneath, and spreading themselves
  outside
Like rocky clouds, build me a gloomy monument of woe:
Will none accompany me in my death? or be a Ransom
  for me

In that dark Valley? I have girded round my cloke, and
   on my feet   20
Bound these black shoes of death, & on my hands,
   deaths iron gloves:
God hath forsaken me, & my friends are become a
   burden
A weariness to me, & the human footstep is a terror to
   me.

Los answerd, troubled: and his soul was rent in twain:
Must the Wise die for an Atonement? does Mercy endure
   Atonement?
No! It is Moral Severity, & destroys Mercy in its Victim.
So speaking, not yet infected with the Error & Illusion,
PLATE 36 [40]
Los shudder'd at beholding Albion, for his disease
Arose upon him pale and ghastly: and he call'd around
The Friends of Albion: trembling at the sight of Eternal
   Death
The four appear'd with their Emanations in fiery
Chariots: black their fires roll beholding Albions House
   of Eternity
Damp couch the flames beneath and silent, sick, stand
   shuddering
Before the Porch of sixteen pillars: weeping every one
Descended and fell down upon their knees around
   Albions knees,
Swearing the Oath of God! with awful voice of thunders
   round
Upon the hills & valleys, and the cloudy Oath roll'd far
   and wide   10

Albion is sick! said every Valley, every mournful Hill
And every River: our brother Albion is sick to death.
He hath leagued himself with robbers: he hath studied
   the arts
Of unbelief: Envy hovers over him! his Friends are his
   abhorrence!
Those who give their lives for him are despised!

Those who devour his soul, are taken into his bosom!
To destroy his Emanation is their intention:
Arise! awake O Friends of the Giant Albion
They have perswaded him of horrible falshoods!
They have sown errors over all his fruitful fields!   20

The Twenty-four heard! they came trembling on watry
    chariots.
Borne by the Living Creatures of the third procession
Of Human Majesty, the Living Creatures wept aloud as
    they
Went along Albions roads, till they arriv'd at Albions
    House.

O! how the torments of Eternal Death, waited on Man:
And the loud-rending bars of the Creation ready to
    burst:
That the wide world might fly from its hinges & the
    immortal mansion
Of Man, for ever be possessd by monsters of the deeps:
And Man himself become a Fiend, wrap'd in an endless
    curse,
Consuming and consum'd for-ever in flames of Moral
    Justice.   30

For had the Body of Albion fall'n down, and from its
    dreadful ruins
Let loose the enormous Spectre on the darkness of the
    deep,
At enmity with the Merciful & fill'd with devouring fire,
A nether-world must have recievd the foul enormous
    spirit,
Under pretence of Moral Virtue, fill'd with Revenge and
    Law.
There to eternity chain'd down, and issuing in red
    flames
And curses, with his mighty arms brandish'd against the
    heavens

Breathing cruelty blood & vengeance, gnashing his teeth
   with pain
Torn with black storms, & ceaseless torrents of his own
   consuming fire:
Within his breast his mighty Sons chaind down & fill'd
   with cursings: 40
And his dark Eon, that once fair crystal form divinely
   clear:
Within his ribs producing serpents whose souls are flames
   of fire.
But, glory to the Merciful-One, for he is of tender
   mercies!
And the Divine Family wept over him as One Man.

And these the Twenty-four in whom the Divine Family
Appeard; and they were One in Him. A Human Vision!
Human Divine, Jesus the Saviour, blessed for ever and
   ever.

Selsey, true friend! who afterwards submitted to be
   devourd
By the waves of Despair, whose Emanation rose above
The flood, and was nam'd Chichester, lovely mild &
   gentle! Lo!   50
Her lambs bleat to the sea-fowls cry, lamenting still for
   Albion.
Submitting to be call'd the son of Los the terrible vision:
Winchester stood devoting himself for Albion: his tents
Outspread with abundant riches, and his Emanations
Submitting to be call'd Enitharmons daughters, and be
   born
In vegetable mould: created by the Hammer and Loom
In Bowlahoola & Allamanda where the Dead wail night
   & day.

(I call them by their English names: English, the rough
   basement.
Los built the stubborn structure of the Language, acting
   against

Albions melancholy, who must else have been a Dumb
   despair.)   60

Gloucester and Exeter and Salisbury and Bristol: and
   benevolent Bath
PLATE 37 [41]
Bath who is Legions: he is the Seventh, the physician
   and
The poisoner: the best and worst in Heaven and Hell:
Whose Spectre first assimilated with Luvah in Albions
   mountains
A triple octave he took, to reduce Jerusalem to twelve
To cast Jerusalem forth upon the wilds to Poplar & Bow:
To Malden & Canterbury in the delights of cruelty:
The Shuttles of death sing in the sky to Islington &
   Pancrass
Round Marybone to Tyburns River, weaving black
   melancholy as a net,
And despair as meshes closely wove over the west of
   London,
Where mild Jerusalem sought to repose in death & be no
   more.   10
She fled to Lambeths mild Vale and hid herself beneath
The Surrey Hills where Rephaim terminates: her Sons
   are siez'd
For victims of sacrifice; but Jerusalem cannot be found!
   Hid
By the Daughters of Beulah: gently snatch'd away: and
   hid in Beulah

There is a Grain of Sand in Lambeth that Satan cannot
   find
Nor can his Watch Fiends find it: tis translucent & has
   many Angles
But he who finds it will find Oothoons palace, for within
Opening into Beulah every angle is a lovely heaven
But should the Watch Fiends find it, they would call it
   Sin

And lay its Heavens & their inhabitants in blood of
    punishment 20
Here Jerusalem & Vala were hid in soft slumberous
    repose
Hid from the terrible East, shut up in the South & West.

The Twenty-eight trembled in Deaths dark caves, in
    cold despair
They kneeld around the Couch of Death in deep
    humiliation
And tortures of self condemnation while their Spectres
    ragd within.
The Four Zoa's in terrible combustion clouded rage
Drinking the shuddering fears & loves of Albions
    Families
Destroying by selfish affections the things that they most
    admire
Drinking & eating, & pitying & weeping, as at a trajic
    scene.
The soul drinks murder & revenge, & applauds its own
    holiness 30

They saw Albion endeavouring to destroy their
    Emanations.

PLATE 38 [43]
They saw their Wheels rising up poisonous against
    Albion
Urizen, cold & scientific: Luvah, pitying & weeping
Tharmas, indolent & sullen: Urthona, doubting &
    despairing
Victims to one another & dreadfully plotting against each
    other
To prevent Albion walking about in the Four Complexions.

They saw America clos'd out by the Oaks of the
    western shore;
And Tharmas dash'd on the Rocks of the Altars of
    Victims in Mexico.

If we are wrathful Albion will destroy Jerusalem with
　　rooty Groves
If we are merciful, ourselves must suffer destruction on
　　his Oaks:
Why should we enter into our Spectres, to behold our
　　own corruptions　　　　　　　　　　　　　　　　10
O God of Albion descend! deliver Jerusalem from the
　　Oaken Groves!

Then Los grew furious raging: Why stand we here
　　trembling around
Calling on God for help; and not ourselves in whom
　　God dwells
Stretching a hand to save the falling Man: are we not
　　Four
Beholding Albion upon the Precipice ready to fall into
　　Non-Entity:
Seeing these Heavens & Hells conglobing in the Void.
　　Heavens over Hells
Brooding in holy hypocritic lust, drinking the cries of
　　pain
From howling victims of Law: building Heavens
　　Twenty-seven-fold.
Swelld & bloated General Forms, repugnant to the
　　Divine-
Humanity, who is the Only General and Universal Form　　20
To which all Lineaments tend & seek with love &
　　sympathy
All broad & general principles belong to benevolence
Who protects minute particulars, every one in their own
　　identity.
But here the affectionate touch of the tongue is closd in
　　by deadly teeth
And the soft smile of friendship & the open dawn of
　　benevolence
Become a net & a trap, & every energy renderd cruel,
Till the existence of friendship & benevolence is denied:
The wine of the Spirit & the vineyards of the Holy-One,

Here: turn into poisonous stupor & deadly intoxication:
That they may be condemnd by Law & the Lamb of
    God be slain!   30
And the two Sources of Life in Eternity[,] Hunting and
    War,
Are become the Sources of dark & bitter Death & of
    corroding Hell:
The open heart is shut up in integuments of frozen
    silence
That the spear that lights it forth may shatter the ribs &
    bosom
A pretence of Art, to destroy Art: a pretence of Liberty
To destroy Liberty, a pretence of Religion to destroy
    Religion
Oshea and Caleb fight: they contend in the valleys of
    Peor
In the terrible Family Contentions of those who love
    each other:
The Armies of Balaam weep – no women come to the
    field
Dead corses lay before them, & not as in Wars of old.   40
For the Soldier who fights for Truth, calls his enemy his
    brother:
They fight & contend for life, & not for eternal death!
But here the Soldier strikes, & a dead corse falls at his
    feet
Nor Daughter nor Sister nor Mother come forth to
    embosom the Slain!
But Death! Eternal Death! remains in the Valleys of
    Peor.
The English are scatterd over the face of the Nations:
    are these
Jerusalems children? Hark! hear the Giants of Albion cry
    at night
We smell the blood of the English! we delight in their
    blood on our Altars!
The living & the dead shall be ground in our rumbling
    Mills

For bread of the Sons of Albion: of the Giants Hand &
    Scofield   50
Scofeld & Kox are let loose upon my Saxons! they
    accumulate
A World in which Man is by his Nature the Enemy of
    Man,
In pride of Selfhood unwieldy stretching out into Non
    Entity
Generalizing Art & Science till Art & Science is
    lost.
Bristol & Bath, listen to my words, & ye Seventeen:
    give ear!
It is easy to acknowledge a man to be great & good
    while we
Derogate from him in the trifles & small articles of that
    goodness:
Those alone are his friends, who admire his minutest
    powers[.]
Instead of Albions lovely mountains & the curtains of
    Jerusalem
I see a Cave, a Rock, a Tree deadly and poisonous,
    unimaginative: 60
Instead of the Mutual Forgivenesses, the Minute
    Particulars, I see
Pits of bitumen ever burning: artificial Riches of the
    Canaanite
Like Lakes of liquid lead: instead of heavenly Chapels,
    built
By our dear Lord: I see Worlds crusted with snows &
    ice;
I see a Wicker Idol woven round Jerusalems children. I
    see
The Canaanite, the Amalekite, the Moabite, the
    Egyptian:
By Demonstrations the cruel Sons of Quality & Negation.
Driven on the Void in incoherent despair into Non
    Entity
I see America closd apart, & Jerusalem driven in terror

Away from Albions mountains, far away from Londons
   spires: 70
I will not endure this thing: I alone withstand to death,
This outrage! Ah me! how sick & pale you all stand
   round me!
Ah me! pitiable ones! do you also go to deaths vale?
All you my Friends & Brothers: all you my beloved
   Companions:
Have you also caught the infection of Sin & stern
   Repentance?
I see Disease arise upon you! yet speak to me and give
Me some comfort: why do you all stand silent? I alone
Remain in permanent strength. Or is all this goodness &
   pity, only
That you may take the greater vengeance in your
   Sepulcher.

So Los spoke. Pale they stood around the House of
   Death: 80
In the midst of temptations & despair: among the rooted
   Oaks:
Among reared Rocks of Albions Sons, at length they rose
PLATE 39 [44]
With one accord in love sublime, & as on Cherubs
   wings
They Albion surround with kindest violence to bear him
   back
Against his will thro Los's Gate to Eden: Four-fold;
   loud:
Their Wings waving over the bottomless Immense: to
   bear
Their awful charge back to his native home: but Albion
   dark,
Repugnant; rolld his Wheels backward into Non-Entity
Loud roll the Starry Wheels of Albion into the World of
   Death
And all the Gate of Los, clouded with clouds redounding
   from

Albions dread Wheels, stretching out spaces immense
 between
That every little particle of light & air, became Opake   10
Black & immense, a Rock of difficulty & a Cliff
Of black despair; that the immortal Wings labourd
 against
Cliff after cliff, & over Valleys of despair & death:
The narrow Sea between Albion & the Atlantic
 Continent:
Its waves of pearl became a boundless Ocean bottomless,
Of grey obscurity, filld with clouds & rocks & whirling
 waters
And Albions Sons ascending & descending in the horrid
 Void.

But as the Will must not be bended but in the day of
 Divine
Power: silent calm & motionless, in the mid-air sublime,
The Family Divine hover around the darkend Albion.   20

Such is the nature of the Ulro: that whatever enters:
Becomes Sexual, & is Created, and Vegetated, and Born.
From Hyde Park spread their vegetating roots beneath
 Albion
In dreadful pain the Spectrous Uncircumcised
 Vegetation. –

Forming a Sexual Machine: an Aged Virgin Form.
In Erins Land toward the north, joint after joint &
 burning
In love & jealousy immingled & calling it Religion
And feeling the damps of death they with one accord
 delegated Los
Conjuring him by the Highest that he should Watch over
 them
Till Jesus shall appear: & they gave their power to Los 30
Naming him the Spirit of Prophecy, calling him Elijah

Strucken with Albions disease they become what they
 behold;

They assimilate with Albion in pity & compassion;
Their Emanations return not: their Spectres rage in the
    Deep
The Slumbers of Death came over them around the
    Couch of Death
Before the Gate of Los & in the depths of Non Entity
Among the Furnaces of Los: among the Oaks of
    Albion.

Man is adjoind to Man by his Emanative portion:
Who is Jerusalem in every individual Man: and her
Shadow is Vala, builded by the Reasoning power in Man   40
O search & see: turn your eyes inward: open O thou
    World
Of Love & Harmony in Man: expand thy ever lovely
    Gates.

They wept into the deeps a little space at length was
    heard
The voice of Bath, faint as the voice of the Dead in the
    House of Death
PLATE 40 [45]
Bath, healing City! whose wisdom in midst of Poetic
Fervor: mild spoke thro' the Western Porch, in soft
    gentle tears

O Albion mildest Son of Eden! clos'd is thy Western
    Gate
Brothers of Eternity: this Man whose great example
We all admir'd & lov'd, whose all benevolent
    countenance, seen
In Eden, in lovely Jerusalem, drew even from envy
The tear: and the confession of honesty, open &
    undisguis'd
From mistrust and suspition. The Man is himself
    become
A piteous example of oblivion. To teach the Sons
Of Eden, that however great and glorious; however
    loving   10

And merciful the Individuality; however high
Our palaces and cities, and however fruitful are our
 fields
In Selfhood, we are nothing: but fade away in mornings
 breath.
Our mildness is nothing: the greatest mildness we can use
Is incapable and nothing: none but the Lamb of God
 can heal
This dread disease: none but Jesus: O Lord descend and
 save:
Albions Western Gate is clos'd: his death is coming
 apace:
Jesus alone can save him; for alas we none can know
How soon his lot may be our own. When Africa in sleep
Rose in the night of Beulah, and bound down the Sun &
 Moon   20
His friends cut his strong chains, & overwhelm'd his dark
Machines in fury & destruction, and the Man reviving
 repented
He wept before his wrathful brethren, thankful &
 considerate
For their well timed wrath. But Albions sleep is not
Like Africa's: and his machines are woven with his life
Nothing but mercy can save him! nothing but mercy
 interposing
Lest he should slay Jerusalem in his fearful jealousy
O God descend: gather our brethren, deliver
 Jerusalem[.]
But that we may omit no office of the friendly spirit
Oxford take thou these leaves of the Tree of Life: with
 eloquence   30
That thy immortal tongue inspires; present them to
 Albion:
Perhaps he may recieve them, offerd from thy loved
 hands.

So spoke, unhear'd by Albion. the merciful Son of
 Heaven

To those whose Western Gates were open, as they stood
   weeping
Around Albion: but Albion heard him not; obdurate!
   hard!
He frown'd on all his Friends, counting them enemies in
   his sorrow

And the Seventeen conjoining with Bath, the Seventh:
In whom the other Ten shone manifest, a Divine Vision!
Assimilated and embrac'd Eternal Death for Albions sake.

And these the names of the Eighteen combining with
   those Ten   40

PLATE 41 [46]
Bath, mild Physician of Eternity, mysterious power
Whose springs are unsearchable & knowledge infinite.
Hereford, ancient Guardian of Wales, whose hands
Builded the mountain palaces of Eden, stupendous
   works!
Lincoln, Durham & Carlisle, Councellors of Los.
And Ely, Scribe of Los, whose pen no other hand
Dare touch: Oxford, immortal Bard! with eloquence
Divine, he wept over Albion: speaking the words of God
In mild perswasion: bringing leaves of the Tree of Life.

Thou art in Error Albion, the Land of Ulro:
One Error not remov'd, will destroy a human Soul
Repose in Beulahs night, till the Error is remov'd
Reason not on both sides. Repose upon our bosoms
Till the Plow of Jehovah, and the Harrow of Shaddai
Have passed over the Dead, to awake the Dead to
   Judgment.
But Albion turn'd away refusing comfort.

Oxford trembled while he spoke, then fainted in the arms
Of Norwich, Peterboro, Rochester, Chester awful,
   Worcester,
Litchfield, Saint Davids, Landaff, Asaph, Bangor, Sodor,
Bowing their heads devoted: and the Furnaces of Los   20

Began to rage, thundering loud the storms began to roar
Upon the Furnaces, and loud the Furnaces rebellow
   beneath

And these the Four in whom the twenty-four appear'd
   four-fold:
Verulam, London, York, Edinburgh, mourning one
   towards another
Alas! – The time will come, when a mans worst enemies
Shall be those of his own house and family: in a Religion
Of Generation, to destroy by Sin and Atonement, happy
   Jerusalem,
The Bride and Wife of the Lamb. O God thou art Not
   an Avenger!

PLATE 42
Thus Albion sat, studious of others in his pale disease:
Brooding on evil: but when Los opend the Furnaces
   before him:
He saw that the accursed things were his own affections,
And his own beloveds: then he turn'd sick: his soul died
   within him
Also Los sick & terrified beheld the Furnaces of Death
And must have died, but the Divine Saviour descended
Among the infant loves & affections, and the Divine
   Vision wept
Like evening dew on every herb upon the breathing
   ground

Albion spoke in his dismal dreams: O thou deceitful
   friend
Worshipping mercy & beholding thy friend in such
   affliction: 10
Los! thou now discoverest thy turpitude to the heavens.
I demand righteousness & justice. O thou ingratitude!
Give me my Emanations back[,] food for my dying soul:
My daughters are harlots! my sons are accursed before
   me.

Enitharmon is my daughter: accursed with a fathers
    curse:
O! I have utterly been wasted! I have given my
    daughters to devils

So spoke Albion in gloomy majesty, and deepest night
Of Ulro rolld round his skirts from Dover to Cornwall.

Los answerd. Righteousness & justice I give thee in
    return
For thy righteousness! but I add mercy also, and bind   20
Thee from destroying these little ones: am I to be only
Merciful to thee and cruel to all that thou hatest[?]
Thou wast the Image of God surrounded by the Four
    Zoa's
Three thou hast slain! I am the Fourth: thou canst not
    destroy me.
Thou art in Error; trouble me not with thy
    righteousness.
I have innocence to defend and ignorance to instruct:
I have no time for seeming; and little arts of compliment,
In morality and virtue: in self-glorying and pride.
There is a limit of Opakeness, and a limit of Contraction;
In every Individual Man, and the limit of Opakeness,   30
Is named Satan: and the limit of Contraction is named
    Adam.
But when Man sleeps in Beulah, the Saviour in mercy
    takes
Contractions Limit, and of the Limit he forms Woman:
    That
Himself may in process of time be born Man to redeem
But there is no Limit of Expansion! there is no Limit of
    Translucence,
In the bosom of Man for ever from eternity to eternity.
Therefore I break thy bonds of righteousness; I crush
    thy messengers!
That they may not crush me and mine: do thou be
    righteous,
And I will return it; otherwise I defy thy worst revenge:

Consider me as thine enemy: on me turn all thy fury   40
But destroy not these little ones, nor mock the Lords
  anointed:
Destroy not by Moral Virtue, the little ones whom he
  hath chosen:
The little ones whom he hath chosen in preference to
  thee.
He hath cast thee off for ever; the little ones he hath
  anointed!
Thy Selfhood is for ever accursed from the Divine
  presence

So Los spoke: then turn'd his face & wept for Albion.

Albion replied. Go: Hand & Hyle! sieze the abhorred
  [fiend]:
As you Have siezd the Twenty-four rebellious
  ingratitudes;
To atone for you, for spiritual death! Man lives by deaths
  of Men
Bring him to justice before heaven here upon London
  stone,   50
Between Blackheath & Hounslow, between Norwood &
  Finchley
All that they have is mine: from my free genrous gift,
They now hold all they have: ingratitude to me:
To me their benefactor calls aloud for vengeance deep.

Los stood before his Furnaces awaiting the fury of the
  Dead:
And the Divine hand was upon him, strengthening him
  mightily.

The Spectres of the Dead cry out from the deeps
  beneath
Upon the hills of Albion; Oxford groans in his iron
  furnace
Winchester in his den & cavern; they lament against
Albion: they curse their human kindness & affection   60
They rage like wild beasts in the forests of affliction

In the dreams of Ulro they repent of their human
  kindness.

Come up, build Babylon, Rahab is ours & all her
  multitudes
With her in pomp and glory of victory. Depart
Ye twenty-four into the deeps! let us depart to glory!

Their Human majestic forms sit up upon their Couches
Of death: they curb their Spectres as with iron curbs
They enquire after Jerusalem in the regions of the dead,
With the voices of dead men, low, scarcely articulate,
And with tears cold on their cheeks they weary repose.   70

O when shall the morning of the grave appear, and when
Shall our salvation come? we sleep upon our watch
We cannot awake! and our Spectres rage in the forests
O God of Albion where art thou! pity the watchers!

Thus mourn they. Loud the Furnaces of Los thunder
  upon
The clouds of Europe & Asia, among the Serpent Temples!

And Los drew his Seven Furnaces around Albions Altars
And as Albion built his frozen Altars, Los built the
  Mundane Shell,
In the Four Regions of Humanity East & West & North
  & South,

Till Norwood & Finchley & Blackheath & Hounslow,
  coverd the whole Earth.   80
This is the Net & Veil of Vala, among the Souls of the
  Dead.

PLATE 43 [29]
Then the Divine Vision like a silent Sun appeard above
Albions dark rocks: setting behind the Gardens of
  Kensington
On Tyburns River, in clouds of blood: where was mild
  Zion Hills

Most ancient promontory, and in the Sun, a Human
  Form appeard
And thus the Voice Divine went forth upon the rocks of
  Albion

I elected Albion for my glory; I gave to him the
  Nations,
Of the whole Earth. He was the Angel of my Presence:
  and all
The Sons of God were Albions Sons: and Jerusalem was
  my joy.
The Reactor hath hid himself thro envy. I behold him.
But you cannot behold him till he be reveald in his
  System   10
Albions Reactor must have a Place prepard: Albion must
  Sleep
The Sleep of Death, till the Man of Sin & Repentance
  be reveald.
Hidden in Albions Forests he lurks: he admits of no
  Reply
From Albion: but hath founded his Reaction into a Law
Of Action, for Obedience to destroy the Contraries of
  Man[.]
He hath compelld Albion to become a Punisher & hath
  possessd
Himself of Albions Forests & Wilds: and Jerusalem is
  taken!
The City of the Woods in the Forest of Ephratah is
  taken!
London is a stone of her ruins; Oxford is the dust of her
  walls!
Sussex & Kent are her scatterd garments: Ireland her
  holy place: 20
And the murderd bodies of her little ones are Scotland
  and Wales[.]
The Cities of the Nations are the smoke of her
  consummation
The Nations are her dust: ground by the chariot wheels

Of her lordly conquerors, her palaces levelld with the
  dust.
I come that I may find a way for my banished ones to
  return
Fear not O little Flock I come: Albion shall rise again.

So saying, the mild Sun inclosd the Human Family.

Forthwith from Albions darkning [r]ocks came two
  Immortal forms
Saying We alone are escaped. O merciful Lord and
  Saviour,
We flee from the interiors of Albions hills and
  mountains!   30
From his Valleys Eastward: from Amalek Canaan &
  Moab:
Beneath his vast ranges of hills surrounding Jerusalem.

Albion walkd on the steps of fire before his Halls
And Vala walkd with him in dreams of soft deluding
  slumber.
He looked up & saw the Prince of Light with splendor
  faded
Then Albion ascended mourning into the porches of his
  Palace
Above him rose a Shadow from his wearied intellect:
Of living gold, pure, perfect, holy: in white linen pure
  he hoverd
A sweet entrancing self-delusion a watry vision of Albion
Soft exulting in existence; all the Man absorbing!   40

Albion fell upon his face prostrate before the watry
  Shadow
Saying O Lord whence is this change: thou knowest I
  am nothing!
And Vala trembled & coverd her face: & her locks were
  spread on the pavement

We heard astonishd at the Vision & our hearts trembled
  within us:

We heard the voice of slumberous Albion, and thus he
    spake,
Idolatrous to his own Shadow words of eternity
    uttering:

O I am nothing when I enter into judgment with thee!
If thou withdraw thy breath I die & vanish into Hades
If thou dost lay thine hand upon me behold I am silent:
If thou withhold thine hand; I perish like a fallen leaf: 50
O I am nothing: and to nothing must return again:
If thou withdraw thy breath, Behold I am oblivion.

He ceasd: the shadowy voice was silent: but the cloud
    hoverd over their heads
In golden wreathes, the sorrow of Man; & the balmy
    drops fell down.
And lo! that son of Man that Shadowy Spirit of mild
    Albion:
Luvah descended from the cloud; in terror Albion rose:
Indignant rose the awful Man, & turnd his back on Vala.

We heard the voice of Albion starting from his sleep:

Whence is this voice crying Enion! that soundeth in my
    ears?
O cruel pity! O dark deceit! can love seek for dominion?   60

And Luvah strove to gain dominion over Albion
They strove together above the Body where Vala was
    inclosd
And the dark Body of Albion left prostrate upon the
    crystal pavement,
Coverd with boils from head to foot: the terrible
    smitings of Luvah.

Then frownd the fallen Man and put forth Luvah from
    his presence
Saying. Go and Die the Death of Man, for Vala the
    sweet wanderer.
I will turn the volutions of your ears outward, and bend
    your nostrils

Downward, and your fluxile eyes englob'd roll round in
    fear:
Your withring lips and tongue shrink up into a narrow
    circle,
Till into narrow forms you creep: go take your fiery way: 70
And learn what tis to absorb the Man you Spirits of Pity
    & Love.

They heard the voice and fled swift as the winters setting
    sun.
And now the human blood foamd high, the Spirits Luvah
    & Vala
Went down the Human Heart where Paradise & its joys
    abounded,
In jealous fears & fury & rage, & flames roll round their
    fervid feet:
And the vast form of Nature like a serpent playd before
    them
And as they fled in folding fires & thunders of the deep:
Vala shrunk in like the dark sea that leaves its slimy
    banks.
And from her bosom Luvah fell far as the east and west.
And the vast form of Nature like a serpent rolld between,   80
Whether of Jerusalems or Valas ruins congenerated, we
    know not:
All is confusion: all is tumult, & we alone are escaped.

So spoke the fugitives; they joind the Divine Family,
    trembling
PLATE 44 [30]
And the Two that escaped; were the Emanation of Los
    & his
Spectre: for whereever the Emanation goes, the Spectre
Attends her as her Guard, & Los's Emanation is named
Enitharmon, & his Spectre is named Urthona: they knew
Not where to flee: they had been on a visit to Albions
    Children
And they strove to weave a Shadow of the Emanation

To hide themselves: weeping & lamenting for the
Vegetation
Of Albions Children: fleeing thro Albions vales in
streams of gore.

Being not irritated by insult bearing insulting
benevolences
They percieved that corporeal friends are spiritual
enemies   10
They saw the Sexual Religion in its embryon
Uncircumcision
And the Divine hand was upon them bearing them thro
darkness
Back safe to their Humanity as doves to their windows:
Therefore the Sons of Eden praise Urthonas Spectre in
Songs
Because he kept the Divine Vision in time of trouble.

They wept & trembled: & Los put forth his hand & took
them in
Into his Bosom: from which Albion shrunk in dismal
pain;
Rending the fibres of Brotherhood & in Feminine
Allegories
Inclosing Los: but the Divine Vision appeard with Los
Following Albion into his Central Void among his Oaks.   20

And Los prayed and said. O Divine Saviour arise
Upon the Mountains of Albion as in ancient time.
Behold!
The Cities of Albion seek thy face, London groans in
pain
From Hill to Hill & the Thames laments along the
Valleys
The little Villages of Middlesex & Surrey hunger & thirst
The Twenty-eight Cities of Albion stretch their hands to
thee:
Because of the Opressors of Albion in every City &
Village:

They mock at the Labourers limbs! they mock at his
    starvd Children!
They buy his Daughters that they may have power to sell
    his Sons:
They compell the Poor to live upon a crust of bread by
    soft mild arts: 30
They reduce the Man to want: then give with pomp &
    ceremony.
The praise of Jehovah is chaunted from lips of hunger &
    thirst:

Humanity knows not of Sex: wherefore are Sexes in
    Beulah?
In Beulah the Female lets down her beautiful Tabernacle;
Which the Male enters magnificent between her
    Cherubim:
And becomes One with her mingling condensing in
    Self-love
The Rocky Law of Condemnation & double Generation,
    & Death.
Albion hath enterd the Loins the place of the Last
    Judgment:
And Luvah hath drawn the Curtains around Albion in
    Vala's bosom
The Dead awake to Generation! Arise O Lord, & rend
    the Veil!   40

So Los in lamentations followd Albion. Albion coverd,
PLATE 45 [31]
His western heaven with rocky clouds of death & despair.

Fearing that Albion should turn his back against the
    Divine Vision
Los took his globe of fire to search the interiors of
    Albions
Bosom, in all the terrors of friendship, entering the
    caves
Of despair & death, to search the tempters out, walking
    among

Albions rocks & precipices! caves of solitude & dark
    despair,
And saw every Minute Particular of Albion degraded &
    murderd
But saw not by whom; they were hidden within in the
    minute particulars
Of which they had possessd themselves; and there they
    take up
The articulations of a mans soul, and laughing throw it
    down   10
Into the frame, then knock it out upon the plank, & souls
    are bak'd
In bricks to build the pyramids of Heber & Terah. But
    Los
Searchd in vain: closd from the minutia he walkd,
    difficult.
He came down from Highgate thro Hackney &
    Holloway towards London
Till he came to old Stratford & thence to Stepney & the
    Isle
Of Leuthas Dogs, thence thro the narrows of the Rivers
    side
And saw every minute particular, the jewels of Albion,
    running down
The kennels of the streets & lanes as if they were
    abhorrd.
Every Universal Form, was become barren mountains of
    Moral
Virtue: and every Minute Particular hardend into grains
    of sand: 20
And all the tendernesses of the soul cast forth as filth &
    mire,
Among the winding places of deep contemplation
    intricate
To where the Tower of London frownd dreadful over
    Jerusalem:
A building of Luvah builded in Jerusalems eastern gate
    to be

His secluded Court: thence to Bethlehem where was
    builded
Dens of despair in the house of bread: enquiring in vain
Of stones and rocks he took his way, for human form was
    none:
And thus he spoke, looking on Albions City with many
    tears

What shall I do! what could I do, if I could find these
    Criminals
I could not dare to take vengeance; for all things are so
    constructed   30
And built by the Divine hand, that the sinner shall
    always escape,
And he who takes vengeance alone is the criminal of
    Providence;
If I should dare to lay my finger on a grain of sand
In way of vengeance; I punish the already punishd: O
    whom
Should I pity if I pity not the sinner who is gone astray!
O Albion, if thou takest vengeance; if thou revengest thy
    wrongs
Thou art for ever lost! What can I do to hinder the
    Sons
Of Albion from taking vengeance? or how shall I them
    perswade.

So spoke Los, travelling thro darkness & horrid solitude:
And he beheld Jerusalem in Westminster & Marybone,   40
Among the ruins of the Temple: and Vala who is her
    Shadow,
Jerusalems Shadow bent northward over the Island white.
At length he sat on London Stone, & heard Jerusalems
    voice.

Albion I cannot be thy Wife, thine own Minute
    Particulars,
Belong to God alone, and all thy little ones are holy
They are of Faith & not of Demonstration: wherefore is
    Vala

Clothd in black mourning upon my rivers currents, Vala
awake!
I hear thy shuttles sing in the sky, and round my limbs
I feel the iron threads of love & jealousy & despair.

Vala replyd. Albion is mine: Luvah gave me to Albion   50
And now recieves reproach & hate. Was it not said of old
Set your Son before a man & he shall take you & your sons
For slaves: but set your Daughter before a man & She
Shall make him & his sons & daughters your slaves for
ever:
And is this Faith? Behold the strife of Albion & Luvah
Is great in the east, their spears of blood rage in the
eastern heaven
Urizen is the champion of Albion, they will slay my
Luvah:
And thou O harlot daughter! daughter of despair art all
This cause of these shakings of my towers on Euphrates.
Here is the House of Albion, & here is thy secluded place   60
And here we have found thy sins: & hence we turn thee
forth,
For all to avoid thee: to be astonishd at thee for thy sins:
Because thou art the impurity & the harlot: & thy
children:
Children of whoredoms: born for Sacrifice: for the meat
& drink
Offering: to sustain the glorious combat & the battle &
war
That Man may be purified by the death of thy delusions.

So saying she her dark threads cast over the trembling
River:
And over the valleys; from the hills of Hertfordshire to
the hills
Of Surrey across Middlesex. & across Albions House
Of Eternity! pale stood Albion at his eastern gate,   70
PLATE 46 [32]
Leaning against the pillars, & his disease rose from his
skirts

Upon the Precipice he stood: ready to fall into
  Non–Entity.

Los was all astonishment & terror: he trembled sitting on
  the Stone
Of London: but the interiors of Albions fibres & nerves
  were hidden
From Los; astonishd he beheld only the petrified
  surfaces:
And saw his Furnaces in ruins, for Los is the Demon of
  the Furnaces;
He saw also the Four Points of Albion reversd inwards
He siezd his Hammer & Tongs, his iron Poker & his
  Bellows,
Upon the valleys of Middlesex, Shouting loud for aid
  Divine.

In stern defiance came from Albions bosom Hand, Hyle,
  Koban,
Gwantok, Peachy, Brertun, Slaid, Huttn, Skofeld, Kock,
  Kotope
Bowen: Albions Sons: they bore him a golden couch
  into the porch
And on the Couch reposd his limbs, trembling from the
  bloody field.
Rearing their Druid Patriarchal rocky Temples around
  his limbs.
(All things begin & end, in Albions Ancient Druid
  Rocky Shore.)

PLATE 47
[*When Albion utterd his last words Hope is banishd from
  me*]
From Camberwell to Highgate where the mighty
  Thames shudders along,
Where Los's Furnaces stand, where Jerusalem & Vala
  howl:
Luvah tore forth from Albions Loins, in fibrous veins,
  in rivers

Of blood over Europe: a Vegetating Root in grinding
  pain.
Animating the Dragon Temples, soon to become that
  Holy Fiend
The Wicker Man of Scandinavia in which cruelly
  consumed
The Captives reard to heaven howl in flames among the
  stars
Loud the cries of War on the Rhine & Danube, with
  Albions Sons,
Away from Beulahs hills & vales break forth the Souls of
  the Dead,
With cymbal, trumpet, clarion; & the scythed chariots of
  Britain.

And the Veil of Vala, is composed of the Spectres of the
  Dead

Hark! the mingling cries of Luvah with the Sons of
  Albion
Hark! & Record the terrible wonder! that the Punisher
Mingles with his Victims Spectre, enslaved and
  tormented
To him whom he has murderd, bound in vengeance &
  enmity
Shudder not, but Write, & the hand of God will assist
  you!
Therefore I write Albions last words. Hope is banish'd
  from me.

PLATE 48
These were his last words, and the merciful Saviour in
  his arms
Reciev'd him, in the arms of tender mercy and repos'd
The pale limbs of his Eternal Individuality
Upon the Rock of Ages. Then, surrounded with a
  Cloud:
In silence the Divine Lord builded with immortal labour,

Of gold & jewels a sublime Ornament, a Couch of repose,
With Sixteen pillars: canopied with emblems & written
    verse.
Spiritual Verse, order'd & measur'd, from whence, time
    shall reveal.
The Five books of the Decalogue, the books of Joshua &
    Judges,
Samuel, a double book & Kings, a double book, the
    Psalms & Prophets   10
The Four-fold Gospel, and the Revelations everlasting
Eternity groan'd & was troubled, at the image of
    Eternal Death!

Beneath the bottoms of the Graves, which is Earths
    central joint,
There is a place where Contrarieties are equally true:
(To protect from the Giant blows in the sports of
    intellect,
Thunder in the midst of kindness, & love that kills its
    beloved:
Because Death is for a period, and they renew tenfold.)
From this sweet Place Maternal Love awoke Jerusalem
With pangs she forsook Beulahs pleasant lovely shadowy
    Universe
Where no dispute can come; created for those who
    Sleep.   20
Weeping was in all Beulah, and all the Daughters of
    Beulah
Wept for their Sister the Daughter of Albion, Jerusalem:
When out of Beulah the Emanation of the Sleeper
    descended
With solemn mourning out of Beulahs moony shades
    and hills:
Within the Human Heart, whose Gates closed with
    solemn sound.

And this the manner of the terrible Separation
The Emanations of the grievously afflicted Friends of
    Albion

Concenter in one Female form an Aged pensive
    Woman.
Astonish'd! lovely! embracing the sublime shade: the
    Daughters of Beulah
Beheld her with wonder! With awful hands she took   30
A Moment of Time, drawing it out with many tears &
    afflictions
And many sorrows: oblique across the Atlantic Vale
Which is the Vale of Rephaim dreadful from East to
    West,
Where the Human Harvest waves abundant in the
    beams of Eden
Into a Rainbow of jewels and gold, a mild Reflection
    from
Albions dread Tomb. Eight thousand and five hundred
    years
In its extension. Every two hundred years has a door to
    Eden
She also took an Atom of Space, with dire pain opening
    it a Center
Into Beulah: trembling the Daughters of Beulah dried
Her tears, she ardent embrac'd her sorrows, occupied in
    labours   40
Of sublime mercy in Rephaims Vale. Perusing Albions
    Tomb
She sat: she walk'd among the ornaments solemn
    mourning.
The Daughters attended her shudderings, wiping the
    death sweat
Los also saw her in his seventh Furnace, he also terrified
Saw the finger of God go forth upon his seventh
    Furnace:
Away from the Starry Wheels to prepare Jerusalem a
    place.
When with a dreadful groan the Emanation mild of
    Albion
Burst from his bosom in the Tomb like a pale snowy
    cloud,

Female and lovely, struggling to put off the Human
    form
Writhing in pain. The Daughters of Beulah in kind arms
    reciev'd   50
Jerusalem: weeping over her among the Spaces of Erin,
In the Ends of Beulah, where the Dead wail night & day.

And thus Erin spoke to the Daughters of Beulah, in soft
    tears

Albion the Vortex of the Dead! Albion the Generous!
Albion the mildest son of Heaven! The Place of Holy
    Sacrifice!
Where Friends Die for each other: will become the
    Place,
Of Murder, & Unforgiving, Never-awaking Sacrifice of
    Enemies[.]
The Children must be sacrific'd! (a horror never known
Till now in Beulah.) unless a Refuge can be found
To hide them from the wrath of Albions Law that
    freezes sore   60
Upon his Sons & Daughters, self-exiled from his bosom
Draw ye Jerusalem away from Albions Mountains
To give a Place for Redemption, let Sihon and Og
Remove Eastward to Bashan and Gilead, and leave
PLATE 49
The secret coverts of Albion & the hidden places of
    America
Jerusalem Jerusalem! why wilt thou turn away
Come ye O Daughters of Beulah, lament for Og & Sihon
Upon the Lakes of Ireland from Rathlin to Baltimore:
Stand ye upon the Dargle from Wicklow to Drogheda
Come & mourn over Albion the White Cliff of the
    Atlantic
The Mountain of Giants: all the Giants of Albion are
    become
Weak: witherd: darkend: & Jerusalem is cast forth from
    Albion.

They deny that they ever knew Jerusalem, or ever dwelt
    in Shiloh[.]
The Gigantic roots & twigs of the vegetating Sons of
    Albion   10
Filld with the little-ones are consumed in the Fires of
    their Altars
The vegetating Cities are burned & consumed from the
    Earth:
And the Bodies in which all Animals & Vegetations, the
    Earth & Heaven
Were containd in the All Glorious Imagination are
    witherd & darkend:
The golden Gate of Havilah, and all the Garden of God,
Was caught up with the Sun in one day of fury and war:
The Lungs, the Heart, the Liver, shrunk away far distant
    from Man
And left a little slimy substance floating upon the tides.
In one night the Atlantic Continent was caught up with
    the Moon,
And became an Opake Globe far distant clad with
    moony beams.   20
The Visions of Eternity, by reason of narrowed
    perceptions,
Are become weak Visions of Time & Space, fix'd into
    furrows of death;
Till deep dissimulation is the only defence an honest man
    has left[.]
O Polypus of Death O Spectre over Europe and
    Asia
Withering the Human Form by Laws of Sacrifice for
    Sin
By Laws of Chastity & Abhorrence I am witherd up.
Striving to Create a Heaven in which all shall be pure &
    holy
In their Own Selfhoods, in Natural Selfish Chastity to
    banish Pity
And dear Mutual Forgiveness; & to become One Great
    Satan

Inslavd to the most powerful Selfhood: to murder the
  Divine Humanity   30
In whose sight all are as the dust & who chargeth his
  Angels with folly!
Ah: weak & wide astray: Ah shut in narrow doleful
  form!
Creeping in reptile flesh upon the bosom of the ground:
The Eye of Man, a little narrow orb, closd up & dark,
Scarcely beholding the Great Light; conversing with the
  ground
The Ear, a little shell, in small volutions shutting out
True Harmonies, & comprehending great, as very small:
The Nostrils, bent down to the earth & clos'd with
  senseless flesh,
That odours cannot them expand, nor joy on them exult:
The Tongue, a little moisture fills, a little food it cloys,   40
A little sound it utters, & its cries are faintly heard.
Therefore they are removed: therefore they have taken
  root
In Egypt & Philistea: in Moab & Edom & Aram:
In the Erythrean Sea their Uncircu[m]cision in Heart &
  Loins
Be lost for ever & ever, then they shall arise from Self
By Self Annihilation into Jerusalems Courts & into
  Shiloh
Shiloh the Masculine Emanation among the Flowers of
  Beulah
Lo Shiloh dwells over France, as Jerusalem dwells over
  Albion
Build & prepare a Wall & Curtain for Americas shore!
Rush on: Rush on! Rush on! ye vegetating Sons of
  Albion   50
The Sun shall go before you in Day: the Moon shall go
Before you in Night. Come on! Come on! Come on! The
  Lord
Jehovah is before, behind, above, beneath, around
He has builded the arches of Albions Tomb binding the
  Stars

In merciful Order, bending the Laws of Cruelty to
    Peace.
He hath placed Og & Anak, the Giants of Albion for
    their Guards:
Building the Body of Moses in the Valley of Peor: the
    Body
Of Divine Analogy; and Og & Sihon in the tears of
    Balaam
The Son of Beor, have given their power to Joshua &
    Caleb.
Remove from Albion, far remove these terrible surfaces.   60
They are beginning to form Heavens & Hells in immense
Circles: the Hells for food to the Heavens: food of
    torment,
Food of despair: they drink the condemnd Soul &
    rejoice
In cruel holiness, in their Heavens of Chastity &
    Uncircumcision
Yet they are blameless & Iniquity must be imputed only
To the State they are enterd into that they may be
    deliverd:
Satan is the State of Death, & not a Human existence:
But Luvah is named Satan, because he has enterd that
    State.
A World where Man is by Nature the enemy of Man
Because the Evil is Created into a State, that Men   70
May be deliverd time after time evermore. Amen.
Learn therefore O Sisters to distinguish the Eternal
    Human
That walks about among the stones of fire in bliss & woe
Alternate! from those States or Worlds in which the
    Spirit travels:
This is the only means to Forgiveness of Enemies
Therefore remove from Albion these terrible Surfaces
And let wild seas & rocks close up Jerusalem away from

PLATE 50
The Atlantic Mountains where Giants dwelt in Intellect;
Now given to stony Druids, and Allegoric Generation

To the Twelve Gods of Asia, the Spectres of those who
  Sleep:
Sway'd by a Providence oppos'd to the Divine Lord
  Jesus:
A murderous Providence! A Creation that groans, living
  on Death.
Where Fish & Bird & Beast & Man & Tree & Metal &
  Stone
Live by Devouring, going into Eternal Death continually:
Albion is now possess'd by the War of Blood! the
  Sacrifice
Of envy Albion is become, and his Emanation cast out:
Come Lord Jesus, Lamb of God descend! for if; O
  Lord!   10
If thou hadst been here, our brother Albion had not
  died.
Arise sisters! Go ye & meet the Lord, while I remain –
Behold the foggy mornings of the Dead on Albions
  cliffs:
Ye know that if the Emanation remains in them:
She will become an Eternal Death, an Avenger of Sin
A Self-righteousness: the proud Virgin-Harlot! Mother
  of War!
And we also & all Beulah, consume beneath Albions
  curse.

So Erin spoke to the Daughters of Beulah. Shuddering
With their wings they sat in the Furnace, in a night
Of stars, for all the Sons of Albion appeard distant stars,   20
Ascending and descending into Albions sea of death.
And Erins lovely Bow enclos'd the Wheels of Albions
  Sons.

Expanding on wing, the Daughters of Beulah replied in
  sweet response

Come O thou Lamb of God and take away the
  remembrance of Sin
To Sin & to hide the Sin in sweet deceit. is lovely!!

To Sin in the open face of day is cruel & pitiless! But
To record the Sin for a reproach: to let the Sun go
   down
In a remembrance of the Sin: is a Woe & a Horror!
A brooder of an Evil Day, and a Sun rising in blood
Come then O Lamb of God and take away the
   remembrance of Sin   30

End of Chap. 2^d.

PLATE 52

Rahab is an ⎱ TO THE DEISTS ⎰ The Spiritual States of
Eternal State ⎰   ⎱ the Soul are all Eternal
                       Distinguish between the
                       Man, & his present State

He never can be a Friend to the Human Race who is the
Preacher of Natural Morality or Natural Religion. he is a
flatterer who means to betray, to perpetuate Tyrant Pride
& the Laws of that Babylon which he forsees shall shortly
be destroyed, with the Spiritual and not the Natural
Sword: He is in the State named Rahab: which State must
be put off before he can be the Friend of Man.

You O Deists profess yourselves the Enemies of Christi-
anity: and you are so: you are also the Enemies of the
Human Race & of Universal Nature. Man is born a   10
Spectre or Satan & is altogether an Evil, & requires a New
Selfhood continually & must continually be changed into
his direct Contrary. But your Greek Philosophy (which is a
remnant of Druidism) teaches that Man is Righteous in his
Vegetated Spectre: an Opinion of fatal & accursed conse-
quence to Man, as the Ancients saw plainly by Revelation
to the intire abrogation of Experimental Theory. and
many believed what they saw, and Prophecied of Jesus.

Man must & will have Some Religion; if he has not the
Religion of Jesus, he will have the Religion of Satan, & will   20
erect the Synagogue of Satan. calling the Prince of this
World, God; and destroying all who do not worship
Satan under the Name of God. Will any one say: Where

are those who worship Satan under the Name of God!
Where are they? Listen! Every Religion that Preaches
Vengeance for Sin is the Religion of the Enemy & Avenger;
and not of the Forgiver of Sin, and their God is Satan,
Named by the Divine Name. Your Religion O Deists:
Deism, is the Worship of the God of this World by the
means of what you call Natural Religion and Natural   30
Philosophy, and of Natural Morality or Self-Righteous-
ness, the Selfish Virtues of the Natural Heart. This was
the Religion of the Pharisees who murderd Jesus. Deism is
the same & ends in the same.

Voltaire Rousseau Gibbon Hume, charge the Spiritually
Religious with hypocrisy! but how a Monk or a Methodist
either, can be a Hypocrite: I cannot concieve. We are
Men of like passions with others & pretend not to be holier
than others: therefore, when a Religious Man falls into
Sin, he ought not to be calld a Hypocrite: this title is more   40
properly to be given to a Player who falls into Sin; whose
profession is Virtue & Morality & the making Men Self-
Righteous. Foote in calling Whitefield, Hypocrite: was
himself one: for Whitefield pretended not to be holier than
others: but confessed his Sins before all the World;
Voltaire! Rousseau! You cannot escape my charge that you
are Pharisees & Hypocrites, for you are constantly talking
of the Virtues of the Human Heart, and particularly of your
own, that you may accuse others & especially the Religious,
whose errors, you by this display of pretended Virtue,   50
chiefly design to expose. Rousseau thought Men Good by
Nature; he found them Evil & found no friend. Friendship
cannot exist without Forgiveness of Sins continually. The
Book written by Rousseau calld his Confessions is an
apology & cloke for his sin & not a confession.

But you also charge the poor Monks & Religious with
being the causes of War: while you acquit & flatter the
Alexanders & Caesars, the Lewis's & Fredericks: who
alone are its causes & its actors. But the Religion of Jesus,
Forgiveness of Sin, can never be the cause of a War nor of   60
a single Martyrdom.

Those who Martyr others or who cause War are Deists,
but never can be Forgivers of Sin. The Glory of Christian-
ity is, To Conquer by Forgiveness. All the Destruction
therefore, in Christian Europe has arisen from Deism,
which is Natural Religion.

I saw a Monk of Charlemaine
Arise before my sight
   I talkd with the Grey Monk as we stood
In beams of infernal light

Gibbon arose with a lash of steel
And Voltaire with a wracking wheel
   The Schools in clouds of learning rolld
Arose with War in iron & gold.

Thou lazy Monk they sound afar
In vain condemning glorious War   10
   And in your Cell you shall ever dwell
Rise War & bind him in his Cell.

The blood, red ran from the Grey Monks side
His hands & feet were wounded wide
   His body bent, his arms & knees
Like to the roots of ancient trees

When Satan first the black bow bent
And the Moral Law from the Gospel rent
   He forgd the Law into a Sword
And spilld the blood of mercys Lord.   20

Titus! Constantine! Charlemaine!
O Voltaire! Rousseau! Gibbon! Vain
   Your Grecian Mocks & Roman Sword
Against this image of his Lord!

For a Tear is an Intellectual thing;
And a Sigh is the Sword of an Angel King
   And the bitter groan of a Martyrs woe
Is an Arrow from the Almighties Bow.

PLATE 53

JERUSALEM

CHAP 3

But Los, who is the Vehicular Form of strong Urthona
Wept vehemently over Albion where Thames currents
    spring
From the rivers of Beulah; pleasant river! soft, mild,
    parent stream
And the roots of Albions Tree enterd the Soul of Los
As he sat before his Furnaces clothed in sackcloth of hair
In gnawing pain dividing him from his Emanation;
Inclosing all the children of Los time after time.

Their Giant forms condensing into Nations & Peoples &
    Tongues
Translucent the Furnaces, of Beryll & Emerald immortal:
And Seven-fold each within other: incomprehensible   10
To the Vegetated Mortal Eye's perverted & single vision
The Bellows are the Animal Lungs. the Hammers, the
    Animal Heart
The Furnaces, the Stomach for Digestion; terrible their
    fury
Like seven burning heavens rang'd from South to North

Here on the banks of the Thames, Los builded
    Golgonooza,
Outside of the Gates of the Human Heart, beneath
    Beulah
In the midst of the rocks of the Altars of Albion. In fears
He builded it, in rage & in fury. It is the Spiritual
    Fourfold
London: continually building & continually decaying
    desolate:
In eternal labours: loud the Furnaces & loud the Anvils   20
Of Death thunder incessant around the flaming Couches
    of

The Twentyfour Friends of Albion and round the awful
    Four
For the protection of the Twelve Emanations of Albions
    Sons
The Mystic Union of the Emanation in the Lord;
    Because
Man divided from his Emanation is a dark Spectre
His Emanation is an ever-weeping melancholy Shadow
But she is made receptive of Generation thro' mercy
In the Potters Furnace, among the Funeral Urns of
    Beulah
From Surrey hills, thro' Italy and Greece, to Hinnoms
    vale.

PLATE 54

In Great Eternity, every particular Form gives forth or
    Emanates
Its own peculiar Light, & the Form is the Divine Vision
And the Light is his Garment. This is Jerusalem in every
    Man
A Tent & Tabernacle of Mutual Forgiveness Male &
    Female Clothings.
And Jerusalem is called Liberty among the Children of
    Albion

But Albion fell down a Rocky fragment from: Eternity
    hurld
By his own Spectre, who is the Reasoning Power in
    every Man
Into his own Chaos which is the Memory between Man
    & Man

The silent broodings of deadly revenge springing from
    the
All powerful parental affection, fills Albion from head to
    foot   10
Seeing his Sons assimilate with Luvah, bound in the bonds
Of spiritual Hate, from which springs Sexual Love as
    iron chains:

He tosses like a cloud outstretchd among Jerusalems
  Ruins
Which overspread all the Earth, he groans among his
  ruind porches
But the Spectre like a hoar frost & a Mildew rose over
  Albion
Saying, I am God O Sons of Men! I am your Rational
  Power!
Am I not Bacon & Newton & Locke who teach
  Humility to Man!
Who teach Doubt & Experiment & my two Wings
  Voltaire: Rousseau.
Where is that Friend of Sinners! that Rebel against my
  Laws!
Who teaches Belief to the Nations, & an unknown
  Eternal Life   20
Come hither into the Desart & turn these stones to bread.
Vain foolish Man! wilt thou believe without Experiment?
And build a World of Phantasy upon my Great Abyss!
A World of Shapes in craving lust & devouring appetite

So spoke the hard cold constrictive Spectre he is named
  Arthur
Constricting into Druid Rocks round Canaan Agag &
  Aram & Pharoh

Then Albion drew England into his bosom in groans &
  tears
But she stretchd out her starry Night in Spaces against
  him, like
A long Serpent, in the Abyss of the Spectre which
  augmented
The Night with Dragon wings coverd with stars & in the
  Wings   30
Jerusalem & Vala appeard: & above between the Wings
  magnificent
The Divine Vision dimly appeard in clouds of blood
  weeping.

PLATE 55

When those who disregard all Mortal Things, saw a
    Mighty-One
Among the Flowers of Beulah still retain his awful
    strength
They wonderd: checking their wild flames & Many
    gathering
Together into an Assembly; they said, let us go down
And see these changes! Others said, If you do so
    prepare
For being driven from our fields, what have we to do
    with the Dead?
To be their inferiors or superiors we equally abhor;
Superior, none we know: inferior none: all equal share
Divine Benevolence & joy, for the Eternal Man
Walketh among us, calling us his Brothers & his Friends: 10
Forbidding us that Veil which Satan puts between Eve &
    Adam
By which the Princes of the Dead enslave their Votaries
Teaching them to form the Serpent of precious stones &
    gold
To sieze the Sons of Jerusalem & plant them in One
    Mans Loins
To make One Family on Contraries: that Joseph may be
    sold
Into Egypt: for Negation; a Veil the Saviour born &
    dying rends.

But others said: Let us to him who only Is, & who
Walketh among us, give decision, bring forth all your
    fires!

So saying, an eternal deed was done: in fiery flames
The Universal Conc[l]ave raged, such thunderous sounds
    as never   20
Were sounded from a mortal cloud, nor on Mount
    Sinai old
Nor in Havilah where the Cherub rolld his redounding
    flame.

Loud! loud! the Mountains lifted up their voices, loud
    the Forests
Rivers thunderd against their banks, loud Winds furious
    fought
Cities & Nations contended in fires & clouds & tempests.
The Seas raisd up their voices & lifted their hands on
    high
The Stars in their courses fought, the Sun! Moon!
    Heaven: Earth.
Contending for Albion & for Jerusalem his Emanation
And for Shiloh, the Emanation of France & for lovely
    Vala.

Then far the greatest number were about to make a
    Separation   30
And they Elected Seven, calld the Seven Eyes of God;
Lucifer, Molech, Elohim, Shaddai, Pahad, Jehovah,
    Jesus.
They namd the Eighth, he came not, he hid in Albions
    Forests
But first they said: (& their Words stood in Chariots in
    array
Curbing their Tygers with golden bits & bridles of silver
    & ivory)

Let the Human Organs be kept in their perfect Integrity
At will Contracting into Worms, or Expanding into Gods
And then behold! what are these Ulro Visions of
    Chastity[?]
Then as the moss upon the tree: or dust upon the plow:
Or as the sweat upon the labouring shoulder: or as the
    chaff   40
Of the wheat-floor or as the dregs of the sweet wine-
    press
Such are these Ulro Visions, for tho we sit down within
The plowed furrow, listning to the weeping clods till we
Contract or Expand Space at will: or if we raise ourselves
Upon the chariots of the morning, Contracting or
    Expanding Time:

Every one knows, we are One Family: One Man blessed
    for ever

Silence remaind & every one resumd his Human
    Majesty
And many conversed on these things as they labourd at
    the furrow
Saying: It is better to prevent misery, than to release
    from misery
It is better to prevent error, than to forgive the
    criminal: 50
Labour well the Minute Particulars, attend to the
    Little-ones:
And those who are in misery cannot remain so long
If we do but our duty: labour well the teeming Earth.

They Plow'd in tears, the trumpets sounded before the
    golden Plow
And the voices of the Living Creatures were heard in the
    clouds of heaven
Crying: Compell the Reasoner to Demonstrate with
    unhewn Demonstrations
Let the Indefinite be explored, and let every Man be
    Judged
By his own Works. Let all Indefinites be thrown into
    Demonstrations
To be pounded to dust & melted in the Furnaces of
    Affliction:
He who would do good to another, must do it in Minute
    Particulars   60
General Good is the plea of the scoundrel hypocrite &
    flatterer:
For Art & Science cannot exist but in minutely organized
    Particulars
And not in generalizing Demonstrations of the Rational
    Power.
The Infinite alone resides in Definite & Determinate
    Identity

Establishment of Truth depends on destruction of
 Falshood continually
On Circumcision: not on Virginity, O Reasoners of Albion

So cried they at the Plow. Albions Rock frowned above
And the Great Voice of Eternity rolled above terrible in
 clouds
Saying Who will go forth for us! & Who shall we send
 before our face?

PLATE 56
Then Los heaved his thund'ring Bellows on the Valley
 of Middlesex
And thus he chaunted his Song: the Daughters of Albion
 reply.

What may Man be? who can tell! But what may
 Woman be?
To have power over Man from Cradle to corruptible
 Grave.
He who is an Infant, and whose Cradle is a Manger
Knoweth the Infant sorrow: whence it came, and where
 it goeth:
And who weave it a Cradle of the grass that withereth
 away.
This World is all a Cradle for the erred wandering
 Phantom:
Rock'd by Year, Month, Day & Hour; and every two
 Moments
Between, dwells a Daughter of Beulah, to feed the
 Human Vegetable   10
Entune: Daughters of Albion, your hymning Chorus
 mildly!
Cord of affection thrilling extatic on the iron Reel:
To the golden Loom of Love! to the moth-labourd Woof
A Garment and Cradle weaving for the infantine Terror:
For fear; at entering the gate into our World of cruel
Lamentation: it flee back & hide in Non-Entitys dark
 wild

Where dwells the Spectre of Albion: destroyer of
  Definite Form.
The Sun shall be a Scythed Chariot of Britain: the
  Moon: a Ship
In the British Ocean! Created by Los's Hammer;
  measured out
Into Days & Nights & Years & Months, to travel with
  my feet   20
Over these desolate rocks of Albion: O daughters of
  despair:
Rock the Cradle, and in mild melodies tell me where
  found
What you have enwoven with so much tears & care? so
  much
Tender artifice: to laugh: to weep: to learn: to know;
Remember! recollect! what dark befel in wintry days

O it was lost for ever! and we found it not: it came
And wept at our wintry Door: Look! look! behold!
  Gwendolen
Is become a Clod of Clay! Merlin is a Worm of the
  Valley!

Then Los uttered with Hammer & Anvil: Chaunt!
  revoice!
I mind not your laugh: and your frown I not fear! and   30
You must my dictate obey from your gold-beam'd
  Looms; trill
Gentle to Albions Watchman, on Albions mountains;
  reeccho
And rock the Cradle while! Ah me! Of that Eternal Man
And of the cradled Infancy in his bowels of compassion:
Who fell beneath his instruments of husbandry & became
Subservient to the clods of the furrow! the cattle and
  even
The emmet and earth-Worm are his superiors & his
  lords.

Then the response came warbling from trilling Looms in
  Albion

We Women tremble at the light therefore: hiding fearful
The Divine Vision with Curtain & Veil & fleshly Tabernacle 40

Los utter'd: swift as the rattling thunder upon the
    mountains
Look back into the Church Paul! Look! Three Women
    around
The Cross! O Albion why didst thou a Female Will
    Create?

PLATE 57
And the voices of Bath & Canterbury & York &
    Edinburgh, Cry
Over the Plow of Nations in the strong hand of Albion
    thundering along
Among the Fires of the Druid & the deep black
    rethundering Waters
Of the Atlantic which poured in impetuous loud loud,
    louder & louder.
And the Great Voice of the Atlantic howled over the
    Druid Altars:
Weeping over his Children in Stone-henge in Malden &
    Colchester.
Round the Rocky Peak of Derbyshire London Stone &
    Rosamonds Bower

What is a Wife & what is a Harlot? What is a Church &
    What
Is a Theatre? are they Two & not One? can they Exist
    Separate?
Are not Religion & Politics the Same Thing?
    Brotherhood is Religion   10
O Demonstrations of Reason Dividing Families in
    Cruelty & Pride!

But Albion fled from the Divine Vision, with the Plow of
    Nations enflaming
The Living Creatures maddend and Albion fell into the
    Furrow, and

The Plow went over him & the Living was Plowed in
   among the Dead
But his Spectre rose over the starry Plow. Albion fled
   beneath the Plow
Till he came to the Rock of Ages. & he took his Seat
   upon the Rock.

Wonder siezd all in Eternity! to behold the Divine
   Vision, open
The Center into an Expanse, & the Center rolled out into
   an Expanse.

PLATE 58
In beauty the Daughters of Albion divide & unite at will
Naked & drunk with blood Gwendolen dancing to the
   timbrel
Of War: reeling up the Street of London she divides in
   twain
Among the Inhabitants of Albion, the People fall around[.]
The Daughters of Albion, divide & unite in jealousy &
   cruelty
The Inhabitants of Albion at the Harvest & the Vintage
Feel their Brain cut round beneath the temples shrieking
Bonifying into a Scull, the Marrow exuding in dismal
   pain.
They flee over the rocks bonifying: Horses: Oxen: feel
   the knife.
And while the Sons of Albion by severe War &
   Judgment, bonify[,]   10
The Hermaphroditic Condensations are divided by the
   Knife
The obdurate Forms are cut asunder by Jealousy & Pity.

Rational Philosophy and Mathematic Demonstration
Is divided in the intoxications of pleasure & affection
Two Contraries War against each other in fury & blood,.
And Los fixes them on his Anvil, incessant his blows:
He fixes them with strong blows. placing the stones &
   timbers.

To Create a World of Generation from the World of
  Death:
Dividing the Masculine & Feminine: for the
  comingling
Of Albions & Luvahs Spectres was Hermaphroditic   20

Urizen wrathful strode above directing the awful
  Building:
As a Mighty Temple; delivering Form out of confusion
Jordan sprang beneath its threshold bubbling from
  beneath
Its pillars: Euphrates ran under its arches: white sails
And silver oars reflect on its pillars, & sound on its
  ecchoing
Pavements: where walk the Sons of Jerusalem who
  remain Ungenerate
But the revolving Sun and Moon pass thro its porticoes,
Day & night, in sublime majesty & silence they revolve
And shine glorious within: Hand & Koban archd over
  the Sun
In the hot noon, as he traveld thro his journey: Hyle &
  Skofield   30
Archd over the Moon at midnight & Los Fixd them
  there,
With his thunderous Hammer; terrified the Spectres
  rage & flee
Canaan is his portico; Jordan is a fountain in his porch;
A fountain of milk & wine to relieve the traveller:
Egypt is the eight steps within, Ethiopia supports his
  pillars;
Lybia & the Lands unknown, are the ascent without;
Within is Asia & Greece, ornamented with exquisite art:
Persia & Media are his halls: his inmost hall is Great
  Tartary.
China & India & Siberia are his temples for entertainment
Poland & Russia & Sweden, his soft retired chambers   40
France & Spain & Italy & Denmark & Holland &
  Germany

Are the temples among his pillars. Britain is Los's Forge;
America North & South are his baths of living waters.

Such is the Ancient World of Urizen in the Satanic Void
Created from the Valley of Middlesex by Londons River
From Stone-henge and from London Stone, from
    Cornwall to Cathnes
The Four Zoa's rush around on all sides in dire ruin
Furious in pride of Selfhood the terrible Spectres of
    Albion
Rear their dark Rocks among the Stars of God: stupendous
Works! A World of Generation continually Creating; out
    of   50
The Hermaphroditic Satanic World of rocky destiny.

PLATE 59
And formed into Four precious stones, for enterance
    from Beulah

For the Veil of Vala which Albion cast into the Atlantic
    Deep
To catch the Souls of the Dead: began to Vegetate &
    Petrify
Around the Earth of Albion, among the Roots of his Tree
This Los formed into the Gates & mighty Wall, between
    the Oak
Of Weeping & the Palm of Suffering beneath Albions
    Tomb.
Thus in process of time it became the beautiful
    Mundane Shell,
The Habitation of the Spectres of the Dead & the Place
Of Redemption & of awaking again into Eternity

For Four Universes round the Mundane Egg remain
    Chaotic   10
One to the North; Urthona: One to the South; Urizen:
One to the East: Luvah: One to the West, Tharmas;
They are the Four Zoas that stood around the Throne
    Divine.

Verulam: London: York & Edinburgh: their English
names
But when Luvah assumed the World of Urizen
Southward
And Albion was slain upon his Mountains & in his Tent,
All fell towards the Center, sinking downwards in dire
ruin,
In the South remains a burning Fire: in the East, a
Void
In the West, a World of raging Waters: in the North;
solid Darkness
Unfathomable without end: but in the midst of these   20
Is Built eternally the sublime Universe of Los &
Enitharmon

And in the North Gate, in the West of the North,
toward Beulah
Cathedrons Looms are builded. and Los's Furnaces in
the South[.]
A wondrous golden Building immense with ornaments
sublime
Is bright Cathedrons golden Hall, its Courts Towers &
Pinnacles

And one Daughter of Los sat at the fiery Reel & another
Sat at the shining Loom with her Sisters attending round
Terrible their distress & their sorrow cannot be utterd
And another Daughter of Los sat at the Spinning Wheel
Endless their labour, with bitter food, void of sleep,   30
Tho hungry they labour: they rouze themselves anxious
Hour after hour labouring at the whirling Wheel
Many Wheels & as many lovely Daughters sit weeping

Yet the intoxicating delight that they take in their work
Obliterates every other evil; none pities their tears
Yet they regard not pity & they expect no one to pity
For they labour for life & love, regardless of any one
But the poor Spectres that they work for, always
incessantly

They are mockd, by every one that passes by, they
   regard not
They labour; & when their Wheels are broken by scorn
   & malice   40
They mend them sorrowing with many tears & afflictions.

Other Daughters Weave on the Cushion & Pillow,
   Network fine
That Rahab & Tirzah may exist & live & breathe & love
Ah, that it could be as the Daughters of Beulah wish!

Other Daughters of Los, labouring at Looms less fine
Create the Silk-worm & the Spider & the Catterpiller
To assist in their most grievous work of pity &
   compassion
And others Create the wooly Lamb & the downy Fowl
To assist in the work: the Lamb bleats: the Sea-fowl
   cries
Men understand not the distress & the labour & sorrow   50
That in the Interior Worlds is carried on in fear &
   trembling
Weaving the shuddring fears & loves of Albions Families
Thunderous rage the Spindles of iron, & the iron Distaff
Maddens in the fury of their hands, weaving in bitter
   tears
The Veil of Goats-hair & Purple & Scarlet & fine
   twined Linen

PLATE 60
The clouds of Albions Druid Temples rage in the eastern
   heaven
While Los sat terrified beholding Albions Spectre who is
   Luvah
Spreading in bloody veins in torments over Europe &
   Asia;
Not yet formed but a wretched torment unformed &
   abyssal
In flaming fire; within the Furnaces the Divine Vision
   appeard

On Albions hills: often walking from the Furnaces in
    clouds
And flames among the Druid Temples & the Starry
    Wheels
Gatherd Jerusalems Children in his arms & bore them
    like
A Shepherd in the night of Albion which overspread all
    the Earth

I gave thee liberty and life O lovely Jerusalem   10
And thou hast bound me down upon the Stems of
    Vegetation
I gave thee Sheep-walks upon the Spanish Mountains
    Jerusalem
I gave thee Priams City and the Isles of Grecia lovely!
I gave thee Hand & Scofield & the Counties of Albion:
They spread forth like a lovely root into the Garden of
    God:
They were as Adam before me: united into One Man,
They stood in innocence & their skiey tent reachd over
    Asia
To Nimrods Tower to Ham & Canaan walking with
    Mizraim
Upon the Egyptian Nile, with solemn songs to Grecia
And sweet Hesperia even to Great Chaldea & Tesshina   20
Following thee as a Shepherd by the Four Rivers of
    Eden
Why wilt thou rend thyself apart, Jerusalem?
And build this Babylon & sacrifice in secret Groves,
Among the Gods of Asia: among the fountains of pitch
    & nitre
Therefore thy Mountains are become barren Jerusalem!
Thy Valleys, Plains of burning sand, thy Rivers: waters
    of death
Thy Villages die of the Famine and thy Cities
Beg bread from house to house, lovely Jerusalem
Why wilt thou deface thy beauty & the beauty of thy
    little-ones

To please thy Idols, in the pretended chastities of
    Uncircumcision[?]   30
Thy Sons are lovelier than Egypt or Assyria; wherefore
Dost thou blacken their beauty by a Secluded place of
    rest,
And a peculiar Tabernacle, to cut the integuments of
    beauty
Into veils of tears and sorrows O lovely Jerusalem!
They have perswaded thee to this, therefore their end
    shall come
And I will lead thee thro the Wilderness in shadow of
    my cloud
And in my love I will lead thee, lovely Shadow of
    Sleeping Albion.

This is the Song of the Lamb, sung by Slaves in
    evening time.

But Jerusalem faintly saw him, closd in the Dungeons of
    Babylon
Her Form was held by Beulahs Daughters, but all within
    unseen   40
She sat at the Mills, her hair unbound her feet naked
Cut with the flints: her tears run down, her reason
    grows like
The Wheel of Hand, incessant turning day & night
    without rest
Insane she raves upon the winds hoarse, inarticulate:
All night Vala hears, she triumphs in pride of holiness
To see Jerusalem deface her lineaments with bitter blows
Of despair, while the Satanic Holiness triumphd in Vala
In a Religion of Chastity & Uncircumcised Selfishness
Both of the Head & Heart & Loins, closd up in Moral
    Pride.
But the Divine Lamb stood beside Jerusalem, oft she
    saw   50
The lineaments Divine & oft the Voice heard, & oft she
    said:

O Lord & Saviour, have the Gods of the Heathen pierced
    thee?
Or hast thou been pierced in the House of thy Friends?
Art thou alive! & livest thou for-evermore? or art thou
Not: but a delusive shadow, a thought that liveth not.
Babel mocks saying, there is no God nor Son of God
That thou O Human Imagination, O Divine Body art all
A delusion. but I know thee O Lord when thou arisest
    upon
My weary eyes even in this dungeon & this iron mill.
The Stars of Albion cruel rise; thou bindest to sweet
    influences: 60
For thou also sufferest with me altho I behold thee not:
And altho I sin & blaspheme thy holy name, thou pitiest
    me:
Because thou knowest I am deluded by the turning
    mills,
And by these visions of pity & love because of Albions
    death.

Thus spake Jerusalem, & thus the Divine Voice replied.

Mild Shade of Man, pitiest thou these Visions of terror
    & woe!
Give forth thy pity & love, fear not! lo I am with thee
    always.
Only believe in me that I have power to raise from death
Thy Brother who Sleepeth in Albion: fear not trembling
    Shade
PLATE 61
Behold: in the Visions of Elohim Jehovah, behold Joseph
    & Mary
And be comforted O Jerusalem in the Visions of Jehovah
    Elohim

She looked & saw Joseph the Carpenter in Nazareth &
    Mary
His espoused Wife. And Mary said, If thou put me away
    from thee

Dost thou not murder me? Joseph spoke in anger & fury.
  Should I

Marry a Harlot & an Adulteress? Mary answerd. Art
  thou more pure

Than thy Maker who forgiveth Sins & calls again Her
  that is Lost

Tho She hates, he calls her again in love. I love my dear
  Joseph

But he driveth me away from his presence, yet I hear the
  voice of God

In the voice of my Husband, tho he is angry for a
  moment, he will not   10

Utterly cast me away, if I were pure, never could I taste
  the sweets

Of the Forgive[ne]ss of Sins: if I were holy: I never
  could behold the tears

Of love! of him who loves me in the midst of his anger
  in furnace of fire.

Ah my Mary: said Joseph: weeping over & embracing
  her closely in

His arms: Doth he forgive Jerusalem & not exact
  Purity from her who is

Polluted. I heard his voice in my sleep & his Angel in
  my dream:

Saying, Doth Jehovah Forgive a Debt only on condition
  that it shall

Be Payed? Doth he Forgive Pollution only on conditions
  of Purity

That Debt is not Forgiven! That Pollution is not
  Forgiven

Such is the Forgiveness of the Gods, the Moral Virtues of the   20
Heathen, whose tender Mercies are Cruelty. But Jehovahs
  Salvation

Is without Money & without Price, in the Continual
  Forgiveness of Sins

In the Perpetual Mutual Sacrifice in Great Eternity! for
  behold!

There is none that liveth & Sinneth not! And this is the
  Covenant
Of Jehovah: If you Forgive one-another, so shall
  Jehovah Forgive You:
That He Himself may Dwell among You. Fear not then
  to take
To thee Mary thy Wife, for she is with Child by the
  Holy Ghost

Then Mary burst forth into a Song! she flowed like a
  River of
Many Streams in the arms of Joseph & gave forth her
  tears of joy
Like many waters, and Emanating into gardens & palaces
  upon   30
Euphrates & to forests & floods & animals wild & tame
  from
Gihon to Hiddekel, & to corn fields & villages &
  inhabitants
Upon Pison & Arnon & Jordan. And I heard the voice
  among
The Reapers Saying, Am I Jerusalem the lost
  Adulteress? or am I
Babylon come up to Jerusalem? And another voice
  answerd Saying

Does the voice of my Lord call me again? am I pure thro
  his Mercy
And Pity. Am I become lovely as a Virgin in his sight
  who am
Indeed a Harlot drunken with the Sacrifice of Idols does
  he
Call her pure as he did in the days of her Infancy when
  She
Was cast out to the loathing of her person. The Chaldean
  took   40
Me from my Cradle. The Amalekite stole me away upon
  his Camels

Before I had ever beheld with love the Face of Jehovah:
    or known
That there was a God of Mercy: O Mercy O Divine
    Humanity!
O Forgiveness & Pity & Compassion! If I were Pure I
    should never
Have known Thee; If I were Unpolluted I should never
    have
Glorified thy Holiness, or rejoiced in thy great
    Salvation.

Mary leaned her side against Jerusalem. Jerusalem
    recieved
The Infant into her hands in the Visions of Jehovah.
    Times passed on
Jerusalem fainted over the Cross & Sepulcher She heard
    the voice
Wilt thou make Rome thy Patriarch Druid & the Kings
    of Europe his   50
Horsemen? Man in the Resurrection changes his Sexual
    Garments at will
Every Harlot was once a Virgin: every Criminal an
    Infant Love:
PLATE 62
Repose on me till the morning of the Grave. I am thy life.

Jerusalem replied. I am an outcast: Albion is dead!
I am left to the trampling foot & the spurning heel!
A Harlot I am calld. I am sold from street to street!
I am defaced with blows & with the dirt of the Prison!
And wilt thou become my Husband O my Lord &
    Saviour?
Shall Vala bring thee forth! shall the Chaste be ashamed
    also?
I see the Maternal Line, I behold the Seed of the
    Woman!
Cainah, & Ada & Zillah & Naamah Wife of Noah.
Shuahs daughter & Tamar & Rahab the Canaanites: 10

Ruth the Moabite & Bathsheba of the daughters of Heth
Naamah the Ammonite, Zibeah the Philistine, & Mary
These are the Daughters of Vala, Mother of the Body of
    death
But I thy Magdalen behold thy Spiritual Risen Body
Shall Albion arise? I know he shall arise at the Last
    Day!
I know that in my flesh I shall see God: but Emanations
Are weak. they know not whence they are, nor whither
    tend.

Jesus replied. I am the Resurrection & the Life.
I Die & pass the limits of possibility, as it appears
To individual perception. Luvah must be Created   20
And Vala; for I cannot leave them in the gnawing Grave.
But will prepare a way for my banished-ones to return
Come now with me into the villages, walk thro all the
    cities.
Tho thou art taken to prison & judgment, starved in the
    streets
I will command the cloud to give thee food & the hard
    rock
To flow with milk & wine, tho thou seest me not a
    season
Even a long season & a hard journey & a howling
    wilderness:
Tho Valas cloud hide thee & Luvahs fires follow thee:
Only believe & trust in me, Lo. I am always with thee:

So spoke the Lamb of God while Luvahs Cloud
    reddening above   30
Burst forth in streams of blood upon the heavens & dark
    night
Involvd Jerusalem, & the Wheels of Albions Sons turnd
    hoarse
Over the Mountains & the fires blaz'd on Druid Altars
And the Sun set in Tyburns Brook where Victims howl
    & cry.

But Los beheld the Divine Vision among the flames of
　the Furnaces
Therefore he lived & breathed in hope. but his tears fell
　incessant
Because his Children were closd from him apart: &
　Enitharmon
Dividing in fierce pain: also the Vision of God was closd
　in clouds
Of Albions Spectres, that Los in despair oft sat, & often
　ponderd
On Death Eternal in fierce shudders upon the mountains
　of Albion   40
Walking: & in the vales in howlings fierce, then to his
　Anvils
Turning, anew began his labours, tho in terrible pains:

PLATE 63
Jehovah stood among the Druids in the Valley of
　Annandale
When the Four Zoas of Albion, the Four Living
　Creatures, the Cherubim
Of Albion tremble before the Spectre, in the starry
　Harness of the Plow
Of Nations. And their Names are Urizen & Luvah &
　Tharmas & Urthona

Luvah slew Tharmas the Angel of the Tongue & Albion
　brought him
To Justice in his own City of Paris, denying the
　Resurrection
Then Vala the Wife of Albion, who is the Daughter of
　Luvah
Took vengeance Twelve-fold among the Chaotic Rocks
　of the Druids
Where the Human Victims howl to the Moon & Thor &
　Friga
Dance the dance of death contending with Jehovah
　among the Cherubim.   10

The Chariot Wheels filled with Eyes rage along the
  howling Valley
In the Dividing of Reuben & Benjamin bleeding from
  Chesters River

The Giants & the Witches & the Ghosts of Albion dance
  with
Thor & Friga, & the Fairies lead the Moon along the
  Valley of Cherubim
Bleeding in torrents from Mountain to Mountain, a
  lovely Victim
And Jehovah stood in the Gates of the Victim, & he
  appeared
A weeping Infant in the Gates of Birth in the midst of
  Heaven

The Cities & Villages of Albion became Rock & Sand
  Unhumanized
The Druid Sons of Albion & the Heavens a Void around
  unfathomable
No Human Form but Sexual & a little weeping Infant
  pale reflected   20
Multitudinous in the Looking Glass of Enitharmon, on
  all sides
Around in the clouds of the Female, on Albions Cliffs of
  the Dead

Such the appearance in Cheviot: in the Divisions of
  Reuben
When the Cherubim hid their heads under their wings
  in deep slumbers
When the Druids demanded Chastity from Woman & all
  was lost.

How can the Female be Chaste O thou stupid Druid
  Cried Los
Without the Forgiveness of Sins in the merciful clouds
  of Jehovah
And without the Baptism of Repentance to wash away
  Calumnies, and

The Accusations of Sin that each may be Pure in their
    Neighbours sight
O when shall Jehovah give us Victims from his Flocks &
    Herds   30
Instead of Human Victims by the Daughters of Albion &
    Canaan

Then laugh'd Gwendolen & her laughter shook the
    Nations & Familys of
The Dead beneath Beulah from Tyburn to Golgotha,
    and from
Ireland to Japan, furious her Lions & Tygers & Wolves
    sport before
Los on the Thames & Medway, London & Canterbury
    groan in pain

Los knew not yet what was done: he thought it was all
    in Vision
In Visions of the Dreams of Beulah among the
    Daughters of Albion
Therefore the Murder was put apart in the Looking-
    Glass of Enitharmon

He saw in Vala's hand the Druid Knife of Revenge & the
    Poison Cup
Of Jealousy, and thought it a Poetic Vision of the
    Atmospheres   40
Till Canaan rolld apart from Albion across the Rhine:
    along the Danube

And all the Land of Canaan suspended over the Valley
    of Cheviot
From Bashan to Tyre & from Troy to Gaza of the
    Amalekite
And Reuben fled with his head downwards among the
    Caverns
PLATE 64
Of the Mundane Shell which froze on all sides round
    Canaan on

The vast Expanse: where the Daughters of Albion
 Weave the Web
Of Ages & Generations, folding & unfolding it, like a
 Veil of Cherubim
And sometimes it touches the Earths summits, &
 sometimes spreads
Abroad into the Indefinite Spectre, who is the Rational
 Power.

Then All the Daughters of Albion became One before
 Los: even Vala!
And she put forth her hand upon the Looms in dreadful
 howlings
Till she vegetated into a hungry Stomach & a devouring
 Tongue.
Her Hand is a Court of Justice, her Feet: two Armies in
 Battle
Storms & Pestilence: in her Locks: & in her Loins
 Earthquake,   10
And Fire, & the Ruin of Cities & Nations & Families &
 Tongues

She cries: The Human is but a Worm, & thou O Male:
 Thou art
Thyself Female, a Male: a breeder of Seed: a Son &
 Husband: & Lo,
The Human Divine is Womans Shadow, a Vapor in the
 summers heat
Go assume Papal dignity thou Spectre, thou Male
 Harlot: Arthur
Divide into the Kings of Europe in times remote O
 Woman-born
And Woman-nourishd & Woman-educated & Woman-
 scorn'd:

Wherefore art thou living? said Los, & Man cannot live
 in thy presence
Art thou Vala the Wife of Albion O thou lovely Daughter
 of Luvah

All Quarrels arise from Reasoning, the secret Murder,
   and   20
The violent Man-slaughter, these are the Spectres double
   Cave
The Sexual Death living on accusation of Sin &
   Judgment
To freeze Love & Innocence into the gold & silver of the
   Merchant
Without Forgiveness of Sin Love is Itself Eternal Death.

Then the Spectre drew Vala into his bosom magnificent
   terrific
Glittering with precious stones & gold, with Garments of
   blood & fire[.]
He wept in deadly wrath of the Spectre, in self-
   contradicting agony
Crimson with Wrath & green with Jealousy dazling with
   Love
And Jealousy immingled & the purple of the violet
   darkend deep
Over the Plow of Nations thundring in the hand of
   Albions Spectre   30

A dark Hermaphrodite they stood frowning upon
   Londons River
And the Distaff & Spindle in the hands of Vala with the
   Flax of
Human Miseries turnd fierce with the Lives of Men
   along the Valley
As Reuben fled before the Daughters of Albion Taxing
   the Nations

Derby Peak yawnd a horrid Chasm at the Cries of
   Gwendolen, & at
The stamping feet of Ragan upon the flaming Treddles
   of her Loom
That drop with crimson gore with the Loves of Albion &
   Canaan
Opening along the Valley of Rephaim, weaving over the
   Caves of Machpelah

PLATE 65

To decide Two Worlds with a great decision: a World of
    Mercy, and
A World of Justice: the World of Mercy for Salvation
To cast Luvah into the Wrath, and Albion into the Pity
In the Two Contraries of Humanity & in the Four
    Regions.

For in the depths of Albions bosom in the eastern
    heaven,
They sound the clarions strong! they chain the howling
    Captives:
They cast the lots into the helmet: they give the oath of
    blood in Lambeth
They vote the death of Luvah, & they naild him to
    Albions Tree in Bath:
They staind him with poisonous blue, they inwove him
    in cruel roots
To die a death of Six thousand years bound round with
    vegetation   10
The sun was black & the moon rolld a useless globe thro
    Britain!

Then left the Sons of Urizen the plow & harrow, the
    loom
The hammer & the chisel, & the rule & compasses; from
    London fleeing
They forg'd the sword on Cheviot, the chariot of war &
    the battle-ax,
The trumpet fitted to mortal battle, & the flute of
    summer in Annandale
And all the Arts of Life. they changd into the Arts of
    Death in Albion.
The hour-glass contemnd because its simple workmanship,
Was like the workmanship of the plowman, & the water
    wheel,
That raises water into cisterns: broken & burnd with
    fire:

Because its workmanship, was like the workmanship of
the shepherd.   20
And in their stead, intricate wheels invented, wheel
without wheel:
To perplex youth in their outgoings, & to bind to labours
in Albion
Of day & night the myriads of eternity that they may
grind
And polish brass & iron hour after hour laborious task:
Kept ignorant of its use, that they might spend the days
of wisdom
In sorrowful drudgery, to obtain a scanty pittance of
bread:
In ignorance to view a small portion & think that All,
And call it Demonstration: blind to all the simple rules
of life.

Now: now the battle rages round thy tender limbs O
Vala,
Now smile among thy bitter tears: now put on all thy
beauty   30
Is not the wound of the sword sweet! & the broken bone
delightful?
Wilt thou now smile among the scythes when the
wounded groan in the field[?]
We were carried away in thousands from London; & in
tens
Of thousands from Westminster & Marybone in ships
closd up:
Chaind hand & foot, compelld to fight under the iron
whips
Of our captains; fearing our officers more than the
enemy.
Lift up thy blue eyes Vala & put on thy sapphire shoes:
O melancholy Magdalen behold the morning over
Malden break;
Gird on thy flaming zone, descend into the sepulcher of
Canterbury.

Scatter the blood from thy golden brow, the tears from
    thy silver locks: 40
Shake off the waters from thy wings! & the dust from
    thy white garments
Remember all thy feigned terrors on the secret couch of
    Lambeths Vale
When the sun rose in glowing morn, with arms of
    mighty hosts
Marching to battle who was wont to rise with Urizens
    harps
Girt as a sower with his seed to scatter life abroad over
    Albion:
Arise O Vala! bring the bow of Urizen: bring the swift
    arrows of light.
How rag'd the golden horses of Urizen, compelld to the
    chariot of love!
Compelld to leave the plow to the ox, to snuff up the
    winds of desolation
To trample the corn fields in boastful neighings: this is
    no gentle harp
This is no warbling brook, nor shadow of a mirtle tree: 50
But blood and wounds and dismal cries, and shadows of
    the oak:
And hearts laid open to the light, by the broad grizly
    sword:
And bowels hid in hammerd steel rip'd quivering on the
    ground.
Call forth thy smiles of soft deceit: call forth thy cloudy
    tears:
We hear thy sighs in trumpets shrill when morn shall
    blood renew.

So sang the Spectre Sons of Albion round Luvahs Stone
    of Trial:
Mocking and deriding at the writhings of their Victim on
    Salisbury:
Drinking his Emanation in intoxicating bliss rejoicing in
    Giant dance;

For a Spectre has no Emanation but what he imbibes from
    decieving
A Victim! Then he becomes her Priest & she his
    Tabernacle,   60
And his Oak Grove, till the Victim rend the woven Veil,
In the end of his sleep when Jesus calls him from his
    grave

Howling the Victims on the Druid Altars yield their
    souls
To the stern Warriors: lovely sport the Daughters round
    their Victims;
Drinking their lives in sweet intoxication; hence arose
    from Bath
Soft deluding odours, in spiral volutions intricately
    winding
Over Albions mountains, a feminine indefinite cruel
    delusion.
Astonishd: terrified & in pain & torment, Sudden they
    behold
Their own Parent the Emanation of their murderd
    Enemy
Become their Emanation and their Temple and
    Tabernacle   70
They knew not, this Vala was their beloved Mother Vala
    Albions Wife.

Terrified at the sight of the Victim: at his distorted
    sinews!
The tremblings of Vala vibrate thro' the limbs of Albions
    Sons:
While they rejoice over Luvah in mockery & bitter scorn:
Sudden they become like what they behold in howlings
    & deadly pain.
Spasms smite their features, sinews & limbs: pale they
    look on one another.
They turn, contorted: their iron necks bend unwilling
    towards

Luvah: their lips tremble: their muscular fibres are
  crampd & smitten
They become like what they behold! Yet immense in
  strength & power,

PLATE 66

In awful pomp & gold, in all the precious unhewn stones
  of Eden
They build a stupendous Building on the Plain of
  Salisbury; with chains
Of rocks round London Stone: of Reasonings: of
  unhewn Demonstrations
In labyrinthine arches, (Mighty Urizen the Architect,)
  thro which
The Heavens might revolve & Eternity be bound in their
  chain.
Labour unparallelld! a wondrous rocky World of cruel
  destiny
Rocks piled on rocks reaching the stars: stretching from
  pole to pole.
The Building is Natural Religion & its Altars Natural
  Morality
A building of eternal death: whose proportions are
  eternal despair
Here Vala stood turning the iron Spindle of destruction   10
From heaven to earth: howling! invisible! but not
  invisible
Her Two Covering Cherubs afterwards named Voltaire
  & Rousseau:
Two frowning Rocks: on each side of the Cove & Stone
  of Torture:
Frozen Sons of the feminine Tabernacle of Bacon,
  Newton & Locke.
For Luvah is France: the Victim of the Spectres of Albion.

Los beheld in terror: he pour'd his loud storms on the
  Furnaces:
The Daughters of Albion clothed in garments of needle
  work

Strip them off from their shoulders: and bosoms, they
    lay aside
Their garments; they sit naked upon the Stone of trial.
The Knife of flint passes over the howling Victim: his
    blood   20
Gushes & stains the fair side of the fair Daug[h]ters of
    Albion.
They put aside his curls; they divide his seven locks upon
His forehead: they bind his forehead with thorns of iron
They put into his hand a reed, they mock: Saying:
    Behold
The King of Canaan whose are seven hundred chariots
    of iron!
They take off his vesture whole with their Knives of
    flint:

But they cut asunder his inner garments: searching with
Their cruel fingers for his heart, & there they enter in
    pomp,
In many tears; & there they erect a temple & an altar:
They pour cold water on his brain in front, to cause   30
Lids to grow over his eyes in veils of tears: and caverns
To freeze over his nostrils, while they feed his tongue
    from cups
And dishes of painted clay. Glowing with beauty &
    cruelty:
They obscure the sun & the moon; no eye can look
    upon them.

Ah! alas! at the sight of the Victim, & at sight of those
    who are smitten,
All who see, become what they behold, their eyes are
    coverd
With veils of tears and their nostrils & tongues shrunk
    up
Their ear bent outwards, as their Victim, so are they in
    pangs
Of unconquerable fear! amidst delights of revenge
    Earth-shaking!

And as their eye & ear shrunk, the heavens shrunk away   40
The Divine Vision became First a burning flame, then a
    column
Of fire, then an awful fiery wheel surrounding earth &
    heaven:
And then a globe of blood wandering distant in an
    unknown night:
Afar into the unknown night the mountains fled away:

Six months of mortality; a summer: & six months of
    mortality; a winter:
The Human form began to be alterd by the Daughters
    of Albion
And the perceptions to be dissipated into the Indefinite.
    Becoming
A mighty Polypus nam'd Albions Tree: they tie the
    Veins
And Nerves into two knots: & the Seed into a double
    knot:
They look forth: the Sun is shrunk: the Heavens are
    shrunk   50
Away into the far remote: and the Trees & Mountains
    witherd
Into indefinite cloudy shadows in darkness & separation.
By Invisible Hatreds adjoind, they seem remote and
    separate
From each other; and yet are a Mighty Polypus in the
    Deep!
As the Mistletoe grows on the Oak, so Albions Tree on
    Eternity: Lo!
He who will not comingle in Love, must be adjoind by
    Hate

They look forth from Stone-henge! from the Cove round
    London Stone
They look on one another: the mountain calls out to
    the mountain:
Plinlimmon shrunk away: Snowdon trembled: the
    mountains

Of Wales & Scotland beheld the descending War: the
   routed flying: 60
Red run the streams of Albion: Thames is drunk with
   blood:
As Gwendolen cast the shuttle of war: as Cambel
   returnd the beam.
The Humber & the Severn: are drunk with the blood of
   the slain:
London feels his brain cut round: Edinburghs heart is
   circumscribed!
York & Lincoln hide among the flocks, because of the
   griding Knife.
Worcester & Hereford: Oxford & Cambridge reel &
   stagger,
Overwearied with howling: Wales & Scotland alone
   sustain the fight!
The inhabitants are sick to death: they labour to divide
   into Days
And Nights, the uncertain Periods; and into Weeks &
   Months. In vain
They send the Dove & Raven: & in vain the Serpent
   over the mountains.   70
And in vain the Eagle & Lion over the four-fold
   wilderness.
They return not: but generate in rocky places desolate.
They return not: but build a habitation separate from
   Man.
The Sun forgets his course like a drunken man; he
   hesitates,
Upon the Cheselden hills, thinking to sleep on the
   Severn
In vain: he is hurried afar into an unknown Night
He bleeds in torrents of blood as he rolls thro heaven
   above
He chokes up the paths of the sky; the Moon is leprous
   as snow:
Trembling & descending down seeking to rest upon high
   Mona:

Scattering her leprous snows in flakes of disease over
  Albion.   80
The Stars flee remote: the heaven is iron, the earth is
  sulphur,
And all the mountains & hills shrink up like a withering
  gourd,
As the Senses of Men shrink together under the Knife of
  flint,
In the hands of Albions Daughters, among the Druid
  Temples,

PLATE 67

By those who drink their blood & the blood of their
  Covenant

And the Twelve Daughters of Albion united in Rahab
  & Tirzah
A Double Female: and they drew out from the Rocky
  Stones
Fibres of Life to Weave for every Female is a Golden
  Loom
The Rocks are opake hardnesses covering all Vegetated
  things.
And as they Wove & Cut from the Looms in various
  divisions
Stretching over Europe & Asia from Ireland to Japan
They divided into many lovely Daughters to be
  counterparts
To those they Wove, for when they Wove a Male, they
  divided
Into a Female to the Woven Male, in opake hardness   10
They cut the Fibres from the Rocks groaning in pain
  they Weave;
Calling the Rocks Atomic Origins of Existence;
  denying Eternity
By the Atheistical Epicurean Philosophy of Albions
  Tree
Such are the Feminine & Masculine when separated
  from Man

They call the Rocks Parents of Men, & adore the
    frowning Chaos
Dancing around in howling pain clothed in the bloody
    Veil.
Hiding Albions Sons within the Veil, closing
    Jerusalems
Sons without; to feed with their Souls the Spectres of
    Albion
Ashamed to give Love openly to the piteous & merciful
    Man
Counting him an imbecile mockery: but the Warrior   20
They adore: & his revenge cherish with the blood of the
    Innocent
They drink up Dan & Gad, to feed with milk Skofeld &
    Kotope
They strip off Josephs Coat & dip it in the blood of
    battle

Tirzah sits weeping to hear the shrieks of the dying:
    her Knife
Of flint is in her hand: she passes it over the howling
    Victim[.]
The Daughters Weave their Work in loud cries over the
    Rock
Of Horeb! still eyeing Albions Cliffs eagerly siezing &
    twisting
The threads of Vala & Jerusalem running from
    mountain to mountain
Over the whole Earth: loud the Warriors rage in Beth
    Peor
Beneath the iron whips of their Captains & consecrated
    banners   30
Loud the Sun & Moon rage in the conflict: loud the
    Stars
Shout in the night of battle & their spears grow to their
    hands
With blood, weaving the deaths of the Mighty into a
    Tabernacle

For Rahab & Tirzah; till the Great Polypus of
  Generation covered the Earth.

In Verulam the Polypus's Head, winding around his
  bulk
Thro Rochester, and Chichester, & Exeter & Salisbury,
To Bristol: & his Heart beat strong on Salisbury Plain
Shooting out Fibres round the Earth, thro Gaul & Italy
And Greece, & along the Sea of Rephaim into Judea
To Sodom & Gomorrha: thence to India, China &
  Japan   40

The Twelve Daughters in Rahab & Tirzah have
  circumscribd the Brain
Beneath & pierced it thro the midst with a golden pin.
Blood hath staind her fair side beneath her bosom.

O thou poor Human Form! said she. O thou poor child
  of woe!
Why wilt thou wander away from Tirzah: why me
  compel to bind thee?
If thou dost go away from me I shall consume upon
  these Rocks[.]
These fibres of thine eyes that used to beam in distant
  heavens
Away from me: I have bound down with a hot iron.
These nostrils that expanded with delight in morning
  skies
I have bent downward with lead melted in my roaring
  furnaces   50
Of affliction; of love; of sweet despair; of torment
  unendurable
My soul is seven furnaces, incessant roars the bellows
Upon my terribly flaming heart, the molten metal runs
In channels thro my fiery limbs: O love! O pity! O fear!
O pain! O the pangs, the bitter pangs of love forsaken
Ephraim was a wilderness of joy where all my wild
  beasts ran
The River Kanah wanderd by my sweet Manassehs side

To see the boy spring into heavens sounding from my
    sight!
Go Noah fetch the girdle of strong brass, heat it red-hot:
Press it around the loins of this ever expanding cruelty   60
Shriek not so my only love! I refuse thy joys: I drink
Thy shrieks because Hand & Hyle are cruel & obdurate
    to me

PLATE 68

O Skofield why art thou cruel? Lo Joseph is thine! to
    make
You One: to weave you both in the same mantle of skin
Bind him down Sisters bind him down on Ebal, Mount
    of cursing:
Malah come forth from Lebanon: & Hoglah from Mount
    Sinai:
Come circumscribe this tongue of sweets & with a screw
    of iron
Fasten this ear into the rock: Milcah the task is thine
Weep not so Sisters: weep not so: our life depends on
    this
Or mercy & truth are fled away from Shechem & Mount
    Gilead
Unless my beloved is bound upon the Stems of
    Vegetation

And thus the Warriors cry, in the hot day of Victory, in
    Songs.   10

Look: the beautiful Daughter of Albion sits naked upon
    the Stone
Her panting Victim beside her: her heart is drunk with
    blood
Tho her brain is not drunk with wine: she goes forth
    from Albion
In pride of beauty: in cruelty of holiness: in the brightness
Of her tabernacle, & her ark & secret place, the
    beautiful Daughter

Of Albion, delights the eyes of the Kings. their hearts &
   the
Hearts of their Warriors glow hot before Thor & Friga.
   O Molech!
O Chemosh! O Bacchus! O Venus! O Double God of
   Generation
The Heavens are cut like a mantle around from the
   Cliffs of Albion
Across Europe; across Africa; in howlings & deadly
   War   20
A sheet & veil & curtain of blood is let down from
   Heaven
Across the hills of Ephraim & down Mount Olivet to
The Valley of the Jebusite: Molech rejoices in heaven
He sees the Twelve Daughters naked upon the Twelve
   Stones
Themselves condensing to rocks & into the Ribs of a
   Man
Lo they shoot forth in tender Nerves across Europe &
   Asia
Lo they rest upon the Tribes, where their panting
   Victims lie[.]
Molech rushes into the Kings in love to the beautiful
   Daughters
But they frown & delight in cruelty, refusing all other
   joy
Bring your Offerings, your first begotten: pamperd with
   milk & blood   30
Your first born of seven years old: be they Males or
   Females:
To the beautiful Daughters of Albion! they sport before
   the Kings
Clothed in the skin of the Victim: blood: human blood:
   is the life
And delightful food of the Warrior: the well fed
   Warriors flesh
Of him who is slain in War: fills the Valleys of Ephraim
   with

Breeding Women walking in pride & bringing forth
    under green trees
With pleasure, without pain, for their food is, blood
    of the Captive
Molech rejoices thro the Land from Havilah to Shur:
    he rejoices
In moral law & its severe penalties: loud Shaddai &
    Jehovah
Thunder above: when they see the Twelve panting
    Victims   40
On the Twelve Stones of Power, & the beautiful
    Daughters of Albion
If you dare rend their Veil with your Spear; you are
    healed of Love!
From the Hills of Camberwell & Wimbledon: from the
    Valleys
Of Walton & Esher: from Stone-henge & from Maldens
    Cove
Jerusalems Pillars fall in the rendings of fierce War
Over France & Germany: upon the Rhine & Danube
Reuben & Benjamin flee; they hide in the Valley of
    Rephaim
Why trembles the Warriors limbs when he beholds thy
    beauty
Spotted with Victims blood? by the fires of thy secret
    tabernacle
And thy ark & holy place: at thy frowns: at thy dire
    revenge   50
Smitten as Uzzah of old: his armour is softend; his
    spear
And sword faint in his hand, from Albion across Great
    Tartary
O beautiful Daughter of Albion: cruelty is thy
    delight
O Virgin of terrible eyes, who dwellest by Valleys of
    springs
Beneath the Mountains of Lebanon, in the City of
    Rehob in Hamath

Taught to touch the harp: to dance in the Circle of
Warriors
Before the Kings of Canaan: to cut the flesh from the
Victim
To roast the flesh in fire: to examine the Infants limbs
In cruelties of holiness: to refuse the joys of love: to
bring
The Spies from Egypt, to raise jealousy in the bosoms of
the Twelve   60
Kings of Canaan: then to let the Spies depart to
Meribah Kadesh
To the place of the Amalekite; I am drunk with
unsatiated love
I must rush again to War: for the Virgin has frownd &
refusd
Sometimes I curse & sometimes bless thy fascinating
beauty
Once Man was occupied in intellectual pleasures &
energies
But now my soul is harrowd with grief & fear & love &
desire
And now I hate & now I love & Intellect is no more:
There is no time for any thing but the torments of love
& desire
The Feminine & Masculine Shadows soft, mild & ever
varying
In beauty: are Shadows now no more, but Rocks in
Horeb   70

PLATE 69
Then all the Males combined into One Male & every
one
Became a ravening eating Cancer growing in the
Female
A Polypus of Roots of Reasoning Doubt Despair &
Death,
Going forth & returning from Albions Rocks to Canaan:
Devouring Jerusalem from every Nation of the Earth.

Envying stood the enormous Form at variance with Itself
In all its Members: in eternal torment of love &
   jealousy:
Driven forth by Los time after time from Albions cliffy
   shore,
Drawing the free loves of Jerusalem into infernal
   bondage;
That they might be born in contentions of Chastity & in   10
Deadly Hate between Leah & Rachel, Daughters of
   Deceit & Fraud
Bearing the Images of various Species of Contention
And Jealousy & Abhorrence & Revenge & deadly
   Murder,
Till they refuse liberty to the Male; & not like Beulah
Where every Female delights to give her maiden to her
   husband
The Female searches sea & land for gratifications to the
Male Genius: who in return clothes her in gems & gold
And feeds her with the food of Eden, hence all her
   beauty beams
She Creates at her will a little moony night & silence
With Spaces of sweet gardens & a tent of elegant
   beauty: 20
Closed in by a sandy desart & a night of stars shining,
And a little tender moon & hovering angels on the wing,
And the Male gives a Time & Revolution to her Space
Till the time of love is passed in ever varying delights
For All Things Exist in the Human Imagination
And thence in Beulah they are stolen by secret amorous
   theft,
Till they have had Punishment enough to make them
   commit Crimes[.]
Hence rose the Tabernacle in the Wilderness & all its
   Offerings,
From Male & Female Loves in Beulah & their Jealousies
But no one can consummate Female bliss in Los's
   World without   30
Becoming a Generated Mortal, a Vegetating Death

And now the Spectres of the Dead awake in Beulah: all
The Jealousies become Murderous: uniting together in
   Rahab
A Religion of Chastity, forming a Commerce to sell
   Loves,
With Moral Law, an Equal Balance, not going down
   with decision
Therefore the Male severe & cruel filld with stern
   Revenge:
Mutual Hate returns & mutual Deceit & mutual Fear.

Hence the Infernal Veil grows in the disobedient Female:
Which Jesus rends & the whole Druid Law removes
   away
From the Inner Sanctuary: a False Holiness hid within
   the Center,
For the Sanctuary of Eden, is in the Camp: in the
   Outline,
In the Circumference: & every Minute Particular is
   Holy:
Embraces are Cominglings: from the Head even to the
   Feet;
And not a pompous High Priest entering by a Secret
   Place.

40

Jerusalem pined in her inmost soul over Wandering
   Reuben
As she slept in Beulahs Night hid by the Daughters of
   Beulah

PLATE 70

And this the form of mighty Hand sitting on Albions
   cliffs
Before the face of Albion, a mighty threatning Form.

His bosom wide & shoulders huge overspreading
   wondrous
Bear Three strong sinewy Necks & Three awful &
   terrible Heads

Three Brains in contradictory council brooding
    incessantly.
Neither daring to put in act its councils, fearing each-
    other,
Therefore rejecting Ideas as nothing & holding all
    Wisdom
To consist, in the agreements & disagree[me]nts of Ideas.
Plotting to devour Albions Body of Humanity & Love.

Such Form the aggregate of the Twelve Sons of Albion
    took; & such   10
Their appearance when combind: but often by birth-
    pangs & loud groans
They divide to Twelve: the key-bones & the chest
    dividing in pain
Disclose a hideous orifice; thence issuing the Giant-
    brood
Arise as the smoke of the furnace, shaking the rocks
    from sea to sea.
And there they combine into Three Forms, named
    Bacon & Newton & Locke,
In the Oak Groves of Albion which overspread all the
    Earth.

Imputing Sin & Righteousness to Individuals; Rahab
Sat deep within him hid: his Feminine Power unreveal'd
Brooding Abstract Philosophy, to destroy Imagination,
    the Divine-
-Humanity A Three-fold Wonder: feminine: most
    beautiful: Three-fold   20
Each within other. On her white marble & even Neck,
    her Heart
Inorb'd and bonified: with locks of shadowing modesty,
    shining
Over her beautiful Female features, soft flourishing in
    beauty
Beams mild, all love and all perfection, that when the
    lips

Recieve a kiss from Gods or Men, a threefold kiss
  returns
From the pressd loveliness: so her whole immortal form
  three-fold
Three-fold embrace returns: consuming lives of Gods
  & Men
In fires of beauty melting them as gold & silver in the
  furnace[.]
Her Brain enlabyrinths the whole heaven of her bosom
  & loins
To put in act what her Heart wills; O who can withstand
  her power   30
Her name is Vala in Eternity: in Time her name is
  Rahab

The Starry Heavens all were fled from the mighty limbs
  of Albion

PLATE 71

And above Albions Land was seen the Heavenly
  Canaan
As the Substance is to the Shadow: and above Albions
  Twelve Sons
Were seen Jerusalems Sons: and all the Twelve Tribes
  spreading
Over Albion. As the Soul is to the Body, so Jerusalems
  Sons,
Are to the Sons of Albion: and Jerusalem is Albions
  Emanation

What is Above is Within, for every-thing in Eternity is
  translucent:
The Circumference is Within: Without, is formed the
  Selfish Center
And the Circumference still expands going forward to
  Eternity.
And the Center has Eternal States! these States we now
  explore.

And these the Names of Albions Twelve Sons, & of his
  Twelve Daughters   10

With their Districts. Hand dwelt in Selsey & had
  Sussex & Surrey
And Kent & Middlesex: all their Rivers & their Hills, of
  flocks & herds:
Their Villages Towns Cities Sea-Ports Temples sublime
  Cathedrals;
All were his Friends & their Sons & Daughters
  intermarry in Beulah
For all are Men in Eternity. Rivers Mountains Cities
  Villages,
All are Human & when you enter into their Bosoms you
  walk
In Heavens & Earths; as in your own Bosom you bear
  your Heaven
And Earth, & all you behold, tho it appears Without it
  is Within
In your Imagination of which this World of Mortality
  is but a Shadow.

Hyle dwelt in Winchester comprehending Hants Dorset
  Devon Cornwall.   20
Their Villages Cities SeaPorts, their Corn fields &
  Gardens spacious
Palaces, Rivers & Mountains, and between Hand & Hyle
  arose
Gwendolen & Cambel who is Boadicea: they go abroad
  & return
Like lovely beams of light from the mingled affections
  of the Brothers
The Inhabitants of the whole Earth rejoice in their
  beautiful light.

Coban dwelt in Bath. Somerset Wiltshire
  Gloucestershire,
Obeyd his awful voice Ignoge is his lovely Emanation;
She adjoin'd with Gwantokes Children, soon lovely
  Cordella arose.
Gwantoke forgave & joyd over South Wales & all its
  Mountains.

Peachey had North Wales Shropshire Cheshire & the
    Isle of Man.   30
His Emanation is Mehetabel terrible & lovely upon the
    Mountains

Brertun had Yorkshire Durham Westmoreland & his
    Emanation
Is Ragan, she adjoind to Slade, & produced Gonorill far
    beaming.

Slade had Lincoln Stafford Derby Nottingham & his
    lovely
Emanation Gonorill rejoices over hills & rocks & woods
    & rivers.

Huttn had Warwick Northampton Bedford Buckingham
Leicester & Berkshire: & his Emanation is Gwinefred
    beautiful

Skofeld had Ely Rutland Cambridge Huntingdon
    Norfolk
Suffolk Hartford & Essex: & his Emanation is Gwinevera
Beautiful, she beams towards the east, all kinds of
    precious stones   40
And pearl, with instruments of music in holy Jerusalem

Kox had Oxford Warwick Wilts: his Emanation is
    Estrild:
Joind with Cordella she shines southward over the
    Atlantic.

Kotope had Hereford Stafford Worcester, & his
    Emanation
Is Sabrina joind with Mehetabel she shines west over
    America

Bowen had all Scotland, the Isles, Northumberland &
    Cumberland
His Emanation is Conwenna, she shines a triple form
Over the north with pearly beams gorgeous & terrible
Jerusalem & Vala rejoice in Bowen & Conwenna.

But the Four Sons of Jerusalem that never were Generated 50
Are Rintrah and Palamabron and Theotormon and
   Bromion. They
Dwell over the Four Provinces of Ireland in heavenly
   light
The Four Universities of Scotland, & in Oxford &
   Cambridge & Winchester

But now Albion is darkened & Jerusalem lies in ruins:
Above the Mountains of Albion, above the head of Los.

And Los shouted with ceaseless shoutings & his tears
   pourd down
His immortal cheeks, rearing his hands to heaven for aid
   Divine!
But he spoke not to Albion: fearing lest Albion should
   turn his Back
Against the Divine Vision: & fall over the Precipice of
   Eternal Death.
But he receded before Albion & before Vala weaving the
   Veil 60
With the iron shuttle of War among the rooted Oaks of
   Albion;
Weeping & shouting to the Lord day & night; and his
   Children
Wept round him as a flock silent Seven Days of
   Eternity

PLATE 72
And the Thirty-two Counties of the Four Provinces of
   Ireland
Are thus divided: The Four Counties are in the Four
   Camps
Munster South in Reubens Gate, Connaut West in
   Josephs Gate
Ulster North in Dans Gate, Leinster East in Judahs
   Gate

For Albion in Eternity has Sixteen Gates among his
   Pillars

But the Four towards the West were Walled up & the
    Twelve
That front the Four other Points were turned Four
    Square
By Los for Jerusalems sake & called the Gates of
    Jerusalem
Because Twelve Sons of Jerusalem fled successive thro
    the Gates
But the Four Sons of Jerusalem who fled not but
    remaind   10
Are Rintrah & Palamabron & Theotormon & Bromion
The Four that remain with Los to guard the Western
    Wall
And these Four remain to guard the Four Walls of
    Jerusalem
Whose foundations remain in the Thirty-two Counties
    of Ireland
And in Twelve Counties of Wales, & in the Forty
    Counties
Of England & in the Thirty-six Counties of Scotland

And the names of the Thirty-two Counties of Ireland
    are these
Under Judah & Issachar & Zebulun are Lowth Longford
Eastmeath Westmeath Dublin Kildare Kings County
Queens County Wicklow Catherloh Wexford Kilkenny   20
And those under Reuben & Simeon & Levi are these
Waterford Tipperary Cork Limerick Kerry Clare
And those under Ephraim Manasseh & Benjamin are
    these
Galway Roscommon Mayo Sligo Leitrim
And those under Dan Asher & Napthali are these
Donnegal Antrim Tyrone Fermanagh Armagh
    Londonderry
Down Managhan Cavan. These are the Land of Erin

All these Center in London & in Golgonooza, from
    whence

They are Created continually East & West & North &
    South
And from them are Created all the Nations of the Earth   30
Europe & Asia & Africa & America, in fury Fourfold!

And Thirty-two the Nations: to dwell in Jerusalems
    Gates
O Come ye Nations Come ye People Come up to
    Jerusalem
Return Jerusalem & dwell together as of old: Return
Return: O Albion let Jerusalem overspread all Nations
As in the times of old: O Albion awake: Reuben
    wanders
The Nations wait for Jerusalem, they look up for the
    Bride

France Spain Italy Germany Poland Russia Sweden
    Turkey
Arabia Palestine Persia Hindostan China Tartary
    Siberia
Egypt Lybia Ethiopia Guinea Caffraria Negroland
    Morocco   40
Congo Zaara Canada Greenland Carolina Mexico
Peru Patagonia Amazonia Brazil. Thirty-two Nations
And under these Thirty-two Classes of Islands in the
    Ocean
All the Nations Peoples & Tongues throughout all the
    Earth

And the Four Gates of Los surround the Universe
    Within and
Without; & whatever is visible in the Vegetable Earth,
    the same
Is visible in the Mundane Shell; reversd in mountain
    & vale
And a Son of Eden was set over each Daughter of
    Beulah to guard
In Albions Tomb the wondrous Creation: & the Four-
    gold Gate

Towards Beulah is to the South[.] Fenelon, Guion,
   Teresa,   50
Whitefield & Hervey, guard that Gate; with all the
   gentle Souls
Who guide the great Wine-press of Love; Four precious
   Stones that Gate:

PLATE 73

Such are Cathedrons golden Halls: in the City of
   Golgonooza

And Los's Furnaces howl loud; living: self-moving:
   lamenting
With fury & despair, & they stretch from South to
   North
Thro all the Four Points: Lo! the Labourers at the
   Furnaces
Rintrah & Palamabron, Theotormon & Bromion, loud
   labring
With the innumerable multitudes of Golgonooza, round
   the Anvils
Of Death. But how they came forth from the Furnaces
   & how long
Vast & severe the anguish eer they knew their Father;
   were
Long to tell & of the iron rollers, golden axle-trees &
   yokes
Of brass, iron chains & braces & the gold, silver &
   brass   10
Mingled or separate: for swords; arrows; cannons;
   mortars
The terrible ball: the wedge: the loud sounding hammer
   of destruction
The sounding flail to thresh: the winnow: to winnow
   kingdoms
The water wheel & mill of many innumerable wheels
   resistless
Over the Four fold Monarchy from Earth to the
   Mundane Shell.

Perusing Albions Tomb in the starry characters of Og &
  Anak:
To Create the lion & wolf the bear: the tyger &
  ounce:
To Create the wooly lamb & downy fowl & scaly serpent
The summer & winter: day & night: the sun & moon
  & stars
The tree: the plant: the flower: the rock: the stone: the
  metal: 20
Of Vegetative Nature: by their hard restricting
  condensations.

Where Luvahs World of Opakeness grew to a period:
  It
Became a Limit, a Rocky hardness without form & void
Accumulating without end: here Los who is of the
  Elohim
Opens the Furnaces of affliction in the Emanation
Fixing the Sexual into an ever-prolific Generation
Naming the Limit of Opakeness Satan & the Limit of
  Contraction
Adam, who is Peleg & Joktan: & Esau & Jacob: &
  Saul & David

Voltaire insinuates that these Limits are the cruel work
  of God
Mocking the Remover of Limits & the Resurrection of
  the Dead   30
Setting up Kings in wrath: in holiness of Natural
  Religion
Which Los with his mighty Hammer demolishes time
  on time
In miracles & wonders in the Four-fold Desart of
  Albion
Permanently Creating to be in Time Reveald &
  Demolishd
Satan Cain Tubal Nimrod Pharoh Priam Bladud Belin
Arthur Alfred the Norman Conqueror Richard John
[*Edward Henry Elizabeth James Charles William George*]

And all the Kings & Nobles of the Earth & all their
   Glories
These are Created by Rahab & Tirzah in Ulro: but
   around
These, to preserve them from Eternal Death Los
   Creates   40
Adam Noah Abraham Moses Samuel David Ezekiel
[*Pythagoras Socrates Euripedes Virgil Dante Milton*]
Dissipating the rocky forms of Death, by his thunderous
   Hammer[.]
As the Pilgrim passes while the Country permanent
   remains
So Men pass on: but States remain permanent for ever

The Spectres of the Dead howl round the porches of Los
In the terrible Family feuds of Albions cities & villages
To devour the Body of Albion, hungring & thirsting &
   ravning
The Sons of Los clothe them & feed, & provide houses
   & gardens
And every Human Vegetated Form in its inward recesses   50
Is a house of ple[as]antness & a garden of delight Built
   by the
Sons & Daughters of Los in Bowlahoola & in Cathedron

From London to York & Edinburgh the Furnaces rage
   terrible
Primrose Hill is the mouth of the Furnace & the Iron
   Door;
PLATE 74
The Four Zoa's clouded rage; Urizen stood by Albion
With Rintrah and Palamabron and Theotormon and
   Bromion
These Four are Verulam & London & York &
   Edinburgh
And the Four Zoa's are Urizen & Luvah & Tharmas &
   Urthona
In opposition deadly, and their Wheels in poisonous

And deadly stupor turn'd against each other loud &
  fierce
Entering into the Reasoning Power, forsaking
  Imagination
They became Spectres; & their Human Bodies were
  reposed
In Beulah, by the Daughters of Beulah with tears &
  lamentations

The Spectre is the Reasoning Power in Man; & when
  separated   10
From Imagination, and closing itself as in steel, in a
  Ratio
Of the Things of Memory, It thence frames Laws &
  Moralities
To destroy Imagination! the Divine Body, by
  Martyrdoms & Wars

Teach me O Holy Spirit the Testimony of Jesus! let me
Comprehend wonderous things out of the Divine Law[.]
I behold Babylon in the opening Streets of London, I
  behold
Jerusalem in ruins wandering about from house to house
This I behold the shudderings of death attend my steps
I walk up and down in Six Thousand Years: their
  Events are present before me
To tell how Los in grief & anger, whirling round his
  Hammer on high   20
Drave the Sons & Daughters of Albion from their
  ancient mountains
They became the Twelve Gods of Asia Opposing the
  Divine Vision

The Sons of Albion are Twelve: the Sons of Jerusalem
  Sixteen
I tell how Albions Sons by Harmonies of Concords &
  Discords
Opposed to Melody, and by Lights & Shades, opposed
  to Outline

And by Abstraction opposed to the Visions of
    Imagination
By cruel Laws divided Sixteen into Twelve Divisions
How Hyle roofd Los in Albions Cliffs by the Affections
    rent
Asunder & opposed to Thought, to draw Jerusalems
    Sons
Into the Vortex of his Wheels, therefore Hyle is called
    Gog   30
Age after age drawing them away towards Babylon

Babylon, the Rational Morality deluding to death the
    little ones
In strong temptations of stolen beauty; I tell how
    Reuben slept
On London Stone & the Daughters of Albion ran around
    admiring
His awful beauty: with Moral Virtue the fair deciever;
    offspring
Of Good & Evil, they divided him in love upon the
    Thames & sent
Him over Europe in streams of gore out of Cathedrons
    Looms
How Los drave them from Albion & they became
    Daughters of Canaan
Hence Albion was calld the Canaanite & all his Giant
    Sons.
Hence is my Theme. O Lord my Saviour, open thou
    the Gates   40
And I will lead forth thy Words, telling how the
    Daughters
Cut the Fibres of Reuben, how he rolld apart & took
    Root
In Bashan, terror-struck Albions Sons look toward
    Bashan
They have divided Simeon he also rolld apart in blood
Over the Nations till he took Root beneath the shining
    Looms

Of Albions Daughters in Philistea by the side of Amalek
They have divided Levi: he hath shot out into Forty
    eight Roots
Over the Land of Canaan: they have divided Judah
He hath took Root in Hebron, in the Land of Hand &
    Hyle
Dan: Napthali: Gad: Asher: Issachar: Zebulun: roll apart   50
From all the Nations of the Earth to dissipate into Non
    Entity

I see a Feminine Form arise from the Four terrible Zoas
Beautiful but terrible struggling to take a form of beauty
Rooted in Shechem: this is Dinah, the youthful form
    of Erin
The Wound I see in South Molton S[t]reet & Stratford
    place
Whence Joseph & Benjamin rolld apart away from the
    Nations
In vain they rolld apart; they are fixed into the Land of
    Cabul

PLATE 75
And Rahab Babylon the Great hath destroyed Jerusalem

Bath stood upon the Severn with Merlin & Bladud &
    Arthur
The Cup of Rahab in his hand: her Poisons Twenty-
    seven-fold

And all her Twenty-seven Heavens now hid & now
    reveal'd
Appear in strong delusive light of Time & Space drawn
    out
In shadowy pomp by the Eternal Prophet created
    evermore

For Los in Six Thousand Years walks up & down
    continually

That not one Moment of Time be lost & every
  revolution
Of Space he makes permanent in Bowlahoola &
  Cathedron.

And these the names of the Twenty-seven Heavens &
  their Churches   10
Adam, Seth, Enos, Cainan, Mahalaleel, Jared, Enoch,
Methuselah, Lamech; these are the Giants mighty,
  Hermaphroditic
Noah, Shem, Arphaxad, Cainan the Second, Salah,
  Heber,
Peleg, Reu, Serug, Nahor, Terah: these are the Female
  Males:
A Male within a Female hid as in an Ark & Curtains.
Abraham, Moses, Solomon, Paul, Constantine,
  Charlemaine,
Luther. these Seven are the Male Females: the Dragon
  Forms
The Female hid within a Male: thus Rahab is reveald
Mystery Babylon the Great: the Abomination of
  Desolation
Religion hid in War: a Dragon red, & hidden Harlot   20
But Jesus breaking thro' the Central Zones of Death &
  Hell
Opens Eternity in Time & Space; triumphant in Mercy

Thus are the Heavens formd by Los within the
  Mundane Shell
And where Luther ends Adam begins again in Eternal
  Circle
To awake the Prisoners of Death; to bring Albion
  again
With Luvah into light eternal, in his eternal day.

But now the Starry Heavens are fled from the mighty
  limbs of Albion

PLATE 77

TO THE CHRISTIANS

Devils are	I give you the end of a
False Religions	golden string,
'Saul Saul'	Only wind it into a ball:
'Why persecutest thou me.'	It will lead you in at
	Heavens gate,
	Built in Jerusalems wall.

We are told to abstain from fleshly desires that we may
lose no time from the Work of the Lord. Every moment
lost, is a moment that cannot be redeemed   every pleasure
that intermingles with the duty of our station is a folly
unredeemable & is planted like the seed of a wild flower
among our wheat. All the tortures of repentance, are
tortures of self-reproach on account of our leaving the
Divine Harvest to the Enemy, the struggles of intanglement
with incoherent roots. I know of no other Christianity and
of no other Gospel than the liberty both of body & mind   10
to exercise the Divine Arts of Imagination   Imagination
the real & eternal World of which this Vegetable Universe
is but a faint shadow & in which we shall live in our
Eternal or Imaginative Bodies, when these Vegetable
Mortal Bodies are no more. The Apostles knew of no other
Gospel. What were all their spiritual gifts? What is the
Divine Spirit? is the Holy Ghost any other than an
Intellectual Fountain? What is the Harvest of the Gospel
& its Labours? What is that Talent which it is a curse to
hide? What are the Treasures of Heaven which we are to   20
lay up for ourselves, are they any other than Mental
Studies & Performances? What are all the Gifts of the
Gospel, are they not all Mental Gifts? Is God a Spirit
who must be worshipped in Spirit & in Truth and are not
the Gifts of the Spirit Every-thing to Man? O ye Religious
discountenance every one among you who shall pretend to

despise Art & Science! I call upon you in the Name of
Jesus! What is the Life of Man but Art & Science? is it
Meat & Drink? is not the Body more than Raiment?
What is Mortality but the things relating to the Body,   30
which Dies? What is Immortality but the things relating to
the Spirit, which Lives Eternally! What is the Joy of
Heaven but Improvement in the things of the Spirit?
What are the Pains of Hell but Ignorance, Bodily Lust,
Idleness & devastation of the things of the Spirit[?]
Answer this to yourselves, & expel from among you those
who pretend to despise the labours of Art & Science which
alone are the labours of the Gospel: Is not this plain &
manifest to the thought? Can you think at all & not
pronounce heartily! That to Labour in Knowledge, is to   40
Build up Jerusalem: and to Despise Knowledge, is to
Despise Jerusalem & her Builders. And remember: He
who despises & mocks a Mental Gift in another; calling
it pride & selfishness & sin; mocks Jesus the giver of every
Mental Gift, which always appear to the ignorance-
loving Hypocrite, as Sins, but that which is a Sin in the
sight of cruel Man, is not so in the sight of our kind God.

Let every Christian as much as in him lies engage
himself openly & publicly before all the World in some
Mental pursuit for the Building up of Jerusalem   50

> I stood among my valleys of the south
> And saw a flame of fire, even as a Wheel
> Of fire surrounding all the heavens: it went
> From west to east against the current of
> Creation and devourd all things in its loud
> Fury & thundering course round heaven & earth
> By it the Sun was rolld into an orb:
> By it the Moon faded into a globe,
> Travelling thro the night: for from its dire
> And restless fury, Man himself shrunk up   10
> Into a little root a fathom long.
> And I asked a Watcher & a Holy-One

Its Name? he answerd. It is the Wheel of Religion
I wept & said. Is this the law of Jesus
This terrible devouring sword turning every way
He answerd; Jesus died because he strove
Against the current of this Wheel: its Name
Is Caiaphas, the dark Preacher of Death
Of sin, of sorrow, & of punishment;
Opposing Nature! It is Natural Religion   20
But Jesus is the bright Preacher of Life
Creating Nature from this fiery Law,
By self-denial & forgiveness of Sin.
Go therefore, cast out devils in Christs name
Heal thou the sick of spiritual disease
Pity the evil, for thou art not sent
To smite with terror & with punishments
Those that are sick, like to the Pharisees
Crucifying & encompassing sea & land
For proselytes to tyranny & wrath.   30
But to the Publicans & Harlots go!
Teach them True Happiness, but let no curse
Go forth out of thy mouth to blight their peace
For Hell is opend to Heaven; thine eyes beheld
The dungeons burst & the Prisoners set free.

England! awake! awake! awake!
  Jerusalem thy Sister calls!
Why wilt thou sleep the sleep of death?
  And close her from thy ancient walls.

      Thy hills & valleys felt her feet,
          Gently upon their bosoms move:
      Thy gates beheld sweet Zions ways;
          Then was a time of joy and love.

    And now the time returns again:
      Our souls exult & Londons towers,   10
    Receive the Lamb of God to dwell
      In Englands green & pleasant bowers.

PLATE 78

JERUSALEM

C 4

The Spectres of Albions Twelve Sons revolve
    mightily
Over the Tomb & over the Body: ravning to devour
The Sleeping Humanity. Los with his mace of iron
Walks round: loud his threats, loud his blows fall
On the rocky Spectres, as the Potter breaks the
    potsherds;
Dashing in pieces Self-righteousnesses: driving them
    from Albions
Cliffs: dividing them into Male & Female forms in his
    Furnaces
And on his Anvils: lest they destroy the Feminine
    Affections
They are broken. Loud howl the Spectres in his iron
    Furnace

While Los laments at his dire labours, viewing Jerusalem,   10
Sitting before his Furnaces clothed in sackcloth of hair;
Albions Twelve Sons surround the Forty-two Gates of
    Erin,
In terrible armour, raging against the Lamb & against
    Jerusalem,
Surrounding them with armies to destroy the Lamb of
    God.
They took their Mother Vala, and they crown'd her with
    gold:
They namd her Rahab, & gave her power over the
    Earth
The Concave Earth round Golgonooza in Entuthon
    Benython,
Even to the stars exalting her Throne, to build beyond
    the Throne

Of God and the Lamb, to destroy the Lamb & usurp
   the Throne of God
Drawing their Ulro Voidness round the Four-fold
   Humanity   20

Naked Jerusalem lay before the Gates upon Mount Zion
The Hill of Giants, all her foundations levelld with the
   dust!
Her Twelve Gates thrown down: her children carried
   into captivity
Herself in chains: this from within was seen in a dismal
   night
Outside, unknown before in Beulah, & the twelve gates
   were fill'd
With blood; from Japan eastward to the Giants causway,
   west
In Erins Continent: and Jerusalem wept upon Euphrates
   banks
Disorganizd; an evanescent shade, scarce seen or heard
   among
Her childrens Druid Temples dropping with blood
   wanderd weeping!
And thus her voice went forth in the darkness of
   Philisthea.   30

My brother & my father are no more! God hath
   forsaken me
The arrows of the Almighty pour upon me & my
   children
I have sinned and am an outcast from the Divine
   Presence!
PLATE 79
My tents are fall'n! my pillars are in ruins! my children
   dashd
Upon Egypts iron floors, & the marble pavements of
   Assyria;
I melt my soul in reasonings among the towers of
   Heshbon;
Mount Zion is become a cruel rock & no more dew

Nor rain: no more the spring of the rock appears: but cold

Hard & obdurate are the furrows of the mountain of wine & oil:

The mountain of blessing is itself a curse & an astonishment:

The hills of Judea are fallen with me into the deepest hell

Away from the Nations of the Earth, & from the Cities of the Nations;

I walk to Ephraim, I seek for Shiloh: I walk like a lost sheep

Among precipices of despair: in Goshen I seek for light 10

In vain: and in Gilead for a physician and a comforter.

Goshen hath followd Philistea: Gilead hath joind with Og!

They are become narrow places in a little and dark land:

How distant far from Albion! his hills & his valleys no more

Recieve the feet of Jerusalem: they have cast me quite away:

And Albion is himself shrunk to a narrow rock in the midst of the sea!

The plains of Sussex & Surrey, their hills of flocks & herds

No more seek to Jerusalem nor to the sound of my Holy-ones.

The Fifty-two Counties of England are hardend against me 20

As if I was not their Mother, they despise me & cast me out

London coverd the whole Earth. England encompassd the Nations:

And all the Nations of the Earth were seen in the Cities of Albion:

My pillars reachd from sea to sea: London beheld me come

From my east & from my west; he blessed me and gave

His children to my breasts, his sons & daughters to my
    knees
His aged parents sought me out in every city & village:
They discernd my countenance with joy! they shewd me
    to their sons
Saying Lo Jerusalem is here! she sitteth in our secret
    chambers
Levi and Judah & Issachar: Ephra[i]m, Manasseh, Gad
    and Dan   30
Are seen in our hills & valleys: they keep our flocks &
    herds:
They watch them in the night: and the Lamb of God
    appears among us!
The river Severn stayd his course at my command:
Thames pourd his waters into my basons and baths:
Medway mingled with Kishon: Thames recievd the
    heavenly Jordan
Albion gave me to the whole Earth to walk up & down;
    to pour
Joy upon every mountain, to teach songs to the shepherd
    & plowman
I taught the ships of the Sea to sing the songs of Zion.
Italy saw me, in sublime astonishment: France was
    wholly mine:
As my garden & as my secret bath; Spain was my
    heavenly couch: 40
I slept in his golden hills: the Lamb of God met me
    there.
There we walked as in our secret chamber among our
    little ones
They looked upon our loves with joy: they beheld our
    secret joys:
With holy raptures of adoration rapd sublime in the
    Visions of God:
Germany; Poland & the North wooed my footsteps they
    found
My gates in all their mountains & my curtains in all
    their vales

The furniture of their houses was the furniture of
my chamber

Turkey & Grecia saw my instr[u]ments of music, they
arose

They siezd the harp: the flute: the mellow horn of
Jerusalems joy

They sounded thanksgivings in my courts: Egypt &
Lybia heard 50

The swarthy sons of Ethiopia stood round the Lamb of
God

Enquiring for Jerusalem: he led them up my steps to my
altar:

And thou America! I once beheld thee but now behold
no more

Thy golden mountains where my Cherubim &
Seraphim rejoicd

Together among my little-ones. But now, my Altars run
with blood!

My fires are corrupt! my incense is a cloudy pestilence

Of seven diseases! Once a continual cloud of salvation,
rose

From all my myriads; once the Four-fold World
rejoicd among

The pillars of Jerusalem, between my winged Cherubim:

But now I am closd out from them in the narrow
passages 60

Of the valleys of destruction, into a dark land of pitch &
bitumen.

From Albions Tomb afar and from the four-fold
wonders of God

Shrunk to a narrow doleful form in the dark land of
Cabul;

There is Reuben & Gad & Joseph & Judah & Levi,
closd up

In narrow vales: I walk & count the bones of my
beloveds

Along the Valley of Destruction, among these Druid
Temples

Which overspread all the Earth in patriarchal pomp &
    cruel pride
Tell me O Vala thy purposes; tell me wherefore thy
    shuttles
Drop with the gore of the slain; why Euphrates is red
    with blood
Wherefore in dreadful majesty & beauty outside appears   70
Thy Masculine from thy Feminine hardening against the
    heavens
To devour the Human! Why dost thou weep upon the
    wind among
These cruel Druid Temples: O Vala! Humanity is far
    above
Sexual organization; & the Visions of the Night of
    Beulah
Where Sexes wander in dreams of bliss among the
    Emanations
Where the Masculine & Feminine are nurs'd into Youth &
    Maiden
By the tears & smiles of Beulahs Daughters till the time
    of Sleep is past.
Wherefore then do you realize these nets of beauty &
    delusion
In open day to draw the souls of the Dead into the light,
Till Albion is shut out from every Nation under
    Heaven.   80
PLATE 80
Encompassd by the frozen Net and by the rooted Tree
I walk weeping in pangs of a Mothers torment for her
    Children:
I walk in affliction: I am a worm, and no living soul!
A worm going to eternal torment: raisd up in a night
To an eternal night of pain, lost! lost! lost! for ever!

Beside her Vala howld upon the winds in pride of
    beauty
Lamenting among the timbrels of the Warriors: among
    the Captives

In cruel holiness, and her lamenting songs were from Arnon
And Jordan to Euphrates. Jerusalem followd trembling
Her children in captivity, listening to Valas lamentation 10
In the thick cloud & darkness, & the voice went forth from
The cloud. O rent in sunder from Jerusalem the Harlot daughter!
In an eternal condemnation in fierce burning flames
Of torment unendurable: and if once a Delusion be found
Woman must perish & the Heavens of Heavens remain no more

My Father gave to me command to murder Albion
In unreviving Death; my Love, my Luvah orderd me in night
To murder Albion the King of Men, he fought in battles fierce
He conquerd Luvah my beloved: he took me and my Father
He slew them: I revived them to life in my warm bosom 20
He saw them issue from my bosom, dark in Jealousy
He burnd before me: Luvah framd the Knife & Luvah gave
The Knife into his daughters hand: such thing was never known
Before in Albions land, that one should die a death never to be reviv'd
For in our battles we the Slain men view with pity and love:
We soon revive them in the secret of our tabernacles
But I Vala, Luvahs daughter, keep his body embalmd in moral laws
With spices of sweet odours of lovely jealous stupefaction:
Within my bosom, lest he arise to life & slay my Luvah
Pity me then O Lamb of God! O Jesus pity me! 30

Come into Luvahs Tents, and seek not to revive the
  Dead!

So sang she: and the Spindle turnd furious as she sang:
The Children of Jerusalem the Souls of those who sleep
Were caught into the flax of her Distaff, & in her Cloud
To weave Jerusalem a body according to her will
A Dragon form on Zion Hills most ancient promontory

The Spindle turnd in blood & fire: loud sound the
  trumpets
Of war: the cymbals play loud before the Captains
With Cambel & Gwendolen in dance and solemn song
The Cloud of Rahab vibrating with the Daughters of
  Albion   40
Los saw terrified, melted with pity & divided in wrath
He sent them over the narrow seas in pity and love
Among the Four Forests of Albion which overspread all
  the Earth
They go forth & return swift as a flash of lightning,
Among the tribes of warriors: among the Stones of
  power!
Against Jerusalem they rage thro all the Nations of
  Europe
Thro Italy & Grecia, to Lebanon & Persia & India.

The Serpent Temples thro the Earth, from the wide
  Plain of Salisbury
Resound with cries of Victims, shouts & songs & dying
  groans
And flames of dusky fire, to Amalek, Canaan and Moab[.]   50
And Rahab like a dismal and indefinite hovering Cloud
Refusd to take a definite form. she hoverd over all the
  Earth
Calling the definite, sin: defacing every definite form;
Invisible, or Visible, stretchd out in length or spread in
  breadth:
Over the Temples drinking groans of victims weeping
  in pity,
And joying in the pity, howling over Jerusalems walls.

Hand slept on Skiddaws top: drawn by the love of
  beautiful
Cambel: his bright, beaming Counterpart, divided from
  him
And her delusive light beamd fierce above the
  Mountain,
Soft: invisible: drinking his sighs in sweet intoxication: 60
Drawing out fibre by fibre: returning to Albions Tree
At night: and in the morning to Skiddaw; she sent him
  over
Mountainous Wales into the Loom of Cathedron fibre
  by fibre:
He ran in tender nerves across Europe to Jerusalems
  Shade,
To weave Jerusalem a Body repugnant to the Lamb.

Hyle on East Moor in rocky Derbyshire, rav'd to the
  Moon
For Gwendolen: she took up in bitter tears his anguishd
  heart,
That apparent to all in Eternity, glows like the Sun in
  the breast:
She hid it in his ribs & back: she hid his tongue with
  teeth
In terrible convulsions pitying & gratified drunk with
  pity   70
Glowing with loveliness before him, becoming apparent
According to his changes: she roll'd his kidneys round
Into two irregular forms: and looking on Albions dread
  Tree,
She wove two vessels of seed, beautiful as Skiddaws
  snow;

Giving them bends of self interest & selfish natural virtue:
She hid them in his loins; raving he ran among the
  rocks,
Compelld into a shape of Moral Virtue against the
  Lamb.
The invisible lovely one giving him a form according to

His Law a form against the Lamb of God opposd to
  Mercy
And playing in the thunderous Loom in sweet
  intoxication   80
Filling cups of silver & crystal with shrieks & cries,
  with groans
And dolorous sobs: the wine of lovers in the Wine-press
  of Luvah

O sister Cambel said Gwendolen, as their long beaming
  light
Mingled above the Mountain[:] what shall we do to keep
These awful forms in our soft bands: distracted with
  trembling

PLATE 81

I have mockd those who refused cruelty & I have
  admired
The cruel Warrior. I have refused to give love to Merlin
  the piteous.
He brings to me the Images of his Love & I reject in
  chastity
And turn them out into the streets for Harlots to be food
To the stern Warrior. I am become perfect in beauty
  over my Warrior
For Men are caught by Love: Woman is caught by Pride
That Love may only be obtain in the passages of Death.
Let us look: let us examine: is the Cruel become an
  Infant
Or is he still a cruel Warrior? look Sisters, look! O
  piteous
I have destroyd Wandring Reuben who strove to bind
  my Will   10
I have stripd off Josephs beautiful integument for my
  Beloved,
The Cruel-one of Albion: to clothe him in gems of my
  Zone
I have named him Jehovah of Hosts. Humanity is
  become

A weeping Infant in ruind lovely Jerusalems folding
    Cloud:

In Heaven Love begets Love! but Fear is the Parent of
    Earthly Love!
And he who will not bend to Love must be subdud by
    Fear,

PLATE 82

I have heard Jerusalems groans; from Vala's cries &
    lamentations
I gather our eternal fate: Outcasts from life and love:
Unless we find a way to bind these awful Forms to our
Embrace we shall perish annihilate, discoverd our
    Delusions.
Look I have wrought without delusion: Look! I have
    wept!
And given soft milk mingled together with the spirits of
    flocks
Of lambs and doves, mingled together in cups and
    dishes
Of painted clay; the mighty Hyle is become a weeping
    infant;
Soon shall the Spectres of the Dead follow my weaving
    threads.

The Twelve Daughters of Albion attentive listen in
    secret shades   10
On Cambridge and Oxford beaming soft uniting with
    Rahabs cloud
While Gwendolen spoke to Cambel turning soft the
    spinning reel:
Or throwing the wingd shuttle; or drawing the cords
    with softest songs
The golden cords of the Looms animate beneath their
    touches soft,
Along the Island white, among the Druid Temples,
    while Gwendolen
Spoke to the Daughters of Albion standing on Skiddaws
    top.

So saying she took a Falsehood & hid it in her left hand:
To entice her Sisters away to Babylon on Euphrates.
And thus she closed her left hand and utterd her Falshood:
Forgetting that Falshood is prophetic, she hid her hand
    behind her,   20
Upon her back behind her loins & thus utterd her
    Deceit.

I heard Enitharmon say to Los: Let the Daughters of
    Albion
Be scatterd abroad and let the name of Albion be
    forgotten:
Divide them into three: name them Amalek Canaan &
    Moab:
Let Albion remain a desolation without an inhabitant:
And let the Looms of Enitharmon & the Furnaces of
    Los
Create Jerusalem, & Babylon & Egypt & Moab &
    Amalek,
And Helle & Hesperia & Hindostan & China & Japan.
But hide America, for a Curse an Altar of Victims & a
    Holy Place.
See Sisters Canaan is pleasant, Egypt is as the Garden
    of Eden: 30
Babylon is our chief desire, Moab our bath in summer:
Let us lead the stems of this Tree let us plant it before
    Jerusalem
To judge the Friend of Sinners to death without the
    Veil:
To cut her off from America, to close up her secret Ark:
And the fury of Man exhaust in War, Woman permanent
    remain
See how the fires of our loins point eastward to Babylon
Look, Hyle is become an infant Love: look! behold! see
    him lie!
Upon my bosom, look! here is the lovely wayward form
That gave me sweet delight by his torments beneath my
    Veil;

By the fruit of Albions Tree I have fed him with sweet
    milk   40
By contentions of the mighty for Sacrifice of Captives;
Humanity the Great Delusion: is changd to War &
    Sacrifice:
I have naild his hands on Beth Rabbim & his [feet] on
    Heshbons Wall:
O that I could live in his sight: O that I could bind him
    to my arm.

So saying: She drew aside her Veil from Mam-Tor to
    Dovedale
Discovering her own perfect beauty to the Daughters
    of Albion
And Hyle a winding Worm beneath [*her Loom upon the
scales.*
Hyle was become a winding Worm :] & not a weeping
    Infant.
Trembling & pitying she screamd & fled upon the wind:
Hyle was a winding Worm and herself perfect in
    beauty: 50
The desarts tremble at his wrath: they shrink themselves
    in fear.

Cambel trembled with jealousy: she trembled! she envied!
The envy ran thro Cathedrons Looms into the Heart
Of mild Jerusalem, to destroy the Lamb of God.
    Jerusalem
Languishd upon Mount Olivet, East of mild Zions Hill.

Los saw the envious blight above his Seventh Furnace
On Londons Tower on the Thames: he drew Cambel in
    wrath,
Into his thundering Bellows, heaving it for a loud blast!
And with the blast of his Furnace upon fishy Billingsgate,
Beneath Albions fatal Tree, before the Gate of Los: 60
Shewd her the fibres of her beloved to ameliorate
The envy; loud she labourd in the Furnace of fire,
To form the mighty form of Hand according to her will.

In the Furnaces of Los & in the Wine-press treading
  day & night

Naked among the human clusters: bringing wine of
  anguish
To feed the afflicted in the Furnaces: she minded not
The raging flames, tho she returnd [*consumd day after
  day*
A redning skeleton in howling woe :] instead of beauty
Defo[r]mity: she gave her beauty to another: bearing
  abroad
Her struggling torment in her iron arms: and like a
  chain,   70
Binding his wrists & ankles with the iron arms of love.

Gwendolen saw the Infant in her siste[r]s arms; she howld
Over the forests with bitter tears, and over the winding
  Worm
Repentant: and she also in the eddying wind of Los's
  Bellows
Began her dolorous task of love in the Wine-press of
  Luvah
To form the Worm into a form of love by tears & pain.
The Sisters saw! trembling ran thro their Looms!
  soften[in]g mild
Towards London: then they saw the Furna[c]es opend,
  & in tears
Began to give their souls away in the Furna[c]es of
  affliction.

Los saw & was comforted at his Furnaces uttering thus
  his voice.   80

I know I am Urthona keeper of the Gates of Heaven,
And that I can at will expatiate in the Gardens of bliss;
But pangs of love draw me down to my loins which are
Become a fountain of veiny pipes: O Albion! my
  brother!
PLATE 83
Corrup[t]ability appears upon thy limbs, and never more

Can I arise and leave thy side, but labour here incessant
Till thy awaking: yet alas I shall forget Eternity:
Against the Patriarchal pomp and cruelty, labouring
   incessant
I shall become an Infant horror. Enion! Tharmas!
   friends
Absorb me not in such dire grief: O Albion, my brother!
Jerusalem hungers in the desart: affection to her children!
The scorn'd and contemnd youthful girl, where shall
   she fly?
Sussex shuts up her Villages. Hants, Devon & Wilts
Surrounded with masses of stone in orderd forms,
   determine then   10
A form for Vala and a form for Luvah, here on the
   Thames
Where the Victim nightly howls beneath the Druids
   knife:
A Form of Vegetation, nail them down on the stems of
   Mystery:
O when shall the Saxon return with the English his
   redeemed brother!
O when shall the Lamb of God descend among the
   Reprobate!
I woo to Amalek to protect my fugitives[.] Amalek
   trembles:
I call to Canaan & Moab in my night watches, they
   mourn:
They listen not to my cry, they rejo[i]ce among their
   warriors
Woden and Thor and Friga wholly consume my Saxons:
On their enormous Altars built in the terrible north: 20
From Irelands rocks to Scandinavia Persia and Tartary:
From the Atlantic Sea to the universal Erythrean.
Found ye London! enormous City! weeps thy River?
Upon his parent bosom lay thy little ones O Land
Forsaken. Surrey and Sussex are Enitharmons Chamber.
Where I will build her a Couch of repose & my pillars
Shall surround her in beautiful labyrinths: Oothoon?

Where hides my child? in Oxford hidest thou with
    Antamon?
In graceful hidings of error: in merciful deceit
Lest Hand the terrible destroy his Affection. thou hidest
    her: 30
In chaste appearances for sweet deceits of love &
    modesty
Immingled, interwoven, glistening to the sickening
    sight.
Let Cambel and her Sisters sit within the Mundane
    Shell:
Forming the fluctuating Globe according to their will.
According as they weave the little embryon nerves &
    veins
The Eye, the little Nostrils, & the delicate Tongue &
    Ears
Of labyrinthine intricacy: so shall they fold the World
That whatever is seen upon the Mundane Shell, the
    same
Be seen upon the Fluctuating Earth woven by the
    Sisters.
And sometimes the Earth shall roll in the Abyss &
    sometimes   40
Stand in the Center & sometimes stretch flat in the
    Expanse,
According to the will of the lovely Daughters of Albion.
Sometimes it shall assimilate with mighty Golgonooza:
Touching its summits: & sometimes divided roll apart.
As a beautiful Veil so these Females shall fold & unfold
According to their will the outside surface of the Earth
An outside shadowy Surface superadded to the real
    Surface;
Which is unchangeable for ever & ever Amen: so be it!
Separate Albions Sons gently from their Emanations,
Weaving bowers of delight on the current of infant
    Thames   50
Where the old Parent still retains his youth as I alas!
Retain my youth eight thousand and five hundred years.

The labourer of ages in the Valleys of Despair:
The land is markd for desolation & unless we plant
The seeds of Cities & of Villages in the Human bosom
Albion must be a rock of blood: mark ye the points
Where Cities shall remain & where Villages[;] for the
    rest:
It must lie in confusion till Albions time of awaking.
Place the Tribes of Llewellyn in America for a hiding
    place:
Till sweet Jerusalem emanates again into Eternity   60
The night falls thick: I go upon my watch: be attentive:
The Sons of Albion go forth; I follow from my
    Furnaces:
That they return no more: that a place be prepard on
    Euphrates
Listen to your Watchmans voice: sleep not before the
    Furnaces
Eternal Death stands at the door. O God pity our
    labours.

So Los spoke, to the Daughters of Beulah while his
    Emanation
Like a faint rainbow waved before him in the awful
    gloom
Of London City on the Thames from Surrey Hills to
    Highgate:
Swift turn the silver spindles, & the golden weights play
    soft
And lulling harmonies beneath the Looms, from
    Caithness in the north   70
To Lizard-point & Dover in the south: his Emanation
Joy'd in the many weaving threads in bright Cathedrons
    Dome
Weaving the Web of life for Jerusalem, the Web of life
Down flowing into Entuthons Vales glistens with soft
    affections.

While Los arose upon his Watch, and down from
    Golgonooza

Putting on his golden sandals to walk from mountain
  to mountain,
He takes his way, girding himself with gold & in his
  hand
Holding his iron mace: The Spectre remains attentive
Alternate they watch in night: alternate labour in day
Before the Furnaces labouring, while Los all night
  watches   80
The stars rising & setting, & the meteors & terrors of
  night.
With him went down the Dogs of Leutha, at his feet
They lap the water of the trembling Thames then
  follow swift
And thus he heard the voice of Albions daughters on
  Euphrates,

Our Father Albions land: O it was a lovely land! & the
  Daughters of Beulah
Walked up and down in its green mountains: but Hand
  is fled
Away: & mighty Hyle: & after them Jerusalem is gone:
  Awake
PLATE 84
Highgates heights & Hampsteads, to Poplar Hackney &
  Bow
To Islington & Paddington & the Brook of Albions River
We builded Jerusalem as a City & a Temple: from
  Lambeth
We began our Foundations; lovely Lambeth! O lovely
  Hills
Of Camberwell, we shall behold you no more in glory &
  pride
For Jerusalem lies in ruins & the Furnaces of Los are
  builded there
You are now shrunk up to a narrow Rock in the midst
  of the Sea
But here we build Babylon on Euphrates, compelld to
  build

And to inhabit, our Little-ones to clothe in armour of
   the gold
Of Jerusalems Cherubims & to forge them swords of
   her Altars   10
I see London blind & age-bent begging thro the Streets
Of Babylon, led by a child, his tears run down his beard
The voice of Wandering Reuben ecchoes from street to
   street
In all the Cities of the Nations Paris Madrid Amsterdam

The Corner of Broad Street weeps; Poland Street
   languishes
To Great Queen Street & Lincolns Inn, all is distress &
   woe.
           [three lines gouged out irrecoverably]
The night falls thick Hand comes from Albion in his
   strength   20
He combines into a Mighty-one the Double Molech &
   Chemosh
Marching thro Egypt in his fury the East is pale at his
   course
The Nations of India, the Wild Tartar that never knew
   Man
Starts from his lofty places & casts down his tents & flees
   away
But we woo him all the night in songs, O Los come
   forth O Los
Divide us from these terrors & give us power them to
   subdue
Arise upon thy Watches let us see thy Globe of fire
On Albions Rocks & let thy voice be heard upon
   Euphrates.

Thus sang the Daughters in lamentation, uniting into
   One
With Rahab as she turnd the iron Spindle of destruction.   30

Terrified at the Sons of Albion they took the Falshood
   which
Gwendolen hid in her left hand, it grew & grew till it

PLATE 85

Became a Space & an Allegory around the Winding
    Worm[.]
They namd it Canaan & built for it a tender Moon
Los smild with joy thinking on Enitharmon & he
    brought
Reuben from his twelvefold wandrings & led him into
    it
Planting the Seeds of the Twelve Tribes & Moses &
    David
And gave a Time & Revolution to the Space Six
    Thousand Years
He calld it Divine Analogy, for in Beulah the Feminine
Emanations Create Space, the Masculine Create Time, &
    plant
The Seeds of beauty in the Space: listning to their
    lamentation
Los walks upon his ancient Mountains in the deadly
    darkness   10
Among his Furnaces directing his laborious Myriads
    watchful
Looking to the East: & his voice is heard over the
    whole Earth
As he watches the Furnaces by night, & directs the
    labourers

And thus Los replies upon his Watch: the Valleys listen
    silent:
The Stars stand still to hear: Jerusalem & Vala cease to
    mourn:
His voice is heard from Albion: the Alps & Appenines
Listen: Hermon & Lebanon bow their crowned heads
Babel & Shinar look toward the Western Gate, they sit
    down
Silent at his voice: they view the red Globe of fire in
    Los's hand
As he walks from Furnace to Furnace directing the
    Labourers   20

And this is the Song of Los, the Song that he sings on
   his Watch

O lovely mild Jerusalem! O Shiloh of Mount Ephraim!
I see thy Gates of precious stones: thy Walls of gold &
   silver
Thou art the soft reflected Image of the Sleeping Man
Who stretchd on Albions rocks reposes amidst his
   Twenty-eight
Cities: where Beulah lovely terminates, in the hills &
   valleys of Albion
Cities not yet embodied in Time and Space: plant ye
The Seeds O Sisters in the bosom of Time & Spaces
   womb
To spring up for Jerusalem: lovely Shadow of Sleeping
   Albion
Why wilt thou rend thyself apart & build an Earthly
   Kingdom   30
To reign in pride & to opress & to mix the Cup of
   Delusion
O thou that dwellest with Babylon! Come forth O
   lovely-one
PLATE 86
I see thy Form O lovely mild Jerusalem, Wingd with
   Six Wings
In the opacous Bosom of the Sleeper, lovely Three-fold
In Head & Heart & Reins three Universes of love &
   beauty
Thy forehead bright: Holiness to the Lord, with
   Gates of pearl
Reflects Eternity beneath thy azure wings of feathery
   down
Ribbd delicate & clothd with featherd gold & azure &
   purple
From thy white shoulders shadowing, purity in holiness!
Thence featherd with soft crimson of the ruby bright as
   fire
Spreading into the azure Wings which like a canopy

Bends over thy immortal Head in which Eternity
   dwells   10
Albion beloved Land; I see thy mountains & thy hills
And valleys & thy pleasant Cities Holiness to the Lord
I see the Spectres of thy Dead O Emanation of Albion.

Thy Bosom white, translucent coverd with immortal
   gems
A sublime ornament not obscuring the outlines of beauty
Terrible to behold for thy extreme beauty & perfection
Twelve-fold here all the Tribes of Israel I behold
Upon the Holy Land: I see the River of Life & Tree of
   Life
I see the New Jerusalem descending out of Heaven
Between thy Wings of gold & silver featherd immortal   20
Clear as the rainbow, as the cloud of the Suns tabernacle

Thy Reins coverd with Wings translucent sometimes
   covering
And sometimes spread abroad reveal the flames of holiness
Which like a robe covers: & like a Veil of Seraphim
In flaming fire unceasing burns from Eternity to
   Eternity
Twelvefold I there behold Israel in her Tents
A Pillar of a Cloud by day: a Pillar of fire by night
Guides them: there I behold Moab & Ammon &
   Amalek
There Bells of silver round thy knees living articulate
Comforting sounds of love & harmony & on thy feet   30
Sandals of gold & pearl, & Egypt & Assyria before me
The Isles of Javan, Philistea, Tyre and Lebanon
Thus Los sings upon his Watch walking from Furnace to
   Furnace.
He siezes his Hammer every hour, flames surround him
   as
He beats: seas roll beneath his feet, tempests muster
Arou[n]d his head, the thick hail stones stand ready to
   obey
His voice in the black cloud, his Sons labour in thunders

At his Furnaces; his Daughters at their Looms sing woes[.]
His Emanation separates in milky fibres agonizing
Among the golden Looms of Cathedron sending fibres of
    love   40
From Golgonooza with sweet visions for Jerusalem,
    wanderer.

Nor can any consummate bliss without being
    Generated
On Earth; of those whose Emanations weave the loves
Of Beulah for Jerusalem & Shiloh, in immortal
    Golgonooza
Concentering in the majestic form of Erin in eternal
    tears
Viewing the Winding Worm on the Desarts of Great
    Tartary
Viewing Los in his shudderings, pouring balm on his
    sorrows
So dread is Los's fury, that none dare him to approach
Without becoming his Children in the Furnaces of
    affliction

And Enitharmon like a faint rainbow waved before him   50
Filling with Fibres from his loins which reddend with
    desire
Into a Globe of blood beneath his bosom trembling in
    darkness
Of Albions clouds, he fed it, with his tears & bitter
    groans
Hiding his Spectre in invisibility from the timorous
    Shade
Till it became a separated cloud of beauty grace & love
Among the darkness of his Furnaces dividing asunder
    till
She separated stood before him a lovely Female weeping
Even Enitharmon separated outside, & his Loins closed
And heal'd after the separation: his pains he soon forgot:
Lured by her beauty outside of himself in shadowy grief.

Two Wills they had; Two Intellects: & not as in times
    of old.   60

Silent they wanderd hand in hand like two Infants
    wandring
From Enion in the desarts, terrified at each others beauty
Envying each other yet desiring, in all devouring Love,
PLATE 87
Repelling weeping Enion blind & age-bent into the
    fourfold
Desarts. Los first broke silence & begun to utter his
    love

O lovely Enitharmon: I behold thy graceful forms
Moving beside me till intoxicated with the woven
    labyrinth
Of beauty & perfection my wild fibres shoot in veins
Of blood thro all my nervous limbs. soon overgrown in
    roots

I shall be closed from thy sight, sieze therefore in thy
    hand
The small fibres as they shoot around me draw out in pity
And let them run on the winds of thy bosom: I will fix
    them
With pulsations, we will divide them into Sons &
    Daughters   10
To live in thy Bosoms translucence as in an eternal
    morning

Enitharmon answerd. No! I will sieze thy Fibres &
    weave
Them: not as thou wilt but as I will, for I will Create
A round Womb beneath my bosom lest I also be
    overwoven
With Love; be thou assured I never will be thy slave
Let Mans delight be Love; but Womans delight be
    Pride[.]
In Eden our loves were the same here they are opposite

I have Loves of my own I will weave them in Albions
   Spectre
Cast thou in Jerusalems shadows thy Loves! silk of liquid
Rubies Jacinths Crysolites: issuing from thy Furnaces.
   While   20
Jerusalem divides thy care: while thou carest for
   Jerusalem
Know that I never will be thine: also thou hidest Vala
From her these fibres shoot to shut me in a Grave.
You are Albions Victim, he has set his Daughter in your
   path

PLATE 88
Los answerd sighing like the Bellows of his Furnaces

I care not! the swing of my Hammer shall measure the
   starry round[.]
When in Eternity Man converses with Man they enter
Into each others Bosom (which are Universes of
   delight)
In mutual interchange, and first their Emanations meet
Surrounded by their Children, if they embrace &
   comingle
The Human Four-fold Forms mingle also in thunders of
   Intellect
But if the Emanations mingle not; with storms &
   agitations
Of earthquakes & consuming fires they roll apart in fear
For Man cannot unite with Man but by their
   Emanations   10
Which stand both Male & Female at the Gates of each
   Humanity
How then can I ever again be united as Man with Man
While thou my Emanation refusest my Fibres of
   dominion?
When Souls mingle & join thro all the Fibres of
   Brotherhood
Can there be any secret joy on Earth greater than this?

Enitharmon answerd: This is Womans World, nor need
    she any
Spectre to defend her from Man. I will Create secret
    places
And the masculine names of the places Merlin &
    Arthur.
A triple Female Tabernacle for Moral Law I weave
That he who loves Jesus may loathe terrified Female
    love   20
Till God himself become a Male subservient to the
    Female.

She spoke in scorn & jealousy, alternate torments; and
So speaking she sat down on Sussex shore singing lulling
Cadences & playing in sweet intoxication among the
    glistening
Fibres of Los: sending them over the Ocean eastward
    into
The realms of dark death; O perverse to thyself,
    contrarious
To thy own purposes; for when she began to weave
Shooting out in sweet pleasure her bosom in milky
    Love
Flowd into the aching fibres of Los, yet contending
    against him
In pride sending his Fibres over to her objects of
    jealousy   30
In the little lovely Allegoric Night of Albions Daughters
Which stretchd abroad, expanding east & west & north
    & south
Thro' all the World of Erin & of Los & all their
    Children

A sullen smile broke from the Spectre in mockery &
    scorn
Knowing himself the author of their divisions &
    shrinkings, gratified
At their contentions, he wiped his tears he washd his
    visage.

The Man who respects Woman shall be despised by
  Woman
And deadly cunning & mean abjectness only, shall
  enjoy them
For I will make their places of joy & love, excrementitious[.]
Continually building, continually destroying in Family
  feuds   40
While you are under the dominion of a jealous Female
Unpermanent for ever because of love & jealousy,
You shall want all the Minute Particulars of Life

Thus joyd the Spectre in the dusky fires of Los's Forge,
  eyeing
Enitharmon who at her shining Looms sings lulling
  cadences
While Los stood at his Anvil in wrath the victim of
  their love
And hate: dividing the Space of Love with brazen
  Compasses
In Golgonooza & in Udan-Adan & in Entuthon of
  Urizen.

The blow of his Hammer is Justice, the swing of his
  Hammer Mercy.
The force of Los's Hammer is eternal Forgiveness;
  but   50
His rage or his mildness were vain, she scatterd his love
  on the wind
Eastward into her own Center, creating the Female
  Womb .
In mild Jerusalem around the Lamb of God. Loud howl
The Furnaces of Los! loud roll the Wheels of Enitharmon
The Four Zoa's in all their faded majesty burst out in
  fury
And fire, Jerusalem took the Cup which foamd in Vala's
  hand
Like the red Sun upon the mountains in the bloody day
Upon the Hermaphroditic Wine-presses of Love &
  Wrath.

PLATE 89

Tho divided by the Cross & Nails & Thorns & Spear
In cruelties of Rahab & Tirzah[,] permanent endure
A terrible indefinite Hermaphroditic form
A Wine-press of Love & Wrath double
    Hermaph[r]oditic
Twelvefold in Allegoric pomp in selfish holiness
The Pharisaion, the Grammateis, the Presbuterion,
The Archiereus, the Iereus, the Saddusaion, double
Each withoutside of the other, covering eastern heaven

Thus was the Covering Cherub reveald majestic image
Of Selfhood, Body put off, the Antichrist accursed   10
Coverd with precious stones, a Human Dragon terrible
And bright, stretchd over Europe & Asia gorgeous
In three nights he devourd the rejected corse of death

His Head dark, deadly, in its Brain incloses a reflexion
Of Eden all perverted: Egypt on the Gihon many
    tongued
And many mouthd: Ethiopia, Lybia, the Sea of Rephaim
Minute Particulars in slavery I behold among the
    brick-kilns
Disorganiz'd, & there is Pharoh in his iron Court:
And the Dragon of the River & the Furnaces of iron.
Outwoven from Thames & Tweed & Severn awful
    streams   20
Twelve ridges of Stone frown over all the Earth in
    tyrant pride
Frown over each River stupendous Works of Albions
    Druid Sons
And Albions Forests of Oaks coverd the Earth from
    Pole to Pole

His Bosom wide reflects Moab & Ammon, on the River
Pison, since calld Arnon, there is Heshbon beautiful
The Rocks of Rabbath on the Arnon & the Fish-pools of
    Heshbon
Whose currents flow into the Dead Sea by Sodom &
    Gomorra

Above his Head high arching Wings black filld with
    Eyes
Spring upon iron sinews from the Scapulae & Os
    Humeri.
There Israel in bondage to his Generalizing Gods   30
Molech & Chemosh, & in his left breast is Philistea
In Druid Temples over the whole Earth with Victims
    Sacrifice,
From Gaza to Damascus Tyre & Sidon & the Gods
Of Javan thro the Isles of Grecia & all Europes Kings
Where Hiddekel pursues his course among the rocks
Two Wings spring from his ribs of brass, starry, black
    as night
But translucent their blackness as the dazling of gems

His Loins inclose Babylon on Euphrates beautiful
And Rome in sweet Hesperia, there Israel scatterd abroad
In martyrdoms & slavery I behold: ah vision of sorrow!   40
Inclosd by eyeless Wings, glowing with fire as the iron
Heated in the Smiths forge, but cold the wind of their
    dread fury

But in the midst of a devouring Stomach, Jerusalem
Hidden within the Covering Cherub as in a Tabernacle
Of threefold workmanship in allegoric delusion & woe[.]
There the Seven Kings of Canaan & Five Baalim of
    Philistea
Sihon & Og the Anakim & Emim, Nephilim &
    Gibborim
From Babylon to Rome & the Wings spread from
    Japan
Where the Red Sea terminates the World of Generation
    & Death
To Irelands farthest rocks where Giants builded their
    Causeway   50
Into the Sea of Rephaim, but the Sea oerwhelmd them
    all.

A Double Female now appeard within the Tabernacle,
Religion hid in War, a Dragon red & hidden Harlot

Each within other, but without a Warlike Mighty-one
Of dreadful power, sitting upon Horeb pondering dire
And mighty preparations mustering multitudes
    innumerable
Of warlike sons among the sands of Midian & Aram
For multitudes of those who sleep in Alla descend
Lured by his warlike symphonies of tabret pipe & harp
Burst the bottoms of the Graves & Funeral Arks of
    Beulah   60
Wandering in that unknown Night beyond the silent
    Grave
They become One with the Antichrist & are absorbd in
    him

PLATE 90
The Feminine separates from the Masculine & both
    from Man,
Ceasing to be His Emanations, Life to Themselves
    assuming:
And while they circumscribe his Brain, & while they
    circumscribe
His Heart, & while they circumscribe his Loins: a Veil
    & Net
Of Veins of red Blood grows around them like a scarlet
    robe,
Covering them from the sight of Man like the woven
    Veil of Sleep
Such as the Flowers of Beulah weave to be their Funeral
    Mantles
But dark! opake! tender to touch, & painful! & agonizing
To the embrace of love, & to the mingling of soft
    fibres
Of tender affection, that no more the Masculine
    mingles   10
With the Feminine, but the Sublime is shut out from
    the Pathos
In howling torment, to build stone walls of separation,
    compelling

The Pathos, to weave curtains of hiding secresy from the
  torment.

Bowen & Conwenna stood on Skiddaw cutting the
  Fibres
Of Benjamin from Chesters River: loud the River; loud
  the Mersey
And the Ribble, thunder into the Irish sea, as the
  Twelve Sons
Of Albion drank & imbibed the Life & eternal Form of
  Luvah
Cheshire & Lancashire & Westmoreland groan in
  anguish
As they cut the fibres from the Rivers he sears them
  with hot
Iron of his Forge & fixes them into Bones of chalk &
  Rock   20
Conwenna sat above: with solemn cadences she drew
Fibres of life out from the Bones into her golden Loom
Hand had his Furnace on Highgate heights & it reachd
To Brockley Hills across the Thames: he with double
  Boadicea
In cruel pride cut Reuben apart from the Hills of
  Surrey
Comingling with Luvah & with the Sepulcher of
  Luvah
For the Male is a Furnace of beryll: the Female is a
  golden Loom

Los cries: No Individual ought to appropriate to
  Himself
Or to his Emanation, any of the Universal
  Characteristics
Of David or of Eve, of the Woman, or of the Lord.   30
Of Reuben or of Benjamin, of Joseph or Judah or
  Levi[.]
Those who dare appropriate to themselves Universal
  Attributes

Are the Blasphemous Selfhoods & must be broken
asunder[.]
A Vegetated Christ & a Virgin Eve, are the
Hermaphroditic
Blasphemy, by his Maternal Birth he is that Evil-One
And his Maternal Humanity must be put off Eternally
Lest the Sexual Generation swallow up Regeneration
Come Lord Jesus take on thee the Satanic Body of
Holiness

So Los cried in the Valleys of Middlesex in the Spirit
of Prophecy
While in Selfhood Hand & Hyle & Bowen & Skofeld
appropriate   40
The Divine Names: seeking to Vegetate the Divine
Vision
In a corporeal & ever dying Vegetation & Corruption
Mingling with Luvah in One, they become One Great
Satan
Loud scream the Daughters of Albion beneath the
Tongs & Hammer
Dolorous are their lamentations in the burning Forge
They drink Reuben & Benjamin as the iron drinks the
fire
They are red hot with cruelty: raving along the Banks
of Thames
And on Tyburns Brook among the howling Victims in
loveliness
While Hand & Hyle condense the Little-ones & erect
them into
A mighty Temple even to the stars: but they Vegetate   50
Beneath Los's Hammer, that Life may not be blotted
out.

For Los said: When the Individual appropriates
Universality
He divides into Male & Female: & when the Male &
Female,

Appropriate Individuality, they become an Eternal
   Death.
Hermaphroditic worshippers of a God of cruelty & law!
Your Slaves & Captives; you compell to worship a God
   of Mercy.
These are the Demonstrations of Los, & the blows of my
   mighty Hammer

So Los spoke. And the Giants of Albion terrified &
   ashamed
With Los's thunderous Words, began to build trembling
   rocking Stones
For his Words roll in thunders & lightnings among the
   Temples   60
Terrified rocking to & fro upon the earth, & sometimes
Resting in a Circle in Malden or in Strathness or Dura.
Plotting to devour Albion & Los the friend of Albion
Denying in private: mocking God & Eternal Life: & in
   Public
Collusion, calling themselves Deists, Worshipping the
   Maternal
Humanity; calling it Nature, and Natural Religion

But still the thunder of Los peals loud & thus the
   thunder's cry

These beautiful Witchcrafts of Albion, are gratifyd by
   Cruelty
PLATE 91
It is easier to forgive an Enemy than to forgive a Friend:
The man who permits you to injure him, deserves your
   vengeance:
He also will recieve it; go Spectre! obey my most
   secret desire:
Which thou knowest without my speaking: Go to these
   Fiends of Righteousness
Tell them to obey their Humanities, & not pretend
   Holiness;

When they are murderers: as far as my Hammer & Anvil
 permit

Go, tell them that the Worship of God, is honouring
 his gifts

In other men: & loving the greatest men best, each
 according

To his Genius: which is the Holy Ghost in Man; there
 is no other

God, than that God who is the intellectual fountain
 of Humanity; 10

He who envies or calumniates: which is murder &
 cruelty,

Murders the Holy-one: Go tell them this & overthrow
 their cup,

Their bread, their altar-table, their incense & their
 oath:

Their marriage & their baptism, their burial &
 consecration:

I have tried to make friends by corporeal gifts but have
 only

Made enemies: I never made friends but by spiritual
 gifts;

By severe contentions of friendship & the burning fire
 of thought.

He who would see the Divinity must see him in his
 Children

One first, in friendship & love; then a Divine Family, &
 in the midst

Jesus will appear; so he who wishes to see a Vision; a
 perfect Whole 20

Must see it in its Minute Particulars; Organized & not
 as thou

O Fiend of Righteousness pretendest; thine is a
 Disorganized

And snowy cloud: brooder of tempests & destructive
 War.

You smile with pomp & rigor: you talk of benevolence
 & virtue:

I act with benevolence & Virtue & get murderd time
    after time:
You accumulate Particulars, & murder by analyzing,
    that you
May take the aggregate; & you call the aggregate Moral
    Law:
And you call that Swelld & bloated Form; a Minute
    Particular.
But General Forms have their vitality in Particulars: &
    every
Particular is a Man; a Divine Member of the Divine
    Jesus.   30

So Los cried at his Anvil in the horrible darkness
    weeping:

The Spectre builded stupendous Works, taking the
    Starry Heavens
Like to a curtain & folding them according to his will
Repeating the Smaragdine Table of Hermes to draw
    Los down
Into the Indefinite, refusing to believe without
    demonstration[.]
Los reads the Stars of Albion! the Spectre reads the
    Voids
Between the Stars: among the arches of Albions Tomb
    sublime
Rolling the Sea in rocky paths: forming Leviathan
And Behemoth: the War by Sea enormous & the War
By Land astounding: erecting pillars in the deepest
    Hell,   40
To reach the heavenly arches; Los beheld undaunted
    furious
His heavd Hammer; he swung it round & at one blow,
In unpitying ruin driving down the pyramids of pride
Smiting the Spectre on his Anvil & the integuments of
    his Eye
And Ear unbinding in dire pain, with many blows,

Of strict severity self-subduing, & with many tears
  labouring.

Then he sent forth the Spectre all his pyramids were
  grains
Of sand & his pillars: dust on the flys wing: & his
  starry
Heavens; a moth of gold & silver mocking his anxious
  grasp
Thus Los alterd his Spectre & every Ratio of his Reason   50
He alterd time after time, with dire pain & many tears
Till he had completely divided him into a separate space.

Terrified Los sat to behold trembling & weeping &
  howling
I care not whether a Man is Good or Evil; all that I
  care
Is whether he is a Wise Man or a Fool. Go! put off
  Holiness
And put on Intellect: or my thundrous Hammer shall
  drive thee
To wrath which thou condemnest: till thou obey my
  voice

So Los terrified cries: trembling & weeping & howling!
  Beholding

PLATE 92
What do I see? The Briton Saxon Roman Norman
  amalgamating
In my Furnaces into One Nation the English: & taking
  refuge
In the Loins of Albion. The Canaanite united with the
  fugitive
Hebrew, whom she divided into Twelve, & sold into
  Egypt
Then scatterd the Egyptian & Hebrew to the four Winds:
This sinful Nation Created in our Furnaces & Looms is
  Albion

So Los spoke. Enitharmon answerd in great terror in
   Lambeths Vale

The Poets Song draws to its period & Enitharmon is no
   more.
For if he be that Albion I can never weave him in my
   Looms
But when he touches the first fibrous thread, like filmy
   dew   10
My Looms will be no more & I annihilate vanish for
   ever
Then thou wilt Create another Female according to thy
   Will.

Los answerd swift as the shuttle of gold. Sexes must
   vanish & cease
To be, when Albion arises from his dread repose O
   lovely Enitharmon:
When all their Crimes, their Punishments their
   Accusations of Sin:
All their Jealousies Revenges, Murders, hidings of
   Cruelty in Deceit
Appear only in the Outward Spheres of Visionary Space
   and Time,
In the shadows of Possibility by Mutual Forgiveness
   forevermore
And in the Vision & in the Prophecy, that we may
   Foresee & Avoid
The terrors of Creation & Redemption & Judgment.
   Beholding them   20
Displayd in the Emanative Visions of Canaan in
   Jerusalem & in Shiloh
And in the Shadows of Remembrance, & in the Chaos
   of the Spectre
Amalek, Edom, Egypt, Moab, Ammon, Ashur,
   Philistea, around Jerusalem
Where the Druids reard their Rocky Circles to make
   permanent Remembrance

Of Sin, & the Tree of Good & Evil sprang from the
  Rocky Circle & Snake
Of the Druid, along the Valley of Rephaim from
  Camberwell to Golgotha
And framed the Mundane Shell Cavernous in Length
  Bredth & Highth

PLATE 93
Enitharmon heard. She raisd her head like the mild Moon
O Rintrah! O Palamabron! What are your dire & awful
  purposes
Enitharmons name is nothing before you: you forget
  all my Love!
The Mothers love of obedience is forgotten & you seek
  a Love
Of the pride of dominion, that will Divorce Ocalythron
  & Elynittria
Upon East Moor in Derbyshire & along the Valleys of
  Cheviot
Could you Love me Rintrah, if you Pride not in my
  Love
As Reuben found Mandrakes in the field & gave them to
  his Mother
Pride meets with Pride upon the Mountains in the
  stormy day
In that terrible Day of Rintrahs Plow & of Satans driving
  the Team.   10
Ah! then I heard my little ones weeping along the Valley:
Ah! then I saw my beloved ones fleeing from my Tent
Merlin was like thee Rintrah among the Giants of Albion
Judah was like Palamabron: O Simeon! O Levi! ye fled
  away
How can I hear my little ones weeping along the Valley
Or how upon the distant Hills see my beloveds Tents.

Then Los again took up his speech as Enitharmon ceast

Fear not my Sons this Waking Death, he is become One
  with me

Behold him here! We shall not Die! we shall be united
   in Jesus.
Will you suffer this Satan this Body of Doubt that
   Seems but Is Not   20
To occupy the very threshold of Eternal Life, if Bacon,
   Newton, Locke,
Deny a Conscience in Man & the Communion of Saints
   & Angels
Contemning the Divine Vision & Fruition, Worshiping
   the Deus
Of the Heathen, The God of This World, & the Goddess
   Nature
Mystery Babylon the Great, The Druid Dragon &
   hidden Harlot[,]
Is it not that Signal of the Morning which was told us
   in the Beginning

Thus they converse upon Mam-Tor, the Graves thunder
   under their feet
PLATE 94
Albion cold lays on his Rock: storms & snows beat
   round him.
Beneath the Furnaces & the starry Wheels & the
   Immortal Tomb
Howling winds cover him: roaring seas dash furious
   against him
In the deep darkness broad lightnings glare long
   thunders roll

The weeds of Death inwrap his hands & feet blown
   incessant
And washd incessant by the for-ever restless sea-waves
   foaming abroad
Upon the white Rock. England a Female Shadow as
   deadly damps
Of the Mines of Cornwall & Derbyshire lays upon his
   bosom heavy
Moved by the wind in volumes of thick cloud returning
   folding round

His loins & bosom unremovable by swelling storms &
   loud rending   10
Of enraged thunders. Around them the Starry Wheels
   of their Giant Sons
Revolve: & over them the Furnaces of Los & the
   Immortal Tomb around
Erin sitting in the Tomb, to watch them unceasing night
   and day
And the Body of Albion was closed apart from all
   Nations.

Over them the famishd Eagle screams on boney Wings
   and around
Them howls the Wolf of famine deep heaves the Ocean
   black thundering
Around the wormy Garments of Albion: then pausing
   in deathlike silence

Time was Finished! The Breath Divine Breathed over
   Albion
Beneath the Furnaces & starry Wheels and in the
   Immortal Tomb
And England who is Brittannia awoke, from Death on
   Albions bosom   20
She awoke pale & cold she fainted seven times on the
   Body of Albion

O pitious Sleep O pitious Dream! O God O God awake
   I have slain
In Dreams of Chastity & Moral Law I have Murdered
   Albion! Ah!
In Stone-henge & on London Stone & in the Oak
   Groves of Malden
I have Slain him in my Sleep with the Knife of the
   Druid O England
O all ye Nations of the Earth behold ye the Jealous
   Wife
The Eagle & the Wolf & Monkey & Owl & the King &
   Priest were there

PLATE 95

Her voice pierc'd Albions clay cold ear. he moved upon
the Rock.
The Breath Divine went forth upon the morning hills,
Albion mov'd
Upon the Rock, he opend his eyelids in pain; in pain he
mov'd
His stony members, he saw England. Ah! shall the Dead
live again

The Breath Divine went forth over the morning hills
Albion rose
In anger: the wrath of God breaking bright flaming on
all sides around
His awful limbs: into the Heavens he walked clothed in
flames
Loud thundring, with broad flashes of flaming lightning
& pillars
Of fire, speaking the Words of Eternity in Human
Forms, in direful
Revolutions of Action & Passion, thro the Four
Elements on all sides   10
Surrounding his awful Members. Thou seest the Sun in
heavy clouds
Struggling to rise above the Mountains, in his burning
hand
He takes his Bow, then chooses out his arrows of flaming
gold
Murmuring the Bowstring breathes with ardor! clouds
roll round the
Horns of the wide Bow, loud sounding winds sport on
the mountain brows
Compelling Urizen to his Furrow; & Tharmas to his
Sheepfold;
And Luvah to his Loom: Urthona he beheld mighty
labouring at
His Anvil, in the Great Spectre Los unwearied labouring
& weeping

Therefore the Sons of Eden praise Urthonas Spectre
  in songs
Because he kept the Divine Vision in time of trouble.

As the Sun & Moon lead forward the Visions of Heaven
  & Earth   20
England who is Brittannia enterd Albions bosom
  rejoicing,
Rejoicing in his indignation! adoring his wrathful
  rebuke.
She who adores not your frowns will only loathe your
  smiles

PLATE 96
As the Sun & Moon lead forward the Visions of Heaven
  & Earth
England who is Brittannia entered Albions bosom
  rejoicing

Then Jesus appeared standing by Albion as the Good
  Shepherd
By the lost Sheep that he hath found & Albion knew
  that it
Was the Lord the Universal Humanity, & Albion saw
  his Form
A Man, & they conversed as Man with Man, in Ages of
  Eternity
And the Divine Appearance was the likeness &
  similitude of Los

Albion said. O Lord what can I do! my Selfhood cruel
Marches against thee deceitful from Sinai & from Edom
Into the Wilderness of Judah to meet thee in his pride   10
I behold the Visions of my deadly Sleep of Six
  Thousand Years
Dazling around thy skirts like a Serpent of precious
  stones & gold
I know it is my Self: O my Divine Creator & Redeemer

Jesus replied Fear not Albion unless I die thou canst not
  live

But if I die I shall arise again & thou with me
This is Friendship & Brotherhood without it Man Is
    Not

So Jesus spoke: the Covering Cherub coming on in
    darkness
Overshadowd them & Jesus said Thus do Men in
    Eternity
One for another to put off by forgiveness, every sin

Albion replyd. Cannot Man exist without Mysterious   20
Offering of Self for Another, is this Friendship &
    Brotherhood
I see thee in the likeness & similitude of Los my Friend

Jesus said. Wouldest thou love one who never died
For thee or ever die for one who had not died for thee
And if God dieth not for Man & giveth not himself
Eternally for Man Man could not exist! for Man is
    Love:
As God is Love: every kindness to another is a little
    Death
In the Divine Image nor can Man exist but by
    Brotherhood

So saying the Cloud overshadowing divided them
    asunder
Albion stood in terror: not for himself but for his
    Friend   30
Divine, & Self was lost in the contemplation of faith
And wonder at the Divine Mercy & at Los's sublime
    honour

Do I sleep amidst danger to Friends! O my Cities &
    Counties
Do you sleep! rouze up! rouze up. Eternal Death is
    abroad

So Albion spoke & threw himself into the Furnaces of
    affliction
All was a Vision, all a Dream: the Furnaces became

Fountains of Living Waters flowing from the Humanity
  Divine
And all the Cities of Albion rose from their Slumbers,
  and All
The Sons & Daughters of Albion on soft clouds Waking
  from Sleep
Soon all around remote the Heavens burnt with flaming
  fires   40
And Urizen & Luvah & Tharmas & Urthona arose into
Albions Bosom: Then Albion stood before Jesus in the
  Clouds
Of Heaven Fourfold among the Visions of God in Eternity
PLATE 97
Awake! Awake Jerusalem! O lovely Emanation of Albion
Awake and overspread all Nations as in Ancient Time
For lo! the Night of Death is past and the Eternal Day
Appears upon our Hills: Awake Jerusalem, and come away

So spake the Vision of Albion & in him so spake in my
  hearing
The Universal Father Then Albion stretchd his hand
  into Infinitude,
And took his Bow. Fourfold the Vision for bright
  beaming Urizen
Layd his hand on the South & took a breathing Bow of
  carved Gold
Luvah his hand stretch'd to the East & bore a Silver
  Bow bright shining
Tharmas Westward a Bow of Brass pure flaming richly
  wrought   10
Urthona Northward in thick storms a Bow of Iron
  terrible thundering.

And the Bow is a Male & Female & the Quiver of the
  Arrows of Love,
Are the Children of this Bow: a Bow of Mercy &
  Loving-kindness: laying
Open the hidden Heart in Wars of mutual Benevolence
  Wars of Love

And the Hand of Man grasps firm between the Male &
    Female Loves
And he Clothed himself in Bow & Arrows in awful state
    Fourfold
In the midst of his Twenty-eight Cities each with his
    Bow breathing

PLATE 98
Then each an Arrow flaming from his Quiver fitted
    carefully
They drew fourfold the unreprovable String, bending
    thro the wide Heavens
The horned Bow Fourfold, loud sounding flew the
    flaming Arrow fourfold

Murmuring the Bow-string breathes with ardor. Clouds
    roll round the horns
Of the wide Bow, loud sounding Winds sport on the
    Mountains brows:
The Druid Spectre was Annihilate loud thundring
    rejoicing terrific vanishing
Fourfold Annihilation & at the clangor of the Arrows of
    Intellect
The innumerable Chariots of the Almighty appeard in
    Heaven
And Bacon & Newton & Locke, & Milton & Shakspear
    & Chaucer
A Sun of blood red wrath surrounding heaven on all
    sides around   10
Glorious incompreh[en]sible by Mortal Man & each
    Chariot was Sexual Threefold

And every Man stood Fourfold, each Four Faces had.
    One to the West
One toward the East One to the South One to the
    North, the Horses Fourfold
And the dim Chaos brightend beneath, above, around!
    Eyed as the Peacock

According to the Human Nerves of Sensation, the Four
  Rivers of the Water of Life

South stood the Nerves of the Eye. East in Rivers of
  bliss the Nerves of the
Expansive Nostrils West, flowd the Parent Sense the
  Tongue. North stood
The labyrinthine Ear. Circumscribing & Circumcising
  the excrementitious
Husk & Covering into Vacuum evaporating revealing the
  lineaments of Man
Driving outward the Body of Death in an Eternal Death
  & Resurrection   20
Awaking it to Life among the Flowers of Beulah
  rejoicing in Unity
In the Four Senses in the Outline the Circumference &
  Form, for ever
In Forgiveness of Sins which is Self Annihilation, it is
  the Covenant of Jehovah

The Four Living Creatures Chariots of Humanity
  Divine Incomprehensible
In beautiful Paradises expand These are the Four
  Rivers of Paradise
And the Four Faces of Humanity fronting the Four
  Cardinal Points
Of Heaven going forward forward irresistible from
  Eternity to Eternity

And they conversed together in Visionary forms dramatic
  which bright
Redounded from their Tongues in thunderous majesty,
  in Visions
In new Expanses, creating exemplars of Memory and of
  Intellect   30
Creating Space, Creating Time according to the
  wonders Divine
Of Human Imagination, throughout all the Three
  Regions immense

Of Childhood, Manhood & Old Age[;] & the all
  tremendous unfathomable Non Ens
Of Death was seen in regenerations terrific or complacent
  varying
According to the subject of discourse & every Word &
  Every Character
Was Human according to the Expansion or
  Contraction, the Translucence or
Opakeness of Nervous fibres such was the variation of
  Time & Space
Which vary according as the Organs of Perception
  vary & they walked
To & fro in Eternity as One Man reflecting each in each
  & clearly seen
And seeing: according to fitness & order. And I heard
  Jehovah speak   40
Terrific from his Holy Place & saw the Words of the
  Mutual Covenant Divine
On Chariots of gold & jewels with Living Creatures
  starry & flaming
With every Colour, Lion, Tyger, Horse, Elephant,
  Eagle Dove, Fly, Worm,
And the all wondrous Serpent clothed in gems & rich
  array Humanize
In the Forgiveness of Sins according to the Covenant
  of Jehovah. They Cry
Where is the Covenant of Priam, the Moral Virtues of
  the Heathen
Where is the Tree of Good & Evil that rooted beneath
  the cruel heel
Of Albions Spectre the Patriarch Druid! where are all
  his Human Sacrifices
For Sin in War & in the Druid Temples of the Accuser
  of Sin: beneath
The Oak Groves of Albion that coverd the whole Earth
  beneath his Spectre   50
Where are the Kingdoms of the World & all their
  glory that grew on Desolation

The Fruit of Albions Poverty Tree when the Triple
  Headed Gog-Magog Giant
Of Albion Taxed the Nations into Desolation & then
  gave the Spectrous Oath

Such is the Cry from all the Earth from the Living
  Creatures of the Earth
And from the great City of Golgonooza in the Shadowy
  Generation
And from the Thirty-two Nations of the Earth among
  the living Creatures

PLATE 99
All Human Forms identified even Tree Metal Earth &
  Stone, all
Human Forms identified, living going forth & returning
  wearied
Into the Planetary lives of Years Months Days & Hours
  reposing
And then Awaking into his Bosom in the Life of
  Immortality.

And I heard the Name of their Emanations they are
  named Jerusalem

              The End of The Song
              of Jerusalem

[PRELIMINARY SECTIONS]

There is not one Moral Virtue that Jesus Inculcated but
Plato & Cicero did Inculcate before him what then did
Christ Inculcate. Forgiveness of Sins This alone is the
Gospel & this is the Life & Immortality brought to light
by Jesus. Even the Covenant of Jehovah, which is This If
you forgive one another your Trespessas so shall Jehovah
forgive you That he himself may dwell among you but if
you Avenge you Murder the Divine Image & he cannot
dwell among you [by his] because you Murder him he
arises Again & you deny that he is Arisen & are blind to   10
Spirit

*

What can this Gospel of Jesus be
What Life & Immortality
What was it that he brought to Light
That Plato & Cicero did not write
The Heathen Deities wrote them all
These Moral Virtues great & small
What is the Accusation of Sin
But Moral Virtues deadly Gin
The Moral Virtues in their Pride
Did oer the World triumphant ride   10
In Wars & Sacrifice for Sin
And Souls to Hell ran trooping in
The Accuser Holy God of All
This Pharisaic Worldly Ball
Amidst them in his Glory Beams
Upon the Rivers & the Streams

Then Jesus rose & said to [*men*] Me
Thy Sins are all forgiven thee
Loud Pilate Howld loud Caiphas Yelld
When they the Gospel Light beheld   20
[*Jerusalem he said to me*]

It was when Jesus said to Me
Thy Sins are all forgiven thee
The Christian trumpets loud proclaim
Thro all the World in Jesus name
Mutual forgiveness of each Vice
And oped the Gates of Paradise
The Moral Virtues in Great fear
Formed the Cross & Nails & Spear
And the Accuser standing by   30
Cried out Crucify Crucify
Our Moral Virtues neer can be
Nor Warlike pomp & Majesty
For Moral Virtues all begin
In the Accusations of Sin
And [*Moral*] all the Heroic Virtues [*all*] End
In destroying the Sinners Friend
Am I not Lucifer the Great
And you my daughters in Great State
The fruit of my Mysterious Tree   40
Of Good & Evil & Misery
And Death & Hell which now begin
On every one who Forgives Sin

*

1   This to come first

If Moral Virtue was Christianity
Christs Pretensions were all Vanity
And Caiphas & Pilate Men
[*Of Moral*] Praise Worthy & the Lions Den
And not the Sheepfold Allegories
Of God & Heaven & their Glories

The Moral Christian is the Cause
Of the Unbeliever & his Laws
The Roman Virtues Warlike Fame
Take Jesus & Jehovahs Name.   10
For what is Antichrist but those
Who against Sinners Heaven close
With Iron bars in Virtuous State
And Rhadamanthus at the Gate

*

Was Jesus Born of a Virgin Pure
With narrow Soul & looks demure
If he intended to take on Sin
The Mother should an Harlot been
Just such a one as Magdalen
With seven devils in her Pen
Or were Jew Virgins still more Curst
And more sucking devils nurst
Or what was it which he took on
That he might bring Salvation   10
A Body subject to be Tempted
From neither pain nor grief Exempted
Or such a body as might not feel
The passions that with Sinners deal
Yes but they say he never fell
Ask Caiaphas for he can tell
He mockd the Sabbath & he mockd
The Sabbaths God & he unlockd
The Evil spirits from their Shrines
And turnd Fishermen to Divines   20
[End] Oerturnd the Tent of Secret Sins
& its Golden cords & Pins
Tis the Bloody Shrine of War
Pinnd around from Star to Star
Halls of Justice hating Vice
Where the Devil Combs his Lice
He turnd the devils into Swine
That he might tempt the Jews to Dine

Since which a Pig has got a look
That for a Jew may be mistook
Obey your Parents what says he   30
Woman what have I to do with thee
No Earthly Parents I confess
I am doing my Fathers Business
He scornd [*his*] Earths Parents scornd [*his*] Earths God
And mockd the one & the others Rod
His Seventy Disciples sent
Against Religion & Government
They by the Sword of Justice fell
And him their Cruel Murderer tell
He left his Fathers trade to roam   40
A wandring Vagrant without Home
And thus he others labour stole
That he might live above Controll
The Publicans & Harlots he
Selected for his Company
And from the Adulteress turnd away
Gods righteous Law that lost its Prey

[NOTEBOOK SECTIONS]

The Vision of Christ that thou dost see
Is my Visions Greatest Enemy
Thine has a great hook nose like thine
Mine has a snub nose like to mine
Thine is the friend of All Mankind
Mine speaks in parables to the Blind
Thine loves the same world that mine hates
Thy Heaven doors are my Hell Gates
Socrates taught what Melitus
Loathd as a Nations bitterest Curse   10
And Caiphas was in his own Mind
A benefactor to Mankind
Both read the Bible day & night
But thou readst black where I read white

*

Was Jesus Chaste or did he
Give any Lessons of Chastity
The morning blushd fiery red
Mary was found in Adulterous bed
Earth groand beneath & Heaven above
Trembled at discovery of Love
Jesus was sitting in Moses Chair
They brought the trembling Woman There
Moses commands she be stoned to death
What was the [words] sound of Jesus breath   10
He laid His hand on Moses Law
The Ancient Heavens in Silent Awe
Writ with Curses from Pole to Pole
All away began to roll
The Earth trembling & Naked lay
In secret bed of Mortal Clay
On Sinai felt the hand Divine
Putting back the bloody shrine
And she heard the breath of God
As she heard by Edens flood   20
Good & Evil are no more
Sinais trumpets cease to roar
Cease finger of God to write
The Heavens are not clean in thy Sight
Thou art Good & thou Alone
Nor may the sinner cast one stone
To be Good only is to be
A [god] Devil or else a Pharisee
Thou Angel of the Presence Divine
That didst create this Body of Mine   30
Wherefore has thou writ these Laws
And Created Hells dark jaws
My Presence I will take from thee
A Cold Leper thou shalt be
Tho thou wast so pure & bright
That Heaven was Impure in thy Sight
Tho thy Oath turnd Heaven Pale
Tho thy Covenant built Hells Jail

Tho thou didst all to Chaos roll
With the Serpent for its soul   40
Still the breath Divine does move
And the breath Divine is Love
Mary Fear Not Let me see
The Seven Devils that torment thee
Hide not from my Sight thy Sin
That forgiveness thou maist win
Has no Man Condemned thee
No Man Lord! then what is he
Who shall Accuse thee. Come Ye forth
Fallen Fiends of Heavenly birth   50
That have forgot your Ancient love
And driven away my trembling Dove
You shall bow before her feet
You shall lick the dust for Meat
And tho you cannot Love but Hate
Shall be beggars at Loves Gate
What was thy love Let me see it
Was it love or Dark Deceit
Love too long from Me has fled.
Twas dark deceit to Earn my bread   60
Twas Covet or twas Custom or
[*Twas*] Some trifle not worth caring for
That they may call a [*crime*] shame & Sin
[*The*] Loves temple [*where*] that God dwelleth in
And hide in secret Hidden Shrine
The Naked Human form divine
And render that a Lawless thing
On which the Soul Expands its wing
But this O Lord this was my Sin
When first I let these Devils in   70
In dark pretence to Chastity
Blaspheming Love blaspheming thee
Thence Rose Secret Adulteries
And thence did Covet also rise
My sin thou hast forgiven me
Canst thou forgive my Blasphemy

Canst thou return to this dark Hell
And in my burning bosom dwell
And canst thou die that I may live
And canst thou Pity & forgive   80
Then Rolld the shadowy Man away
From the Limbs of Jesus to make them his prey
An Ever devo[u]ring appetite
Glittering with festering Venoms bright
Crying [*Ive found*] Crucify this cause of distress
[*You*] Who dont keep the secrets of Holiness
All Mental Powers by Diseases we bind
But he heals the Deaf & the Dumb & the Blind
Whom God has afflicted for Secret Ends
He comforts & Heals & calls them Friends   90
But when Jesus was Crucified
Then was perfected his glittring pride
In three Nights he devourd his prey
And still he devours the Body of Clay
For dust & Clay is the Serpents meat
Which never was made for Man to Eat

*

Seeing this False Christ In fury & Passion
I made my Voice heard all over the Nation
What are those &c

*

Did Jesus teach doubt or did he
Give any lessons of Philosophy
Charge Visionaries with decieving
Or call Men wise for not Believing

*

Was Jesus gentle or did he
Give any marks of Gentility
When twelve years old he ran away
And left his Parents in dismay

When after three days sorrow found
Loud as Sinai's trumpet sound
No Earthly Parents I confess
My Heavenly Fathers business
Ye understand not what I say
And angry force me to obey   10
Obedience is a duty then
And favour gains with God & Men
John from the Wilderness loud cried
Satan gloried in his Pride
Come said Satan come away
Ill soon see if youll obey
John for disobedience bled
But you can turn the stones to bread
Gods high king & Gods high Priest
Shall Plant their Glories in your breast   20
If Caiaphas you will obey
If Herod you with bloody Prey
Feed with the Sacrifice & be
Obedient fall down worship me
Thunders & lightnings broke around
And Jesus voice in thunders sound
Thus I sieze the Spiritual Prey
Ye smiters with disease make way
I come Your King & God to sieze
Is God a Smiter with disease   30
The God of this World raged in vain
He bound Old Satan in his Chain
And bursting forth [with] his furious ire
Became a Chariot of fire
Throughout the land he took his course
And traced diseases to their source
He cursd the Scribe & Pharisee
Trampling down Hipocrisy
Where eer his Chariot took its way
There Gates of Death let in the day   40
Broke down from every Chain & Bar
And Satan in his Spiritual War

Dragd at his Chariot wheels loud howld
The God of this World louder rolld
The Chariot Wheels & louder still
His voice was heard from Zions hill
And in his hand the Scourge shone bright
He scourgd the Merchant Canaanite
From out the Temple of his Mind
And in his Body tight does bind   50
Satan & all his Hellish Crew
And thus with wrath he did subdue
The Serpent Bulk of Natures dross
Till he had naild it to the Cross
He took on Sin in the Virgins Womb
[*And on the Cross he Seald its doom*]
And put it off on the Cross & Tomb
To be Worshipd by the Church of Rome

*

Was Jesus Humble or did he
Give any proofs of Humility
When but a Child he ran away
And left his Parents in dismay
When they had wanderd three days long
These were the words upon his Tongue
No Earthly Parents I confess
I am doing my Fathers business
When the rich learned Pharisee
Came to consult him secretly   10
He was too Proud to take a bribe
He spoke with authority not like a Scribe
Upon his heart with Iron pen
He wrote Ye must be born again
He says with most consummate Art
Follow me I am meek & lowly of heart
As that is the only way to Escape
The Misers net & the Gluttons trap
He who loves his Enemies hates his Friends
This is surely not what Jesus intends   20

He must mean the meer love of Civility
And so he must mean concerning Humility
But he acts with triumphant honest pride
And this is the Reason Jesus died
If he had been [*the*] Antichrist Creeping Jesus
Hed have done any thing to please us
Gone sneaking into the Synagogues
And not used the Elders & Priests like Dogs
But humble as a Lamb or an Ass
Obey himself to Caiaphas   30
God wants not Man to humble himself
This is the Trick of the Ancient Elf
Humble toward God, Haughty toward Man
This is the Race that Jesus ran
And when he humbled himself to God
Then descended the cruel rod
[*Why dost thou humble thyself to me*
Thou Also dwelst in Eternity]
If thou humblest thyself thou humblest me
Thou also dwelst in Eternity   40
Thou art a Man God is no more
Thine own Humanity learn to Adore
And thy Revenge Abroad display
In terrors at the Last Judgment day
Gods Mercy & Long Suffering
Are but the Sinner to Judgment to bring
Thou on the Cross for them shalt pray
[*Whom thou shalt Torment at the Last Day*]
And take Revenge at the last Day

Do what you will this Lifes a Fiction   50
And is made up of Contradiction

THE EVERLASTING GOSPEL

Was Jesus Humble or did he
Give any Proofs of Humility
Boast of high Things with Humble tone
And give with Charity a Stone

When but a Child he ran away
And left his Parents in dismay
When they had wanderd three days long
These were the words upon his tongue
No Earthly Parents I confess
I am doing my Fathers business   10
When the rich learned Pharisee
Came to consult him secretly
Upon his heart with Iron pen
He wrote Ye must be born again
He was too proud to take a bribe
He spoke with authority not like a Scribe
He says with most consummate Art
Follow me I am meek & lowly of heart
As that is the only way to escape
The Misers net & the Gluttons trap   20
What can be done with such desperate Fools
Who follow after the Heathen Schools
I was standing by when Jesus died
What I calld Humility they calld Pride
He who loves his Enemies [hates] betrays his Friends
This surely is not what Jesus intends
But the sneaking Pride of Heroic Schools
And the Scribes & Pharisees Virtuous Rules
For he acts with honest triumphant Pride
And this is the cause that Jesus died   30
He did not die with Christian Ease
Asking pardon of his Enemies
If he had Caiphas would forgive
Sneaking submission can always live
He had only to say that God was the devil
And the devil was God like a Christian Civil
Mild Christian regrets to the devil confess
For affronting him thrice in the Wilderness
He had soon been bloody Caesars Elf
And at last he would have been Caesar himself   40
Like dʳ Priestly & [Sir Isaac] Bacon & Newton
Poor Spiritual Knowledge is not worth a button

[*As*] For thus the Gospel Sr Isaac confutes
God can only be known by his Attributes
And as for the Indwelling of the Holy Ghost
Or of Christ & his Father its all a boast
And Pride & Vanity of the Imagination
That disdains to follow this Worlds Fashion
To teach doubt & Experiment
Certainly was not what Christ meant   50
What was he doing all that time
From twelve years old to manly prime
Was he then Idle or the Less
About his Fathers business
Or was his wisdom held in scorn
Before his wrath began to burn
In Miracles throughout the Land
That quite unnervd Caiaphas hand
If he had been [*the*] Antichrist Creeping Jesus
Hed have done any thing to please us   60
Gone sneaking into Synagogues
And not usd the Elders & Priests like dogs
But Humble as a Lamb or Ass
Obeyd himself to Caiaphas
God wants not Man to Humble himself
This is the trick of the ancient Elf
This is the Race that Jesus ran
Humble to God Haughty to Man
Cursing the Rulers before the People
Even to the temples highest Steeple   70
And when he Humbled himself to God
Then descended the Cruel Rod
If thou humblest thyself thou humblest me
Thou also dwellst in Eternity
Thou art a Man God is no more
Thy own humanity learn to adore
For that is my Spirit of Life
Awake arise to Spiritual Strife
And thy Revenge abroad display
In terrors at the Last Judgment day   80

Gods Mercy & Long Suffering
Is but the Sinner to Judgment to bring
Thou on the Cross for them shalt pray
And take Revenge at the Last Day
[*All Corporeal lifes a*/*This Corporeal*
(*All*) *lifes a fiction*
And is made up of Contradiction]

Jesus replied & thunders hurld
I never will Pray for the World
Once [I] did so when I prayd in the Garden
I wishd to take with me a Bodily Pardon   90
Can that which was of woman born
In the absence of the Morn
When the Soul fell into Sleep
And Archangels round it weep
Shooting out against the Light
Fibres of a deadly night
Reasoning upon its own dark Fiction
In doubt which is Self Contradiction
Humility is only doubt
And does the Sun & Moon blot out   100
Rooting over with thorns & stems
The buried Soul & all its Gems.
This Lifes dim Windows of the Soul
Distorts the Heavens from Pole to Pole
And leads you to Believe a Lie
When you see with not thro the Eye
That was born in a night to perish in a night
When the Soul slept in the beams of Light.

*

I am sure This Jesus will not do
Either for Englishman or Jew

FOR THE SEXES
THE GATES OF PARADISE

[PROLOGUE]
Mutual forgiveness of each Vice
Such are the Gates of Paradise
Against the Accusers chief desire
Who walked among the Stones of Fire
Jehovahs Finger Wrote the Law
Then Wept! then rose in Zeal & Awe
And the Dead Corpse from Sinais heat
Buried beneath his Mercy Seat
O Christians Christians tell me Why
You rear it on your Altars high   10

THE KEYS
The Catterpiller on the Leaf
Reminds thee of thy Mothers Grief

OF THE GATES
1 My Eternal Man set in Repose
   The Female from his darkness rose
   And She found me beneath a Tree
   A Mandrake & in her Veil hid me
   Serpent Reasonings us entice
   Of Good & Evil: Virtue & Vice
2 Doubt Self Jealous Watry folly
3 Struggling thro Earths Melancholy   10
4 Naked in Air in Shame & Fear
5 Blind in Fire with shield & spear
   Two Horn'd Reasoning Cloven Fiction
   In Doubt which is Self contradiction

A dark Hermaphrodite We stood
Rational Truth Root of Evil & Good
Round me flew the Flaming Sword
Round her snowy Whirlwinds roard
Freezing her Veil the Mundane Shell

6   I rent the Veil where the Dead dwell   20

When weary Man enters his Cave
He meets his Saviour in the Grave
Some find a Female Garment there
And some a Male, woven with care
Lest the Sexual Garments sweet
Should grow a devouring Winding sheet

7   One Dies! Alas! the Living & Dead
    One is slain & One is fled

8   In Vain-glory hatcht & nurst
    By double Spectres Self Accurst   30
    My Son! my Son! thou treatest me
    But as I have instructed thee

9   On the shadows of the Moon
    Climbing thro Nights highest noon

10   In Times Ocean falling drownd
    In Aged Ignorance profound

11   Holy & cold I clipd the Wings
    Of all Sublunary Things

12   And in the depths of my Dungeons
    Closed the Father & the Sons   40

13   But when once I did descry
    The Immortal Man that cannot Die

14   Thro evening shades I haste away
    To close the Labours of my Day

15   The Door of Death I open found
    And the Worm Weaving in the Ground

16   Thou'rt my Mother from the Womb
    Wife, Sister, Daughter to the Tomb
    Weaving to Dreams the Sexual strife
    And weeping over the Web of Life   50

[EPILOGUE]

TO THE ACCUSER WHO IS THE GOD OF THIS WORLD

Truly My Satan thou art but a Dunce
And dost not know the Garment from the Man
Every Harlot was a Virgin once
Nor canst thou ever change Kate into Nan

Tho thou art Worshipd by the Names Divine
Of Jesus & Jehovah: thou art still
The Son of Morn in weary Nights decline
The lost Travellers Dream under the Hill

THE GHOST OF ABEL

A Revelation In the Visions of Jehovah

Seen by William Blake

PLATE I

    To LORD BYRON in the Wilderness

                      What doest thou here Elijah?

Can a Poet doubt the Visions of Jehovah? Nature has
no Outline: but Imagination has. Nature has no Tune:
but Imagination has! Nature has no Supernatural &
dissolves: Imagination is Eternity

*Scene. A rocky Country. Eve fainted over the dead body
of Abel which lays near a Grave. Adam kneels by her
Jehovah stands above.*

JEHOVAH: Adam!

ADAM: I will not hear thee more thou Spiritual
    Voice

  Is this Death?

JEHOVAH: Adam!

ADAM: It is in vain: I will not hear thee

  Henceforth! Is this thy Promise that the Womans
    Seed

  Should bruise the Serpents head: Is this the
    Serpent? Ah!

  Seven times, O Eve thou hast fainted over the Dead.
    Ah! Ah!

Eve revives.

EVE: Is this the Promise of Jehovah! O it is all a vain
    delusion

  This Death & this Life & this Jehovah!

JEHOVAH: Woman: lift
    thine eyes

A Voice is heard coming on.

VOICE: O Earth cover not thou my Blood! cover not
   thou my Blood

Enter the Ghost of Abel.

EVE: Thou Visionary Phantasm thou art not the real
   Abel.
ABEL: Among the Elohim a Human Victim I wander I
   am their House
   Prince of the Air & our dimensions compass Zenith
   & Nadir
   Vain is thy Covenant O Jehovah I am the Accuser &
   Avenger
   Of Blood O Earth Cover not thou the Blood of
   Abel
JEHOVAH: What Vengeance dost thou require
ABEL: Life for
   Life! Life for Life!
JEHOVAH: He who shall take Cains life must also Die
   O Abel   20
   And who is he? Adam wilt thou, or Eve thou do
   this
ADAM: It is all a Vain delusion of the all creative
   Imagination
   Eve come away & let us not believe these vain
   delusions
   Abel is dead & Cain slew him! We shall also Die a
   Death
   And then! what then? be as poor Abel a Thought: or
   as
   This! O what shall I call thee Form Divine! Father
   of Mercies
   That appearest to my Spiritual Vision: Eve seest thou
   also.
EVE: I see him plainly with my Minds Eye. I see also
   Abel living:

Tho terribly afflicted as We also are, yet Jehovah sees him

PLATE 2

Alive & not Dead: were it not better to believe Vision
With all our might & strength tho we are fallen & lost

ADAM: Eve thou hast spoken truly. let us kneel before his feet.

They Kneel before Jehovah.

ABEL: Are these the Sacrifices of Eternity O Jehovah, a Broken Spirit

And a Contrite Heart. O I cannot Forgive! the Accuser hath

Enterd into Me as into his House & I loathe thy Tabernacles

As thou hast said so is it come to pass: My desire is unto Cain

And He doth rule over Me: therefore My Soul in fumes of Blood

Cries for Vengeance: Sacrifice on Sacrifice Blood on Blood

JEHOVAH: Lo I have given you a Lamb for an Atonement instead

Of the Transgres[s]or, or no Flesh or Spirit could ever Live

ABEL: Compelled I cry O Earth cover not the Blood of Abel

*Abel sinks down into the Grave from which arises Satan
Armed in glittering scales with a Crown & a Spear.*

SATAN: I will have Human Blood & not the blood of Bulls or Goats

And no Atonement O Jehovah the Elohim live on Sacrifice

Of Men: hence I am God of Men: Thou Human O Jehovah.

10

By the Rock & Oak of the Druid creeping Mistletoe &
Thorn

Cains City built with Human Blood, not Blood of Bulls
& Goats

Thou shalt Thyself be Sacrificed to Me thy God on
Calvary

JEHOVAH: Such is My Will. *Thunders.*

that Thou Thyself go to
Eternal Death

In Self Annihilation even till Satan Self-subdud Put
off Satan

Into the Bottomless Abyss whose torment arises for
ever & ever.

20

*On each side a Chrous of Angels entering Sing the
following:*

The Elohim of the Heathen Swore Vengeance for Sin!
Then Thou stoodst

Forth O Elohim Jehovah! in the midst of the darkness
of the Oath! All Clothed

In Thy Covenant of the Forgiveness of Sins: Death O
Holy! Is this Brotherhood

The Elohim saw their Oath Eternal Fire; they rolled
apart trembling over The

Mercy Seat: each in his station fixt in the Firmament
by Peace Brotherhood and Love.

The Curtain falls.

NOTES

Blake's Works are abbreviated in the Notes as follows:

PS	*Poetical Sketches*
SI	*Songs of Innocence*
SE	*Songs of Experience*
SIE	*Songs of Innocence and of Experience*
FR	*The French Revolution*
MHH	*The Marriage of Heaven and Hell*
SL	*A Song of Liberty*
VDA	*Visions of the Daughters of Albion*
Eur	*Europe*
SL	*The Song of Los*
BU	*The First Book of Urizen*
BA	*The Book of Ahania*
BL	*The Book of Los*
FZ	*Vala, or the Four Zoas*
M	*Milton*
J	*Jerusalem*
OED	refers to the *Oxford English Dictionary*.

For references to Bentley, Damon, Erdman, Frye and Stevenson, see Further Reading.

Terms printed in small capitals in the Notes are more fully defined in the Dictionary of Proper Names.

Poetical Sketches

A collection of Blake's earliest known work, printed for him by his wealthier friends John Flaxman and the Rev. A. S. Mathew in 1783 but not publicly distributed. There are twenty-two known copies, some containing corrections in B.'s hand. The 'Advertisement' (p. ii) reads:

'The following Sketches were the production of untutored youth, commenced in his twelfth, and occasionally resumed by the author till his twentieth year; since which time, his talents having been wholly directed to the attainment of excellence in his profession, he has been deprived of the leisure requisite to such a revisal of these sheets, as might have rendered them less unfit to meet the public eye.

'Conscious of the irregularities and defects to be found in almost every page, his friends have still believed that they possessed a poetic originality, which merited some respite from oblivion. These their opinions remain, however, to be now reproved or confirmed by a less partial public.'

B.'s literary models include Elizabethan poetry, Shakespearean drama, Milton, Thomson's *Seasons* (1726–30), Percy's *Reliques of Ancient Poetry* (1756), Gray, Collins and the then popular archaic forgeries of 'Ossian' and Chatterton. His antipathy is the elegant Augustan couplet and its imitations.

MISCELLANEOUS POEMS

TO SPRING
The metre of this and the following five lyrics is irregular blank verse.

13–16 *pour . . . modest tresses* The imagery recalls Collins's 'Ode to Evening': 'While Spring shall pour his showers, as oft he wont/And bathe thy breathing tresses, meekest Eve.'

15 *languish'd head* A phrase from Milton: *Comus* 744 and *Samson Agonistes* 119.

TO SUMMER
6 *thy ruddy limbs and flourishing hair* Reappears in the Notebook epigram 'Abstinence sows sand all over/The ruddy limbs & flaming hair,' p. 153 below.

TO AUTUMN

The close of this poem parallels that of Milton's *Lycidas*: 'Thus sang the uncouth swain . . .'

TO WINTER

11 *and his hand*] Printed 'and in his hand', corrected by B. in some copies.

16 *mount Hecla* An Icelandic volcano mentioned in Thomson's *Winter* 888.

TO MORNING

1 In Spenser's *Epithalamion* 151, Phoebe rises at dawn 'Clad all in white, that seems a virgin best'.

FAIR ELENOR

This poem and 'Gwin' (p. 32 below) are in the archaizing and sensational 'Gothic' style popular in the late eighteenth century. Both are ballads.

34-5 *the arrows that fly . . . destruction* Psalm 91: 5-6: 'the arrow that flieth . . . the destruction that wasteth'.

61 *behold*] Printed 'I am', corrected by B. in some copies.

68 *to bereave my life* The usage occurs in Spenser, *Faerie Queene* I.iii.36.2: 'He to him leapt, in mind to reave his life'.

SONG: 'HOW SWEET I ROAM'D . . .'

B. is supposed to have written this lyric before the age of fourteen (Bentley, *Blake Records*, 428). The 'prince of love' is Eros or Cupid, and the winged victim suggests Psyche (Gr. 'soul'), who was depicted as a young woman with butterfly wings, or simply as a butterfly, in books B. might have seen during his apprenticeship.

SONG: 'MY SILKS AND FINE ARRAY . . .'

This poem is a pastiche of Elizabethan imagery. For example, the clown's song in *Twelfth Night*, II.iv.52, 'Come away, come away, death,' has a dying lover, yew, and a true lover weeping over a tomb. The grave-digger in *Hamlet* (v.i.94–5) sings of 'A pickax, and a spade, a spade,/For and a shrouding sheet'. The female lover, however, is not typically Elizabethan.

SONG: 'LOVE AND HARMONY COMBINE...'

16 *his*] Printed 'her', corrected by B. in one copy.

MAD SONG

Percy's *Reliques* contained six 'Mad Songs' and a note that 'madness' seemed to be a peculiarly English theme.

2 *the night is a-cold* In *King Lear* III.iv.152, 'Poor Tom's a-cold.'

4 *infold*] Printed 'unfold', altered by B. in one copy.

7 *birds*] Printed 'beds', corrected by B. in some copies.

17 *Like a fiend in a cloud* This line reappears in 'Infant Sorrow', *SE*, p. 129 below, and the image of the 'cloud' as the fleshly body which hides and imprisons the essential spirit is also in 'The Little Black Boy', *SI*, p. 106 below.

SONG: 'WHEN EARLY MORN...'

1 Resembles *Lycidas* 187, 'While the still morn went out with Sandals gray.'

TO THE MUSES

Solicitations to the muses were an eighteenth-century commonplace, probably derived from the unsatisfied search in *Lycidas* 50–55, 'Where were ye Nymphs ... For neither were ye playing on the steep ... Nor on the shaggy top of *Mona* high,/Nor yet where *Deva* spreads her wisard stream'.

GWIN, KING OF NORWAY

13 *Gordred the giant* Probably from Chatterton's 'Gordred Covan' (printed in 1778 in Chatterton's *Miscellanies*, but in magazine form earlier).

65 *like balances* The image of heavenly scales as a sign before a conflict is from *Paradise Lost* IV.1011–14.

75-88 Addison's *The Campaign* 11-12 has 'Rivers of blood . . . and hills of slain,/An Iliad rising out of one campaign'. 'Hills of slain' is a repeated phrase in Chatterton.

83 *Like blazing comets* In *1 Henry IV* 1.i.10-13, armies 'like the meteors of a troubled heaven . . . Did lately meet in the intestine shock/ And furious close of civil butchery'.

AN IMITATION OF SPEN[S]ER

An early attempt on B.'s part to define his poetic vocation. The title is printed 'Spencer', and is uncorrected. B. uses Spenserian archaisms and a nine-line stanza, but does not attempt to reproduce Spenser's rhyme scheme.

10-15 *brutish Pan . . . Midas* Midas carelessly judged Pan superior to Apollo in a singing contest, and was rewarded with ass's ears.

13 *leesing* B. takes Spenser's 'lesing' or 'leasing' (lie, falsehood) as an adjectival form.

18 *tinkling rhimes, and elegances terse* Criticism of the 'elegant' eighteenth-century couplet.

19 *Mercurius* Mercury, messenger of the gods, and god of Eloquence.

33 B. idealistically attributes to Eloquence what Richard Glover in *London: or, the Progress of Commerce* (1739) attributed to Commerce: 'Thou, gracious Commerce, from his cheerless caves/In horrid rocks and solitary woods/The helpless wand'rer, man, forlorn and wild/Did charm to sweet society.'

46 *Pallas, Minerva* Greek and Latin names for the goddess of Wisdom.

BLIND-MAN'S BUFF

Metre, tone and opening image are from the song in *Love's Labour's Lost* v.ii.922-3, 'When icicles hang by the wall/And Dick the shepherd blows his nail'.

KING EDWARD THE THIRD

An unfinished dramatic fragment inspired by Shakespeare's history plays, especially *Henry V*. The metre is blank verse, but extremely loose. The play combines an ironic treatment of military values urged in the name of high ideals, with an attempt at Shakespearean 'sympathy' even for villains and misled men, and an apparently genuine admiration for bravery. B. might have found both the historical details and his critical approach to Edward and his conquests in Thomas Cooke's *Life of King Edward III of England* (1734), which saw Edward as a 'gallant and illustrious Murderer'.

SCENE 1

9 *Liberty* The major ideal invoked by patriotic English poets throughout the eighteenth century. In the most famous example, Thomson's poem *Liberty* (1735), 'Cressy, Poitiers, Agincourt proclaim/ What Kings supported by almighty love/And people fired with liberty can do' (IV.865–7).

19 *triple steel* The demons in *Paradise Lost* II.569 are armed 'with stubborn patience as with triple steel'.

SCENE 2

16 *first to commerce?* The virtues of Commerce were celebrated in a large body of eighteenth-century Whig poetry, including Young's *The Merchant* (1729), dedicated to 'His grace the Duke of Chandos' (Chandos is one of B.'s characters here), Glover's *Progress of Commerce* (1739) and Thomson's *Liberty*.

36–7 The Druids of ancient England are supposed to have worshipped in oak groves. Hence the Bishop's 'wisdom' is ironically more heathen than Christian.

52 *'tis with princes as 'tis with the sun* King Henry gives Prince Hal similar advice in *I Henry IV* III.ii.29–91.

SCENE 3

154ff. Dagworth's conversations with the common soldiers parallel those of the young King in *Henry V* IV.i.

272–4 *but the pure soul . . . heaven of glory* The headstrong Hotspur in *I Henry IV* I.iii.201–2 cries: 'By heaven, methinks it were an easy leap/To pluck bright honour from the pale-faced moon'.

SCENE 4

Stage direction *William his Man* Presumably the mouthpiece of
William Blake; hence the scene is ironic.

SCENE 6

1 *Trojan Brutus* The legendary Brutus who was supposed to have
escaped the fallen Troy and founded the British nation.

51 *prevented* Prefigured and eclipsed.

DRAMATIC FRAGMENTS

PROLOGUE . . . KING EDWARD THE FOURTH

1 *O For a voice* Parallels the prologue to *Henry V*.

4 *Who can stand?* The 'who shall stand' formula is used in Nahum
1:6, Malachi 3:2, Revelation 6:17.

PROLOGUE TO KING JOHN

The form of the prose-poem was popular in B.'s day. B. wrote five other
experimental pieces in the same style: 'The Couch of Death', 'Con-
templation' and an unfinished 'Samson' (not reprinted here) which
conclude *PS*; and the MS. fragments 'Then She Bore Pale Desire' and
'Woe Cried the Muse'.

1 *Albion's breast* Albion here is female: she is the soul of England
which must be redeemed from Tyranny and War. In B.'s later work
Albion is a male figure whose female counterpart is named 'Jerusalem'.

A WAR SONG TO ENGLISHMEN

Possibly the second mistrel's song promised to Dagworth in *King
Edward the Third* sc. 4. If so, the promise of 'glorious' death should be
taken ironically.

POEMS WRITTEN IN A COPY OF *POETICAL SKETCHES*

These three poems were written in a copy of *Poetical Sketches* inscribed 'from Mrs Flaxman May 15, 1784'. 'Song 2nd by a Young Shepherd' is an early version of 'Laughing Song', *SI*, p. 109 below.

SONG BY AN OLD SHEPHERD

1 Compare the opening of 'Blind-man's Buff', *PS*, p. 37 and n.

Songs from 'An Island in the Moon'

Date of composition: *c.* 1784. 'Island' is an untitled and unfinished MS. burlesque on a lunar society which 'seems to have some affinity to England'. The characters, parodies of Blake himself and his circle of friends, meet in a salon-type setting and occasionally break – sober or drunk – into song. The 'three philosophers' are Quid the Cynic (William Blake), Suction the Epicurean (Robert Blake) and Sipsop the Pythagorean (probably the Platonist Thomas Taylor). Steelyard the Lawgiver is B.'s friend John Flaxman. There is a full discussion of the work by M. W. England, 'Apprenticeship at the Haymarket?' in D. V. Erdman and J. E. Grant (eds.), *Blake's Visionary Forms Dramatic*, Princeton University Press, 1970.

CHAP 3

12 *Honour & Genius* Parody of a song in James Harris's *Daphnis and Amaryllis* (1762).

CHAP 6

13 *When old corruption* Suggested by John Gay's 'On Quadrille' (1727), 'When as Corruption hence did go/And left the nation free ... Then Satan, thinking things went ill/Sent forth his spirit, call'd Quadrille.' As a satire on the medical profession, this song may have been suggested by the play *The Devil Upon Two Sticks*, currently on stage. It also parodies the genealogy of Sin and Death in *Paradise Lost* 11.

CHAP 8

4 *John Taylor* Probably the dissenting minister (1694–1761), author of *The Scripture Doctrine of Original Sin*, 1740.

CHAP 9

3 *Lo the Bat* A combined parody of Pope's 'Lo, the poor Indian' (*Essay on Man* 1.99) and Collins's 'Weak-eyed bat' which 'with short shrill shriek flits by on leathern wing' ('To Evening' 9–10).

58 *This frog* From a popular nursery-rhyme.

116–17 *Doctor South/Or Sherlock* Dr Robert South (1634–1716) and Dr William Sherlock (1641–1707), author of *A Practical Discourse concerning Death* (1689), were writers of religious tracts. They are here contrasted with the philanthropist Thomas *Sutton* (1532–1611), founder of Charterhouse, a charitable boys' school and hospital for the aged.

147 *This city & this country* A parallel to the popular song 'The Roast Beef of Old England' from Fielding's *Grub Street Opera*.

CHAP 11

1 *Upon a holy thursday* First version of 'Holy Thursday', *SI*, p. 111 below.

20 *When the tongues of children* First version of 'Nurse's Song', *SI*, p. 114 below.

38 *O father* First version of 'The Little Boy lost', *SI*, p. 109 below.

103 *A crowned king* This song is unfinished; a leaf is missing from the MS.

There is No Natural Religion [a, b]; All Religions are One

These three series of aphorisms, etched in 1788 on tiny copperplates, form B.'s earliest work in illuminated printing. They also constitute his first attack on deism, and his first apologia for the Poetic or Prophetic Character as the source of all religion and philosophy. The ideas, the mockery of rationalism and the insistence on Man's potential infinitude are further developed in *MHH*.

The Book of Thel

Date: 1789 for most of the text, but Erdman and others agree that
'Thel's Motto' and the conclusion (Pl. 6) are no earlier than 1791.
Fifteen copies of this illuminated book are known.

Thel (Gr. 'wish' or 'will') may be understood equally as descending
to earthly life, to death or to the state of Experience. Like the virgin-
goddess Persephone, she undertakes a descent to the underworld; but
she fears and rejects the impending transformation. The metre is iambic
septenary, B.'s adaptation of ballad form into long lines.

THEL'S MOTTO

Pl. i   Ll. 3–4 form a deleted line in *Tiriel*, and appear to allude to 'Or
ever the silver cord to be loosed, or the golden bowl be broken',
Ecclesiastes 12:6. But the silver rod and golden bowl here evidently
stand for male and female sexual organs.

I

Pl. I.1   *Mne Seraphim*   An obscure name, not used again. The term
'Bne Seraphim' ('Sons of the Seraphim') occurs in the *Occult Philo-
sophy* of the alchemist philosopher Cornelius Agrippa (1486–1535), and
is associated with concord, cure of melancholy and barrenness, and
increase of fruitfulness in men and animals. Alteration to 'Mne' puns
on 'Mnetha' (see *Tiriel*) to produce ironic associations. Thus Thel
remains lonely and virginal, rejecting fruitfulness for herself.

4   *river of Adona*   Probably from the river Adonis in *Paradise Lost*
1.450–52, hence associated with rituals of fertility and of death and
rebirth.

13–14   *the voice/Of him that walketh*   'And they heard the voice of the
Lord God walking in the garden in the cool of the day,' Genesis 3:8.

Pl. 2.1   *the vales of Har*   See *Tiriel* 2.4ff., *The Song of Los* 4.5–16.

II

Pl. 3.8   *Luvah*   A sun-god of Love. This is the first mention of any
of the FOUR ZOAS.

IV

Pl. 6.1 In the cave of the Naiads (*Odyssey*, XIII) there are two gates, one towards the north, for men; one to the south, for gods. The neo-Platonists explained this passage allegorically as a descent of the soul to matter. In Spenser's *Faerie Queene* III.vi.31 the Garden of Adonis, in which all souls grow, also has 'Double gates . . . th'one fair and fresh, the other old and dried,' and a porter, 'Old Genius, the which a double nature had'.

9 *her own grave plot* Her own body, or her own potential Experience. In neo-Platonic theory, what we call 'life' should be understood as death or imprisonment to the soul.

& there she sat down 'By the rivers of Babylon, there we sat down, yea, we wept, when we remembered Zion,' Psalm 137:1.

19–20] Lines deleted in two copies.

Tiriel

Date: *c.* 1789. An eight-page manuscript, never published, written in a fair hand except for the conclusion (8.4ff.), which is hastily written and may be some years later. Deletions of lines and passages occur throughout. The theme is Tyranny. The manner is Gothic. The metre is septenary.

1

1 *Aged Tiriel* The name is found in Agrippa's *Occult Philosophy*, associated with the planet Mercury and the base elements sulphur and mercury. It also suggests 'tyrant', 'ritual' and the Prince of Tyre denounced by Ezekiel for assuming the role of God. Analogues to Tiriel's obsessively tyrannical and blind personality include Oedipus, King Lear and possibly George III of England, some years later described by Shelley as 'An old, mad, blind, despised and dying King'.

3 *Myratana . . . western plains* In the antiquarian Jacob Bryant's *New System* (1774–6), *Myrina* is a queen of *Mauretania* (West Africa).

22 *Serpents not sons* 'Tigers, not daughters,' *King Lear* IV.ii.40.

25 *Heuxos or Yuva* The source of these names is unknown.

35 *son of Zazel* Zazel, a rejected and enslaved brother of Tiriel (section 7). The name occurs in Agrippa's *Occult Philosophy*, associated with discord and loss of honours (Damon), and in occult Hebraic–Christian tradition as an earth demon who presides over corpses (Stevenson). *Azazel* is Heb. 'scapegoat'.

2

4 *vales of Har* Since *Har* is Heb. 'mountain', 'vales of Har' is ironic or pathetic.

5 *Har & Heva* Tiriel's parents, a degenerated and senile Adam and Eve representing the failure of Natural Law.

6 *Mnetha* Compound of Athena (Wisdom) and Mnemosyne (Memory, mother of the muses), the nurse or foster-mother of Har and Heva.

3

14 *the cage of Har* This and ll. 22–3 are literary satire, with 'great cage' suggesting the heroic couplet and 'our singing birds' and 'fleeces' suggesting domesticated neo-classical lyric and pastoral.

4

3 *Ijim* In Isaiah 13:21, this is a collective term meaning 'creatures of the wilderness' or 'satyrs'. The figure here represents savage superstition – an alternative to Tiriel's civilization, but not an acceptable one. He may be a satire on Rousseau's 'noble savage'.

40 *bore him on his shoulders* Ironic inversion of Aeneas bearing his father Anchises on his shoulders *from* the burning Troy (*Aeneid* II.705–29).

50–61 The transformations resemble those of Proteus in Ovid's *Metamorphoses* VIII.734–8.

59 *toad . . . in my ears* Satan is found 'Squat like a toad, close at the ear of Eve' in *Paradise Lost* IV.800.

87 *Orcus* A Latin name for Hell.

5

18 *five daughters* Five senses.

24 *Hela* A Norse goddess of Hell in Gray's 'Descent of Odin'.

33 *Thirty . . . sons* Compare the degeneration of the thirty cities of Africa in *BU* IX, p. 257 below.

6

5 *This is the right & ready way* Possible ironic allusion to Milton's *The Ready and Easy Way to Establish a Free Commonwealth* (1660), comparably written in desperation during a political collapse.

43 *Let snakes rise* Medusa was thus accursed by Athena.

8

10 *one law* 'One Law for the Lion & Ox is Oppression' (conclusion of *MHH*). See also *VDA* 4.22.

37–41 *Compelld to pray . . . my thirsty hissings* Tiriel's story parallels that of Satan in *Paradise Lost*. Satan is compelled to worship, and rebels. He becomes a subtle serpent in Paradise. In *PL* x.504–77 Satan and his followers are transformed unwillingly into serpents, and forced to chew a seeming fruit of knowledge which turns to ashes: 'Thus were they plagued/And worn with famine long, and ceaseless hiss.'

Songs of Innocence and of Experience

The Songs of Innocence were composed *c.* 1784–90. Drafts of 'Nurse's Song', 'The Little Boy lost' and 'Holy Thursday' appear in *An Island in the Moon*. The illuminated volume was first published alone (1789), later incorporated in the combined volume *Songs of Innocence and of Experience* (1794), but also sometimes issued separately thereafter.

The *Songs of Experience* were composed for the most part between 1790 and 1792 (see Notebook drafts, pp. 134–61 below). But 'The Little Girl Lost', 'The Little Girl Found', 'The School Boy' and 'The Voice of the Ancient Bard' first appeared in *Innocence* and were then transferred to *Experience*. 'To Tirzah' does not appear in five copies, and may be from 1805 or later (Erdman). There are twenty-one known copies of *SI* and twenty-seven of *SIE*. The order of the poems within each group varies, but eight copies follow the arrangement given here.

The form of these songs may suggest Tudor and Jacobean lyric, Wesleyan hymns, and nursery rhymes. In part, the form also derives from Isaac Watts (1674–1748), whose *Divine and Moral Songs in Easy Language* (1715), a chapbook of short poems intended for children, was still popular in B.'s day. Several of B.'s poems implicitly criticize Watts's religion and morality.

SONGS OF INNOCENCE

THE ECCHOING GREEN

Title A village common.

The scene, the day–night cycle and the images of animated nature corresponding with human activity all parallel Spenser's *Epithalamion*.

THE LAMB

Title 'The next day John seeth Jesus coming unto him, and saith, "Behold the Lamb of God, which taketh away the sin of the world"' (John 1:29). See also the conclusion of B.'s prose tract *There is No Natural Religion*: 'Therefore God becomes as we are, that we may be as he is,' p. 76 above.

THE LITTLE BLACK BOY

The Society for the Abolition of the Slave Trade was formed in 1787, and many artists and writers were involved in this movement. B. too opposed slavery, but the plea of this poem is more fundamentally against doctrines of racial and religious superiority. Immediate targets may have been Watts's lyrics 'Praise for Birth and Education in a Christian Land' and 'Praise for the Gospel', in both of which a little English boy thanks God for making him born a Christian, and pities the heathen.

14 *to bear the beams of love* cf. Watts's 'Grace Shining and Nature Fainting' (*Horae Lyricae*, 1709): 'Nor is my soul refined enough/To bear the beaming of his love,/And feel his warmer smiles./When shall I rest this drooping head?/I love, I love the sun, and yet I want the shade.'

16 *but a cloud* Dante's *Purgatorio* XXVIII.90 compares the body to a cloud.

25 *Ill shade him* The two boys will be 'free' of their bodies – yet one is still darker, one whiter and needing assistance. Why? The paradox is adumbrated by Job 19:26: 'though after my skin worms destroy this body, yet in my flesh shall I see God'.

THE CHIMNEY SWEEPER

This poem may be read in two contrary ways: 1. As an indictment of a society which enslaves children both physically and spiritually, promising heaven hereafter in exchange for obedient suffering here, its conclusion in favour of 'duty' is bitterly ironic (see 'An answer to the parson', p. 155 below). 2. As a celebration of the boys' imagination, the conclusion is positive, the happiness and warmth are not delusive but real, and 'duty' means seeing and feeling the delightful reality of spiritual life. See B.'s letter to Hayley, Oct. 1803: '. . . now I have lamented over the dead horse let me laugh and be merry . . . for as Man liveth not by bread alone I shall live altho I should want bread – nothing is necessary to me but to do my Duty and to rejoice in the exceeding joy that is always poured on my Spirit' (*Letters*, ed. Keynes, 100–101).

3 *weep weep* Ironically foreshortened pronunciation of the street-cry 'Sweep!'

THE LITTLE BOY LOST

A draft of this poem appears in *An Island in the Moon*.

8 *the vapour* A will-o'-the-wisp; the 'wand'ring light' of the next poem. The design shows the boy pursuing a light, perhaps mistaking it for his father.

LAUGHING SONG

An earlier version of this poem is on p. 61; the girls' names are different.

A CRADLE SONG

In part a reaction to Watts's metrically similar 'Cradle Hymn', where the mother congratulates her infant on being materially better off than the infant Jesus: 'How much better thou'rt attended/Than the Son of God could be . . . Here's no ox anear thy bed,' etc. B.'s mother sings of spiritual rather than material grace, and perceives the closeness of infant and Creator rather than the distinction.

THE DIVINE IMAGE

17 *all must love* Both an imperative, 'all *should* love', and a declarative, 'all *do* (logically, of necessity) love'.

HOLY THURSDAY

Title Charity children were brought to annual services at St Paul's on the first Thursday in May. A first draft of this poem appears in *An Island in the Moon*, where the children wear 'grey' instead of 'red'.

9 *mighty wind* In Acts 2:1–4 the sound of a 'rushing mighty wind' comes from heaven, and the congregation, filled with the Holy Ghost, begins to speak in tongues.

NIGHT

31 *each mild spirit* The angels receive the spirits of predators as well as victims.

42 From the vision of the peaceable kingdom in Isaiah 11:6.

45 *lifes river* 'And he showed me a pure river of water of life, clear as crystal, proceeding out of the throne of God and of the Lamb,' Revelation 22:1.

INFANT JOY

2–5 The repetition of 'I am' in connection with the query 'What shall I call thee?' suggests Moses' first encounter with the God who identifies Himself as 'I AM'. By implication the infant is divine and divinity is 'joy'.

A DREAM

Watts's song 'The Ant, or Emmet' is metrically similar.

1 *a shade* Shadow or protection.

ON ANOTHERS SORROW

22 *Wiping all our tears away* 'and God shall wipe away all tears from their eyes', Revelation 7:17, 21:4.

SONGS OF EXPERIENCE

INTRODUCTION

Interpretation of this poem depends upon whether the call of stanzas 2–4 is that of the Bard, or that of the Holy Word. It also depends upon whether the Holy Word and this call are to be conceived as generous and merciful or tyrannical and punitive. Unlike the tender God of *Innocence*, the God of *Experience* is the repressive father-figure of institutional religion.

4–7   Adam and Eve, having sinned, 'heard the voice of the Lord God walking in the garden in the cool of the day: and . . . hid themselves . . . amongst the trees of the garden,' Genesis 3:8.

8   *That*   may refer to 'voice', 'Holy Word' or 'lapsed soul'.

8–9   *controll*   Restrain, curb (*OED* 4.b).
   The starry pole   The north pole, or region of the pole star. In B. this image is associated with war and monarchy.

11   From Jeremiah 22:29: 'O earth, earth, earth, hear the word of the Lord.' Milton, in *The Ready and Easy Way to Establish a Free Commonwealth*, complaining that England was choosing 'a Captain back for Egypt', declares, 'Thus much I should perhaps have said, though I were sure I should have spoken only to Trees and Stones; and had none to cry to, but with the Prophet, "O Earth, Earth, Earth!" to tell the very Soil itself, what her perverse inhabitants are deaf to.'

18   *starry floor*   An image of Reason. Stars in B. are associated with the rational God who created a Newtonian cosmos. As in ancient metaphysics, the stars are symbols or agents of Necessity, which rules the world of Nature.

19   *watry shore*   An image of Materialism, elsewhere in B. called the dead 'sea of Time and Space'.

EARTH'S ANSWER

The Notebook draft for this poem is on p. 142 below.

7   *Starry Jealousy*   The Jealous God, who created the stars in conformity with Reason and Law, demands obedience from the soul, and keeps Earth imprisoned. Elsewhere in Blake this God is called URIZEN.

13-15 Can a creative or procreative impulse fulfil itself when repressed?

21 *this heavy chain* Reason; repressive Moral Law; the flesh itself.

23 *vain* (1) Self-admiring; (2) futile.

HOLY THURSDAY

A 'contrary' poem to that of *Innocence*. The Notebook draft is on p. 155 below.

4 *usurous hand* (1) Economically, the supposed benefactors of the charity children are rich citizens of London; (2) spiritually, the citizens expect a return of gratitude on their investment of charity.

THE LITTLE GIRL LOST

In this and the following poem, Lyca (like the heroine of *The Book of Thel*) may be understood as the soul entering mortal life, or the Innocent entering Experience – specifically sexual experience. Though the new state seems a decline (a sleep), she does not fear it, and is protected. Details derive from neo-Platonic interpretations of the myth of Persephone, as well as the 'Sleeping Beauty' and 'Snow White' of fairy tales.

3-4 (1) Sleep is the 'sentence' passed on earth (and all mankind). It is both serious ('grave') and profound ('deep'). (2) It is a sentence of death. (3) 'Grave' also means 'engrave'.

7-8 *the desart . . . a garden* In Isaiah 35:1 'the desert shall rejoice, and blossom as the rose'. In the myth of Persephone, the earth grows barren when the virgin-goddess is captured by the King of Hades, but resumes its fertility at her annual return each spring.

13 *Seven Summers old* The design, however, shows an adolescent maiden embracing a youth.

THE LITTLE GIRL FOUND

2 *Lyca's parents* In the myth, the earth-goddess Ceres seeks her abducted daughter through the world, and finally bargains for her annual return. B., however, gives *two* parents and has them remain with the child.

36 According to some classical sources, Pluto (god of the underworld) and Zeus (god of heaven) are one. Here, 'beast' and 'spirit' are one.

THE CHIMNEY SWEEPER

The 'contrary' poem to that of *Innocence*. Notebook draft, p. 151.

NURSES SONG

The 'contrary' poem to that of *Innocence*. Notebook draft, p. 144.

THE SICK ROSE

Notebook draft, p. 149.

THE FLY

Notebook draft, p. 156.

5–6 From Gray's 'Ode on the Spring': 'Poor moralist! and what art thou? A solitary fly.'

THE ANGEL

Notebook draft, p. 155. An allegory on Chastity.

THE TYGER

See *MHH* 8.7, p. 184 below: 'The roaring of lions, the howling of wolves, the raging of the stormy sea, and the destructive sword. are portions of eternity too great for the eye of man.' 'Contrary' poem to 'The Lamb', *Innocence*. Notebook draft, p. 145.

2 *forests of the night* The dark woods of Dante's *Inferno* and Milton's *Comus* represent Nature. Both contain beasts which symbolize the dangerous passions. B.'s tyger is (1) God's wrath, as the Lamb is His Love; (2) a ruthless natural predator; (3) man's own 'burning' passion shut in his natural body. The questioner – throughout the poem – cannot understand how such things come to be.

4 *frame* (1) Construct, fabricate; (2) place within a restrictive border.

6 *fire of thine eyes* (1) Fiery eyes; (2) fire itself, before it was seized and used for eyes.

17–18 *the stars . . . their spears . . . their tears* The fading of the first stars, falling of the first dew? In *FZ* v.64.26–8 the god of Reason, URIZEN, describes the Fall: 'I called the stars around my feet in the night of councils dark/The stars threw down their spears & fled naked away/We fell.' Here, too, the suggestion is that Reason, having created a 'frame' for primordial Energy, is still inadequate to deal with it.

MY PRETTY ROSE TREE

Notebook draft, p. 134.

AH! SUN-FLOWER

In Ovid's *Metamorphoses* the nymph Clytie pines away for love of the scornful sun-god Hyperion, and is transformed to a flower whose face follows the path of the sun all day.

THE LILLY

Notebook draft, p. 144.

THE GARDEN OF LOVE

Notebook draft, p. 135.

THE LITTLE VAGABOND

Notebook draft, p. 153.

LONDON

Watts's 'Praise for Mercies' begins, 'Whene'er I take my walks abroad,/ How many poor I see.' Watts's comfortable child–speaker, noting the starvation, ragged clothing, ill-housing and criminal tendencies of others, promises to love the God who has created these pleasant inequities.

1 *charter'd* The charters of London were ancient guarantees of the city's liberties. B.'s use is ironic.

10 *appalls* (1) Horrifies, frightens; (2) casts a pall over.

15–16 The harlot to whom a young man resorts may infect both him and his family. But all are victimized by the deadening institution of the 'Marriage hearse', which prohibits free love.

THE HUMAN ABSTRACT

'Contrary' poem to 'The Divine Image', *Innocence*. Notebook draft, p. 147.

5 *mutual fear brings peace* A summary description of the Social Contract.

14 *Mystery* B.'s first mention of the TREE OF MYSTERY.

INFANT SORROW

'Contrary' poem to 'Infant Joy', *Innocence*. Notebook draft, p. 139.

A POISON TREE

Notebook draft, p. 138.

A LITTLE BOY LOST

'Contrary' poem to 'The Little Boy lost' and 'Found', *Innocence*. Notebook draft, p. 150. Watts's 'Obedience to Parents' reads: 'Have ye not heard what dreadful plagues/Are threatened by the Lord,/To him that breaks his father's law/Or mocks his mother's word? . . . The ravens shall pick out his eyes,/And eagles eat the same.'

A LITTLE GIRL LOST

'Contrary' poem to 'The Little Girl Lost', originally in *Innocence*.

TO TIRZAH

This poem is only in later copies of *SIE* and cannot be earlier than mid-1803 in its style of lettering. Tirzah, an important figure in *Milton* and *Jerusalem*, is the individual's mortal mother, or Mother Nature herself. The design shows a dead body being anointed by an old man, on whose robes appear the words, 'It is raised a spiritual body', from Paul's discussion of the resurrection of the body (1 Corinthians 15:44).

16 *what have I to do with thee?* Jesus says to Mary (John 2:4) 'Woman, what have I to do with thee?'

Notebook Poems and Fragments, c. 1789–93

B.'s much-used Notebook (also known as the Rossetti MS., since it was owned for a time by D. G. Rossetti) was apparently inherited from his brother Robert, who died in 1787. From *c.* 1789 until as late as 1818, he made this notebook a major repository for drawings and sketches, drafts and fair copies of poems, miscellaneous squibs, and prose writings.

The group of poems here consists of drafts for most of the lyrics in *Songs of Experience*, plus other lyrics written at the same period and on similar themes; two political pieces datable to 1792–3 (all this work is clustered at the back of the Notebook, which was reversed to make a new beginning); and an epigram on marriage inscribed near the front of the volume, but not dated.

'A FLOWER WAS OFFERD TO ME . . .'

Becomes 'My Pretty Rose Tree', *SE*, p. 126.

'LOVE SEEKETH NOT ITSELF TO PLEASE . . .'

Becomes 'The Clod & the Pebble', *SE*, p. 118.

'I WENT TO THE GARDEN OF LOVE . . .'

Becomes 'The Garden of Love', *SE*, p. 127.

'I HEARD AN ANGEL SINGING . . .'

An attempted 'contrary' to 'The Divine Image', *SI*, p. 111.

11–14   Slightly revised, these lines become the opening of 'The human image' (Notebook, p. 147), finally entitled 'The Human Abstract' in *SE*, p. 128.

A CRADLE SONG

An attempted 'contrary' to 'A Cradle Song', *SI*, p. 110, but not finally used in *SE*.

CHRISTIAN FORBEARANCE

Becomes 'A Poison Tree', *SE*, p. 129.

INFANT SORROW

B. kept only the first two stanzas for the poem of this name in *SE*, p. 129. It is a 'contrary' to 'Infant Joy', *SI*, p. 115.

36–7 This couplet also concludes 'In a mirtle shade' (Notebook, p. 142) and 'The Angel' (Notebook, p. 155; *SE*, p. 124).

'SILENT SILENT NIGHT'

Possibly intended as a 'contrary' to 'Night', *SI*, p. 112.

'O LAPWING ...'

The lapwing is a kind of plover, noted for a slow, irregular flapping flight and a shrill wailing cry. Probably a sexual *double entendre*; see 'Thou hast a lap full of seed'.

'THOU HAST A LAP FULL OF SEED ...'

The term is used bawdily in *Hamlet* III.ii.121: 'Shall I lie in your lap? – No, my lord. – I mean, my head upon your lap?'

EARTHS ANSWER

Used, with the deleted stanza at the centre retained, in *SE*, p. 118.

IN A MIRTLE SHADE

Keys in after stanza 6 of 'Infant Sorrow', p. 140.

LONDON

The final form of this poem is in *SE*. p. 128.

TO NOBODADDY

'Nobodaddy' is Daddy Nobody, Blake's coinage for God the Father.

'THE MODEST ROSE ...'

Becomes 'The Lilly', *SE*, p. 126.

'WHEN THE VOICES ...'

Becomes 'Nurses Song', *SE*, p. 123. 'Contrary' to that of *SI*, p. 114.

THE TYGER

First version: stanza 5 ('When the stars threw down their spears') was written later than the rest, and added on the following page of the Notebook.

Second version: this is a fair draft, written on the later page, of stanzas 1, 3, 5, 6, with stanza 2 then added to the left. But stanza 4 was now missing, and B. was apparently dissatisfied with this version. It was crossed out with several heavy strokes, and the previous rough draft was used as the basis for the final text in *SE*, p. 125.

THE HUMAN IMAGE

With the last six lines omitted, this becomes 'The Human Abstract', *SE*, p. 128.

THE SICK ROSE

Used, almost unchanged, in *SE*, p. 123.

'NAUGHT LOVES ANOTHER ...'

Becomes 'A Little Boy Lost', *SE*, p. 130.

THE CHIMNEY SWEEPER

Used unchanged in *SE*, p. 123.

MERLINS PROPHECY

In Geoffrey of Monmouth's *History of the Kings of Britain*, 'Merlin's Prophecy' is a series of gnomic verses which move from historic matters to apocalyptic imaginings. In *King Lear* the Fool concludes his set of satiric tetrameter couplets with a laconic 'This prophecy Merlin shall make; for I live before his time' (III.ii.95).

'ABSTINENCE SOWS SAND . . .'

2 *The ruddy limbs & flaming hair* Adapted from the 'ruddy limbs and flourishing hair' of 'To Summer', *PS*, p. 21.

THE LITTLE VAGABOND

Used, slightly altered, in *SE*, p. 127.

RICHES

1 *a merry heart* Stock ballad phrase, as in 'A merry heart goes all the day, Your sad heart tires in a mile-a' (*Winter's Tale* IV.iii.134), or 'And drink unto the leman mine, And a merry heart lives long-a' (*2 Henry IV* v.iii.48).

HOLY THURSDAY

Used, slightly altered, in *SE*, p. 119; 'contrary' to that of *SI*, p. 111.

THE ANGEL

In *SE*, p. 124. Ll. 15–16 are from 'In a mirtle shade', above, p. 142.

'LITTLE FLY . . .'

Becomes 'The Fly', *SE*, p. 124.

9–10 *The cut worm Forgives the plough* Deleted here, this becomes a Proverb of Hell in *MHH*, p. 183.

AN ANCIENT PROVERB

1–2 *blackning church . . . marriage hearse* Phrases from 'London', p. 128.

'LET THE BROTHELS OF PARIS BE OPENED . . .'

This and the following poem are both in very rough draft form, and were presumably written between October 1792 (the fall of La Fayette) and January 1793 (the execution of Louis XVI).

9 *Nobodaddy* 'God the Father'; see 'To Nobodaddy', note, p. 891.

20 An ironic rejoinder to Edmund Burke's famous paean on Marie Antoinette in *Reflections on the Revolution in France* (1790): 'Surely never lighted on this orb, which she scarcely seemed to touch, a more delightful vision. I saw her just above the horizon, decorating and cheering the elevated sphere she just began to move in . . . little did I dream that I should have lived to see such disasters fallen upon her in a nation of gallant men . . . but the age of chivalry is gone.'

26 *a great many suckers* Shoots growing at a plant's foot, parasites.

'FAYETTE BESIDE KING LEWIS STOOD . . .'

At the outset of the French Revolution, the Marquis de La Fayette (1757–1834) was a 'hero of the people' for his past defence of liberty in the American war, and for his gallant soldiery and statesmanship. As commander of the national guard, La Fayette became the King's *de facto* warder when the royal family was brought from Versailles to Paris by the army in October 1789. He consistently attempted to defend limited monarchy, and by 1792 was attacked by royalists as a revolutionary and by radicals (including Blake) as not revolutionary enough. After the Paris rising of August 1792 he was relieved of his command, abandoned by his army and proscribed by the Assembly. He fled France, and was arrested and imprisoned by the Austrians (1793–7). The poem is a response to his imprisonment.

The French Revolution

This poem exists as a set of page proofs, dated 1791, probably written 1790, commissioned by the radical publisher and bookseller Joseph Johnson. It was never published, and probably never continued beyond Book the First, despite the Advertisement.

The poem is a quasi-mythological treatment of events surrounding the fall of the Bastille (14 July 1789). On 17 June 1789, the Third Estate of France constituted itself a National Assembly. On 20 June it issued the 'tennis-court oath' defying the Monarchy. The King met in council on 19 and 21 June, and had several confrontations with the Assembly and Estates General in the following weeks. The much-resented troops which had been brought to Paris were ordered to withdraw on 15 July, the day after the Bastille fell.

B. condenses events of several weeks into one day, and invents some others. After a portentous opening and evocation of the Bastille as a symbol of tyranny, the royal council deliberates. 'Burgundy' and 'Archbishop' give anti-revolutionary militaristic speeches. 'Orleans' and 'Sieyes' give revolutionary and generous visionary addresses. The King (spoken for by 'Burgundy') refuses to remove the troops. But the Assembly successfully orders their withdrawal, leaving the King and peers helpless.

The metre is a loose anapestic septenary, which B. did not attempt elsewhere.

2 *the Prince* Louis XVI of France.

7 *Necker* Jacques Necker (1732–1804), the popular French–Swiss minister of finance under Louis. An anti-aristocratic economic reformer, he was dismissed 11 July 1789, recalled after the storming of the Bastille, and finally resigned 1790.

8 *five thousand years* B. uses a tradition that the world was created in 4004 BC, and that 6,000 years – now nearly concluded – would bring the Millennium (see l. 90). Five thousand years is the period of Monarchy.

13 *Forty men* (B.'s invention) the Royal Council.

16 *the Commons* B.'s term for the Third Estate, which met in May and June 1789 at Versailles. B. intends this session to be understood as simultaneous with the Royal Council meeting.

18 *the Bastile* The fortress and State prison in the centre of Paris, soon to be stormed by the populace. The thousand troops and seven towers are B.'s invention, though the fortress did hold seven prisoners when seized. Damon (314) interprets the prisoners as: (1) the poet; (2) imprisoned royalty (from the seventeenth-century story of the Man in the Iron Mask); (3) the schismatic, representing religious liberty; (4) true religion, denying the power of the State; (5) the upholder of free speech; (6) the good man turned court parasite; (7) the patriot driven to madness by hopes of liberty.

59 *heavy brow'd jealousies* A thundercloud figure opposed to 'light' (l. 53) and 'spirits of fire' (l. 54): Aristocracy opposes the Third Estate. The Royal Council, however, met at Versailles, not in the Louvre.

62 *The voice ceas'd* i.e., 'the loud voice of France', l. 15.

68ff. The following council scene is B.'s invention.

74–8 *Hide from the living . . . in the dust* In Revelation 6:15–16, kings, great men, rich men and captains 'hid themselves in the dens and in the rocks of the mountains, And said to the mountains . . ., Fall on us, and hide us . . . from the wrath of the Lamb.'

83 *Burgundy* B.'s invention. The last Duke of Burgundy died in 1714. B. uses the name (1) for association with vineyards and the wine-press of War (Isaiah 63, Revelation 14:19); (2) for a pun on Edmund Burke, whose conservative ideas in *Reflections on the Revolution in France* (1790) are reflected in Burgundy's speech.

89–90 *mowers . . . starry harvest* Imagery of stars swept to earth is found in Revelation 16:13 and 12:3–4. A last harvest of the earth is prophesied in Rev. 14:15–16.

Atlantic mountains: see Dictionary of Proper Names. Burgundy's question means: shall revolutionaries subdue the armies which defend our traditions?

99 *To enrich the lean earth* Refers to a tradition that earth soaked in blood from battles would be fruitful.

100 *starry hosts* Armies.

104 *Till Fayette point his finger* Burgundy expects Fayette to attack the Assembly (La Fayette was not in fact put in charge of the National Guard until 15 July).

109 *Necker rise, leave the kingdom* Louis dismissed the liberals from his cabinet, and exiled Necker, on 11 July 1789.

116–20] These lines follow l. 104 in the original text. W. F. Halloran argues convincingly for the present reading.

126–7 *the Archbishop . . . sulphurous smoke* The Archbishop, repre-senting clerical privilege, has Satanic attributes. His vision (ll. 130–50) resembles the dream of Eliphaz in Job 4:13–21, in which a voice asks, 'Shall mortal man be more just than God? Shall a man be more pure than his maker?' The Archbishop fears popular godlessness as portend-ing the overthrow of royal and clerical privilege.

159 *Aumont* The Duke of Aumont refused to accept command of the newly formed National Guard on the eve of 14 July.

163 *The Abbe de Sieyes* A liberal leader who sat as representative of Paris in the Third Estate, rather than as ecclesiastic in the First Estate. He represents the liberal element in the clergy, and is 'the voice of the people' (l.204).

165 *King Henry the Fourth* The great popular monarch of the sixteenth century appears to accompany Sieyes in spirit.

168–9 *Bourbon . . . Bretagne . . . Borgogne* Invented personalities.

175 *Orleans* The Duke of Orleans (1747–93) made himself popular in Paris by large gifts to the poor in time of famine, and by airing democratic views. His bust, with Necker's, was carried through the streets before the storming of the Bastille.

177 *instead of words harsh hissings* Taken from the humiliation of Satan in *Paradise Lost* x.517–19.

187–8 *Fayette . . . Mirabeau . . . Target . . . Bailly . . . Clermont* All revolutionary figures active in the National Assembly.

200 *Great Henry's soul* Henry IV (l. 165).

211–14 *When the heavens . . . inslav'd* A condensed account of the material creation as identical with the decline of Man. This doctrine becomes central in B.'s major prophecies.

216ff. A prophecy of Man's resurrection and redemption.

240 Mirabeau (not Sieyes) demanded the removal of the royal troops on 8 July 1789.

246 *blood ran down* The same image is in 'London', *SE*, p. 128.

251 *black southern prison* Probably L'Abbaye, in St Germain des Près, which a mob attacked on 29 June, releasing eleven imprisoned soldiers (Stevenson).

261 *the General of the Nation* La Fayette. The following episode (withdrawal of troops under Fayette on the Assembly's command) is B.'s invention.

294ff. An allegorical rendition of Louis's failure to maintain military control over Paris. Creatures of the slime are released, and the bottoms of the world opened, as repressed elements begin to emerge.

306 *morning's beam* A sunny peaceful morning, in contrast to the clouded morning which opens the poem.

The Marriage of Heaven and Hell

Date: *c.* 1790 ('A Song of Liberty', 1792–3). An illuminated book. Nine complete copies are known.

In part, *MHH* records B.'s reaction to Emanuel Swedenborg, a Swedish engineer-turned-visionary, whose many works were being translated into English in the 1780s. B. met John Flaxman, a fervent Swedenborgian, in about 1780, and attended the first General Conference of London Swedenborgians in 1789. There was much to attract him. Swedenborg was an enthusiast, believed in 'Divine Humanity', in the Bible as God's dictation to inspired men, in minute and total correspondences between the natural world and the world of the spirit, and in the possibility of ordinary people attaining spiritual revelation. Swedenborg also exalted sexuality and formulated the image of a 'Grand Man' whose bodily form was the form of Heaven. Blake's marginal comments on Swedenborg's *Wisdom of Angels Concerning Divine Love* (pub. 1789) are sympathetic and include the remark, 'Heaven and Hell are born together.' But further reading persuaded B. that Swedenborg's theology and morality were conventional at heart, and his imagination limited. On *Divine Providence* he annotates 'Cursed Folly!' and calls S. a 'Spiritual Predestinarian'. *MHH* attacks S. as inflated and pompous; B.'s 'Memorable Fancies' parody S.'s 'memorable relations' of spiritual experiences.

Aside from its attack on Swedenborg, *MHH* constitutes B.'s first full-scale foray on religious, political, social and literary orthodoxy, and a self-confidently exuberant announcement of his own principles.

Pl. 2 *The Argument* The first piece of free verse in English. It is a condensed history of the birth and growth of Orthodoxy in this world, and a promise of impending upheaval.

1 *Rintrah* A figure vaguely suggesting Wrath; but see the Dictionary of Proper Names.

2 *swag* Sag, sway pendulously.

4–5 *The just man . . . death* In *Pilgrim's Progress* Christian treads a perilously thin path through the Valley of the Shadow of Death.

10–13 *And a river . . . Red clay* Examples of miracles: God makes springs flow in the desert (Exodus 17:1–7) and clothes dry bones with flesh (Ezekiel 37). 'Adam' is Heb. for 'red clay'. These miracles then attract the 'villain' of false orthodoxy which drives out justice.

19-20 *the just man ... lions roam* The angry Elijah, Isaiah, Ezekiel or B. himself are all suggested as outcast voices of truth crying in the wilderness.

Pl. 3.1-2 *a new heaven ... advent* A private joke. Swedenborg had announced that a 'last Judgment was commenced in ... 1757', which happened to be the year of B.'s birth. B. in 1790 was now thirty-three – Christ's age at His death and resurrection.

3-4 *Swedenborg is the Angel ... linen clothes folded up* The angel and grave-clothes left neatly behind at the resurrection of Christ.

4-5 *dominion of Edom* Edom was the land of the despised children of Esau, a 'just man' who lost his birthright to his trickster-brother Jacob. In Genesis 27:40 the patriarch Isaac promises Esau an eventual 'dominion, that thou shalt break his yoke from off thy neck'.

5-6 *Isaiah* XXXIV prophesies a 'day of the Lord's vengeance' on 'all nations'.
Isaiah XXXV prophesies the return of 'the ransomed of the Lord', when 'The desert shall rejoice and blossom as the rose.'

11 *Good & Evil* A succinct summary of the principles of morality here follows. B. makes the following associations:

Good	Evil
Passive	Active
Reason	Energy
Angels	Devils
Heaven	Hell
Soul	Body

He proceeds to advocate (and illustrate, in his style of writing) the latter set.

Pl. 5.4-5 *And being restraind ... desire* The modern version of this idea is Freud's theory of psychic repression in which super-ego ('good' reason) subdues id ('evil' energy).

7 *the Governor or Reason is call'd Messiah* In Milton's *Paradise Lost* the son of God defeats Satan and his hosts and casts them out of Heaven. He is also the judge of Adam and Eve's guilt.

10 *Sin & Death* From *Paradise Lost* 11.648ff.

11 *in the Book ... Satan* Milton's 'Son' is an accuser and punisher. So is the 'Satan' of the Book of Job.

Pl. 6.3-4 *he prays . . . comforter* Jesus in John 14:16-17, 26, promises a comforter who is 'the spirit of truth' and the 'Holy Ghost' to inspire and sustain the disciples. But the identification of the Comforter with Desire is B.'s own.

6 *he, who dwells*] Mended in the copper from 'The Devil who Dwells'.

10-11 *Milton wrote in letters . . . and at liberty* Wrote badly and wrote well. Critics have agreed that the 'heavenly' passages of *Paradise Lost* are duller than those dealing with Satan. B. accounts for this by the assumption that Poetic Genius is always more allied to Lawless Desire, represented by Satan, than to Law and Reason, represented by God and angels.

Pl. 7.1 *corroding fires* *MHH*, like B.'s other illuminated books, was etched, a process whereby corrosive acids are used to produce a design.

5 *Proverbs of Hell* The biblical Book of Proverbs endorses conventional prudence, wisdom and morality. B.'s Proverbs of Hell are Anti-Proverbs. The form also imitates Lavater's *Aphorisms on Man* (1788), which B. read and annotated with sympathy.

11 Used in a deleted stanza of 'Little fly . . .', Notebook, p. 156.

Pl. 9.14 *The soul of sweet delight* Repeated in *VDA* 1.9, *America* 8.14.

Pl. 12.1 *The Prophets Isaiah and Ezekiel* Swedenborg's *Relations* were commonly encounters with heavenly spirits; but B. mocks S.'s solemnity.

14 *this firm perswasion removed mountains* In Matthew 17:19-20, the disciples fail to exorcise the devil from a child, and Jesus succeeds. The disciples ask, 'Why could not we cast him out?' The reply is, 'Because of your unbelief: for verily I say unto you, If ye have faith as a grain of mustard seed, ye shall say unto this mountain, Remove hence to yonder place; and it shall remove.'

Pl. 13.3 *our great poet King David* The supposed author of the Psalms.

17-18 *naked and barefoot three years* An episode in Isaiah 20.

19 *Diogenes* Greek cynic philosopher, *c.* 412-323 BC, who elected a life of virtuous poverty and lived in a tub. When Alexander asked what he might do for him, Diogenes replied, 'Step out of my light.'

20–21 *eat dung . . . left side* An episode in Ezekiel 4 connected with the captivity prophesied for Israel. Eating bread baked over dung signified defilement.

Pl. 14.1 *The ancient tradition* A tradition, pre-dating Christianity but accepted by many Christians, that the world was limited to 6,000 years. B. also accepts the tradition established by Archbishop James Ussher (1581–1656) of dating the Creation at 4004 BC.

4 *the cherub with his flaming sword* 'Cherubim, and a flaming sword' (Genesis 3:24) are set by God to prevent Adam's return to Eden.

12 *the infernal method. by corrosives* B.'s method of etching designs by acid. This is also a metaphor for the literary form of satire.

15 *the doors of perception* The five senses (see 'inlets of Soul', 4.9).

17–18 *For man has closed . . . cavern* Plato's allegory of the cave (*Republic* VII) is the major source of this image in western literature and philosophy. In B. the cave or cavern of ignorance is often literally man's skull. Cf. also Boehme's *Aurora* x.96 (quoted by Damon, 324): 'But if God did once put away that Duskiness, which moves about the Light, and that thy Eyes were opened, then in that very place where thou standest, sittest, or liest, thou shoudst see the glorious Countenance or Face of God and the whole Heavenly Gate.'

Pl. 16.1–2 *The Giants . . . in chains* Man's Energies, subdued by Reason, are like the Titans overthrown by the Olympians, or Prometheus chained to a mountain by Zeus for giving fire to mankind.

Pl. 17.4–6 *Jesus Christ . . . Sword* See Matthew 25:32–3 and 10:34.

9 *An Angel* Angels represent conventional 'good' theology and morality. This one shows B. 'Hell' from his own point of view. B. reciprocates by showing him theology from a Blakean point of view.

16–19 *stable . . . church . . . vault . . . mill . . . cave . . . void* A logical descent from the place of Jesus' birth progressively downwards, to institutional Religion, Dogma, analytical Reason, the imprisoned Mind, and the blankness which fills it (in Locke's theory of the *tabula rasa*). An Inferno vision follows but is interrupted.

Pl. 19.3–4 *My friend the Angel . . . mill* A retreat to the safer regions of philosophy and argument. 'Mills' in B. always symbolize a mechanical use of Reason.

23 *between saturn & the fixed stars* In pre-Copernican astronomy, Saturn was the outermost planetary sphere.

27 *a deep pit* For the theologian and scholar, the Bible is not a source of inspiration but a dark mystery requiring analysis. The seven houses are the schools of established religion, each with its own theologians and philosophers, which to B. are monkeys.

Pl. 20.18 *Opposition is true Friendship*] Deleted by pigment in six copies.

Pl. 22.14 *Paracelsus* Swiss physician and alchemist, 1493-1541, author of numerous medical and occult works.

15 *Behmen* Jakob Boehme (1575-1624), German shoemaker, religious mystic and visionary. Both men influenced B. Boehme in particular believed in a God who, in Himself, contains all antithetical principles.

Pl. 23.10 *bray a fool in a morter* Quotes Proverbs 27:22.

14-15 *did he not mock at the sabbath* The Devil cites scriptural evidence that Jesus scorned the Commandments. Passages referred to are Mark 2:27, John 8:2-11, Matthew 27:13-14. This view of a rebellious Jesus is further developed in *The Everlasting Gospel, c.* 1818, p. 848.

23 *Jesus was all virtue* From Lat. 'vir', man. 'Superiority or excellence, unusual ability, merit, distinction; physical strength or energy; manliness' (*OED*).

A SONG OF LIBERTY

As a topical piece, the 'Song' refers to the advent of the French Revolution in the fall of the Bastille (1789), and the hostility of the other European powers, culminating in an attempted invasion of France which was repulsed in September 1792. Most likely, the 'Song' was completed before England declared war on France in February 1793.

The allegory is as follows: In a Europe burdened by oppression, Nature gives birth to Revolution. Tyranny casts out the newborn child, but his fall rouses mankind and Tyranny collapses temporarily. In the ensuing confrontation between 'gloomy king' and 'son of fire', the former lacks morale and the latter anticipates an apocalyptic liberation.

Pl. 25.1 *The Eternal Female groand!* Nature is about to give birth. This figure is developed in B.'s later work.

7 *thy dungeon* The Bastille, sacked in 1789.

9 *thy keys* Traditional emblems of Papal authority.

11 *And weep* Line shortened from 'And weep and bow thy reverend locks,' to echo the shortest verse in the Bible, 'Jesus wept' (John 11:35) from the story of Lazarus. The old Europe, like Lazarus, is dying.

12-15 *the new born terror . . . the new born fire* This is the first appearance in Blake of ORC, spirit of Revolution, represented as a flaming youth. The 'terrible babe' figure also occurs in 'The Mental Traveller', Pickering MS., p. 499.

14-15 *mountains . . . atlantic sea* Atlantis, legendary utopian island, overcome by flood, also figures in *America*.

16 *starry king* Elsewhere developed as URIZEN, B.'s archetypal tyrant. Stars in B. are associated with rationalism and a fixed Newtonian universe.

Pl. 26.10 *the hoary element* The sea.

17 *Urthona's dens* The earth; see URTHONA. ORC, URIZEN and URTHONA are among the FOUR ZOAS who later become major figures in B.'s mythology.

Pl. 27.7 *the stony law* The Ten Commandments, inscribed on tablets of stone.

15 *For every thing that lives is Holy* Repeated in *VDA* 8.10, *America* 8.13.

Visions of the Daughters of Albion

Date of publication: 1793. An illuminated book in iambic septenary metre. Seventeen complete copies are known.

The story is simple: OOTHOON loves and offers herself to THEO-TORMON, but is raped and held captive by BROMION. Maintaining her spiritual purity and liberty, she continues to offer her love to Theo-tormon, but he does not respond.

As a tract on Free Love, the poem is a 'contrary' response to Milton's *Comus*, which idealizes Chastity. But other issues are also central to this poem: the slave trade with its sexual abuse of female slaves, the exploitation of child labour, political and religious tyranny, and the rationalism which justifies such evils. For B., all these issues are one – Slavery *versus* Liberty – and all are dramatized by the opposition between closed human possessiveness and will to power, as against open human generosity and will to love. For full discussion of the political allegory see Erdman, 226-42.

Pl. 1.1–2 Oppressed British women may look to America longingly as a symbol of political and social liberty, but also pityingly as a symbol of the slave trade.

11 *Oothoon pluck'd* The plucking of a flower traditionally symbolizes sexual initiation.

16 *Bromion rent her* Bromion rapes the newly aroused Oothoon, who hereafter is both captive woman and captive slave.

21 *Stampt with my signet* Slaves were commonly branded by their owners.

Pl. 2.3 *storms rent Theotormons limbs* Theotormon is emotionally devastated by the rape of Oothoon, but remains passive.

5 Bromion and Oothoon are 'bound' together, for the master is not truly free but dependent upon his victim.

8–10 Slaves and exploited children are kept subdued by cold religion while their masters exercise 'volcanic' lust for both sex and power.

13 *Theotormons Eagles* In Greek myth, Prometheus the fire-bringer was preyed on by the eagles of Zeus as punishment.

30–34 Body, mind and emotions, which should all be free, are rigidly limited. This destroys the individual's true life.

35–6 *Instead of morn . . . an eye/. . . instead of night a . . . charnel house* Morn should bring fresh life and energy, but now the sun is only a judging eye. Night should bring rest and renewal, but now is deadly.

Pl. 4.12–24 Bromion is troubled by a bad conscience and dim stirrings of awareness that Oothoon's vision is correct. But he quickly returns to his original position of rigid materialism and moralism.

22 *one law for both the lion and the ox?* 'One Law for the Lion & Ox is Oppression' (conclusion of *MHH*, p. 194).

Pl. 5.1ff. *her lamentation renewd* The remainder of the poem is Oothoon's rhapsody on Liberty. Its argument is as follows: (1) The god of Reason (URIZEN, l. 3) is wrong, for all individuals are unique and have their own forms, visions, joys. These are truly holy. The false holiness of State and Church wastes and exploits human energy. It also enforces loathsome marriages which in turn produce monstrous children. (2) Childhood should begin in erotic (pleasure-loving) infancy and move freely towards a mature sexuality which would bring vigour and bliss. The teachings of modesty distort this process and produce hypocrisy, self-righteousness and shame. Oothoon, having escaped these distortions, is perpetually virginal. Conventional virginity, however, is only repressed desire which must lead to auto-eroticism, a fruitless perversion. (3) True love is free. Possessiveness is not love. To prove her conviction, Oothoon offers complete liberty to Theotormon. She concludes with images of life-denying selfishness contrasted to the bliss of accepting all life as holy.

10 *contemns poverty* Disdains, despises the poor.

14–15 *the fat fed hireling . . . wastes* The gamekeeper who serves the rich at the expense of the poor; or the recruiting sergeant who lures young men away from the land.

17 *the parson* The collector of tithes, a mandatory church-tax.

Pl. 5.41–Pl. 6.3 (1) Mortality for Man means life for worms; (2) the fact of mortality reminds Man to 'seize the day'.

Pl. 7.1 *In happy copulation* Copulation between the eye and its object. Oothoon declares that even visual perception is an erotic act.

12 *Father of Jealousy* URIZEN, the god of Reason, is also the traditional 'Jealous God' of the Old Testament.

America

Date of publication: 1793. Fifteen copies of this illuminated book are known. Proofs of three cancelled plates also exist: [a] is almost identical with Pl. 3, [b] was replaced by Pl. 4, [c] fits between Pls. 8 and 9. A fourth fragment [d] was apparently rejected from this poem. The metre is iambic septenary.

Like *The French Revolution*, *America* treats history mythologically. But now B. concentrates less on day-to-day events, and more on the spiritual significance of the American revolt. The plot is as follows: Washington and his friends complain of oppression and are confronted by a wrathful Albion's angel (spirit of Repression). At this moment ORC (revolution) explodes from the mid-Atlantic, defies England and promises human liberation. The angel sounds to war, but the thirteen colonies refuse to obey and the thirteen governors are helpless. The angel sends spiritual troops armed with plagues, but the plagues recoil upon England. URIZEN the tyrant-god intervenes and freezes the action for twelve years, but it is promised that the light of revolt will reach France and set Europe aflame.

PRELUDIUM

Title added (by a small extra plate) in all but two copies.

Pl. 1.1 *The shadowy daughter ... Urthona ... red Orc* See Dictionary of Proper Names for these. Nature sustains Rebellious Energy until he is ready to seize her in a 'fierce embrace' (l. 10) which will bring liberty. The story is retold in greater detail and less optimistically in *FZ* 7 [a] 85.12–22 and 7 [b] 91.1–93.31.

2 *fourteen suns* Fourteen years.

13–15 *eagle, lion, whale, serpent* Emblems of Liberty in North and South America. In Nature, they represent powers of air, earth, water, fire.

Pl. 2.18–21 *The stern Bard ... lamentings*] These lines were omitted from almost all copies of *America*.

A PROPHECY

Pl. 3.1 *The Guardian Prince of Albion* Also called 'Albion's Angel', Pl. 5ff.

4 *Washington, Franklin, Paine & Warren, Gates, Hancock & Green* The first three were leaders of the American Revolution in military, political and ideological spheres respectively. The latter four held positions in the American army and the first Continental Congress.

14 *wrathful*] Pl. [a]: fiery.

15 *dragon* An epithet for Pharaoh in Ezekiel 29:3.

16 *red*] Pl. [a]: fierce.

Pl. 4.2–11 *Solemn heave ... murky atmosphere* A volcano explodes. Its flames and red clouds gradually take the form of Orc.

Pl. 5.2, 6 *the terror ... The Spectre* Epithets for Orc.

Pl. 6 Like the American Declaration of Independence, the speech on this plate promises life (ll. 1–5), liberty (6–11) and the pursuit of happiness (12–15).

2 Allusions to the scene at Christ's resurrection.

3–4 *The bones of death ... Reviving* In Ezekiel 37:1–10 God makes dry bones into living men.

15 *Empire is no more* Repeats the conclusion of 'A Song of Liberty', *MHH*, p. 195.

Pl. 7.3 *Orc ... serpent-form'd* See Preludium 1.15. The Angel correctly perceives that Orc is the Serpent of Rebellion against the Law of the State and the Law of God. In Pl. 8.1, Orc is wreathed around the 'accursed tree' of Good and Evil.

4–5 *the gate of Enitharmon ... Antichrist* In Revelation 12:1–4, a dragon (Satan or Antichrist) stands ready to devour the child of the 'woman clothed with the sun'.

Pl. 8.3 In B.'s reading of the Book of Exodus, the motive of the exodus was Liberty. This was perverted into Law when the Ten Commandments were issued during the wandering in the wilderness.

8 *To make the desarts blossom* 'The desert shall ... blossom as the rose,' Isaiah 35:1.

10–14 *pale religious letchery ... defil'd* These lines amalgamate phrases and ideas in *MHH* Proverb 53, 'A Song of Liberty' (Chorus), and *VDA* 1.9–10, 8.10.

15–17 The fires purify humanity. B. combines the stories of Daniel unharmed in Nebuchadnezzar's furnace (Dan. 3:25–7) and the King's dream of an image with gold head, silver breast and arms, brass belly and thighs, and feet of clay (Dan. 2:32–3). Orc's image is of noble metals without feet of clay.

Pl. 9.1–2 Albion's Angel calls to arms.
Thirteen Angels Minions of ideological repression in the colonies. But in 12.2–3 they relinquish authority and turn rebellious.

Pl. 10.6–10 *Atlantean hills ... Ariston* See Dictionary of Proper Names.

Pl. 11.12–15 Boston's Angel denounces the Church which preaches peace, pity and abstinence, but supports war, oppression and greed. Boston was a leading city in the pre-war opposition to English control.

Pl. 13.1–2 *convene/In Bernard's house* Sir Francis Bernard, Governor of Massachusetts Bay 1760–69. This incident is B.'s invention.

Pl. 14.3–4 *thunderous command ... plagues obedient* Satan and his followers are attacked by 'thunders' which inflict spiritual 'plagues' in *Paradise Lost* VI.836–8. Plagues are a common instrument of God's wrath in the Old Testament.

17 The fabled Atlantis was lost by flood; this might have happened to America also. Compare Psalm 124:2–4: 'If it had not been the Lord who was on our side, when men rose up against us: Then they had swallowed us up quick, when their wrath was kindled against us: Then the waters had overwhelmed us, the stream had gone over our soul.'

20 *the plagues recoil'd!* As in Hosea 8:7, 'They have sown the wind, and they shall reap the whirlwind.' The spiritual attack, intended to demoralize the Americans, recoils to produce civil disaffection in England. See next note.

Pl. 15.1–15 *the Pestilence began . . . shame & woe* Actual conditions referred to include riots in Bristol and London, a high desertion rate, and the mental depression of George III, later to develop into insanity.

16 *the Bard of Albion* William Whitehead, who as poet laureate (1757–85) wrote in defence of British policy.

19 *The doors of marriage are open* The revolution brings sexual liberation also (cf. *VDA*, *passim*).

26 *a vine . . . the tender grape* From the springtime image in Song of Solomon 2:13, 'the vines with the tender grape'.

Pl. 16.2 *Urizen* The god of Reason and Law (see Dictionary of Proper Names). His snows are the propaganda of counter-revolutionary writers.

14 *twelve years* The dates referred to are disputed among commentators. Possibly from 1777, the decisive defeat of Burgoyne and the endurance of Washington's troops through the cruel winter of Valley Forge, to 1789, the fall of the Bastille.

19 *the five gates* The five senses.

20 *blasting . . . mildews* Two terms in the famous curse uttered in Deuteronomy 28:22.

Europe

Date of publication: 1794. Twelve copies of this illuminated book are known, ten without the prefatory 'fairy' poem. The metre is predominantly iambic septenary, but varied by free-verse lines of shorter length.

Europe continues and extends the mythological mode of *America*. The poem takes place in a single 'night', in which the goddess ENITHAR-

MON has dominion over her consort LOS and all their children. On earth this night is the 1800 years of spiritual error from the time of Christ to the advent of the French Revolution. Enitharmon's dream – a poem within the poem – concentrates on the efforts of England to resist revolution. This takes up where *America* left off. At the conclusion, dawn comes and the inevitable final apocalypse approaches.

Pl. iii.1 *Five windows* Five senses.

6 *stolen joys . . . pleasant* 'Stolen waters are sweet, and bread eaten in secret is pleasant' is the invitation of the 'foolish woman' seductress in Proverbs 9:17.

PRELUDIUM

Pl. 1.1–2.11 Nature in the Preludium laments her own endless but meaningless fertility. Her union with ORC (in *America*) has not yet brought redemption or transcendence for the world. She is forced to produce life, but all her creations exist in pain and mutual destruction, and even their natural vigour is thwarted by the doctrines of Enitharmon.

A PROPHECY

Pl. 3.1–4 The birth of Christ (identified with Orc in this poem). The lines parallel and parody Milton's 'On the Morning of Christ's Nativity' in metre and theme. Milton celebrates the peace which descends on Nature, and the rout of paganism, at the nativity. B. acknowledges these events (l. 4) but to him it is a false dawn.

7 *Los, possessor of the moon* The proper roles of the sexes are reversed. Los should be a vigorous sun-god. Here he is only Enitharmon's consort, indulging in irresponsible hedonism.

Pl. 4.10–13 *Arise O Orc . . . thou art bound* Orc (Rebellion), son of Los and Enitharmon, has been 'bound' by his parents (the full story is in *FZ* v, pp. 59–62). The allusions are to Christ crucified. Thus, to crown him with garlands is a mockery; the 'hour of bliss' is blissful for Los, not Orc.

Pl. 6.5 Following the death of Christ, Enitharmon directs her sons to establish official Christianity, a religion in which female principles will dominate through the teaching of virgin-worship, repression of sexuality and promises of heaven for the passively virtuous.

Pl. 9.6-Pl. 13.8 The 'episode' of Enitharmon's dream, which in this world is historical reality for 1,800 years.

Pl. 9.8 *Albions Angel smitten* Takes up where *America* leaves off (*c.* 1780). Britain is responding to the American war and the threat of revolution.

12 *the council house; down rushing* Parliament collapses.

Pl. 10.2-5 *his ancient temple serpent-form'd . . . Verulam* Conservative policy reverts to the ancient spirit of DRUIDISM, supposedly the archaic religion of England. In the following passage, B. describes a supposed Druid temple, then traces this religion to man's fall from 'the infinite' into a finite material world.

10-15 *the five senses whelm'd . . . infinite* B. interprets the biblical Flood as a flood of materialism. With limited material senses, man can no longer behold 'the infinite', and so his world too becomes finite.

21-3 Druid religion was the outcome and image of Man's fallen and limited world after the Flood.

26-30 *the Stone of Night . . . attractive north* Man's mind, once free and open to light and warmth (south), is now enclosed in a cave-like skull and sunk in wintry rationality (north). We are cosmically inverted, like Nature in the Preludium, mistakenly thinking that 'north' is 'up' and 'south' is 'down'.

Pl. 12.4 *For Urizen unclaspd his Book!* As in *VDA* and *America*, URIZEN is the tyrant-god of Reason, ultimately responsible for all earthly repression.

5-13 The young are taught repressive doctrines, but they know the old order is failing.

15 *The Guardian of the secret codes* Chancellor Thurlow, dismissed 17 June 1792 (Erdman).

23-4 *Palambron shot . . . Rintrah hung* Enitharmon's sons have become Burke and Pitt, defending the old order (Erdman).

Pl. 13.1 *The red limb'd Angel* Albion's Angel, now desperate.

5 *Newton . . . enormous blast!* Newtonian rationalism is the true philosophical basis for anti-radical policy.

6-8 A surprise ending. The radicals are not suppressed. Instead, the counter-revolutionary forces are revealed to be dead leaves awaiting extinction. These lines ironically parallel the rout of the pagan gods in Milton's 'Nativity Ode'.

Pl. 13.9–Pl. 14.32 *Then Enitharmon woke . . . She ceas'd* Enitharmon is unaware of the approaching apocalypse. Her song invokes, in her children, sexual attributes intended to maintain the dominion of 'lovely Woman' (6.3).

Pl. 14. 32 *for All were forth at sport*] Mended in the copper from 'and all went forth to sport'.

35–6 The advent of dawn ends Enitharmon's dominion.

35 *the eastern gate*] Variant proof sheet adds: 'and the angel trumpet blew!'

Pl. 14.37–Pl. 15.2 Orc is released from Enitharmon's power. The French Revolution begins.

Pl. 15.1 *of Enitharmon*] Variant proof sheet adds: 'before the Trumpet blew'.

9 *Then Los arose* Los as sun-god and prophet resumes his rightful role.

The Song of Los

Date of publication: 1795, but probably composed before *The Book of Urizen* (dated 1794). An illuminated book known in five copies.

The poem is in two parts, 'Africa' and 'Asia'. *America* and *Europe* should be understood as coming between them, in historical sequence.

'Africa' outlines religious and intellectual history from Adam and Noah to Rousseau and Voltaire, and concludes with a world ripe for revolution. 'Asia' presents the cynical self-justification of kings, describes a retreating URIZEN (Tyranny) and an advancing ORC (Revolution), and concludes with a resurrection of the dead. 'Africa' is in free verse, 'Asia' primarily in a rough trimeter.

AFRICA

Pl. 3.2 *four harps* The four continents Africa, Asia, Europe, America.

8–9 LOS is the 'Spirit of Prophecy'. His children embody the evolution of that spirit through history. The tyrant-god URIZEN imposes his will through their means, as they shape men's thoughts. In the following passage, Rintrah, Palamabron, Oothoon and Leutha, Sotha and Diralada are the children of Los. See Dictionary of Proper Names for their individual characters.

11 *Abstract Philosophy to Brama* In Sir William Jones's *Asiatic Researches* (1788), Brahma is abstract and logical (Raine).

18-19 *Trismegistus . . . Pythagoras Socrates & Plato* Hermes Trismegistus, supposed divine author of the Hermetic Books (treating magic, astrology and alchemy), is grouped with the major mystic or idealist Greek philosophers.

20 *the sons of Har* All Mankind. See *Tiriel*.

20-21 *time after time . . . chain'd down* ORC is the Promethean rebel and sufferer. The 'Orc cycle' (Frye's term), in which revolutionary energy is thwarted and punished, repeats time after time in history.

22-4 Jesus hears the cry of liberty and love, but accepts a gospel of passive suffering (see *VDA*).

29 *a loose Bible* The Koran.

30 *Odin . . . a Code of War* This completes the catalogue of repressive philosophies and religions given to the nations – the East, the Hebrews, the Greeks, Christian Europe, the Mohammedans and the Germanic tribes.

Pl. 4.21] This line opens *America* which should sequentially follow.

ASIA

Pl. 6.1-2 This takes up where *Europe* leaves off. The revolutionary impulse is spreading from Europe to Asia.

3-4 *Web . . . Den* The Web of Religion; the Den of Materialism.

9 *Shall not the King call* Hereafter follows a catalogue of English devices, some publicly discussed, some actually enforced, for quelling dissent and the ambitions of the poor. (See Erdman, 284-5.)

Pl. 7.9-23 Urizen retreats to his stronghold, Hebrew Religion, but finds it dead. Books of brass, iron and gold are texts of Law, War and Economics.

27-8 *pillar of fire . . . serpent of fiery flame* Symbols of escape from tyranny (Exodus 13:21-2) and healing of plague (Numbers 21:5-9).

29 *sullen Earth* 'Like to the lark at break of day arising/From sullen earth,' Shakespeare, Sonnet 29.

31-2 *rattling bones to bones/Join* From the resurrection of the dry bones in Ezekiel 37.

35-6 As life is renewed, the grave becomes sexually procreative.

42 *Urizen Wept* 'Jesus wept' (John 11:35, shortest verse in the Bible) before the raising of Lazarus. Cf. 'A Song of Liberty', *MHH* 25.8.

The (First) Book of Urizen

Date of publication: 1794. This illuminated book is known in seven copies containing from twenty-four to twenty-eight plates, with some variation in the order. Copies [a] and [g] delete 'First' from the poem's title. Copy [a] has several significant deletions and emendations.

The Book of Urizen is B.'s ironic version of the biblical Book of Genesis. It is also the locus for his mythology in 'A Song of Liberty', *VDA*, *America*, *Europe*, *The Song of Los*, *The Book of Ahania* and *The Book of Los*, all of which rest on the ideas presented in this poem. The story is as follows: URIZEN – a god of Reason who separates himself from the other Eternals, demands obedience to his self-proclaimed principles, and falls into Chaos – is an abstract, vain and punitive deity. A body is created for him by LOS, 'the Eternal Prophet' or Divine Imagination. But Los, exhausted, divides into male (Los) and female (ENITHARMON). Their child ORC (Rebellious Energy) is born but immediately chained to a rock. Urizen then explores his deadly world, and mankind shrinks up from Eternity. Finally, some of Urizen's children begin an exodus.

It is important to note that the Creation and the Fall are, for B., one event. This event occurs in stages, each of which shows unity lapsing into duality and spiritual energy lapsing into material passivity. Humanity as we know it appears only at the very end of a long cataclysmic process, and is – from the point of view of Eternity – almost wholly pathetic.

Many of the ideas in this poem also occur in neo-Platonic, gnostic and alchemic teachings, and in the work of Jacob Boehme. There are numerous verbal echoes of Milton's *Paradise Lost*, mostly ironic in intent.

The metre of this and the following two poems is a rough anapestic trimeter.

CHAPTER I

The Fall of Urizen; his formation of Chaos.

Pl. 3.1–20 *Unknown, unprolific, repelling, void, vacuum, unseen, secret,* etc. The character of Urizen is defined by abstractions and negations for two reasons: (1) From the point of view of Eternity, Urizen is unreal; (2) only an isolated 'Reason' can invent abstract and negative terms. In a full reality, such terms would have no meaning. Note that Milton's God is praised by the angels for being 'invisible' and 'thron'd inaccessible' (*Paradise Lost* III.375–7). B. condemns such qualities in a deity, and mocks them by exaggeration.

11 *In his*] Changed from 'Like' in copy [g].

27–8 *His cold horrors . . . Urizen/Prepar'd* Urizen is always seen by B. as a winter god, like the Winter of *PS*, p. 23.

CHAPTER II

Eternity before the Fall; its initial disruption by Urizen's announcement of his principles.

36 In Eternity there are no spheres (such as planets, moons, stars, etc.) subject to the law of gravity.

37–8 Eternity is non-Newtonian. Expansion and contraction are by will, not by the law of gravity.

40–41 Details from the mustering of angelic armies in *Paradise Lost* VI.55–60.

44 *myriads of Eternity* Myriads of Eternals. Line deleted in copy [a].

Pl. 4] This plate is lacking in four copies.

10–13 This speech gives Urizen's motivation. It is intended to sound reasonable, as Urizen is Reason. *Why will you die O Eternals?* is from 'Why will ye die, O house of Israel?' (Ezekiel 18:31, 33:11). But he does not see that joy and pain are necessary contraries for a living existence, that 'a solid without fluctuation' is dead, and that the burning fires of 'the enjoyments of Genius' only appear like 'torment and insanity' to those who do not understand them (*MHH*, p. 182).

14 *I fought with the fire* Urizen fights the fire of passion within himself.

18 *self balanc'd stretch'd o'er the void* 'And the earth was without form and void' (Genesis 1:2); 'And Earth self-balanc'd on her Center hung' *Paradise Lost* VII.242.

19 *I alone, even I!* The egotism of Urizen echoes at once the biblical Jehovah ('I am the Lord thy God,' Exodus 20:2) and the Miltonic Satan.

30 *Seven deadly Sins* Urizen's own invention. Line deleted in copy [c].

34–5 A *Law* of peace, or of love, etc., is a contradiction.

40 'Thou shalt have no other gods before me' (Exodus 20:3). Milton's God promises, after 'long obedience ... One Kingdom' (*Paradise Lost* VII.159–61).

CHAPTER III

Urizen is rejected by Eternity and confined in a black globe (Chaos).

49 *All the seven deadly sins*] Line deleted in copy [a].

Pl. 5.1–2] Lines deleted in copy [a].

3–4 *Sund'ring ... Rent away* The Fall (of God or Man) is always understood by B. as a division. The *division* of Urizen from the hosts of Eternity has ironically resulted from his attempts to enforce a fixed and static *unity*.

16 Line erased in copy [a].

17 *no light from the fires* Detail from Milton's Hell, *Paradise Lost* I.61–3.

20 *he*] Changed from 'they', here and in ll. 21, 22, 23, 29, all copies. Capitalized only in copy [a]. The alteration gives Urizen sole responsibility.

21 *combining* Re-uniting with the 'self-begotten armies', l. 16 above.

22 *He dug mountains* Detail from Milton's war in Heaven, *Paradise Lost* VI. 639–69.

28–37 *a roof ... like a womb ... like a black globe ... like a human heart ... world of Urizen* The images are confused because Urizen's world is 'unorganiz'd' (6.8) and 'formless' (7.9).

Pl. 6.2-4 *Los wept . . . Urizen was rent* Los is the power of poetic imagination. If Imagination is separated from Reason, both are drastically wounded. Los is in anguish because he has lost his Mind.

CHAPTER IV [A]

Pl. 8 Composed after Pl. 10, probably originally intended to replace it.

1-2 *Los . . . Frightend* Los took fright.

2-4 *hurtling bones . . . surging . . . raging* Urizen is asleep or dead from the point of view of Eternity. This means he has become a chaos of disorganized motion. His elements (sulphur, pitch, nitre) suggest that he has become a hell; his mind is 'sulphureous' (8.3, 10.14, 10.21) because sulphur is a primal formative element in alchemical theory.

CHAPTER IV [B]

Los creates a body for Urizen. This is a parody of the seven days of creation in Genesis. Though necessary to save Urizen from Chaos, it constricts and shrinks his original powers.

Pl. 10.15 Los is now for the first time called 'the Eternal Prophet'. In Eternity there is no need for Prophecy because there is no Time. Time belongs to the fallen world, and is a necessity for it. Hence Los divides the night into 'watches' and creates 'hours, days and years' by the repeated beat of his blacksmith's hammer – which is a metaphor for the metre of poetry.

19-23 *The eternal mind . . . White as the snow* An allusion to the *tabula rasa* of Lockean psychology, a 'blank slate' empty of intrinsic ideas, capable only of receiving and combining external impressions. Urizen's mind should not be blank, but is becoming so.

33 *a roof shaggy wild* The skull covered with hair.

Pl. 11.2-6 *a red/Round globe . . . ten thousand branches* The heart and blood vessels.

11 *brain shot branches* The nervous system.

Pl. 13.6 *A craving Hungry Cavern* The digestive system.

CHAPTER V

The division into male and female.

40 Los falls into exhaustion and despair with Urizen.

51-2 *Pity began . . . dividing* As Urizen divided himself from the other Eternals, so now Los will divide into male (strong, active) and female (weak, passive). This division does not exist in Eternity. Here it indicates passive helplessness in the face of disaster.

Pl. 18.1 *The globe of life blood* The female is created from a fluid, rather than a solid rib.

CHAPTER VI

The world of Generation and the birth of Orc.

Pl. 19.13 *She fled* Eve at first flees Adam in *Paradise Lost* IV.477-82.

20 *a Worm* An embryo.

44 *Delving earth . . . resistless* Digging through the mother's body . . . irresistible.

CHAPTER VII

The binding of Orc; the rousing of Urizen.

Pl. 20.9 *A tight'ning girdle* Los feels heart-constricting jealousy.

23 The infant Oedipus was abandoned on a mountainside because of an oracle that he would kill his father and marry his mother. B.'s version of the Oedipus myth combines the theme of incest-threat with the idea of adult authority restricting youthful energy.

CHAPTER VIII

Urizen explores his dens, curses his children, and establishes Religion.

Urizen's dens signify the world of Materialism. His exploration parallels the journey of Satan through Chaos, *Paradise Lost* II. The Web of Religion he leaves trailing behind him parallels the highway built by Sin and Death in Satan's track, *Paradise Lost* II.1024-9. The episode is greatly expanded in *FZ* Night the Sixth.

Pl. 23.11–17 *Thiriel . . . Utha . . . Grodna . . . Fuzon* Urizen's four sons are the four elements air, water, earth, fire.

27 *life liv'd upon death* In a fallen world, everything lives on something else (the Ox is food) and what one appropriates, another lacks (the Dog goes hungry). Laws of unity are impossible in such a world.

Pl. 25.18 *the Web is a Female in embrio* That is, a nascent Church? B. consistently makes Churches female. The line is deleted in copy [a].

22 *The Net of Religion* A second enclosure for mankind, like the Tent of Science (Pl. 19).

CHAPTER IX

Human history begins.

23–39 *the Inhabitants . . . shrunk up* Primitive mankind recapitulates the constriction and shrinking of Urizen's divine senses.

32–3 *woven hipocrisy . . . streaky slime* The 'Net of Religion'.

38 *seven feet stature* 'There were giants in the earth in those days' (Genesis 6:4).

43–4 *thirty cities . . . human heart* 'Heart-form'd Africa' (*SL* 3.3) is the cradle of civilization.

Pl. 28.19–22 Fuzon is Moses leading the Exodus from Egypt.

The Book of Ahania

Date of publication: 1795. Only one copy of this book (printed in intaglio rather than B.'s usual relief etching) and some scattered prints of individual plates are known.

Ahania is Blake's version of the biblical Book of Exodus. This ironic and bitter narrative, which tells the failure of Man's first attempt to rebel against the god of Reason, follows directly from *The Book of Urizen*. Fuzon (Moses) attacks God, is slain by a rock which then becomes Mt Sinai, and is crucified on a Tree of Mystery. His corpse, seemingly alive, sheds pestilence throughout the forty years' wandering in the wilderness, until the Israelites reach the Promised Land (here called Asia, 4.41). The impulse to liberty has been thwarted successfully, and the poem concludes with the lament of Urizen's female 'soul', the once-beloved, now-deserted Ahania.

CHAPTER I

The rebellion of Fuzon (Exodus).

Pl. 2.1 *Fuzon* URIZEN's fiery rebel-son (*BU* 23.17-18) is Moses in the historical allegory. He also recalls Prometheus; Christ; David attacking Goliath; David's own rebellious son Absalom; and Blake's contemporary, the revolutionary Robespierre, whose policy of violence against the enemies of freedom was ultimately turned against himself.

30-34 As Urizen is wounded in the loins, his female aspect, Ahania, divides from him (cf. the division of Los and Enitharmon, *BU* v). Instantly lustful and jealous, but also anguished by this revelation of his own sexuality, he calls her Sin. In *Paradise Lost* Sin springs from Satan's brow and he afterwards copulates with her.

45 *a pillar of fire* Orc is a pillar of fire in *SL* 7.27; see note.

CHAPTER II

The revenge of Urizen (foundation of Mt Sinai).

Pl. 3.16 *Oak* Associated with the Druids and their cult of human sacrifice.

38 *I am God. said he* As in 'The Grey Monk', Pickering MS., p. 505: 'The iron hand [i.e., of rebellion] crushd the Tyrants head/And became a Tyrant in his stead.'

CHAPTER III

Crucifixion of Fuzon on the Tree of Mystery.

54-62 *A Tree . . . Mystery* The first appearance in B.'s prophetic books of the TREE OF MYSTERY.

64 *book of iron* A code of war.

CHAPTER IV

The wandering in the wilderness.

Pl. 4.9-10 *Forth flew the arrows . . . tree* Fuzon is dead, but the pestilence-emitting parasites that live on his body, as on an originally vital religion, are 'alive'. Their origin is explained (in ll. 11-35, which re-tell the story of the binding of Urizen, from *BU* IV): they are 'effluvia' of Urizen's brain.

CHAPTER V

The lament of Ahania concludes the poem. She recalls life in Eternity, where male and female were one. Then, Reason was vigorous and fructifying, and Ahania was fertile. Now she is deserted and barren. The conclusion recalls 'Earth's Answer', *SE*, p. 118.

The Book of Los

Date of publication: 1795. Printed by the same method as *Ahania*. One copy – plus a single print of Pl. 4 – is known. The poem begins with a prelude on a Golden Age when 'sins' were not sinful because they were not forbidden. At 3.27, the narrative is interrupted, and the story intersects with *BU* IV, to give another treatment of the Creation from Los's point of view.

CHAPTER I

Prelude; the rage of Los.

Pl. 3.31–Pl. 4.10 *The Eternal Prophet . . . senses* LOS is surrounded by flames of desire (his desire to act) but is chained and forced to guard the fallen Urizen. As he rejects the fires, they turn cold and congeal around him like marble.

CHAPTER II

The fall of Los; creation of the elements.

19 *The Prophetic wrath* Los's wrath is impatient and forceful, but lacks form and direction (he repelled his flames of desire), hence he falls.

42 *his downward-borne fall chang'd oblique* In Lucretius' *De Rerum Natura*, creation starts when indefinitely falling atoms go through a *clinamen* or swerve.

47 *wafting* Floating on water or air. In *Paradise Lost* 11.1041-2 Satan, emerging from chaos 'with less toil, and now with ease/Wafts . . .'

50-52 *the Vacuum/Became element . . . to rise . . . fall . . . swim . . . fly* The four elements fire, earth, water, air, appear in the vacuum.

CHAPTER III

Material creation continues: solid, liquid and fire divide.

57 *Polypus* A floating, formless sea-creature such as a jellyfish.

Pl. 5.3 *He rose on the floods* 'the spirit of God moved upon the face of the waters', Genesis 1:2.

CHAPTER IV

Light appears; Los forges the sun; the binding of Urizen.

10 *Then Light first began* 'And there was light', Genesis 1:3.

34-5 *An immense Orb of fire . . . he quench'd it* Los creates the sun and starts it on its cycle of rising and setting.

44-5 *the sun . . . self-balanc'd* 'And Earth self-balanc'd on her Center hung', *Paradise Lost* VII.242.

48 *the Deep fled away* 'The loud misrule of Chaos far remov'd', *Paradise Lost* VII.271-2.

53 *four rivers* The four rivers of Paradise (Genesis 2:10-14) are also Urizen's major blood vessels.

56 *Human Illusion* Our reality is only illusion from the point of view of Eternity.

Vala, or the Four Zoas

Blake's first attempt at a long epic poem exists in the form of a much-revised manuscript of 132 pages inscribed on seventy large sheets (mostly drawing paper or proof sheets for Young's *Night Thoughts*, which B. was commissioned to illustrate in 1794) plus two small sheets and a fragment. Its theme is a cosmic history of Mankind and his universe, from initial collapse and division among his primal energies, to final regeneration. In its first form the poem was called *Vala*, was in nine 'Nights' like Young's *Night Thoughts*, and may be dated *c.* 1797-1803. Revisions, including both major and minor deletions, erasures, transpositions and additions, sometimes written in margins or squeezed between lines or in stanza-breaks, seem to have continued until 1808 or beyond, during which time the poem also became a quarry of ideas and passages for *Milton* and *Jerusalem*. Night VIII, and the alteration of the title to *The Four Zoas*, date at least from 1804, and may be considerably later. In general, the revisions reflect an expanded mythology and symbolism. The splicings, however, are not always smooth, and the correct order of the leaves is still conjectural in places. In the present text, although most of the legible deleted material is retained (in brackets and italicized), it is impossible to indicate the complexity of layers and phases of B.'s re-writing. For full discussion of this manuscript, see the following editions:

H. M. Margoliouth (ed.), *Vala* (Oxford University Press, 1956); an attempt to disentangle the poem's initial version from the later additions.

G. E. Bentley, Jr (ed.), *Vala, or The Four Zoas* (Oxford University Press, 1963); a facsimile, transcript and commentary.

David V. Erdman (ed.), *The Poetry and Prose of William Blake* (Doubleday, New York, 1970).

NIGHT THE FIRST

The Fall of Man: Chaos.

The basic mythology behind *The Four Zoas* is as follows: Man (the Ancient Man, or ALBION) lives in Eternity or EDEN, as one of a divine family of Eternals who collectively compose One Man, Christ. Man himself is composed of four ZOAS: URIZEN (his Reason), LUVAH (his Passion), THARMAS (his Sensation) and URTHONA (his Instinct). Each of these figures has a female counterpart or EMANATION, but in Eden male and female are one, and the Zoas live in unity.

Prior to the poem's opening, Man's separation from Eden has already begun. Man has become passive instead of active. His Zoas are divided. Urizen and Luvah each have tried to seize absolute power – Urizen by refusing to serve Man, Luvah by seducing him with the female counterpart VALA, and by usurping Urizen's steeds of light. Tharmas and Urthona are also drawn into the disastrous conflict. All four Zoas 'fall' and carry Man with them. Furthermore, Man and his Zoas become separated from their female counterparts. The whole of *The Four Zoas* will be occupied with the results of this initial trauma – periodically recalled in various versions by various figures involved – from which issues our entire cosmos, and all of human history until Man's final regeneration and return to divine unity at the close of the final Night.

It should be emphasized that the Fall is not a moral lapse from 'good' to 'evil'. Morality, for Blake, is merely something Urizen attempts to impose on others. Rather, the Fall means a lapse from unity, vigour and the life of the imagination, to alienation, compulsion or passivity, and the deadness of material objects. Thus one final set of names must be mentioned: the names of those levels of human consciousness or potential which B. treats spatially as realms or lands, and through which his characters may ascend or descend. EDEN is his Heaven, Man's permanent home. It is 'fourfold' and 'human'. BEULAH, a step below, is a lower paradise, a passive resting place from the energetic life of Eden, humanity's dreamland and the source of all poetic inspiration. It is 'threefold' and 'sexual'. GENERATION is the cycle of life and death for all living things – our normal world. It is 'twofold' and 'vegetative'. ULRO, finally, is Hell: the condition of dead and barren mechanism and materialism, inorganic, meaningless and hopeless.

The poem itself begins in midst of catastrophe with the quarrelling division and fall of THARMAS and ENION. Tharmas becomes a sea of incoherence. Enion weaves the SPECTRE of Tharmas, while the Daughters of Beulah create a space for the Circle of Destiny and close Tharmas's Gate of the Tongue. Enion, ravished by the spectre, gives birth to LOS and ENITHARMON. They are the fallen form of Urthona, and represent Prophecy and the Muse in the fallen world. They quarrel, she taunting him with a song of Vala which hints that Luvah and Vala have caused Man's fall, and claiming female dominance. Los strikes her and prophesies suffering and punishment, but she allies herself with Urizen, who then assumes Godhead and presides over their discontented nuptial feast. The song at this feast celebrates War and prophesies future events. Meanwhile, the rejected Enion laments the sufferings endured by all natural creatures.

The Night concludes with a full account of Man's Fall given to the Council of God in Eternity, and the election of the SEVEN EYES OF GOD who are to guard Man, while Beulah guards Man's emanation, JERUSALEM. Historically, this entire Night is to be understood as occurring prior to the Creation in Genesis 1.

P. 3.6 *Four Mighty Ones* The Four Zoas, Man's Energies. John 17:21-3: 'That they all may be one; as thou, Father, art in me, and I in thee, that they also may be one in us: that the world may believe that thou hast sent me. And the glory which thou gavest me I have given them; that they may be one, even as we are one: I in them, and thou in me, that they may be made perfect in one; and that the world may know that thou hast sent me, and hast loved them, as thou hast loved me.' John 1:14: 'And the Word was made flesh, and dwelt among us, (and we beheld his glory, the glory as of the only begotten of the Father), full of grace and truth.' The Greek quotation repeats: 'and dwelt among us'.

Four signifies perfection in B.'s numerology: Man is composed of four Zoas, Eden is fourfold, and 'fourfold vision' is the 'supreme delight' available to the visionary. The immediate reference is to the four beasts which surround the chariot of the Almighty in Ezekiel, and the four living creatures (Ζῶα) around the throne of God in Revelation. But similar symbolism occurs in other traditions; for example, the sacred quaternion which is the source of eternal nature in Pythagoras, the fourfold worlds based on the Tetragrammaton (sacred name of God, composed of four letters) in Kaballah, the fourfold systems of Ptolemy's gnosticism, of Rosicrucianism, and of Boehme, the four suits of the Tarot deck, the four elements, the four humours; and there are obvious correspondences to the four seasons and the four compass points.

11 *Los was the fourth immortal starry one* In Daniel 3:25 'the form of the fourth is like the Son of God', and is sent to save the three men cast into the fiery furnace. So Urthona-Los, the spirit of Poetry in this fallen world, will work to save it.

Pl. 3.13-Pl. 4.1 *Urthona ... In Eden* In Eden, Man's original home, Urthona was the creator of playful inventions ('Fairies of Albion') which were received by Man's ear ('Auricular Nerves') as by a fertile earth. But in the fallen world these fairies become awesome and dreadful gods, systematically worshipped.

4 *Daughter of Beulah Sing* The epic invocation of the Muse.

5 B. here announces the theme of his epic.

8 *Begin with Tharmas* An epic opening *in medias res*. The quarrel between Tharmas and Enion is a by-product of the greater Fall of Man in which they are involuntarily trapped. Left to themselves Tharmas and Enion are Earth Father and Earth Mother, honest, simple, receptive and coherent. Beyond their ken, Urizen (Reason) and Luvah (Passion) are striving to control Man. Man is divided, and his feminine portions have fled to Tharmas for refuge. This produces panic in Tharmas and jealousy in Enion; their love turns to analysis and accusation, their self-respect to masochism, and they too are divided – not to reunite until the end of the epic.

19 *Thy fear ... surrounded me* (repeated in *J* 21.1) An ironic speech. Tharmas himself is fearful, and has infected Enion with fear. But she believes him to be a God, as in Psalm 88:14-17: 'Lord, why castest thou off my soul? why hidest thou thy face from me? ... while I suffer

thy terrors I am distracted ... thy terrors have cut me off. They came round about me daily like water; they compassed me about together.' An additional irony is that Tharmas will degenerate into water as a result of this quarrel.

20-35 Portions of these lines reappear in *J* 22.

26 *Hide me some shadowy semblance* Enion begs a retreat from reality to illusion. Autobiographically the issue is B.'s confusion about publishing radical writings, and Catherine's (or his own) fear of repercussions if he does so openly. 'Shadowy semblance' would mean a 'literary' disguise less terrifying and dangerous than plain speech (see Erdman, 272-8).

P. 5.6 *So saying* Enion divides from Tharmas, and hereafter is purely passive.

6-7 *weaving soft ... A tabernacle* Enion weaves the generated body on a 'Loom of Vegetation' (6.1-2); the loom is a neo-Platonic symbol for generation.

11 *Turnd round the circle of Destiny* Tharmas accepts his fate, sets Destiny in motion, and collapses from coherence into a formless sea. Hereafter he is Chaos or the Flood.

17 *lacteal* Lymph vessel.

23 *Nine days* In neo-Platonic commentary, 'nine' is a number of incompletion. Blake consistently uses 'three', 'nine' and their multiples to indicate phases of a fallen world.

25-6 *Round rolld the Sea ... appeard* 'And God said, let the waters ... be gathered together unto one place, and let the dry land appear' (Genesis 1:9); 'And Earth self-balanc'd on her Center hung' (*Paradise Lost* VII.242).

29-43 This passage, introducing Beulah, is a late addition. It is rewritten and expanded in *M* 30.

35 *Creating Spaces* The creation of protective spaces for fallen beings is the work of females throughout B.'s prophecies.

38-9 *The Spectre ... Deformd* The idea is repeated in *FZ* VII [a] 84.36-7, *J* 33.4.

39 *the three heavens* Beulah is 'threefold' and restful and has three heavens. Eden, in contrast, is 'fourfold' and energetic.

P. 7.21 *they join in burning anguish* The copulation of Enion and the spectre of Tharmas is a monstrous mingling of unlike physical bodies, rather than the complete union enjoyed by male and female in Eden.

22 *high she soard* Compare Eve's Satan-inspired dream of soaring to heaven (*Paradise Lost* v.86–7).

31 *Enion brooded* She (1) pondered, (2) prepared children for birth. This ambiguous usage is from *Paradise Lost* 1.21: 'Dove-like satst brooding on the vast abyss.'

P. 8.2 *Behold two little Infants* The birth of Los and Enitharmon.

8 *But those in Great Eternity*] This deleted scene returns on P. 21.

12–19 Enion as Earth Mother produces 'tree yielding fruit', 'winged fowl' and 'beasts of the earth', as in Genesis 1:12–24.

P. 9.9–13 This act recurs in *J* 48.30–39.

19 *But Los & Enitharmon delighted* Los and Enitharmon now represent Creative Energy perverted by lack of social purpose. As a gloss on their characters at this stage one may consider the incestuous or quasi-incestuous, sullen and destructive lovers in such novels as *Wuthering Heights*, *Women in Love* and *The Sound and the Fury*.

P. 10.9 *Hear! I will sing a Song of Death!* Enitharmon taunts Los with her version of Man's Fall, in which the female takes dominance over the male.

10 *The Fallen Man* Albion. His sleep of Reason, turning away from 'the Universal Vision' (l. 23), allowed Passion to triumph. His following speech shows submission to the female.

13 *Luvah siez'd the Horses of Light* The usurpation of the head (Reason) by the heart (Passion) parallels the myth of Phaethon disastrously driving the chariot of the Sun.

P. 11.21–3 *I see ... Luvah ... the shower of blood* Los prophesies the incarnation and crucifixion of Christ in the form of Luvah.

30–31 *Descend O Urizen ... Threaten not me O visionary* Enitharmon invokes Reason as ally, and rejects Prophecy.

P. 12.8 *Now I am God* Here begins Urizen's reign, confirming the Fall of Man.

14 *The prince of Love the murderer* Urizen claims that Luvah has slain Man.

32–3 *Ten thousand thousand . . . hosts . . . Chariots* In *Paradise Lost* VI.767–70, God's victory over the rebel angels is 'Attended with ten thousand thousand Saints . . . And twenty thousand . . . Chariots'.

35 *Rejoicing in the Victory* The victory of Urizen over the other Zoas, and his dominance of Man.

37 *the golden feast* The marriage feast of Los and Enitharmon.

38–9 *But the bright Sun . . . blue shell* '. . . for yet the Sun/Was not; she in a cloudy Tabernacle/Sojourn'd the while' (*Paradise Lost* VII.247–9).

44 A black and cannibalistic Mass; Los and Enitharmon are feasting upon Humanity.

P. 13.8–9 *Eternity . . . One Man . . . In Luvahs robes of blood* A vision of Christ incarnate and crucified.

P. 14.6 *And This the Song!* The wedding feast of Los and Enitharmon is celebrated by a song of the values of War triumphant.

7 *Ephraim . . . Zion* The two mountains represent the northern kingdom of Israel and the southern kingdom of Judah. Biblical allusions are a relatively late addition to *FZ* and develop from B.'s idea that all nations were originally one in Albion. Thus the 'Promised Land' of the Bible becomes a separate geographical entity only because of the Fall.

20 *plat* Plait.

P. 15.7–8 *Luvah & Vala ride/Triumphant* War is Passion uncontrolled.

8 *the Human form is no more* This concludes the rejoicing of Mount Ephraim. The Demons of the Deep then continue the song, first with their version of strife and collapse among the Zoas, then with a prophecy of the future.

9–19 *The listning Stars . . . dark confusion* A condensed and confused version of the Fall: the Stars (Urizen's troops) hear the rejoicing at Luvah's War. Urizen prepares for battle (the sun prepares to rise). Tharmas the shepherd ('Mighty Father') angrily swings his sheephook through the sky, and all rushes downwards to devastation.

11–12 *his Horse . . . smelt the battle/Afar off* In Job 39:25 the horse 'smelleth the battle afar off'.

P. 15.20–P. 16.12 *Hark I hear the hammers . . . . rage in vain* The song now predicts the suffering of Luvah in the 'Furnaces of Affliction'

(11 Pp. 25–40); his birth in the form of Orc from Enitharmon's womb (v.P.58.17); and his subsequent fettering (v.P60.6–P61.9).

15–16 *Urizen/With faded radiance sighed* Parallels the description of the fallen Satan, *Paradise Lost* I. 591–602.

P. 18.11–12 *Now Man was come ... Beulah* A palm tree (Judges 4:5) and an Oak of Weeping (Genesis 35:8) are mentioned in connection with Bethel, where the journeying patriarch Jacob rested his head on a stone, dreamed of the ladder of angels, and received God's promise to him. Man at the edge of Beulah is likewise at the border of the land of divine dreams. He sinks outside it into Generation.

13–15 Albion's decline to the Rock of Ages is also in *J* 48. 1–4.

P. 21.2–6 *As one Man ... in Eden the land of life* A parallel description of the Divine Family is in *J* 34.17–20.

7 *Snowdon* A mountain in Wales, home of traditional bards. Erdman (288, n. 9) notes that a group of English radicals retired under pressure to Wales in 1797. (The rejected reading, 'Mount Gilead', indicates that in Eternity the holy nations of Albion and Israel were one. Thus British and biblical place-names are interchangeable.)

12 *Luvah & Urizen contend in war* The Fall of Man was produced by conflict between Reason and Passion. However, here and hereafter, so far as the political allegory of *The Four Zoas* is concerned, one sense of Luvah is 'France', one sense of Urizen is 'England'. The two nations were at war almost continuously from 1793 to 1815.

15 *Conways Vale* The setting of Gray's 'The Bard', also in Wales.

16 *The Eternal Man wept* The messengers here give B.'s 'Authorized Version' of Albion's Fall. While Man is passive, Urizen and Luvah contend for dominance over him; Urthona in shock falls, dividing into Los, Enitharmon and the Spectre; the jealousy between Tharmas and Enion takes place; all the Zoas fall together; this also constitutes the 'ruin' of Jerusalem, Albion's emanation.

19 *& thus conferrd* Details of the Urizen–Luvah belligerencies may derive from English–French negotiations and mutual demands of 1796–7, and Napoleon's assumption of power (Erdman, 284–6).

23 *deep in the North* Urizen's proper realm in Eternity is the South. His plan to usurp the North follows the account of Satan in *Paradise Lost* V.689 and Isaiah 14:13.

P. 22.25-6 *such thing was never known . . . revivd* Repeated with alterations in *J* 80.23-4.

P. 19.9-10 *Seven/Eyes of God . . . lamps* These are guardians of fallen mankind, each presiding over a historic cycle. The imagery derives from Zachariah 4:10 and Revelations 4:5. The idea is systematically developed in Night VIII and in *M* 13.14-27, *J* 55.31-8.

13 *mount Ephraim . . . a Sepulcher* The region of Ephraim, in north central Palestine, revolted against Solomon and formed, with Israel, the northern kingdom. In Psalm 78 God is praised for his persistent forgiveness despite the persistent rebellion of the people, and Ephraim is singled out as a ringleader of apostasy. Another possible reference may be to Jesus' flight to Ephraim after the raising of Lazarus. Ironically, Albion 'wanders' – the term implies 'strayed' – in Ephraim seeking death.

P. 20.1 *The Daughters of Beulah beheld the Emanation* Albion's emanation, Jerusalem, has fallen with him.

4 *Three gates within* Enitharmon has perversely closed the gates of her heart, brain and loins against Los. These gates lead to Beulah and thence to Eternity. A turning point in the poem therefore will be the bursting of her heart gate, beginning in v.63.11-12.

12-13 *the Eternal Wheels . . . living creatures* The vision of the heavenly wheels of four living creatures is in Ezekiel 1.

NIGHT THE SECOND

The rule of Reason; creation of the Mundane Shell.

Albion surrenders all his power to Urizen. Urizen creates the MUNDANE SHELL (the heavens), while Man degenerates. The nations of the world become geographically separated from Albion, in whom they were one, and Jerusalem falls in ruins. Luvah is melted in the furnaces of affliction. The stars and skies are geometrically created. Urizen's palace is built to house his emanation AHANIA, but cannot heal their separation. Urizen is troubled by visions of futurity. Meanwhile, Enitharmon continues to elude and mock Los. The conclusion of this Night is a second lament of Enion which now reaches Ahania.

P. 23.5 *Take thou possession!* The weakened Albion relinquishes his power to Reason alone.

12-13 *The Human Brain . . . its golden porches* Albion's brain and senses.

14 *No more Exulting* Urizen now has the power he wanted, but perceives it – too late – as a void. All his 'creative' deeds hereafter are compensatory.

P. 24.5 *the great Work master* A phrase used by Bacon (*The Advancement of Learning*) and Milton (*Paradise Lost* III.696) for the god of Reason, creator of the stars. A commonplace of rationalist philosophy is that the orderly courses of the stars perfectly represent the Godhead of Reason. In the following account of Reason building the Mundane Shell, there are echoes of Plato's *Timaeus*, Milton's *Paradise Lost* VIII, and gnostic tradition, in which the demiurge who creates this inferior material world is identified, as here, with the Jehovah of the Hebrews.

P. 25 The symbolism of this page is that developed in *J*. The basic ideas are as follows: Mankind's rule by Reason is a 'petrifying' of the human imagination. Hence 'Albion' as a geographical location suffers, and is separated from the 'Nations of the Earth' which in Eternity were one with him. *Reuben* and *Levi* (l. 21), two sons of the Patriarch Jacob, represent the natural man and priestcraft in this world. In Eternity they are Albion's sons (and Albion and Jacob are one). Now they become remote from him. *The Daughters of Albion* here listed (ll. 29-30) are enemies of Jerusalem – his true Liberty – and Jerusalem goes into Babylonian captivity. *Nimrod* (l. 32) is the first hunter of men, and Mankind's first king. The *druid stones* are sacrificial.

40 *Luvah was cast into the Furnaces of affliction* Reason casts Passion into Hell. In Isaiah 48: 10 'the furnace of Affliction' is God's instrument for refining transgressing Israel. This episode also appears in *J* 7.30-37.

41 *Vala fed* Here and hereafter, Vala is Nature. She feeds the fires whereby Passion suffers.

P. 26.4 *Hear ye the voice of Luvah* The lament of Passion when repressed by Reason. Luvah's perceptions are in part reliable, in part distorted by his sufferings.

P. 27.9-10 *Lamb/Of God clothed in Luvahs garments* Christ shall experience the 'Passion' and become the dying God of which Luvah is here the archetype.

19 *Urizen . . . thy stern ambition* Luvah recognizes Urizen's error, but not his own.

P. 28.11–21 A parenthetical passage. Individual human beings retain the imagination to be appalled at the sufferings imposed by Urizen. But the rest, closed off from brotherhood, occupy themselves domestically (self-contained family life is selfishness) or deny vision and instead engage in pursuit of rational but barren Science or Commerce.

25 *Then siez'd the Lions of Urizen their work* Urizen's creation of the Mundane Shell continues: Luvah's molten substance becomes stars; the golden looms weave the atmosphere; nets trap souls into material forms. A heavenly palace of Reason (the Zodiac) is built with Vala's ashes and slave labour.

32 *the strong scales* The constellation Libra.

P. 29.3 *Caverns . . . Looms* The loom within a cave is a neo-Platonic symbol of Generation.

4 *First spun, then wove the Atmospheres* From *Paradise Lost* VII.241: 'between spun out the Air'.

P. 30.8 *the Architect divine* A common eighteenth-century Deist epithet for God.

10 *Quadrangular the building rose the heaven squared by a line* This is a palace or temple of Reason; the line is the horizon. Compare 'Behold, the heaven of heavens cannot contain thee; how much less this house that I have builded' (1 Kings 8:27).

15 *Twelve halls . . . twelve sons* The twelve signs of the zodiac form the Palace of Reason.

17 *three daughters* These resemble the Fates. They reappear in Nights VI, VII and IX.

23 *His Shadowy Feminine Semblance* Urizen's emanation, Ahania – his Idealism, now separate from him.

P. 31.9–10 *I see not Luvah . . . pillars of fire* God's glory took the form of a pillar of fire and a pillar of smoke to guide the Israelites through the wilderness.

P. 32.14 The Saviour takes on the body of Luvah.

P. 33.6 *the World of Tharmas* Beyond Reason's constructed realm is Chaos, here identified with the 'sea' of incoherence into which Tharmas collapsed in Night I.5.13. This follows Milton's cosmology in *Paradise Lost* II.895ff., and VII.212, where Chaos is seen outside the gates of Heaven, 'Outrageous as a Sea, dark, wasteful, wild'.

16 *a golden chain* From *Paradise Lost* 11.1052, where it sustains this 'pendant world'. Urizen's chain both sustains and imprisons Man.

P. 34.5 *Urizen . . . envied* Urizen's rational but rigid heaven, now complete, brings him not joy but anxiety. He *envies* the greater flexibility of Los and Enitharmon.

9-10 *For Los & Enitharmon . . . Contracting or expanding* The ability to contract or expand the senses voluntarily, perceiving with a free imagination, is a divine attribute in Blake. Hence Los and Enitharmon have not fallen so far as the rigid Urizen, the passive Luvah or the chaotic Tharmas.

16-47 Torments of love and jealousy between Los and Enitharmon, as she frustrates his desires and is jealously possessive. The relationship here is sexual, but is also that of the Muse to her Poet: she will not obey him, yet she will not allow him any other mistress.

24-30 *If the God enraptured . . . the bright God* Urizen here seen as Apollo. Inspiration, which should properly give itself to the Prophet, surrenders instead to Reason.

40 *the flocks of Tharmas* In Eden Tharmas is a shepherd.

57 *But thus she sang* Enitharmon's song of female will triumphant; see her two comparable songs in *Europe* Pls. 6-8, 13-14, pp. 229, 233-6 above.

62 *nine . . . spheres of harmony* The harmony of the spheres (sun, moon and seven known planets) is a symbol of cosmic order from Pythagoras and Plato to Dante and Milton; but here it is under female control.

78-80 *Arise . . . holy* These lines quote Oothoon in *VDA*, 8.9-10. But where Oothoon's motive was generosity, Enitharmon's is power.

93 *Rapturous delusive trance* Enitharmon enraptures and deludes herself as well as Los.

98 *Vortex* A Cartesian term (see *M* 15.21, n., p. 972 below) which B. adapts to mean a system of thinking or feeling which attracts other things into itself. By driving Ahania into Enion's vortex of sorrow, Los will divide her from Urizen. This occurs, with disastrous effects for Urizen's rational 'heaven' – which cannot allow for sorrow – in Night III.

P. 35.3-4 Taken from *VDA* 5.8-9, p. 202 above.

9 *My heavens are brass my earth is iron* From Deuteronomy 28:23: 'thy heaven . . . shall be brass, and the earth . . . shall be iron'.

11 *What is the price of Experience* From Job 28:12–13: 'Where shall wisdom be found? and where is the place of understanding? Man knoweth not the price thereof.'

P. 36.4 Taken from *BU* 25.1–2, p. 256 above.

13 *it is not so with me!* From the cry in Job 9:34–5: 'Let him take his rod away ... Then would I speak, and not fear him; but it is not so with me.'

NIGHT THE THIRD

The Flood.

Urizen enthroned is rebuked by Ahania (his idealism). Unable to suffer this, he casts her out – and inadvertently produces a cataclysm which destroys the Circle of Destiny and unlooses the Flood of Tharmas hitherto (since Night I) contained by it. In this cataclysm, Urizen himself falls with all his hosts, and is dashed to pieces.

P. 38.2 Los (the Prophet) was born from Tharmas (Ocean) in Night I. Reason sees this and fears to yield his tyranny – like Pharaoh in Exodus 1, Herod in Matthew 2 and Zeus in the myth of Prometheus.

8–10 *Vala ... Luvah* Urizen predicts the descent to birth in the fallen world of LUVAH and VALA as the lower forms ORC and the SHADOWY FEMALE. Orc's birth occurs in Night V, the Shadowy Female's in Night VIII.

P. 39.4 *Why didst thou listen ... Luvah* Ahania's version of the Fall begins here. It is accurate, except that it places entire blame on Passion, seeing Reason as merely passive. The account in Night I (Pp. 21–2) blames both, and Urizen's self-condemning soliloquy in Night V (Pp. 64–5) will show that he too knows better.

8 *the wine presses of Luvah* Love and War.

10 *They* Urizen's horses, now disobedient and perverse.

12 *but O how unlike* From *Paradise Lost* 1.84: 'But O how fallen! how changed.'

15 *The vision of Ahania* In Ahania's vision, Albion – being intellectually asleep – worships his own shadow as a god, is smitten with boils by Luvah, then rejects Luvah. This follows the Job story backwards; for Job is initially virtuous (B. would interpret this as a rejection of Luvah–Passion), then is smitten, and concludes by worshipping. The episode recurs in *J* 43.33–82.

P. 41.16 'Satan . . . smote Job with sore boils' (Job 2:7), and B. here is identifying the biblical Satan with Luvah.

17 *the Fallen Man . . . presence* This is the rejection of Passion, or Desire, complained of in *MHH* Pl. 5, p. 182 above.

P. 42.18-19 A pencil addition, possibly made only in connection with B.'s intended transfer of the passage to *J* where it fits better.
   we alone are escaped The messengers of disaster to Job each say 'I only am escaped alone to tell thee.'

22 *Do I not stretch the heavens* God 'alone spreadeth out the Heavens', Job 9:8.

P. 43.14 *A cavern shaggd with horrid shades* 'By grots and caverns shagg'd with horrid shades,' Milton, *Comus* 429.

27 *The bounds of Destiny were broken* Tharmas set the Circle of Destiny in motion in Night I. Its destruction wrecks Urizen's world, and unlooses the Flood. This is B.'s version of Genesis 7. Tharmas–Chaos–Flood emerges, struggles to assume Man's image, but remains a watery incoherence.

NIGHT THE FOURTH

The post-deluvian world; the binding of Urizen.

This Night opens with Tharmas–Chaos–Flood triumphant yet despairing. He commands Los to rebuild the ruined world, and when Los defies him, he rips Los and Enitharmon apart. At this, the crippled Spectre of Urthona (Urthona was the unfallen Los) appears, and gives his version of the Fall. Tharmas confides in the spectre, and forces Los to rebuild the ruined furnaces of Urizen. Los does so, then proceeds to the 'binding of Urizen' into a solid bodily form – of which the miserably limited anatomy is our own – in seven ages of woe.
   At this low point in the action, B. adds a passage of specifically Christian import, based on the story of Lazarus. The Daughters of Beulah worship the Saviour while Albion's corpse becomes like a polypus beaten by the sea of time and space. The Saviour promises regeneration and finds the lower limits of Opacity and Contraction in Albion. Following this interpolation, Los, terrified by the results of his labours, 'becomes what he beholds' – that is, his body too becomes solid.

P. 48.3-4 *But thou My Son . . . Rebuild this Universe* Tharmas gives Los the task of reconstruction.

12 Los becomes God's voice to the sea in Job 38:11: 'Hitherto shalt thou come, but no further: and here shall thy proud waves be stayed.'

21 *Doubting stood Tharmas* The pun on 'doubting Thomas' reflects Tharmas's condition as the physical 'sea' of perpetual flux and destructiveness. The Apostle Thomas could not believe in the risen Christ until he had touched him physically.

P. 49.8 *griding* Piercing, wounding, cutting painfully; from Milton's 'griding sword' (*Paradise Lost* VI.329).

11 *the Dark Spectre* Urthona has now divided into Los, Enitharmon and the Spectre of Urthona. Unlike Los, the Spectre of Urthona remembers the goodness of life in Eternity, and wills to restore it.

P. 50.1 *I well remember* The Spectre of Urthona recounts his own fall into division.

10-17 A similar version of the birth of Enitharmon is in *BU* 18, p. 252 above.

31 *O I could tell thee tales* From *Hamlet* I.v.15-16: 'I could a tale unfold, whose lightest word/Would harrow up thy soul.'

P. 51.2-3 *this Son/Of Enion* Los must now 'bind the fallen King' Urizen. The Eternal Prophet's task is to embody, and thus at once define and limit, in artistic form, fallen Reason.

7 *the terror ... drave ... the tide* The Spectre parts the waves to permit Enitharmon's return, as an engraver digs a channel in metal.

P. 52.2 From Deuteronomy 30:19: 'I have set before you life and death . . . therefore choose life.'

P. 52.28-P. 53.3 *the thundering/Hammer . . . pulsative furor* Los's hammer, by its regular beat, produces (1) periodic clock time; (2) the metre of poetry.

24 *he became what he beheld* Repeated 55.22. According to B., all beings are defined by their perceptions. Thus the Prophet embodies his age, and is also limited by it. Los, binding Urizen, also binds himself.

P. 54.1-P. 55.9 The binding of Urizen, which parodies the seven days of creation, is also told in *BU* IV [b], p. 247 above.

P. 55.10-P. 56.27 The Council of God passage is a later interpolation in the text.

P. 55.14 *a Double female form* Mary and Martha in the story of Lazarus.

P. 56.1-3 *if thou hadst been here . . . thee* From the story of Lazarus, John 11:21-2, 'Then said Martha unto Jesus, Lord, if thou hadst been here, my brother had not died. But I know, that even now, whatsoever thou wilt ask of God, God will give it thee.' Albion, like Lazarus, will be raised from death. This is repeated in *J* 50.11.

8-10 *In which . . . we shall consume* Repeated in *M* 30.25-7.

8 *hidden under the Shadow of wings* From Psalm 17:8, 'hide me under the shadow of thy wings'.

18 *If ye will Believe your Brother shall rise again* From the words of Jesus to Martha, John 11:23-6, 'Thy brother shall rise again . . . he that believeth in me, though he were dead, yet shall he live . . . Believest thou this?'

19 *the Limit of Opacity . . . Satan* Opacity is impermeable to the Divine Light. SATAN represents the greatest possible 'hardness' of heart and mind which can still sustain life.

21 *the Limit of Contraction . . . Adam* Contraction is shrinkage from infinity. ADAM represents the greatest possible 'smallness' or 'narrowness' of heart and mind which can still sustain life. Humankind as we know it is as 'hard' and 'narrow' as it can be without lapsing into an inorganic state. SATAN and ADAM in this context are labels, not characters.

23 *the Starry Wheels* The orbiting stars of Urizen's purely rational universe.

25 *the Seventh furnace* Los has reconstructed Urizen's ruined furnaces. The seventh and last corresponds to the Seventh Eye of God, Jesus; Divine Mercy points to salvation. Compare *J* 48.45.

P. 55 (second pt.) The exhaustion of Los repeats *BU* v, p. 250 above.

NIGHT THE FIFTH

Rebellion is generated: The birth of Orc.

Los and Enitharmon stiffen into huge but rock-like forms, as the fires of creation fade. Enitharmon gives birth to ORC (the 'terrible child' who represents Rebellious Energy and is the fallen form of Luvah). When Orc reaches the age of fourteen, Los binds him to a mountain with the chain of Jealousy. Despite his chains Orc is fiery and spiritually free. Los and Enitharmon repent their deed but find they cannot undo it, and Enitharmon's previously closed heart begins to break. Finally, Urizen hears Orc struggling and reso lves to explore his dens in hope of finding him.

P. 57.1 *Infected Mad he dancd* The dance of Los suggests that of a shaman, who in primitive societies is at once priest, prophet and healer, curing diseases by absorbing them into himself during fits of hallucinatory ecstatic dancing.

P. 58.3–4 *But the soft pipe ... silver voices* Orc is born like Christ, in mid-winter, attended by music. Details all parallel Milton's 'Nativity Ode'; but the event is demonic, not divine.

8 *Earth convulsed with rending pangs* In *Paradise Lost* IX.1000–1001, 'Earth trembl'd from her entra ils, as again/In pangs' at the advent of original sin.

P. 58.22–P. 59.20 The Demons of the Deep sing a 'carol' for Orc's birth. In 58.23–5 they recapitulate Night I.22.12–15. Then, since Luvah is born in the form of Orc, they call for the birth of Vala, his counterpart. This occurs in Night VII [a].

P. 59.11–16 *Torn by black storms ... flames of fire* Repeated with alterations in *J* 40.39–42.

P. 60.3–4 *He builded Golgonooza ... Luban* The image of the City of Prophecy, and its Gate looking out on darkness, becomes a major symbol in *Jerusalem*.

6 *fourteen summers & winters* The puberty of Orc precipitates an Oedipal triangle. Rebellion challenges his father but is repressed by a Chain of Jealousy. The episode is repeated with alterations from *BU* 20.9–24.

26–8 *the iron mountains top ... naild him down* The infant Oedipus was left by his parents to die with pierced ankles on a mountain.

P. 61.2 *the Demons rage flamd* Orc's element is fire.

10 *Storgous Appetite* From Gr. *storge*, instinctive parental affection for the young.

11 *His limbs bound down mock* Youthful rebellion is spiritually free and alive, despite repression.

18–20 *His eyes ... Vala* Orc sees into the secrets of Nature. (Note that the objects of Orc's expansive perceptions, as well as the images of his own being, are all from Nature; such is his kingdom in this world.)

P. 62.22–P. 63.3 *Lo the young limbs . . . one with him* Repression begins as an external force, but soon is internalized by the individual. Then it is too late to undo.

P. 62.30 Neither instinct nor passion can defeat repression. (Note the echo of Humpty-Dumpty.)

P. 63.11 *Enitharmon on the road of Dranthon* Enitharmon's conversion begins. The term 'road of Dranthon' is not developed elsewhere, but in Acts 9 the future Apostle Paul is converted by a vision of Jesus on the road to Damascus.

11–12 *the inmost gate . . . burst open* Enitharmon's previously 'hard' heart begins to break. Suffering begins the process of redemption, and she sees true visions.

23 Urizen lies enclosed in the world constructed by Urthona–Los (in Night IV) after his own world fell in ruins when he rejected Ahania (idealism) in Night III. The distant struggles of incipient Rebellion awaken him to memory of his former eternal state and realization of his error.

26 *the sons of wisdom* Urizen's sons in Eternity.

27 *the Virgins sang* The Muses sang (Urizen as 'Prince of Light' in Eternity was identical with Apollo, parent of the Muses).

P. 64.3 *Nine virgins* The nine Muses.

14 *O I refusd the Lord of day* Intellect (day) refused to serve his Lord, the Divine Vision who created him.

21–2 *the mild & holy voice . . . shine* The voice of the Divine Vision saying 'Let there be light' (Genesis 1:3).

24 *guide my Son* Intellect was supposed to have been the guide of Mankind, Albion.

26 *the night of councils dark* The negotiations between the Prince of Light and Luvah, each desiring dominance over Man. Urizen's version of the Fall corresponds with that told by the Ambassadors in Night I, P. 21.

27 *The stars . . . their spears* From 'When the stars threw down their spears', 'The Tyger', *SE*, p. 125 above.

29–31 *Luvah . . . the golden cup* Luvah was the vintner of Eternity, as Urizen was the ploughman with his horses. Urizen made the bread of communion, Luvah the wine; they should not have changed places (see 65.5-7).

P. 65.12 The closed intellect rejects divine Love, thus forcing it into a hellish form. Luvah has been born as Orc – a demon – because Love's only outlet now is Rebellion.

NIGHT THE SIXTH

Urizen explores his dens.

Urizen sets out in search of Orc. He is now no longer the cosmic Creator, but a fallen mind wandering through its own ruins. He begins badly, by cursing his daughters at the Water of Life. He travels through the realm of Tharmas (west), sees but cannot heal the sufferings of men in his own realm (south) who have inherited his curse, and falls into the void of Luvah's world (east). Here he undergoes repeated falls, deaths and resurrections, which represent successive civilizations in history, but his intellectual confusion persists. Desperate to gain control, he creates fixed 'Sciences' and a Web of Religion. Still sorrowing, he approaches the world of Urthona–Los (north) and the chained Orc.

P. 67.1 *Urizen . . . explord his dens* The journey of Urizen parallels that of Satan through Hell and Chaos (*Paradise Lost* II).

1-3 *his Spear . . . helmet* Weapon and armour indicate that Urizen's repentance (close of Night v) was incomplete.

5 *three terrific women* Urizen's daughters may recall the Fates, the Furies, the Three Witches in *Macbeth* or – since he soon curses them – the three daughters of King Lear. They rain, gather into a spring, and divide into rivers, the water of life.

P. 68.3 *dry the rocky strand* Reason dries up the waters of life.

16-19 *I will reverse . . . stinking corruptibility* Thus God curses the daughters of Zion (Isaiah 3:24): 'Instead of sweet smell there shall be stink; and instead of a girdle a rent; and instead of well set hair baldness . . . and burning instead of beauty.'

P. 70.21-48 *The horrid shapes . . . ruind world* The sufferings inflicted in Urizen's world include torture, slavery, industrial labour, prisons, servitude of the weak to the strong, and the dominance of materialism – iron, brass and gold.

P. 71.18-19 *he stood a while . . . voyage* Thus Satan in *Paradise Lost* II.918-19 'Stood on the brink of Hell and look'd a while/Pondering his Voyage'.

23 *bottomless vacuity* Thus Satan in *Paradise Lost* II.932 falls through 'vast vacuity'.

32–4 *flight . . . another resurrection* Urizen's voyage now spans the history of mankind. His repeated births, growths and deaths are the rises and falls of civilizations.

35 *But still his books he bore* Urizen's scriptures are the dogmas of successive civilizations. They remain unconsumed – though perpetually augmented with scholarly commentary – throughout history. Although the 'death clothes' of particular dogmas may rot as a particular civilization declines, dogmatism in itself persists.

P. 73.14 *Here will I fix my foot* Urizen resolves to systematize the intellectual confusion of his kingdom. The compass image is a dominant emblem of the god of Reason, and one which B. dwelt on persistently, as in the frontispiece to *Europe* and the Notebook epigram 'To God' (p. 628): 'If you have formd a Circle to go into/Go into it yourself & see how you would do.'

15 *Mountains of Brass promise much riches* Mammon argues similarly to his fellow demons in *Paradise Lost* II.270–73.

21 *the Sciences were fixd* An 'Age of Enlightenment' tyrannizes over mankind more strictly than any previous age. Possibly B. is thinking of 'classical' Graeco–Roman culture, which he despised.

31 *a dire Web* See the 'Net of Religion', *BU* VIII, p. 257 above. Urizen's systematic rationalism connects one 'vortex' of intellect to another, and further imprisons mankind.

P. 74.8 *rending the web* Mankind's spiritual agony causes rips in the web of religion, but does not destroy it.

12 *Four Caverns* The four Zoas now have four mental prisons, and their regions (except for Urthona's) are dislocated from those of Eternity. In ll. 14–19, Orc is fire, Urizen is air, Urthona is earth, and Tharmas is water, assailing the rest.

P. 75.6 *the Shadow of Urthona* Urizen meets the Spectre of Urthona, last seen in Night IV. Pp. 49–51. He is now a crude warrior-figure combining attributes of Orion, Hercules and the Norse god Thor.

19–21 *Four winged heralds . . . fifty two armies* The four seasons, and the weeks in a year, are the troops of Urthona–Los, who is Time. The passage is taken with alterations from *America*, cancelled Pl. [c] 14–17.

25-6 *Urizen . . . Retiring* Time forces Reason into temporary retreat. Compare the confrontation between Satan and the Angel Gabriel with his troops in *Paradise Lost* IV.877-1015.

NIGHT THE SEVENTH [a]

The lapse of Orc; birth of the Shadowy Female; reunion of Los and Enitharmon.

This night divides into three episodes, of which the first two trace the consolidation of Urizen's power and the 'horrible' birth of a goddess of Nature. But in the third, out of the depths of grief and despair, the positive activity of prophetic art at last gets under way. The episodes are as follows:

1. Reason (Urizen) at last encounters Revolution (Orc), with envious snowstorms trying to cool Orc's fires. Urizen now has degenerated to simple tyranny. He is the God–priest–king–politician–intellectual authoritarian, desperately resisting change. The Tree of Mystery shoots up around him. Urizen pretends to pity Orc, is confused by his incomprehensible 'joy'. Orc scorns his pity and mocks his rigidity. Urizen compels his daughters to knead the bread of sorrow as a demonstration of his power, and reads a cynical sermon on how to control the poor. His hypocrisy weakens Orc, who lapses into a worm or serpent, and is made by Urizen to climb the Tree of Mystery.

2. The Los–Enitharmon story resumes (81.7). At the close of Night V they had failed to free Orc, and 'all their after life was lamentation'. Now Enitharmon's Shadow (her life force, 'spirit' or vitality) leaves her each night to mourn for Orc beneath the Tree of Mystery, and Los is left with an unresponsive wife. Urthona's Spectre (remnant of unfallen Los) courts and embraces Enitharmon's Shadow, and a 'wonder horrible' is born. This is the earthly form of Vala, later called the SHADOWY FEMALE. She is the seductive goddess of Nature.

3. At this point (85.13) Enitharmon's heart finally breaks completely, while mankind declines, lured by Nature. Los reunites with the Spectre, who promises another better world within, and they work together to build GOLGONOOZA (City of Art). Los eats the fruit of the Tree of Mystery, but resists self-destruction and begins to create living works of Art, with Enitharmon's help.

P. 77.5 *But Urizen . . . Caves of Orc* Reason encounters Revolution, aflame. In the all-consuming fires of revolutionary passion, reason's horses of instruction and lions and tygers of wrath can only suffer. The Scales of Justice are melted by the oil-burning Lamps of revolutionary mercy. The plough and harrow of Eternity become mired in bloody fields, among scenes of battle instead of agriculture.

18 *Urizen approachd not near* Reason dares not deal directly with Revolution.

P. 78.2 *His book of iron* Urizen's code of war.

5-6 *the root of Mystery . . . Branches* The Tree of Mystery grows from Reason's hostility to Revolution. Reason – trying to maintain the *status quo*, or to damp the fires of Rebellion – is forced to take the position that sacred truths must remain incomprehensible to men.

9-12 These lines are repeated from *The Book of Ahania*, 3.68-74.

17-32 *Image of dread . . . Yet thou dost laugh* Reason cannot understand the terrible joy of Revolution, which persists despite Promethean tortures.

30 *Pity for thee movd me* Urizen is hypocritical or self-deluding. He sought Orc out of nervous dread about the future (III.38.10-11, V.65.10-12).

P. 79.3 *Thou art not chaind Why shouldst thou sit* Revolution, in turn, cannot understand the rigidity of Reason.

23 *bread of Sorrow* From God's punishment of Adam (Genesis 3:17-19): 'cursed is the ground for thy sake: in sorrow shalt thou eat of it . . . In the sweat of thy face shalt thou eat bread.'

25 *Eleth, Uveth, Ona* Urizen's daughters.

P. 80.1 *Urizen Read in his book of brass in sounding tones* Urizenic economics, in tones of 'sounding brass' that 'have not charity' (1 Corinthians 13:1).

9-14 *Compell the poor . . . with temper* William Pitt as Lord of the Treasury in the 1800 Bread Bill debate countered complaints of scarcity and proposals for lowered prices with an insistence that the poor should be encouraged 'to diminish the consumption' and that Parliament should 'act with proper temper, firmness and sobriety' (see Erdman, 341-2). The principles of ll. 9, 16 recur in *J* 44.30-31.

12-14 *And when his children . . . arts* The economist Malthus in a 1798 *Essay on Population* pointed out that war, famine and pestilence were effective checks on population growth.

28-9 *thou beginnest to weaken/My divided spirit* Revolution begins to degenerate into a passive worm (such as English radicalism) or a powerful but hypocritical serpent (such as French radicalism subverted by Napoleon). See Erdman, 348.

31 *Am I a worm* 'But I am a worm, and no man' (Psalm 22:6).

P. 81.3-5 *Orc/In Serpent form . . . submission* Revolution has now hardened and lost its true nature. Thus it is crucified, and thus ends a historical cycle. The images are from John 3:14: 'And as Moses lifted up the serpent in the wilderness, even so must the Son of man be lifted up,' and John 12:32: 'And I, if I be lifted up from the earth, will draw all men unto me.'

7 The Los–Enitharmon story resumes.

P. 82.23 The following episode takes place 'beneath the Tree of Mystery'. The Spectre woos and seduces the Shadow, in desperate hopes of reunion and return to Eternity. But in their conscious life above the Tree, Los and Enitharmon are unaware that this is happening.

P. 83.4-34 *I will tell . . . my fierce boy* The Shadow of Enitharmon gives her feminine version of the Fall. She blames everything on Vala, and wants Vala punished, subjected to her son Orc. (She does not know that Orc is the fallen Luvah and thus the proper mate for Vala.)

P. 84.5-35 *Where thou & I . . . unite again in bliss* The Spectre of Urthona recalls Eternity and the Fall, and promises (1) to cause Vala's birth and subjection to Orc in this world; (2) to destroy Los (his own fallen form); and (3) to reunite with Enitharmon's shadow.

P. 85.6-7 *Enitharmons shadow . . . a wonder horrible* Vala is born on earth as the Shadowy Female: seductive Material Nature. The results are terrible (War in Night VIII) yet necessary to the process of Man's salvation.

11-12 *then she ran . . . Elements* Enitharmon's subdued desire, having given birth to the Shadowy Female, returns to Enitharmon's 'upper' or conscious life, producing havoc.

13 *She burst . . . heart* Suffering finally completes Enitharmon's heartbreak; hereafter she has the 'broken and contrite heart' required for salvation.

18-21 *Till many . . . lovely shadow* In neo-Platonic doctrine, immortal souls are lured to descend into fleshly bodies by the attraction of Nature, who is commonly described as a 'shadow' of reality. Here, many in the fallen world sink lower still, seduced by Nature. Lacking ideals (feminine counterparts), they are wholly destructive.

22 Nature becomes the guardian of Revolution. See Orc and the Shadowy Female in the preludium to *America*, pp. 208-10 above; and the Babe and Woman Old in 'The Mental Traveller', Pickering MS., p. 499 below.

P. 87.9 *new heavens & a new Earth* From Revelation 21:1-2: 'And I saw a new heaven and a new earth: for the first heaven and the first earth were passed away . . . And I John saw the holy city, new Jerusalem, coming down from God out of heaven.'

11-13 *A Threefold Atmosphere . . . Translucence* The sky of the City of Art extends upward into the 'threefold' realm of Beulah. But the City's lower limit is that of Opacity and Contraction (see IV.56.19-21, n.). In other words, the range of Art is from divine dreams at its best to malice and stupidity at its worst.

16 Enitharmon confesses her sin (made known to her by eating the fruit of the Tree of Mystery) and despairs. She hopes Los, likewise eating the fruit, will resist the effects of guilt. But Los despairs. The idea is from Romans 7:7-9: 'I had not known sin, but by the law: for I had not known lust, except the law had said, Thou shalt not covet . . . For I was alive without the law once: but when the commandment came, sin revived, and I died.'

29 *six thousand Years* The fruit of the tree having been eaten, as in Genesis, recorded human history begins. At the end of this period apocalypse and redemption will occur.

P. 90.8-9 *Stern desire . . . semblances* Los announces the will to create works of Art in which 'the dead' of this world will find their true lives.

27-8 *the loud roaring flames/He vanquishd* Los uses the hitherto barren flames of Reason in conflict, and Revolution enchained, for his Art.

36-7 *And first he drew . . . tincturd it* Catherine Blake commonly coloured B.'s engravings for him.

45 *Rintrah . . . Palamabron* Sons of Los representing Wrath and Pity (or sublime and pathetic art).

57 *soft silken veils* Bodies covering the spirit.

58 *his . . . spirit drew Urizen* Los recreates even Urizen as a form of Art, and thus is able to love him.

63 Thiriel, Urizen's oldest son, is the element of air (see *BU* VIII). Reason enters sublime art; his son enters pathetic art.

NIGHT THE SEVENTH [b]

Empire, War and the dominion of Nature.

A separate fragment, partially tallying with the situation at the close of VII [a], although [a] was written later than [b] and may have been intended to replace it. Pp. 95.15–98 follow 91.1–95.14 in the MS., but B. indicates that the two halves of this Night should be transposed. In the transposed reading, events are as follows:

Urizen develops an empire, builds a temple and prepares for conquest. Los opposes him. Tharmas allies himself with Los. Finally Orc breaks loose and rends the Shadowy Female. Thus all the Zoas have become involved in destruction. The elemental gods celebrate this with a cruel war song. Orc has now become fully serpentine – Revolution subverted – and the Shadowy Female triumphs in the war. She tries, unsuccessfully, to make Tharmas her ally. She remains, despite her triumph, a 'howling melancholy'. Amid the devastation, the Daughters of Beulah remember the divine promise of regeneration, even while men sink lower into a Satanic state.

P. 95.20 Urizen triumphs as God, 'Who coverest thyself with light as with a garment: who stretchest out the heavens like a curtain' (Psalm 104:2).

32-3 *Urizen ... Builded a temple in the image of the human heart* Worship of the 'selfish virtues of the natural heart' is condemned in *J* 52.

P. 96.1-2 *And in the inner part ... Secret place* B. here condemns the mysteries of priestcraft and ritual. The Tabernacle of the Temple, in Old Testament times, could be entered only by the High Priest. B. interprets this 'secret place' sexually, claiming that the priests pretend to worship purity and repress sexuality, yet practise 'secret lust'.

9 *they took the Sun ... Los* The light of Prophecy is exploited to justify the temple of Empire.

18 *The day ... religion* War and Religion mutually support each other.

19 *Urizen namd it Pande* Pandemonium, the demonic abode of *Paradise Lost* 1.756.

20 *Los reard his mighty stature* Prophecy prepares to oppose Empire. Los here is a primitive bard (of epic poetry or heroic ballad) who 'follows War' (97.21).

P. 98.22 *The Prester Serpent* The legendary medieval priest–tyrant Prester John. His cowl is a cobra's head.

P. 91.2 *The nameless shadowy Vortex* This is the SHADOWY FEMALE, fallen form of VALA, the Nature-goddess born in Night VII [a] 85 and set to guard Orc.

17–19 *The hairy shoulders ... nameless shadow* Revolution at last breaks loose, and ravishes Nature.

P. 91.21–P. 93.19 The long war song of the 'elemental Gods' concerns the conflict between Urthona–Los of the north, and Urizen ('the rising ... King', 91.30) of the south. It modulates between rhapsodic celebration and prophetic narrative. Comparable songs by 'Demons of the Deep' are in Night 1.14.7ff., Night v.58.22ff. Most of this song is repeated in *J* 65.6–55.

P. 92.3 *darts of wintry hail ... black bow* Artillery, cannon.

9–13 *clarions of Victory ... death of Luvah* The Druid practice, reported by Caesar, of sacrificing prisoners before a battle to ensure victory, is identified with the Crucifixion (which will occur in Night VIII.P.106). We are not told which side wins this battle, for it does not matter. The victim is always Love.

17–33 *Then left the Sons ... rules of life* An interruption in the song. Blake associates warfare, industrialism and rationalism as mutually necessary parts of one system.

34 In the following passage, Vala is the seductress, at once Nature-goddess and *femme fatale*, whose worship is responsible for War.

P. 93.6 *Remembers all thy feigned terrors* By feigning chastity the seductress encourages her lovers to be warriors. War is the sublimation of thwarted sexual energy.

33 *The Shadowy Female* Vala has seduced both Orc and Urizen. She now turns to Tharmas, appealing to his pity. Though triumphant in the war, she is a 'howling melancholy' (94.48) because she cannot reunite with Luvah.

P. 94.16–17 *Enitharmon & Ahania ... Enion/Hid him* A lie. Vala wants Tharmas to pity her, not blame her for Man's Fall.

P. 95.6 *If ye will believe ... rise again* Repeats the promise given at the close of Night IV (56.18).

11 Repeats the decline of Night VII [a] (85.18).

NIGHT THE EIGHTH

The dark before the dawn; Mankind submerged in War; Incarnation and Crucifixion of the Lamb.

The Council of God meets to create fallen Man on the limit of contraction. Man begins to wake. The activity of Prophecy goes on, as Los–Enitharmon continue receiving spectres of the dead from Urizen's wars through Enitharmon's broken heart gate, and Enitharmon makes looms to weave them bodies. The Divine Countenance shines on them. Urizen is perplexed by this sight (the Lamb of God in Luvah's robes), for he thought he had conquered Luvah (Passion) by subverting Orc (Revolution). Meanwhile Orc in serpent form keeps eating the bread of sorrow, which breaks out in jewels all over him.

Urizen at last makes war directly against Los (P. 100, second portion). His artillery is described. The battle takes the form of a HERMAPHRO-DITE called SATAN. Los and Enitharmon respond not by violence but by inspired contemplation, their prophecies receiving and humanizing the victims of war. Urizen augments his armaments, makes martial music to pervert souls, propagates his books. But Vala, begging him to return Luvah, soaks with her tears the Web of Religion until it falls, altering all the vortexes of knowledge and entangling Urizen himself. Meanwhile, Enitharmon's opus, collectively, is JERUSALEM, the EMANATION of ALBION. The Lamb of God emerges from Jerusalem (P. 104). SATAN emerges from the hermaphroditic war. They meet. The synagogue of Satan, concealing the Great Whore RAHAB and the cruel TIRZAH within, judges and crucifies the Lamb. Los tries to teach Rahab, but she turns away. Urizen is transformed into a dragon – his final degeneration.

The close of the book (P. 108) begins with a hopeful dialogue between Ahania and Enion, who anticipates regeneration, while the body of the Lamb is placed in a sepulchre. P. 111 gives the history of Rahab in the Christian era, down to the eighteenth century.

P. 99.2 *Gilead & Hermon* Mountains on the frontiers of the Holy Land.

16-17 *Man began/To wake ... sneezed seven times* The prophet Elisha revived a dead child by lying upon his body, 'and the child sneezed seven times and ... opened his eyes' (2 Kings 4:35).

P. 101.8 *a Serpent . . . among the Constellations* Serpens is the constellation adjoining Ophiocus.

17–18 *Orc devourd the food . . . gems & gold* Degenerated Revolution feeds on the Bread of Sorrow – made from the fruit of the Tree of Mystery – and becomes encrusted with emblems of wealth. Thus Revolution turns into Reaction.

20–21 *the dark shadowy female . . . food* See *America*, preludium.

P. 100.34 *Synagogue of Satan* A term in Revelation 3:9 denoting blasphemous religious hypocrisy.

   Sanhedrim Jewish councils or courts; in the Gospels, they are opposed to Jesus.

P. 101.33–4 *Urizen beheld the battle . . . hermaphrodite* The hermaphrodite contains both sexes in contradiction without synthesis and is thus a Blakean symbol of monstrous absurdity. War is hermaphroditic because it is self-contradictory; note the idea that Reason never intends to produce contradiction, but always does.

P. 101.43–P. 102.11 *Feeling the hand of Los . . . beastial length* A description of the lives of soldiers. While inspired by heroic ideals (works of Los) they may be temporarily 'human'. But they soon relapse to bestiality.

P. 102.15–16 *linked chains . . . boring screws* Chain-shot, and instruments for sinking enemy ships.

P. 102.26 *the Shadowy Female* The Shadowy Female is Vala, now not a *femme fatale* but a *dolorosa*: the beloved who craves her lover.

P. 103.3 *the murderer of my Luvah* Vala's error: she does not see the Divine Vision except as her lover's murderer.

18 *For he was source* Love was a reality; Theology is a mockery.

26 *the . . . Web of Religion . . . fell* Rational Religion – a flimsy web – cannot sustain the weight of Sorrow's tears. It falls, and entangles even Reason in its collapse.

P. 104.1 *Jerusalem the holy* The 'family' (103.37) of lost souls given form by Enitharmon collectively becomes Jerusalem, Albion's emanation and bride.

7 *put off the dark Satanic body* From Colossians 3:9–10, 'ye have put off the old man . . . And have put on the new man, which is renewed in knowledge after the image of him that created him.'

P. 113 A 'set piece' on life, death and the resurrection is inserted here. The Sons of Eden sing of Los and Enitharmon creating life, then of Tirzah and Rahab, Satan and Beelzeboul creating death, and finally of the Lamb's triumph over death.

1 *Looms . . . Forges* Painting and Poetry to create Man.

2 *Spindles . . . Mills* Fate and Logic to destroy Man.

4–5] Deleted lines used in *M* 24.63–4.

16 Souls put on their bodies, at the brink of earthly life.
Arnon A river at the border of the Holy Land.

35 *She smites with her knife of flint* The knife used for circumcision (lit. 'cutting-round') destroys the body of the Lamb. But the body is removed ('put off') like a husk, and the spirit remains.

39 *They anoint his feet* Mary does so for Jesus in John 12:3.

P. 104.17 From Revelation 22:20: 'Surely I come quickly: Amen. Even so, come, Lord Jesus.'

23–7 *Satan . . . A male . . . Yet hiding the shadowy female Vala* The apotheosis of Satan, concealing Vala (Nature) as his guiding power, immediately precedes the Nativity.

32 *the Lamb of God Descended* The Nativity takes place.

P. 105.5 *the Synagogue of Satan in dire Sanhedrim* The congregation of Hypocrisy (Revelation 3:9) in the court of the Commandments will condemn Jesus.

7 From Isaiah 53:12, fulfilled in Mark 15:28 and Luke 22:37.

11 *A False Feminine Counterpart* In the trial against Jesus, the guiding power is RAHAB, a 'vegetated' form of Vala. She is the final apotheosis of Nature which torments Spirit, and the Church of worldly corruption.

27 *Tirzah* See Dictionary of Proper Names.

31–54 *O thou poor human form . . . Vegetation* This song of female cruelty is repeated in *J* 67.44–68.9.

42–3 *Ephraim . . . Manasseh* Regions in the north of the Holy Land (as are Shechem and Gilead, l. 52), of which Tirzah was a secessionist capital, competing with Jerusalem.

45–55 *Noah, Malah, Hoglah, Milcah, Tirzah* Daughters of Zelophehad who successfully demanded female inheritance in the absence of sons (Numbers 27:1–7). B. makes them an example of cruel female will.

48 *Ebal* The site of a ritual curse laid on Israel (Deuteronomy 27:13–26).

49 *Lebanon* Famous for forests (thus representing 'error').
sinai The site of the law.

56 *the twelve portions of Luvah* Implies the twelve tribes of Israel.

P. 106.26 *the Sepulcher which Los had hewn* Los fills the role of Joseph of Arimathea, who gave Jesus burial in his own tomb and who – according to legend – afterwards became the apostle of Britain.

P. 113.50–51 Los likewise announces himself in *M* 22.15–16.

P. 115 Catalogue of the children of Los and Enitharmon. The male and female lists both begin in myth and end in recorded history. Damon (387–8) considers this an intended catalogue of all human types through the ages, and interprets many of the names.

Male list: In the Bard's Song of *M*, *Rintrah, Palambron, Theotormon, Bromion* are Los's 'good' sons. *Antamon, Ozoth, Sotha* are in minor roles. *Satan* is Los's bad son. *Har* and *Ijim* are 'law' and 'superstition' in *Tiriel*. *Adam* is the first 'historic' hero, followed by the twelve tribes of Israel, then *David* and *Solomon* as Israel's great kings. *Paul, Constantine, Charlemaine, Luther* represent the Churches of the Christian era. Finally, *Milton* is the most modern embodiment of the spirit of Prophecy.

Female list: the first four are emanations of the first four males, and represent various aspects of female sexuality. The second four are mentioned in *BU* and *Europe* and represent the elements air, earth, fire, water. *Moab* and *Midian* were nations hostile to Israel. *Adah, Zillah, Naamah, Tamar* are biblical wives and sisters. *Rahab* and *Tirzah* are the temptresses and torturers of mankind. Finally, *Mary* perhaps pairs with *Milton* as the most recent female receptacle of the Holy Spirit.

12 *But Satan accusd Palamabron* This story, here only sketchily suggested, is told in full in the Bard's song of *M* Pls. 3–13. The main point is that Satan as a child of Los precipitated a quarrel which ended in his exclusion from Los's family, and that the sacrifice of Jesus is a final result.

42–50 *Lucifer ... Jesus* The successive guardians of mankind are also named in *M* 13.17–27 (see note). They are the 'eyes of God' or 'lamps of the Almighty' given in Night 1.19.9–10. See SEVEN EYES OF GOD.

P. 106.29 *Urizen sitting in his web* The Web of Religion fell and entangled Urizen himself in 103.26.

36-42 *His eyes shot outwards ... the Abyss* Attempting to embrace Nature, Urizen becomes a beast, falling prone like Satan in *Paradise Lost* x. 511-12. Reason has now collapsed to its opposite.

P. 107.21-31 *Then Tharmas & Urthona ... strength* The stupefying poison of Nature affects Tharmas and Urthona-Los. But Tharmas and Urthona sacrifice themselves to strengthen Los.

P. 108.8 *And thus Ahania cries aloud* The lament of the fertile earth, now barren.

11-12 Taken in modified form from *VDA* 5.41-6.1.

21 A conflation of Romans 7:24: 'O wretched man that I am! who shall deliver me from the body of this death?' and 1 Corinthians 15:53: 'For this corruptible must put on incorruption, and this mortal must put on immortality.'

P. 109.13 *Enion replies ... Grave* Enion herself is 'the grave', now anticipating resurrection.

21 *Awake the bridegroom cometh* In the parable of the wise and foolish virgins, Matthew 25:6, the bridegroom is Christ.

32-3 *cast away/The former things* 'There shall be no more death, neither sorrow, nor crying, neither shall there be any more pain: for the former things are passed away' (Revelation 21:4).

P.111.4 *John Saw these things Reveald* 'John of Patmos' is the author of Revelation. The references are to Revelation 6:9-11 (the souls of the martyrs) and Revelation 17:3-5 (the triumph of the harlot).

10-11 *She secretly left ... Orc* B. outlines the history of Theology and the Church in the Christian era, alternating between legalism and radicalism.

11 *She hid him with the flax* The harlot Rahab in Joshua 2:6 protected two Jewish spies by hiding them in the flax on her roof.

20 *To burn Mystery* The old theology dies, but is renewed again in deism, the 'rational' religion of the eighteenth century.

NIGHT THE NINTH

The Last Judgement.

Los in final desperation tears down the sun and moon, and the fires of Orc begin to consume the whole world. The dead awake to judgement, and Tyranny is cut off.

Man awakes (119.24) and commands Urizen to resume his true form. Urizen weeping rejects 'futurity', accepts the present, gives up the effort to curb all the Zoas, and immediately rises into heaven as a radiant haloed youth. Ahania simultaneously rises, like a bubble – but bursts from excess of joy and is buried for the duration of winter. Man tells Urizen to plough and await the spring, and the remainder of Night IX follows a seasonal cycle.

122.26: In winter, the universe explodes, the dead are resurrected and oppressors are punished by their victims, as flames roar. Man gets up from his rock, walks, tries to meet the Lord in the flames, but is driven back. Urizen ploughs, sows, harrows, awaits the harvest. The continual flames make the seeds grow. Ahania (spring) returns. Man again tries to enter the flames, is again driven back.

P. 126: The advent of summer. As Orc is consumed in his own flames, Luvah and Vala appear, and enter a pastoral golden age. Tharmas and Enion are born as children in Vala's garden. As autumn arrives (P. 132), Urizen reaps the last harvest. Tharmas and Enion reunite at a feast of the Eternals. Urizen threshes and winnows the nations: this is the end of Mystery and the liberation of slaves. Finally, Luvah presses the human grapes of the last vintage. Urthona (137. 34) rises and grinds the corn (the nations) in his mills. Tharmas sifts it, and the bread bakes in the last winter. Final chorale.

P. 117.8–11 *the Sun . . . the Moon . . . Sound of Loud Trumpet* 'Immediately after the tribulation of those days shall the sun be darkened, and the moon shall not give her light . . . And he shall send his angels with a great sound of a trumpet' (Matthew 24:29–31).

14–18 *Folding like scrolls . . . Kings are shaken* 'And the heaven departed as a scroll . . . and every mountain and island were moved out of their places. And the Kings of the earth . . . hid themselves' (Revelation 6:14–15).

16 'The earth shook and trembled; the foundations of heaven moved and shook' (2 Samuel 22:8).

P. 118.9 *Orc began to Consume . . . fire* Orc is consuming both 'the whole creation' and himself. The fires continue until P. 125.

P. 119.3-4 *twenty Seven/Folds* M and J develop the image of a MUNDANE SHELL of twenty-seven heavens (successive Churches) encrusted round the material earth.

15 *the Dragon form . . . stony form* Urizen was transformed to a prone dragon, while his human form petrified, in Night VIII.

32 'But I see another law in my members, warring against the law of my mind' (Romans 7:23). 'From whence come wars and fightings among you? come they not hence, even of your lusts that war in your members?' (James 4:1).

P. 119.33-P. 120.3 This passage, somewhat altered, appears in J 19.1-14.

P. 120.10 *Yet will I look . . . morning* 'Though he slay me, yet will I trust in him' (Job 13:15). 'My soul waiteth for the Lord more than they that watch for the morning' (Psalm 130:6). Albion at last begins his renewal.

50 A 'line of scarlet thread in the window' (Joshua 2:18) was the sign to save Rahab and her family.

P. 121.26 Urizen at last sees the light. The Reason which fears Passion and Sensation is only Doubt. When it relinquishes this fear it becomes Faith.

35-7 *Ahania rose in joy . . . She fell down dead* Idealism cannot be sustained by Faith alone. The full restoration of Ahania will depend on Works. Ahania in VIII. Pp. 108-9 was 'the furrowd field', abandoned and barren. She now becomes a spirit of springtime, like Persephone, who rests in the underworld through the winter, and returns in new growth after the plough.

P. 122.17-18 *Jerusalem . . . out of heaven* 'And I John saw the holy city, new Jerusalem, coming down from God out of heaven, prepared as a bride adorned for her husband' (Revelation 21:2).

21 *my Error remains with me* The results of Error remain, even after repentance. They must be destroyed ('All things reversd', l. 27) and new works of Truth performed.

27-8 *rattling bones/To bones Join, shaking* The resurrection of the dead. In Ezekiel's valley of dry bones (37.7), 'there was a noise, and behold a shaking, and the bones came together, bone to his bone'.

P. 123.5 *They shew their wounds . . . opressor* The idea of a period of human retaliation and vengeance following the general resurrection occurs in the Koran.

20 'Every eye shall see him, and they also which pierced him: and all . . . shall wail because of him' (Revelation 1:7).

27–8 *the Cloud of the Son . . . Glory* 'They shall see the Son of man coming in a cloud with power and great glory' (Luke 21:27).

33–8 'A throne was set in heaven . . . And round about the throne were . . . four and twenty elders sitting . . . and in the midst of the throne, and round about the throne, were four beasts full of eyes before and behind' (Revelation 4:2–6). The Greek for 'beasts' is Ζωα, which may also be translated 'living creatures' or 'lifes'.

P. 124.5 *the Redeemd Man . . . Consummation* It is not enough for Christ to pay for (redeem) Man's sins. Man himself must act.

6 *Then siezd the Sons . . . Plow* Man's Reason begins the final cycle which ends in a last harvest and vintage, and a feast of bread and wine.

19–21 'They shall beat their swords into ploughshares, and their spears into pruning hooks: nation shall not lift up sword against nation, neither shall they learn war any more' (Isaiah 2:4).

30 *the Seed of Men* Ploughing is finished; sowing begins. The seeds are all men's souls; and 'that which thou sowest is not quickened, except it die' (1 Corinthians 15:36).

P. 125.8–10 *warriors . . . Kings & Princes* Soldiers and nobility have no place in Eternity. Therefore they fall on infertile ground, as in the Parable of the Sower (Luke 8:5–15).

P. 126.4 *the flaming Demon & Demoness* As Orc at last is consumed in his own flames, Luvah and Vala reappear.

29 *And thus . . . renewd* Luvah and Vala return to their original lives as the Eros and Psyche of Man. *Their* golden age is also the 'golden age' of Arcadian Mankind. Thus the style of the following interlude is 'idyllic', and the details follow the story of Cupid and Psyche in Apuleius' *Golden Ass*.

34 B.'s retranslation of *Aeneid* VII. 808–9. Pope's more famous version is '. . . when swift Camilla scours the Plain/Flies o'er th'unbending corn, and skims along the Main' (*Essay on Criticism*, 372–3).

P. 127.6 *O thou creating voice* Luvah is Vala's creator, just as Eros is in principle the creator as well as the lover of Psyche.

14-27 *thou art as the grass . . . survive* An apparent inconsistency, not a real one. Luvah first addresses Vala as a mortal body, and teaches her that 'All flesh is grass.' As body, she has been wakened by the sun, is nourished by it, but will die. Vala mourns for herself. But Luvah then addresses her as immortal 'Soul' (l. 24). As soul, she does not depend on the sun, and will live for ever.

P. 128.3 *a new song arises to my Lord* 'Sing unto the Lord a new song' (Psalm 96:1; 98:1).

P. 130.7 Tharmas and Enion appear in the first stage of their renewal. Vala (Nature) is the foster-mother of Sensation.

P. 131.30-31 *Then Urizen . . . Cried Times are Ended* The angel in Revelation 10:6 swears 'that there should be time no longer'. Urizen returns to his work of the Last Harvest.

P. 132.23 *For Lo the winter melted away* 'For, lo, the winter is past, the rain is over and gone' (Song of Solomon 2:11).

P. 133.21 In Ephesians 3:10 Paul says his task is to show God's wisdom to the heavenly powers through the church. Thus the Eternals learn brotherhood by seeing Man grouped into families.

25 *Man liveth not by Self alone* 'Man shall not live by bread alone' (Matthew 4:4).

P. 134.1 *And all Nations were threshed* The flail threshes the harvest and separates good grain from worthless chaff; the winnowing fan blows away the chaff. The scene suggests Matthew 3:12, where Christ's 'fan is in his hand, and he will thoroughly purge his floor, and gather his wheat into the garner; but he will burn up the chaff with unquenchable fire'.

5 The fate of the 'chaff'. *Mystery* is the Rahab of Night VIII, whose cup is 'full of abominations' (Revelation 17:4). She is overthrown, as in Revelation 18, along with all who serve her.

18-24 Lines repeated from *America* 6.6-12. As the chaff is cast off, the wheat is uncovered. As the oppressors vanish, the oppressed are liberated.

31 *Sing a New Song* 'Sing unto the Lord a new song' (Psalm 96:1; 98:1).

P. 135.5 *the Vintage is ripe* The vintage follows the harvest in Revelation 14:19-20: 'And the angel thrust in his sickle into the earth, and gathered the vine of the earth, and cast it into the great winepress of the wrath of God. And the winepress was trodden . . . and blood came out of the winepress.'

P. 136.16–P. 137.4 The Vintage of Love is a Dionysiac orgy of ecstatic ruthlessness, reminding us that 'passion' means 'suffering'. The passage is repeated, with additions and alterations, in *M* 27.3–41.

P. 138.20–21 Two lines taken from *America* 6.13–14 begin this final chorale.

ADDITIONAL FRAGMENTS

These passages appear on two small sheets of paper, and are not incorporated in the text of *The Four Zoas*.

Three Poems, ? c. 1800

'A FAIRY SKIPD UPON MY KNEE . . .'

An undated lyric, written on the blank side of a drawing depicting the infant Hercules.

'AROUND THE SPRINGS OF GRAY . . .'; TO MRS ANN FLAXMAN

Two sets of verses inscribed in a volume of B.'s water-colour illustrations to Gray's poems, presented to Mrs Flaxman. The illustrations may have been done in 1797, but the 'transplantation' image apparently refers to Flaxman's influence on Blake's move to Felpham in 1800 (see Poems from Letters, p. 481 below).

Poems from Letters

TO JOHN FLAXMAN, 12 SEPTEMBER 1800

According to Gilchrist, B. met Flaxman, a Swedenborgian and fellow-artist, *c.* 1780, and Henry Fuseli, a painter and intellectual, at about the same time. Flaxman was in Italy from 1787 to 1794. In January 1800 he introduced B. and his work to William Hayley, poet and connoisseur of art. At the time of this letter, the Blakes were preparing to move to Hayley's cottage in Felpham. They did so on 18 September.

TO MRS FLAXMAN, 14 SEPTEMBER 1800

Written at the close of a letter from Catherine Blake to Mrs Flaxman, again just before the Blakes' departure for Felpham.

7 *the Turret* Hayley's house.

15 *the blessd Hermit* Hayley himself.

TO THOMAS BUTTS, 22 NOVEMBER 1802

The vision of Los recorded in this poem may also be a basis for that of B.'s prophetic poem *Milton*.

14-15 *Brother Robert* B.'s favourite, ten years his junior, whom he nursed on his deathbed in 1787, and with whose spirit he said he conversed often afterwards. B.'s Notebook was originally Robert's.

   Brother John According to Tatham, John was a rival of William, 'a dissolute disreputable youth' who 'lived a few reckless days, enlisted as a soldier, and died' (*Blake Records*, 508-9).

27 *double the vision* B. cultivated 'double vision', 'threefold vision' and 'fourfold vision', states of altered perception which would commonly be considered hallucinatory.

29 *an old Man grey* An image of Prudence, which B. despised.

31 *If thou goest back* B. was considering a return to London, to escape his patron's insistence that he confine himself to 'the meer drudgery of business' (letter to Butts, 10 January 1802).

88 *Newtons sleep* Both the kind of sleep Newton had, and the kind which his philosophy would impose on us.

TO THOMAS BUTTS, 16 AUGUST 1803

Written just before B.'s return to London, in September 1803. The opening line comes from 'Mary', Pickering MS., p. 503 below.

Notebook Poems, c. 1800–1806

This period of Notebook writing covers Blake's association with Hayley, his trial for sedition and his depression over the Napoleonic Wars, which were raging both before and after the temporary Peace of Amiens

(1802–3), and for which B. had given up hope of a political solution. Concurrently, he was writing *Milton*, and (*c.* 1804) beginning *Jerusalem*.

'WHEN KLOPSTOCK ENGLAND DEFIED . . .'

The German poet Friedrich Gottlieb Klopstock (1724–1803) was critical of English poetry, which he considered coarse, and blamed this on Swift's influence. In an article in the London journal *The German Museum*, August 1800, which Hayley might have shown to B., he compared German and English translations of Homer, deprecating the English. Blake's counter-attack may date from 1800 or earlier, and is of a super-Swiftian crudity.

3–4   Lines quoted from 'Let the brothels . . .', Notebook, p. 159.

ON THE VIRGINITY OF THE VIRGIN MARY & JOHANNA SOUTHCOTT

Johanna Southcott (1750–1814) was a semi-literate servant girl turned prophetess. She announced in 1802 that she was the woman in Revelation 12 who would be the mother of the coming Messiah, in 1813 claimed to be pregnant with this child, and in 1814 died of a dropsy. B.'s squib probably dates from 1802.

'BENEATH THE WHITE THORN LOVELY MAY . . .'

A finished copy, entitled 'The Golden Net', is in the Pickering MS., p. 498 below.

'I SAW A MONK . . .'

Possibly dates *c.* 1804, the period of Blake's sedition trial; also the year of Richard Warner's famous pacifist sermon (see *J*, Pl. 40, n.) which the Monk seems to echo. From this rough and much-revised draft, B. extracted seven stanzas for *J* Pl. 52, and nine stanzas for 'The Grey Monk' in the Pickering MS., p. 505 below.

18   A line drawn in the MS. connects the poem at this point to stanza 12 ('Untill the Tyrant himself relent') omitting the interlude with the Mother.

28–31   In part an autobiographical complaint. B.'s patron Hayley did not appreciate his writing, and tried to bend him towards more conventional pursuits. See Bentley, *Blake Records*, 72-120 *passim*. There is some evidence that Hayley tried to work through Catherine; B. may have associated Catherine's illness at Felpham with this spiritual brow-beating as well as with the bad climate.

36 A reminiscence of 'Gwin, King of Norway', *PS*, p. 32 above. There, too, vengeance is enacted on a tyrant, yet the conclusion implies that vengeance is sad, not sweet.

MORNING

West, in B.'s symbolism, always implies liberation and the opening of a new world. At sunrise, the sun is moving westwards with the speaker.

7-9 *The war of swords & spears ... Exhales* The stars (of Reason) fade as the dew falls. The same imagery is in 'The Tyger', *SE*, p. 125 above.

EACH MAN IS IN HIS SPECTRES POWER

Ll. 1-4 appear in *J* Pl. 32, in mirror-writing.

'MOCK ON MOCK ON ...'

Thus Job (21:3) to his comforters: 'Suffer me that I may speak; and after that I have spoken, mock on.'

1 *Voltaire Rousseau* Attacked by B. as rationalists and Deists.

9 *Atoms of Democritus* The Greek philosopher Democritus (*c*. 460-370 BC) held that all things were composed of tiny atoms in constant motion. He is the first consistent materialist in western thought, and hence offensive to Blake.

10 *Newtons Particles* In Newton's optics, light takes the form of tiny corpuscles or particles emitted from a luminous body.

'MY SPECTRE AROUND ME ...'

Dialogue with a coy mistress – or wife. The man speaks stanzas 1-8, the woman stanzas 9-10, the man stanzas 11-12, and both together may speak the final two stanzas.

1-3 *My Spectre ... My Emanation* These are B.'s terms for 'male' and 'female' fragments of a human personality, here enacting a drama of pursuit and rejection.

34 *Seven ... loves* The 'loves' conceived as Cupids here and in the following stanzas, are the man's own amorous desires and impulses.

58 *Female Love* Mistaken adoration of the female. Compare Milton's condemnation of courtship, with its 'starved Lover' and 'proud fair, best quitted with disdain' (*Paradise Lost* IV.770).

59 *root up the Infernal Grove* From Micah 6:14: 'I will pluck up thy groves out of the midst of thee.' 'Groves', throughout the Authorized Version, occur in connection with worship of the Canaanite goddess Asherah, condemned by the prophets.

'GROWN OLD IN LOVE ...'

B. here is presumably forty-nine, and the year is 1806.

Poems from the Pickering Manuscript

This MS. (owned by B. M. Pickering in 1866) consists of eleven leaves containing fair copies of lyric and ballad pieces, primarily on the themes of sexuality, politics and the nature of visionary experience. Most editors date it *c.* 1803; Stevenson conjectures 1805.

THE GOLDEN NET

An allegory of male entrapment by females. A draft of this poem is in the Notebook, p. 489.

THE MENTAL TRAVELLER

This is one of B.'s most difficult short poems. It is an allegory of mankind's history, represented as a process of alternating dominance of male and female principles. The male, beginning as a babe and becoming a youth, mature man, old man and finally babe again, is a Jesus–Prometheus–Everyman figure who embodies the potential genius and energy of Mankind. The female, variously manifested as old woman, virgin, female babe and finally old woman again, embodies all that may control, thwart or reject him. Comparable figures in B.'s longer works are ORC (Revolution) and VALA (Nature).

In the opening sequence, the babe is nailed down and tormented by Mother Nature, who may also represent any Church or State founded on Nature. He subdues her as he grows to maturity, and becomes a source of joy to others, but in old age is driven out by a female babe sprung from his hearth – possibly a Church founded on his deeds, which gains ascendancy and forgets its source. In the final sequence, his pursuit of a new maiden returns him to infancy and her to old age. A whole civilization has been formed from their distress, and the whole cycle resumes.

7–8 *Reap in joy . . . sow* In Psalm 126:5, 'They that sow in tears shall reap in joy.' But a joyous birth after a woeful begetting implies that something is sexually amiss in this world.

11–16 These torments suggest the fate of Prometheus, that of Jesus, and that of sacrificial victims in Mexico. Similar tortures are inflicted by females on male victims in *FZ* VIII.105.31–53, IX.136.21–137.1, *M* 19.44–55, 27.30–38, *J* 67.24–5, 67.41–62, 80.81–2.

23–4 *he rends up . . . binds her down* See the story of Orc and the 'shadowy female' in the preludium to *America*, p. 208 above.

51 *aged Host* Puns on the 'Host' of the Eucharist, Christ's body, now rejected.

56 *a Maiden* The Maiden resembles the elusive mistress of 'My Spectre around me', Notebook, p. 494, and the artful virgins of 'The Golden Net'; in the end she is revealed as another manifestation of the Woman Old.

57 *to allay his freezing Age* Similarly, when King David 'was old and stricken in years; and . . . gat no heat', his counsellors brought him a fair damsel to 'lie in thy bosom, that my lord the king may get heat' (1 Kings 1:1–2). What follows, however, is squabbling over David's throne among his heirs; as here, the world is turned to a hostile desert.

63–4 As male vitality and all that it represents declines, perceptions become narrow and the world becomes alien. B. thought that the flatness or roundness of the earth depended on one's vision, and believed that a flat earth implied expansiveness in an 'infinite plane', while a round globe separated from other globes implied limitation.

69–81 The infant lovers Los and Enitharmon, *FZ* I.9.24, p. 284 above, are likewise tormented by 'Alternate Love & Hate . . . Scorn & Jealousy'.

95 *the Babe is Born* Blake proposes that the birth into this world of Jesus, or any form of human energy, is greeted by society with terror, not love, for it is a true threat to the *status quo*.

MARY

21 Blake uses this line, but applies it to himself, in the verse conclusion of a letter to Butts, 16 August 1803, p. 487 above.

THE CRYSTAL CABINET

The experience of love as a delightfully beautiful yet imprisoning enclosure first appears in 'How sweet I roam'd . . .', *PS*, p. 26 above, supposedly written before B. was fourteen. 'I saw a chapel all of gold . . .', Notebook, p. 136, employs similar enclosure imagery to describe sexuality.

15 *Threefold* Blake consistently associates 'threefold vision' (a physiological possibility for him) with the state of lovely and dreamy sexuality he called BEULAH. Perception is heightened in this state, yet it remains inferior to the 'fourfold vision' he considered fully human. In other words: sexual love can take one only so far, and no further. Another autobiographical treatment of altered states of vision – 'twofold', 'threefold' and 'fourfold' – occurs in the poem 'With happiness stretchd across the hills . . .', which concludes a letter to Butts, 22 November 1802, p. 485 above.

24 *like a weeping Babe became* Desire is physically gratified, but full union has not been achieved. The 'Babe' and 'Woman' are also in 'The Mental Traveller', above, p. 499.

THE GREY MONK

A rough draft, with additional stanzas, is in the Notebook, p. 491.

AUGURIES OF INNOCENCE

These couplets were written as a fair copy, although the organization and grouping of ideas seem erratic. Editors have suggested other arrangements of the lines, but B.'s apparent failure to organize may have been deliberate.

17 *The Game Cock clipd* Cockfighting was not legally prohibited in England until 1849.

35 *Chafers sprite* A chafer is a kind of beetle.

126 Seeing 'through' rather than 'with' the eye constituted true vision for B. The conclusion to his prose tract, *A Vision of the Last Judgment*, reads:

'I assert for My self that I do not behold the Outward Creation & that to me it is hindrance & not Action it is as the Dirt upon my feet No part of Me. What it will be Questiond When the Sun rises do you not see a round Disk of fire somewhat like a Guinea O no no I see an Innumerable company of the Heavenly host crying Holy Holy Holy is the Lord God Almighty I question not my Corporeal or Vegetative Eye any more than I would Question a Window concerning a Sight I look thro it & not with it.'

127 *Born in a Night . . . Night* Jonah's gourd 'came up in a night and perished in a night' (Jonah 4:10). The moral is that material things are less important than spiritual.

129-30 *God is Light . . . Night* Ironic commentary on Milton's 'since God is light', *Paradise Lost* III.3.

WILLIAM BOND

28 From the words of Jesus to Mary at Cana: 'Woman, what have I to do with thee?' (John 2:4).

Milton

An illuminated poem known in four copies. Title page date: 1804. Two copies, on paper watermarked 1808, contain forty-five plates, eight of which are full-page designs without text. A third copy, on the same paper, adds five pages of text (3, 4, 10, 18, 32) but omits the Preface. The last copy, on paper dated 1815, omits the Preface and adds one more page (5). The present text follows the page-arrangement of this copy.

B. originally intended *Milton* to be a 'Poem in 12 Books' but altered the title page '12' to '2'. As it now stands, the poem is just half the size of *Jerusalem*, and is something like a prelude to it. It tells the story of the poet Milton's descent to earth and entry into William Blake, an event at once intimately personal and of cosmic reverberation.

B. assumes that the poet's task is no less than the salvation of Mankind. He acts through divine inspiration and conveys – as best he can, within his historic and personal limitations – divine truth. As history proceeds, poets embody more and more of truth, and expose more and more of error. The final result of this process will be the Coming of Jesus. Now, as B. sees it, Milton was a true poet, but did not escape error. His self-righteous religion interfered with his vision. To correct this, Milton must return to earth, annihilate his moralistic selfhood, and reunite with his rejected inspiration, which takes the form of a female 'emanation' Ololon. He is aided in this quest by all the powers of divine imagination, and assailed by all the powers of mundane error. His ultimate success brings the entire universe a step nearer to its final fulfilment in Jesus.

It seems clear that B. experienced a moment of revelation in which he 'saw' all this happening, one day in his Felpham garden, and fainted. His recording of this central event is placed in a mythological and doctrinal context, so that the narrative is interrupted by sub-narratives and digressions, which 'explain' the story. Thus, as in *The Four Zoas*, all earthly action occurs within the form of Albion, the sleeping giant who has fallen away from union with the divine family of Eternals who are one with Jesus. Again, as in *FZ*, there is descent from higher to lower realms of potential human consciousness and imagination: Eden to Beulah to Generation to Ulro. Third, a geographical symbolism is developed in which British and biblical places and historical events are equivalents of each other. This rests on Blake's assumption that all nations were originally one within Albion, and allows him to place Milton's journey simultaneously in England and in Palestine. Finally, there is the highly developed figure of Los, the 'Eternal Prophet' or spirit of poetry, father of all individual poets and intellectuals throughout history, whose task is the creation of a City of Art in the midst of the fallen world. Los plays various roles in this poem. Sometimes he is in the background behind the action, sometimes he is interceding in it. A Bard's Song concerning troubles in the family of Los inspires Milton's descent to earth. Los himself watches over this descent; and he as well as Milton enters into William Blake. In other words, throughout this poem, wherever an act of the human imagination is occurring, there one finds Los.

In epic literature, the closest parallels to *Milton* are John Milton's *Paradise Regained*, Dante's *Purgatorio* and Homer's *Odyssey*.

Title *To Justify the Ways of God to Men* From Milton's prayer in the Invocation to *Paradise Lost* (1.26):

> What in me is dark
> Illumine, what is low raise and support;
> That to the highth of this great argument
> I may assert eternal Providence,
> And justify the ways of God to Men.

PREFACE

Pl. 1.6 *consciously & professedly Inspired Men* The authors of the Bible.

7-8 *Daughters of Memory . . . Daughters of Inspiration* The classical Muses are daughters of Mnemosyne (Memory). B.'s own Muses resemble Milton's 'Heav'nly Muse' (*Paradise Lost* 1.6).

9-10 *malady and infection . . . Sword* Malady and infection derived from classical writers who celebrated War.

BOOK THE FIRST

Invocation. Milton, unhappy though in heaven, hears a Bard's Song (Pls. 2-13) concerning LOS, the Eternal Prophet, and his family. In this song, which allegorizes Blake's difficulties with his patron Hayley, SATAN(Hayley) precipitates a quarrel with PALAMABRON(Blake) which results in Satan's exclusion from Los's family and his identification with URIZEN (the god of Reason and Moral Law).

Hearing the song, Milton (Pl. IV) realizes that he himself is a Satanic selfhood, and he resolves to go down to Eternal Death. In the following action, he enters something like a dream state. His 'real self' remains asleep in EDEN, guarded by the seven angels of the Presence. But subjectively he enters his shadow and begins a descent from BEULAH (the dreamland of poetic inspiration) to ULRO (our earth, B.'s equivalent of hell). Approaching earth (Pl. 15), he sees ALBION asleep on the rock of ages, then drops like a shooting star into B.'s foot. He passes his six females, who tempt him with all his former errors as a poet. He journeys about the MUNDANE SHELL. The FOUR ZOAS see him, and Los – misunderstanding his purpose – tries to stop him. The SHADOWY FEMALE (Nature) responds to his advent with a promise of cruelty (Pl. 18) which Orc begs her to change. Urizen and Milton meet and struggle on the shores of Arnon (Pl. 19). Albion stirs in sleep as Milton descends through his heart. Meanwhile 'the real Milton' and his guardians are driven out of heaven by a group of wrathful Eternals.

Then Los realizes Milton's true mission is the liberation of Orc (Revolutionary Energy). The Eternals in OLOLON, who drove Milton out, realize this also (Pl. 21), and repentantly resolve to follow him to Ulro. The Divine Family, united in Jesus, is with them in this quest.

Los descends and becomes one with Blake (Pl. 22). His sons Rintrah and Palamabron express fear of Milton and his religion. Los tries to reassure them and urges patience, but they are unconvinced. Here the narrative of Book 1 ends. The conclusion of the Book (Pls. 24-9) describes the works of Los, which include all creative effort both within the human organism and within society.

Pl. 2.1-15 The Invocation, highly condensed like that of Milton's *Paradise Lost*.

1 *Daughters of Beulah* B.'s Muses dwell in the dreamland of Beulah which is a realm of reposeful sexuality and artistic inspiration. These things are 'delusions' compared with man's 'real' life in Eternity, but they are nevertheless far superior to our ordinary experience. Asking their help B. implies an anatomy of poetic creation, traced back to its divine source. This final source is 'The Eternal Great Humanity Divine' (l. 8), Jesus, of whom all men are members.

9 *the Spectres of the Dead* Fallen human beings, who in the poet's imagination become true images of God.

10 *the False Tongue* The voice of Satan, and of all religious doctrine which accuses men of sin and demands atonement. 'What shall be done unto thee, thou false tongue? Sharp arrows of the mighty, with coals of juniper' (Psalm 120).

17 *One hundred years* An approximate figure. Milton died in 1674.
intricate mazes 'mazes intricate' (*Paradise Lost* v.622).

19 *Sixfold Emanation* Milton's three wives and three daughters; but also the 'female' qualities which he condemned and rejected within himself and his art.

25 *Mark well my words!* Here begins the Bard's Song. This line is repeated as a periodic refrain in it.

26 *Three Classes are Created* Three classes of Mankind exist in this world. The Reprobates are rebels, the Elect are orthodox and self-righteous (like the 'devils' and 'angels' of *MHH*). The Redeemed are mid-way, uncertain of what is right. The definitions are given in 7.1-3 (which originally followed Pl. 2 directly) and 25.31-7.
the Hammer of Los LOS, the Eternal Prophet, labours as a blacksmith, creating permanent and definite forms for indefinite ideas. He and his sons create the intellectual history of Mankind, which for B. is its *real* history.

Pl. 3 This plate is a late addition. It gives background on the Fall of Man, the creation of the material body and the development of the family of Los.

1 *Enitharmon's looms* ENITHARMON is the EMANATION of Los. She and her daughters, throughout the poem, 'weave' the generated bodies of men. The looms symbolize motherhood.

Albion was slain ALBION (mankind) lies in a death-like sleep throughout the course of this poem. The full story of his fall is in *FZ*, *passim*.

6 *Urizen lay in darkness* The following passage retells *BU* 10.31–13.20. The creation of a limited physical body, beginning with an enclosed skull and heart, is an essential part of the Fall of Man.

33 *separated into a Female* The creation of Enitharmon. See *BU* 13.50–19.1.

36 *separated into a Male* The creation of the Spectre of Los.

39 *They Builded Great Golgonooza* Los and his Spectre built the City of Art.

41–3 *Satan ... Miller of Eternity ... Prince of the Starry Wheels* SATAN, Los and Enitharmon's youngest son, is a miller; the Starry Wheels turn like mill wheels and are associated with Urizenic Reason. Satan is, in fact, a form of URIZEN.

Pl. 4] This plate is a late addition.

1–2 *Beneath ... Rintrah & ... Palamabron* Satan should be subservient to his brothers RINTRAH and PALAMABRON; their plough and harrow are more important than his mill.

3 *the Mundane Shell* The sky. For its creation by Urizen, see *FZ* 11.23.8–31.15.

6–14 Los's speech to Satan, who wants to tend the harrow instead of his own mills.

11 *Newtons Pantocrator* A bitter pun. Panto crator means: (1)'Omnipotent Lord' (a traditional epithet for Christ); (2) 'A copying machine' (a coinage of Newton's).

12 *Shaddai* Heb. 'Almighty'.

21 *South Molton Street* where B. lived at No. 17 after leaving Felpham in 1803, and *Stratford Place* are at the foot of Tyburn Hill. B. identifies Tyburn gallows with Calvary.

22 *the Victims ... their Cherubim* Cherubim usually signify prohibition in B., but the victims here are turning the tables on their guardians. Probably this is autobiographical. B. is taking the courage to write.

Pl. 5 This plate is a late addition, found only in one copy of the poem. It contains the lament of the Daughters of Albion over Man's limited perceptions. The Daughters create the three classes of men, and offer consoling delight to two (the Reprobate and Redeemed, who are 'contraries'), but not to the Elect, who are the 'reasoning negative'.

1-3 The fiery harrow, artillery and Sin are equated; Palamabron and Christ could bear the heat; Satan could not.

19-26 Repeated with alterations in *J* 49.32-41.

27 Limited perceptions produce restrictive moral codes; these reinforce worship of Babylon.

39-40 *Charles . . . Cromwell . . . James* Historical examples of the three classes of men.

James calls for fires because the Catholics were popularly blamed for starting the great fire of London (1666); James II was Catholic.

Pl. 6] This plate is an interpolation, but is contained in all copies of the poem.

1 *Golgonooza . . . London* The City of Art is a spiritual and fully realized version of the city of this world.

6 *Enitharmons Loom* The weaving of Enitharmon parallels the hammering of Los as creative labour.

12 *Rintrah, Palamabron, Theotormon, Bromion* Four sons of Los.

14 *Lambeths Vale* The area of London where B. lived 1791-1800. B. insists that Jerusalem was 'builded here' before the fall of Albion.

16 *Oak Groves rooted* Druidism substituted for the ruined original City of God, Jerusalem.

23-4 *Babel . . . glory & war* England has grown to be an empire instead of a sacred land.

Pl. 7 Here begins the main line of the Bard's story, the conflict between Satan and Palamabron. This in part allegorizes the quarrel between Blake (Palamabron) and his patron Hayley (Satan). Hayley considered himself an important poet and Blake an eccentric dependant. Blake disagreed.

4-6 *Satan . . . soft intreated Los* Hayley wished to be considered a major poet.

10   *blamable*   May refer to Los, who should not have succumbed to Satan–Hayley's nagging; or to Palamabron–Blake, who should not have suppressed his anger.

Pl. 8.4–5   *Satan . . . found all confusion*   For Blake, trying to do the trivial work Hayley recommends, has 'marred' it with his own ideas.

26   *the cliffs of the Dead*   The brows of mortal men.

27–8   *Jehovahs rain, & Molechs/Thick fires*   Epic epithets; a storm of rain and lightning. (Molech was a Canaanite god of fire and child-sacrifice.)

30   *Theotormon & Bromion*   Sons of Los, they also appear in *VDA* as a pair with limited vision. Here, they possibly represent artist-friends of Hayley's.

31   *trembling at eternal death*   See 4.17. Satan's 'work is Eternal Death'.

32–4   *Michael, Thulloh, Rintrah*   Sons of Los opposed to Satan. Possibly they all represent artist-acquaintances of Blake and Hayley, sympathetic to Blake.

43   *She form'd a Space*   The formation of spaces around offending figures is in B. always an act of female mercy, which protects and encloses the offender, and at the same time prevents the infection from spreading to others.

46   *Palamabron called down*   Palamabron at last takes action; Blake quarrels publicly with Hayley.

Pl. 9.8   *the Two Witnesses*   A theological pun. One may 'witness' in a law court or 'witness' for Christ. The prophecy of two martyred witnesses of God is in Revelation 11:3–10.

10   *it fell on Rintrah*   This judgement is explained below, 11.15–26

10–11   *his rage . . . against Palamabron*   Satan–Hayley at last loses his temper; an Elect behaving like a Reprobate.

19–29   Satan insisting on principles of sin and punishment reveals himself as 'the Accuser who is the God of this world'. Hayley is a representative of these principles, though until now disguised in mild politeness.

32–3   *the stones becoming opake/Hid him*   Satan has 'hardened his heart'.

46 *Satan not having ... Wrath* Satan not knowing how to express the emotion of anger simply and directly. Cf. 'A Poison Tree', *SE*, p. 129 above: 'I told my wrath, my wrath did end.'

50 *the seven mountains of Rome* The seven Churches.

51 The COVERING CHERUB guards Paradise and prevents Man's re-entry. B. identifies this figure with the false religions of Rome, Babylon and Tyre. The symbolism suggested here is further developed in *J*.

Pl. 10] This plate is a late addition.

8–10 *Satan ... Became Canaan* Satan is becoming a god of this world, and Canaan is becoming his exclusive holy land. A false and divisive holiness will necessarily precipitate War (l. 11). The geographical symbolism here is further developed in *J*.

12–13 *their God ... nor King* Neither Church nor State can be worshipped by Poetry.

14–19 *Elynittria ... And Ocalythron* Here begins a new theme, that of sexual jealousy and possessiveness as the source of human conflict. ELYNITTRIA is Palamabron's emanation (Catherine Blake). OCALYTHRON is mentioned in *Europe*, but not developed.

Pl. 11.1 *Eon* Another word for 'emanation'. JERUSALEM is Albion's emanation.

13 *the Spectres of the Dead* Misguided mortal men.

14 *the Unutterable Name* The Tetragrammaton, the name of God which it was forbidden to pronounce aloud; another sign of falsely 'holy' divinity, since God and Man should be one.

17–18 *If the Guilty ... Eternity* To punish the guilty prevents them from reforming themselves, and perpetuates a cycle of punishment.

28 *Leutha* In *Europe*, a temptress-figure. Here she is Satan's emanation (i.e., Inspiration). Her plea is that Satan–Hayley must not be blamed for a false Inspiration.

Pl. 12.10–41 Leutha's version of Satan–Hayley's attempts to be a great poet. He cannot handle the fires of creativity (ll. 10–23), his doctrines are anti-libertarian (to devour Albion and Jerusalem, l. 27), he adds insult to injury (the Serpent is the subtle liar and reasoner of *PL.* IX) in criticizing Blake (ll. 29–34). When contradicted, he retracts (l. 36). When he cannot succeed in writing, he continues to lecture (ll. 37–8). When Blake returns to the scene, full of his own inspiration (ll. 40–42), Hayley at first keeps his ideas to himself, then disclaims them.

10 *I sprang out of the breast of Satan* As Sin sprang from Satan's brow in *Paradise Lost* 11.752–60.

39 *And call'd me ... held me* Quotes *Paradise Lost* 11.760–61.

Pl. 13.2 Hayley's egotism is still agitated.

8 *All is my Fault ... Spectre of Luvah* In an excess of contrition, Leutha incorrectly identifies herself and Satan with Luvah (who in *FZ* has his own part to bear in the ruin of Albion).

17 *Six Thousand years* From 4004 BC, the supposed date of creation, to an anticipated apocalypse.

17–23 *Lucifer ... Jehovah* The SEVEN EYES OF GOD, a succession of deities presiding over periods of fallen history, each inadequate until the coming of the Lamb. See Dictionary of Proper Names.

35 *the fatal Brook* Tyburn (identified with Calvary).

43–4 *Leutha lived/In Palamabrons Tent* Blake studied and came to understand what Hayley represented in Art and Doctrine.

Pl. 14.9 Milton understood and believed the Bard, and was instantly inspired to act upon what he had heard.

18 *O when Lord Jesus wilt thou come?* The final promise and prayer of the New Testament was Revelation 22:20: 'He which testifieth these things saith, Surely I come quickly: Amen. Even so, come, Lord Jesus.'

30–32 The key moral statement of the poem. All selfhood is Satanic. Milton had created a hell in *Paradise Lost* for his 'Satan'. Now he must recognize that Satan is a part of himself. He must also recognize that fire is not 'Hell', but the proper element of the poet labouring at his 'furnaces' of creation. 'Eternal Death' is the 'life' of this world.

36 *he beheld his own Shadow* (1) His lower self; (2) the influence of his writing in the world.

37 *hermaphroditic* The hermaphroditic form in B. is a sterile parody of humanity in Eden, which transcends divided sexuality and is androgynous.

39 *twenty-seven-fold* For the 'twenty-seven heavens and their churches', see 37.35ff. and Dictionary of Proper Names.

40 *direst Hell* Ulro, the world of complete dead mechanism.

42 *Seven Angels of the Presence* The term is from Isaiah 63:7-9, speaking of God's love for his children: 'In all their affliction he was afflicted, and the angel of his presence saved them.' Thus these are figures of compassion, one for each of the Eyes of God named on Pl. 13. The Seven, joined by Milton (15.5), make Eight, and at the close of the poem (42.10-11) 'the Starry Eight became/One Man, Jesus the Saviour'.

Pl. 15.8 *Polypus* Octopus or jellyfish; a symbol of poisonous vagueness, later developed by B. as a major image for the material body. Milton now exists in three forms: walking about as a divine image in Eden, sleeping in Beulah, and descending lonely to the world of Generation.

19 *a comet* Mortal men (here called Spectres) see Milton as a comet or falling star.

21-35 'Vortex' is a term in Cartesian cosmology meaning 'sphere of influence' around a star (Stevenson). In B.'s adaptation, a vortex is any idea or philosophy which makes a whole world to itself, and each is a form of human experience. The traveller, while *within* a vortex, sees it as we see our own world – our little circle of cornfields and valleys with the heavenly bodies above – i.e., partially. Having *left* a vortex, he may see it from the outside as a closed system, a globe separated from him, or he may see it (more truly) as a human form, a friend.

45-7 *so Milton's shadow fell ... falling star* Compare the fall of Mulciber in *Paradise Lost* 1.742-5: 'From morn/To noon he fell, from noon to dewy eve/A summer's day; and with the setting sun/Dropp'd from the zenith like a falling star.'

Pl. 15.51-Pl. 17.1 *the Three Heavens ... three females* Milton's mortal loves had represented the whole of female beauty (in head, heart and loins) to him.

Pl. 16 A full-page design shows Milton striving with Urizen. Inscription reads: 'To Annihilate the Self-hood of Deceit & False Forgiveness'.

Pl. 17.2-3 *that they ... Selfhood* In order that they (the twice three females, Milton's emanation) might be renewed to life and reassumed as a part of Milton's being, by his surrender of his narrower selfhood.

7 *Female forms* Temptations which now surround him.

11 *Rahab and Tirzah* The Whore of Babylon and her daughter the cruel Virgin collectively come to represent female will embodied in false religions.

Tirzah, Milcah, Malah, Noah, Hoglah Daughters of Zelophehad who became his heirs. For B. they represent the materialism of the five senses, and a triumph of female will. Thus the idea here is: Milton's wives and daughters (his collective emanation) contain the beauty of his poetic inspiration derived from Beulah, but they also contain the error of his false puritanic doctrines of Moral Law derived from Ulro. Mt Horeb or Sinai is the site of the Commandments and Law.

13-14 *they wrote ... His dictate* Milton's daughters were his secretaries in his old age, when he was blind.

16 *Hor ... Hermon* Mountains and mountainous regions in and around Palestine.

20 *Edom ... Amalek* Tribes bordering Palestine.

31 *Los the Vehicular terror* Los is the vehicle of all poetry and prophecy. But he and Enitharmon here misunderstand Milton's mission, and resist it.

Pl. 18 This plate is a late addition. Further implications of Milton's descent are explored through an interchange between the SHADOWY FEMALE and ORC. The full story of these two figures (not important here) occurs in the preludium to *Europe*, and in *FZ* VII [a] and VIII.

2 *The Shadowy Female* Vala, bride of Luvah–Orc, in her fallen form becomes a brutalized Nature. Here she represents primitive hardships of natural existence and the Natural Religion that results.

26 *Take not the Human Form* Orc replies that the female, which is but half of humanity, should not pretend to be the whole. Nature, which is but a passive and fallen material aspect of the universe, should not pretend to be its totality.

39-41 *Oothoon & Leutha* parallel *Jerusalem & Babylon* as contrary aspects of female character – one representing Liberty, one representing Bondage. They are both 'within' the Shadowy Female as potential developments.

Pl. 19 A climax of the first part of the poem. Milton encounters URIZEN, and is tempted by RAHAB and TIRZAH. His response is to give warm life and human form to the cold and death-dealing god of Reason, and to ignore the temptations. In the geographical symbolism,

Arnon (l. 6) is a river of birth, *Jordan* (l. 8) a river of deathly baptism. *Mahanaim* (l. 7) is the plain where Jacob had his vision of the angels. *Succoth* (l. 10) is on the border of Jordan, and had 'clay ground' (1 Kings 7:46). *Red clay* is what Adam was made of, and is the Hebrew meaning of his name. *The Valley of Beth Peor* (l. 14) is the burial place of Moses, just short of the promised land which he never entered. In the 'enticement' passage below (19.36-20.6), Milton must resist crossing the river into a promised land of self-righteous holiness.

15-24 *Four Universes . . . without end* A brief recapitulation of the fall of the Four Zoas, and the cosmic geography through which Milton presently travels. *South* (Intellect) is the region abandoned by Urizen and wrongly appropriated by Luvah. *East* was abandoned by Luvah. *West* is Tharmas, *North* is Urthona. They are also the four elements fire, air, water, earth. (See also 34.32-9, *J* 59.10-17.)

27-8 *Rahab . . . and Tirzah* form the sum of Milton's temptations to holiness, which was his former error as a poet.

36-7 *Come thou to Ephraim . . . Canaan . . . Amalekites* A temptation to political power over the Promised Land and its enemies. (B. is thinking here of Milton's career as propagandist for Cromwell.)

39 *The banks of Cam* The site of Cambridge University, where Milton studied.

41-3 *Ahania . . . Enion . . . Vala* The estranged emanations of Urizen, Tharmas and Luvah. Their sufferings are detailed in *FZ*.

46 A temptation to subject Christian art (Jerusalem) to pagan art (the Grecian lyre). B. evidently felt that Milton had compromised himself on this issue by his use of classical mythology.

48 *Let her be Offerd up to Holiness!* A temptation to sacrifice true faith to impersonal 'Holiness' and analytic theologizing; here again, B. is criticizing Milton's poetry.

55 *She ties the knot* Tirzah ties the brain, heart and genitals into limited forms. This is a temptation to believe in the reality of the material world and the material body.

58-9 *Hand, Hyle & Coban, Scofield, Reuben* See ALBION, SONS OF, and ISRAEL, SONS OF. These figures are important in *J* but not here.

Pl. 20.3-6 A concluding temptation to be a spiritual dictator.

Ephraim & Manasseh In biblical history, secessionist (hence faithless) regions of which Tirzah was capital.

Hazor A Canaanite town whose king unsuccessfully led twelve tribes against the conquering Israelites.

15–18 Blake interrupts himself at the daunting prospect of the high things to come in his narrative, as Milton does for the Invocation to Light which opens *Paradise Lost* III.

16 *the Four-fold Man* The Divine Humanity, Albion with his Four Zoas.

33 *Og & Anak* Biblical giants, foes of Israel who suffered crushing defeats. The implication is that they seem more dangerous than they are.

43–5 *the Eternals ... wrathful* at the sight of Milton, not understanding the reason for his descent, drive his human form into Ulro. Thus begins a new major action in the poem. See 21.16–44.

46 *the Watchers* The seven angels guarding Milton.

47 *the Shadowy Eighth* Milton's sleeping Humanity.

52 *Rintrah & Palamabron* Honest Wrath and Pity, Los's sons. See the Bard's Song, Pl. 14 above; see also the Dictionary of Proper Names.

53 *Reuben, Gad* In Joshua 22 their apparent rebellion against God proves unreal; they are faithful. But in *FZ* VIII these are faithless sons of Los.

Pl. 21.16 *Ololon* is a region, but also its inhabitants. It will later be identified with Milton's emanation.

those who Milton drove Those who drove Milton are the wrathful Eternals of 20.43. Here they are identified as Ololon.

20 *sulphur Sun* The material sun. Sulphur is a 'base' element in alchemical theory.

24 *Providence began* The family of Eden now became aware of Milton's self-sacrifice, and began to gather its forces to help.

45 *Ololon* The dwellers in Ololon, who will later unite with Milton's divided emanation, and reunite with Milton at the close of the poem.

47–50 Ololon attempts to understand 'this world of Sorrow'. Is the sorrow a form of punishment? It is a refuge from the strenuous mental wars of Eternity, but an unnatural one. Is it, then, a form of repentance? Ololon resolves to 'enter into' the suffering of the world: to investigate and to participate.

51–7 This is the guiding speech of Providence, which implicitly 'began' on l. 24.

60 From Matthew 26:64: 'Hereafter shall ye see the Son of man ... coming in the clouds of heaven.'

Pl. 22 Los enters Blake and triumphantly announces the role of prophetic art. But working against his confident assurance is the fear of his sons that 'Miltons Religion' will perpetuate all the old errors.

31 *Whence is this Shadow* Los's sons identify the shadow of Milton with his self-righteous puritanism. They fear that (ll. 32-3) 'he/Will unchain Orc' (instigate War), and will 'let loose Satan, Og, Sihon & Anak' (a quaternary of vague threat-figures). Sihon, like Og and Anak (20.33), was a giant king 'utterly destroyed' (Joshua 2:10) by Israel.

38 *Jealousy of Theotormon* The sexual jealousy and craving for purity (see *VDA*) which underlies all religions of virtue.

41 *Voltaire ... Rousseau* Though traditional religions and Churches seem dead, their errors are perpetuated. Voltaire's worldly scepticism and Rousseau's Natural Religion still encourage self-righteousness, deny the value of enthusiasm and self-sacrifice, support the State, are legalistic, are able to pervert true vision, condemn true liberty, and allow divine matters to remain in the hands of Mystery, when they should be the province of all men's capacity for spiritual vision.

50-54 A critique of Swedenborg's writings (cf. *MHH* Pl. 21).

Pl. 22.55–Pl. 23.2 *Whitefield ... Westley* For B., the great eighteenth-century English evangelists were men of true vision unperverted by rationalism. He identifies them with the martyred 'witnesses' of Revelation 11:3-10.

Pl. 23.6 *Lo Orc arises* Political revolutions have already begun.

11-12 *How long ... How long* In Revelation 6:9-11 the souls of the martyrs 'cried with a loud voice, saying, How long, O Lord, holy and true, dost thou not judge and avenge ...? and it was said unto them, that they should rest yet for a little season' (as in Los's reply (l. 32), 'be patient yet a little').

15-16 *Hand, Hyle & Coban ... Gwendolen & Conwenna* Sons and daughters of Albion who deny faith and liberty. These figures are further developed in *J, passim*.

32 *O noble Sons, be patient* This scene is Los's Gethsemane – he begs, 'watch with me one hour' (Matthew 26:40).

39 *These lovely Females* Daughters of Beulah. Los is reminding his sons that they have allies in the task.

51 *powers fitted to circumscribe* Los explains that the work of art at once defines and places limits on the experience of fallen Mankind.

53 Compare the speech of the Clod of Clay in *Thel* 5.5; and the speech of Jesus in Matthew 26:42: 'O my Father, if this cup may not pass away from me, except I drink it, thy will be done.' Also see Mark 13:24-33, where the Lord's return in glory is promised soon, 'But of that day and that hour knoweth no man, no, not the angels . . . neither the Son . . .Take ye heed, watch and pray: for ye know not when the time is.'

62 *Twelve Sons* The twelve tribes of Israel.

Pl. 24.2-3 *Reuben . . . Judah* Seven of the twelve tribes of Israel.

3-4 *Generated . . . with Tirzah* Became mere mortals subject to Nature.

6 *We called him Menassheh* (From Hebrew *Nasheh*, 'cause to forget'.) Joseph's son, born in Egypt, so named because 'God . . . hath made me forget all my toil, and all my father's house' (Genesis 41:51).

20 *Ephraim & Menassheh* Egyptian-born sons of Joseph.

27 *the Vehicular Body* The emblem.

29 *the Sleeping Body* of Albion.

35 *Cathedrons Looms weave only Death* The looms of Enitharmon are uncreative when not working in conjunction with the labours of Los and his sons.

47 *no hope of an end* Here the narrative of Book I ceases. The remainder of Book I describes the sorrow and joy of the labours of Los. See Dictionary of Proper Names for GOLGONOOZA; BOWLAHOOLA; ALLAMANDA; LUBAN.

71 *the ever apparent Elias* The prophet Elijah, traditionally herald of the Messiah, is identified with Los.

76 *the Throne Divine* From Revelation 4:2-6 'and behold a throne was set in heaven . . . and round about the throne, were four beasts [lit. Zῶα, 'living creatures'] full of eyes before and behind'. Los is the fourth Zoa.

Pl. 25] In two copies of the poem, Pls. 25-7 are arranged 26, 27, 25.

1 *the Wine-presses* B.'s image for 'war on earth', derived from imagery of the violent last harvest and vintage in Revelation 14:14-20 and 19:15, where the winepress is identified with the wrath of God, crushing the nations of the earth. In *FZ* IX.135.21-137.23, the last vintage and the winepress of Luvah are apocalyptic. Here the image refers specifically to the Napoleonic wars as harbingers of apocalypse.

22 *The Awakener* From 21.33, 'Milton the Awakener'. The meaning is (1) one who himself wakes up; (2) one who wakes others.

23 Albion himself begins to awake.

42 *the Mundane Egg* Our 'three-dimensional world of time and space, in which fallen Man incubates until he hatches and re-enters Eternity' (Damon, *Dictionary*). It is surrounded by the Mundane Shell, the sky.

44 *you sowed in tears* From Psalm 126:4-6: 'Turn again our captivity, O Lord, as the streams in the south. They that sow in tears shall reap in joy. He that goeth forth and weepeth, bearing precious seed, shall doubtless come again with rejoicing, bringing his sheaves with him.'

48-50 *Lambeth ruin'd ... Apollo ... Asylum ... Hercules* Blake complains of the use of classical names (and the spirit implied by the names) in his English neighbourhood, Lambeth. His house was in 'Hercules Buildings', near by lay 'Apollo Gardens' and the Royal Asylum for Female Orphans.

55 *Jerusalem ... all Nations* From Isaiah 2:2-4: 'And it shall come to pass in the last days, that the mountain of the Lord's house shall be established in the top of the mountains ... and all nations shall flow unto it ... for out of Zion shall go forth the law, and the word of the Lord from Jerusalem ... and they shall beat their swords into plowshares ...'

61 *the Lamb & his Bride* From Revelation 21:2: 'And I John saw the holy city, new Jerusalem ... prepared as a bride adorned for her husband.'

71 *the calm Ocean joys beneath & smooths* From Milton's 'Nativity Ode', 64-6: 'The Winds, with wonder whist/Smoothly the waters kiss't/Whispering new joys to the mild Ocean.'

Pl. 26.11 *the hem of their garments* In Matthew 14:35-6 all the diseased were brought to Jesus 'that they might only touch the hem of his garment: and as many as touched were made perfectly whole'.

13 *Two Gates* The cave of the nymphs (*Odyssey* XIII) had two gates, the north for men, the south for gods. In neo-Platonic interpretation the cave was mortal life, the northern gate was for souls ascending from bodies after death.

14–15 The locations are cliffs facing the ocean at the far north and far south of Britain.

18 *Los against the east* East is the realm abandoned and left 'void' by Luvah. Los has his back to it.

19 *Hounslow to Blackheath* West to east of London.

23–5 The place-names are locations in and around Golgonooza, Los's City of Art.

31–2 *every Generated Body . . . Is a garden . . . & a building* The body is a garden in the Song of Solomon 4:12, 'A garden inclosed is my sister, my spouse,' and both a garden and a building in 1 Corinthians 3:9–16: 'Ye are God's husbandry, ye are God's building . . . know ye not that ye are the temple of God?'

Pl. 27.2 *Luvah laid the foundation & Urizen finish'd it* Wars begin in hot passion and end in cold reasoning.

3–41 Most of this is from *FZ* IX.136.16–137.4.

60] Line deleted in copper in two copies.

Pl. 28.3 Theseus in *A Midsummer Night's Dream* v.i.16–17 remarks that the poet 'gives to airy nothing/A local habitation and a name'. In the remainder of this plate, the craft of prophecy is described as a giving of form to unborn spectres, and to time itself.

21 *Theotormon & Sotha* Sons of Los, whose function is to catch the unborn spectres so that they can be given forms. The spectres, like small children, must be tempted or frightened into moving.

35–6 *like the black pebble . . . like the diamond* The rough diamond looks from the outside like a black pebble, but is beautiful within; so, too, mortal men.

Pl. 29 This plate makes a final distinction between the visionary world created by Los, and the delusion and death of the vegetated world.

25–6 *Bowlahoola & Allamanda . . . Pulsation* The digestive, nervous and circulatory systems in men's bodies.

30–31 *every Man . . . is Orc* All men have an element of Revolt within them, which unites them; but on earth Revolt remains formless.

34 *Satan ... Orc ... Luvah* Luvah is Passion in Eternity, but only Rebellion in this world; furthermore, Rebellion in this world regularly produces a spectre of self-righteous Reaction.

35-6 *Accident being Formed ... Demonstration* Empirical science treats 'accident' (Matter) as if it were 'substance' (Spirit). But to *see* existence this way is to *make* it so.

43 *Death to delude* In order to delude (beguile) Death.

57 *Horeb* The desert surrounding Mt Sinai.
Rephaim 'Valley of the shades of the dead'.

58 *Zelophehads Daughters* were five in number (corresponding to the five senses) and had no brothers. See 17.11 above.

65 *the Science of the Elohim* The knowledge or skill of the Elohim. This is a collective plural term for 'God', used in Genesis and elsewhere.

BOOK THE SECOND

The land of Beulah is described (Pls. 30–31). Ololon descends to Beulah. The sleeping Milton is instructed by his seven angels (Pl. 32). The songs of Beulah include God's promise of redemption to the Female (Pl. 33). The songs welcome Ololon (Pl. 34). Ololon descends to Ulro and asks forgiveness of the Starry Eight (Pl. 35), who rejoice. Ololon continues the descent to Los and Enitharmon, and B. describes the wild thyme and the larks as messengers of Los at the crucial moment of Ololon's appearance in female form in Blake's garden (Pls. 35–6). Milton's shadow condenses into the covering Cherub of all religious error (Pl. 37). Milton and Satan meet (Pl. 38). The Starry Seven appear with Milton in Blake's garden, and call on Albion to wake (Pl. 39). Milton and Ololon meet and Milton at last declares his true vocation as a poet (Pl. 41). The six-fold female divides from Ololon and dives into Milton's shadow; Ololon unites with the Starry Eight, and they appear as the Saviour (Pl. 42). Blake's vision concludes as the Saviour prepares to enter Albion's bosom, and the earth is prepared for the Last Judgement.

Pl. 30 An inscription in mirror-writing around the words 'Milton Book the Second' reads 'How wide the Gulf & Unpassable! between Simplicity & Insipidity/Contraries are Positives/A Negation is not a Contrary'. Then the narrative picks up from 21.60: 'Jesus the Saviour appeard coming in the Clouds of Ololon.'

Pl. 31.10-17 In Isaiah 63:9 the Saviour suffers with Mankind: 'In all their affliction he was afflicted.' Here, the idea is reversed: As the Saviour approaches with lamentation, all spheres of the creation respond sympathetically.

20 *Fairies, Nymphs, Gnomes, Genii* Folklore divinities, not high in the scale of the divine imagination. They belong to air (Urizen), water (Tharmas), earth (Urthona) and fire (Luvah).

24 *Element against Element, opposed in War* The natural warfare of the four elements is a staple of natural philosophy from Lucretius down to the seventeenth century.

49 *Og & Anak* Threat-figures. See 20.33n.

62 *sick with Love* From Song of Solomon 2:5: 'Stay me with flagons, comfort me with apples: for I am sick of love.'

Pl. 32] This plate is a late addition.

1 *And Milton ... Couch of Death* The narrative picks up from 15.1-7.

4 *My Spectre ... my Emanation* The cruel ideology of courtship. See 'My Spectre around me . . .', Notebook, p. 494.

8 *Hillel . . . Lucifer* Lucifer ('morning star') is the first eye of God (13.17). In Isaiah 14:12, translated 'Lucifer, son of the morning', Lucifer is 'Helel'. The Jewish Rabbi Hillel, who lived just before Christ, taught love of God and one's brother, and hence was also a 'morning star'.

10-22 The Seven Angels are 'states' or conditions which individuals may pass through (as in common usage we speak of a 'state' of happiness or a 'state' of sin). In the service of Divinity they are angels in human form. But in the service of Satan they are shapeless rocks, and their 'holiness' is that of 'Length: Bredth & Highth'. Such 'holiness' can only admire itself, and thinks Imagination is a blasphemy against it. But these qualities (length, breadth and height) should obviously be Man's servants, not his gods.

14 כרכים Not a correct Hebrew word, but a cross between *Kerabim* ('as multitudes') and *Cherubim*.

23 *States Change* Individuals may pass from one state to another, without losing their permanent individuality.

34-5 *Reason is a State . . . Created* One systematic philosophy wears out and is succeeded by another. But eternal forms – such as the prophet perceives – remain.

Pl. 33.1-23 God's song to Babylon – the Unholy City – as a jealous bride who has alienated her beloved. No people should set themselves up as the one Chosen People of God, denying his love to others. But even Babylon may be redeemed if she generously gives her handmaiden Jerusalem to her husband. This polygamous ideal of true love derives from several Old Testament stories in which wives give their hand-maidens to their husbands. Oothoon offers such love in *VDA*, and Milton's emanation is about to do the same.

16 *intirely abstracting . . . loves* Compare 'Let us agree to give up Love,' 'My Spectre around me . . .', Notebook, p. 494.

Pl. 34 Ololon, who was a 'Fiery Circle' of Eternals in 20.43-50, is about to descend to Ulro, which is seen from above as a chaotic Polypus.

12-13 *Alla . . . Al-Ulro . . . Or-Ulro* These names are sub-classifica-tions of the fallen world, which are never used again.

26 *Twenty-seven fold* For the twenty-seven evil Churches (see 35.63-4 and Dictionary of Proper Names) which encrust fallen Mankind.

27 *Five Females* Five senses; Zelophehad's five daughters.

30 *The River Storge* A river of mortal birth. *Storge* is Gr. 'parental affection'.

41 *Chasms of the Mundane Shell* Gaps left within the perimeters of the circles, when Man shrunk to his egg shape. See Diagram.

42 *Southward & by the East* Equally in the realms of Reason and Passion.

45 *Four Immortals* Four Zoas.

50 *They said* Ololon said.

50-52 *Wars of man . . . Interior Vision* Wars, which in Eternity are mental sport, are taken seriously by mortals.

Pl. 35.7-13 *Female forms . . . the dark Woof* The females are Zelo-phehad's five daughters (17.11, 27.58) plus Rahab. The place-names are locations in the environs of London. The dark woof of the loom of Death opposes Enitharmon's life-giving loom.

18–25 Immortals such as Ololon cannot see the City of Art until they descend to the material world, although those who dwell in the material world already can see it.

31–3 The crime of Ololon was to drive Milton into the Ulro.

42 *There is a Moment* The moment of inspiration in which an individual's fragmentary understanding suddenly becomes integrated and unified. This is the crucial moment in which 'the Poets Work is done' (29.1). Here it is the moment in which Ololon, Los, Milton, and all the forces which oppose them, finally converge in Blake's garden.

59 *Luvahs empty Tomb* associates Luvah with the crucified and risen Christ.

60 *Ololon . . . on the Rock* associates Ololon with the women who waited at Christ's tomb.

63–4 *Twenty-seven churches* (see Dictionary of Proper Names) fill the firmament in concentric folds of increasing opacity. The SEVEN EYES OF GOD each preside over four Churches – but the count of Churches is incomplete (should amount to twenty-eight, a more 'perfect' number). The place of the twenty-eight, then, is taken by Truth in the form of Ololon (and Jesus) whom the twenty-eighth lark meets (36.9–10).

Pl. 36.16–17 *One Female . . . a Virgin of twelve years* Ololon is now the embodiment of Milton's lost emanation.

31–2 *my Shadow of Delight . . . is sick* Catherine Blake, who was often ill while at Felpham.

Pl. 37.6–8 *Milton's Shadow* becomes the condensation of his errors as a thinker, here identified with the COVERING CHERUB which keeps men expelled from Paradise and separated from God.

11 *the Wicker Man of Scandinavia* Caesar's *Commentaries* mention a Druid form of human sacrifice, burning men within a huge wicker image.

15–18 Milton's erroneous puritanism contains and implies all religious errors throughout history, including those that Milton himself denounced.

20–34 The twelve gods of Ulro are pagan deities, their names taken from Milton's list in *Paradise Lost* 1.392–521.

50 *Og . . . Sihon* These lands, hostile to Israel, exist also among the stars.

54 *Forty-eight deformed Human Wonders* The constellations.

57–9 *none can pass . . . Entuthon Benython* The passage to Eternity is not through contemplation of the stars but through the labours of Prophecy.

Pl. 38 The meeting of Milton and Satan is Milton's final temptation.

10 *Milton within his sleeping Humanity* Milton has descended to this world, and so is asleep compared to his waking life in Eternity.

23–6 *Mystery Babylon . . . her Cup . . . her scarlet Veil* Within Satan is the Whore of Babylon, who in Revelation 17:4 has 'a golden cup in her hand full of abominations', and is 'arrayed in purple and scarlet colour'.

28 *the Eastern porch* The gate of Passion.

29–32 Compare 'The iron hand crushd the Tyrants head/And became a Tyrant in his stead,' 'The Grey Monk', Pickering MS, p. 506 above. Milton's triumph over temptation means renunciation of the self-righteous virtue exhibited in his literary and political careers.

50 *Satan . . . Coming in a cloud* As does God over Mt Sinai.

52 *Fall therefore down & worship me* So Satan tempts Jesus in Luke 4:7, 'If thou therefore wilt worship me, all shall be thine,' and in *Paradise Regained* IV.166–7, 'if thou wilt fall down/And worship me as thy superior Lord'.

Pl. 39.11 *Cast him . . . into the Lake* From Revelation 20:10: 'And the devil . . . was cast into the lake of fire and brimstone.'

32 *Then Albion rose* B. describes Albion's attempt to rise and walk in terms of place-names throughout Great Britain and in the City of London.

43–4 *York . Norwich* Cathedral cities of England. In *J* the theme of the cathedral cities as 'Albion's Friends' is developed.

53 *Urizen faints* The narrative picks up from Pl. 19, the struggle between Milton and Urizen.

Pl. 40.9 *those who contemn Religion* Those such as Milton who consciously oppose religious tyranny, yet unconsciously support it.

12 *Voltaire & Rousseau . . . Hume & Gibbon & Bolingbroke* all mocked Christianity and were felt by Blake to believe only in a 'dead' Newtonian universe.

17 *Rahab* Moral Virtue, of which Milton had approved. Moral Virtue is a two-fold monster because it promotes self-righteous War and because it hides suppressed Lust.

Pl. 41.5 *Bacon, Locke & Newton* B.'s trinity of Reasoners.

25 *the Sexual Garments* The clothing of flesh worn by mortals.

27 *Which Jesus rent* The rending of the veil of the Temple when Jesus died (Matthew 27:51) and the old Law died with him.

28 *Generation . . . swallowd up in Regeneration* From Isaiah 25:7-8: 'And he will destroy . . . the face of the covering cast over all people, and the veil that is spread over all nations. He will swallow up death in victory.'

Pl. 42.3-6 *the Virgin divided . . . Miltons Shadow* Error splits from Truth and gives herself to annihilation with the shadow.

7 *a Moony Ark* The ark of Noah was shaped like a crescent moon.

18 *the Immortal Four* The Zoas, or the four cities named in *J* as Albion's faithful friends: Verulam, London, York, Edinburgh.

28 *Shadow of Delight* Catherine Blake.

Pl. 43.1 *the Great Harvest & Vintage of the Nations* Described in Revelation 14:14-20, and by B. in *FZ* IX. Pp. 131-5.

Dedication to Blake's Illustrations to Blair's Grave

TO THE QUEEN

Dedication to the illustrations for Cromek's edition of Blair's *Grave* (1808), designed by B. and engraved by Schiavonetti.

Notebook Epigrams and Satiric Verses, c. 1808-12

Most of these pieces vent B.'s spleen against fools and foes in the world of art. After his return from Felpham B. was having difficulty making a living, felt himself surrounded by misunderstanding and malice, and believed that bad artists and bad principles of art were ruining the culture of England. See Bentley, *Blake Records*, 166-223 *passim*.

His prose works of this period – including the Advertisement of his Exhibition (15 May 1809), his *Descriptive Catalogue* (1809), 'Public Address' (*c*. 1810) and *A Vision of the Last Judgment* (1810) – more fully enunciate his artistic theories and opinions on public taste, as do his Annotations (*c*. 1808) to the *Discourses on Art* of Sir Joshua Reynolds.

'YOU DONT BELIEVE ...'

11 *Only Believe Believe & try* A collation of Jesus' words to Jairus, whose daughter had died, 'Be not afraid, only believe' (Mark 5:36), and the episode of Doubting Thomas (John 20:24–9). However, no-where in the Gospels does Jesus use the word 'try'.

'NO REAL STYLE OF COLOURING ...'

3 *Sʳ Joshuas Colouring* Sir Joshua Reynolds (1723–92), President of the Royal Academy from 1769 to 1790. His *Discourses on Art* (published 1798) enraged Blake; see the verses written among B.'s marginalia, p. 632. As to 'colouring', B. disapproved of painting in oils, which he considered muddy and inclined to yellow. He also disapproved of emphasis on colouring, rather than firm drawing and outline in art.

'AND HIS LEGS CARRIED IT ...'

The opening of this poem is missing. It is written in a fair hand, then emended. The matters referred to are: 1. In 1803 B. was accused of sedition by Private John Scholfield, a dragoon whom he had ejected from his Felpham garden. His patron, Hayley, retained a lawyer, Samuel Rose, to defend him. B. was tried and acquitted January 1804. Rose died shortly afterwards. 2. In 1805, the publisher Cromek asked B. to design forty illustrations to Blair's *Grave*, promised he could do half the engravings for this volume, then gave all the engraving work to the more fashionable Schiavonetti. Schiavonetti died in 1810, Cromek in 1812. 3. In 1806, Cromek took B.'s idea for a painting of Chaucer's 'Canterbury Pilgrims' and suggested it to Stothard, who exhibited the ensuing work in 1807 – to B.'s fury. 4. In 1809 B. held an unsuccessful exhibition of his own paintings. *The Examiner*, edited by Leigh and Robert Hunt, called him 'an unfortunate lunatic'.

In the present poem, the supposed speaker is Stothard ('Stewhard'). The soul-stealer of the opening lines is Cromek (called 'Screwmuch' in the closing lines). 'Yorkshire Jack Hemp' and 'daw' are John and

Ann Flaxman, by whom B. during this period did not feel sufficiently appreciated. 'Felpham Billy' is William Hayley. 'Billy's lawyer' was Samuel Rose. 'Cur' and 'Dady' have not been identified. 'Assassinetti' is Schiavonetti. 'Death' is Blake himself.

17 *Hare* Puns on Hunt.
weakly Puns on 'weekly'.

'WAS I ANGRY . . .'

4-5 *Flaxman, Cromek, Stothard, Schiavonetti* See note to previous poem.

6 *Macklin, Boydel, Bowyer* All had employed Blake as an engraver.

'THE SUSSEX MEN ARE NOTED FOOLS . . .'

3 *H[aines] the painter* Blake and Samuel Haines both did illustrations for Boydell's *Shakespeare* (1802) and Hayley's *Romney* (1809).

TO H[UNT]

1 *Fuseli* B.'s artist-friend and supporter Henry Fuseli (1741–1825) was attacked along with Blake in Hunt's *Examiner* in 1808 (see Bentley, *Blake Records*, 195).

'HE IS A COCK WOULD . . .'

Private Cock supported the charge of sedition made against B. in 1803-4.

FLORENTINE INGRATITUDE

Sir Joshua Reynolds was elected in 1775 to the Florentine Academy, which required him to send a self-portrait.

15 *an English Fetch* An English trick.

26 *Ghiottos Circle or Appelles Line* Giotto (1266–1377), when asked to send Pope Benedict IX a sample of his work, drew a perfect circle freehand. Apelles (4th century BC) challenged Protogenes in drawing freehand straight lines.

A PITIFUL CASE

8 *Michael Angelo* Reynolds's concluding words in the *Discourses* are in praise of Michael Angelo.

'IF IT IS TRUE WHAT THE PROPHETS WRITE . . .'

5 *Bezaleel & Aholiab* The two master craftsmen who designed the Hebrew Tabernacle, its furnishings and ornaments (Exodus 31:1-11, 35:30-35).

'P[HILLIPS] LOVED ME, NOT . . .'

Thomas Phillips did the portrait of B. for Cromek's edition of Blair's *Grave* (see note to 'And his legs carried it . . .' above).

ON H[AYLE]YS FRIENDSHIP

5 *act upon my wife* Did Hayley try to make Catherine influence her husband in the direction of greater conventionality?

6 *Hired a Villain* No evidence exists to connect Hayley with Schol-field, and Hayley did his best to support Blake through his sedition trial. Perhaps Blake considered Rose, the lawyer Hayley got to defend him, 'a villain'. The line is from 'Fair Elenor', *PS*, p. 24 above.

'COSWAY FRAZER & BALDWIN OF EGYPTS LAKE . . .'

Richard Cosway, a fashionable miniature painter and Swedenborgian; ?Alexander Fraser, a painter (who, however, came to London only in 1813); George Baldwin, a traveller, mystic and one-time consul-general n Egypt.

'I RUBENS . . .'

Peter Paul Rubens (1577-1640) was a sometime diplomat as well as pro-lific painter.

'SWELLD LIMBS WITH NO OUTLINE . . .'

Rubens's figures are consistently large and opulent.

4 *an hundred Journeymens how dye do* Many paintings issued from Rubens's studio were executed mainly by assistants.

'THE CRIPPLE EVERY STEP DRUDGES & LABOURS . . .'

6 *Newton & Bacon* B. uses the two great English scientists here as advocates of careful 'labour' in scientific experiment, hence approving 'labour' in an artistic cripple.

9 *high labourd* A term for a carefully finished and polished work of art.

ON THE GREAT ENCOURAGEMENT GIVEN ... DUCROWE & DILBURY DOODLE

Pierre Ducros (1745–1810) was a Swiss landscape artist. 'Dilbury Doodle' is a nonsense name; 'doodle' means simpleton, noodle; but as a verb means to fool, cheat.

5 *Colonel Wardle* Gwyllym Lloyd Wardle, soldier and Member of Parliament who assailed the Duke of York for corruption in 1809.

6 *a dose of Cawdle* Medicinal drink; but also: to lecture, harangue; and a 'hempen caudle' means hanging (obs.).

THE CUNNING SURES & THE AIM AT YOURS

'Connoisseurs and amateurs', a phrase from 'Public Address', p. 634.

'ALL PICTURES THATS PANTED ...'

'Panted' and 'pant' are presumably Cromekian mispronunciations; see also 'English Encouragement of Art' and 'I ask'd my Dear Friend Orator Prigg . . .', below.

ENGLISH ENCOURAGEMENT OF ART

A much-revised piece. B. added the subtitle and altered the language to burlesque Cromek's speech. In the final reading:

2 *Menny wouver* Manoeuvre.

3 *a great Conquest are Bunglery* A great congress? corpus? are bunglers.

4 *Jenous looks to ham* Genius looks to them.

9–12 These lines may belong to the close of the following poem, but the sense suits this one.

'WHEN YOU LOOK AT A PICTURE ...'

4 *Jenny suck awa'* Je ne sais quoi.

'I GIVE YOU THE END OF A GOLDEN STRING...'

Used in *J* Pl. 77 (p. 797, below) and entitled 'To the Christians'.

WILLIAM COWPER ESQRE

The poet Cowper (1731–1800) was a religious enthusiast, and was sub-ject to fits of depression and madness. B. accuses Hayley (the name can be made out in the erased first stanza) – who tried to help Cowper, and wrote his posthumous biography – of helping too late, and understand-ing too little. His own identification with Cowper is clear. Annotating Spurzheim's *Observations on Insanity* (1817), he commented on the assertion that 'religion is another fertile cause of insanity', as follows: 'Cowper came to me & said. O that I were insane always I will never rest. Can you not make me truly insane. I will never rest till I am so. O that in the bosom of God I was hid. You retain health and yet are as mad as any of us all – over us all – mad as a refuge from unbelief – from Bacon Newton & Locke.'

1–4] The first stanza is an afterthought written over an erased original opening.

3 *Fuseli . . . both Turk & Jew* Fuseli was actually Swiss.

'I WILL TELL YOU WHAT JOSEPH OF ARIMATHEA...'

Joseph of Arimathea, according to legend, brought the Holy Grail to Britain. B. sets him against the Roman scholar Pliny and the Roman Emperor Trajan.

TO VENETIAN ARTISTS

1 Newton did major work in optics and the phenomenon of colour.

BLAKES APOLOGY FOR HIS CATALOGUE

These verses exist in a much-revised first draft in Notebook, pp. 62–3, where they follow a passage in 'Public Address', and where the title and first couplet are squeezed in at the bottom. A fair copy is on p. 65. The present text follows the line-arrangement of the latter.

4 *Bartolloze* Francesco Bartollozi (1727–1815), a popular engraver who worked in a 'soft' style while B. continued to do old-fashioned 'hard-line' engraving.

7 *Dryden in Rhyme* Dryden's rhymed closet-opera *The State of Innocence* (1674) was based on *Paradise Lost*, and Nat Lee's prefatory poem praises Dryden as a refiner of Milton's rough ore. B. comments: 'Stupidity will prefer Dryden because it is in Rhyme and monotonous sing song sing song from beginning to end' ('Public Address').

9 *Tom Cooke cut Hogarth down* The engraver Thomas Cook (1744–1818) created 'Hogarth Restored', laborious copies of Hogarth's works, first in the same size as the originals, then reduced.

FROM CRATETOS

A literal translation of this epigram, ascribed to Crates of Thebes, is: 'Time has bent me; though a skilled craftsman, yet he makes all things weaker.'

'THE CAVERNS OF THE GRAVE...'

A poem for the Earl of Egremont's wife, who had commissioned a painting of the Last Judgement, which B. completed in 1808. The opening lines refer to B.'s illustrations for Blair's *Grave*, which he had dedicated to the Queen (see p. 608 above).

Miscellaneous Verses and Epigrams

VERSE FROM THE MARGINALIA TO REYNOLDS'S *DISCOURSES*

Blake commented lengthily and splenetically in his copy of the *Works* of Sir Joshua Reynolds, ed. Edmund Malone, 1798, and included several bits of verse. Some were written at B.'s first reading, others *c*. 1809–10 – the same period in which he was writing Notebook epigrams against Reynolds and other figures in the world of art.

ADVICE OF THE POPES

Written on the title page of Reynolds's *Works*, with the comment: 'This Man was Hired to Depress Art.'

'SOME LOOK. TO SEE THE SWEET OUTLINES . . .'

Sardonic response to Reynolds's admission that he did not at first appreciate Raphael.

'WHEN FRANCE GOT FREE . . .'

Malone in a footnote praises Reynolds's disapproval of the French Revolution, and quotes Pope: 'They led their wild desires to woods and caves,/And thought that all but SAVAGES were slaves.'

ON THE VENETIAN PAINTER

This and the next two pieces deal with painters such as Titian, whose 'elegance' Reynolds praises.

VERSE FROM THE ADVERTISEMENT TO BLAKE'S EXHIBITION OF PAINTINGS, 1809

An insertion in B.'s advertisement (dated 15 May 1809), following notice of one of his major paintings: 'THE ANCIENT BRITONS – Three Ancient Britons overthrowing the Army of armed Romans; the Figures full as large as Life – From the Welch Triads'. The lines have been traced (Damon, *Dictionary*, under 'Welsh') to an item in the *Myvyrian Anthology* (1801–7) which tells of Arthur's last battle against the Saxons. B.'s first stanza is an adaptation which alters Saxons to Romans, the second stanza is his own invention. The Welsh nationalist Owen Pugh, friend of the Blakes, may have shown him the poem.

EPIGRAMS FROM *A DESCRIPTIVE CATALOGUE* AND 'PUBLIC ADDRESS'

Blake published the *Descriptive Catalogue* to accompany his unsuccessful exhibition of paintings in 1809. It is a polemical work which not only lists and describes the paintings for sale, but defends B.'s ideas and attacks his foes. The first epigram attacks Thomas Stothard, whose 'reserve and modesty' were praised in a prospectus for his rival painting of the Canterbury Pilgrims, and the second attacks Flaxman and Stothard together. Rhymed versions of both appear in the Notebook, pp. 618, 617.

'Public Address' (an editorially given title) consists of disconnected fragments of an essay on art and artists scattered through the Notebook. Again, B. attacks his foes and defends himself and his own principles as an artist. In addition to the two epigrams given here, there is a shorter version of 'Blakes apology for his Catalogue' (see p. 627).

Jerusalem

An illuminated book of 100 plates, including four full-page designs, known in five copies printed by Blake, and three printed posthumously. Although the 1804 title-page may indicate the beginning of composition, most of the poem was probably written between 1809 and 1815, and etched between 1815 and 1820. The arrangement of plates is uniform except for Chapter 2, in which the order of plates 29-46 varies in two copies.

Jerusalem, Blake's final epic poem, is his monumental equivalent of Milton's *History of England*. Incorporating B's various earlier mythologies into a single self-consistent myth, it tells the story of the Fall of ALBION – who is Blake's Mankind – from union with Jesus, the Divine Vision; Albion's rejection of his EMANATION, JERUSALEM, and his seduction by the lower female principle of VALA; the labours of the prophet LOS – who embodies man's visionary and creative powers – to save him from the violent and cruel nightmare of his ensuing history; and his final regeneration and reunion with Jesus.

Jerusalem is more complicated in its personages and actions than any of B.'s other works, in part because it is an 'intellectual allegory' in the Dantean sense of pursuing several different levels or types of meaning simultaneously. Among these are:

1. Historical–geographical. Albion is both a giant man who incorporates all men from the beginning to the end of time, and a place. In Eternity, Albion contained all nations within himself. In his fall, the nations separate into mere physical geographical locations. Most tragically, the lands of the Bible become separated from those of Great Britain. This gives B. several significant sub-themes.

(a) Place-names within and around London and throughout Great Britain become loci for much of the poem's action, and are sometimes personified. In an important episode of Chapter 2, the cathedral cities of Great Britain become 'Friends' who try to aid him, but fail.

(b) A system of correspondences exists between British and biblical locales. For example, Tyburn Hill equals Calvary, Lambeth equals Bethlehem, mountains in Derbyshire are identified with mountains in the Holy Land, and the counties of England, Scotland and Wales are identified with the regions belonging to the twelve tribes of Israel.

(c) The history handed down to us by the Old and New Testaments is really Albion's history. The Patriarchs are identified with the DRUIDS, who according to Blake worshipped nature and practised human sacrifice. The conquest of Canaan by the twelve tribes means a binding of man to material nature, and a confirmation of self-righteous moral law. The apostasy of the secessionist northern kingdom of Israel, whose capital was Tirzah, corresponds to Albion's further plunge into materialism. And the sufferings of Jerusalem, culminating in Babylonian captivity, reflect Great Britain's stubborn rejection of the Divine Vision.

(d) Albion has TWELVE SONS and TWELVE DAUGHTERS, corresponding to the twelve tribes of Israel. They enact the *secular* history of Britain, as the tribes enact *religious* history. The Sons (sometimes called Spectres) are motivated by rationalism and militarism, and have names taken from Blake's personal enemies. The Daughters (their Emanations) have names of queens and princesses in British legend, and personify Female Will. These groups are:

Hyle	Cambel–Boadicea
Hand	Gwendolen
Coban	Ignoge
Gwantok	Cordella
Peachey	Mehetabel
Brereton	Ragan
Slayd	Gonorill
Hutton	Gwinefred
Skofield	Gwineverra
Kox	Estrild
Kotope	Sabrina
Bowen	Conwenna

2. Religious–sexual. Religious and sexual symbols are closely associated throughout B.'s work, from the short lyrics 'The Garden of Love' and 'I saw a chapel all of gold . . .' onwards. In *J* Mankind's lapse into false religion continues to be presented in terms of dominance by females.

(a) The 'body' of the faithful is to Blake a human body, in which male and female are one, and both are one in Jesus. All historical Churches and religions form impediments to such union. Instead of uniting Man and God, they divide them. All restrictions on human sexuality, too, form barriers. For sexual impulses, however 'sinful', must be expressed to be transcended. To show the identity of these issues, Blake presents temples and tabernacles, arks, veils and guardian cherubim – all that is 'secret', 'sacred', 'holy' and untouchable – through imagery of a chaste feminine body. As the veil of the temple was rent when Jesus died, so must organized religion, and the moral laws it enforces, fall before the higher union of man, woman and God.

(b) Like the author of Revelation, Blake sees Jerusalem as both a city and a woman who is the bride of Jesus. But at the outset of the poem, Albion jealously refuses to give Jerusalem to Jesus, moralistically rejects her as sinful and allows her to be cast out by his sons and daughters. Further, he allows himself to be seduced by Vala, Jerusalem's 'shadow'. Vala is the seductive goddess of Nature (of whom the sub-manifestations RAHAB and TIRZAH are, respectively, the Whore and the Virgin), and she is also the unholy city, Babylon. Worship or 'love' of Vala is what Blake calls 'Natural Religion'. It means division between man and God, submission to corporeal limitations, allegiance to the kingdoms of this world and devotion to war and human sacrifice.

(c) Blake posits a succession of twenty-seven churches in man's history, and describes them as combinations of male and female principles, such that the first third are 'hermaphroditic', the second third 'male within female', the last group 'female within male'.

3. Political. The specifically political portions of *Jerusalem* are those connected with LUVAH. As in earlier works, Luvah is the Zoa of Passion within Albion; he is also France. Rejection and sacrifice of Luvah means both suppression of domestic radicalism and hostility towards revolution abroad. The theme of vengeance enacted against Luvah treats the Napoleonic wars, and embodies Blake's plea that even an offensive nation should not be punished but forgiven. Beyond these episodes, however, we are to remember that Jerusalem is named 'Liberty', and that throughout the poem rejection of her means rejection of political liberty as well as of sexual and spiritual fulfilment.

4. Psychological. The fallen Albion may be seen as an individual human being in a condition of mental illness, variously described as asleep, diseased or dead. By renouncing Jesus and Jerusalem, he renounces his own humanity. His sleep is the sleep of Reason – a barren

rationalism which demands physical demonstration, and causes doubt and despair. His disease is the disease of Moral Virtue which sets up laws of purity, demands righteousness and punishes the sinful. Devoured by his own selfhood, he is dead to the promise of salvation. Until he wakes from his sleep in Chapter 4, he is portrayed as tortured but stubborn in his errors, and dominated by his rational spectre, the *femme fatale* Vala and the cruel Sons and Daughters who express his selfishness. He is – the reader must understand – each of us, as we live in this world.

5. Visionary. The prophet LOS, throughout *Jerusalem*, strives to build GOLGONOOZA, a 'fourfold' city of art or imagination which is simultaneously a human body. Working within ULRO – the hell of a material world or of a material body – he and his sons labour perpetually at his furnaces, while his female counterpart ENITHARMON labours with her daughters at their looms, giving permanent form to all things on earth. His one desire is to save Albion, who is unaware of his existence. He must also struggle against his own Spectre – all the forces within the artist which urge him against creativity – and force the Spectre to work with him. Finally, he must persist despite the rebellion of his Emanation, who is both female counterpart and muse. Although Blake speaks in his own voice on occasion, Los is certainly a projection of his character, desires and struggles as an artist. Los, keeper of the Divine Vision throughout the 'time of troubles' which we call human history, is the hero of the poem; in the finale, however, he disappears, having been re-absorbed into the fulfilled Albion.

Pl. 1 [*Frontispiece*]   This depicts a man in a hat and coat, carrying a shining globe, as he enters a darkened doorway under a pointed arch. The text is seen only on an early proof of the plate; it was afterwards deleted by further engraving.

CHAPTER I

This opening chapter, prefaced with an address 'To the Public', presents the issues of the poem in the relatively simple terms of unity *v.* division, love *v.* jealousy, faith *v.* despair, forgiveness *v.* accusation. At the outset, Albion rejects the love of the Saviour, and hides Jerusalem from his 'vision and fruition'. The rest of the chapter has two major movements, one showing the internal struggles of Los (and Blake) to maintain hope, the other showing the decline of Albion to a state of despair. At the centre of the chapter is a vision of Golgonooza. The sections are as follows: Pl. 4: The Saviour rejected by Albion. Pl. 5: Blake announces his 'great task', and sees the 'starry wheels' of mechanical Reason, driven by the sons of Albion, drawing Jerusalem eastwards into non-entity. Pls. 6-11: A long dialogue between Los and his Spectre. Los forces the reluctant Spectre to labour at the furnaces. Erin comes forth from the furnaces with the Daughters of Beulah and the Sons and Daughters of Los, and all commiserate over the sufferings of Jerusalem.

Pls. 12-14: Vision of Golgonooza.

Pl. 15: Blake sees the sleeping Albion, the present state of Europe, and the original division of the twelve tribes from Albion. Pl. 16: The geographical labours of Los and his sons. Pl. 17: Los communes with himself concerning female temptation and love.

Pls. 18-19: The Sons of Albion denounce Jerusalem, and their starry wheels rend Albion's loins.

Pls. 20-24: Dialogue of Albion, Jerusalem and Vala, concludes in Albion's despair.

Pl. 25: Beulah laments over Albion.

Pl. 3.3 *Giants & Fairies* Epic and lyric poems.

28-9 *Sinais . . . art of writing* A tradition that phonetic writing began with Moses.

36-58 The first free-verse manifesto in English. It is modelled on Milton's prefatory note to *Paradise Lost* justifying blank verse.

40-41 $E\delta o\theta\eta$ . . . $\epsilon\pi\iota$ $\gamma\eta s$ 'All power is given to me in heaven and in earth.' B.'s argument is that the power of the poet derives ultimately from Jesus.

43-5 *Monotonous Cadence . . . derived from . . . Rhyming* Sense unclear. An extension of rhyming? Liberated from rhyming? 'The modern bondage of Rhyming' is Milton's phrase.

Pl. 4 *Movos ὁ Iεsous* In John 8:9 'only Jesus' remains with the woman found in adultery, when her accusers depart. In Luke 9:36 the slightly different phrase 'ὁ Iεςους μονος' gives us 'Jesus alone' at the Transfiguration, after the vision and cloud vanish. Both passages have application to the theme of *Jerusalem*.

6 *Awake . . . O sleeper* Jesus addresses Albion, who is both England and Mankind.

14 In Proverbs 8:30 'Wisdom' is co-eternal with God, 'and I was daily his delight, rejoicing always before him'.

17 *the vision and fruition of the Holy-one* The phrase implies mutual perceiving and sexual union or birth-giving between Jerusalem and her Saviour. Jealous Albion, because he will not accept the Saviour as one with himself but sees him as a rival, has cut off this union.

18 *I am not a God afar off* In Deuteronomy 30:11–13 the command-ment of God 'is not hidden ... neither is it far off ... But the word is very nigh to thee'.

29 Albion's reply to the Saviour echoes Pharaoh in Ezekiel 29:3: 'My river is mine own and I have made it for myself.'

30 *Malvern, Cheviot, Plinlimmon, Snowdon* Mountains in England and Wales.

Pl. 5.1–15 Albion's jealous dissembling means psychic disintegration. His parts are randomly scattered, given up to conflict, and shrunken, while his emanation is sacrificed.

3 *Cambridge & Oxford & London* Albion's seats of imaginative leadership are lost in the errors of rationalist philosophy; their 'starry Wheels' (l. 4) represent the dead Newtonian universe. These wheels, which become a major negative symbol, are driven – we soon discover – by the Sons of Albion.

16 *Trembling I sit* Blake speaks of his task as a poet. The following passage introduces GOLGONOOZA and the furnace of Los, set against the destructive SONS and DAUGHTERS OF ALBION.

25–7 *Hand ... Bowen* See ALBION, SONS OF.

31–2 *Southward ... Northward ... time after time* See *Milton* 26.13n. The northern entrance is for mortals, the southern for immortals. The Sons of Albion are representative immortals who are recurrently born into history, as on a wheel.

34 *Male ... Furnace; Female ... loom* The Sons and Daughters of Albion represent destructive furnace and loom, opposed to the creative furnace and loom of Los and Enitharmon.

39 *they controll our Vegetative powers* The Daughters of Albion control our mortal life-cycle. Their names are listed in ll. 40–45.

46–53 Newtonian starry wheels, turning in vacuum, create a draught which disperses JERUSALEM and VALA in smoke rising from the chim-neys of Los's furnaces. The idea is that Error is a vacuum which sucks in Truth: 'Mighty was the draught of Voidness to draw Existence in' (*FZ* 11.23.18).

Pl. 5.66–Pl. 6.2 Los's SPECTRE (masculine) and EMANATION (feminine) divide from him. A 'Spectre' in B. is the purely male portion of a divided personality. It may be identified with mechanical 'reasoning power', with self-preservation instinct or with physical potency. In itself, it is pathological – caring only for survival at all costs – yet it is a powerful ally. In *J* Los forces his reluctant spectre to labour with him at the furnaces.

Pl. 7.2 *He stood over the Immortal* Los's Spectre stood over Los. His following speech is an attempt to discourage Los–Blake's creativity.

11 *He drinks thee up* The Spectre charges that Albion exploits and scorns Los, who is dedicated to saving him (England does not appreciate B.'s art).

14 *thy stolen Emanation* May refer to B.'s quarrel with Stothard over the 'Canterbury Pilgrims' (1806).

18–25 *Hand has peopled Babel . . . Schofield is Adam* Albion's cruel sons are the powers behind the patriarchs, from Adam, to the flood, to the first established monarchy. The biblical lineage goes as follows: *Adam* is seven generations from *Enoch*. Enoch is the great-grandfather of *Noah*. Noah's sons are *Shem, Ham* and *Japheth*, his grandsons include *Cush, Ashur* and *Aram*. *Nimrod* is his great-grandson, and the first King. *Babel* and *Ninevah* were early post-deluvian cities.

30–37 A re-telling of *FZ* 11.25.40–27.20, the sufferings of Passion in the fires of Nature.

38–41 *Luvah . . . Forming the Spectres of Albion* The Spectre of Los, lost in paranoia by this time, mistakenly thinks the suffering Luvah is a foe. Hence Los's reply 'I know not this.'

Pl. 8.2 *Ranelagh, Strumbolo, Cromwells gardens* Places of public entertainment.
    Chelsea Hospital was for wounded soldiers.

32 *Uncircumcised pretences to Chastity* Circumcision in B. means relinquishment of selfhood.

Pl. 9.17–28 *I took the sighs . . . tears flow down* All the injustices of this world, just catalogued, are formed by Los into (tragic, indignant) Art.

Pl. 10] An added plate.

Pl. 10.8 *Two Contraries* See *MHH, passim.* All reality is organized into contraries, and the contraries are equally valid. But the Sons of Albion reduce everything to dead moralistic abstraction.

37–8 *thy Sins/That thou callest thy Children* The creative acts of Los, the prophets and visionaries throughout history, are called sins.

Pl. 11.8 *Then Erin came forth* Erin (Ireland) is a figure of faith and hope for liberty throughout *J.*

19–20 *Sabrina & Ignoge . . . light and love* An ironic image.

22 *mandrake . . . before Reubens gate* Mandrakes were supposed to make those who ate them sexually desirable. Reuben's mandrakes were a source of jealous contention between his mother Leah, and Rachel, Jacob's other wife (Genesis 30).

24–5 To the children of Los, anything in Nature is but a reflection of Eternity.

Pl. 12.1 *Why wilt thou give to her a Body* Los answers this question in l. 13 : all falsehoods must be given bodies – must be fully realized and encountered in order to be disproved.

5 *the finger of God* God's finger will touch the seventh furnace which is the seventh eye of God – Jesus – as in *FZ* VIII.

7 *I feel my Emanation also dividing* The division of Enitharmon from Los is not occurring for the first time just now; it is co-incident with the initial Fall and is a fact throughout the history of lapsed mankind. Los 'feels' his pain afresh, as if it were new – a sign of his strong memory of Eternity and desire for wholeness.

14 *Appollyon* (Gr., 'destroyer'.) A tormenting angel of the bottomless pit in Revelation 9:11; and the 'foul fiend' whose reasons and darts Christian meets and overcomes in the Valley of Humiliation in *Pilgrim's Progress.*

16 *Such were the lamentations* The lamentations are in fact full of hope.

Pl. 12.25–Pl. 13.29 The City of Golgonooza is described, parallel to the description of the Temple in Ezekiel 40–43 and of new Jerusalem in Revelation 21.

Pl. 12.26 *Ethinthus* A vague 'Queen of Waters' in *Europe.*
  Tyburn The site of the gallows in London.

28 *Paddington* A slum district, adjacent to Tyburn. The sense is that of the Beatitudes. Can it be, B. asks, that blessed are the poor in spirit, and they that mourn, and they that are persecuted? Do we see the Kingdom of Heaven being built for them?

43-4 *Jerusalem wanders ... among the dark Satanic wheels* Jerusalem was dispersed among the Starry Wheels (a rational universe of Newtonian vacuity) in 5.46-53.

45 *fourfold* Four and its multiples represent human perfection in B. (Four Zoas, four directions of the compass, four elements, four worlds of Eden, Beulah, Generation, Ulro, and 'fourfold vision' as the highest possible to attain.) To visualize Golgonooza one would need four dimensions, as one also needs to describe the infinite yet closed universe of post-Einsteinian cosmology.

54-60 The correspondences are:

West – Tongue – Circumference	Eden
South – Eyes – Zenith	Beulah
East – Nostrils – Centre	Ulro
North – Ear – Nadir	Generation

58 *Ezekiel ... by Chebars flood* Ezekiel (1:1-14) saw 'visions of God' beginning with 'the likeness of four living creatures ... they had the likeness of a man. And every one had four faces, and every one had four wings ... Their wings were joined ... they went every one straight forward ... they ... had the face of a man ... a lion ... an ox ... an eagle.'

Pl. 13.22-3 *but the third Gate ... threefold curtain* Three and its multiples always represent imperfection or incompleteness in B. The curtain here suggests the veil of sexuality.

26-9 *sixty-four thousand* $4^3 = 64$, a perfect number; multiplication by 1000 implies merely 'a great multitude'.
  Genii, Gnomes, Nymphs, Fairies These are elemental servants of the Four Zoas.

32 *Twenty-seven Heavens* A vision of the celestial firmament as twenty-seven concentric spheres of religious error within the *Mundane Shell* (the sky). See *M* 37.35, and Dictionary of Proper Names.

36 *And there it meets Eternity again* 'Eternity' exists in the furthest reaches beyond ourselves, and in the furthest reaches within ourselves: the two are one.

56 *the City of Golgonooza, & its smaller Cities* The 'suburbs' of Golgonooza include all the spiritual enemies of Israel. Art must include and express the doctrines even of its foes, in order to give Error a body.

Pl. 14.2-10 Los sees the COVERING CHERUB which guards the tree of life, and the fallen forms of the other three Zoas: ORC (fallen Luvah) as serpent, URIZEN as dragon, THARMAS as false tongue; and their lost emanations, as well as his own, ENITHARMON.

19-24 The *gates* in *loins*, *heart* and *head* are 'doors of perception' as in *MHH* Pl. 14, p. 187 above.

26 *the western gate . . . is clos'd* As is the western gate of Golgonooza which faces Eden.

34] Concluding line originally followed by: 'End of the 1st Chap:'; later deleted.

Pl. 15.5 *such is my awful Vision* Blake now enters the poem and speaks personally. What Los sees, he sees. There follows an analysis of the present state of Europe.

18-20 *wheel without wheel* An emblem of Machinery, opposed to the *Wheel within Wheel* emblem of Vision (as in Ezekiel's 'wheel in the middle of a wheel' belonging to the 'four living creatures').

22 *the Four Sons of Los* Rintrah, Palambron, Theotormon, Bromion.

24-9 In Eternity, Albion and Israel are one. In our world, they are geographically divided. Abram, twelve generations after Noah, entered into covenant with God, left his native Chaldea, was re-named Abraham, 'father of many nations', and given Canaan as the promised land for his seed When the covenant is renewed after the exile in Egypt, Reuben, Jacob-Israel's eldest son, representing all twelve sons, settles in Canaan. This settlement in 'a little & dark Land' (*FZ* 11.25.24) is simultaneously a curse and a blessing: it perpetuates division (between the chosen people and the rest of Mankind) yet is the fulfilment of prophecy, and so is part of the redeeming labours of Los's sons.

34 *the Valley of the Son of Hinnom* Place just outside Jerusalem where children were supposedly sacrificed by fire (2 Chronicles 28:3, 33:6; Jeremiah 7:31-2). Los's redemptive work goes on even here.

Pl. 16.1-27 The sons of Los, Bromion, Theotormon, Palambron, Rintrah, labouring in London's suburbs, London itself, and throughout England.

28-60 A catalogue of correspondences between the counties of Great Britain and the lands of the twelve tribes of Israel, established when Mankind was divided.

Pl. 17.6-15 Probably personal: Blake can contend with male opposition, but against female temptation he must harden his heart and act brutally, or he will become softened and unfit for work. He therefore responds to flirtation with open lust, and the ladies then take refuge in seeming chastity. Compare the brutality of Tamburlaine to the four virgins of Egypt who sue for pity (*Tamburlaine the Great* v.i.64-190), and the association of this with his poetic love for Zenocrate like that of Los–Blake for Enitharmon–Catherine.

22 *Tormented with sweet desire* Los–Blake admits that he is tempted, but knows the temptresses cannot really love him, since they hate his inspiration–wife. Vala likewise tempts Albion, Pls. 20-23.

33 *Negations are not Contraries* Los–Blake now turns on his spectre, calls it a mere negation and warns it against vainglorious ambition. This is a necessary warning because the spectre is so useful to Los.

51-6 The division of Enitharmon in a globe of blood is from *BU* v. The separation of his spectre from his back is in *Milton* 3.34-6.

59 *Go thou to Skofield . . . Bath . . . Canterbury* Ask the Accuser if he is a physical or spiritual healer. Bath and Canterbury are developed Pls. 41-6.

Pl. 18 The hateful conclave of Albion's sons rejects Jerusalem–Liberty.

Pl. 18.2 *Outside* Outside of reality. This term always means 'void' in Blake. Eternity is always 'within' and makes true definite forms defined by an 'outline of identity'. The Outside meets itself four-dimensionally here, as Eternity meets itself in 13.35-6.

8 *Three Immense Wheels* The twelve Sons of Albion group themselves as Accuser, Judge, Executioner, against Jerusalem.

26 *the Perfect*: Albion's sons justify the morally 'pure' or 'good', called 'Angels' in *MHH* and 'Elect' in *Milton*.

30 *She is our Mother! Nature!* Vala, Nature, is not in fact their real mother. 'Sinful Jerusalem' is, but they disown her.

32 *the Potters field* A burial place for paupers and criminals.

33 *Her little-ones* implies vessels of Christ: 'Whoso shall receive one such little child in my name receiveth me. But whoso shall offend one of these little ones which believe in me, it were better for him that a millstone were hanged about his neck, and that he were drowned in the depth of the sea.' (Matthew 18:5–6; see also Mark 9:42, Luke 17:2.)

39 *Hand ... absorb'd Albions Twelve Sons* The rational man leads the rest.

Pl. 19.1–14] Repe ated almost unchanged from *FZ* IX.119.33–120.3.

16 *His Eon* His emanation.

17–20 *his Sons ... Spectres of the Twentyfour* Albion's sons are spectres of his twenty-four 'friends' (the cathedral cities of Pl. 36ff.).

36 Albion's heart was hardened against his friends (l. 30), thanks to his sons. Resisting help, he grows solid (clos'd) and opaque (darkning).

41–2 *Vala/The Lilly of Havilah* Pure and sterile beauty. 'Havilah' means 'sand'.

Pl. 20.5 *Wherefore hast thou shut me* Jerusalem addresses Albion, but is answered instead by Vala.

11 *Vala replied* The reply appears sympathetic, but implies that Jerusalem has deserved her present exile.

21 *Jerusalem answer'd* Jerusalem understands the implied accusation and replies that the answer to 'Sin' is love and forgiveness. She reminds Vala also of the mutual former love among herself, Vala and Albion.

36 *Albion lov'd thee! he rent thy Veil!* Sexually, Albion took Vala's virginity. Spiritually, he destroyed the barrier to the Holy of Holies, thus making possible access to God. The rending of the veil of the Temple at the death of Jesus signified the New Dispensation, ending the Dispensation of Law.

Pl. 21 Deluded Albion takes on the role of Job, revels in his suffering and blames all on female lack of chastity.

Pl. 22 Vala claims that she has suffered under accusations of sin (Albion's sons) and been saved only by war (Nimrod). Albion too, she says, is secretly sinful.

Pl. 22.19 *Then spoke Jerusalem* Jerusalem alone does not share Albion's and Vala's obsession with sin and accusation.

Pl. 23   Albion, in a frenzy of accusation and self-accusation, collapses.

Pl. 23.5   *Hast thou again . . . Vala*   Jerusalem's sustained love, which is still willing to offer Vala to Albion without jealousy, is her re-knitting of Vala's veil. To Albion this is sinful.

7   *O wretched Father!*   Albion in self-pity addresses himself.

20   *he bore the Veil whole away*   Instead of rending the veil, Albion maintains it as a trap for mortal souls (l. 23) and a shroud for himself (l. 35).

26   *These were his last words*   Albion's final monologue parallels Satan's introspective soliloquy on Mt Niphates (*Paradise Lost* IV.32–113). Like Satan, Albion convinces himself of his own turpitude and distance from God.

Pl. 24.3   *Two bleeding Contraries*   Contraries such as 'good' and 'evil' are necessary for life (see *MHH* Pl. 3). But these contraries have been wounded by Albion's 'Reasoning Negation', thanks to the destructive work of Albion's sons, 10.8.

4–7   *We reared mighty Stones . . . Shame siezd us*   A primitive Druid rite ends in shame at nakedness, like that of the fallen Adam and Eve.

17–50   *O Jerusalem Jerusalem . . . were there*   Albion temporarily remembers his true union with Jerusalem, when even the arch-foe Babylon paid homage to her, and all nations were one in Jesus.

52   *Yet why these smitings of Luvah*   Luvah has smitten Albion with boils (21.4, 43.64) like those of Job.

53–4   *O Lamb of God/Thou art a delusion*   Albion retracts his repentance in doubt.

57–9   *Dost thou appear . . . merciful upon me*   The Lamb suddenly appears to Albion, as God does to Marlowe's Faustus *in extremis*. The cry of Faustus is (v.ii.191) 'My God, my God, look not so fierce on me!' Albion paradoxically is *refusing* salvation.

Pl. 25.8   *not one sparrow can suffer*   'Are not two sparrows sold for a farthing? and one of them shall not fall on the ground without your Father' (Matthew 10:29).

13   *the Creation of States & the deliverance of Individuals*   The doctrine of States – B.'s means of loving the sinner while hating the sin – is explained in *M* 32.10–32 and *J* 49.65–75. A state such as the 'state of sin' may be merely occupied temporarily by an individual.

CHAPTER 2

This chapter, prefaced by an address 'To the Jews', focuses on the opposition between Moral Virtue, which is seen as a disease, and Mercy. As narrative, it pursues the decline of Albion into righteousness and vengeance, but promises ultimate deliverance in the Saviour. The episodes are as follows:

Pls. 28–30: Albion establishes Sin, Moral Virtue and the Law of God. His rejection of Humanity is confirmed by his spectre and by Vala's domination over him.

Pls. 30–32: The conquest of the Holy Land by the twelve tribes of Israel (represented by Reuben) takes place. The 'binding down' of Reuben's senses to earth and materialism also affects the gentile nations, the sons of Albion and the Zoas, all of whom degenerate. But the Divine Hand establishes limits to this decline.

Pls. 33–42: Albion is pursued and exhorted to awake by Los, the Divine Family, the Friends (his cathedral cities) and the Zoas. But he rejects all help and falls into non-entity. The Friends are infected by Albion's disease; Los alone remains as watchman.

Pls. 43–4: The promise of the Divine Vision; the tale of Albion's original fall; the prayer of Los.

Pls. 45–8: Los as watchman explores Albion's interior. He sees Man's sufferings, Vala condemning Jerusalem and glorifying War, the defiant sons of Albion building Druid temples, and the vengeful strife of Albion against Luvah. Albion repeats his last words (of Pl. 24), 'Hope is banish'd from me,' but the Saviour places him upon the Rock of Ages and builds for him the couch of the scriptures.

Pls. 48–50: Erin creates a protective space for Jerusalem. Communing with the Daughters of Beulah, she laments Man's degeneration to materialism and promises regeneration.

Pl. 27.2–3 *Was Britain the Primitive Seat . . .?* A number of eighteenth-century antiquarians argued that the Druids of Britain were actually the Patriarchs of the Old Testament.

17 *You have a tradition* The Cabbalistic tradition of Adam Kadmon (lit. 'Ancient Man') whom B. identifies with Albion.

25 *the Elohim* The name of God in Genesis 1.

41–3 The direction of Jerusalem's fall is eastwards from London (as in *J* 5.48) towards Palestine.

77–8 B. denounces the doctrine of a chosen people as selfish and Satanic.

Pl. 28 Albion establishes Sin, Moral Virtue and the Law of God.

Pl. 28.15 *A deadly Tree* See TREE OF MYSTERY.

21–2 *Albion began to erect . . . rocks* An altar of unhewn stones inscribed with the Law is raised in Joshua 8:30–32.

Pl. 29] Pls. 29–46 are found in two arrangements. The present sequence follows that of copies [a, c, f]; bracketed numbers indicate the order of copies [d, e].

Pl. 29.7 The gourd in Jonah 4:10 'came up in a night, and perished in a night'.

26–7 *Albions Emanation . . . Appeard* The 'appearance' is Vala, not Jerusalem, and Albion now worships Vala.

Pl. 29.36–Pl. 30.1 Vala's memory of Eternity and her assertions about the present are equally delusive. She exalts her past position falsely, indulges in unjustified self-pity for her 'love' of Jerusalem and wrongly but seductively claims that Beauty is superior to Brotherhood.

Pl. 30.2–16 The awesomeness of Vala's beauty has emasculated Albion, though in part against his better judgement.

3–4 *milky fear!/A dewy garment* The ejaculation and perspiration of Albion's sexual dream.

10 *why have thou elevate inward* Why have you usurped a position which you should not have?

15 *they neither marry nor are given in marriage* Quotes Matthew 22:30. In B.'s Eternity, humanity is not separated into sexes, and so has no need of marriage.

27–8 *There is a Throne . . . her own* The doctrine is from 1 Corinthians 11:3–9: 'But I would have you know, that the head of every man is Christ; and the head of the woman is the man . . . Neither was the man created for the woman; but the woman for the man.' Vala has destroyed this order.

36 Hand is the leader of Albion's sons; Reuben, called 'unstable as water' (Genesis 49:3), the eldest of the sons of Israel. The following passage concerns the settlement of the Promised Land (from Joshua

13–21), which Los–Blake deplores. Los from *Mam-Tor*, a hill in Derbyshire, sees Reuben in *Bashan*, a territory east of the river Jordan. (Reuben, Gad and Manesseh were given lands east of the Jordan.) *Succoth* and *Zaretan* are cities east and west of the Jordan. *Bohan* is a boundary stone.

46 *the Daughters of Albion divided Luvah* This story does not occur elsewhere and is never developed.

47 *Los bended his Nostrils down* Reuben, as he gains earthly territory, loses his perceptive powers. His eyes, tongue, ears follow (Pl. 32). In each case Reuben's limited perceptions also affect the Gentile nations.

58 *Consider Sexual Organization* Sexual organization – any organism in the state of Generation – is by nature limited.

Pl. 31 An interruption in the story. The Saviour establishes limits to Albion's fall, and promises ultimate deliverance.

Pl. 31.1 *the Two Limits, Satan and Adam* The lower limits of Opacity and Contraction in Mankind's collapse.

11 *No individual can keep these Laws* Albion's promulgation of Law was the opening act of Chapter 2 (Pl. 28).

13 *Albion hath enterd the State Satan!* Albion has become – for the time being – 'Satanic'; that is, as mentally opaque as it is possible to be. The doctrine of States is examined *M* 32.10–38, *J* 49.65–75. A State may be accursed; an individual cannot be.

Pl. 32 The story of the settlement of the Promised Land continues.

Pl. 32.10 *Heshbon ... Moab* These lands border the territory assigned to Reuben, on the north and south.

12 *Mount Gilead ... Gilgal* Reuben faces the Promised Land from the east.

14 *The Seven Nations* The Gentiles.

25–42 Cosmic disruption within and around Albion accompanies the foregoing appropriation of territory by the tribes of Israel. The Zoas sink into lower material forms: Urizen–air–fairies; Luvah–fire–genies; Tharmas–water–nymphs; Urthona–earth–gnomes.

29 *Urizen ... East, Luvah ... South* They reverse their proper stations.

34] Conjectural reading of deeply gouged deletion (Erdman).

39 *The Atlantic Continent* Fabled Atlantis, sunk beneath the Atlantic ocean in the Flood; a myth employed also in *America*.

41 *Reuben is Merlin* Reuben, like Merlin, was led astray by a woman.

Pl. 33.1] Line added by engraving on the etched plate.

10 *blue death*] Mended in all copies from *pale* death, to suggest that Albion is Druidic; but 'pale' is restored in one copy.

Pl. 34.29 *I behold London* Here begins the evocation of Albion's Friends, his cities in human form, who guard and try to help him. This treatment of geography contrasts with the dehumanizing conquest and partition of the Promised Land in the preceding episode. The Friends (listed in 36.47–61, 41.1–19) are the twenty-seven cathedral cities of England, plus Edinburgh. London, Verulam–Canterbury, York and Edinburgh are chief 'guardian cities'. In effect, as centres of moral leadership, the cities constitute Albion's conscience.

55–6 The Gate of Luban, limit of Los's redeeming power, invisible to mortal men. Just outside this gate is the threat of Eternal Death (35.8), equated with the system of Moral Virtue (35.10). Albion, fleeing his would-be saviours, enters this gate (35.11).

Pl. 35.12–13 *Los . . . In Cambridgeshire . . . is the twenty-eighth* Cambridge was Milton's university, and Milton was the last great representative of Los on earth, hence *twenty-eighth*. There are twenty-eight Friends in all, as also twenty-eight heavens in *M*. As a multiple of four, twenty-eight is a 'perfect' number.

Pl. 36.3 *The Friends of Albion* Albion's cathedral cities (see note on 34.29). There are twenty-eight in all, of which four appear in 34.40–51, and the rest arrive in 36.21.

45 *And these the Twenty-four* (See previous note.) The list of Albion's Friends begins here and is continued on Pl. 41.

48 *Selsey* Threatened by coastal erosion, Selsey's village and church were moved inland to Chichester in 1075.

Pl. 37.1–2 *Bath . . . the physician and/The poisoner* In Geoffrey of Monmouth's *History*, Merlin prophesies that Bath's healing waters will 'bring forth death'. B.'s meaning possibly is that physical healing may be spiritual harm.

5-6 *To cast Jerusalem . . . to Poplar & Bow . . . Malden & Canterbury* East London and east England – the direction of Jerusalem's 'fall' (as in 5.48 and 27.41).

7-8 *Islington & Pancrass, Marybone . . . Tyburn* Moves in an arc from north to west London.

11 *She fled to Lambeths mild Vale* Blake lived in Lambeth from 1791 to 1800. The following passage allegorizes the 'protection' of Jerusalem by Blake's love. The encroaching *Rephaim* (l. 12) is Philistine territory.

15 *There is a Grain of Sand* 'To see a World in a Grain of Sand' ('Auguries of Innocence', Pickering MS., p. 506 above).

The design at the foot of this plate shows a man with his head on his knees. At his side is a scroll of mirror-writing: 'Each Man is in/his Spectres power/Untill the arrival/of that Hour,/When his Humanity/awake/And cast his Spectre/Into the Lake.' A draft of these lines is in the Notebook, p. 494.

Pl. 38 The general theme of this plate is the destructive effect of Albion's fall, especially in producing war and enmity among men.

Pl. 38.1 The Zoas are acting their worst selves, though in self-defence.

5 *the Four Complexions* A phrase not used elsewhere: the qualities or humours of the Four Zoas?

6 *Oaks* Associated with human sacrifice. See DRUIDS.

7 *Tharmas dash'd on the Rocks . . . in Mexico* Tharmas, when disorganized, is water. The reference is to Aztec human sacrifice, associated for B. with Druidism.

37 *Oshea and Caleb fight* Joshua and Caleb were stoned by their brothers for insisting that Canaan could be conquered and settled (Numbers 14:7-10).

39 *Balaam* A Moabite who was converted to the side of the Israelites.

48 *We smell the blood of the English!* From the folk-tale giant's chant: 'Fe Fi Fo Fum/I smell the blood of an Englishman.'

65 *Wicker Idol* Druid figure in which men were supposedly burned alive, according to Caesar's *Commentaries*.

66 *Canaanite . . . Egyptian* Nations hostile to Israel.

74 *All you my Friends & Brothers* Los addresses his fellow Zoas, now associated with the Friends of Albion.

Pl. 39.5-6 *Albion dark,/Repugnant* Albion repels his Zoas, resists being returned to Eden and rolls backwards into Ulro.

Pl. 40.1-2 *Bath ... mild spoke* In 1804, Richard Warner of Bath preached and published a radically pacifist sermon, *War Inconsistent with Christianity*. Here, the 'healing city' preaches that man can be healed only by Jesus.

17 *Albions Western Gate is clos'd* This is the entrance to Eden. It has been closed since the poem's beginning.

19 *When Africa in sleep* This story that 'Africa' once rebelled like 'Albion' is not mentioned elsewhere.

40] Line added by engraving on the etched plate.

Pl. 41.7 *Oxford, immortal Bard!* Possibly Edward March, Fellow of Oriel, referred to by B. as 'Edward the Bard of Oxford' (letter to Hayley, 27 January 1804).

Pl. 42 Albion now is confirmed in error, and opposes 'Righteousness' and 'Justice' to Los's mercy.

Pl. 42.3-4 *He saw ... own beloveds* Albion has cursed his own free impulses, hereafter referred to as his 'little ones'.

29 *a limit of Opakeness ... a limit of Contraction* imply, respectively, 'hardness' of heart and 'narrowness' of perception. These limits were established by the Saviour in Pl. 31.

32-3 *the Saviour ... forms Woman* The creation of sexes is necessary for Generation; Generation is necessary for progress towards redemption. Without it, humanity would remain static and doomed.

41 *these little ones ... the Lords anointed* Albion's own impulses, which he seeks to destroy, are favoured by God.

47 *fiend]* Etched 'friend', probably in error.

51 *Blackheath & Hounslow ... Norwood & Finchley* London's east, west, south, north.

76 *Serpent Temples* Druid temples.

80 *Norwood & Finchley & Blackheath & Hounslow* See l. 51 above.

Pl. 43 The scene is sunset, preceding Albion's Dark Night.

Pl. 43.9 *The Reactor* That part of Albion which believes in Sin and Repentance? The term is not used elsewhere.

14-15 *Reaction ... Action* Newton's famous Third Law is that 'every Action must have an equal but opposite Reaction'. This fits B.'s theory of the necessary contraries in human life (*MHH* Pls. 3-4). But Albion has allowed his Reaction (his Morality) to dominate him totally.

18 *Ephratah* Bethlehem.

28 *rocks*] Etched 'locks', probably in error (see l. 2).
   two Immortal forms Los's Spectre and Emanation flee from Albion's mind.

29 *We alone are escaped* The messengers of disaster to Job each repeat, 'I only am escaped alone to tell thee.' In the remainder of this plate, the 'two forms' relate the initial Fall of Albion (a version similar to that in *FZ* III). Albion's errors are, first, the worship of his own Shadow, and second, the rejection of Luvah.

Pl. 44.2 *Spectre* In this episode the Spectre of Los is his friend, not his foe. Ll. 9-15 seem autobiographical, referring to Blake's Felpham troubles.

11 *Uncircumcision* Always a negative term in Blake, signifying retention of selfhood.

18 *Feminine Allegories* Also a negative term. 'Allegory' in B. usually means 'Church-propagated Lie'.

34-5 *Tabernacle ... Cherubim* The Tabernacle of the Female is like that described in Exodus 25, with a veiled inner room called the Holy of Holies. See CHERUBIM.

38 Albion's submission to Vala brings him to his nadir. But this is necessary for salvation, just as Generation is necessary for Regeneration.

Pl. 45 Los begins his exploration of Albion's interior life.

Pl. 45.7 *Minute Particular* Usually a term B. uses to refer to the details of a work of art. Here it means 'Englishmen'.

12 *Heber & Terah* Ancestors of Abraham. The imagery of the previous lines is that of making bricks from a mould.

14-16 *Highgate ... Rivers side* Los walks the fringes of London, from north (Urthona's realm) to east (Luvah's realm).
   the Isle/Of Leuthas Dogs The Isle of Dogs, a district famous for vice.

18 *kennels* Open drains, gutters.

25 *Bethlehem* Bedlam, the madhouse (lit. 'house of bread').

32   The revenger acts against Providence, which works by forgiveness rather than punishment.

37-8   *hinder the Sons/Of Albion from taking vengeance*   Specifically political: hinder England from punishing France (here represented by Luvah).

40   *Westminster & Marybone*   Los now moves westwards, the direction of Liberty and the closed gate towards Eden.

Pl. 46.1   *his disease*   Albion's disease is Moral Virtue.

Pl. 47.9   *the cries of War on the Rhine & Danube*   The Napoleonic wars.

Pl. 48.1   *These were his last words*   Picks up from Albion's collapse, Pl. 24, but now a comfort is added: the couch of the scriptures is built for Albion's repose.

13-14   *Beneath the bottoms of the Graves . . . a place*   Beulah is at the joining-place of Eden, Ulro and Generation. Here begins a movement of comfort, as Erin and the Daughters of Beulah create a protective space for exiled Jerusalem. This parallels the couch of the scriptures built by the Saviour for Albion, mentioned above.

27   *the . . . Friends of Albion*   His cities, who were unable to save him (Pl. 39).

28   *an Aged pensive Woman*   Erin.

30-38   *she took/A Moment of Time . . . an Atom of Space*   The opening-up of times and spaces for recovery of lost souls is an essential labour of Beulah. See *FZ* 1.5.29-37; *M* Pl. 28.

35   *a Rainbow*   A promise that Mankind will not be destroyed, no matter how sinful.

44   *his seventh Furnace*   Los's seventh furnace corresponds to the final cycle of history, before the apocalypse.

Pl. 49.4-5   *Rathlin . . . Drogheda*   Irish place-names.

9   *Jerusalem . . . Shiloh*   The two sacred cities of the Holy Land.

15   *Gate of Havilah*   The land of Havilah was encompassed by the Pison, first of the four rivers of Eden. Vala is the Lily of Havilah.

31   *who chargeth his Angels with folly*   Quotes Job 4:18.

32–41 Erin's lament over man's fallen senses is taken from *M* 5.19–26.

42 *Therefore they are removed* The Sons of Albion have made themselves into Gentiles.

44 *the Erythrean Sea* The Red Sea, which swallowed up Pharaoh's army.

45 *then they shall arise* The Sons of Albion will recover.

53–9 Erin sees the omnipresence of Jehovah as guaranteeing that enemy forces shall be turned into allies.

65 *Yet they are blameless* As in Lear's exclamation (IV.vi.172), 'None does offend, none, I say none!' The doctrine is that of separating the Sinner from his Sin, in order to accomplish 'Forgiveness of Enemies' (l. 75).

Pl. 50.10 *Come Lord Jesus* The final prayer of the New Testament (Revelation 22:20).

11 *If thou hadst been here* From the Lazarus story: 'Lord, if thou hadst been here, my brother had not died' (John 11:21).

27 *to let the Sun go down* 'Let not the sun go down upon your wrath' (Ephesians 4:26).

30 *O Lamb of God … Sin* 'Behold the Lamb of God, which taketh away the sin of the world' (John 1:29). Note, however, the difference between removing sin itself, and B.'s idea of removing *remembrance* of sin.

CHAPTER 3

This chapter, prefaced by an address 'To the Deists', develops the opposition between Rationalism and Revelation. Albion is now basically inactive, submerged by his rational Spectre. Thus the primary movement of the poem shows all the forces of Rationalism consolidating. These forces are devoted to War and to religions of human sacrifice, from the Druids to the 'Natural Religion' of Blake's contemporaries. Their worship of a cruel female Nature is gradually revealed, and this movement culminates in the apotheosis of Rahab–Babylon and her twenty-seven Churches. In the counter-movement, we have Los continuing to build Golgonooza, acting as messenger of the Eternal Conclave, labouring at his furnaces, but helpless to influence outward events. The one hopeful moment comes close to the centre of the chapter, as the Divine Vision tries to comfort a despairing Jerusalem with a vision of Joseph and Mary and the forgiveness of sins. The episodes are as follows:

Pls. 53–6: Los builds Golgonooza amid Albion's stone altars, while Albion's Spectre teaches rationalism. The Eternal Conclave elects the Seven Eyes of God, then returns to the plough, declaiming against rationalism and seeking a messenger. Los – responding as messenger – unsuccessfully entreats the Daughters of Albion, as mothers of mankind, to forsake female will. Pl. 57: Albion, fleeing the Divine Vision, is ploughed under by the plough of nations. Pls. 58–9: The daughters of Albion rejoice at war; Luvah's and Albion's spectres mingle. Urizen builds his world – mundane shell and mundane egg – while the daughters of Los work in Cathedron, weaving life.

Pls. 60–62: The Divine Vision tries to comfort Jerusalem.

Pls. 63–70: A series of related episodes involving war, vengeance, human sacrifice and the shrinking and binding of Man, dominated by seductive goddess-figures, is seen by Los in his furnaces. He periodically comments and exhorts, but goes unheeded.

Pls. 71–2: Geographical catalogues: the counties of England assigned to Albion's children in Eternity; the thirty-two counties of Ireland assigned to the tribes of Israel; the thirty-two nations once contained within Albion.

Pl. 73: Natural Religion creates kings. Los creates prophetic visionaries. Pl. 74: Blake begs the help of the Saviour. The form of Dinah–Erin appears to him. Pl. 75: Apotheosis of Rahab, the Whore of Babylon.

Pl. 52. (prose) 1 *To the Deists* B. labels all religion and philosophy which dispenses with spiritual inspiration 'Deist'.

6 *He is in the State named Rahab* B. asserts that the preacher of Natural Religion is a worshipper of the kingdoms of this world, allying himself with the Whore of Babylon.

13–15 *your Greek Philosophy … Vegetated Spectre* B. attacks the belief that man is 'naturally' good.

43 *Foote* Samuel Foote, 1720–77, author of *The Minor*, an anti-Methodist satire.

44 *Whitefield* George Whitefield, 1714–70, famous Methodist evangelist.

Pl. 52. (poem) 1 *I saw a Monk* A longer draft of this poem is in the Notebook, p. 491.

Pl. 53.4 *Albions Tree* The Tree of Moral Virtue which began to grow at the opening of Chapter 2. See TREE OF MYSTERY.

10 *Seven-fold* Los has seven furnaces, each corresponding to an Eye of God or period of human history.

22 *The Twentyfour ... Four* Albion's twenty-four cathedral cities, led by Verulam, Edinburgh, London and York.

29 *Hinnoms vale* Site of potters' workshops just outside Jerusalem; also reputedly a place of idolatry and child sacrifice.

Pl. 54.5 *Jerusalem is called Liberty* 'Liberty' is the quality Englishmen have always prized as uniquely English.

11 *Seeing his Sons assimilate with Luvah* See 58.19–20, n.

21 *turn these stones to bread* Thus the Devil tempts Jesus in the wilderness, 'If thou be the Son of God, command that these stones be made bread' (Matthew 4:3).

25 *he is named Arthur* B. makes King Arthur, the first monarch of England, a warlike Druid. His love of a false queen, as well as the legend of his death-sleep and promised return, associate him with Albion.

27 *England* Albion is Great Britain; England is one portion of him. In 32.28 she 'divided into Jerusalem and Vala'.

Pl. 55.12–16 *the Princes of the Dead ... Into Egypt* Kings and priests on earth teach their followers to worship phallic aggressiveness, to exalt a chosen people instead of universal brotherhood, and to enforce order. Since order on command is impossible, Joseph is sold by his jealous brothers into slavery. All this is made possible by the veil which separates man and woman, man and man, man and God.

20 *Conclave*] Etched 'Concave'.

27 *The Stars in their courses* 'The stars in their courses fought against Sisera' (Judges 5:20).

31 *the Seven Eyes of God* See *M* 13.17–26, notes, and Dictionary of Proper Names.

33 *They namd the Eighth* In *M*, the 'Eighth' is the Edenic form of the poet Milton.

42-6 *tho we sit down . . . we are One family* The curse of Ulro is the separation of one person from another. But in Eternity, Man is divinely One. Idea and phrasing are from Psalm 139:7-10: 'Whither shall I go from thy spirit? or whither shall I flee from thy presence?/If I ascend up into heaven, thou art there: if I make my bed in hell, behold, thou are there./If I take the wings of the morning, and dwell in the uttermost parts of the sea;/Even there shall thy hand lead me, and thy right hand shall hold me.'

65-6 *Establishment of Truth . . . Virginity* Falsehood must be cut away, for Truth to be revealed.

69 *Who will go forth for us!* When God asks (Isaiah 6:8) 'Whom shall I send, and who will go for us?' Isaiah replies, 'Here am I; send me.' Thus Los, in the next plate, is responding like Isaiah.

Pl. 56 Los attempts to persuade the Daughters of Albion towards 'mildness'. Their replies (ll. 26-8, 39-40) are self-pitying and devious.

5-7 Jesus, born of woman, knows all in human life, including woman's role in weaving the flesh. 'All flesh is grass, and all the goodliness thereof is as the flower of the field. The grass withereth, the flower fadeth' (Isaiah 40:6-7).

8 *the erred wandering Phantom* Mankind.

11-14 The Daughters of Albion, says Los, must make the garment of flesh attractive, or no unborn soul will be willing to enter it.

18 *The Sun . . . a Scythed Chariot . . . the Moon: a Ship* Los ironically promises to create a world of images suitable to the warlike inclinations of the Daughters.

42 *Look back into the Church Paul!* (1) The Pauline Church, which became woman-dominated through worship of the Virgin; (2) St Paul's Cathedral, in which the three Marys mourn around the Cross.

Pl. 57.7 *Rosamonds Bower* Subterranean labyrinth in Oxfordshire's Blenheim Park, supposedly built by Henry II for his mistress, Rosamond Clifford. A ballad on Fair Rosamond and her bower is in Percy's *Reliques.*

Pl. 58.2-3 *Gwendolen dancing to the timbrel/Of War* In triumph after the drowning of Pharaoh's hosts in the Red Sea, 'Miriam . . . took a timbrel in her hand; and all the women went out after her with timbrels and with dances' (Exodus 15:20).

3-4 *she divides in twain . . . the People fall around* In time of war (such as the Napoleonic wars) the English people are divided. Those who support the war and those who oppose it both suffer.

11 *The Hermaphroditic Condensations* Supporters of war (hermaphroditic because monstrous and barren).

12 *The obdurate Forms* Opposers of war.

19-20 *the comingling . . . Hermaphroditic* May refer (1) to the meaningless Truce of Amiens between England and France, 1802; (2) to the rationalist (Deist) philosophy shared by England and France.

21-51 Los still labours, but Urizen for the time being directs. It is a time of false peace; hence the building has the illusion of restoring the divine order in which all nations are within Albion. But this unity is enforced only by the logic of empire.

Pl. 59.10 *Four Universes round the Mundane Egg* See *M* 34.32-9. The Mundane Egg is the material world in a state of contracted collapse which will nevertheless incubate Eternity. The four universes are the places of the Zoas, left chaotic when the world collapsed inwards.

23 *Cathedrons Looms* The workshop of Enitharmon and her daughters, who are also daughters of Los. Their work is redemptive, as they weave the flesh.

55 In Exodus 35:5-6, 25-6, Moses asks 'whosoever is of a willing heart' to bring offerings for the tabernacle of 'blue, and purple, and scarlet, and fine linen, and goats' hair', and 'all the women whose hearts stirred them up in wisdom' spun these gifts. The point is that the gifts are offered freely, not by command.

Pl. 60.10-37 The Lamb's song to Jerusalem mildly rebukes her for giving way to despair (she was subdued by Vala in Pl. 45; despairing, she burst away from Albion's bosom with a groan, and was given a space in Erin on the verge of Beulah, in Pl. 48).

18 *Nimrods Tower* The Tower of Babel.
 Mizraim Egypt.

20 *Tesshina* Unexplained; possibly B.'s misreading of Shinar, which is near Chaldea.

36 *I will lead thee thro the Wilderness* God led the Hebrews through the wilderness by a pillar of fire and a pillar of cloud.

42-3 *her reason grows like/The Wheel of Hand* Jerusalem's reason becomes controlled by doubt instead of certainty, as is shown in her next speech.

67 *lo I am with thee always* The close of the first Gospel: 'Lo I am with you alway, even unto the end of the world' (Matthew 28:20).

68 *Only believe* From the story of the raising of Jairus' dead daughter: 'Be not afraid, only believe . . . the damsel is not dead, but sleepeth' (Mark 5:36, 39).

69 *Thy Brother* Lazarus–Albion.

Pl. 61 An interpolation. Jerusalem has been condemned for impurity. So, too, was Mary, when found pregnant out of wedlock. Blake re-interprets the story of Joseph's doubt(cleared up by an angel in Matthew 1:19-20). In his version, Mary is indeed 'impure' but is freely forgiven by both God and Joseph.

61.2 *And be comforted O Jerusalem* 'Comfort ye, comfort ye my people, saith your God. Speak ye comfortably to Jerusalem, and cry unto her, that her warfare is accomplished, that her iniquity is pardoned' (Isaiah 40:1-2).

6 *Art thou more pure* 'Shall a man be more pure than his maker?' (Job 4:17).

16 *his Angel in my dream* In the gospel story, the angel tells Joseph that Mary has conceived of the Holy Ghost. Here, the angel insists on forgiveness of sin, implying that Mary has sinned; attribution to the Holy Ghost (l. 27) in this context is ambiguous; perhaps the Holy Ghost has inspired Mary to sin so that she can be forgiven.

30-33 *Emanating into gardens . . . Jordan* Mary's joy at being forgiven fills all the known world with joy. *Euphrates, Gihon, Hiddekel* and *Pison* are the four rivers of Eden. *Arnon* and *Jordan* flow into the Dead Sea.

33 *And I heard the voice* Blake hears the voice of Jerusalem, exiled like Ruth among the reapers.

34-5 *or am I/Babylon come up to Jerusalem?* 'Arise, shine; for thy light is come . . . And the Gentiles shall come to thy light' (Isaiah 60:1-3).

35 *And another voice answerd* The voice of Vala–Babylon, 'with whom the Kings of the earth have committed fornication, and the inhabitants of the earth have been made drunk with the wine of her fornication' (Revelation 17:2), realizing the possibility of forgiveness.

39–40 *in the days of her Infancy . . . person* 'Thus saith the Lord God unto Jerusalem . . . thou was cast out in the open field, to the loathing of thy person. And when I passed by thee, and saw thee polluted in thine own blood, I said unto thee . . . Live' (Ezekiel 16: 3–6). The remainder of Ezekiel 16 catalogues the abominations of Jerusalem, and the punishments to follow, but promises in the end a renewed covenant.

52 *Every Harlot was once a Virgin* In 'To The Accuser who is The God of This World' (p. 863): 'Every Harlot was a Virgin once/Nor canst thou ever change Kate into Nan.'

Pl. 62.7 *Shall Vala bring thee forth!* Shall the Saviour be born of woman in the state of Nature?

8–12 *the Maternal Line . . . Mary* The twelve women named are all biblical mothers, but the lineage is B.'s invention, fashioned to include 'heathen' daughters as ancestresses of Christ. *Cainah*, 'wife of Cain', *Ada, Zillah*, Cain's daughters-in-law. *Naamah*, Zillah's daughter, Noah's wife. *Shuah's daughter, Tamar, Rahab, Ruth*, all were alien women who became linked to the Hebrews. *Bathsheba*, mistress of David, mother of Solomon. *Naamah*, wife of Solomon, mother of apostate King Jehoash. *Mary*, mother of Jesus.

15 From the Lazarus story: 'Jesus saith unto her, Thy brother shall rise again. Martha saith unto him, I know that he shall rise again in the resurrection at the last day. Jesus said unto her, I am the resurrection and the life' (John 11:23–5).

16 *I know that in my flesh I shall see God* 'though . . . worms destroy this body, yet in my flesh shall I see God' (Job 19:25).

29 *Lo. I am always with thee* See 60.67 n.

30 *Luvahs Cloud* The imagery returns to war and human sacrifice.

38–9 *the Vision of God . . . Spectres* The Vision was obscured by Rationalism.

Pl. 63 The remaining episodes in Chapter 3 are visions in Los's furnaces helplessly perceived by Los.

5 *Luvah slew Tharmas* Revolutionary France suppressed free speech and simple honesty.

6 *To justice in . . . Paris* British troops occupied France in 1814 and again, after Napoleon's Hundred Days, in 1815.

7 *Vala ... the Daughter of Luvah* Vala is Luvah's emanation; figuratively, his daughter. She takes vengeance on Albion by producing a Walpurgisnacht of superstition.

9 *Thor & Friga* Norse gods of War and Love.

12 *the Dividing of Reuben & Benjamin* A re-enactment of the separation between Albion and Israel. Reuben is Israel's oldest son, Benjamin his youngest.

21 *the Looking Glass of Enitharmon* A Platonic image for this world as a mere reflection of eternity. In B.'s *Vision of the Last Judgment*: 'There exist in the eternal world the permanent realities of everything which we see reflected in this vegetable glass of Nature.'

38 *the Murder was put apart* The murder of Luvah by Albion.

Pl. 64.6 The following episode is the triumph of Vala–Nature as a goddess of War.

31 *A dark Hermaphrodite they stood* Vala–Nature united with Albion's Spectre–Reason. See *For the Sexes: The Gates of Paradise*, l. 15 (p. 862 below).

35 *Derby Peak yawnd a horrid Chasm* This peak and underground caverns are in the Pennines.

38 *Caves of Machpelah* Burial place of Abraham, Isaac and Jacob, and their wives.

Pl. 65.1 *To decide Two Worlds* Vala and the Spectre decide *between* two worlds, and choose 'Justice' or 'Wrath' (punishment) for Luvah–France, and 'Mercy' or 'Pity' (military impunity) for Albion.

5–56] Adapted and expanded from *FZ* VII [b] 92.9–53. In this and the following passages, the Napoleonic wars incorporate and recapitulate all past wars.

9 *poisonous blue* The woad with which the ancient British warriors painted their bodies.

21–2 *intricate wheels ... To perplex youth* The factory system of the Industrial Revolution, and the rationalism on which it is founded. Technology here is handmaiden of War.

33–4 *We were carried away ... in ships closd up* Pressgangs and the Navy.

47 Luvah–France's usurpation of the horses of the sun: Passion trying to be Reason. The Phaethon story here refers specifically to the failure of the French Revolution.

56–7 The sacrifice of Luvah–France is a Druid act.

Pl. 66.2 *They build a stupendous Building* Stonehenge is built as the justification for 'punishment' of France. The axis of Stonehenge points directly to the rising sun on midsummer's day (see l. 5). Hence it represents 'Natural Religion' – Nature-worship – and 'Natural Morality' (l. 8).

12 *Her Two Covering Cherubs* Stonehenge is here identified with the Hebrew Tabernacle, which had two cherubim covering the mercy seat in the Holy of Holies.

13 *Cove & Stone of Torture* The horseshoe structure surrounding the central 'altar stone' at Stonehenge.

20–28 *The Knife of flint . . . his heart* The sacrifice of Luvah continues, combining elements of circumcision (in which flint knives were used), crucifixion, flaying and Aztec sacrifice, in which the priests cut out the hearts of their victims.

41–3 *The Divine Vision . . . globe of blood* Chronological sequence of visions: Moses' burning bush, the pillar of fire which led the Hebrews in Exodus, Ezekiel's wheel. A 'globe of blood' divides from Los and develops into Enitharmon in *BU* Pls. 13–18, *M* 3.29–33, *J* 86.50–58.

46–8 *The Human form . . . Albion's Tree* B. elsewhere treats Nature as a vast, spreading poisonous polypus, and Morality as a vast, spreading, poisonous tree. These symbols now coalesce, and become further identified with the branches of Man's nervous system, circulatory system and reproductive organs. In brief, the agents of human sacrifice become like their victims: their own humanity is sacrificed.

55 *As the Mistletoe grows on the Oak* Parasitically.

59 *Plinlimmon . . . Snowdon* Mountains in Wales.

62 *Gwendolen . . . shuttle . . . Cambel . . . beam* The daughters of Albion are weaving at the loom of War. The fibres used are human tissues, and the cutting of the fibres (67.11) continues the imagery of human sacrifice.

79 *high Mona* From *Lycidas* 54, 'the shaggy top of Mona high', a supposed Druidic site.

Pl. 67.1 *the blood of their Covenant* From Exodus 24:8 and Hebrews 13:20, 'the blood of the everlasting covenant'.

2 *Rahab & Tirzah* These two figures collectively represent female cruelty, Rahab as mistress–whore, Tirzah as mother.

12 *Calling the Rocks Atomic Origins* The philosophy of Epicurus and Lucretius.

23 *Josephs Coat* Joseph's brothers stripped off his coat of many colours and dipped it in goat's blood to simulate his death (Genesis 37:31-3).

26-7 *the Rock/Of Horeb* Mt Sinai.

29 *Beth Peor* The burial place of Moses, adjacent to the Promised Land.

41-2 The slaying of Philistine Sisera by Jael, who drove a nail through his head, epitomizes female control of man's mind, supposedly 'for his own good'.

67.44-68.9 Tirzah's speech: her cruelty to Man is all in the name of Love. The passage is adapted from *FZ* VIII.105.30-53.

Pl. 68.3 *Ebal, Mount of cursing* The stones of the Law were placed in Mt Ebal, and a curse pronounced on offenders (Deuteronomy 27).

17-18 *Thor & Friga ... Generation* Norse, Gentile and Greek gods of War (male) and Love (female) are worshipped by the warriors. B. mistakenly treats Chemosh (associated with Molech) as female.

22-3 *Ephraim ... Valley of the Jebusite* Place-names within Israel, approaching Jerusalem. *Olivet* is the Mount of Olives.

30 *Bring your Offerings* The Daughters of Albion adore 'strong men' and will give their love only to warriors who slay the innocent.

38 *Havilah to Shur* Region of the outcast Ishmaelites (Genesis 25:18).

43-4 *Camberwell, Wimbledon, Walton, Esher* Suburbs of London; *Stonehenge* is west, *Malden* east.

51 *Smitten as Uzzah* Uzzah was struck dead for touching the ark of God (1 Chronicles 13:10). B.'s interpretation of *ark* and *spear* is sexual.

53-70 The Warrior–lover's speech to the Daughter(s) of Albion makes clear B.'s major point that war is a sublimation of unsatisfied sexuality.

55-61 *Rehob in Hamath ... Meribah Kadesh* The latter was a stopping-place for the Hebrews in the wilderness whence spies were sent to survey Canaan. They surveyed the land up to 'Rehob, as men come to Hamath' (Numbers 13:21). B. interprets this episode as a provocation to war.

Pl. 69.6 The One Male is not a unity, for all the men who compose him are in competition with each other.

11 *Leah & Rachel* Jacob's two competing jealous wives.

14-31 *Beulah ... Vegetating Death* The sacred tabernacle of the Israelites was an image of sexuality, as experienced in the dream-world in Beulah. But in the physical world sexuality binds men down to the cycle of life and death.

32 *the Spectres of the Dead awake in Beulah* Beulah becomes infected by the lower world.

38-44 (1) A final opposition between the conventional sexuality of 'a Secret Place' *versus* true embracings of whole beings; (2) a final opposition between the conventional religion of a veiled sanctuary accessible only to the High Priest *versus* the true holiness embodied in all God's people. The tabernacle of the Hebrews in the wilderness was surrounded by their tents, yet the common people were forbidden to enter it. The veil of this tabernacle was rent when Jesus died.

45 *Wandering Reuben* The 'wandering Jew'.

Pl. 70.1 *mighty Hand* Leader of the Sons of Albion, and representing them all. He is three-headed like Cerberus, for the brothers Robert, John and Leigh Hunt, publishers of *The Examiner*; and for the rational trinity, Bacon, Newton and Locke.

17-18 *Rahab/Sat deep within him* Rahab, the whore, controls Hand by promises of sensual delight. She has a heart where a brain should be.

Pl. 71.10-49 A catalogue of the territories belonging to the children of Albion in Eternity. (Wiltshire and Staffordshire are named twice; Lancashire is omitted.)

50-51 *the Four Sons of Jerusalem . . . Bromion* In *Milton* and in *J* 15.22, these are the four loyal sons of Los. Their loyalty unites them also to Jerusalem.

Pl. 72.1-27 A catalogue of correspondences between the counties of Ireland and the twelve tribes of Israel. The *Four Camps* (l. 2) corresponding to the *Four Provinces* of Ireland were the historic groupings of the Hebrews in the wilderness.

32 *And Thirty-two the Nations* The design in this plate shows two angels weeping next to a globe on which is inscribed: 'Continually Building. Continually Decaying because of Love & Jealousy.'

50-51 *Fenelon, Guion, Teresa* The seventeenth-century quietist theologian; his female disciple, imprisoned for her opinions; Teresa of Avila, the renowned sixteenth-century mystic and leader in the Catholic Reformation. *Whitefield*, the Methodist evangelist; *Hervey*, author of *Meditations Among the Tombs*. All are praised for retaining and propagating their faith despite opposition.

53 Mirror-writing: 'Women the comforters of Men become the Tormentors & Punishers'.

Pl. 73.16 Los's four sons examine the constellations ruled by these biblical giants.

28 *Peleg & Joktan* were the two sons of Eber; in their day 'was the earth divided' (Genesis 10:25). *Esau & Jacob* were the competing sons of Isaac. *Saul* tried to kill *David*, who later succeeded him as king. The three pairs of men represent the enmities caused by 'contraction' of human vision.

29 *Voltaire* An attack on Voltaire's scorn of Christianity.

35-7] A list of kings and conquerors spiritually descended from Satan. B. deleted l. 37.

41-2] A list of spiritual, philosophical and poetic leaders, opposites of the kings. B. deleted l. 42.

54 *Primrose Hill* This was on the outskirts of London. B. told Crabb Robinson, 10 Dec. 1825, 'I have conversed with the Spiritual Sun – I saw him on Primrose Hill.'

Pl. 74.24-6 In music, Blake preferred melody to harmony; in painting, clear outline to chiaroscuro; and in literature (or philosophy), vision of particulars rather than generalizing abstraction.

28 *Hyle roofd Los* as Hayley patronizingly restricted Blake.

30 *Gog* The defeat of Gog in the last days is prophesied in Ezekiel 38-9 and Revelation 20:8.

41-57 *how the Daughters ... Cabul* The separation of the twelve tribes of Israel from Albion, and the lands apportioned to each.

54 *Dinah ... Erin* Dinah was the one daughter of Jacob. As her lover Shechem was murdered by her brothers, so England 'murdered' Ireland's faith by religious intolerance.

Pl. 75.2 Merlin and Bladud are associated with King Arthur. Bladud was supposed to have founded Bath, practised magic, and died attempting to fly.

3 *The Cup* Babylon's 'cup ... full of abominations' (Revelation 17:4).

10–20 *Twenty-seven Heavens ... War* See Dictionary of Proper Names. This list of successive erroneous religions leading towards apocalypse is adapted from *M* 37.35–43.

CHAPTER 4

This final chapter, prefaced by an address 'To the Christians', divides into two parts. The first (Pls. 78–93) depicts Los's culminating struggles as he approaches the realization of his vision, and the Covering Cherub–Antichrist is revealed. The second (Pls. 94–9) brings the awakening of Albion, his reunion with Jesus, and the renewal of his full humanity. The episodes are:

Pls. 78–80: While the Sons of Albion besiege Erin and Jerusalem, ruined Jerusalem laments, as does – surprisingly – triumphant Vala.
Pls. 80–82: The turning-point of the poem comes as the seductive Daughters of Albion begin unwittingly to serve Los's purposes.
Pls. 83–8: Los, with renewed confidence, becomes a watchman of the night. As the Daughters of Albion create the allegory of Canaan, he makes it into divine analogy, planting seeds of future truth and beauty. He sees a vision of the true Jerusalem, and steadfastly continues his labours. At this point, however, his emanation, Enitharmon, rebels.
Pl. 89: The apotheosis of the Covering Cherub, identified as Antichrist.
Pls. 90–93: Destructive efforts continue by the Sons and Daughters of Albion, the Spectre of Los, and Enitharmon. But Los contends against them with increasing certitude.
Pls. 94–5: Time finishes; Albion awakes and reunites with England–Britannia. Pl. 96: Albion meets Jesus in friendship, and as the Covering Cherub comes on, sacrifices himself for Jesus. At this moment, the nightmare of the poem ceases, for 'all was a dream'. Pl. 97–9: A final description of regenerate Man.

Pl. 77. (epigraph) 1 *I give you the end of a golden string*] From lines in the Notebook (p. 624).

3–4 *'Saul Saul'/'Why persecutest thou me'* The words of Jesus in Saul's vision on the road to Damascus (Acts 9:4). In the following argument, B. reminds nominal 'Christians' that they too are in need of conversion.

(prose) 5 *seed of a wild flower* From the parable of the tares sown among the wheat, Matthew 13:24-30.

19 *What is that Talent* From the parable of the talents, Matthew 25.

20 *What are the Treasures* From Matthew 6:19-21.

22 *What are all the Gifts* From Matthew 7:7-11.

(poetry) 1 *I stood among my valleys* B. places himself in the south, or intellectual region. His vision contains a devouring wheel, implicitly opposed to the wheel of 'living creatures' in Ezekiel 1:16, 21.

12 *a Watcher ... Holy-One* From Daniel 4:13. John in Revelation similarly converses with angels.

18 *Caiaphas* The high priest who condemned Jesus for blasphemy.

31 *Publicans & Harlots* Jesus is several times in the Gospels named as friend of 'publicans and sinners' or 'publicans and harlots', for 'They that be whole need not a physician, but they that are sick' (Matthew 9:12). Publicans were Jewish tax-collectors for Rome, hence despised by their fellow-Jews.

Pl. 78.12 *Forty-two Gates of Erin* A mistake? Ireland has thirty-two counties, as in Pl. 72.

26 *the Giants causway* Headland composed of basalt columns in the north of Ireland.

31 *My brother and my father* Albion is both brother and father to Jerusalem.
    God hath forsaken me Christ's words on the cross: 'My God, why hast thou forsaken me?' (Matthew 27:46).

32 *arrows of the Almighty* From Job 6:4.

Pl. 79 The lament of Jerusalem is that Albion and the Holy Land, once identical, have become divided and merely geographical places.

68 *Tell me O Vala thy purposes* Jerusalem once again questions Vala–Nature's separation of humanity into sexes.

78 *Wherefore then do you realize these nets* Why do you make these nets (of sexuality) real, when they should be accepted as illusions.

Pl. 80.3 *I am a worm* 'I am a worm, and no man' (Psalm 22:6).

6-7 *Vala . . . Lamenting* We expect Vala to triumph. She laments (1) because she wishes Albion to remain 'dead', and fears he will be reborn; (2) she knows inwardly that her role of murderer is not her true role, and hopes, unconsciously, for a return to Eternity.

16 *My Father* Luvah is both father and beloved of Vala.

27 *I . . . keep his body* Vala keeps Albion's body.

35-6 *To weave Jerusalem . . . A Dragon form* Vala hopes to clothe Jerusalem in War, thus creating 'a dragon red and hidden harlot' – another Church for men to worship.

51-2 *Rahab . . . Refusd to take a definite form* Rahab refused to reveal, openly, what she was.

57 *Skiddaws top* A mountain in the Lake District.

61 *Drawing out fibre by fibre* Cambel is (1) alluring Hand; (2) using his substance as thread for her loom.

82 *the Wine-press of Luvah* At once Love and War. It presses the juice from 'human grapes' in *FZ* IX.

Pl. 81.2 *Merlin the piteous* Merlin was undone by love of a woman, Vivian.

8 *is the Cruel become an Infant* The female will seeks to reduce Man to infantile dependence.

11 *Josephs beautiful integument* (1) His coat of many colours; (2) his skin.
  my Beloved Hyle.

Pl. 82.17 *So saying she took a Falsehood* The design for Pl. 81 shows the nude Gwendolen pointing to the following lines in mirror-writing while holding her left hand behind her:

> In Heaven the only Art of Living
> Is Forgetting & Forgiving
> Especially to the Female
> But if you on Earth Forgive
> You shall not find where to Live.

29 *But hide America* America represents potential liberty.

33 *the Friend of Sinners* Epithet for Jesus, here applied to Jerusalem.

34 *close up her . . . Ark* Make Jerusalem chaste by force, so that Man, sexually (and spiritually) frustrated, will exhaust himself in War.

43] All copies give 'hands' twice in this line, but the sense is clear. In the Song of Solomon 7:4, 'Thy neck is as a tower of ivory; thine eyes like the fish-pools in Heshbon, by the gate of Bath–Rabbin.' Gwendolen makes the song of love into a song of crucifixion of her lover Hyle.

44 'O that thou wert as my brother, that sucked the breasts of my mother! . . . Set me as a seal upon thine heart, as a seal upon thine arm' (Song of Solomon 8:1, 6).

47 *And Hyle a winding Worm* At this crucial point in the poem, female will is shown to be ultimately self-defeating. The winding worm is (1) a further degeneration of helpless infancy – Gwendolen's wish has come true, as in fairy tales, beyond her intention; (2) the phallic worm; (3) the devouring worm. Gwendolen's 'perfect' beauty (l. 50) is now useless to her, and the entire episode – reduction of 'warrior' to 'worm' – recalls Shakespeare's *Antony and Cleopatra*. But instead of a tragic close, this metamorphosis will bring the possibility of genuine love to the Daughters of Albion.

56–7 Here begins a turn for the better. Los's wrath gives him new strength. In the following passages the Daughters of Albion begin despite themselves to serve Los's redemptive purposes.

59 *Billingsgate* The London fish-market, famous for foul and abusive language; also a term for foul, vituperative language itself. Thus: Blake–Los is angry at Cambel and releases a 'blast' of Billingsgate at her.

81–2 *I know . . . I can at will expatiate* Los knows that in his eternal form he can (1) wander freely; (2) speak or write freely.

Pl. 83.5 *I shall become an Infant . . . Enion! Tharmas!* Los feels he is in danger of losing his strength and vision. In *FZ* Los and Enitharmon, in their fall, entered the world of Generation as the infant children of Tharmas and Enion.

9–13 *Sussex . . . Hants, Devon & Wilts . . . Mystery* Sussex rejects the unwed mother. Los demands that the other three counties (supposed Druid sites) must make definite forms for the cruelties of Vala and Luvah, nailing them to their own error as they have sacrificed other victims.

34–7 The indefinite and always changing form of this earth, believed at some times to be the centre of the universe, at other times to be a globe in space, and at still others to be flat. The appearances alter as mortal perceptions – controlled by the Daughters of Albion – alter. But realities are permanent.

51 *the old Parent* Father Thames; perhaps Tharmas, as in *FZ*.

59 *the Tribes of Llewellyn* The Welsh.

61 *The night falls thick* Possibly an echo of *Macbeth* III.ii.50-51: 'Light thickens, and the crow/Makes wing to th' rooky wood.' Los now becomes Watchman of London as Ezekiel was made 'watchman unto the house of Israel' (3:17). Like the watchman of God in Isaiah 21:9, he will ultimately see that 'Babylon is fallen, is fallen'.

76-7 *Putting on his golden sandals . . . girding himself* In Acts 12:8 an angel frees the Apostle Peter from prison, saying, 'Gird thyself, and bind on thy sandals . . . and follow me.'

82 *the Dogs of Leutha* The Isle of Dogs in the Thames; the dogs of Diana, the virgin huntress, which destroyed Actaeon. Here they seem tame.

Pl. 84.31-Pl. 85.9 *they took the Falshood . . . in the Space* See 82.17. The Daughters of Albion, still hoping to subdue their threatening male counterparts, unintentionally imitate the protective activities usually performed by Daughters of Beulah and by Enitharmon. (In *M* 8.39-44, Enitharmon creates a space for Satan and Michael and 'clos'd it with a tender moon'.) The Space created by the Daughters is an 'Allegory' – a theological lie. But Los uses this falsehood to plant seeds of truth. Thus: the idea of a 'Chosen People' is based on a 'Jealous God'. This is a falsehood. Yet from this falsehood springs the truth of the Gospels.

85.22 *O lovely mild Jerusalem!* Los now sees the 'New Jerusalem' of Revelation 21-2.

Pl. 86.1 *Six Wings* From Isaiah 6:2.

4 *Holiness to the Lord* From the description of Aaron's sacred vestments (Exodus 28). These words were graved on a gold plate for his brow. Jerusalem's *immortal gems, gold & azure & purple*, and *bells* are also from Aaron's vestments. *Gates of pearl* are from Revelation 21:21.

18 *The River of Life & Tree of Life* From Revelation 22:1-2.

19 'And I John saw the holy city, new Jerusalem, coming down from God out of heaven, prepared as a bride adorned for her husband' (Revelation 21:2).

32 *Javan* Progenitor of the inhabitants of Greece (Genesis 10:2).

50 On the verge of realizing his vision, Los must contend with a final obstacle: the rebellion of his own emanation. This episode (Pls. 86-8,

92–3) recapitulates the division and jealousies between Los and Enitharmon developed in B.'s earlier works, notably *BU* and *FZ*, where the division formed a part of Man's original Fall. Here, however, the rebellion of Ehitharmon comes at the end of history instead of the beginning, and is the final sexual split which precipitates the coming of Antichrist.

Pl. 86.62–Pl. 87.2 In *FZ* I.Pp.8–9, Enion gives birth to Los and Enitharmon, who then repel her, as here.

Pl. 88.23 *Sussex shore* Felpham, where Blake and Catherine lived under Hayley's patronage.

56 *Jerusalem took the Cup* The 'cup of abominations' in Revelation 17:4, held by Vala in *J* 63.39 and Rahab in *J* 75.3. Jerusalem is about to poison herself.

58 *Hermaphroditic* Self-contradictory, barren.

Pl. 89.4 *Love & Wrath* These are contraries and should be opposed. When united in the 'Wine-press' of false religion, both are meaningless.

6–7 *Pharisaion . . . Saddusaion* Pharisees, scribes, elders, high priest, priest, sadducees.

9 *the Covering Cherub* The whole ruling body of the old Church, just catalogued, and identified as Antichrist. The ensuing description of his head, heart and loins is in perverse parallel to the vision of Jerusalem (Pl. 86). For the sexual symbolism of the Covering Cherub, see Dictionary of Proper Names.

13 *In three nights* Three nights between Crucifixion and Resurrection.

15 *Gihon* One of the four rivers of Paradise; identified with the 'perverted Nile' here. The other rivers are Pison–Arnon (l. 25), Hiddekel–Tigris (l. 35), and Euphrates (l. 38).

19 *the Dragon* Pharaoh is a river dragon in Ezekiel 29:3.

21 *Twelve ridges of Stone* Twelve lines on the Covering Cherub's brow, one for each of the twelve tribes and twelve Sons of Albion, compose a Druid temple.

33–4 The power of the Covering Cherub spreads north around the rim of the Mediterranean, thence to Europe.

43 The Holy City absorbed and hidden by the Covering Cherub as if devoured.

46 *Seven Kings . . . Five Baalim* For the number of Canaanite tribes, and of Philistine towns, opposing Israel. *Baalim*, 'idols'.

47 Legendary giants of Canaan.

55 *Horeb* Sinai, the site of the Law.

57 *Midian* Tribe named for a son of Abraham.
Aram Syria.

58 *Alla* A region of Ulro.

Pl. 90 The Sons and Daughters of Albion are seen once again at their destructive work, dividing the tribes of Israel from their rightful places in Albion.

25 *Reuben . . . Surrey* An error? Reuben (16.44) belongs in Suffolk, not Surrey.

28–37 A complex and condensed argument. Universal attributes or characteristics (such as womanliness or lordship) belong to no single individual but to Man. Private persons who consider themselves as self-sufficient units, rather than as members of a Universal Man or Divine Body, are 'Blasphemous Selfhoods'. The notion of Christ's incarnation through virgin birth is both blasphemous and barren. For Jesus, born of impure woman, is another potential egocentric Satan or selfhood. His divinity consists in *casting off* his selfhood, not in *lacking* it.

38 *Come Lord Jesus* The last cry of the New Testament, Revelation 22:21: 'Even so, come, Lord Jesus.'
take on . . . Body of Holiness Jesus is to take on a Satanic form, as a garment to shed and a burden to be put off.

58 *Giants of Albion* Sons of Albion.

59 *rocking Stones* Natural rock formations in which a large broad rock balances on a narrow one. B. associates them with the Druid trilithons.

62 *a Circle in Malden or in Strathness or Dura* Malden has some pre-historic remains, though no stone circles. Strathness, the valley of Loch Ness, is near stone circles at Muir of Ord and Cononbridge. Dura, an island off Scotland, has rocky caves.

Pl. 91.7–10 *the Worship of God . . . there is no other/God* Adapted from *MHH* Pl. 29. But the new definition of God as 'the intellectual fountain of humanity' alters the meaning radically.

32   *The Spectre*   The spectre of Los. His 'buildings' are last-gasp rationalizations of the *status quo*, and Los destroys them.

32–3   *Heavens/Like to a curtain*   From Psalm 104:2.

34   *Smaragdine Table of Hermes*   A famous text in occult tradition and alchemy. B. apparently rejects occultism as too materialistic.

38–9   *Leviathan ... Behemoth*   The great sea-monster and land-monster of Job 40:15, 41:1; associated in two paintings of B.'s 1809 exhibition, and in the Job engravings, with Nelson and Pitt.

50   *every Ratio of his Reason*   Every systematic rationale.

Pl. 92.1   *What do I see?*   The following vision is one of *unification* of nations within Albion, instead of division and dispersion.

12   *Then thou wilt Create another Female*   Eve's fear in *Paradise Lost* IX.826–9 is similar.

15–17   Los promises that the crimes, punishments, accusations, jealousies, revenges, murders and deceits of present life – the major facts of life – will in Eternity become things merely to be imagined or recalled as a caution.

Pl. 93   The design here shows three Accusers crouching and pointing. Their bodies bear the inscription: 'Anytus Melitus & Lycon thought Socrates a Very Pernicious Man. So Caiphas thought Jesus'.

1–16   Enitharmon selfishly pleads with her sons. She wants them to love her alone.

5   *Ocalythron & Elynittria*   Emanations of Rintrah and Palamabron.

6   *East Moor ... Cheviot*   Both part of the highlands of England which run north to south and 'divide' the country.

8   *Reuben ... Mandrakes*   Reuben gave his mother, Leah, mandrakes to make her attractive to Jacob.

10   *Rintrahs Plow ... Satans ... Team*   In the Bard's Song in *M* Pls. 7–8 Satan usurped Palamabron's harrow. This is either the same story mis-remembered, or a similar one.

17–26   Los makes a counter-argument, as in *M* 23.32, where he similarly tries to reassure his sons.

26   *that Signal of the Morning*   The darkest hour is just before the dawn. In Revelation the appearance of all the forces of evil in their strength – Satan, the Beast and Babylon – immediately precedes the Second Coming of Christ in glory.

27 *Mam-Tor* The peak in Derbyshire whence Los denounced female will (30.41).

Pl. 94.5 *The weeds of Death* Seaweed; shrouds.

18 *Time was Finished!* The sounding of the seventh trumpet in Revelation 10:6 announces that there is 'time no longer', and the remainder of the book occurs outside of time.

20 *England who is Brittannia* 'Brittannia' is the conventional female personification, as in Thomson's 'Rule Britannia' (1740), 'England' her guiding portion.

Pl. 95.10 *The Four Elements* Albion's Four Zoas (ll. 16-20).

Pl. 96.35 Albion at last sacrifices himself for his friend Jesus, and the nightmare of history is finished immediately.

Pl. 97.3-4 'Rise up, my love, my fair one, and come away, for, lo, the winter is past, the rain is over and gone' (Song of Solomon 2:10-11).

Pl. 98.1-11 The annihilation of the Spectre by the living bow and arrows of Love.

98.9 *Bacon & Newton & Locke* The rational trinity, now included among the 'Chariots of the Almighty'. The chariots – vehicles of human genius – are 'Sexual Threefold', not Human Fourfold, because all these men were mortals, working within the limits of the world of generation.

11 *Sexual Threefold*] Mended from 'Sexual Twofold'.

12-27 The description of the Fourfold Man.

28-56 The creative life of Man.

39-40 *clearly seen/And seeing* 'For now we see through a glass, darkly; but then face to face: now I know in part; but then shall I know even as ... I am known' (1 Corinthians 13:12). In Plotinus, 'They see themselves in others. For all things are transparent, and there is nothing dark or resisting, but every one is manifest to every one ... For every one has all things in himself ... and the splendour is infinite.'

44 The serpent of Sin, being forgiven, becomes human.

45 *the Covenant of Jehovah*] Mended from 'thy Covenant Jehovah'; restored to 'thy' in copy [f].

46 *the Covenant of Priam* The classic set of values which encourages military might and conquest, instead of mutual love and forgiveness. This 'Covenant' is then linked to Graeco-Roman 'virtue', Hebraic-

Christian 'Good & Evil', Druidic human sacrifice, and finally British colonial practices.

52–3 *the Triple Headed Gog–Magog . . . Nations* 'Gog and Magog' were to be overthrown in the last days (Revelation 20:8–9). Hand, the leader of Albion's sons, is triple-headed in 70.4. Statues of Gog and Magog stood outside London's Guildhall. Thus: Commerce, the exploitation of the many poor by the few rich, was responsible for British imperialism.

53 *the Spectrous Oath* Albion's reasoning spectre, having overthrown him, announced (54.16) 'I am God.'

The Everlasting Gospel

This late and fragmentary work consists of nine scattered entries in B.'s Notebook, and three sections on a separate scrap of paper watermarked 1818, which were probably – though not necessarily – intended for a single poem defining Blake's unorthodox view of Jesus and the Christian Gospel. The present text follows Erdman's conjecture that the prose and verse on the separate paper constitute a preliminary handling of the theme, and that the section on Notebook p. 120 (sewn in at the end of the Notebook) is probably also early. Though the work as it now stands is 'rough' in both tone and organization, it is well to remember that more 'finished' works such as *The Marriage of Heaven and Hell* and the fair draft of 'Auguries of Innocence' cultivate a not dissimilar air of spontaneous flourish. 'The Everlasting Gospel' is, in fact, an expanded version of ideas initially stated almost thirty years earlier in *MHH* Pl. 23.

'IF MORAL VIRTUE WAS CHRISTIANITY . . .'

14 *Rhadamanthus* In classic mythology, a son of Zeus and Europa, noted in life for justice, and made a judge in Hades.

'WAS JESUS BORN OF A VIRGIN PURE . . .'

4–5 In *J* Pl. 61, B. makes Mary an adulteress, though not a harlot, and she is forgiven by God. Mary Magdalene, from whom Jesus cast out seven devils (Mark 16:9), is also traditionally considered a 'fallen' woman.

16 Caiaphas was the Jewish High Priest in Jesus' time. In the following lines (17–48), B. has him list Jesus' offences against the Law. But ll. 21–6, inserted from the bottom and margin of the page, are clearly Blake's voice, not Caiaphas'.

17 Jesus antagonized the Pharisees on several occasions by performing 'unlawful' acts such as healing on the Sabbath.

20 The disciples Simon (called Peter), Andrew, James and John were fishermen. The idea that common men could be spiritual leaders would, of course, antagonize a priest.

27 From the episode of the Gadarene swine, Luke 8:27–37, Mark 5:1–19.

32 Jesus' words to his mother at Cana (John 2:4).

34 From the episode of young Jesus staying to question the doctors in the Temple instead of returning home with his parents (Luke 2:41–51).

37 From Luke 10:1–20.

47–8 From the episode of the woman taken in adultery (John 8:3–11).

'THE VISION OF CHRIST THAT THOU DOST SEE . . .'

3–4 *a great hook nose . . . mine* On Notebook p. 64 B. remarked: 'I always thought Jesus Christ was a snubby or I should not have worshipd him if I had thought he had been one of those long spindle-nosed rascals.'

9 *Melitus* One of the accusers in the trial of Socrates.

'WAS JESUS CHASTE . . .'

4 The adulteress of John 8 is not named, but B. identifies her with Mary Magdalene and perhaps with the Virgin Mary.

29 Jehovah in Exodus 33:14 promises to accompany Moses with 'my presence', to show his favour. B. elsewhere calls Jehovah, the law-given and punisher of the Old Testament, 'leprous'.

47–8 Quotes John 8:10–11. The remainder of the colloquy is of course B.'s invention.

54 From the curse on the serpent in Genesis 3:14: 'dust shalt thou eat all the days of thy life'.

64 From 1 Corinthians 6:19: 'your body is the temple of the Holy Ghost which is in you'.

81 *the shadowy Man* Revealed in l. 96 as the serpent, Satan, who demands punishment rather than forgiveness, and who devours Man's material body.

'SEEING THIS FALSE CHRIST ...'

Brief fragment written below the previous section, and apparently referring to another passage, now lost.

'DID JESUS TEACH DOUBT ...'

Written sideways in the margin of p. 52, possibly related to the note at the top of the page: 'This was spoke by My Spectre to Voltaire Bacon etc.'

'WAS JESUS GENTLE ...'

3 From the episode in Luke 2:41–51.

15 From the temptation of Jesus by Satan in the wilderness, Matthew 4, Luke 4. Satan bids Jesus turn stones to bread, Matthew 4:3, and offers him the Kingdoms of the world 'if thou wilt fall down and worship me', Matthew 4:9.

17 John the Baptist was killed by King Herod.

32 From the vision in Revelation 20:2.

48 From the scourging of merchants and money-changers in the temple, John 2:13–16.

'WAS JESUS HUMBLE ...'

A first draft followed by an expanded second draft.

THE EVERLASTING GOSPEL, 'WAS JESUS HUMBLE ...'
REVISED

4 From Matthew 7:9, Luke 11:11: 'what man ... if his son ask bread, will he give him a stone?'

11 *the rich learned Pharisee* Nicodemus, in John 3:1–21, to whom Jesus declares, 'Ye must be born again.'

16 From the response of the congregation in Capernaum, Matthew 7:29.

18 From Matthew 11:28–9.

41 *d^r Priestly* Joseph Priestley, the discoverer of oxygen.

83 Jesus on the cross prayed, 'Father, forgive them; for they know not what they do' (Luke 23:34).

86 *I never will Pray for the World* From John 17:9: 'I pray not for the world, but for them which thou hast given me; for they are thine.'

89 Refers to Jesus' prayer in Gethsemane, 'O my Father, if it be possible, let this cup pass from me,' immediately retracted with 'nevertheless, not as I will, but as thou wilt' (Matthew 26:39, Mark 14:36, Luke 22:42). B.'s sense in this passage may be that Jesus rejects God's interpretation of the Crucifixion as an act of humility to be followed by revenge. Instead, he scorns the death of the body – which is only a 'fiction' – and thus does not need to be either humble now or vengeful at Judgement Day.

103–6 These final lines are adapted from 'Auguries of Innocence', ll. 125–8, p. 510.

'I AM SURE THIS JESUS WILL NOT DO ...'

A couplet written marginally near the end of the previous section.

For the Sexes: The Gates of Paradise

In 1793 B. published an emblem-book entitled *For Children: The Gates of Paradise*, consisting of a frontispiece and sixteen designs with brief legends, symbolically depicting the sufferings and limitations of mortal life. Years later (estimates of the date range between 1806 and 1818) he reissued this book with a new title, expanded inscriptions, a prologue and three new pages of text. Five complete copies, and seven incomplete, are known. The designs are reproduced in Keynes and Erdman, among other editions, as well as in J. Beer, *Blake's Humanism*, with a commentary. Facsimiles may be found in the Blake Trust edition (1969).

PROLOGUE

8 The 'corpse' (a pun on *corpus*?) of the Law: the Ten Commandments, placed beneath the Mercy Seat in the Temple.

THE KEYS OF THE GATES

The Keys The numbers to the left of the lines refer to the designs on which they comment.

1 The frontispiece design depicts a caterpillar above a baby-faced chrysalis.

5 Emblem 1 depicts a woman plucking an infant from under a tree-root.

9-12 Emblems 2-5 depict water, earth, air and fire. Their inscriptions form another quatrain:
Water: Thou waterest him with Tears
Earth: He struggles into Life
Air: On Cloudy Doubts and Reasoning Cares
Fire: That end in endless strife.

15 The female and her child constitute a hermaphrodite pair because they cannot unite in transcendence of sexuality.

20 Emblem 6 depicts a winged child emerging from a shell. The inscription reads 'At length for hatching ripe he breaks the shell' (from Dryden's *Palamon and Arcite*, 1069).

21 When Man is born in a mortal body. The cave, grave and garments of flesh are all neo-Platonic symbols of birth.

27 Emblem 7 depicts a boy catching small winged figures in his hat. One lies on the ground, and one is fleeing. The source of the design may well be *King Lear* (IV.i.38): 'As flies to wanton boys are we to the Gods/ They kill us for their sport.' The inscription reads: 'What are these? Alas! the Female Martyr/Is She also the Divine Image?'

31 *My Son! my Son!* This is the inscription to Emblem 8, which depicts a youth aiming a spear at an old man. The words are King David's (2 Samuel 18:33) at the death of his rebel son: 'Would God I had died for thee, O Absalom, my son, my son!'

33 Emblem 9 depicts a man preparing to climb a ladder to the moon. The inscription reads: 'I want! I want!'

35   Emblem 10 depicts a man drowning with arm upraised. The inscription reads: 'Help! Help!'

37   Emblem 11 depicts an old bespectacled man, with closed eyes, clipping the wings of a young boy who tries to escape towards the sun. The inscription reads: 'Aged Ignorance/Perceptive Organs closed, their Objects close.'

39   Emblem 12 depicts Ugolino and his sons in prison. The inscription reads: 'Does thy God, O Priest, take such vengeance as this?'

42   Emblem 13 depicts an old man's spirit rising from his deathbed while his family watches. The inscription reads: 'Fear and Hope are – Vision.'

43   Emblem 14 depicts a traveller with walking stick. The inscription reads: 'The Traveller hasteth in the Evening.'

45   Emblem 15 depicts an old man entering a stone doorway. The inscription reads: 'Death's Door'.

47   Emblem 16 depicts a hooded woman sitting in shadow with a worm winding about. The inscription reads: 'I have said to the Worm:/Thou art my mother and my sister.'

TO THE ACCUSER . . .

1   From Young's *Night Thoughts* VIII.1417: 'Satan, thy master, I dare call a dunce.'

8   *The lost Travellers Dream*   The lost traveller is man, and Satan is but his dream.

The Ghost of Abel

B.'s final etched work, dated 1822, responds to Byron's romantic drama *Cain, A Mystery*, which had appeared in 1821. Byron dwells at length on the despair and the agonized guilt of Cain, and indicts the God responsible for death. If life ends in death, it is meaningless. But B. argues in effect that a poet should see beyond the sufferings of this world: spiritual vision should reveal Eternity, in which there is no death – hence no cause for despair. The central issues in *The Ghost of Abel* are Faith *versus* Doubt and Vengeance for sin *versus* Forgiveness for sin. The central action is that the ghost of Abel, inspired by Satan, demands vengeance, while Jehovah offers the covenant of forgiveness.

Pl. 1.1 *What doest thou here Elijah?* B. addresses Byron in the words of God to Elijah (1 Kings 19:9, 13), when the prophet had fled to the wilderness out of fear for his life, and was lapsing into despair. As God commands Elijah to resume his prophetic labours, so, B. implies, should Byron. As a poet, Byron should have faith in 'Visions of Jehovah' which are one with his own imagination.

6 *I will not hear thee . . . Voice* Adam rejects Jehovah, as Albion in the opening of *Jerusalem* rejects Jesus. He refuses to believe in the spiritual, insisting it is 'delusion'.

8–9 *the Womans Seed . . . head* From Genesis 3:15, God's promise to Adam and Eve.

15 *Among the Elohim . . . I wander* Elohim is the title for the Creator-God in Genesis 1. It is a plural form, implying a polytheistic creation. On Pl. 2 of *The Ghost of Abel*, we find that both Jehovah and Satan are Elohim.

16–17 *Prince of the Air . . . Avenger* Satan (who appears on Pl. 2) has entered into Abel, and speaks through him.

Pl. 2.19–20 *that Thou Thyself . . . Self Annihilation* To go down to eternal death in self-annihilation is the heroic task Milton sets for himself in *M* Pls. 14, 38, 41. Does Jehovah imply that by willingly sacrificing himself on Calvary, he will teach even Satan to do the same, so that Satan too may eventually be redeemed? The Chorus of Angels at the close of the drama suggests that the vengeful Elohim are converted to peace, brotherhood and love.

The design at the foot of the text shows a figure rising from Abel's body, inscribed 'The Voice of Abels Blood'.

Dictionary of Proper Names

THE ABOMINATION OF DESOLATION: A Biblical phrase signifying unutterable heathen idols (Old Testament) and the ANTICHRIST (New Testament).

ABRAM: The first Hebrew Patriarch. A native of CHALDEA, he was led to CANAAN by God, who changed his name to Abraham ('father of multitudes') and promised blessing to his seed.

ADAM: Heb. 'red earth'. The 'limit of contraction' created at a late stage of the Fall to prevent further degeneration of the Universal Man. See SATAN.

AHANIA: Athena? The emanation of URIZEN. Idealism, true Wisdom. See FOUR ZOAS; EMANATION.

ALBION: Archaic and poetic name for Great Britain. In B. he is a giant, sometimes England, but usually Mankind or 'Eternal Man'. Originally a member of the DIVINE FAMILY of Eternals who are one with Jesus, he sinks into a deadly sleep in which he becomes divided from Eternity. The FOUR ZOAS – his Reason, Passion, Sensation and Instincts – once integrated, divide and war against each other and against him. This Fall is in B. identical with the formation of the created universe. Its effects form the substance of his prophetic books.

ALBION, DAUGHTERS OF: In *VDA*, Englishwomen enslaved by social convention. In *J*, Albion's twelve daughters typify the 'female will', beautiful but cruel. Their names derive from ancient queens and princesses (except Gwinifred, from the virgin-martyr Winifred) in Geoffrey of Monmouth's *Historia Britonum* and Milton's *History of Britain*. Most are ruthless and ambitious characters. The first five, Cambel (EMANATION of Hand), Gwendolen (Hyle), Conwenna (Bowen), Cordella (Gwantok), Ignoge (Coban), collectively comprise TIRZAH. The last seven, Gwineverra (Scofield), Gwinefred (Hutton), Gonorill (Slade), Sabrina (Kotope), Estrild (Kox), Mehetabel (Peachey), Ragan (Brereton), collectively comprise RAHAB. Boadicea appears in *FZ* list of Daughters and in *J* is identified with Cambel. All the daughters, as well as Rahab and Tirzah, are aspects of VALA.

ALBION, FRIENDS OF: The twenty-eight cathedral cities of the Church of England (Edinburgh is included to represent Presbyterian Scotland), acting as Albion's conscience. The four chief cities are Canterbury–Verulam, Edinburgh, London and York.

ALBION, SONS OF: Albion's twelve sons are treacherous rationalist destroyers. They are associated in *J* with figures from Hebrew history. They have modern names, derived from B.'s personal enemies: Hand (the brothers Hunt, whose

Examiner editorials – signed with a hand-insignia – ridiculed B. and his art. Hand is the chief son, and at times represents them all); Hyle (Hayley, B.'s patron, and *hyle*, Gr. 'matter'); Coban or Koban (not identified); Guantok or Kwantok (John Guantock, a judge at B.'s sedition trial); Peachey (John Peachey, a judge at B.'s trial); Brereton (William Brereton, an assisting justice at B.'s trial); Slade or Slayd (not identified); Hutton (Lt George Hutton, a soldier involved in B.'s trial); Scofield (Private John Scholfield, who accused B. of treason); Kox (Private Cock, Scholfield's friend and fellow-accuser of B.); Kotope (not identified); Bowen (possibly Thomas Bowen, a Sussex lawyer who might have assisted at B.'s trial).

ALLAMANDA: A workshop of LOS in GOLGONOOZA; Man's circulatory system; Commerce. Associated with BOWLAHOOLA, the digestive system.

AMALEK: Biblical heathen nation south of Palestine, foe of Israel. Amalekite females in B. symbolize sexual temptation and cruelty. Commonly coupled with CANAAN and MOAB, or CANAAN, MOAB and EGYPT.

AMERICA: Symbol of Liberty, unfortunately separated from England by the Atlantic. In *VDA*, symbol of Liberty Enslaved.

AMMON: Biblical heathen nation east of the River JORDAN.

ANAK: See OG.

ANNANDALE: Valley of the river Annan in Dumfries, Scotland. In B., a place of Druid worship.

ANTAMON: A son of LOS and ENITHARMON, 'prince of the pearly dew', probably the Cloud in *Thel*, seminal fluid, youthful gratified desire, shaper of bodies for the unborn.

ANTICHRIST: In Christian tradition, the Beast of Revelation 13:17, Christ's great opponent who will be conquered at the Second Coming.

ARAM: Biblical son of Cush, grandson of NOAH, ancestor of the Arameans; also a Hebrew name for Syria.

ARISTON: In Herodotus, a Spartan king who stole his bride from his best friend. In B., a 'king of beauty' in legendary Atlantis.

ARNON: A Jordanian river which runs through a great gorge into the Dead Sea. In B., the female sexual tract (Damon, *Dictionary*), hence a symbol of birth.

ARTHUR: Legendary British king who established the Round Table and the code of chivalry which idealized war and womankind. He was deceived by his queen (Gwineverra) and slain in treacherous battle, but is supposed one day to return. He is identified with the northern constellation Boötes, which circles around the Pole Star (associated with war in B.).

ASHER: See ISRAEL, SONS OF.

ATLANTIC: The ocean which separates Britain from America. In B. the two were once united in a single golden continent (ATLANTIC MOUNTAINS or ATLANTIC HILLS), now flooded and lost like the legendary Atlantis. The sea is 'the Sea of Time and Space'.

BABEL: City founded by the warrior-monarch Nimrod on the plain of Shinar (Mesopotamia). Site of the Tower of Babel.

BABYLON: Capital city of the Babylonian (Mesopotamian) Empire, a chief foe of Israel, by which Jerusalem was sacked, her Temple destroyed and the Hebrews taken into captivity. In Christian apocalyptic literature, Babylon, with its luxurious living, stands for Rome, persecutor of Christianity. She is 'Mystery, Babylon the Great, the mother of harlots and abominations of the earth' and will be overthrown at the Second Coming. B. also identifies her with Rahab. See MYSTERY; RAHAB.

BACON, FRANCIS: 1561–1626. First Baron Verulam, statesman and philosopher, a founder of modern scientific method. 'Bacon Newton & Locke' constitute B.'s false trinity of English rationalists.

BATH: A popular spa in the eighteenth century, site of an unfinished Norman cathedral. Bath's Rev. Richard Warner was a famous pacifist preacher in B.'s day.

BENJAMIN: See ISRAEL, SONS OF.

BETH PEOR: See PEOR.

BEULAH: 1. Heb. 'married land', the name which will be given Palestine when returned to God's favour (Isaiah 62:4).

2. In *Pilgrim's Progress*, a happy land where the pilgrims dwell until crossing the river JORDAN (Death) into eternal life. 3. In B., a dream-world paradise presided over by the moon, and by beautiful comforting females. It is a resting-place from the vigorous life of EDEN (Eternity), but too-prolonged rest may lead to ULRO (Materialism). For fallen Mankind, Beulah is the way back to Eden: it is the subconscious, and the source of poetry. See EDEN; GENERATION; ULRO.

BEULAH, DAUGHTERS OF: B.'s Muses.

BEULAH, CHURCHES OR HEAVENS OF: The *lower* border of Beulah consists of churches, which to fallen man seem like heavens *above* him. There are three (brain, heart, loins); twelve (Paganism); or twenty-seven (official Judeo-Christianity).

BOADICEA: See ALBION, DAUGHTERS OF.

BOWEN: See ALBION, SONS OF.

BOWLAHOOLA: A workshop of LOS in GOLGONOOZA; Man's digestive system; a region of anvils and furnaces where unborn souls receive bodies; Law. Associated with ALLAMANDA, the circulatory system.

BRERETON: See ALBION, SONS OF.

BRITANNIA: In *J*, England, wife of Albion, who divided at the Fall into VALA (the dominant female) and Jerusalem (the true but rejected female).

BROMION: Gr. *bromios*, 'roaring'. In *VDA*, a self-justifying rapist: rational science or technology brutally applied. Elsewhere, a son of LOS: the artist's science. See also RINTRAH; PALAMABRON; THEOTORMON.

CAMBEL: See ALBION, DAUGHTERS OF.

CANAAN: The Biblical Promised Land, conquered by the Israelites.

CANTERBURY: Seat of the English Church. B. at times guardedly refers to it as VERULAM, which was within its ecclesiastical province.

CATHEDRON: Cathedral? Catherine? A building in GOLGONOOZA, where

ENITHARMON and her daughters weave the web of life. The womb; possibly the art of painting.

CHALDEA: Biblical nation hostile to the Hebrews. The Patriarch Abraham's original native land.

CHARLEMAINE: 742–814. Founder of the Holy Roman Empire.

CHEMOSH: Moabite god, worshipped by burning children alive.

CHERUB: See COVERING CHERUB.

CHERUBIM: In the Old Testament, winged beings or figures associated with the majesty and inaccessibility of God. Cherubim guard the Garden of Eden after Man's expulsion. Carved cherubim guard the Ark of God within the Holy of Holies. Embroidered, they adorned the veil of the Temple. Elsewhere, they bear God's throne or chariot. Ezekiel identifies them with his visionary 'living creatures'. In Christian literature they become the high angelic order (Wisdom) second only to seraphim (Love).

In B. cherubim are sometimes angelic spirits and merciful intercessors, sometimes representatives of Pagan or Norse mythology, but most often guardians of Holiness, separating Man from union with the Divine. As sexual symbols the two cherubim which cover the Ark are female labia; the cherubim depicted on the Veil constitute the hymen. See COVERING CHERUB.

CHEVIOT: Hills on the English–Scottish border, location of the war-ballad 'Chevy Chase'.

CHURCHES: See TWENTY-SEVEN CHURCHES.

CIRCLE OF DESTINY: In FZ, set in motion at the Fall, it crashes at the Flood. Historically corresponds to the Olympian period in mythology, in which even Zeus is subject to Destiny.

COBAN: See ALBION, SONS OF.

CONSTANTINE THE GREAT: 288?–337. Roman ruler, founder of Christian Empire.

CONWENNA: See ALBION, DAUGHTERS OF.

CORDELLA: See ALBION, DAUGHTERS OF.

COVERING CHERUB: In Ezekiel (28:1–19) the blasphemous Prince of Tyre who says 'I am a God' is identified with the 'cherub that covereth'. In B. this figure represents Churches throughout history, and is identified as ANTI-CHRIST at the close of J. See CHERUBIM.

DAN: See ISRAEL, SONS OF.

DAUGHTERS OF ALBION: See ALBION, DAUGHTERS OF.

DIVINE FAMILY: (Universal Family; Eternal Family; the Eternals) The community of perfect beings in Eternity (Eden). Seen close by, they are multitudes of individuals. Seen from afar, they are One Man, Jesus. ALBION is originally a member of this family, and ultimately reunites with it.

DIVINE HUMANITY: God; Jesus.

DRAGON: B.'s symbol of Empire.

DRUIDS: The priests and judges of primitive Britain and Gaul. According to B. and his eighteenth-century sources, they: (1) Originated in Britain and formed the first patriarchal religion. B. identifies them with the Hebrew

Patriarchs. (2) Practised human sacrifice, burning victims or slaying them alive on stone altars. (3) Worshipped the oak. (4) Built huge stone serpent-temples at Stonehenge on Salisbury Plain, Avebury, Verulam and elsewhere.

EDEN: Dwelling-place of the Divine Family of Eternals; region of perfectly fulfilled 'fourfold' humanity. Lesser and lower realms are BEULAH, GENERA-TION and ULRO.

EDOM: Another name for Esau, son of Jacob, who lost his birthright and blessing. A nation hostile to Israel.

EGYPT: The nation from which Moses led the Jews; symbol of hostility, cruelty and slavery.

ELOHIM: Heb. 'God'. A name for God used in Genesis 1 and elsewhere; a collective plural form. See SEVEN EYES OF GOD.

ELYNITTRIA: A daughter of LOS and ENITHARMON, emanation of PALAM-ABRON.

EMANATION: B.'s term for the female portion of Man. In Eternity, where Man is bisexual, the Emanation is a part of any being, and is experienced as his inspiration and dwelling-place. In the Fall, she becomes a separate being, and the reunion of Man and his emanation is necessary for re-entry to Eternity. The Four Zoas each have emanations, as do other male figures. See also SHADOW, SPECTRE.

ENION: Anyone? Emanation of THARMAS, Man's sensation, and power of coherence. In the Fall, as he becomes chaotic Flood, she becomes water vapour, tears and the 'watery grave', an aged and helpless Demeter-figure. She is the parent of LOS and ENITHARMON.

ENITHARMON: Enion + Tharmas; In Harmony; Gr. *anarithmon*, 'number-less'. The emanation of LOS, the Eternal Prophet; his Muse; his Pity; in fallen form, an archetypal jealous, elusive and cruel Female Will. In *BU*, the first female. In *Europe*, a selfish sky-goddess. Insofar as they work for Man's regeneration, Los is Time, Enitharmon is Space; Los is Sun, Enitharmon is Moon; Los is Poetry, Enitharmon is Painting; Los is the blacksmith of souls, Enitharmon is the weaver of bodies. At times: Los is Blake, Enitharmon is Catherine Blake.

ENO: Eon; One. The undefined 'aged Mother' who speaks *The Book of Los*, sings *The Four Zoas* and is a nurse of souls in BEULAH.

ENTUTHON BENYTHON: A gloomy forest of error in ULRO. It surrounds the city of GOLGONOOZA (Art) and contains the black lake UDAN-ADAN (Form-lessness).

EPHRAIM: See ISRAEL, SONS OF. Son of JOSEPH, younger brother of MANA-SSEH. The land allotted to his tribe included the sanctuary-city SHILOH in Mt Ephraim, as well as the city of Shechem. Its powerful capital, TIRZAH, became the capital of the secessionist Northern Kingdom of Israel.

ERIN: Archaic name for Ireland; in B., symbolizes hope for Liberty.

ERYTHREAN SEA: B.'s name, following the antiquarian Bryant, for the Indian Ocean.

ESAU: See EDOM.

ESTRILD: See ALBION, DAUGHTERS OF.

ETERNAL PROPHET: See LOS.

ETERNALS: See DIVINE FAMILY.

ETHINTHUS: Daughter of LOS and ENITHARMON; a moon-goddess, her consort is Manathu-Vorcyon.

EUPHRATES: The river which flows by Babylon.

EYES OF GOD: See SEVEN EYES OF GOD.

FELPHAM: Coastal village in Sussex, where B. lived under William Hayley's patronage 1800–1803.

FEMALE, SHADOWY: See SHADOWY FEMALE.

FOUR ZOAS: From Gr. Zῶα, 'living creatures'. The energies of Mankind, or of any individual man. In Eternity they are integrated as the members of a single divine being. In the Fall, they divide and war against Man and each other, split from their EMANATIONS (female counterparts) and degenerate in character. They are the agents of Man's history, and re-unite at the final apocalypse.

Name (Emanation) Title	URIZEN (AHANIA) 'Prince of light'	LUVAH (VALA) 'Prince of love'	THARMAS (ENION)	URTHONA (ENITHARMON)
Faculty	Reason	Passion	Sensation	Instinct
Eternal Role	Ploughman	Vintner	Shepherd	Blacksmith
Eternal Virtue	Faith, certainty	Love	Coherence, receptivity	Creativity
Fallen Form	'God, Priest, King'	ORC (SHADOWY FEMALE) 'Demon Red'	'Parent Power'	LOS (ENITHARMON) 'Eternal Prophet'
Fallen Character	Doubt, Tyranny	Rebellion, Revolution	Flood, Chaos	Poetry, Prophecy
Element	Air (light)	Fire (heat)	Water	Earth
Region	S. (zenith)	E. (centre)	W. (circum-ference)	N. (nadir)

Note: Los and Enitharmon are born from Tharmas and Enion and in turn become the parents of Orc and the Shadowy Female.

FUZON: A son of URIZEN (BU, BA); symbolizes Rebellion against Law; fills roles of Moses, Prometheus, Christ.

GAD: See ISRAEL, SONS OF.

GENERATION: The state of nature in its continuing cycle of life and death; a 'vegetative' world. Above it are EDEN (human perfection) and BEULAH (the dream-paradise); below it is ULRO (dead matter).

GILEAD: A region in eastern Palestine known for its balm; also Mt Gilead.

GOLGONOOZA: From Golgotha, 'hill of skulls'. The City of Art built by Los throughout human history in the midst of the fallen material world of ULRO.

GONORILL: See ALBION, DAUGHTERS OF.

GUANTOK: See ALBION, SONS OF.

GWENDOLEN: See ALBION, DAUGHTERS OF.

GWINIFRED: See ALBION, DAUGHTERS OF.

GWINEVERRA: See ALBION, DAUGHTERS OF.

HAND: See ALBION, SONS OF.

HAR and HEVA: From Heb. *har*, 'mountain', and Lat. *Eva*, 'Eve'. Parents of Mankind, in B.'s early and transitional prophetic books; a senile and helpless Adam and Eve; a representation of the failure of natural law and classical culture.

HAVILAH: Heb. 'sand'. Land supposed to have been compassed by the Pison, one of the four rivers of the Garden of Eden; Havilah and Shur bounded the Ishmaelite territory.

HEAVENS, TWENTY-SEVEN: See TWENTY-SEVEN CHURCHES.

HERMAPHRODITE: A being with both male and female sexual organs. In B., a major symbol of monstrous sterility and contradiction evolving at the end of a process of error, usually associated with war and Churches.

HERMON: Highest mountain in Palestine.

HESPERIA: Italy.

HOREB: Heb., 'mountain of God'. The place where God revealed Himself to Moses in the burning bush. Also another name for Mt Sinai, where God issued the Ten Commandments.

HUTTON: See ALBION, SONS OF.

HYLE: See ALBION, SONS OF.

IGNOGE: See ALBION, DAUGHTERS OF.

ISRAEL: Jacob's name was changed by God to Israel, and he became ancestor of the Israelites. In B., Albion and Israel were one nation in Eternity. In the Fall, they are divided.

ISRAEL, SONS OF: Jacob–Israel had twelve sons: Reuben, Simeon, Levi, Judah, Dan, Naphtali, Gad, Asher, Issachar, Zebulon, Joseph and Benjamin. Each founded one tribe, except for Joseph, who founded two: MANASSEH and EPHRAIM. After the Exodus from Egypt and the conquest of Canaan, each tribe received a portion of land, except for the Levites (the priest-caste) who received forty-eight 'cities of refuge'. After the Babylonian captivity, only two tribes – Judah and Benjamin – returned to the Holy Land; the rest were 'Lost Tribes'.

In B., the Sons of Jacob–Israel are lost portions of Albion, who erroneously flee him and become incorporated in material bodies. Their conquest and settlement of Canaan confirm this tragic separation. Redeemed, they will return to Albion. Meanwhile, they correspond in spirit to the twelve SONS OF ALBION.

ISSACHAR: See ISRAEL, SONS OF.

JEHOVAH: The personal 'name' of God, told to Moses at Horeb. In B., sometimes a symbol of Moral Law, sometimes a symbol of Forgiveness. See SEVEN EYES OF GOD.

JERUSALEM: The Holy City of the Bible. In B., the emanation of Albion; Liberty; the intended bride of the Lamb.

JORDAN: River forming the eastern boundary of the Promised Land; the place of Jesus' baptism; traditionally, to 'cross the Jordan' means to die and enter Paradise.

JOSEPH: See ISRAEL, SONS OF. Because he was his father's favourite, his jealous brothers stripped his 'coat of many colours', sold him as a slave into Egypt and pretended he was dead.

JUDAH (JUDEA): See ISRAEL, SONS OF. Judah's lands formed the Southern Kingdom, whose capital was Jerusalem. He was also the ancestor of David and Jesus.

KOBAN: See ALBION, SONS OF.
KOTOPE: See ALBION, SONS OF.
KOX: See ALBION, SONS OF.
KWANTOK: See ALBION, SONS OF.

LAMBETH: Beth is Heb. 'house'; hence for B., 'house of the Lamb'. London district containing B.'s home, 1791–1800.

LEBANON: Fertile mountain region north of the Holy Land.

LEUTHA: A daughter of LOS and ENITHARMON, EMANATION of BROMION; sometimes paired with ANTAMON and SATAN. She represents female exotic impulse and allure, miscalled 'Sin'. Her vale (valley) is the female genital region.

LEUTHA'S DOGS, ISLE OF: The Isle of Dogs, a dock area of London known for vice.

LEVI: See ISRAEL, SONS OF.

LOCKE, JOHN: 1632–1704. Most popularly accepted English philosopher of the eighteenth century. In B., he is objectionable for the belief that the human mind at birth is a blank slate without innate ideas, and that all knowledge and motivation must thus derive ultimately from sense-experience. 'Bacon, Newton & Locke' constitute B.'s false trinity of English rationalists.

LONDON STONE: A Roman milestone set in central London. In B., a symbol of Druid human sacrifice and the errors of rationalism.

LOS: (Loss; Sol) 'The Eternal Prophet', fallen form of the Zoa Urthona (see FOUR ZOAS). He is Prophecy, Poetry, the creative impulse throughout human history; Time; the sun of Imagination. He is the blacksmith of Man; at times he is William Blake. His major works are: (1) the binding of Urizen (*BU, BL, FZ*); (2) the building of GOLGONOOZA (*FZ, M, J*).

LUBAN: The gate of GOLGONOOZA, City of Art, which faces on this world. Site of CATHEDRON, where bodies are woven, and Los's palace, furnaces and forge, where souls are wrought. The omphalos or vagina (Damon, *Dictionary*) of this world.

LUCIFER: 'Light-bearer', morning star. Traditionally identified with the fallen SATAN. See SEVEN EYES OF GOD.

LUTHER, MARTIN: 1483–1546. Founder of the German Reformation; for B., a father of militant (and military) Protestantism. See TWENTY-SEVEN CHURCHES

LUVAH: Love, lover, lava. 'Prince of Love'; Man's passions, both active and suffering. In *FZ*, his struggle with URIZEN for control of Man produces the Fall. In this world he is manifested as ORC (active Rebellion) and the incarnate and crucified Lamb (passive Suffering). In political allegory (*J*) he is France, Urizen is England. Redeemed (*FZ* IX), he becomes first Eros, then the Dionysian ruler of the Last Vintage whose wine-press is war on earth, and finally a servant. See FOUR ZOAS.

MALDEN (MALDON): A port in south-east England; B. associates it with Druidism.

MANASSEH: See ISRAEL, SONS OF. Older son of JOSEPH, brother of EPHRAIM. His lands became part of the apostate Northern Kingdom, whose capital was TIRZAH.

MEDWAY: A river emptying into the Thames.

MEHETABEL: See ALBION, DAUGHTERS OF.

MERLIN: Legendary magician and prophet at King Arthur's court, ultimately betrayed by his mistress.

MIDIAN: A desert region south of MOAB, whose daughters tempted the Israelites during their wanderings.

MILTON, JOHN: 1608–74. English poet; B.'s most immediate model. Note the following correspondences between works of Milton and works of B. which treat similar themes:

MILTON	BLAKE
L'Allegro and *Il Penseroso*	*Songs of Innocence and of Experience*
Lycidas	*Thel*
Comus	*Visions of the Daughters of Albion*
Political Tracts	*French Revolution, America*
Nativity Ode	*Europe*
On Christian Doctrine	*Marriage of Heaven and Hell*
Paradise Lost	*Four Zoas*
Paradise Regained	*Milton*
History of Britain	*Jerusalem*

MOAB: Heathen nation east of Palestine, whose daughters tempted the wandering Israelites. Worshippers of the god Chemosh. Commonly coupled in B. with AMALEK and CANAAN.

MOLECH: Ammonite deity worshipped by burning children alive. See SEVEN EYES OF GOD.

MOSES: Leader of the Exodus from Egypt, promulgator of God's law from Mt Sinai; supposed author of the Pentateuch. See TWENTY-SEVEN CHURCHES.

MUNDANE EGG: The material world of time and space which Man inhabits like an incubating bird. It is surrounded by the MUNDANE SHELL.

MUNDANE SHELL: The visible sky above and around Man. It is an incrustation of Error, which contains the forty-eight constellations and twelve signs of the zodiac, the twelve gods of Asia and the twenty-seven opaque layers of heavens and their churches (official Judeo-Christianity). It is a mirror of our perishing world. Chaos surrounds it, and beyond Chaos, Eternity. Immortals can descend through it, but mortals cannot ascend. The SEVEN EYES OF GOD are guardians throughout it. See also TWENTY-SEVEN CHURCHES.

MYSTERY: Blake's term for all State religion, which by definition separates Man from God. Its two symbols are a multiply-enrooting tree (of Good and Evil, and of Crucifixion), and a great whore created from the tree's fruit. See BABYLON; RAHAB; TREE OF MYSTERY.

NAPHTALI: See ISRAEL, SONS OF.

NATURAL RELIGION: Any worship of nature instead of divine humanity; any religion which dispenses with revelation.

NEWTON, SIR ISAAC: 1642–1727. Greatest of English physicists; inventor of calculus; founder of the laws of dynamics. 'Bacon, Newton & Locke' constitute B.'s false trinity of English rationalists.

NIMROD: Legendary first king; founder of the Babylonian Empire; builder of the Tower of Babel; traditionally a 'hunter of men'.

NOAH: Biblical patriarch who survived the Flood and fathered the subsequent races of mankind. See TWENTY-SEVEN CHURCHES.

NOAH (female): See TIRZAH.

NOBODADDY: Daddy Nobody, B.'s coinage for God the Father.

OCALYTHRON: Daughter of LOS and ENITHARMON, EMANATION of RINTRAH (Wrath).

OG and ANAK: Legendary heathen giants defeated in the conquest of the Promised Land. In B., OG and ANAK, OG and SIHON, or OG, ANAK, SIHON and SATAN are threat-figures opposing man's self-fulfilment.

OLIVET: Mount of Olives, just outside Jerusalem, scene of Jesus' agony in the Garden before the Crucifixion.

OLOLON: In *M*, the sixfold EMANATION of Milton; his three wives and three daughters; in Eden, a river region and its multitudes of dwellers; descended to earth, a virgin.

OOTHOON: A daughter of LOS and ENITHARMON; female desire for free love; heroine of *VDA*.

ORC: Lat. *orcus*, 'hell'. The 'Demon Red'; Rebellion; Revolution; Libido. He is the fallen, earthly form of the Zoa LUVAH (Passion), born to LOS (Prophecy). He is typically a babe or a pubescent flaming youth; he is fettered but ultimately frees himself. His two forms are fire or pillar of fire, and serpent.

PADDINGTON: A slum district of London, in B.'s time being redeveloped.

PAHAD (PACHAD): A name of God, commonly translated 'fear' or 'terror'. See SEVEN EYES OF GOD.

PALAMABRON: A son of LOS: the artist's Pity. In the 'Bard's Song' of *M* he represents Blake, the genuine artist, whose labours at the harrow make it possible for seeds to grow. His antagonist SATAN represents Blake's patron William Hayley, the self-deluding bad artist whose proper labour is at the mills of logical reasoning, but who wishes to appropriate the harrow. See also RINTRAH; BROMION; THEOTORMON.

PAUL, ST: The Apostle to the Gentiles; preacher of Man's union with Christ; founder of the Church Militant. See TWENTY-SEVEN CHURCHES.

PEACHEY: See ALBION, SONS OF.

PEOR: A mountain peak in MOAB. BETH-PEOR: a valley, burial place of Moses, just outside the Promised Land.

PHARAOH: Title of kings of Egypt.

PHARISEES: Legalistic Jewish sect, rejecters of Jesus.

PHILISTEA: Heathen nation hostile to Israel.

POLYPUS: General name for a variety of tentacled sea-creatures including the jellyfish, sea anemone and hydra; colonial organisms such as the Portuguese man-of-war, formed by budding; also a kind of tumour. In B., symbol of the meaninglessly breeding physical world, and human society within it.

PRIAM: King of Troy in the *Iliad*. In B., associated with war and paganism.

RAGAN: See ALBION, DAUGHTERS OF.

RAHAB: 1. Biblical harlot of Jericho who aided Israelite spies. 2. In Psalms and Isaiah, identified with Egypt and 'the dragon'. In B., she becomes the Whore of Babylon, also called MYSTERY (Revelation 17), the seductive, cruel and corrupt Church opposed to true Christianity. She and TIRZAH are degenerate forms of VALA. Together they comprise the DAUGHTERS OF ALBION. Their triumph is the triumph of female will.

REPHAIM: Heb. 'giants' or 'ghosts'. A general name applied to several pre-Israelite tribes. VALE OF REPHAIM: a valley near Jerusalem, supposed to harbour those ghosts. SEA OF REPHAIM: Blake's invention.

REUBEN: See ISRAEL, SONS OF. Eldest son of Jacob–Israel, in B. commonly used to represent them all. Also represents the 'average sensual man'.

RINTRAH: In the Argument to *MHH*, a vague figure of impending upheaval. Elsewhere specified as a son of LOS; the artist's Wrath or Indignation; in the 'Bard's Song' of *M*, an ally of PALAMABRON. See also BROMION; THEOTORMON.

ROCK OF AGES: Traditional epithet for God and, more popularly, Christ. In B. it is the place where Albion is left to sleep.

ROUSSEAU, JEAN JACQUES: 1712–78. French philosopher praised by B. in *FR* as a precursor of revolution, but elsewhere rejected for his deism and belief in the virtue of the Natural Man.

SABRINA: See ALBION, DAUGHTERS OF.

SALISBURY PLAIN: See DRUIDS.

SATAN: 1. The 'God of this world', worshipped in all forms of self-righteous morality.

2. A 'state' rather than a character: (a) the 'limit of Opacity' beyond which Man cannot fall, and live; (b) the selfhood in every man.

3. In 'the Bard's Song' of *M*, Satan (Hayley) is the self-righteous and self-deluded artist, antagonist of PALAMABRON (Blake) the genuine artist. Both are sons of LOS.

4. A degenerate form of the Zoa URIZEN.

SCOFIELD: See ALBION, SONS OF.

SEVEN EYES OF GOD: A succession of guardian deities corresponding to periods of human history and religious development, each inadequate until the end. Their names and periods are as follows:

LUCIFER: Silver age: period of wars of Titans and Olympians, wars of Jotans on Odin in the *Eddas*.

MOLOCH: Bronze age: period of Druidism, human wars, human sacrifice.

ELOHIM: Iron Age: creation of Adam and Eve, and of the physical universe as we know it, from 4004 BC. Here begin the TWENTY-SEVEN CHURCHES.

SHADDAI: period of the nine patriarchs Adam to Lamech (Genesis 5) and their Churches.

PACHAD: period of the eleven patriarchs Noah to Terah (Genesis 11:10–26), and their Churches.

JEHOVAH: period of the First Covenant: Abraham (end of Druidism and human sacrifice), Moses (the Ten Commandments and the Law), Solomon (consolidation of Kingdom; Judgement; Wisdom), and their Churches.

JESUS: period of Christianity: Paul, Constantine, Charlemaine, Luther, and their Churches.

SHADDAI: A name of God commonly translated 'the Almighty'. See SEVEN EYES OF GOD.

SHADOW: 1. An individual's suppressed vitality or desires.

2. The inferior and dim projection of any reality. For example, VALA (Nature) is a 'shadow' of JERUSALEM (Spirit).

SHADOWY FEMALE: An earth-figure, fallen form of VALA (Nature), born to ENITHARMON. Her rape by ORC (Revolution) precipitates war.

SHILOH: Biblical sanctuary-town, northern sister-city to JERUSALEM. In B.'s political allegory, the EMANATION of France.

SIHON: See OG.

SIMEON: See ISRAEL, SONS OF.

SINAI, MT: The mountain on which God gave Moses the Ten Commandments.

SLADE, SLAYD: See ALBION, SONS OF.

SOLOMON: King of Israel following David; consolidated rule, built the Temple, is supposed to have written Proverbs, Ecclesiastes, Song of Songs.

SOTHA: Soothe. A son of LOS and ENITHARMON associated with sexual fantasy or dream. Frustrated, he helps cause war; labouring, he helps create bodies. His EMANATION is Thiralatha or Diralada (*Eur*, *SL*).

SLAYD: See ALBION, SONS OF.

SPECTRE: The masculine principle which may divide from a being when his feminine portion (EMANATION) separates, to assume independent life. Usually 'the reasoning power in man', it is brutal, obsessive and selfish, and must be reintegrated.

SPECTRES OF THE DEAD: Unborn spirits in need of bodies, or mortals in need of the 'body' of Art, without which they die.

SONS OF ALBION: See ALBION, SONS OF.

STONEHENGE: See DRUIDS.

SURREY: County in south-east England; in B.'s time included LAMBETH, the district of London in which B. lived 1791–1800.

SUSSEX: County in south of England. B. lived near the seashore in the village of FELPHAM, 1800–1803.

SWEDENBORG, EMANUEL: 1688–1772. Swedish engineer-turned-mystic philosopher, founder of the New Church. B. embraced his visionary elements, attacked his pedantry and conventional morality.

TABERNACLE: A shrine. In Old Testament, the veiled shrine containing a Holy of Holies in which was the Ark of the Covenant, and the Presence of God, carried by the Israelites through the wilderness. May symbolize protection of a true ideal, or concealment of a false one. In sexual symbolism: the female body or genitals.

THAMES: Chief river of England, flowing through London.

THARMAS: The arms, Father Thames, doubting Thomas. 'Parent Power', Man's sensation. In EDEN, he is that which enfolds and maintains Man's coherence, hence a shepherd. He is also Man's means of self-communication, hence the tongue. In the Fall, he becomes Chaos, the Flood, an incoherent and hence false tongue. His leading qualities throughout are simplicity, honesty, guilelessness. See FOUR ZOAS.

THEOTORMON: God-fear? In *VDA*, the too-meek lover, broken by jealousy and prudishness. Elsewhere, a son of LOS: the artist's care or conscientiousness. A Hamlet-figure. See also RINTRAH; PALAMBRON; BROMION.

THOR: Norse thunder-god.

TIRZAH: Heb. 'delight'. 1. One of Zelophehad's five daughters who succeeded in becoming his heirs (the others were Milcah, Hoglah, Noah, Zillah); hence, 'Female Will'. 2. Canaanite city on Mt EPHRAIM which became a secessionist northern capital, rival to JERUSALEM. In B., a beautiful and cruel virgin mother, or Mother Nature, who binds Man to a physical world. She and RAHAB are degenerate forms of VALA. Together they comprise all the DAUGHTERS OF ALBION.

TREE OF MYSTERY: A multiply-enrooting tree of obscure and esoteric knowledge, guarded by priests, which divides Man from God. It derives from the tree of forbidden knowledge in Genesis, the banyan, the deadly upas tree of Java described in Erasmus Darwin's *Loves of the Plants*, and the Norse world ash, Yggdrasil, whose branches and roots extended through heaven, earth and underworld, and which was to be destroyed at the doom of the Gods. It is also the Cross of Christ.

TYBURN: Hill, near a brook, site of the London gallows.

TYRE: Prosperous Phoenician port city. See COVERING CHERUB.

TWELVE TRIBES OF ISRAEL: See ISRAEL, SONS OF.

TWENTY-SEVEN CHURCHES, or HEAVENS: Official Judeo-Christianity: an incrustation surrounding Man's imagination in successive layers or folds (see MUNDANE SHELL) which to him seem like 'heavens'. Each is a historic period.

DRUIDS 1–9   Adam–Lameth (from geneologies in Genesis 5). These are HERMAPHRODITIC, self-contradictory.

     10–20   Noah–Terah (from Genesis 11:10–26). These are 'Male within female', patriarchal authority.

HEBREWS

     21–3   Abraham – end of human sacrifice, beginning of chosen people. Moses – Exodus' Ten Commandments of Moral Law.

           Solomon – Temple; consolidation of Empire.

CHRISTIANS

     24–7   Paul – Church Militant begins.

           Constantine – Christianity becomes State religion.

           Charlemaine – foundation of Holy Roman Empire.

           Luther – Reformation.

           All these are 'female within male', religion within war: increasing aggressiveness but also increasing worship of female (mariolatry leads to Natural Religion).

UDAN-ADAN: Lake of Formlessness or Indefiniteness in the Forest of Error (ENTUTHON BENYTHON).

ULRO: Ur + low. The world of pure materialism and delusion, the basest condition to which Man can sink. See GENERATION; BEULAH; EDEN.

URIZEN: Horizon; your reason. 'Prince of Light', Man's intellect. In Eternity he is Faith and Certainty. In the Fall he is Doubt, Authoritarianism, Limitation, Abstraction. He is the supreme tyrant–god–priest–king–father figure. In political allegory, he is England, LUVAH is France. See FOUR ZOAS.

URTHONA: Earth owner. Man's instinct, intuition, a cave-dwelling blacksmith in EDEN. Manifests primarily in the form of LOS. See FOUR ZOAS.

URTHONA, SHADOWY DAUGHTER OF: See SHADOWY FEMALE.

VALA: Vale, veil, Valhalla. EMANATION of LUVAH. In Eternity, he is Love, she is the Beloved. In the Fall she is the seductress Nature triumphant over spirit, cruel yet herself suffering, the *femme fatale*. Her degenerate forms include RAHAB, TIRZAH and the SHADOWY FEMALE. Her VEIL is 'the film of matter which covers all reality' (Damon, *Dictionary*), and is variously identified as the Veil of the Temple which separates Man from God; the Moral Law; the MUNDANE SHELL; the body itself; and the female hymen.

VERULAM: Ruined Roman town in southern England. The rationalist philosopher Francis Bacon was Baron Verulam. The town is in the province of Canterbury, and B. at times identifies the two.

VOLTAIRE: 1694–1778. French philosopher admired (in *FR*) by Blake for his attacks on hypocrisy and organized religion, but rejected for his deism.

ZEBULON: See ISRAEL, SONS OF.

ZOAS, FOUR: See FOUR ZOAS.

ZOA: A Greek plural, 'living creatures', used by B. as a singular.

ZION: Heb. 'fortress'. The Temple hill in JERUSALEM, at times identified with the whole city.

Note to the Indexes

Manuscript deletions and emendations are reproduced in both indexes but ignored for purposes of alphabetization, except where they constitute a major part of the entry. Blake's works are abbreviated throughout as follows:

SI	*Songs of Innocence*
SE	*Songs of Experience*
NPF	Notebook Poems and Fragments, *c.* 1789–93
NP	Notebook Poems, *c.* 1800–1806
NESV	Notebook Epigrams and Satiric Verses, *c.* 1808–12
MVE	Miscellaneous Verses and Epigrams

Index of Titles

Index of First Lines

THE STORY OF PENGUIN CLASSICS

Before 1946 ...'Classics' are mainly the domain of academics and students, without readable editions for everyone else. This all changes when a little-known classicist, E. V. Rieu, presents Penguin founder Allen Lane with the translation of Homer's *Odyssey* that he has been working on and reading to his wife Nelly in his spare time.

1946 *The Odyssey* becomes the first Penguin Classic published, and promptly sells three million copies. Suddenly, classic books are no longer for the privileged few.

1950s Rieu, now series editor, turns to professional writers for the best modern, readable translations, including Dorothy L. Sayers's *Inferno* and Robert Graves's *The Twelve Caesars*, which revives the salacious original.

1960s The Classics are given the distinctive black jackets that have remained a constant throughout the series's various looks. Rieu retires in 1964, hailing the Penguin Classics list as 'the greatest educative force of the 20th century'.

1970s A new generation of translators arrives to swell the Penguin Classics ranks, and the list grows to encompass more philosophy, religion, science, history and politics.

1980s The Penguin American Library joins the Classics stable, with titles such as *The Last of the Mohicans* safeguarded. Penguin Classics now offers the most comprehensive library of world literature available.

1990s The launch of Penguin Audiobooks brings the classics to a listening audience for the first time, and in 1999 the launch of the Penguin Classics website takes them online to a larger global readership than ever before.

The 21st Century Penguin Classics are rejacketed for the first time in nearly twenty years. This world famous series now consists of more than 1300 titles, making the widest range of the best books ever written available to millions – and constantly redefining the meaning of what makes a 'classic'.

The Odyssey continues ...

The best books ever written

PENGUIN (🐧) **CLASSICS**

SINCE 1946

Find out more at www.penguinclassics.com